VICTORIAN AND EDWARDIAN RECEIPT BOOK CAKES

COMPILED BY:
THE CURIOSITY SHOP AND CHEF R.J. AITKEN
1ˢᵗ EDITION

"I request you will prepare
To your own taste the bill of fare;
At present, if to judge I'm able,
The finest works are of the table.
I should prefer the cook just now
To Rubens or to Gerard Dow."

This volume is a Dedication to all those Chefs and Cooks who gone before and are now seated at the great table.

Disclaimer: Every effort has been made to ensure that the information in this book is complete and accurate. As such the publishers are not liable for any resulting injury or loss or damage to property whether directly or consequential due to mistakes or omissions in the publication. The publishers have accepted these recipes in good faith from the various contributing sources and therefore accept no responsibility for any breach of copyright belonging to third parties.

Copyright © (2017) R.J. Aitken and The Curiosity Shop

This book is copyright. Except for the purpose of fair review, no part may be stored or transmitted in any form or by any means, electronic or mechanical, including recording or storage in any information retrieval system, without permission in writing from the publishers. No reproduction may be made, whether by photocopying or by any other means, unless a license has been obtained from the publisher or its agent.

ISBN:

978 – 0 – 473 – 45004 – 5

INTRODUCTION

Victorian and Edwardian Receipt Book
CAKES

Here is a Book that has it all – from the past

The Recipe Book covers everything you need to know when it comes to making Cakes from the 1800's through to 1920.

As a reader of old cookbooks (Receipt's as they were known back then) this one has it all. From how to handle the way Cakes were made back in the 1800 and how those traditional ways changed all the way through to the 1920.

How to remove the cake for an old Coal Ranges and what temperature they should be kept ensuring the quality remains.

As the times changer (just like they do today)

Back in the day it was prudent to have several receipts for the same Cake. This was to assist with the price or perhaps what was in the cupboard in some of the backwaters of where people life.
There are several recipes for the same Cake taken which you can choose to experiment with.

Go ahead and make a Cake that was part of our Heritage.

The Victorian and Edwardian Receipt Book really is a must read.

Graham Hawk: President

Compilers Note

This book covers the period from 1800 to 1940.

It is in no way a complete collection of the products that were produced in the many styles of kitchens throughout this period as I am still collecting and collating them.

The dates beside each receipt is the first publication date.

Some receipts only list the ingredients. This was apparently due to the original author(s) assuming that the person(s) using the receipts knew what they were doing and how to produce the products.

Many products used within these dishes may no longer be available and therefore a substitute can be found and used.

I have also included within this volume original notes and these will be included in possible future books.

It should be noted by the reader that the baking powders and the yeasts that are called for in many of the receipts were made in the kitchens.

Crisco and Cottolene may be substituted by any vegetable-based shortening that is available in supermarkets etc.

Lard and dripping may be obtained from the butcher.

Isinglass may be substituted with gelatine although it may be obtained through specialty stores.

Saleratus is Sodium Bicarbonate an ingredient in Baking Powder and is a raising agent along with Bakers Ammonia, Harts Horn, Potash and Pearl Ash can be all be substituted with Baking Soda.

RECEIPTS LIST

Part 1: Notes
Part 2: 0 – A
Part 3: B
Part 4: C
Part 5: D
Part 6: E
Part 7: F
Part 8: G
Part 9: H
Part 10: I
Part 11: J
Part 12: K
Part 13: L
Part 14: M

Part 15: N
Part 16: O
Part 17: P
Part 18: Q
Part 19: R
Part 20: S
Part 21: T
Part 22: U
Part 23: V
Part 24: W
Part 25: Y
Part 26: Z
Part 27: Index

Part 1: Notes

Cake – Baking Powder (1894)
Weights and Measures (1913)
Reliable Weights and Measures as used (1922)
Cakes (1922)
Cakes (1899)
Cakes (1913)
Cakes and Icings (1876)
Cakes, Etc. General Observations (1840)
Cakes, Great and Small (1913)

Remarks on Making and Baking Cake (1869)
Cakes (Remarks on) (1898)
Things to be Remembered in Mixing and Baking Cake (1912)
Cakes, General Directions (1820)
Cakes. General Directions (1904)
Observation on Torten Forms (1873)
Kuchen
New Receipts and Points on Cake Making (1922)

Notes

Cake – Baking Powder (1894)

Three rounding teaspoons baking powder are equal to one level teaspoon of soda and two full teaspoons of cream tartar.

Weights and Measures (1913)

4 Teaspoonfuls equal 1 tablespoonful liquid.
4 Tablespoonfuls equal 1 wineglass, or half a gill.
2 Wineglasses equal 1 gill, or half a cup.
2 Gills equal 1 coffee-cupful, or 16 tablespoonfuls.
2 Coffee-cupfuls equal 1 pint.
2 Pints equal 1 quart.
4 Quarts equal 1 gallon.
2 Tablespoonfuls equal 1 ounce, liquid.
1 Tablespoonful of salt equals 1 ounce.
16 Ounces equal 1 pound, or a pint of liquid.
4 Coffee-cupfuls of sifted flour equal 1 pound.
1 Quart of unsifted flour equals 1 pound.
8 or 10 ordinary sized eggs equal 1 pound.
1 Pint of sugar equals 1 pound. (White granulated.)
1 Tablespoonful of soft butter, well rounded, equals 1 ounce.
An ordinary tumblerful equals 1 coffee-cupful, or half a pint.
About 25 drops of any thin liquid will fill a common-sized teaspoon.
1 Pint of finely chopped meat, packed solidly, equals one pound.
A set of tin measures (with small spouts or lips), from a gallon down to half a gill, will be found very convenient in every kitchen; though common pitchers, bowls, glasses, etc., may be substituted.

Reliable Weights and Measures as used. (1922)

Are equal to:

Flour:	1 quart or 4 teacups.	1 lb.
Flour (sifted):	3 coffee cups, level.	1 lb.
Flour:	2 tablesps., well-rounded.	1 oz.
Flour:	1 teaspoonful. heaped.	½ oz.
Sugar, granulated:	2 measuring cups, level.	1 lb.
Sugar, "A" coffee:	1¾ coffee cups, level.	1 lb.
Sugar, powdered:	2½ coffee cups, level.	1 lb.
Sugar, powdered:	2 tablesps., well-rounded.	1 oz.
Sugar, best Brown:	2 coffee cups, level.	1 lb.
Sugar, granulated, "A" or brown:	1 tablesp., well-heaped.	1 oz
Butter, soft:	2 full cups, well-pressed.	1 lb.
Butter, soft:	1 tablesp., well-rounded.	2 ozs.
Butter, soft:	Piece size of an egg.	1 oz.
Lard:	2 cups.	1 lb.
Eggs:	10, but if quite large 9.	1 lb.
Cornstarch:	3 cups.	1 lb.
Indian Meal:	2¾ coffee cups, level.	1 qt.
Coffee, ground:	4 cups.	1 lb.
Chocolate, sweet:	3 grated tablespoons.	1 oz.

Rice:	2 cups, heaped.	1 lb.
Rice:	2 tablespoons.	1 oz.
Sago:	2 cups, heaped.	1 lb.
Barley:	4 cups.	1 lb.
Bread crumbs:	1 cup, grated.	2 ozs.
Chopped meat:	2 cups, heaped.	1 lb.
Suet:	1 pint.	1 lb.
Nutmeg:	2 cups.	1 lb.
Almonds:	5 medium-sized.	1 oz.
Figs:	2 cups.	1 lb.
Dates:	2 cups.	1 lb.
Raisins:	2 cups.	1 lb.
Prunes:	2 cups.	1 lb.
Citron:	2 cups, heaped.	1 lb.
1 cup:		4 ozs.
2 rounded tablespoons:		1 oz.

Cakes (1922)

There are five principal ways of making cakes.

The first method is used for plain cakes. The shortening is rubbed into the flour in the same way as for short pastry; then the dry ingredients, such as sugar, fruit, and spice, are added, and lastly the eggs and milk. Then all are mixed well together.

The second way is used for fruit, pound, and seed cakes. The shortening and sugar are creamed together, the eggs beaten in one at a time, and the fruit and flour stirred in lightly and quickly at the last.

In the third way the eggs and sugar are beaten together until thick and creamy, then the flour is stirred in lightly and quickly. This is used chiefly for sponge cakes and cakes of that texture.

For the fourth way the sugar, shortening, milk, and syrup or molasses are melted together, then cooled slightly and added to the dry ingredients. This method is used for gingerbreads.

In the fifth way the sugar and eggs are beaten thoroughly over boiling water, then cooled before the melted shortening and dry ingredients are added. This method is used for Gennoise cake and some kinds of layer cakes. Care must be taken to insure the right consistency of cakes. The mixture should be fairly stiff. If too moist the fruit will sink to the bottom. For rich cakes the tins should be lined with paper, the paper coming a short distance above the tins, so that the cake is protected as it rises. For very rich fruit cakes, experience has shown that it is best not to grease the paper or tin. The cake is not so liable to burn, and the paper can be removed easily when the cake is done without injuring it. On the other hand, if tins are lined for sponge cakes or jellyrolls, the paper should be greased.

When making cakes in which baking powder, carbonate of soda, cream of tartar or tartaric acid are used, almost everything depends upon the handling, which should be as light and as little as possible. The more rapidly such cakes are made the better they will be. Two cooks working from the same recipe will often produce entirely different results, if one kneads her mixture as if it were household bread, while the other handles it with due lightness of touch. As soon as the baking powder or other rising medium is added to the mixture, the cake should be put into the oven as quickly as possible. Soda alone is never good in a cake where there is shortening, unless some substance containing acid is used along with it. Molasses is one of the substances containing acid.

The greatest care and cleanliness must be exercised in all cake making; and accuracy in proportioning the materials to be used is indispensable. The flour should be thoroughly dried and sifted, and lightly stirred in. Always sift flour before measuring, then sift it again with the baking powder to insure a thorough blending. Good cakes never can be made with indifferent materials. Eggs are used both as an aerating agent and as one of the "wetting" materials. It is not economy to buy cheap eggs, for such eggs are small, weak, colourless, and often very stale. Eggs should be well beaten, yolks and whites separately, unless other directions are given. The yolks must be beaten to a thick cream and the whites until they are a solid froth. Sugar tends to improve the texture of cakes, and when cheap cakes are made, plenty should be used, provided that the cake is not made too sweet. It should be dissolved before being added to the fat and the flour.

For best cakes, and all that are required of a light colour, fine-grained sugar should be used. With coarse-grained sugar there is danger of producing specks which show on the cakes after baking unless they have been made by the method of beating up the eggs and sugar together with a beater over hot water. This method will dissolve the grains of sugar.

Always buy the best fruits for cake making, as they are sweetest and cleanest. Currants and sultana raisins for cakes should not be too large, but of medium size, sweet and fleshy. Cheap dry sultanas should not be used. Though there is no need to wash sultanas, yet if the fruit is inclined to be very dry, it will be better to do so than to put them in to spoil the appearance and the flavour of the cake. Currants always should be washed, cleaned, and dried before using. Orange, lemon, and citron peel should be of good colour and flavour. They should not be added to cake mixture in chunks, as often is done, but should be in long shredded pieces. Large pieces of peel are sometimes the cause of a cake cutting badly. In making fruit cakes add the fruit before the flour, as this will prevent it falling to the bottom.

If a cake cracks open while baking, the recipe contains too much flour. There are two kinds of thick crusts which some cakes have. The first of these is caused by the cake being overbaked in a very hot oven. Where this is so, the cake, if a very rich one, has a huge crack in the top caused by the heat of the oven forming a crust before the inside has finished aerating; then as the interior air or gas expands, it cracks the crust to escape. This crack spoils the appearance of the cake, and when cut it generally will be found to be close and heavy in texture. To guard against this, it is necessary to bake them at a suitable temperature, noting that the richer the cake the longer the fruit takes to bake.

The second kind of thick crust referred to may only be on top of the cake, and in this case, may be caused by an excess of fat and sugar being mixed together, or otherwise insufficient flour. In this case the mixture will not bake, but only forms a kind of syrup in the oven, and the cake sinks in the center. A cake made under such conditions would have a thick shiny crust and be liable to crumble when touched. The inside of the cake would be heavy, having more the appearance of pudding than cake.

Successful cake making means constant care. In recipes in which milk is used as one ingredient, either sweet or buttermilk may be used but not a mixture of both. Buttermilk makes a light, spongy cake, and sweet milk makes a cake which cuts like pound cake. In creaming shortening and sugar, when the shortening is too hard to blend easily warm the bowl slightly, but do not heat the shortening, as this will change both the flavour and texture of the cake. For small cakes have a quick oven, so that they set right through, and the inside is baked by the time the outside is browned. For all large cakes have a quick oven at first, to raise them nicely and prevent the fruit sinking to the bottom. The oven then should be allowed to become slower to fire the cakes thoroughly.

Cake must not be hurried. Keep the oven steady though slow, and after putting a large cake into it do not open the door for at least twenty minutes. During baking, do not open the door unnecessarily, or in fact do anything to jar the cake lest the little bubbles formed by the action of the baking powder burst, causing the gas to escape and the cake to sink. This produces what is known as a "sad" cake but refers probably to the state of mind of the cook. A very light cake put into a quick oven rises rapidly round the sides but leaves a hollow in the middle.

If a cake is made too light with eggs or powder and an insufficient quantity of flour is added it will drop in the center. Another frequent cause is the moving of cakes while in the oven before the mixture has set properly. The same defect is produced if the cakes are removed from the oven before being baked sufficiently. When a cake batter curdles, the texture will not be so even as if the curdling had not taken place. Sometimes the mixture will curdle through the eggs being added too quickly, or if the shortening contains too much water. This forms a syrup with the sugar, and after a certain quantity of eggs have been added the batter will slip and slide about and will not unite with the other ingredients. Weak, watery eggs are another cause of this happening; and although this may be checked by adding a little flour at the right time, yet the cake would be better if it were unnecessary to add any flour until all the eggs had been beaten in, that is, if the batter had not curdled. Before turning out a cake allow it to remain in the tin for a few minutes. It is best to lay it on a wire cake stand or lay it on a sieve; but if you do not possess these, a loosely made basket turned upside down will do. If the cake will not turn out of the tin easily, rest it on its side, turning it round in a couple of minutes and it may loosen, if not, pass a knife round the edge, turn the cake over on a clean cloth, and let it stand a few minutes.

Do not place cakes in a cold place or at an open window, or the steam will condense and make them heavy, A rich cake improves in flavour and becomes softer with keeping (from 2 to 6 weeks, according to quality) before cutting. Wrap, when cold, first in a clean towel, then in paper. After a week remove the paper and put the cake into a tin wrapped in the towel. Small cakes may be baked in tiny molds or tins, or baked in a flat sheet, and then cut out into squares, diamonds or rounds. Then they can be frosted or coated with cream and decorated with cherries or other crystallized fruits. If a real distinction is desired, they may be placed in tiny crinkled paper cases, bought by the hundred at a trifling cost.

Cake tins should be greased with Crisco and dredged with flour, the superfluous flour shaken out, or they can be fitted with paper which has been greased with Crisco. When creaming Crisco and sugar, do not grudge hard work; at this stage of manufacture the tendency is to give insufficient work, with the result that the lightness of the cake is impaired.

Cakes (1899)

Feed sparingly, and defy the physician. - Sel.

Who lives to eat, will die by eating. - Sel.

Whoever eats too much, or of food which is not healthful, is weakening his powers to resist the clamors of other appetites and passions. - Christian Temperance.

The best seasoning for food is hunger. - Socrates.

Reason should direct, and appetite obey. - Ciceto.

Men should be temperate in eating as well as drinking. - Dr. Brandreth.

To make cake, get everything in readiness before beginning. Mix the ingredients in a granite-ware, enamelled, or earthen basin. Sift the flour before using. If baking-powder is used, sift together with the flour two or three times. Use white sugar unless brown is called for.

Beat the whites and yolks of the eggs separately; the yolks until they cease to foam, and the whites to a stiff froth. Eggs will beat to a stiffer froth if cold, and beaten in a cold dish, and in a cool room. Use earthen or china bowls or plates to beat eggs in - a bowl if an egg-beater is employed, and a plate when a fork or egg-whip is used. The Dover eggbeater is doubtless the best.

First rub the butter and sugar to a cream, then add the beaten yolks of the eggs, and beat and stir well; then the milk and flour, and lastly the beaten whites of the eggs.

Have the oven less hot for cake than for bread, but hotter for thin cake than for loaf cake. A cake is baked when a clean broom-straw may be passed through the thickest part without any dough adhering to it. If it is necessary to move the cake about after putting it in the oven, it should be done carefully, as jarring it in any way is liable to make it fall and become heavy.

A tube cake pan, as shown in the accompanying cut, is very good for baking ordinary cakes, as the tube causes the cake to bake more evenly and renders it less liable to fall.

To prevent cake from sticking to the pan, rub the pan with cold butter, and sprinkle with flour before turning in the batter.

If raisins or dried currants are used, they should first be carefully looked over, washed and dried, and then dusted with flour. The raisins should also be seeded. A good way to wash these fruits is to put them into a colander, set the colander in a pan of warm water for a short time until they become plump, which will loosen the sand and grit, and then rinse by dipping the colander in and out of clean water several times. Then spread the fruit on a clean cloth to dry. The raisins may easily be seeded just after being washed in this way.

Cakes (1913)

In baking cake, the oven should be kept at an even heat. For light, thin cakes a hot oven is used. After the cake begins to rise it should not be moved.

For fruit cakes and other heavy, dark cakes the oven should be moderately hot. Thick cakes are baked in pans lined with buttered paper.

Cakes and Icings (1876)

Always have good flour and sift it. Be careful to have fresh eggs and beat them light. Use good sugar and sweet butter, as poor butter will give the cake a bad flavour. Beat cake in an earthen bowl, with a wooden spoon, or paddle. Have the oven at the right heat when it is ready to put in - too cold an oven will - make cake heavy.

Wash currants (after picking them over) in a sieve set in a large pan of water; rub them well with the hands, changing the water two or three times; drain dry, then pour them on a coarse towel, and rub well; put back into a sieve and set out to dry. A quantity of currants can be prepared at once and used whenever you wish. Raisins should be stoned before using. Citron should be sliced very thin for cake and put in alternate layers with the dough.

For fried cakes, dissolve the sugar in the milk, to prevent the cakes from absorbing the fat. In using baking powder, sift it in a half-cup of flour; mix well and sprinkle in the last thing.

Cakes, Etc. General Observations (1840)

Unless you are provided with proper and convenient utensils and materials, the difficulty of preparing cakes will be great, and in most instances a failure; involving disappointment, waste of time, and useless expense. Accuracy in proportioning the ingredients is indispensable; and therefore, scales and weights, and a set of tin measures (at least from a quart down to a gill) are of the utmost importance. A large sieve for flour is also necessary; and smaller ones for sugar and spice. There should be a marble mortar, or one of lignum vitae, (the hardest of all wood;) those of iron (however well, tinned) are apt to discolour the articles pounded in them. Spice may be ground in a mill kept, exclusively for that purpose. Every kitchen should be provided with spice-boxes. You should have a large grater for lemon, cocoa-nut, &c., and a small one for nutmeg. Butter and sugar cannot be stirred together conveniently without a spaddle or spattle, which is a round stick flattened at one end; and a deep earthen pan with sides nearly straight. For beating eggs, you should have hickory rods or a wire whip, and broad shallow earthen pans. Neither the eggs, nor the butter and sugar should be beaten, in tin, as the coldness of the metal will prevent them from becoming light.

For baking large cakes, the pans (whether of block tin or earthen) should have straight sides; if the aides slope inward, there will be much difficulty in icing the cake. Pans with a hollow tube going up from the centre, are supposed to diffuse the heat more equally through the middle of the cake. Buns and some other cakes should be baked in square shallow pans of block tin or iron. Little tins for queen cakes, &c. are most convenient when of a round or oval shape. All baking pans, whether large or small, should be well greased with butter or lard before the mixture is put into them, and should be filled but little more than half. You should have at least two dozen little tins, that a second supply may be ready for the oven, the moment the first is taken out. You will also want tin cutters for cakes that are rolled out in dough.

All the utensils should be cleaned and put away as soon as they are done with. They should be all kept together, and, if possible, not used for any other purposes.

[**Footnote**: All the utensils necessary for cake and pastry-making, (and for the other branches of cooking,) may be purchased in Philadelphia; at Gideon Cox's household store in Market street, No. 335, two doors below Ninth. Everything of the sort will be found there in great variety, of good quality, and at reasonable prices.]

As it is always desirable that, cake-making should be commenced at an early hour, it is well on the day previous to ascertain if all the materials are in the house; that there may be no unnecessary delay from sending or waiting for them in the morning. Wastefulness is to be avoided in everything; but it is utterly impossible that cakes can be good (or indeed anything else) without a liberal allowance of good materials. Cakes are frequently rendered hard, heavy, and uneatable by a misplaced economy in eggs and butter; or tasteless and insipid for want of their due seasoning of spice, lemon, &c.

Use no flour but the best superfine; if the flour is of inferior quality, the cakes will he heavy, ill-coloured, and unfit to eat. Even the best flour should always be sifted. No butter that is not fresh and good; should ever be put into cakes; for it will give them a disagreeable taste which can never be disguised by the other ingredients. Even when of excellent quality, the butter will be improved by washing it in cold, water, and squeezing and pressing it. Except for gingerbread, use only white sugar, (for the finest cakes the best loaf,) and have it pulverized by pounding it in a mortar, or crushing it on the paste-board with the rolling-pin. It should then be sifted. In mixing butter and sugar, sift the sugar into a deep pan, cut up the butter in it, set it in a warm place to soften, and then stir it very hard with the spaddle, till it becomes quite light, and of the consistence of cream. In preparing eggs, break them one at a time, into a saucer, that, in case there should be a bad one among them, it may not spoil the others. Put them into a broad shallow pan and beat them with rods or with a wire whisk, not merely till they froth, but long afterwards, till the froth subsides, and they become thick and smooth like boiled custard. White of egg by itself may be beaten with small rods, or with a three-pronged fork, or a broad knife. It is a very easy process and should be continued till the liquid is all converted into a stiff froth so firm that it will not drop from the rods when held up. In damp weather it is sometimes difficult to get the froth stiff. The first thing to be done in making cake, is to weigh or measure all the ingredients. Next sift the flour, powder the sugar, pound or grind the spice, and prepare the fruit; afterwards mix and stir the butter and sugar, and lastly beat the eggs; as, if allowed to stand any time, they will fall and become heavy. When all the ingredients are mixed together, they should be stirred very hard at the last; and (unless there is yeast in the cake) the sooner it is put into the oven the better. While baking, no air should be admitted to it, except for a moment, now and then, when it is necessary to examine if it is baking properly, for baking; cakes, the best guide is practice and experience; so much depending on the state of the fire, that it is impossible to lay down any infallible rules.

If you bake in a Dutch oven, let the lid be first heated by standing it up before the fire; and cover the inside of the bottom with sand or ashes, to temper the heat. For the same purpose, when you bake in a stove, place bricks under the pans. Sheets of iron without sides will be found very useful for baking small flat cakes. For cakes of this description, the fire should be brisk; if baked slowly, they will spread, lose their shape, and run into each other. For all cakes, the heat should be regular and even; if one part of the oven is cooler than another, the cake will bake imperfectly, and have heavy streaks through it. Gingerbread (on account of the molasses) is more apt to scorch and burn than any other cake; therefore, it should be baked with a moderate fire.

It is safest, when practicable, to send all large cakes to a professional baker's; provided they can be put immediately into the oven, as standing will spoil them. If you bake them at home, you will find that they are generally done when they cease to make a simmering noise; and when on probing them to the bottom with a twig from a broom, or with the blade of the knife, it comes out quite clean. The fire should then be withdrawn, and the cake allowed to get cold in the oven. Small cakes should be laid to cool on an inverted sieve. It may be recommended to novices in the art of baking, to do everything in little tins or in very shallow pans; there being then less risk than with a large thick cake. In mixing batter that is to be baked in small cakes; use less proportion of flour.

Small cakes should be kept' closely covered in stone jars. For large ones, you should have broad stone pans with close lids, or else tin boxes. All cakes that are made with yeast should be eaten quite fresh; so also, should sponge cake. Some sorts may be kept a week; black cake much longer.

Cakes, Great and Small (1913)

The very queen among cake makers sums her secret of success in a sentence: "The best of everything." Cake will never be better than the things whereof it is made, no matter how skilled the maker. But it can be, and too often is, dismally worse, thus involving a waste of heaven's good gifts of sugar, butter, eggs, flour and flavours. Having the best at hand, use it well. Isaac Walton's direction for the bait, "Use them as though you loved them," applies here as many otherwheres. Unless you love cake-making, not perhaps the work, but the results, you will never excell greatly in the fine art. Better buy your cake, or hire the making thereof, else swap work with some other person better gifted in this special branch.

Here are a few cardinal helps. Have the eggs very cold, butter soft but not oily, flour dry and light - sun or oven-dry it in muggy weather. Sift it three times for ordinary cakes, twice for tea cakes, and so on, four to five times for very light things, sponge cake, angel's food, and measure it before sifting, and don't forget the needed amount - then you will be in no danger of putting in too much or too little. Always put a pinch of fine salt in the bottom of the mixing bowl, which ought to be freshly scalded and wiped very dry. A damp bowl clogs with either sugar or flour, making the stirring much harder. Unless specifically directed otherwise, separate the eggs, set the whites on ice till time to whip them, beat the yolks very, very light - to a pale, frothy yellow, add the sugar, free of lumps, a cupful at a time, then the butter washed and beaten to a creamy froth, beat hard together for five minutes, then add alternately the flour and the egg-whites beaten to the stiffest possible froth. Add a pinch of salt as beating begins, and if the egg supply is scant, a teaspoonful of cold water to each white. This will increase the quantity, and help to make the cake lighter, as it is the air-bubbles imprisoned in the froth which give it its raising virtue. Add fruit and flavouring last thing. Fruit should be well floured but never clotted. If batter appears to be too stiff a little whiskey thins it excellently and helps to make it lighter. Put in two tablespoonfuls to six eggs, using more in proportion. Rose water or a liqueur have the same effect but give their own flavour - which whiskey does not.

If strong butter needs must be used, it can be mitigated to a degree, by washing and kneading well in cold water barely dashed with chloride of lime solution, then rinsing well in cold water, and afterward in sweet milk. The milk may be half water. Rinse it out clean. Let the butter soften well before undertaking to cream it. A stout, blunt wooden spoon is the best for creaming, along with a deep bowl very narrow at the bottom. Grease deep cake tins plentifully, with either lard or butter - using only the best. For heavy cakes such as fruit, spice and marble cake, line them with double thicknesses of buttered paper and either set shallow pans of water in the oven while baking or stand the pans themselves in other pans with a quarter inch of water in the bottoms. If cakes brown too fast, open the oven door, a trifle, and lay over the pan a thick, well buttered paper until the oven cools. Never jar the oven while cake is baking in it--neither by banging the doors, nor dumping heavy vessels on top of it. Beware likewise slamming kitchen doors or bumping things about in the room. Fine cake demands as many virtues of omission as of commission. Indeed, the don'ts are as essential as the doings.

Layer cakes need to be mixed thinner than deep ones. The batter must run freely. Half fill the tins and set in a hot oven, taking care not to scorch before rising is finished. Butter tins very freely - it is economy in the end. Be sure the tins sit level in the oven - thus you escape an ungainly final loaf. Get filling ready as baking goes forward so as to put your layers together while still warm and pliable. Let cool before frosting, so as to trim sides smooth. Take care fillings are not too watery, also that they are mixed smooth. Spread evenly, and press down a layer firmly all over, before putting filling on top. Layers simplify greatly the problem of baking, but to my mind, no layer cake, not even the famous Lady Baltimore, is equal to a fine deep loaf, well frosted, and meltingly rich throughout.

Remarks on Making and Baking Cake (1869)

The materials for making cake should be of the best quality, as your success very much depends on it. Flour should be dried and sifted, sugar rolled fine, spices pounded and sifted. Where brown sugar is used, it should be spread on a dish and dried before rolling it. I have known very good pound cake made with brown sugar; also jumbles, &c. Persons that make their own butter sometimes use it fresh from the churn, which prevents the necessity of washing the salt out of it for cake, and it mixes more readily than hard butter. Currants should be picked over, washed and dried; raisins should be stemmed and stoned. When these preparations are made the day before, it is a great assistance. Eggs should be fresh, or they will not beat light: in beating the whites, take a broad flat dish, and beat them until you can hold the dish upside down, - this is a test of their lightness. A large bowl is best for mixing and beating cake. You must use your hand for mixing the sugar and butter, and as you add the other ingredients, you may take a large wooden spoon; beat it sometime after all is mixed. The oven should be ready to bake immediately, as standing makes cake heavy. A brick oven is the most certain, - and over your pans of cake, you should spread several layers of newspaper, to prevent its browning too suddenly. Cake requires more time than bread: a large cake should stay in the oven from an hour and a half to two hours, turning and looking at it from time to time; when you think it is sufficiently baked, stick a broad bright knife in the centre; if it is dry and free from dough when drawn out, the cake is likely to be done, though sometimes this is not a certain test, and you will have to draw a little from the centre of the cake with the knife. A broom straw will sometimes answer in a small cake instead of a knife. A large stone pan, with a cover, is the best for keeping cake, or a large covered bowl.

Cakes (1898)
(Remarks on)

All cakes should be thoroughly cooked in a tin lined with buttered paper and should have a buttered paper laid over them as soon as they are nicely browned on top.

It will be observed that I have generally given directions that the butter is to be melted with as slight a degree of heat as will suffice to liquify it, and beaten in, a tea-spoonful at a time, the last thing before the cake is put into the oven. This will be found much less trouble than beating the butter to a cream and mixing the other ingredients with it. In a few instances, such as pound cake, I have adhered to the old-fashioned way as being suited to that particular composition. In these cases, the butter should be put into a small, hot basin, and beaten with a wooden spoon until it becomes smooth and creamy.

Eggs must always be beaten and strained before they are added to the cake, and any other liquid, such as milk or brandy, should be added to the eggs before they are mixed with the dry ingredients, so that the whole cake is moistened at once.

Currants should be washed and picked, then spread out on a large dish (which should be put on the kitchen fender), and very slowly dried. They must be quite dry before they are used, or the cakes will be heavy.

Sugar should be pounded, but brown sugar may be used in plain cakes.

Great care must be taken in the baking of cakes. Further directions for the heat of oven, etc., may be found under " Remarks on Baking."

Only really fresh eggs and fruit of fine quality should be used.

Things to be Remembered in Mixing and Baking Cake (1912)

Always sift the flour and sugar before measuring.

Use light coloured butter, rich yellow butter does not make good cake, it is too oily. If yellow butter must be used, bleach by washing well with cold water, in summer use ice water. Pour off water and add lemon juice.

For delicate cake where butter is used, line the bottoms of the pans with oiled paper, or manila paper brushed over with lard. For muffin or little mould cakes, grease the pans and dust lightly with flour. Bake with an increasing heat; avoid having the oven hot at first.

When cake rises too high in the middle too much flour has been used; when it cracks, too much heat.

Use a round bottom porcelain bowl and wooden slotted spoon for mixing.

In very cold weather warm the bowl in which you mix the cake, also the flour and sugar. Use a good quality of fine granulated sugar and winter wheat flour is preferable.

In putting batter in pans allow from one-half to three inches for rising. Allow space according to the size of cake and shape of pans.

Layer cakes are cooked from twenty to thirty-five minutes, according to the thickness of the layers.

Mould cakes from forty minutes to two hours.

Do not remove mould cakes from pan until cold.

In mixing fruit cake, prepare the browned flour, nuts .and fruit before beginning to make the cake.

Never stir or beat sponge or angel food cake batter.

If your oven cooks too quickly for cakes and puddings wrap greased paper around the moulds or pans.

In making chocolate glaze melt the chocolate and add to glaze when cool, it will cloud if added while hot.

In cutting small cakes from sheet, dip your knife in warm water first and in cutting rounds or crescents ice or glaze over before cutting.

How to Mix and Bake Fruit Cake.

Cream the butter, add sugar, then the lightly beaten yolks of eggs, sift the spices, raising material and flour together and add next, unless molasses is used; in that case, the molasses first, then the flour, etc. Beat the whites of eggs very stiff and stir in, add the nuts and fruit last. If brandy or wine is used, add just before the fruits and nuts are stirred in.

Put the batter or mixture into a pan or mould, large enough to allow two or three inches for the rising. Set this into a pan deep enough to hold several inches of water; have the water hot and put in a rather slow oven. Cover over the top of cake mould with tin top. Set a pan of hot water on upper grate. Cook in this way until the cake has risen to the top of pan; remove the top and continue the cooking until the cake is done but not browned. Take pan of water from upper grate and cook until the cake browns.

Cakes can be cooked without the hot water but are much more moist and tender cooked in this way. Leave in the pan until perfectly cold. Run a spatula around the sides of pan and then invert the pan and the cake will slip out. Cook from three to four hours according to size of cake and the quantity of fruit used.

How to Mix and Bake Angel Food and Sponge Cake.
Beat the whites of eggs until light, add cream of tartar and continue the beating until the eggs are very stiff. Beat in the sugar lightly, add the flavouring and fold in the flour as lightly as possible. Never stir or beat the batter, it breaks the enfolded air and the batter falls, and the cake will be tough. Bake in ungreased pans in a. moderate oven and with an increasing heat. If nuts or fruits are used, add with the sugar.

Sponge cake is mixed and baked very much in the same way as angel food, generally adding the sugar to the yolks of eggs and beating together until light, the flour is folded in last, then the stiffly beaten whites (add rising material, with flour if any is used); the flavouring is added with yolks and sugar. There are some variations in mixing sponge cake, but these are the general rules.

Cakes, General Directions (1820)

Since perfection in the completed cake does not depend alone on the ingredients and their proper proportions, it is advisable that all who use this booklet read the following suggestions:

Utensils: A few well selected pieces of equipment are absolutely necessary to the best success of these recipes. It is true that edible cakes and cookies can be obtained with the make shift of the average kitchen, but not the successful product intended.

To insure success and enjoyment while working you should own the following:

Standard tablespoon (16 to 1 cup).
Standard teaspoon (3 to 1 tbsp.)
Wooden spoon for mixing.
Steel case knife for removing baked cakes.
(Spatula not best for this.)
Glass measuring cup.
Aluminum measuring cup.
Egg whip or wire whisk.
Egg beater of the wheel or Dover type (Not a cheap one.)
Crockery bowls.
Limber spatula to remove cake batter. (Not necessary, but a great convenience.)
Flour sifter.
Cake rack on which to cool cakes, bread, etc.
The wire shelf of the refrigerator is a good substitute.
"Turk's Head" cake pan for large cakes, as fruit or sponge. (Has hole in center.)
Tin or aluminum cake pan about 7x11x2 inches. (Suitable for cakes of the "Novelty type.")
Square cake pan with removable bottom.
Loaf cake pan about 4x8x3 inches.
Layer cake pans.
Russian iron or aluminum cookie sheet.
Oven thermometer.
Pair of scissors for cutting fruit, marshmallows, etc.
Brush for oiling pan, though a piece of clean paper may be used.
Double boiler, one-quart size.

Collect all ingredients and utensils before starting the cake.

Abbreviations:
tsp. teaspoon,
tbsp. tablespoon.
c. cup.
lb. pound,
pt. pint.
oz. ounce.

Equivalents: All measurements are levelled by knife moved forward at right angles to spoon or cup. Do not pack. Flour is sifted once before measuring. Use no favorite "coffee" or "tea" cups or dessertspoons!

3 tsp. equals 1 tbsp.
16 tbsp. equals 1 cup.

(When measuring molasses, sour milk, or other liquids and fat, always remove surplus clinging to spoon before calling it a measured table spoon.)

2 c. liquid equals 1 pt.
2 c. sugar equals 1 lb.
2 c. fat equals 1 lb.
4 c. flour equals 1 lb.
16 oz. equals 1 lb.

Mixing: With the exception of true sponge, cakes depend for their lightness upon the gas generated when the baking powder combines with liquid ingredients. Therefore, do not beat the batter any longer than to thoroughly mix it, or the gas will be lost and a heavy, compact mass results. A better method is to reserve two tablespoons of the flour and sift it with the baking powder into the well beaten batter before the whites are folded in. Long beating before addition of the leavener tends to make a more even grained texture.
Flour: To obtain a fine even texture, use one of the especially prepared cake flours on the market, or make your own pastry flour by substituting two tablespoons of cornstarch for two of flour in each cup of sifted flour. This always gives better results than bread flour though the cake dries out more readily. Effects of Various Ingredients In making an untested recipe for the first time it is interesting to know that:
1. If the cake has a gummy surface with a tendency to fall, an excess of sugar was used.
2. If there are heavy streaks and a friable crumb, too much fat was used.
3. A dry, bready cake is the result of too much flour.
4. An excess of baking powder makes a porous cake which falls easily.
5. An excess of egg gives tendency to toughness and produces "tunnels."
Baking: If all else has been observed and the cake is carelessly baked, failure is usually the reward.
One should learn the good and bad points of the oven used and act accordingly.
The cake is usually placed in the center of the oven. A large square of asbestos insures against burning on the bottom. The top shelf of the oven is used for browning.
An over thermometer, purchasable for a small sum, does away with guess work if one records results of each baking.
Temperatures:

Plain Cake (sheet or cup) 375 F. 30 minutes.
Plain Cake (loaf) 350 F 45 minutes.
Plain Cake (layer) 375F. 20 minutes.
Fruit Cake (cheap) 235F. 1¼ hours.
Fruit Cake (very large) 275 F. 3 to 4 hours.
Sponge Cake 320 1 hour.
Angel Cake 320 F. 1 hour.

Baking Powder Biscuit 450F. 12 to 15 min.
Muffins 400F. 25 minutes.
Corn Cake 400 F. 20 to 25 minutes.
Pop-Overs 450F. 30 min., and 350 F. 15 min.
Gingerbread 325 F. 45 minutes.
Bread 350 F. 45 minutes to one hour.
Biscuits (yeast) 400 F. 425F. 20 minutes.
Rolled Vanilla Cookies 450 F. 10 minutes.
Filled Cookies 450 F. 11 minutes.
Drop Bran Cookies 425 F. 12 minutes.
Soft Molasses Cookies 375 F. 18 minutes.
Ginger Snaps 350 F. 7 minutes.
Tests When Done
A cake may be tested in three ways:
a. When it shrinks from the sides of the pan.
b. When a straw inserted comes out without any dough adhering.
c. When lightly touched the dent does not remain.

Leave sponge cakes in pan till cold. Other cakes may be removed to cake rack to cool.
All cakes cut best with a wet knife.

Cakes: General Directions. (1904)

To be successful with cakes, pastry, etc., their ingredients should be put into a warm place for a few hours - in the Winter for a night - to get them to the proper temperature, and the stirring and working should also be done in a warm place where there is no draught. With pie crust and puff paste this is not necessary. When the whites of eggs are to be frothed, they should not be brought where it is warm before they are to be used.
The flour and cornstarch used must always be of the best quality. As soon as warm both the flour and sugar should be sifted; for very fine cakes the addition of some rice flour is recommended. Flour and sugar are more or less moist and should then be sifted after warming and drying.
The butter used should be of the best and unsalted. Cream the butter, put it on boiling water or on top of the stove until soft, but it must not melt, then with a wooden ladle rub it to a cream.
The eggs must be perfectly fresh; a single slightly stale egg will be sufficient to spoil the cake, and for this reason eggs should be broken into a separate dish. The extract of lemon can often be substituted for lemon peel and juice. Lemon peel used in too large a quantity will impart an unpleasant taste to any dish, and the same is the case with cardamom seeds, which are not liked by everybody. Cakes in which yeast is used can be nicely flavoured with rose water. Before the dough is put into the mould be sure that the latter has been properly prepared, nicely cleaned, rubbed with butter and dredged with rolled crackers or grated bread so that it will not be necessary to first get the mould ready while the dough is waiting for it. Many a cake is spoiled through this cause. Puff paste does not require a buttered mould.
Puff paste must never be kneaded, because this will make it heavy. To have it light and flakey put the butter into the middle of the flour, stir and work the dough with a knife at first, then with the ball of the hand, turning the dough frequently and folding it from the sides to the center, often dusting with flour and continue in this manner until flour and butter are thoroughly mixed; then set aside in a cool place for a few hours.
The addition of baking powder in biscuits, bread and almond cakes and the like will tend to make them lighter. When using yeast be cautious to get it fresh and sweet. For baking with yeast, the milk must be luke-warm and the flour, butter, sugar and the baking dish should also be slightly warm. When using baking powder all of the ingredients should be cold. After the dough has been well stirred, it will be greatly improved, smoother and finer if the mass is vigorously and uninterruptedly beaten for a while. To beat a soft dough, use the flat side of a ladle. Firm doughs are beaten on the moulding board; fold the dough and continue the beating and folding as long as indicated in the several receipts. Afterwards set the dough in a warm place where there is no draught, cover with a clean cloth and let it raise for 1½ - 2 hours. Slow fermentation produces a mild dough, whereas if it raises too quickly the dough will be tough.

The degree of heat in the oven can be tested by means of a piece of paper. If the paper soon turns to a yellow (not black) colour in the oven, this indicates the first degree of heat and is sufficient for puff paste and yeast doughs; if it turns yellow slowly it indicates the second degree of heat, fit for most kinds of baking; the third degree must be still lower for cakes, etc., that should dry more than bake.

In the receipts for the cakes, the time for baking is given as precisely as possible, but the length of time to finish the baking depends largely upon the heat of the oven; there are various tests for determining how near the cake is done, such as piercing it with a straw or something similar, which, if dry when drawn Out, indicates that the cake is done. Leaving the cake in the oven unnecessarily long is very detrimental to it, particularly if it is a yeast cake.

After the cake has been taken out of the oven let it stand in the mould for about 10 minutes where there is no draught. Then take it out of the mould but do not bring it into a cold room at once. Cake moulds made so that the outer rim is removable are the best, because then the cake can be taken out without shaking, which causes spongy cakes to fall. All kinds of cakes should be turned out of the mould onto a wire cake cooler, which will allow them to cool more readily. The mould should be cleaned with soft paper or a cloth immediately after being used.

Cakes will keep best in a tightly covered porcelain or glass dish. Tin cake boxes are also very good but must be cleaned from time to time with hot water and frequently aired. Yeast or fruit cakes are the best when fresh, although they are good after a few days when placed in the oven for a few moments before serving. If it should happen that a fruit cake is not baked until done at first, it will not lose in taste if it is finished the next day in a hot oven.

Observation on Torten Forms (1873)

When the round shallow tins used for so many kinds are not at hand, paper ones may be substituted. Make them by straining white foolscap paper over a large plate. Fold up the sides in plaits at regular distances and tack them round with needle and thread; then cut them round evenly, from one to two inches deep. They must always be buttered. The cakes baked in them are mostly light masses poured in thin, so that there will be no strain upon the paper to put the shape out of place.

Kuchen:

In different localities several kinds of Kuchen are called Torten, and these are as frequently called Kuchen elsewhere. Those about to be described hereafter have, with some exceptions, a tart paste for their foundation. They are baked in shallow tins, or on the large sheet tins used in the baker's oven. These are covered with very thin tart paste, the edge of which is raised a little by moulding with finger and thumb. They are spread over with whatever they are named after, and when baked they are cut into square, oblong, or three-cornered pieces, as they are taken off the tin. The better kinds are baked in round tins with rims an inch deep. The following pastes are used:

Mürber Teig - Short Crust for Savoury Pasties (No. 1)
Mürber Teig - Short Crust (No. 2)
Mürber Teig - Short Crust (No. 3)
Mürber Teig - Common Short Crust (No. 4)
Blätter Teig - Puff Paste (No. 1)
Blätter Teig - Puff Paste (No. 2.
Hefen Teig - Yeast Dough

New Receipts and Points on Cake Making (1922)

In making up a new receipt a little study of the materials is required, to obtain proper results; and notice should be taken how they work in the mixtures.

The same goods do not always work alike. The flours differ greatly in their water-absorbing power; and so, do the different brands of starch. These qualities of flour and starch cause the mixtures, cakes or creams, getting too firm or too soft as the case may be; and more or less should be used, or liquid added to obtain the right consistency.

The baking and boiling process also causes the evaporation of the liquids, and if continued too long, causes the drying out of the articles made.

The best pastry and cake flours are the red winter wheat flours of Missouri and Illinois. The Michigan and Ohio flours are more starchy, and a little strong patent flour may be used with these flours for cake mixtures. Flour merchants sell cake flours which are blended specially for cake baking.

If baking powder or cream of tartar is used it should be sifted in the flour; and all the flour should be sifted before using it in the mixtures.

For cake and meringues, the sugar should be dry and sifted before using.

A good tough butter makes the best cream and the lightest cake. Very salty butter should be washed before using.

The eggs should be as fresh as possible and the breaking and separating be done carefully, because one egg is liable to spoil the whole batch. The safest way is to break the eggs one by one in a cup; or, if separating the whites, in two cups, before adding them to the other eggs.

When mixing cakes, it is best to have all the materials ready which into the mixture, so the mixing can proceed without interruption. Begin by preparing the pans in which the cake is to be baked; then weigh the sugar. (if butter is used put it on top of the sugar, adding the additional weight: this prevents the sticking of the butter to the scales. Next weigh the flour and add the baking powder or cream of tartar and sift it with the flour into a pan or on a paper. Then break up or separate the eggs and measure eggs and milk. If soda is used dissolve it in the milk. Ammonia should be powdered very fine and may be dissolved in milk or added dry. Grated lemon rind and spices may be added to the sugar. The liquid extracts are added after the butter is creamed with the sugar and eggs before the flour.

Put the sugar and butter in the mixing bowl, (it is best for creaming to have the butter a little soft, but not too soft, as it becomes oily). Cream the butter and sugar light before adding the eggs. Have the eggs cold and them two at a time; work them in well; add more again, till they are all worked in.

Some bakers add a little flour during the mixing to prevent the curdling of eggs and butter; and others cream flour and butter to prevent oiling in the hot season, adding the sugar and eggs well beaten together in the mixture.

If milk is used in the mixture it is added after the eggs are creamed with the butter; also, the extracts; then the flour is worked in. It is best to leave a little of the milk out, if not sure of the strength of the flour, to prevent getting the mixture too slack, and add it after the flour is all in if required.

If fruits or peels are used, they should be added when the flour is about half mixed in. For heavy fruit cakes, the fruits and spices may be mixed with syrup or liquor the day before using and put in the mixture. For lighter cakes the fruit should be soft but dry, to prevent sinking in the cakes during baking.

The baking of pastry and cakes requires different degrees of heat. Puff Paste from 400 to 450 degrees Fahrenheit; Pie Paste 350 to 400 degrees Fahrenheit; also, cream puffs, lady-fingers, layer cakes and light cookies, from 300 to 350 degrees Fahrenheit; the large cakes, which contain milk and baking powder, from 250 to 300 degrees Fahrenheit; and heavy pound and fruit cake, about 200 degrees Fahrenheit. Hard cakes which consist of sugar and eggs only, or with little flour, also the meringues, require still less heat in baking. Large sheet and layer cakes, also heavy large cakes, should be moved as little as possible during the time they are coming up in the oven, as moving causes the mixture to fall.

Sometimes it is advisable to bake the cakes on double pans when the oven has got to much bottom heat; and large cakes require covering with paper to prevent baking too much colour.

When a large cake is fully baked, it shrinks slightly from the sides, and feels elastic to the touch of thee fingers. The cakes may also be tested by sticking a splinter of wood in the center: if it comes out dry the cake is done.

Substitutes for butter are used in form of butterine, lard and Cottolene, for commercial cake making.

Cakes of the cheaper kind are made without eggs. Coloring is used in place of eggs; and a strong flour is used with baking powder to make large cakes.

It is advisable to use always the best materials and, when making up a new receipt, figure out the cost, note the amount got out of the receipt, and use it for reference the next time.

To make this book suitable for all classes of the trade, I give a variety of receipts for caters, and also for the general cake trade, where lower prices obtain.

The most difficult cakes to prepare properly are the mixtures which contain no baking powder – the rich pound and sponge cakes.

The lightening agent in the sponge mixtures is the air beaten into the eggs.

In some mixtures the sugar and eggs are beaten together, mostly warm till light and then cold; in others the eggs are separated, the yolks are stirred light with the sugar, and the whites are beaten to a firm froth; both are put together before the flour is added.

For the rich pound and lady cake mixtures the creaming of the butter and sugar should be done carefully. It is best to have the butter a little soft, but do not let it become oily. If the cream gets too warm it injures the rich cakes. The mixtures which contain baking powder are not so easily affected by this, because they are lightened by the powder.

The rich fruit cake mixtures are made from the pound and white cake preparations. The fruit is added for the heavy wedding and Christmas cakes in proportions of two pounds of mixed peel and fruit to one pound of cake batter; sometimes with less sugar. The lighter cakes contain from six ounces to one pound of fruit to one pound of batter.

Caterers prepare the holiday fruit cakes a month or more before they are used; this makes the cake mellow and they are greatly improved by age.

Many of the lighter cake mixtures can be used for a stock mixture to make several kinds of cake from, by changing or adding to the ingredients. For instance, take the mixture of the New York Pound Cake No.2 and the Plain Genoa Pound Cake. The mixture will make a plain Pound or Wine cake, or, with a little more flour and fruit added, a light Citron, Sultana, Currant or Nut Cake. If the mixture is worked more after the flour has been added it will make nice Cup and Drop Cakes. By adding a little more milk, it can be made into layer or sheet cake. By using whites of eggs instead of whole eggs, this makes Silver cake or White Mountain Cake. If coloured partly chocolate and red it makes Chocolate cake. And all three colours combined makes Marble Cake.

Pound Cakes: The old pound to pound mixtures have changed in recent years into many combinations, and given other names as Madeira and Genoa cakes etc. Most all plain cakes which contain no fruit are termed pound cakes, and the lighter kinds of these cakes contain milk and baking powder, less eggs and butter and more flour.

Wine Cakes: Wine cakes are baked generally in the small round or square tins, five- and ten-cent size.

Sponge Cakes: These cakes are best baked in wooden frames, as generally used for large square cakes, or in rings. Take the frames and rub lightly with butter or lard and dust with powdered sugar. Put a sheet of paper on the pan, dust also and set on the frame. Fill in the mixture and bake in a medium heat.

Angel cake: Angel Cake or Angel Food is a cousin of the sponge cake made from the whites of eggs only. The quality differs according to how much more or less flour is used in the mixture. The cornstarch is added to make the cake eat short; the cream of tartar to whiten the mixture. (If the latter is left out the cakes get a dull dark colour like as if a very dark flour has been used; and the cake feels dry and tough).

The cakes are best baked in the round pans with a wide center tube.

The moulds are not lined with paper or greased like for other cakes. On the contrary, they should be dry and free from grease, so the cake sticks to the moulds when baked.

Bake the cake in a medium heat of 300 degrees Fahrenheit. When done turn upside down and let cool. This prevents the cake from shrinking and keeps it light. When cold loosen the cake around the edge, knock the pan on the table and the cake should drop out. Brush off the brown crumbs and ice with vanilla.

From the Angel Cake mixture is made a variety of fancy flavoured cakes, as Rose, Violet, Pistachio, Strawberry, Raspberry, etc., using the proper colours and icings.

Fruit cakes: The fruit cakes are divided into heavy and light cakes.

The black fruit cakes and the English wedding cakes contain the most fruit.

Some bakers add burned sugar to the cake or brown flour to darken the mixture; but this custom is detrimental to the good flavour of the cakes.

The heavy cakes should be baked at a low temperature of about 200 degrees Fahrenheit and made about two and one-half inches thick. A cake of this thickness, about a foot square will bake in two and one half to three hours' time. The pans should have a double lining of strong paper, well buttered, to prevent too much colour in baking.

Many of the English FRUIT, BRIDES and CHRISTMAS CAKES are iced with the almond paste while warm, right after they are baked; and when the paste is dry, a coat of Royal or Fondant Icing is put over the almond icing and then decorated.

Another way is to put the Almond Paste on with a bag and star tube, put it back in the oven and brown it lightly in a quick heat, instead of using two coats, and decorate with French fruit.

Nut Cakes: From the pound and white cake mixtures a variety of Nut Cakes may be made with the different kinds of nut meats.

The best way to bake these cakes is to bake them in small round, oval or square tins which hold from eight ounces to one pound. The Angel Cake moulds may also be used to advantage.

By using the different nuts, you get:

Walnut Cake

Pecan Cake

Brazilian Cake

Peanut Cake

Filbert Cake and Pistachio Cake

Other combinations of this kind are made of mixed nuts and almonds; nuts and sultanas, nuts and orange peel, or nuts and French cherries, etc.

Use either of the mixtures; flavour with lemon, orange or vanilla, or vanilla with a drop of bitter almond.

Use about one ounce or more of the chopped nut meat to one pound of cake batter, and when the cakes are baked, ice fully and sprinkle with chopped nuts before the icing gets dry; or ice and sprinkle the sides with chopped nuts, and use some half walnuts or other kinds, or split almonds to decorate the top.

For less expensive cake put only a broad strip of icing in the center and decorate with a few half nuts.

Chocolate, caramel and vanilla, also nut-flavoured icings are the most suitable for Nut Cake.

With different shapes of tins, various icing and mixtures you can evolve many more cakes of this kind.

A nice cake deserves a nice name and sells better, so you may call your cake Princess or Victoria or Duchess Nut Cake, etc.

Notes on Layer Cakes: The mixtures from Marble Cakes (1922) to Layer Cake, White Mixture (No.2) are standard Layer Cake receipts of different quality, as generally used for white and yellow layers.

They are prepared like the other cakes which contain milk.

A baking temperature of 350 degrees, and for the plainest mixtures 400 degrees Fahrenheit, is the most suitable for these cakes.

For the best and richest kind of these cakes the Butter, Sponge, Genoise and Pound Cake mixtures are used by caterers; and other special mixtures are made as occasion demands.

All of the following fillings and several of the tart fillings, and also the icings may be used for the layer cakes:

Almond and Nut Cream Filling

Chocolate Nut Cream, or Caramel Nut Cream

Almond Filling (No.1)

Almond Filling (No. 2)

Nut Filling (No. 1)

Nut Filling (No. 2)

Cocoanut Filling

Orange Filling

Plain Lemon Filling

Lemon and Orange Butter Filling

Pineapple Filling

Vienna Cream Filling (No. 1)

Vienna Cream Filling (No. 2)

Fruit Pastes for Filling Layer Cakes

Tartlet Crumb Filling

Pastry Creams

Cream Puff Filling

Pastry Cream

Pastry Cream (Water Cream)

The fruit jellies and jams make another variety of fillings.

The Nut Cake recipes and suggestions, as given, can be made into Layers and iced as suggested.

The Layer Cakes are made in two or three layers. When they are baked and cool, the filling is put between, pressed together, trimmed straight, and iced on top and sides.

The jelly cakes are often sprinkled thickly with cocoanut, which makes the use of a thin icing possible and looks nice.

Some caterers use the square pound cake, and split it in two or three layers, put the filling between and ice. This makes very attractive Layer Cakes which are given special names. The cakes are named either after the flavours they contain or are named after prominent persons or localities.

In many of the best cakes a double icing is used. Either a firm fruit jam, or almond paste icing is put on and followed with another coat of Royal or Fondant. The English method of icing Loaf and layer Cake in this manner, is to take a thin almond or macaroon mixture, spread it over the cake, sprinkle or dip in shredded almonds or nuts, and put the cake into the oven for a minute to get a nice colour; or take a firmer paste which keeps its shape and put it on with bag and star tube in a decorative way; or, spread the paste over plain, and take a fork and make it rough looking, then put the cake in the oven to colour. When cold the cake is finished with fondant or royal icing or decorated with French fruits glacés.

The Layer Cakes are also baked in large sheets, two layers put together with filling and iced in one whole sheet; or, cut up in small squares or diamonds before icing and dipped in the icing like cream candies; or, set nearly touching each other on a wire grate and the icing poured over. The icing used may be soft royal icing or a fondant icing.

To make the small cakes attractive, prepare a batch of white icing and divide it into four or five parts; colour one part pink, flavour rose or maraschino; one part yellow, flavour orange; one part chocolate; one part pale green, flavour pistachio; and leave one part white. Dip the cakes in the different colours, and before the icing becomes dry, put a slice of fruit glace, and a half an almond, walnut or hickory nut on each piece; or a dot of icing of reverse colours.

Another form of decorating is to use ornamenting icing in different colours, and with a cornet, pipe on patterns of any description, setting it off with dots or bright fruit jelly.

Another way is to prepare tiny flowers and stars beforehand from royal icing; or, buy small berry candies, dragees, etc., of different colours and drop them on the small cakes as soon as they are iced.

The coloured sugars may also be used in these cakes.

Many bakers utilize stale cakes in this manner without any filling, only they use different coloured icing and sprinkle the cake with chopped nuts. The plainer kinds are called Nougatines. The others, made from black fruit cakes or ginger bread, are general iced chocolate, and called Negritos, or Negro Nougatinas. Of cause, there are many other ways of decorating and a skilful inventive workman can devise thousands of them to make the cake look decorative.

Cakes and Cookies (1897)
(Kakor och Bakelser)

All sugar and flour to be used should be sifted and weighed. Very hard butter should be warmed a little but not melted; if salted and packed, freshen it with cold water since first broken in pieces. It is only when sour milk is used that soda can be used, but with sweet milk cream of tartar must be used or baking powder. For all white and fine kinds of cake, use powdered sugar; for so called "rich cakes", use crushed sugar and powdered mixed, and for dark cakes, use brown sugar. Old cake makers with experience are in the habit of beating the milk and all the minor ingredients with the butter and the sugar, then the yolks of the eggs, then the whites and lastly the flour.

Part 2: 0 – A

1-2-3-4 Cake (1922)
A Caramel Cake (1893)
A Caramel Cake Chocolate Filling (1893)
A Caramel Cake Filling (1893)
A Charlotte Polonaise (1840)
A Cheaper Fruit Cake (1869)
A Composition Cake (1869)
A Nice Apple Cake (1904)
A Rich Fruit Cake (1869)
A Sally Lunn (1840)
A Virginia Hoe Cake (1869)
Abgeriebener Napfkuchen (1910)
Africans (1920)
(Africains)
Aepfel Kuchen (No. 1) (1873)
(Common Apple Kuchen)
Aepfel Kuchen (No. 2) (1873)
(Apple Cake)
Aepfel Kuchen (No. 3) (1873)
(Apple Cake)
Aepfel Kuchen (No. 4) (1873)
(Apple Cake)
Aepfel Kuchen (No. 5) (1873)
(Apple Cake)
Air Cake (1913)
Alliance Tourte (1922)
Allianz Torte (1873)
Alliance Cake
Almond and Citron Cake (1922)
Almond Biscuit (1920)
(Biscuit aux Amandes)
Almond Cake No. 1 (1904)
Almond Cake with Wheat Bread No. 2 (1904)
Almond Cake No. 1 (1904)
Almond Cake No. 2 (1904)
Almond Cake (1912)
Almond Cake (1898)
Almond Cake (1840)
Almond Cake (1869)
Almond Cake (1920)
(Gâteau d'Amandes)
Almond Cake (1898)
Almond Cake (1876)
Almond Cake 1 (1894)
Almond Cake 2 (1894)
Almond Cake 3 (1894)
Almond Cakes (1890)
Almond Cakes (1914)
Almond Cakes (1911)
Almond Cakes (1898)
(Small for Afternoon Tea)
Almond Cakes (1914)
Almond Cakes Candy (1894)
Almond Cheese Cake (1840)
Almond Cheese Cakes (1911)
Almond Cheese Cakes (1898)
Almond Cream Cake (1893)
Almond Custard Cake (1876)
Almond Gingerbread (1898)
Almond Marzapan (1904)
Almond or White Cake (1894)
Almond Silver Cake (1894)
Almond Roll (1922)
Almond Torte (1820)
Altdeutscher Napfkuchen (1910)
American Fruit Cake (1922)
Angel Cake (1922)
Angel Cake (No. 1) (1922)
Angel Cake (No. 2) (1922)
Angel Cake (No. 3) (1922)
Angel Cake (No. 4) (1922)
Angel Cake (No. 5) (1922)
Angel Cake (1893)
Angel Cake (1920)
(Gâteau des Anges)
Angel Cake (1894)
Angel Cake 1 (1893)
Angel Cake 1 (1893)
Angel Cake (1893)
Angel Cake (1911)
Angel Cake (1889)
Angel Cake (1912)
(With Nut and Whipped Cream Filling)
Angel Food (1820)
Angel Food (1893)
Angel Food Cake (1912)
Angel Marshmallow Cake (1912)
Angel Sponge Cake (1820)
Aniskuchen (1910)
(Aniseed Cakes)
Another Pretty Cake (1876)
Apees (1840)
Apfelkuchen I (1910)
(Apple Cake)
Apfelkuchen II (1910)
(Apple Cake)
Apfelkuchen mit Blätterteig (1910)
(Apple Cake with Puff Paste)
Apfelsinen Torte (No.1) (1873)
(Orange Tart or Cake)
Apfelsinen Torte (No. 2) (1873)
(Orange Cake)

Apfel-Torte (1910)
Apple Cake (1904)
Apple Cake (1920)
Apple Cake (1920)
(Gâteau aux Pommes)
Apple Cake (1898)
Apple Cake with Lemon Sauce (1913)
Apple Cakes (1878)
Apple Cake made of puff paste (1904)
Apple Cake with Almond Icing (1904)
Apple Cheese Cakes (1898)
Apple Gems (1876)
Apple Griddle Cakes (1902)
Apple Roll (1922)
Apple Sauce Cake (1820)

Apple Sauce Cake (1912)
Apple Sauce Cake (1911)
Apple Sauce Cake (1917)
(Without Butter, Eggs, or Milk)
Apple Sauce Fruit Cake without Milk (1922)
Apple-Sauce Torte (1922)
Apple and Cranberry Shortcake (1917)
Apricot Cake (N.D)
Arrow Root Cakes (Small) (1898)
Arrowroot Cake (1898)
Ash Cake (1913)
(Pioneer)
Aunt Amy's Cake (1911)
Aunt Rachel's Flannel Cakes (1876)

1-2-3-4 Cake (1922)

1 cup butter
1 cup sour cream
2 cups sugar
1 teaspoon soda

3 cups flour
Spices
4 eggs

Cream butter and sugar; add eggs and stir until creamy. Add the sour cream and soda dissolved in cream and lastly the flour containing the spices.

A Caramel Cake (1893)
(To be baked in layers)

Four eggs
Three-fourths of a cup of butter
One-half cup of milk

Three and one-half cups of flour
Two teaspoonfuls of baking powder
Flavour to suit taste

Filling:

Two cups of brown sugar
One cup of rich cream

Size of a walnut of butter

Boil one-half hour well stirred; spread between the layers of the cake while hot.

Chocolate Filling:

Six tablespoonfuls of grated chocolate
One and one-half cups of pulverized sugar

Two tablespoonfuls of cream

Put the chocolate in the pan with the cream and one-half the sugar and let dissolve; add the remainder of the sugar to the whites of two eggs well beaten; flavour with vanilla for four layers of cake.

A Caramel Cake Chocolate Filling (1893)

Six tablespoonfuls of grated chocolate
One and one-half cups of pulverized sugar

Two tablespoonfuls of cream

Put the chocolate in the pan with the cream and one-half the sugar and let dissolve; add the remainder of the sugar to the whites of two eggs well beaten; flavour with vanilla for four layers of cake.

A Caramel Cake Filling (1893)

Two cups of brown sugar
One cup of rich cream

Size of a walnut of butter

Boil one-half hour well stirred; spread between the layers of the cake while hot.

A Charlotte Polonaise (1840)

Boil over a slow fire a pint and a half of cream. While it is boiling have ready six yolks of eggs, beaten up with two table-spoonfuls of powdered arrow-root, or fine flour. Stir this gradually into the boiling cream, taking care to have it perfectly smooth and free from lumps. Ten minutes will suffice for the egg and cream to boil together. Then divide the mixture by putting it into two separate sauce-pans.

Then mix with it, in one of the pans, six ounces of chocolate scraped fine, two ounces of powdered loaf-sugar, and a quarter of a pound of maccaroons, broken up. When it has come to a hard boil, take it off, stir it well, pour it into a bowl, and set it away to cool.

Have ready, for the other sauce-pan of cream and egg, a dozen bitter almonds, and four ounces of shelled sweet almonds or pistachio nuts, all blanched and pounded in a mortar with rose-water to a smooth paste and mixed with an ounce of citron also pounded. Add four ounces of powdered sugar; and to colour it green, two large spoonfuls of spinach juice that has been strained through a sieve. Stir this mixture into the other half of the cream, and let it come to a boil. Then put it aside to cool.

Cut a large sponge-cake into slices half an inch thick. Spread one slice thickly with the chocolate cream and cover another slice with the almond cream. Do this alternately (piling them evenly on a china dish) till all the ingredients are used up. You may arrange it in the original form of the sponge-cake before it was cut, or in a pyramid. Have ready the whites of the six eggs whipped to a stiff froth, with which have been gradually mixed six ounces of powdered sugar, and twelve drops of oil of lemon. With a spoon heap this meringue (as the French call it) all over the pile of cake, &c., and then sift powdered sugar over it. Set it in a very slow oven till the outside becomes a light brown colour.

Serve it up cold, ornamented according to your taste.

If you find the chocolate cream too thin, add more maccaroons. If the almond cream is too thin, mix in more pounded citron. If either of the mixtures is too thick, dilute it with more cream.

A Cheaper Fruit Cake (1869)

Four pounds of flour
Three of butter
Three of sugar
Two of raisins
One of currants

Two dozen eggs
An ounce of mace
Three nutmegs
A half pint of brandy

If you want it dark, put in a little molasses
Mix the ingredients together, as the above fruit cake, and bake it from two to three hours.

A Composition Cake (1869)

One pound of sugar
One of flour
Half a pound of butter
Six eggs

Two and a half wine-glasses of milk
One tea-spoonful of soda
One of tartaric acid

Warm the milk and butter; add the sugar, then the yolks of the eggs beaten light, then the whites and the flour alternately, then the soda, (to be dissolved in half a wine-glass of water;) season with nutmeg, mace, or a little essence of lemon, and add lastly, the tartaric acid, dissolved in half a wine-glass of water. Bake it one hour in an oven, as hot as is usual for bread; when brown at the top, cover it with paper. A pound of dried currants is an agreeable addition.

A Nice Apple Cake (1904)

Make a crust as given, take some nice cooking apples of uniform size, 1 cupful of white wine, 1 lemon, plenty of sugar and some pounded almonds.

Roll the dough or else put it into a round mould and press it as given under Plum Cake (1904). In the meantime, peel the apples, halve them, and on the round side hack them with a knife (but this must be done quickly so that they will not discolour), and dip them into a mixture made of the wine, grated lemon peel and their juice, almonds and sugar. Lay the cut side of the apple to the bottom of the cake and bake in a moderate oven for

1¼ hours. When wished the cake can be dotted with any kind of preserved fruits and make an edge of sugared orange slices. It can also be served without any further additions.

A Rich Fruit Cake (1869)

Have the following articles prepared before you begin the cake: dry and sift four pounds of flour, four pounds of butter with the salt washed out, two pounds of loaf-sugar pounded, one ounce of nutmegs grated, an ounce of mace pounded; wash four pounds of currants; dry, pick, and rub them in flour; stone and cut two pounds of raisins; slice two pounds of citron, blanch a pound of sweet almonds and cut them in very thin slices; break thirty eggs, separate the whites and yolks, and beat them till very light; work the butter with your hand till it is soft as cream; put in alternately the flour, sugar and eggs. When all are mixed in, and the cake looks very light, add the spice, fruit, almonds, and half a pint of brandy; set it in a well-heated oven to bake; when it has risen, and the top is beginning to brown, cover it with paper; let it bake four hours, and when it is nearly cool, ice it. This will keep a long time in a stone pan, covered close.

A Sally Lunn (1840)

This cake is called after the inventress.
Sift into a pan a pound and a half of flour. Make a hole in the middle and put in two ounces of butter warmed in a pint of milk, a salt-spoonful of salt, three well-beaten eggs, and two table-spoonfuls of the best fresh yeast. Mix the flour well into the other ingredients and put the whole into a square tin pan that has been greased with butter. Cover it, set it in a warm place, and when it is quite light, bake it in a moderate oven. Send it to table hot and eat it with butter.
Or, you may bake it on a griddle, in small muffin rings, pulling the cakes open and buttering them when brought to table.

A Virginia Hoe Cake (1869)

Pour warm water on a quart of Indian meal, stir in a spoonful of lard or butter, some salt, make it stiff, and work it for ten minutes, have a board about the size of a barrel head, (or the middle piece of the head will answer,) wet the board with water, and spread on the dough with your hand, place it before the fire, prop it aslant with a flat-iron, bake it slowly, when one side is nicely brown, take it up and turn it, by running a thread between the cake and the board, then put it back, and let the other side brown. These cakes used to be baked in Virginia on a large iron hoe, from whence they derive their name.

Abgeriebener Napfkuchen (1910)

1¼ lb. flour	10 oz. butter
½ lb. sugar	4 oz. sultanas
4 eggs	3 oz. yeast
4 extra yolks	The rind of 1 lemon

Prepare the yeast as in preceding recipe, with a gill of the milk and 3 tablespoonsful flour. Cream the butter, beat it up with the eggs and sugar, add the sultanas and grated lemon peel and stir in the risen yeast. Add the milk and flour alternately and knead the dough well. Fill, half full, a well-buttered earthenware mould (Napfkuchenform) lined with breadcrumbs, stand in a warm place, covered over, till the dough has well risen, and bake 1 hour.
¼ lb. grated sweet almonds may be substituted for the sultanas and lemon peel.

Africans (1920)
(Africains)

Make a small lady finger preparation; pour it in a linen bag furnished with a quarter of an inch socket and lay the cakes on paper in the shape of small rounds an inch and a quarter in diameter; place this paper on a baking sheet and bake the cakes in a slow oven. As soon as they are done remove them from the sheet and let get cold on the paper, then take the biscuits off, scoop them out on the flat side, and fill in the empty space with pastry cream; fasten them together in pairs and dip them entirely in icing flavoured with vanilla, rose, coffee or chocolate, removing them with a fork. Drain well on a wire grate, then set them at the oven door an instant to gloss.

Aepfel Kuchen (No. 1) (1873)
(Common Apple Kuchen)

Line a shallow tin with tart-paste (Hefen Teig - Yeast Dough), or baker's bread dough if you have no yeast to make one; peel, quarter, and core apples; cut them in half-quarters; lay these close together sideways over the paste till it is covered. Mix a custard of a cup of milk, two eggs, a good teaspoonful of arrowroot or corn-flour, some grated or shred lemon peel or nutmeg, and sugar enough to sweeten; pour it over the apples, mix powdered sugar and cinnamon, and strew this over. Bake it in a moderate oven; slice a little butter over before baking.

Aepfel Kuchen (No. 2) (1873)
(Apple Cake)

A better one is of apples cut in half-quarters, laid on a thin paste. Mix a cup of grated bread-crumbs, an ounce of almonds blanched and either pounded coarse or cut in thin slices, a few sultana or other raisins, powdered cinnamon, and sugar. Beat three eggs well, mix them with the above, and spread the mass over the apples; slice a little butter over, and bake.

Aepfel Kuchen (No. 3) (1873)
(Apple Cake)

The apple-quarters are to be laid on good paste, as above, the yolks of four eggs, a tablespoonful of flour, a handful of almonds cut small, sugar, cinnamon, and the egg-whites whipped to a froth; must he all well mixed and spread over the apples; slice a little butter over, and bake.

Aepfel Kuchen (No. 4) (1873)
(Apple Cake)

Peel and slice apples enough for a tart; put them in an earthen or enamelled stew-pan with two ounces of raisins, the same of currants, sugar, cinnamon, two or three cloves, and a glass of wine; stew soft, and put them to cool. Mix a grated stale roll with an ounce of warmed butter, and two ounces of pounded almonds. Have a shallow tin lined with a thin paste; spread on this the apple mass a good half-inch thick, cover this with the crumb-mixture, and bake till the paste is nicely done.

Aepfel Kuchen (No. 5) (1873)
(Apple Cake)

Cut up apples to the size of hazel nuts, strew sugar among them; grate two small stale rolls, heat a quarter of a pound of butter to a cream, then the yolks of five eggs with it; add three ounces of almonds pounded or sliced thin, a quarter of a pound of sugar, some grated lemon-peel or powdered cinnamon, and lastly mix in the egg-whites, whipped to a snow, and bake on thin good paste.

Air Cake (1913)

Cream together a cupful of sugar and a rounding tablespoonful of butter. Add a well beaten egg and a cupful of sweet milk. Sift a large cupful of flour with a rounding teaspoonful of baking powder and a little salt. Mix well and add a little flour if necessary for a medium stiff batter.

Alliance Tourte (1922)
Bake three layers

One layer of the Brod Tourte (1922)
One layer of the Vienna Almond Tourte (1922)
One layer of the Mixture Plain Sponge Cake (1922)

Spread one layer with apricot marmalade, one layer with raspberry marmalade, put together, spread with almond icing and put in the oven to dry. Let cool and ice with fondant in three colours. Decorate with royal icing and fruit glace.

Allianz Torte (1873)
(Alliance Cake)

Bake three torten, one brod, one mandel, and one biscuit; which are the brown bread, almond, and sponge cakes, already described. They must be of the size directed for the Punsch Torte. Cover the brod torte with raspberry, or other fine preserve. Lay on this the sponge cake, and spread over it a layer of orange marmalade, or another kind of preserve. Put the almond cake on the top and cover the whole with a white or chocolate icing. The cakes must be baked a day or two before the finishing.

Almond and Citron Cake (1922)

1 cupful sugar
2 cupfuls flour
1 cupful Crisco
1 teaspoonful baking powder
5 eggs
½ wineglass brandy
½ lb. blanched chopped almonds
¼ teaspoonful powdered mace
¼ lb. shredded candied citron peel
1 teaspoonful salt

Cream Crisco and sugar thoroughly together, beat in yolks of eggs one by one, add almonds, citron, brandy, mace, flour, baking powder, salt, mix well and fold in whites of eggs beaten to a stiff froth. Turn into a papered cake pan and bake in a moderate oven for one hour. Cover with boiled frosting if liked.
Sufficient for: one large cake.

Almond Biscuit (1920)
(Biscuit aux Amandes)

Beat one pound of sugar in a basin with fifteen egg-yolks, obtaining a very light mixture; add five ounces of sweet and one of bitter almonds, pounded finely with two egg-whites; continue to whip together for a few minutes longer, then add five ounces of flour, five ounces of fecula, two ounces of melted fresh butter and lastly twelve stiffly whipped egg-whites. Pour this preparation into a pound cake or "manqué" mold lined with paper and bake in a very slow oven. Turn out the cake as soon as done, transferring it to a grate to cool; mask the surface with apricot marmalade and ice with almond milk fondant. After this icing is dry slip the cake on a round board covered with lace paper and decorate the top with royal icing. Surround the base with a circle of fine large preserved cherries and lozenges of angelica.

Almond Cake No. 1 (1904)

1 pound of fresh sweet and ½ ounce of bitter almonds
¾ pound of sifted sugar
12 - 15 eggs
1 lemon, a slip of mace
2 heaping spoonfuls of finely grated and sifted potato flour, or better still rice flour

The almonds are hulled, washed, dried and grated, the yolks of the eggs stirred with the sugar on which half of the lemon is grated, then add the juice, mace and the almonds, constantly stirring for ½ hour (see General Directions (1904)). Mix the whites of the eggs lightly through this, then the flour and baking powder, pour into a form, put into a moderately hot oven and bake for 1¼ hours. Do not jar the form; the heat must not be stronger from the bottom than from the top. To make this cake look prettier pour over it a frosting, and dot this with preserved or candied fruit sliced as thin as paper.

Almond Cake with Wheat Bread No. 2 (1904)

10 ounces of sifted sugar
8 ounces of fresh sweet and 1 ounce of bitter almonds, grated
12 - 14 eggs
6 ounces of not too stale grated and sifted wheat bread
1 lemon

Grate some of the lemon peel on the sugar, stir it with the juice and the yolks of the eggs for ¼ hour as directed under General Directions (1904), add the almonds to this and stir for ¼ hour longer. When this is done mix the wheat bread quickly through the mass and lightly stir through it the beaten whites of the eggs. The cake is baked and frosted the same as the above cake. It can also, be baked in layers and spread with jelly. A very pretty way is to colour one part green, one part red and one part brown.

Almond Cake No. 1 (1904)

½ pound of flour
¼ pound of butter
¼ pound of sifted sugar
¼ pound of sweet almonds
6 grated bitter almonds
2 fresh eggs

Melt the butter, then add the eggs one by one, sugar, almonds, and stir for ¼ hour, stir through this the flour, put into the pan, press out quite thin and bake to a nice yellow colour. Spread the cake with jelly; if sugar is preferred, cut the cake into pieces of the size required and sprinkle with sugar.

Almond Cake No. 2 (1904)

Puff paste (Good Batter for large Cakes 1904)
½ pound of sifted sugar
½ pound of pounded almonds
A few lemons
The whites of 2 eggs
2 - 2¼ ounces of crushed rock candy

Put the sugar into water, let it dissolve, stir in the almonds and the finely cut peel of a lemon with its juice, and then set aside to cool.
Make a puff paste, divide it into 2 parts, rolling it into an upper and lower crust, making the lower 1 inch wider than the upper crust, spread on the lower crust the almond syrup, leaving about 1 inch for an edge, put the top on this and bake the cake not too slowly. As soon as taken from the oven, spread over it the beaten whites of the eggs, cut the lemon into small cubes, taking out the seeds, lay the cubes on the cake together with a few whole lemon slices, sprinkle over it the rock candy, set in the oven for a few moments to dry.

Almond Cake (1912)

One pound of pulverized sugar
One pound of almonds chopped fine and roasted
Four eggs
One pound of citron

One teaspoon each of cinnamon and cloves
Two teaspoons baking powder

Two or more cups of flour

Roll out, cut and cook quickly.

Almond Cake (1898)

6 eggs
4 oz. pounded sweet almonds
½ oz. pounded bitter almonds
6 oz. sifted sugar

6 oz. flour
6 oz. butter
Finely grated rind of 1 lemon

Method: Whisk and strain the eggs, mix them with the almonds and sugar, and sift in the flour, beating constantly all the time. Then add the butter, which must be melted, but not hot, a small portion at a time, beating very thoroughly as each portion is added, and lastly the lemon rind. Line a cake tin with buttered paper, and rather more than half fill it with the mixture.
Bake the cake in a well-heated oven, covering the top with a buttered paper when sufficiently coloured. Test it with a small skewer or knife in the usual way.
Time: About 1 hour.

Almond Cake (1840)

Blanch, and pound in a mortar, four ounces of shelled sweet almonds and two ounces of shelled bitter ones; adding, as you proceed, sufficient rose-water to make them light and white. Sift half a pound of flour and powder a pound of loaf-sugar. Beat thirteen eggs; and when they are as light as possible, stir into them alternately the almonds, sugar, and flour; adding a grated nutmeg. Butter a large square pan; put in the mixture and bake it in a brisk oven about half an hour, less or more, according to its thickness. When cool, ice it. It is best when eaten fresh.

Almond Cake (1869)

Ten eggs
One pound of loaf-sugar
Half a pound of almonds

Half a pound of flour
One nutmeg

Beat the yolks first, then put in the sugar, beating them very light; blanch the almonds and pound them in a mortar, with rose water or the juice of a lemon; add them alternately with the flour, and the whites of the eggs well beaten. If you bake in one large cake, it will require an hour and a half in a slow oven; in small pans, it will take less time, and in either case, will require watching.

Almond Cake (1920)
(Gâteau d'Amandes)

From some parings of puff paste roll out a round flat twelve inches in diameter and three-sixteenths of an inch in thickness; lay it on a slightly dampened tart plate; cover this flat with an even layer of almond cream a quarter of an inch thick, placed half an inch inside the border; moisten the edge lightly and cover over with another layer of the paste of the same diameter and thickness as the lower one, only making it of puff paste prepared to six turns; press the edges well to attach the two flats together, and scallop this border with a small knife; egg the top, decorate it by making incisions in the shape of a rosette with the tip of a kitchen knife, then push the cake into a brisk oven to bake. As soon as done remove to the oven door, bestrew lightly with powdered sugar and return it again to the oven to have the top well glazed.

Almond Cake (1898)

6 eggs
4 oz. pounded sweet almonds
½ oz. pounded bitter almonds
6 oz. sifted sugar

6 oz. flour
6 oz. butter
Finely grated rind of 1 lemon

Method: Whisk and strain the eggs, mix them with the almonds and sugar, and sift in the flour, beating constantly all the time. Then add the butter, which must be melted, but not hot, a small portion at a time, beating very thoroughly as each portion is added, and lastly the lemon rind. Line a cake tin with buttered paper, and rather more than half fill it with the mixture.
Bake the cake in a well-heated oven, covering the top with a buttered paper when sufficiently coloured. Test it with a small skewer or knife in the usual way.
Time: About 1 hour.

Almond Cake (1876)

Beat one pound of sugar with the yolks of twelve eggs; whip the whites of nine eggs to a stiff froth and add to the above; then add one pound of flour, a half-pound of sweet almonds, a half-pound of bitter almonds, blanched and pounded with rose water to a cream, and six tablespoons of thick cream. Use the reserved whites of the eggs for frosting. This makes one large or two small cakes.

Almond Cake 1 (1894)

One and a half cups sugar
Half-cup butter
Two-thirds cup milk
Three cups flour
Whites of seven eggs

One teaspoon cream tartar
One- half teaspoon soda
Small cup almonds blanched and pounded
One large teaspoon of almond essence

Flavour frosting with rose water.

Almond Cake 2 (1894)

One cup butter
Two cups sugar
Three and one-half cups flour
One-half cup milk

Whites eight eggs
Two teaspoons cream tartar
One teaspoon soda
Flavour with almond

Almond Cake 3 (1894)

Two cups sugar
One cup butter
Whites six eggs
One cup milk
Three and a half cups flour

Heaping teaspoon cream tartar
Half teaspoon soda
Three teaspoons almond extract
Half-pound blanched almonds on top

Sprinkle with sugar.

Almond Cakes (1890)

One cupful of butter

1 cupful of sugar

1 egg
1 cupful of flour

¼ of a pound of grated almonds

Work with the hand and place in tart molds the thickness of pie crust. Bake in a slow oven.

Almond Cakes (1914)

Two cupfuls of rice flour
One quarter cupful of almond oil
One half cupful of chopped almonds

One and one half cupfuls of powdered sugar
Two eggs

Mix thoroughly two cupfuls of rice flour, one and one half cupfuls of powdered sugar, and half a cupful of blanched almonds, chopped very fine, with a quarter of a cupful of almond oil. Moisten with two beaten eggs. Use no water, and if too stiff, add more egg. Roll about quarter of an inch thick and cut in fanciful shapes. Place half an almond in the centre of each cake and bake them for one hour in a moderate oven. These cakes are certain to keep for a long time if they are placed in a tin box.

Almond Cakes (1911)

One-pound sifted flour
One-half pound butter
Three-fourths pound sugar
Two eggs

One-half teaspoon ground cinnamon
Four ounces of almonds blanched and chopped very fine
Two ounces of raisins finely chopped

Mix all the dry ingredients together, then rub in the butter, add eggs and spices last of all, roll out half an inch thick, cut in fancy shapes and bake in a slow oven.

Almond Cakes (1898)
(Small for Afternoon Tea)

3 eggs
2 oz. pounded sweet almonds
¼ oz. pounded bitter almonds
3 oz. sifted sugar

3 oz. flour
3 oz. butter
Finely grated rind of ½ a lemon

Method: Whisk and strain the eggs, mix them with the almonds and sugar, and sift in the flour, beating constantly all the time. Then add the butter, which must be melted, but not hot, a small portion at a time, beating very thoroughly as each portion is added; lastly add the lemon rind, and beat all well together. Butter some patty pans, and rather more than half fill each with the mixture. Bake in a well-heated oven, taking care that they are nicely browned but not burnt.
Time: 20 to 30 minutes.
Sufficient for: 12 small cakes.

Almond Cakes (1914)

½ cup butter
¼ tablespoon clove
1 egg
¼ tablespoon grated nutmeg
⅓ cup blanched almonds

Grated rind ½ lemon
½ cup sugar
2 tablespoons brandy
½ tablespoon cinnamon
2 cups flour

Cream the butter, add eggs well beaten, and almonds finely chopped; then add remaining ingredients. Toss on a floured board and roll to one-fourth inch in thickness. Shape with a round cutter, first dipped in flour, and bake in a slow oven until delicately browned.

Almond Cakes Candy (1894)

Whites five eggs, stir in sugar enough to make it stiff, with just a little pinch of flour, half pound almonds scalded and pounded. Drop on buttered tins and bake in a quick oven.

Almond Cheese Cake (1840)

This though usually called a cheese cake, is in fact a pudding.
Cut a piece of rennet about two inches square, wash off the salt in cold water, and wipe it dry. Put it into a tea-cup, pour on it sufficient lukewarm water to cover it, and let it soak all night, or at least several hours. Take a quart of milk, which must be made warm, but not boiling. Stir the rennet-water into it. Cover it and set it in a warm place. When the curd has become quite firm, and the whey looks greenish, drain off the whey, and set the curd in a cool place. While the milk is turning, prepare the other ingredients. Wash and dry half a pound of currants and dredge them well with flour. Blanch three ounces of sweet and one ounce of bitter almonds, by scalding and peeling them. Then cool them in cold water, wiping them dry before you put them into the mortar. If you cannot procure bitter almonds, peach kernels may be substituted. Beat them, one at a time, in the mortar to a smooth paste, pouring in with every one a few drops of rose water to prevent their being oily, dull-coloured, and heavy. If you put a sufficiency of rose water, the pounded almond paste will be light, creamy, and perfectly white. Mix, as you do them, the sweet and bitter almonds together. Then beat the yolks of eight eggs, and when light, mix them gradually with the curd. Add five table-spoonfuls of cream, and a tea-spoonful of mixed spice. Lastly, stir in, by degrees, the pounded almonds, and the currants alternately. Stir the whole mixture very hard. Bake it in buttered dishes, laying puff paste round the edges. If accurately made, it will be found delicious. It must be put in the oven immediately.

Almond Cheese Cakes (1911)

Blanch and pound to a fine paste, one cupful almonds. As you pound them add rose water, a few drops at a time to keep them from oiling. Add the paste to one cupful milk curd, together with a half-cup cream, one cupful sugar, three beaten egg yolks and a scant teaspoonful of rose water. Fill patty pans lined with paste .and bake in hot oven ten minutes.

Almond Cheese Cakes (1898)

3 eggs
4 oz. pounded sweet almonds
3 oz. sugar
2 oz. butter

1 dessert-spoonful lemon juice
Short crust, made with 8 oz. flour, other ingredients in proportion

Method: Whisk and strain the eggs, beat in the almonds and sugar, add the butter, which must be melted, but not hot, and the lemon juice, and beat the mixture for five minutes. Line 12 patty pans with the paste made as directed above; put some of the mixture into each and bake in a quick oven.
Time: About 15 minutes.
Sufficient for: 12 cheese cakes.

Almond Cream Cake (1893)

Two cupfuls of pulverized sugar
One-quarter cupful of butter

One cupful of sweet milk
Three cupfuls of flour

Two and a half teaspoonfuls of baking powder
Whites of four eggs, beaten very light

One-half teaspoonful of vanilla

Bake in four layers. Whip one cupful of sweet cream to a froth, stirring gradually into it half a cupful of pulverized sugar, a few drops of vanilla, one pound of almonds, blanched and chopped fine. Spread thick between layers; frost top and sides.

Almond Custard Cake (1876)

One pound of butter
One pound of sugar
One pound of flour

The whites of twelve eggs
And the yolks of seven

Custard:

One pint of sweet cream
One pound of soft shell almonds blanched

Whites of four eggs beaten to a froth with four spoons of sugar

Beat the cream to a froth with four spoons of sugar; then mix cream and eggs; chop almonds and add them the last thing. Flavour with almond or vanilla.

Almond Gingerbread (1898)

½ lb. golden syrup
¼ lb. butter
¼ lb. sugar

½ lb. flour
2 oz. candied orange peel
¼ lb. pounded sweet almonds

Method: Warm the golden syrup in a lined saucepan and melt the butter in it. Pour the hot syrup and butter into a basin, and beat the flour into it, then add the candied peel, cut into very small pieces, and the sugar, and lastly, the almonds. Mix very thoroughly. Butter a tin, pour in the mixture, and bake in a moderate oven. A few whole almonds may be sprinkled on the top of the cake if liked.
Time: About 45 minutes.
Sufficient for: 1 moderate sized cake.

Almond Marzapan (1904)

1 pound of the best sweet and ½ ounce of bitter almonds

1 pound of powdered sugar and rosewater

The almonds are prepared as in the Lubec Marzapan receipt. Then grate as fine as flour, mix with the sugar and rosewater to a stiff dough, which must not be too soft when rolling it out. Dust the bread board with sugar, divide the dough into round pieces, roll out to about the thickness of a table knife and cut into small round cakes or any other desired shape. In making the edge, roll the dough quite long, cut into narrow strips and brush with rosewater, and indent the edge with the thumb or with a knife. At this stage heat the cover of a tart pan with glowing coals, put the cakes on some paper, place the hot cover over them and bake to a light yellow. Let them cool on the paper and lay on a flat dish. In the meantime, stir 1 pound of powdered sugar with rosewater for ¾ hour, fill the marzapan to the edge with this and as soon as the sugar is hard lay over it some preserved fruits.

Almond or White Cake (1894)

Whites of six eggs
Two cups sugar

One cup butter
One cup milk

Three cups flour
One teaspoon cream tartar

Half teaspoon soda dissolved in the milk
Two teaspoons almond essence

Almond Silver Cake (1894)

One coffee cup sugar
One-half cup butter
beaten together to a cream

One-half cup milk
One-half teaspoon cream tartar
One-quarter teaspoon soda

Add whites four eggs, beaten to a stiff froth, and two full cups flour. Flavour with almond.

Almond Roll (1922)

1 cake yeast
½ oz. teaspoon almond extract
1 tablespoon sugar
½ cup chopped almonds
¼ cup water
3 tablespoons butter

1 cup milk
1 teaspoon salt
3½ or 4 cups flour
1 egg
½ of orange peel, grated

Dissolve yeast and sugar in lukewarm water. Scald and cool milk. Mix these with 1 cup of the flour. Let rise in a warm place until bubbly. Add beaten egg, melted butter, salt, extract, and flour. Work well into soft dough; let rise to double its height; roll out into a sheet, brush with melted butter, sprinkle peel and almonds on it and roll up; form into a roll and butter the top. Let rise again until light and bake 30 minutes at 400° F.

Almond Torte (1820)

4 eggs
½ c. almonds blanched finely chopped
1 c. powdered sugar

⅓ c. ground chocolate
¾ c. fine cracker crumbs
1 tsp. baking powder

Beat yolks of eggs until thick and lemon-coloured; add sugar gradually, then fold in whites of eggs beaten until stiff and dry. Add chocolate, almonds, baking powder and cracker crumbs. Bake in a moderately slow oven. Cool, split, and put whipped cream, sweetened and flavoured, between and on top. Garnish with angelica and candied cherries. This makes a most attractive dessert when baked in individual tins. When cool remove centres and fill with whipped cream.

Altdeutscher Napfkuchen (1910)

1 lb. clarified butter
1¼ lb. sifted flour
½ oz. baking powder
A little cardamom

8 eggs
¾ lb. sugar
¾ lb. currants
Grated rind of a lemon

Cream the butter and the sugar and then add the yolks of eggs. Beat ¾ hour to a froth, then add the grated lemon peel and cardamom and alternately the whites of eggs, whisked to a snow, and the sifted flour, mixed with the baking powder. Finally stir in the currants lightly. Bake about 1¼ hour.

American Fruit Cake (1922)

2 lbs. Sugar
2 lbs. butter

2 lbs. flour
16 eggs

½ pt. molasses
½ pt. brandy
4 lbs. currants
2 lbs. seeded raisins
2 lbs. sultanas
12 oz. citron
4 oz. orange peel

1 oz. allspice
1 oz. cinnamon
½ oz. ginger
½ oz. cloves
½ oz. mace
2 oz. lemon peel

Soak the prepared fruit mixed with the spices in the brandy and molasses overnight. Before using, cream the butter, sugar and eggs the same as for Pound Cakes. Mix in the flour, and when half mixed add the fruit; finish and bake as directed.

Angel Cake (1922)

Angel Cake or Angel Food is a cousin of the sponge cake made from the whites of eggs only. The quality differs according to how much more or less flour is used in the mixture. The cornstarch is added to make the cake eat short; the cream of tartar to whiten the mixture. (If the latter is left out the cakes get a dull dark colour like as if a very dark flour has been used; and the cake feels dry and tough).
The cakes are best baked in the round pans with a wide center tube.
The moulds are not lined with paper or greased like for other cakes. On the contrary, they should be dry and free from grease, so the cake sticks to the moulds when baked.
Bake the cake in a medium heat of 300 degrees Fahrenheit. When done turn upside down and let cool. This prevents the cake from shrinking and keeps it light. When cold loosen the cake around the edge, knock the pan on the table and the cake should drop out. Brush off the brown crumbs and ice with vanilla.
From the Angel Cake mixture is made a variety of fancy flavoured cakes, as Rose, Violet, Pistachio, Strawberry, Raspberry, etc., using the proper colours and icings.
Mixture Angel Cake (No. 4) is a very light mixture - the old original angel food. The whites should not be beaten up fully for this one mixture, only till the eggs stand up on the beater.
The others are standard mixtures, generally used.

Angel Cake (No. 1) (1922)

One quart of whites
One and three quarters pounds of sugar
Eighteen ounces of flour

Two ounces of cornstarch
A half-ounce of cream of tartar

Angel Cake (No. 2) (1922)

One quart of whites
One and one quarter pounds of sugar
Eight ounces of flour

Eight ounces of cornstarch
A half-ounce of cream of tartar

Angel Cake (No. 3) (1922)

One quart of whites
Two pounds of sugar
Fourteen ounces of flour

Two ounces of cornstarch
A half of cream of tartar

Angel Cake (No. 4) (1922)

One quart of whites
Two pounds of sugar

Twelve ounces of flour
Two ounces of cornstarch

A half-ounce of cream of tartar

Angel Cake (No. 5) (1922)

One quart of whites
One pound of sugar
Fourteen ounces of flour

Two ounces of cornstarch
A half-ounce of cream of tartar

Mix the flour, starch, sugar and cream of tartar well together; sifting it three or four times. Beat the whites firm same as for meringues. Add a handful of the mixed sugar and flour and beat it in with the flavour; then add the flour and sugar; mix and fill into the mould, and bake.

Angel Cake (1893)

The whites of eleven eggs beaten to a stiff froth; add one and one- half cups of pulverized sugar and one teaspoonful of vanilla extract; take one even cup of flour and one teaspoonful cream of tartar and sift with flour four times; beat lightly but thoroughly; bake fifty minutes in an ungreased pan; cut out when cold.

Angel Cake (1920)
(Gâteau des Anges)

Pour twenty egg-whites into a basin and whip them till quite firm; at once add ten ounces of sugar, part of it flavoured with vanilla, and continue whipping the whole until quite smooth, then add half a pound of flour into which has been mixed half a teaspoonful of cream of tartar and sifted several times through a sieve; mix all together lightly till smooth. With this preparation fill some angel cake molds, eight to nine inches in diameter, three-quarters full; these should be quite dry. without any buttering. Push the cakes into a very slack oven to cook for forty to fifty minutes, then take them out and keep them in their molds for two hours; now pass a small kitchen knife between the pan and the cake, knock the edges of the former gently on the table to detach the cake and turn it on a grate; pare the tops very straight, ice with royal icing and dress on a lace-paper-covered board or dish; after the icing is dry decorate with more of the royal icing.

Angel Cake (1894)

Whites of eleven eggs
One and one-half cups granulated sugar
One cupful flour, measured after being sifted four times

One teaspoon cream tartar
One teaspoon vanilla extract

Sift the flour and cream tartar together; beat the whites to a stiff froth; beat the sugar slowly into the eggs, adding the seasoning and flour, stirring quickly and lightly; bake for forty minutes in a moderate oven. Do not grease the pan and use a new tin or a bright one.

Angel Cake 1 (1893)

Put into one tumbler of flour
one teaspoon cream tartar, sift five times

Sift 1½ glasses white powdered sugar
Beat to stiff froth the whites of 11 egg

Stir the sugar into the eggs by degrees, very lightly, carefully adding 3 teaspoons vanilla extract, then add flour, stirring quickly and lightly. Pour it into a clean, bright tin cake dish, which should not be buttered or lined. Bake at once in moderate oven about 40 minutes. When done, let it remain in tin, turning it upside down with the sides resting on the top of two saucers, so that the current of air will pass under it.

Angel Cake 2 (1893)

Whites of 9 eggs,
1 teaspoon cream tartar, beaten stiff
Add 1¼ cups sugar, sifted 4 times, beat to a stiff froth

Fold in 1 cup of flour, with Crystaline salt, sifted 7 times

Bake in unbuttered angel cake tin 40 minutes in moderately hot oven.

Angel Cake (1893)

Whites 10 eggs, whipped stiff
1 cup flour
1½ cups sugar

½ cup cream tartar
1 teaspoon vanilla
Chrystaline salt

Angel Cake (1911)

1 ½ cups of sugar
½ cup of butter
½ cup of milk
2 ½ cups of flour

1 teaspoon of cream tartar
¼ teaspoon of soda
5 eggs (the whites only)

Put all the parts together and then add the whites of the eggs beaten to a froth. The same recipe, using the yolks, makes a very nice cake.

Angel Cake (1889)

Whites of eight eggs, well beaten
One cup pulverized sugar
Half-cup flour
Half cup corn starch

One teaspoonful baking powder, sifted with flour, sugar, and starch
Add eggs
Flavour with lemon

Angel Cake with Nut and Whipped Cream Filling (1912)

Make angel food and bake in layers or bake in mould and split. Whip cream very stiff, sweeten and flavour to taste and add chopped almonds; put between layers; it can be iced with marshmallow icing if desired and nuts sprinkled over.

Angel Food (1820)

1½ c. sugar
1 c. flour
11 eggs

1 tsp. vanilla
1 tsp. cream tartar

Sift flour four or five times. Sift sugar the same. Beat whites until stiff. Add cream of tartar to whites when beating. Sift into the whites a little of the sugar at a time and beat. Fold in the flour a little at a time and fold just enough to mix flour. Do not beat. Vanilla may be added to whites. Bake in a Turk's Head pan in a slow oven for one hour. Invert to cool. Frost with any white frosting.

Angel Food (1893)

Whites of fifteen eggs
One and one-half cups of powdered sugar
One cup of flour
One teaspoon of cream of tartar

Sift sugar three times; mix cream of tartar with flour, sift seven times; beat eggs stiff, add sugar gradually, beating all the time with egg beater; take out; stir the flour quickly with wooden spoon; do not grease or line the tin; bake slowly and steadily; turn out on platter for frosting.

Angel Food Cake (1912)

The whites of eleven large or twelve small eggs beaten stiff
One and one-half scant cups of flour
one and three-fourths cup of Sugar
One scant teaspoon of cream of tartar

Following above directions for mixing and baking.

Angel Marshmallow Cake (1912)

Whites of thirteen eggs beaten one-half. Then add one teaspoon of cream of tartar and beat until very stiff. Sift in gradually one and three-fourths cups of sugar, flavour with one teaspoon of vanilla, fold in one and one-half cups of flour previously sifted several times. Bake in layer cake pans about twenty minutes. When cool fill with marshmallow frosting. Ornament the top with marshmallow, cut in triangles.

Angel Sponge Cake (1820)

3 eggs
1⅓ c. flour
1 c. sugar
½ c. boiling water
½ tsp. baking powder
1 tsp. flavouring

Beat whites until stiff. Beat yolks, adding a pinch of salt. Add to whites and beat. Add sugar beating with egg beater. Add boiling water, then flour and lastly baking powder. Add flavouring. Bake in ungreased cake tin, in a hot, then moderate oven for 35-45 minutes. When done turn the cake tin upside down between two dishes until cold.

Aniskuchen (1910)
(Aniseed Cakes)

4 oz. sugar
4 eggs
1 teaspoonful aniseed
4 oz. flour

Beat the eggs and sugar ½ hour to a froth, then add the pounded aniseed, and gradually the sifted flour. Put into little heaps (with at least 6 inches between each) on a well-buttered sheet of tin and bake in a moderate oven, after standing 2 hours.

Another Pretty Cake (1876)

Bake white cake in three layers, with pink frosting. Cut it in small squares of about two inches and alternate it in the basket with chocolate cake made as follows:
Bake the gold cake in corresponding thin layers. Scrape fine two tablespoons of chocolate; put it into a tin cup and pour over it just enough hot water to dissolve it into a cream, setting it on the stove for a moment. Stir this into the frosting, making it just a pretty shade of brown. Cut this cake into diamonds. I always bake my thin cakes in square tin pans. Half the receipt for gold cake makes two thin ones. The white of one egg is enough for one cake. The amount of chocolate given is intended for two.

Apees (1840)

Rub a pound of fresh butter into two pounds of sifted flour, and mix in a pound of powdered white sugar, a grated nutmeg, a table-spoonful of powdered cinnamon, and four large table-spoonfuls of carraway seeds. Add a wine glass of rose water and mix the whole with sufficient cold water to make it a stiff dough. Roll it out into a large sheet about a third of an inch in thickness and cut it into round cakes with a tin cutter or with the edge of a tumbler. Lay them in buttered pans, and bake them in a quick oven, (rather hotter at the bottom than at the top) till they are of a very pale brown.

Apfelkuchen I (1910)
(Apple Cake)

Prepare as Pflaumenkuchen, allowing 3 lbs. apples, cut into slices.

Apfelkuchen II (1910)
(Apple Cake)

½ lb. flour
½ oz. yeast
½ teaspoonful castor sugar
Cinnamon
3 oz. butter

½ gill lukewarm milk
A little cream
1 egg
Apples or other fruit

Put ½ pound of flour in a basin, make a hole in the middle and pour in 3 ounces butter (melted), a little cream, ½ ounce yeast, and ½ teaspoonful castor sugar; mix with the yeast ½ gill lukewarm milk and 1 beaten up egg.
Strain this into the middle of the flour, mix and knead all well together, cover the basin over and put it away to rise till it is twice its original size.
Then take the dough, roll it out thinly, and lay it on buttered tins or plates, spreading all over it melted butter, a good sprinkling of castor sugar and powdered cinnamon; cover thickly with apples peeled, cored, and cut into thick slices. Bake in a quick oven.
Other kinds of fruit may be used thus.

Apfelkuchen mit Blätterteig (1910)
(Apple Cake with Puff Paste)

Make some puff paste with ½ lb. butter and ½ lb. flour. Roll out thinly in two layers. Place one upon a buttered sheet of tin. Peel ¾ lb. apples, cut them into slices, stew them in ½ lb. sugar and ¼ pint water. Drain superfluous water off. Sprinkle over the paste on the tin with breadcrumbs, place the apples on it, cover with the other layer of paste, brush over with egg, sprinkle with sugar and bake in a moderate oven for ½ hour. Cut into squares and eat with whipped cream.

Apfelsinen Torte (No.1) (1873)
(Orange Tart or Cake)

Make a paste as directed for linzer torte, using threequarters of a pound of flour, half a pound of butter, quarter of a pound of sugar, quarter of a pound of almonds blanched and pounded, three well-beaten eggs, and the yolks of three or four hard-boiled ones. Roll out the paste as thin as possible, so that it will hold together when moved; it must not be more than the third of an inch thick. Lay a large plate on it to cut it round by. Form the cuttings of the paste into a small cord, either plaited threefold or twisted in two; moisten the edge of the cake and lay this round. Then bake it a rich yellow in a moderate oven. It must be baked on buttered paper; indeed, it may be rolled out partly on this, so laid on the flat baking-tin, and slid off by the aid of large knives when done. During the baking, thoroughly beat the yolks of eight eggs and whites of two; stir in a quarter of a pound of powdered sugar, the grated peel of three oranges and their juice. Stir this with a wire whisk over the fire till it thickens; then take it from the fire. When the cake and cream are both partly cooled, mix into the cream the whites of four eggs whisked to a stiff snow, with a tablespoonful of sifted sugar. Spread the cream over the cake; the former must have boiled to the thickness of jam. Peel and divide an orange into its separate half-moons, without breaking their skins. When the torte is cold, lay these on its centre in the form of a star or other device, and sift sugar over them.

Apfelsinen Torte (No. 2) (1873)
(Orange Cake)

Bake the same form of cake, of an ordinary tart paste. Make a cream as above, with three well-beaten eggs, three oranges, a quarter of a pound of sugar, and a piece of butter the size of a walnut. The whites of three eggs whipped to a snow may be added, as above, or dispensed with. Finish and ornament with orange slices as above.

Apfel-Torte (1910)

6 oz. butter	4 oz. currants
1 egg	10 oz. flour
2 yolks	2 tablespoonsful sour cream
2 lbs. apples	2 oz. sweet almonds
6 oz. sugar	

In addition:

½ gill sour cream	4 yolks
A little extra sugar,	

Cream the butter, add 1 egg, 2 extra yolks, 2 oz. sugar, 1 tablespoonful water and then the flour and mix to a paste. Roll out and line the bottom and sides of a shallow, broad, cake tin. Bake a few minutes, but not completely. Grate the almonds and mix with 2 tablespoonsful of sour cream. Spread on the cake and sprinkle over with grated breadcrumbs.
Peel the apples, cut them into thin slices and mix with the currants and 4 oz. sugar. Place these on the breadcrumbs and pour over them ½ gill of slightly sour cream, beaten up with 4 yolks and a little sugar. Place in the oven and finish baking.

Apple Cake (1904)

For the dough take:

¾ pound of flour	Good apples
½ pound of freshened butter	Wine
3 ounces of sifted sugar	Sugar
1 egg	Lemon peel
2 spoonfuls of water	Whole cinnamon
2 spoonfuls of rum	

Stir the butter to a cream, then add sugar, egg, rum, water and flour, stir all for a short time, put into a cake pan, and with a flat wooden ladle press out the dough, having it a little thicker on the sides so as to form an edge; sprinkle some grated bread over the bottom. In the meantime, cook thickly sliced apples in wine, sugar, lemon peel and whole cinnamon until half done, and after they are cold lay them neatly on the cake and bake to a golden - not brown - colour. Boil down the juice until quite thick, and when the cake is served pour it over the apples.

Apple Cake (1920)

Prepare a dough the same as for Butter Cakes and divide it into 6 parts, as the dough for Apple Cake has to be thinner than for Butter Cakes; line 6 shallow tin pans with the dough and set it to rise to double its height; in the meantime pare, core and cut into eighths some large, tart apples and lay them together closely in long rows over the cake; drop 1 tablespoonful melted butter over each cake, sprinkle over some granulated sugar and bake in a hot oven; when done dust with powdered sugar.

Apple Cake (1920)
(Gâteau aux Pommes)

Prepare a frolle paste; keep it in a cool place on ice for twenty minutes. Cut about fifteen good apples in four, peel, shred them small and cook partially, while tossing them over a brisk fire, in a pan with some butter, sugar and vanilla added, then set aside to cool. Roll out two-thirds of the paste, not too thin, four inches wide and about the length of the baking sheet on a floured table; roll it over the rolling-pin to unroll on a baking sheet and cut it away straight; surround the edges with a narrow-raised rim and put in a moderate oven to half bake and leave till quite cold. Then fill the center with the cooked apples and finish exactly the same as the gooseberry cakes.

Apple Cake (1898)

Ingredients:

3 lbs. apples
¾ lb. sugar
2 tablespoonfuls water
3 oz. butter

Juice and chopped rind of a lemon
Paste, made with 1 lb. flour, and other ingredients in proportion

Method: Pare, core, and quarter the apples, and boil them with the sugar, water, chopped lemon rind and juice, until quite tender. Then take them off the fire, stir in the butter, which must be melted, and set the mixture aside to cool.
Well butter a cake tin. Roll the paste about ¼ inch thick and cut out a piece to fit the bottom of the tin, and a long strip to line the sides. Fit them in carefully and cut an inch strip of paste to cover the join round the bottom of the tin. Damp this slightly with a paste brush dipped in warm water before fixing it, so as to make it stick firmly and strengthen the mould. Fill with the preparation of apple, roll out the cover of paste and lay it over the top.
Bake in a moderately quick oven and cover the top with a sheet of buttered paper should it seem inclined to burn or take too deep a colour.
Turn out carefully, sprinkle with sifted sugar, and serve very hot.
Time: About 1 hour.
Sufficient for: 5 or 6 persons.

Apple Cake with Lemon Sauce (1913)

2 cups flour
1/2 teaspoon salt
1/2 teaspoon soda
1 teaspoon cream of tartar
3 tablespoons Cottolene

1 egg well beaten
7/8 cup milk
4 tart fine flavoured apples
3 tablespoons granulated sugar
1/4 teaspoon cinnamon

Process: Mix and sift the dry ingredients in the order given; rub in Cottolene with tips of fingers; add beaten egg to milk and add slowly to first mixture stirring constantly, then beat until dough is smooth. Spread dough evenly in a shallow, square layer cake pan to the depth of one inch. Core, pare and cut apples in eighths, lay them in parallel rows on top of dough, pressing the sharp edge into the dough half the depth of apples. Sprinkle sugar and cinnamon over top. Bake in hot oven twenty-five to thirty minutes. Serve hot with butter as a luncheon dish, or as a dessert for dinner with Lemon Sauce.

Apple Cakes (1878)

Pare, core, and slice a quart of apples, (price five cents)
Stew them with half their weight in sugar, about one pound, (cost about twelve cents)
The grated rind and juice of a lemon, (cost two cents)
One ounce of batter, (cost two cents)
A very little grated nutmeg

When they are tender beat them with an egg whisk until they are light, drop them by the dessert-spoonful on buttered paper laid on a baking sheet, and bake them in a cool oven until they are firm, which will be in about fifteen minutes. When they are cool put them in a tin box until wanted for use. The cost will be about twenty cents.

Apple Cake made of puff paste (1904)

Make a puff paste
Take nice apples
2 ounces of almonds neatly sliced
1 - 2 lemons
Sugar
Cinnamon
A few spoonfuls of grated bread

Roll one-half of the dough for an under, crust and strew over it some grated bread and then put on the sliced and cored apples with the almonds, lemon slices, cinnamon and the necessary sugar; over the top put a crust, or a lattice as given for gooseberry pie.
The cake is baked in a quick oven to a nice yellow colour.

Apple Cake with Almond Icing (1904)

Take 18 - 20 nice cooking apples of medium size and for the filling nicely washed currants, sugar, cinnamon, citron and a little butter.

For icing: 6 fresh eggs, ¼ pound of sugar, ¼ pound of grated almonds and ½ teaspoonful of mace.
Pare the apples, take out the core and leave the apples whole, put them into a pan side by side and fill with currants, sugar, cinnamon, citron and a small piece of butter. Then take the yolks of the eggs, sugar, almonds and mace, stir together for ¼ hour, mix with the beaten whites of the eggs, pour over the apples and bake for 1 – 1 ¼ hours.
Serve this if possible when warm; if made the day before set in the oven for ½ hour before serving.

Apple Cheese Cakes (1898)

Ingredients:

½ lb. apples
4 oz. sugar
2 oz. butter
2 eggs
The rind and juice of ½ a lemon
1 dessert-spoonful water
Paste, made with 8 oz. flour, and other ingredients in proportion

Method: Pare and core the apples and cut them into quarters. Boil them with the sugar and water until they become a smooth marmalade. Take them off the fire and leave them until lukewarm. Then beat in the lemon juice and grated rind and the butter, which must be melted. Beat the eggs thoroughly, and strain them slowly into the mixture, beating all the time, and continue beating for 2 minutes. Line some patty pans with the paste. Put some of the mixture in each and bake in a moderately quick oven.
Time: 20 to 30 minutes.
Sufficient for: 1 2 cheese cakes.

Apple Gems (1876)

Rich flavoured, tart apples, pared, cored and grated, mixed with gem dough, are nice if one wants a simple fruit cake. Take three good sized apples to one mold of gems; make the dough nearly thick enough to roll.

Apple Griddle Cakes (1902)

Put 1 cup finely chopped apple in 1 qt. of any griddle batter; stir well to keep the apple evenly distributed.

Apple Roll (1922)

2 cups flour
2 teaspoons baking powder
4 tablespoons sugar
½ teaspoon salt
5 tablespoons shortening
⅔ cup sweet milk

Sift dry ingredients, then cut in the shortening, add the milk, stirring all together. Roll dough on board about ¼ of an inch thick, keeping dough in oblong shape; spread with melted butter, then a generous layer of finely chopped apples and sugar. Sprinkle cinnamon over this and roll tightly into a long roll. Cut slices about 2 inches thick and place in greased pan. Keep slices close together; on top of each slice place ⅓ of an apple. Bake in oven until apples on top are brown.
Serve hot with rich sauce.

Apple Sauce Cake (1820)

2 c. flour
½ c. nuts, chopped
1 c. sugar
½ c. raisins
2 tsp. soda
1½ c. apple sauce medium thick, (unsweetened)
2 tsp. spice
3 tbsp. chocolate
½tsp. salt
½ c. melted fat
1 tbsp. cornstarch

Sift all dry materials. Add nuts, raisins, applesauce, and lastly melted fat. Bake as a shallow loaf in moderate oven about 45-60 minutes. The nuts and raisins may be increased to 1 c. each for a richer cake. Apricot, prune or peach sauce of similar consistency may be used.

Apple Sauce Cake (1912)

Two cups of unsweetened apple sauce
Two cups of white sugar
One-half cup of butter
One cup of raisins
One cup of currants, citron and almonds, if you like
Four cups of flour
One teaspoon of soda dissolved in one-third cup of hot water
One-half teaspoon each of cinnamon, cloves and nutmeg

Bake as fruit cake in moderate oven.

Apple Sauce Cake (1911)

1 cup sugar
1 cup apple sauce
½ cup shortening

1½ cups flour (full measure)
1 teaspoon saleratus
Raisins and spice of all kinds

Apple Sauce Cake (1917)
(without Butter, Eggs, or Milk)

1 cup unsweetened apple sauce
1/4 teaspoon salt
1/2 cup melted shortening
1 teaspoon cinnamon
1 cup sugar

1/2 teaspoon nutmeg
1 teaspoon soda
1/4 teaspoon clove
2 cups flour
1 cup raisins seeded and chopped

Mix in order given, sifting dry ingredients together, beat well, pour into a deep pan, and bake about one hour in a slow oven.

Apple Sauce Fruit Cake without Milk (1922)

1 cupful brown sugar
1 teaspoonful powdered cinnamon
1½ cupfuls apple sauce
2½ cupfuls flour
1 teaspoonful grated nutmeg
½ cupful Crisco

2 teaspoonfuls baking soda
1 lb. raisins
½ teaspoonful salt
1 teaspoonful powdered cloves
3 tablespoonfuls vinegar

Cream Crisco and sugar thoroughly together, add apple sauce, flour, raisins, spices, salt, and soda mixed with vinegar. Mix and pour into greased and floured cake tin and bake in moderate oven one and a half hours.
Sufficient for one cake.

Apple-Sauce Torte (1922)

4 eggs
2 cups apple-sauce (unsweetened)
1 can evaporated milk

Juice of 1 lemon
½ cup melted butter

Mix yolks of eggs, apple-sauce, lemon juice and milk together; add stiffly beaten whites. Line sides and bottom of torte pan with one package of ground graham crackers, mixed with scant cup melted butter. Bake in a slow oven. Reserve some of the graham cracker mixture to sprinkle on top of cake. Serve with whipped cream.

Apple and Cranberry Shortcake (1917)

4 apples
2 teaspoons cornstarch
1/2 cup cranberries
2 tablespoons sultana raisins

1/2 cup water
A few gratings of orange peel
1/2 cup sugar

Core and slice apples, add cranberries and water; cook ten minutes, and press through a sieve; mix sugar and cornstarch, stir into fruit; add raisins and grated rind, and simmer ten minutes; spread between and on top of shortcake, and garnish with a few raisins.

Apricot Cake (N.D)

1 cup flour
1 teaspoon baking powder

½ cup sugar
¾ cup of milk

Pour into small buttered pan about size of bread tin, lay cooked apricots on top (as many as you wish). Sprinkle with sugar, little cinnamon and chunks of butter. Bake in moderate oven, and serve with whipped cream.

Arrow Root Cakes (Small) (1898)

Ingredients:

1 oz. arrowroot
2 oz. flour
2 oz. castor sugar

Rind of ½ a lemon
2 oz. butter
2 eggs

Method: Beat and strain the eggs, and beat into them by degrees the arrowroot, flour, sugar, and finely-grated lemon rind. Melt the butter and add it very gradually to the mixture, beating all the time. Continue beating for 3 minutes. Butter some patty-pans, and half fill each with the mixture. Bake in a moderate oven.
Time: 15 to 20 minutes.
Sufficient for: 12 small cakes.

Arrowroot Cake (1898)

Ingredients:

3 oz. arrowroot
3 oz. castor sugar
3 oz. flour, rind of 1 lemon

4 oz. butter
4 eggs

Method: Beat and strain the eggs, then beat into them by degrees the arrowroot, sugar, flour, and finely-chopped lemon rind. Melt the butter and add it very gradually to the mixture, beating thoroughly all the time. Continue beating for 3 minutes, then pour the mixture into a cake tin, lined with buttered paper, and bake very carefully a nice light brown.
Time: About 1 hour.
Sufficient for: 1 cake of moderate size.

Ash Cake (1913)
(Pioneer)

This is possible only with wood fires - to campers or millionaires. Make dough as for plain bread, but add the least trifle of salt, sweep the hot hearth very clean, pile the dough on it in a flattish mound, cover with big leaves - cabbage leaves will do at a pinch, or even thick clean paper, then pile on embers with coals over them and leave for an hour or more, according to size. Take up, brush off ashes, and break away any cindery bits. Serve with new butter and fresh buttermilk. This was sometimes the sole summer supper of very great families in the old time. Beyond a doubt, ash cake properly cooked has a savoury sweetness possible to no other sort of corn bread.

Aunt Amy's Cake (1911)

Two eggs
One and one-half cups of sugar
One cup of sour milk
One-half cup of butter

Two cups of flour
One teaspoonful of soda
Spice to taste

This is a good cake and one which is also inexpensive in baking. Use a moderate oven and bake in loaves rather than sheets.

Aunt Rachel's Flannel Cakes (1876)

One-quart warm water, a little more than lukewarm
One cup yeast

One cup corn meal and flour enough to make very stiff

Let it rise overnight for breakfast or mix at noon for tea. When light, or just before baking, put in one egg., one scant cup of milk or cream, one teaspoon soda and one of salt. The batter will be very thin. Bake on griddles as pancakes.

Part 3: B

Baba (1881)
Baba (1920)
Baba Syruped or Iced (1920)
(Baba au Sirop ou Glacé)
Baba with Marsala (1920)
(Baba au Marsala)
Babas with Rum-Small (1920)
(Petits Babas au Rhum)
Baked Rice Cake (1902)
Bakers' Lemon Snaps (1876)
Baltimore Cake 1 (1911)
Baltimore Cake 2 (1911)
Banana Cake (N.D.)
Banana Cake (1920)
Banana Cream Cake (1922)
Banana Shortcake (1917)
Banbury Cakes (1913)
Banbury Cakes (1898)
Bangor Corn Cake (1894)
Barneys (1905)
Batter Cakes 1 (1876)
Batter Cakes 2 (1876)
Batter Cakes 3 (1876)
Batter Cakes (1913)
(Old Style)
Baum-Torte (1910)
(Tree Spongecake)
Bavarian Cheese Cake (1908)
Beautiful Cake (1893)
Beef and Bacon Cakes (1917)
Beef and Sausage Cakes (1913)
Beef Cake (1898)
Beef Cakes (1840)
Beef Hash Cakes (1911)
Berliner Pfannkuchen (1910)
(Berlin Pancakes)
Berliner Waffeln (1910)
(Berlin Wafers)
Berry Muffins (1911)
Berwick Cake (1893)
Berwick Sponge Cake (1876)
Best Jumbles (1922)
Birthday Cake (1897)
(Födelsedags-kaka)
Biscuit à la Hernani (1920)
(Biscuit à la Hernani)
Biscuit-Torte (1910)
(Spongecake)
Biscuit Torte (No.1) (1893)
(A Sponge Cake)
Biscuit Torte (No.2) (1893)
(Sponge Cake)
Blackberry Jam Cake (1820)
Black Cake (1876)
Black Cake (1840)
Black Cake (1869)
Black Cake No. 1 (1889)
Black Cake No. 2 (1889)
Black Cake with Prune Filling (1922)
Black Chocolate Cake (1922)
Black Cake Icing (1840)
Black Clouds (1876)
Black Molasses Fruit Cakes (1922)
(Cheap)
Blackberry Roll (1922)
Blätter Teig (No. 1) (1873)
(Puff Paste)
Blätter Teig (No. 2) (1873)
(Puff Paste)
Blätter Torte, von Linzerteig (1873)
(Linzer Leaves)
Blätterteig-Bretzel (1910)
(Puff Paste Twists)
Blechkuchen (1910)
Blitzkuchen (1910)
(Lightning Cake)
Blitzkuchen (1873)
(Blitz Cake)
Blueberry Cake (1893)
Blueberry Cake (1893)
(For breakfast)
Blueberry Cake (1894)
Blueberry Cake (1890)
Blueberry Cake 1 (1894)
Blueberry Cake 2 (1894)
Blueberry Muffins (1917)
Blueberry Muffins (1911)
Blueberry Muffins (1922)
Blueberry Muffins (N.D.)
Blueberry Tea Cake (1913)
Boiled Raisin Cake (1912)
Boiled Rice Muffins (1911)
Boiling Water Cake (1922)
Boston Cream Cakes 1 (1876)
Boston Cream Cakes 2 (1876)
Boston Flat Cake (1913)
Boston Gingerbread (1894)
Boston Pound Cake (1876)
Boswell Cake (1889)
Bran Muffins (1917)
Bran Muffins (1922)
Bran Muffins 1 (N.D.)

Bran Muffins 2 (N.D.)
Braune Pfeffernüsse (1910)
(Mecklenburgische)
Braunschweiger Kuchen (1873)
(Brunswick Cake)
Braut Torte (1873)
(Bride Cake)
Bread Batter Cakes (1869)
Bread Cake (1904)
Bread Cake (1894)
Bread Cake (1840)
Bread Cake (1893)
Bread Cake (1911)
Breakfast Cake (1894)
Breakfast Cake (1893)
Breakfast Cakes (1876)
Breakfast Cakes (1911)
Breakfast Cakes (1893)
Breakfast Gems (1876)
Bremen Butter Cake (1904)
Breton Cake (1920)
(Gâteau Breton)
Brick House Bride's Cake (1911)
Bride Cake (1864)
Bride's Cake (1904)
Bride's Cake (1913)
Bride's Cake (1911)
Bride's Cake 1 (1894)
Bride's Cake 2 (1894)
Bridgeport Cake (1876)
Bridgeport Cake (1876)
Bridgewater Cake (1894)
Brioche, or Propheten Kuchen (1873)
(Brioche)
Brioche Cake (1920)
Brod Kuchen (1912)
Brod Torte (1873)
(Brown Bread Cake No. 1)
Brod Torte (1873)
(Brown Bread Cake No. 2)
Brod Torte mit Chocolade (1873)
(Bread Cake with Chocolate)
Brown Nut Cake (N.D.)
(Brown Sugar Cake 1893)
Bublanina Cherry Cake (1920)
Buckwheat Cakes (No. 1) (1904)
Buckwheat Cakes (No, 2) (1904)
Buckwheat Cakes (1922)
Buckwheat Cakes (1864)
Buckwheat Cakes (1913)
Buckwheat Cakes (1840)
Buckwheat Cakes (1869)
Buckwheat Cakes (1894)
Buckwheat Cakes with Baking Powder (1920)
(Galettes de Sarrasin à la Levure en Poudre)
Buckwheat Cakes with Sour Milk (1876)
Buckwheat Cakes with Yeast (1920)
(Galettes de Sarrasin à la Levure)
Butter Cakes (1920)
Butter Cakes (with Baking Powder) (1920)
Butterkuchen (1910)
Butterless-Milkless-Eggless Cake (1922)
Butter-Mandel-Torte (1910)
(Almond Spongecake)
Butter-milk Batter Cakes (1869)
Butter-milk Cake (1911)
Butter-milk Cakes (1869)
Butter-milk Cakes (1869)
Buttermilk Muffins (1911)
Butter Sponge Cake (No. 1) (1922)
Butter Sponge Cake (No.2) (1922)
Butter Sponge Cake (No.3) (1922)
Butter-Zopf (1910)
(Butter Twist)

Baba (1881)

One pound of flour; take one quarter of it and make a sponge with half an ounce of compressed yeast and a little warm water, set it to rise, make a hole in the rest of the flour, add to it ten ounces of butter, three eggs, and a dessert-spoonful of sugar, a little salt, unless your butter salts it enough, which is generally the case. Beat all together well, then add five more eggs, one at a time, that is to say, add one egg and beat well, then another and beat again, and so on until the five are used. When the paste leaves the bowl it is beaten enough, but not before; then add the sponge to it, and a large half ounce of citron chopped, the same of currants, and an ounce and a half of sultana raisins, seedless. Let it rise to twice its size, then bake it in an oven of dark yellow paper heat; the small round babas are an innovation of the pastry-cook to enable him to sell them uncut. But the baba proper should be baked in a large, deep, upright tin, such as a large charlotte russe mold, when they keep for several days fresh, and if they get stale, make delicious fritters, soaked in sherry and dipped in frying batter.

In some cases, however, it may be preferred to make them as usually seen at French pastry cooks; for this purpose you require a dozen small-sized *round* charlotte russe molds, which fill half full only, as they rise very much; bake these in a hotter oven, light brown paper heat; try with a twig as you would any other cake, if it comes out dry it is done; then prepare a syrup as follows: Boil half pound of sugar in a pint of water, add to this the third of a pint of rum, and some apricot pulp - peach will of course do - and boil all together a few minutes; pour this half an inch deep in a dish, and stand the cake or cakes in it; it should drink up all the syrup, you may also sprinkle some over it. If any syrup remains, use it to warm over your cake when stale, instead of the sherry.

Baba was introduced into France by Stanislas Leczinski, king of Poland, and the father-in-law of Louis XIV.; and his Polish royal descendants still use with it, says Carême, a syrup made of Malaga wine and one sixth part of *eau de tanaisie*.

But, although our forefathers seemed to have relished tansy very much, to judge from old recipe books, I doubt if such flavouring would be appreciated in our time.

Baba (1920)

¾ pound flour
½ pound butter
5 eggs
2 ounces sugar
The finely chopped peel of ½ lemon
¼ teaspoonful salt

1 yeast cake dissolved in ¼ cup warm milk
2 ounces well washed and dried currants
1½ ounces seedless raisins
1½ ounces finely cut citron
A little finely cut candied orange peel

Mix yeast, milk and ½ cup flour together and set it in a warm place to rise; stir the butter to a cream, add the sugar and next the eggs, 1 at a time, stirring a few minutes between each addition; next add the yeast which was set in a warm place to rise, then the flour and fruit; beat the whole thoroughly with the right hand for 15 minutes; cover with a clean cloth and let it rise to double its size; press it down and let it rise again; then put it into a well buttered form with a tube in center, which should be ¾ full; let it rise till form is full; paste with the white of egg a strip of buttered paper around the top edge of form and bake the cake about 1 hour; when done turn the cake out of form and set it for a few minutes in the oven to dry; in the meantime put ½ cup sugar with ¾ cup Madeira wine over the fire; let it get hot and pour all over the baba; serve either hot or cold on a napkin. Small babas are made of the same dough and baked in small deep forms, otherwise treated the same as above. Instead of Madeira any other kind of wine may be used; also, vanilla or pineapple syrup.

Baba Syruped or Iced (1920)
(Baba au Sirop ou Glacé)

With some baba paste fill a well-buttered baba mold three-quarters full; stand this in a moderately heated place, cover and leave until the paste has reached to the upper edges of the mold, then set it on a pie plate in a slow oven to bake; this operation ought to take from an hour and a quarter to an hour and a half; as soon as baked cut away any surplus paste overreaching the top and invert the baba on a grate. Prepare a thirty-two-degree hot syrup flavoured with good rum; soak the baba with this, applying it with a brush, and let drain well. It can be served simply soaked with this syrup or else iced with a light layer of water icing or fondant well flavoured with rum. After the icing has dried remove the baba carefully from the grate and lay it on a dish; should it be iced decorate the icing with angelica lozenges, halved cherries and cuts of orange peels, surrounding the base with a circle of marchpane in small cases; serve.

Baba with Marsala (1920)
(Baba au Marsala)

Fill a buttered baba mold to half its height with a baba paste without any raisins; set it to rise in a rather mild temperature until the mold is nearly full, then bake it in a moderate oven. As soon as done cut it off even with the top of the mold. Unmould, and pour over a rum syrup, flavoured with vanilla and orange peel; drain it well and glaze it with lemon icing. Dress it on a very hot dish and fill up the inside of the hollow space with fruits prepared as follows, serving the surplus of them in a sauce-boat:

Preparation of Fruits: Put in a saucepan a quarter of a pound of well-cleaned sultana raisins, two ounces of candied orange peel, two ounces of candied green almonds and two ounces of candied pineapple, the whole to be cut in small three-sixteenths inch squares; two gills of Marsala wine, three gills of syrup at thirty-two degrees, the peel of half a lemon and the peel of half an orange; put the saucepan on the fire and take it off at the first boil.

Babas with Rum-Small (1920)
(Petits Babas au Rhum)

Cut two ounces of candied fruits into small dice, such as citron, orange peel, preserved pears and a few cherries; add to them as many currants and raisins well washed in hot water, picked and cleaned. Prepare a small baba paste as described, and when ready to mold stir in the fruits. Butter some small baba molds, fill them half full with the paste, and leave to rise; when entirely full push into a hot oven to bake; unmould as soon as done, and dip them into a hot thirty-two-degree syrup well flavoured with vanilla and rum.

Baked Rice Cake (1902)

One pt. of cold boiled rice	About 1/2 a pt. of flour just sufficient to hold it together
Mixed with a cup of cold milk	
1 egg	

Put into a deep pan and bake 1/2 an hour.

Bakers' Lemon Snaps (1876)

Two pounds of sugar	Eight eggs and two and a half pounds of flour
Twelve ounces of lard	Flavour with lemon
A fourth of an ounce of hartshorn	

Roll thin and cut into small, round cakes.

Baltimore Cake 1 (1911)

Beat one cupful of butter to a cream, using a wood cake spoon. Add gradually while beating constantly two cupfuls fine granulated sugar. When creamy add a cupful of milk, alternating with three and one-half cupfuls pastry flour that has been mixed and sifted with two teaspoonfuls of baking powder. Add a teaspoonful of vanilla and the whites of six eggs beaten stiff and dry. Bake in three buttered and floured shallow cake tins and spread between the layers and on top the following icing: Put in a saucepan three cups sugar, one cup water. Heat gradually to the boiling point and cook without stirring until the syrup will thread. Pour the hot syrup gradually over the well beaten whites of three eggs and continue beating until of the right consistency for spreading. Then add one cupful chopped and seeded raisins, one cup chopped pecan meats and five figs cut in strips.

Baltimore Cake 2 (1911)

One cupful butter
Two cupfuls sugar
Three and one-half cupfuls flour
One cupful sweet milk

Two teaspoonfuls baking powder
The whites of six eggs
A teaspoonful of rose water

Cream the butter, add the sugar gradually, beating steadily, then the milk and flavouring, next the flour sifted with the baking powder, and lastly the stiffly beaten whites folded in at the last. Bake in three-layer cake tins in an oven hotter than for loaf cake. While baking, prepare the filling. Dissolve three cupfuls sugar in one cupful boiling water and cook until it spins a thread. Pour over the stiffly beaten whites of three eggs, stirring constantly. Add to this icing one cupful chopped raisins, one cupful chopped nut meats, preferably pecans or walnuts, and a half-dozen figs cut in fine strips. Use this for filling and also ice the top and sides with it.

Banana Cake (N.D.)

1½ cups sugar
⅔ cup of butter
2 egg yolks (beat whites separately)
4 tablespoons sour milk
1 teaspoon soda

½ teaspoon baking powder
1 scant teaspoon salt
1 teaspoon vanilla
1 cup mashed bananas
1½ cups of flour

Cream butter and sugar, add egg yolks. Then add baking soda to sour milk and add to sugar mixture. Then add salt, vanilla, mashed bananas and flour, and fold in beaten whites, Follow the order of mixing exactly.

Banana Cake (1920)

Three bananas
1 cup of currant jelly
½ pint of whipped cream
3 ounces butter
¾ cup sugar

1½ cups of flour
1 teaspoonful baking powder
The whites of 3 eggs beaten to a stiff froth
½ cup milk
The juice and grated rind of ½ lemon

Sift flour and baking powder together, stir butter and sugar to a cream, add the lemon, then alternately flour, milk, and the white of egg; butter 2 jelly tins of medium size, dust them with flour, divide the cake mixture evenly in the tins, and bake in a medium-hot oven. When done and cold, spread half of the jelly over one layer, cover with banana slices, lay over the second layer, put on the remaining jelly and bananas; mix the whipped cream with 1 tablespoonful fine sugar and a little vanilla, cover the whole cake with cream, or take 1 pint of whipped cream and put half of the cream between the layers and the remaining over the top, and serve.

Banana Cream Cake (1922)

⅔ cup shortening
4 tablespoons of sour milk
1½ cups sugar

2 cups flour
2 eggs
1 teaspoon soda

1 cup mashed bananas   ½ cup chopped walnut

Cream shortening; add sugar gradually and cream again; add unbeaten eggs one at a time, beating thoroughly after each addition. Then add mashed bananas with sour milk; stir well.
Fold in sifted dry ingredients and bake in layers in hot oven, 375 degrees F., 20 to 25 minutes.
Makes 2 layers.

Banana Shortcake (1917)

Prepare Shortcake, slice two small bananas over layer of hot shortcake, and sprinkle with lemon juice and powdered sugar; put on upper layer, cover with two more sliced bananas, sprinkle with lemon juice and sugar, and garnish with bits of jelly.

Banbury Cakes (1913)

"Take a pound of dough, made for white bread, roll it out and put bits of butter upon the same as for puff paste, till a pound of the same has been worked in; roll it out very thin, then cut it into bits of an oval size, according as the cakes are wanted. Mix some good moist sugar with a little brandy, sufficient to wet it, then mix some clean-washed currants with the former, put a little upon each bit of paste, close them up, and put the side that is closed next the tin they are to be baked upon. Lay them separate, and bake them moderately, and afterward, when taken out, sift sugar over them. Some candied peel may be added, or a few drops essence of lemon."

Banbury Cakes (1898)

Ingredients:

½ lb. currants
¼ lb. mixed candied peel
2 oz. beef suet
2 oz. Pounded macaroons
Small pinch mixed spice

Chopped rind of ½ a lemon
½ tea-spoonful salt
Short crust, made with 12 oz. flour, and other ingredients in proportion

Method: Wash and pick the currants, chop the suet finely, cut the candied peel into very small pieces, and crumble the macaroons. Mix these thoroughly together, and add the lemon rind, spice, and salt. Make the crust, roll it out to a thin sheet, and divide in half. Spread the mixture evenly on one portion, and cover it with the other. Close the edges carefully, sift sugar over it, and mark it with the back of a knife in divisions, about 3 inches long and 2 wide. Bake the cakes in a moderate oven, and, when quite cooked, cut through the divisions whilst still hot. Set them aside to cool, and serve cold, piled on a silver or glass dish.
Time: 30 to 35 minutes.
Sufficient for: 12 Banbury cakes.

Bangor Corn Cake (1894)

One tablespoon butter
Two tablespoons sugar
One egg
One cup flour

One-half cup corn meal
Two-thirds cup milk
One teaspoon cream tartar
One-half teaspoon soda

Barneys (1905)

4 cups of whole wheat flour   3 teaspoonfuls of baking-powder

1 teaspoonful of salt   Enough water to make it seem like cake batter

Drop with a spoon into hot buttered muffin-pans and bake in a hot oven about fifteen minutes.

Batter Cakes 1 (1876)

One quart of sweet milk   Whites of four eggs
One-half tablespoon of salt   Two and one-half teaspoons of baking powder

Stir the salt in the milk, add the flour till you have a pretty stiff batter, next stir in the baking powder and add the whites, beaten to a stiff froth the last thing, mixing the whole gently.

Batter Cakes (1913)
(Old Style)

Sift together half-cup flour, cup and a half meal, add pinch of salt, scald with boiling water, stir smooth, then add two eggs well beaten, and thin with sweet milk - it will take about half a pint. Bake by spoonfuls on a hot, well-greased griddle - the batter must run very freely. Serve very hot with fresh sausage, or fried pigs' feet if you would know just how good batter cakes can be.

Batter Cakes 2 (1876)

One pint of sour milk   The whites and yolks beaten separately
One teaspoon of soda   Two tablespoons of butter or lard or one of each
Two eggs   A little salt

Stir in the whites of the eggs, beaten light, the last thing, with flour sufficient to make a batter.

Batter Cakes 3 (1876)

One-half pint of sour cream   One teaspoon of soda
One-half pint of sweet milk   Nearly one quart of sifted flour
Two eggs

Baum-Torte (1910)
(Tree Spongecake)

1 lb. sugar   14 oz. flour
10 eggs   4 oz. potato flour or cornflour
2 to 3 grains cardamom   4 oz. sweet almonds
A little vanilla   10 bitter almonds
The grated rind of a lemon   1 tablespoonful rum
A small piece of mace

Cream the butter, add the sugar and beaten-up yolks of eggs and stir all for ¾ hour. Then add the grated lemon peel, the almonds (grated in their skin), and the ground spice, adding then, alternately, the flour, sifted and mixed with baking powder and the whites of eggs whisked stiffly. Mix well. Butter a broad, shallow cake tin (Tortenform), line it with buttered paper, and pour sufficient of the mixture in to thinly cover the bottom. Place in the oven for a few minutes till slightly brown, then pour in enough to make another layer and bake as before, placing the tin now, however, on a pan of cold water, which must be renewed with fresh cold water immediately it begins to boil. This is to prevent the cake becoming overdone at the bottom. A few sheets of tin may also be placed under the cake tin. As each layer is baked, add another, until all of the mixture has been used up.

Chocolate, or any other, icing may be spread over the cake, which may also be ornamented with marzipan, etc. A richer cake is obtained by baking three-quarters of the mixture on layers as described and then taking out of the tin. The rest of the mixture is then baked in two layers. Spread on the thicker portion a layer of good jam, cover with a layer of marzipan, and place the thinner layer of cake on this. Glaze with lemon icing and ornament with marzipan fruit or preserved fruit.

For the layer of marzipan reckon ½ lb. sweet almonds, ½ lb. castor sugar and ½ gill rose water.

Bavarian Cheese Cake (1908)

Make a rich biscuit dough; roll out and place on a well-buttered pie-dish.
Then mix:

1/2 pound of cottage cheese with a pinch of salt	1/2 lemon grated
1/4 cup of melted butter	2 yolks of eggs
1/2 cup of sugar	1/2 cup of currants

Add the whites beaten stiff. Fill the pie with the cheese. Serve hot or cold with coffee.

Beautiful Cake (1893)

Two cups sugar	3 eggs, yolks and whites beaten separately
½ of butter	1 teaspoon cream tartar
1 cup milk	½ soda; flavour to taste
3 cups flour	

Beef and Bacon Cakes (1917)

1-pound flank of beef	1/4 teaspoon salt
1/2 cup water	1/4 cup dried bread crumbs
3 slices bacon	Dash of cayenne

Put meat and bacon through chopper; add crumbs, water, and seasonings; mix well, form into small flat cakes, and sauté in bacon fat.

Beef and Sausage Cakes (1913)

Have the butcher grind together one pound of beef and a quarter of a pound (or more) of pork sausage. Then mix together two slices of stale bread (crumbed), a chopped celery stem, a pinch or more of dried sage, a slice of onion (minced) and a beaten egg. Mix all thoroughly with the sausage and make into small balls and fry in drippings.
(The egg may be omitted.)

Beef Cake (1898)

Ingredients:

1½ lbs. rump steak	Seasoning pepper and salt
¼ lb. Suet	1 egg
½ lb. streaky bacon	½ pint brown gravy
½ tea-spoonful dried sweet herbs	

Method: Remove all skin and fat from the steak and chop it and the suet finely. Mix the seasonings thoroughly with them, beat and strain the egg and stir it into the mixture. Butter a cake tin, line it with the bacon, cut into very thin slices, put in the minced beef, and cover it with the rest of the bacon. Bake in a good but not fierce oven, taking care it should not become dry by cooking too quickly. When done turn it out of the mould and take off the bacon. Have ready ½ pint of brown gravy very hot, pour it over the cake and serve.
This is an excellent dish served cold without the gravy.
Time: About 1½ hours.
Sufficient for: 5 or 6 persons.

Beef Cakes (1840)

Take some cold roast beef that has been under-done and mince it very fine. Mix with it grated bread crumbs, and a little chopped onion and parsley. Season it with pepper and salt and moisten it with some beef-dripping and a little walnut or onion pickle. Some scraped cold tongue or ham will be found an improvement. Make it into broad flat cakes and spread a coat of mashed potato thinly on the top and bottom of each. Lay a small bit of butter on the top of every cake and set them in an oven to warm and brown.
Beef cakes are frequently a breakfast dish.
Any other cold fresh meat may be prepared in the same manner.
Cold roast beef may be cut into slices, seasoned with salt and pepper, broiled a few minutes over a clear fire, and served up hot with a little butter spread on them.

Beef Hash Cakes (1911)

Chop cold corned beef fine and add a little more than the same measure of cold boiled potatoes, chopped less fine than the beef. Season with onion juice, make into small cakes, and brown in butter or beef drippings; serve each cake on a slice of buttered toast moistened slightly.

Berliner Pfannkuchen (1910)
(Berlin Pancakes)

1 lb. flour	8 bitter almonds
2 oz. sugar	1 tablespoonful rum
4 eggs	½ pint milk
4 oz. butter	1½ oz. yeast

Crumble the yeast, sprinkle a little sugar over it and stir it with ½ gill milk and 3 tablespoonsful flour. Stand on one side for 10 minutes to rise.
Beat the sugar and eggs to a froth, stir into them by degrees the grated almonds, rum, flour, butter (melted), prepared yeast, and remaining milk, mixing thoroughly. Knead and beat the dough and place in a covered pan near the fire to rise. Then take a piece of the dough, place it on a floured pasteboard and draw out a strip to about ½ inch in thickness. On this, at intervals of about 2 inches from one another and from the edge, place with a teaspoon, small heaps of jam, mixed with a little rum. Fold the edges of the strip of dough together, so that the jam is completely covered, and press together a little round each heap of the jam. Then with a wine glass cut out the doughnuts, leaving a good margin round the jam. Press the edges together firmly and place on another floured board to rise. Continue in this manner until the whole of the dough has been made into doughnuts. When they have well risen, slide them carefully, three or four at a time, into a large saucepan of steaming hot fat and leave them in till brown on all sides. To test if done, insert a wooden skewer; if dry when withdrawn, the doughnuts are ready to take out. Place them then on a sieve, on blotting paper, to absorb all fat and afterwards on a dish, rolling them first in fine castor sugar.
Instead of the sugar, a thin icing may be poured over them, composed of 1 lb. castor sugar mixed with a gill of rosewater.

Berliner Waffeln (1910)
(Berlin Wafers)

8 oz. flour
3 eggs
A little salt

½ pint sour cream
2 tablespoonsful Kümmel liqueur

Mix all ingredients and proceed as in Waffeln. (Wafers; French: Gaufres (1910)) recipe.

Berry Muffins (1911)

Mix two cups sifted flour, one-half teaspoon salt and two rounded teaspoons baking powder. Cream one-quarter cup of butter with one-half cup sugar, add well beaten yolk of one egg, one cup milk, the flour mixture and white of egg beaten stiff. Stir in carefully one heaped cup blueberries which have been picked over, rinsed, dried and rolled in flour. Bake in muffin pans twenty minutes.

Berwick Cake (1893)

Beat 6 eggs 2 minutes
Add 3 cups powdered sugar, beat 3 minutes
Add 2 cups flour with 2 teaspoons cream tartar mixed with it, beat 1 minute

1 cup cold water with 1 teaspoon soda in it, beat 1 minute
Add 2 cups flour, beat 1 minute

Flavour
Never fails.

Berwick Sponge Cake (1876)

Beat three eggs two minutes
Add a cup and a half of sugar and beat five minutes
Then add one cup of flour
One teaspoon of baking powder mixed in the flour

A half-cup of cold water
Another cup of flour
A little salt
The grated rind of a lemon and half the juice

Best Jumbles (1922)

2 cupfuls sugar
3 tablespoonfuls milk
1 cupful Crisco
1 teaspoonful salt
4 eggs

3 teaspoonfuls baking powder
4 cupfuls flour
1 teaspoonful almond extract
1 teaspoonful rose extract

Cream Crisco and sugar thoroughly together, then gradually add eggs well beaten, now add milk, extracts, flour, salt and baking powder. Mix and roll out lightly on floured baking board; cut into circles with doughnut cutter, lay on Criscoed tins and bake in moderate oven from seven to ten minutes or till light brown. These cookies will keep fresh two weeks, and if milk is left out, a month.
Sufficient for: seventy jumbles.

Birthday Cake (1897)
(Födelsedags-kaka)

1½ pound fine sugar

The same amount of butter

Three and a half pounds of dried currants
2 pounds of flour
Half a pound candied peel
Half a pound almond

2 ounces spices
And the grated rind of 3 lemons
18 eggs
And a gill of brandy

Bake in oven 3 hours.

Biscuit à la Hernani (1920)
(Biscuit à la Hernani)

Bake a Savoy biscuit in a dome-formed mould eight inches in diameter by four inches high. Turn it out and let stand till cold, then put it back again in the mould and pare it straight; cut around the top at about two inches from the bottom a cover by means of a small knife held on a slant, to have the cut form a bevel (this is to prevent the cover falling in the biscuit), and empty it, leaving the outer crust only half an inch in thickness. Place it on a grate with its cover on and cover with reduced apricot marmalade, and glaze with fondant to which melted chocolate is added. At serving time fill the empty biscuit with whipped cream, into which mix a few chocolate pastilles, some finely shredded pistachios and a few preserved cherries cut in two. Lay the biscuit on a frolle paste foundation, coated with egg whites, and dredged over with white granulated sugar; slide the whole on a cold dish and surround the base with a wreath of Africans glazed with chocolate.

Biscuit-Torte (1910)
(Spongecake)

1 teaspoonful grated lemon peel
8 oz. sugar
8 eggs

4 oz. cornflour or potato flour
1 tablespoonful lemon juice

Stir the beaten-up eggs with the sugar, lemon juice and grated lemon peel, in a double milk saucepan, to a froth. Then sprinkle in the cornflour or potato flour, stirring briskly all the time. Fill at once a wide, shallow tin, well-buttered and bake 1 hour in a moderate oven. Ten minutes after taking out of the oven, turn out and glaze with icing. The cake may be cut through when cold into two layers, jam spread on the under half and the top then placed on it again.

Biscuit Torte (No. 1) (1893)
A Sponge Cake

Half a pound of sifted sugar and the yolks of ten eggs must be stirred a quarter of an hour. Add six ounces of butter beaten to a cream, the grated peel of a lemon and its juice, half a pound of fine flour, and, when these are well stirred, add the whites of the ten eggs whipped to a snow. Stir all well together. Butter either one or two moulds, to fill three parts full. Strew thin slices of almonds and some coarsely pounded sugar on the top and bake in a moderate oven.

Biscuit Torte (No. 2) (1893)
Sponge Cake

A pound of sifted sugar and eighteen eggs must be stirred one way for nearly an hour, then mix in by degrees a pound of fine flour and the grated peel of a lemon. Butter the moulds, and bake the cakes in a quick oven.

Blackberry Jam Cake (1820)

1 c. sugar
3 eggs

⅔ c. fat
2 c. flour

1 c. sour milk
1/2 tsp. spice
1 tsp. soda

½ c. blackberry jam
1 tsp. baking powder

Mix as for butter cakes only mix the soda with the jam. Bake in layers and put together with icing or butter cream filling. Sweet milk may be substituted for the sour by using 1/2 tsp. soda instead of one tsp.

Black Cake (1876)

One pound of flour
One pound of butter
One and a half pounds of sugar
Three pounds of raisins
Two pounds of currants
Ten eggs

Two nutmegs
A half-ounce of cloves
A half-ounce of mace
Three-fourths of an ounce of cinnamon
A half teaspoon of saleratus

Black Cake (1840)

Prepare two pounds of currants by picking them clean, washing and draining them, through a cullender, and then spreading them out on a large dish to dry before the fire or in the sun, placing the dish in a slanting position. Pick and stone two pounds of the best raisins and cut them in half. Dredge the currants (when they are dry) and the raisins thickly with flour to prevent them from sinking in the cake. Grind or powder as much cinnamon as will make a large gravy-spoonful when done; also, a table-spoonful of mace and four nutmegs; sift these spices and mix them all together in a cup. Mix together two large glasses of white wine, one of brandy and one of rose water, and cut a pound of citron into large slips. Sift a pound of flour into one pan, and a pound of powdered loaf-sugar into another. Cut up among the sugar a pound of the best fresh butter and stir them to a cream. Beat twelve eggs till perfectly thick and smooth, and stir them gradually into the butter and sugar, alternately with the flour. Then add by degrees, the fruit, spice and liquor, and stir the whole very hard at the last. Then put the mixture into a well-buttered tin pan with straight or perpendicular sides. Put it immediately into a moderate oven and bake it at least four hours. When done, let it remain in the oven to get cold; it will be the better for staying in all night. Ice it next morning; first dredging the outside all over with flour, and then wiping it with a towel. This will make the icing stick.
Icing: A quarter of a pound of finely powdered loaf-sugar, of the whitest and best quality, is the usual allowance to one white of egg. For the cake in the preceding receipt, three quarters of a pound of sugar and the whites of three eggs will be about the proper quantity. Beat the white of egg by itself till it stands alone. Have ready the powdered sugar, and then beat it hard into the white of egg, till it becomes thick and smooth; flavouring it as you proceed with a few drops of oil of lemon, or a little extract of roses. Spread it evenly over the cake with a broad knife or a feather; if you find it too thin, beat in a little more powdered sugar. Cover with it thickly the top and sides of the cake, taking care not to have it rough and streaky. To ice well requires skill and practice.
When the icing is about half dry, put on the ornaments. You may flower it with coloured sugar-sand or nonparels; but a newer and more elegant mode is to decorate it with, devices and borders in white sugar; they can be procured at the confectioners and look extremely well on icing that has been tinted with pink by the addition of a little cochineal.
You may colour icing of a pale or deep yellow, by rubbing the lumps of loaf-sugar (before they are powdered) upon the outside of a large lemon or orange. This will also flavour it finely.
Almond icing, for a very fine cake, is made by mixing gradually with the white of egg and sugar, some almonds, half bitter and half sweet, that have been pounded in a mortar with rose water to a smooth paste. The whole must be well incorporated and spread over the cake near half an inch thick. It must be set in a cool oven to dry, and then taken out and covered with a smooth plain icing of sugar and white of egg.
Whatever icing is left, may be used to make maccaroons or kisses.

Black Cake (1869)

Rub a pound and a half of softened butter in three pounds of flour, add a pound of brown sugar, rolled fine, a pint of molasses, a table-spoonful of rose brandy, a nutmeg or some mace, four eggs well beaten, a pound of raisins stoned and chopped; mix the whole well, and before baking add a tea-cup of sour cream with a tea-spoonful of soda dissolved in it - beat it up again, have the pans well-buttered, and put in about three parts full; this quantity will make about six cakes, in bread pans; bake as bread and if it brown too much, put paper on it, if it seems too stiff, add a little more molasses or cream. It will keep several weeks in cold weather.

Black Cake No. 1 (1889)

Two pounds butter
Two pounds sugar
Two pounds flour
Five pounds raisins
Five pounds currants
Two pounds citron

Twenty eggs
One tumblerful brandy
One tumblerful wine
One tablespoonful cloves
Two tablespoonfuls cinnamon
Two tablespoonfuls mace

Black Cake No. 2 (1889)

Thirteen pounds raisins
Three pounds preserved lemon peel
Three pounds citron
Five pounds currants
Four pounds butter
Six pounds sugar
Four pounds flour

Thirty-six eggs
Two ounces mace, ground
Half-ounce nutmeg
Half box cinnamon, ground
Half box cloves
One-pint molasses
Two and a half pints whiskey and wine

This is absolutely perfect cake and has been tried many times. The receipt given makes about fifty pounds. One-quarter of the receipt is enough for ordinary occasions. Do not attempt to bake it in the house but send to a baker.

Black Cake with Prune Filling (1922)

1½ cupfuls sugar
½ teaspoonful baking soda
½ teaspoonful salt
2 cupfuls flour
3 eggs

1 teaspoonful baking powder
½ cupful Crisco
½ teaspoonful vanilla extract
1 cupful milk
⅓ cake chocolate

For Filling:

1 cupful sugar
½ cupful stoned stewed prunes
⅓ cupful boiling water

⅓ cupful blanched chopped almonds
1 white of egg

For cake: Beat 1 egg in double boiler, add ½ cupful milk, ½ cupful sugar and chocolate; mix well and cook until it thickens. Cool and set aside. Cream Crisco with remainder of sugar, add salt, eggs well beaten, soda mixed with remainder of milk, flour, baking powder and vanilla. Mix well and add chocolate paste and divide into two Criscoed and floured layer cake tins. Bake twenty minutes in moderate oven.
For filling: Boil sugar and water together without stirring until it forms a soft ball when tried in cold water, or 240° F., then pour it over the beaten white of egg, beating all the time. Now add chopped prunes and almonds and beat well. Put between layers of cake.
Sufficient for: One good-sized layer cake.

Black Chocolate Cake (1922)

1¼ cups sugar
2 eggs
¼ cup Crisco
4 squares chocolate
1½ cups flour, measured after sifting

3 teaspoons baking powder
1 teaspoon salt
½ cup milk
1 teaspoon vanilla

Cream Crisco and sugar, add well beaten eggs, then chocolate melted, beat thoroughly. Sift salt and baking powder with flour and add alternating with milk to previous mixture. Add flavouring last and beat thoroughly before pouring into a pan well-greased with Crisco. Bake in a moderate oven about 40 minutes.

Black Cake Icing (1840)

A quarter of a pound of finely powdered loaf-sugar, of the whitest and best quality, is the usual allowance to one white of egg. For the cake in the preceding receipt, three quarters of a pound of sugar and the whites of three eggs will be about the proper quantity. Beat the white of egg by itself till it stands alone. Have ready the powdered sugar, and then beat it hard into the white of egg, till it becomes thick and smooth; flavouring it as you proceed with a few drops of oil of lemon, or a little extract of roses. Spread it evenly over the cake with a broad knife or a feather; if you find it too thin, beat in a little more powdered sugar. Cover with it thickly the top and sides of the cake, taking care not to have it rough and streaky. To ice well requires skill and practice. When the icing is about half dry, put on the ornaments. You may flower it with coloured sugar-sand or nonparels; but a newer and more elegant mode is to decorate it with, devices and borders in white sugar; they can be procured at the confectioners and look extremely well on icing that has been tinted with pink by the addition of a little cochineal.

You may colour icing of a pale or deep yellow, by rubbing the lumps of loaf-sugar (before they are powdered) upon the outside of a large lemon or orange. This will also flavour it finely.

Almond icing, for a very fine cake, is made by mixing gradually with the white of egg and sugar, some almonds, half bitter and half sweet, that have been pounded in a mortar with rose water to a smooth paste. The whole must be well incorporated and spread over the cake near half an inch thick. It must be set in a cool oven to dry, and then taken out and covered with a smooth plain icing of sugar and white of egg.

Whatever icing is left, may be used to make maccaroons or kisses.

Black Clouds (1876)

One cup of brown sugar
A half-cup of molasses
A half-cup of butter
A half-cup of sour milk
Two cups of flour

A half teaspoon of soda
Yolks of five egg and white of one
Two teaspoons of cinnamon
A half teaspoon each of cloves and nutmeg

Black Molasses Fruit Cakes (1922) (Cheap)

One-half pound of sugar
One quart of molasses
One quart of milk
A half-ounce of soda
One pound of lard
Five pounds of flour

Four eggs
Two ounces of mixed spices
Four pounds of currants
Two pounds of raisins
A half-pound of citron

Cream sugar, spices and lard; add molasses; milk with the soda dissolved; add the flour and beat in the eggs; last, mix in the fruit. Bake like the other fruit cakes.

Blackberry Roll (1922)

1-pint flour	1 tablespoon butter
2 teaspoons baking powder	A small pinch of salt

Add milk enough to make the dough the thickness of biscuit dough. Roll about one-half inch thick and powder with flour and sugar mixed, half and half.
Drain from one pint to one quart of cooked blackberries, sweeten to taste and place on dough with bits of butter specked over berries. Roll quickly (to keep dough from splitting) and place in a deep pan into which a half pint of cold water has been placed. Dust top with two parts of flour to one part of sugar, place in hot oven and bake about thirty minutes.

Blätter Teig (No. 1) (1873)
(Puff Paste)

Rub into a pound of flour a quarter of a pound of butter and a little salt. If the weather is warm, chop it in with a knife instead of handling. Mix with water to form a smooth paste, roll it out half an inch thick. Flatten with the rolling pin three-quarters of a pound of butter; lay this in the middle of the paste and fold its edges over. Roll it out thin again; cut it into four, and lay each part on the other, dredge it a little with flour, and roll it out again; repeat the cutting and rolling out three times.

Blätter Teig (No. 2) (1873)
(Puff Paste)

To a pound of fine flour on a pasteboard add, in small pieces, a quarter of a pound of butter. Beat up an egg in half a teacupful of milk and add to this half a wineglass of brandy. Make a hollow in the flour, pour in the mixture, and work it together with a knife to a smooth paste, sprinkling with milk if it is not moist enough. Finish moulding lightly with the hand to bring it quite smooth; roll it out, flatten half a pound of butter on it, and over this fold the paste. Roll out and fold it four times, keeping it as cool as possible.

Blätter Torte, von Linzerteig (1873)
(Linzer Leaves)

A pound and a quarter of flour	The yolks of eight hardboiled eggs rubbed smooth
Three-quarters of a pound of butter	Three well-beaten eggs
Half a pound of sweet almonds	Cream or milk enough to make a paste as before directed
Half an ounce of bitter ones	
Half a pound of sugar	

Divide the mass into six parts; roll them out very thin, to about the size of a pudding plate. Lay these on a buttered baking-tin; brush them over with egg and bake them in a cool oven a yellow colour. Slide them carefully off the tins while warm, the first one on to the dish in which it will be served. Spread over it any nice preserve or marmalade; place a cake on it; then another layer of preserve; then alternate cake and preserve, till the last cake is on the top. Cut it even all round, and sift sugar over, or ice it with a snow of sugar and white of egg.

Blätterteig-Bretzel (1910)
(Puff Paste Twists)

Make some puff paste, leave it in a cool place for some time, then roll it out and cut into strips about ½ inch thick and wide. Roll each strip on the well-floured board and twist into the shape of a Bretzel or double loop. Bake a pale golden colour on a buttered tin.

Blechkuchen (1910)

1 lb. flour
2 eggs
4 oz. butter

3 oz. sugar
½ pint milk
1½ oz. yeast

Crumble the yeast into the lukewarm milk, mix well, pour into the centre of the flour in a basin, add the beaten-up eggs, the butter (melted) and sugar, and mix and knead well, beating with the rolling-pin till the paste no longer sticks to the latter. Stand in a covered pan in a warm place to rise. When well risen, cover with it - about ½ inch thick, or less - a well-buttered sheet of tin and let it rise a little longer before covering with fruit, etc., to make Obst-, Butter-, Streussel- or Käsekuchen.

Blitzkuchen (1910)
(Lightning Cake)

½ lb. sugar
½ lb. butter
½ lb. potato flour mixed with ½ oz. baking powder

6 eggs
½ lb. flour
Grated rind and juice of a lemon

Cream the butter and stir into it the beaten-up eggs, sugar, lemon juice and grated lemon peel, and lastly add the flour, sifted, and mixed with baking powder. When thoroughly mixed, fill at once a well-buttered tin and bake 1 hour.

Blitzkuchen (1873)
(Blitz Cake)

Stir nine ounces of butter to a cream. Add nine ounces of sifted sugar, eight eggs, leaving out half the whites, ten ounces of fine flour, and the grated rind of a lemon. Stir altogether briskly for a quarter of an hour. Butter a mould well. Strew it with raspings and bake it at once in a quick oven.

Blueberry Cake (1893)

One cup sugar
1 cup milk
1 egg
1 tablespoon lard

Crystaline salt
2 heaping teaspoons baking powder
1-pint flour
1-pint berries

Blueberry Cake (1893)
(For breakfast)

One cup milk
1 cup sugar
1 spoon butter
1 cup blueberries

1 teaspoon of soda
1 teaspoon cream tartar
3 cups of flour

Blueberry Cake (1894)

One-half cup butter creamed

One cup sugar

Two eggs
One cup milk
One teaspoon soda

Two teaspoons cream tartar in one and one-half pints of flour
Little salt

Roll one-pint blueberries in two handfuls of flour

Blueberry Cake (1890)

Three pints of sifted flour
1 cupful of sugar
One-half cupful of butter
1 pint of sweet milk

2 eggs
1 pint of blueberries
1 teaspoonful of soda in the milk
2 teaspoonfuls of cream of tartar in the flour

Rub the butter, sugar and eggs together, then add the milk with soda, then the flour with cream of tartar, and lastly, stir the blueberries in gently, and bake three-quarters of an hour in two long pans. Very nice.

Blueberry Cake 1 (1894)

One-quart flour
Half a cup butter
One and a half cups white sugar
One cup sweet milk

Two teaspoons cream tartar
One teaspoon soda
Two eggs
Blueberries

Blueberry Cake 2 (1894)

One cup milk
Three cups flour
One egg, salt
Two tablespoons sugar

One of butter
Two teaspoons cream tartar
One of soda
One cup blueberries

Blueberry Muffins (1917)

Follow recipe for Cambridge Muffins; add one cup of blueberries just before putting into the pans. If canned blueberries are used, drain, and dredge with flour before adding to batter.

Blueberry Muffins (1911)

1 egg
¾ cup sugar
2 tablespoons butter
1 cup sweet milk

2 even cups flour
½ teaspoon soda
1 teaspoon cream tartar
2 cups blueberries

Blueberry Muffins (1922)

Sift and mix thoroughly:

1 1/2 cups flour
1 cup sugar

2 teaspoonfuls baking powder

To the above then add:

4 tablespoons melted butter

2 eggs well beaten

1 cup milk

1 box blueberries that have been dredged in ½ cup flour

Bake in hot oven 12 to 15 minutes.

Blueberry Muffins (N.D.)

1 egg
2 rounding teaspoons tartar
1 teaspoon soda sifted with 2 cups flour
½ teaspoon salt

½ cup sweet milk cream
½ cup cream
2 tablespoons sugar

Fold in half cup blueberries. Have tins hot and bake in moderately hot oven.

Blueberry Tea Cake (1913)

3 tablespoons Cottolene
1/2 cup sugar
1 egg
2 ⅔ cups bread flour

4 teaspoons baking powder
1 teaspoon salt
1 cup milk
3/4 cup berries

Process: Cream Cottolene, add sugar gradually, stirring constantly. Add egg beaten thick and light. Mix and sift flour (except three tablespoons), baking powder and salt; add to first mixture alternately with milk. Sprinkle remaining flour over berries and fold them in quickly. Bake in well-greased shallow pan thirty minutes in a moderate oven. Serve hot with Hard Sauce or cream, or with butter.

Boiled Raisin Cake (1912)

Cover one and one-half cups of seeded raisins with boiling water and simmer twenty minutes. Cream three-fourths cup of sugar and one-fourth cup of butter together, add one and one-half cups of flour, one-half cup of the raisin water and one egg beaten lightly but not separated. One teaspoon of soda should be sifted in the flour. Add one teaspoon each of nutmeg and cinnamon, the raisins well dredged with flour, bake thirty or forty minutes.

Boiled Rice Muffins (1911)

To make muffins with cooked rice, sift two and one-quarter cups of flour twice with five level teaspoons of baking powder, one rounding tablespoon of sugar, and a saltspoon of salt. Put in one well beaten egg, half a cup of milk, and three-quarters cup of boiled rice mixed with another half-cup of milk, and two tablespoons of melted butter. Beat well, pour into hot gem pans and bake.

Boiling Water Cake (1922)

1 cupful boiling water
1 cupful sultana raisins
1 cupful sugar
2½ cupfuls flour
½ cupful Crisco
½ teaspoonful salt

1 egg
2 teaspoonfuls baking powder
¼ cupful chopped candied citron peel
¼ teaspoonful grated nutmeg
½ teaspoonful lemon extract

Put Crisco and sugar into basin, pour boiling water over them; let stand till cold, then add egg well beaten, sift in flour, salt, baking powder, and nutmeg, add peel, raisins, and lemon extract, and mix well. Turn into

greased and floured small square tin and bake in moderate oven half hour. Cool and cover with boiled frosting.
Sufficient for: one small cake.

Boston Cream Cakes 1 (1876)

Boil one-fourth of a pound of butter in one tumbler of water; stir in one and a half tumblers of flour while boiling; take it from the fire, and when cool add five eggs, then add a half teaspoon of soda. Drop by spoonfuls on buttered tins and bake in a quick oven fifteen minutes. When done, make a hole in the side of the cakes and put in the following:

Cream: Two tumblers of milk, one and a half coffee cups of sugar, a half coffeecup of flour and two eggs. Beat the sugar, eggs and flour together; add a little flavour and stir in the milk while boiling; let it boil until of the consistency of custard.

Boston Cream Cakes 2 (1876)

A half-pound of butter
Three-fourths of a pound of flour
Ten eggs

One pint of water
One small teaspoon of soda

Boil butter and water together, sprinkle in flour while boiling; let it boil for two or three minutes, stirring all the while. When cool, add eggs and soda; beat well together. Drop the batter on tins, a tablespoon at a time, and bake in a quick oven.

Cream for filling:

One quart of milk
Four eggs

One cup of white sugar
One cup of flour

Boil the milk. Beat eggs, flour and sugar together and stir in while boiling. Flavour with vanilla. When cool open one side of the cakes and fill with the cream.

Boston Flat Cake (1913)

Sift together a cupful of flour and a rounding teaspoonful of baking powder, add half an even teaspoonful of salt. Dissolve an even teaspoonful of saleratus in a little water. Stir all with a dessert spoonful of olive oil and sour milk to make a dough. Stir with a large spoon and shape (with the spoon) into biscuits the size of cookies. Put them into a greased pie pan, dot with a bit of butter or a few drops of oil and sprinkle lightly with brown sugar. Bake for ten or twelve minutes and serve hot.

Boston Gingerbread (1894)

One-pound sugar
One-pound butter
Two pounds flour
Six eggs
One-pint molasses

One gill of water
One teaspoon soda
Two teaspoons each allspice, cloves and mace
One quart of fruit
Half-pound of citron

Bake in two loaves three hours.

Boston Pound Cake (1876)

One pound of sugar

Three-fourths of a pound of butter

One pound of flour
Six eggs
One cup of cream or rich milk

One teaspoon of soda
The grated rind of one lemon

Put in the soda the last thing.

Boswell Cake (1889)

Ten cups of flour
Six cups of sugar
Three cups of butter
Eight eggs
Three cups warm milk and one wineglass of rum in it

One teaspoonful of soda, dissolved in a little of the milk
Two pounds of raisins
Nutmeg, or mace

Bake an hour and a half.

Bran Muffins (1917)

2 cups bran
1/2 cup molasses
1 cup flour
1-3/4 cups milk

1/2 teaspoon salt
1 tablespoon melted shortening
1 teaspoon soda

Mix in order given; beat well and bake in moderate oven about twenty-five minutes. These muffins are moist, keep well, and may be reheated successfully in a covered pan, either over steam or in the oven.

Bran Muffins (1922)

1 cup bran flour
2 tablespoons molasses
2 cups graham flour

1 teaspoon soda
1½ cups milk
½ teaspoon salt

Mix milk and molasses, add the dry ingredients. Bake in a very hot oven for one hour. This recipe should make a dozen muffins.

Bran Muffins 1 (N.D.)

1 cup of sugar
1 cup of milk in which 1 teaspoon of baking powder has been added (sweet or sour milk may be used)
1 tablespoon each of butter and Crisco

1 teaspoon of baking
1 pinch of salt
1 egg
1½ cups of flour
½ cup of bran and a few raisins

Method: Mix in order given, will make 16 buns. Bake in moderate oven for ½ hour.

Bran Muffins 2 (N.D.)

1 egg (do not separate)
2 tablespoons sugar
1⅓ cups flour

2 tablespoons butter (melt the butter)
1 teaspoon salt
1 teaspoon baking powder

1 cup sour milk (thick)
1 cup Pillsbury's bran

½ teaspoon soda

Beat egg, add sour milk and beat together, then add flour, salt, baking powder, soda, and sugar, which have been sifted together three times. Add melted butter and bran and bake in muffin pans. (The batter should be thick).

Braune Pfeffernüsse (1910)
(Mecklenburgische)

1 lb. syrup
½ lb. sugar
1½ oz. butter.
½ oz. potash dissolved in
4 tablespoonsful rosewater
1 teaspoonful ground coriander

2 lbs. flour
½ oz. ground cinnamon
10 oz. ground cloves
1 tablespoonful chopped candied orange peel
4 oz. chopped citron
A pinch of baking powder

Boil up the syrup, sugar and butter. Mix 1½ lb. flour (mixed with the baking powder) with the ground spices and chopped candied peel. Add the cooled syrup and the potash, dissolved in rosewater. Then stir in the remaining flour and knead to a dough. Cover over and leave in a warm place for 3 days, kneading it again on the second day. Make up into rolls, slice them up slantingly and bake on a buttered tin in a moderate oven.

Braunschweiger Kuchen (1873)
(Brunswick Cake)

Ingredients:

Two pounds and a half of flour
A pound of butter
Six eggs, and the yolks of six others
Six ounces of sugar
A grated lemon-peel
An ounce of sweet almonds, and a dozen bitter ones, blanched and pounded

Half a pound of raisins
Half a pound of currants
Half a nutmeg grated
Two or three ounces of yeast, or two ounces of dried yeast
A pint of milk

First stir the butter to a cream; add by degrees the other ingredients. Let the milk be lukewarm and stir the yeast into it; add this to the butter, and, by degrees, the flour. Beat the whole to a light dough, and lastly add the currants and raisins. Dredge with flour a flat baker's tin, that has an edge turned up all round; turn the dough on to this and spread or roll it out half an inch thick or less. Set it in warmth to rise. When it is somewhat risen, make dents with the finger here and there; put into each hollow a little piece of butter, the size of a nut: sprinkle thickly with sugar, and bake it in a rather quick oven. Or, bake it without the sugar on the top, and when it is drawn from the oven brush it over with a glazing of sifted sugar, moistened with rose-water, and set it back in the oven a few minutes to harden this.

Braut Torte (1873)
(Bride Cake)

For this excellent cake blanch and pound in a marble mortar a pound of almonds quite fine, using white of egg to prevent their clogging together. Beat a pound of fresh butter to a cream; add to it, by degrees, a pound of sifted sugar, then the yolks of twelve eggs, the grated peel of a lemon, and a small teaspoonful of grated nutmeg. Next add the almonds, and a pound of fine flour well dried. Stir all briskly for half an hour; after which add the egg-whites, whipped to a snow. Bake four cakes of the mass in flat round tins with inch-deep rims, which these must be lined with buttered paper, rising an inch above the tins. Bake them in a moderate oven a deep yellow colour, not brown. Meantime, warm, in a small enamelled saucepan, a quarter of a pound of fresh butter; stir into it a quarter of a pound of powdered sugar, the grated peel of a lemon, the yolks of four eggs, and the juice of four lemons. Stu' it quickly until it thickens; then take it from the fire and continue the stirring until it cools. Spread this over three of the cakes, as you lay one over the other. Lay the fourth on the top. Next day, if the cake is not even and smooth all round, make it so with a sharp knife. Ice it all over with lemon icing and ornament it according to taste.

Bread Batter Cakes (1869)

Soak slices of stale bread in cold sweet milk for half an hour, then put it over the fire, and let it come to a boil; and mash it well, when nearly cool, add wheat flour enough to make a stiff batter, beat this together with two eggs, a tea-spoonful of salt, and a table-spoonful of good yeast, let it rise and bake as buckwheat cakes, if light before you are ready, set them in a cold place.

Bread Cake (1904)

16 eggs
1 pound of sifted sugar
1 pound of fresh grated almonds
2 ounces of grated and sifted chocolate
2 ounces of, finely cut candied citron
$\frac{1}{8}$ ounce of cloves

$\frac{1}{8}$ ounce of cardamom
$\frac{1}{4}$ ounce of cinnamon
the juice of a lemon
$\frac{1}{2}$ pound of toasted, rolled and sifted brown bread
1 cupful of arrac

The yolks of the eggs, and the sugar, almonds and spices are stirred for $\frac{1}{2}$ hour, then stir through it the brown bread and the beaten whites of 12 eggs and at last the arrac. This is put into a well-buttered mould, sprinkled with wheat bread crumbs and baked for 1½ hours, the same as almond cake. Pour over it an icing seasoned with lemon juice or chocolate. The bread cake can also be made without an icing; in this case use a little more chocolate.

Bread Cake (1894)

Three cups of raised dough
Two cups sugar
One-half cup butter

One cup raisins
Teaspoon soda
Spice to taste

Bread Cake (1840)

When you are making wheat bread, and the dough is quite light and ready to bake, take out as much of it as would make a twelve-cent loaf, and mix with it a tea cup full of powdered sugar, and a tea-cup full of butter that has been softened and stirred about in a tea-cup of warm milk. Add also a beaten egg. Knead it very well, put it into a square pan, dredged with flour, cover it, and set it near the fire for half an hour. Then bake it in a moderate oven and wrap it in a thick cloth as soon as it is done. It is best when fresh.

Bread Cake (1893)

Three cups of very light dough
Three cups sugar
One cup butter
Three eggs

One nutmeg
One teaspoonful cinnamon, raisins
A teaspoon of salaratus dissolved in a little hot water

Bread Cake (1911)

Cream one cup of sugar and one-half cup of butter, add one-half cup of milk, two cups of flour sifted with three teaspoons of baking powder and last the stiffly beaten whites of three eggs and half a teaspoon of vanilla flavouring. Bake in one loaf

Breakfast Cake (1894)

Sift together:

Two cups flour
Two tablespoons Indian meal
Two tablespoons sugar
Four even teaspoons baking powder

One cup sweet milk
Two well beaten eggs
A pinch of salt

Bake in large or small tins.

Breakfast Cake (1893)

2 eggs
½ cup butter
½ cup meal
1 cup milk

1 cup flour
2 tablespoons sugar
2 teaspoons baking powder

Breakfast Cakes (1876)

One pint of meal
One pint of sour milk
One (tea) spoon of soda sifted in the meal

Two eggs
One ~~tea~~spoon of sugar

All thoroughly beaten. Bake quickly. If preferred, sweet milk and baking powder can be used.

Breakfast Cakes (1911)

Sift one cup of corn meal, one-quarter teaspoon of salt and two-level teaspoons of sugar together, stir in one cup of thick sour milk, one-half tablespoonful melted butter, one well beaten egg and one-half teaspoon of soda, measured level. Beat hard and bake in gem pans in a quick oven.

Breakfast Cakes (1893)

1¼ cups milk
¼ sugar
1 egg
2 cups flour
1 tablespoon Indian meal

1 tablespoon melted butter
1 teaspoon cream tartar
½ soda
Crystaline salt

Bake in quick oven in gem pan.

Breakfast Gems (1876)

Beat two eggs thoroughly and mix with a pint of sweet milk. Add a teaspoon of baking powder to flour enough to make a stiff batter. Stir into the batter a tablespoon of melted lard or butter, and bake in gem pans, first well heated. This receipt makes first-rate cakes with corn meal instead of flour.

Bremen Butter Cake (1904)

For the dough:

3 pounds of sifted flour
1 pound of washed and stoned raisins
½ pound of sifted sugar
1½ pints of milk

3 ounces of yeast
1 teaspoonful of salt
1 pound of freshened butter
Spices according to taste

For filling take:

¾ pound of washed and warmed currants
¼ pound of sugar

2 ounces of cut almonds
1 ounce of citron

Make the dough, warming all ingredients as given in Roll Cake (1904), let it raise slowly for about 1½ hours, roll into along narrow strip about 1 inch thick, press with the rolling pin in the center of this so as to have the sides thicker, fill with currants, citron, almonds, then fold the two sides together so as to have the cake shaped like a half moon, put into the pan, make a few incisions into the cake, let it raise, spread with egg, and bake in a moderate oven for 1 hour.

Breton Cake (1920)
(Gâteau Breton)

Set in a basin one pound and a quarter of sugar, eighteen eggs and a small pinch of salt; beat continuously for twenty-five to thirty minutes so as to have it very light, then add six ounces of almonds, including an ounce of bitter ones, these to be pounded very finely with one egg. Continue the beating process for a few minutes longer and then mix in a pound and a half of sifted flour and finally ten ounces of melted butter. Distribute this preparation into a set of six Breton molds, having these buttered and floured; fill them up to the top and bake in a slack oven. Remove as fast as they are done, unmould on a grate, let cool and then pare very straight. Ice the smallest as well as the fourth one in size with white vanilla fondant; the second and fifth with pink strawberry fondant and the third and sixth with chocolate fondant. Dry the icings well then dress the cakes on an office paste foundation in a pyramid, one on the other, alternating the colours and graduating the various sizes. Fill the hollow formed in the cake with Quillet cream and decorate with more of this pushed through a cornet. Keep the cake in a cool place until required for serving.

Brick House Bride's Cake (1911)

Whites of 5 eggs
1½ cups of sugar
½ cup of butter
½ cup of milk

2 cups flour
1 teaspoonful cream tartar
½ teaspoonful of soda
Flavour to taste; almond is best

Bride Cake (1864)

The bridal came; great the feast, And good the bride cake and the priest. SMART.

Take four pounds of fresh butter, two pounds of loaf sugar, pounded and sifted fine, a quarter of an ounce of mace and the same quantity of nutmegs; to every pound of flour put eight eggs; wash and pick four pounds of currants, and dry them before the fire; blanch a pound of sweet almonds, and cut them lengthways very thin, a pound of citron, a pound of candied orange, a pound of candied lemon, and half pint of brandy; first work the butter to a cream; then beat in your sugar a quarter of an hour; beat the white of your eggs to a very strong froth; mix them with your sugar and butter; beat the yolks half an hour at least, and mix them with your cake; then put in your flour, mace, and nutmeg; keep beating it till your oven is ready; put in your brandy; beat the currants and almonds lightly in; tie three sheets of paper round the bottoms of your hoops, to keep it from running out; rub it well with butter; put in your cake and the sweetmeats in three layers, with cake between every layer; after it is risen and coloured, cover it with paper.

It takes three hours baking.

Bride's Cake (1904)

1 pound of fresh butter
1 pound of fresh grated almonds
1 pound of powdered sugar
1 pound of warmed flour

12 eggs,
The grated rind of a lemon
A teaspoonful of mace

For brushing the cakes use:

1 the yolks of 4 eggs
¼ pound of powdered sugar
¼ pound of freshened butter

The juice of 4 lemons, using the grated rind of one of them

Cream the butter (see Cakes, General Directions (1904)) add sugar, spices, the yolks of eggs and almonds under constant stirring, and stir for ½ hour as directed Cakes, General Directions (1904). Then slowly add the flour, also the beaten whites of the eggs, and bake four cakes of equal size with a moderate fire to a dark yellow, not brown, colour.

Cover the cakes with a lemon cream, letting the butter melt on a slow fire, stir sugar, lemon peel, yolks of eggs and lemon juice to the butter until it is thick, take from the fire, stir for a while longer, spread three cakes with this, pour over the top the frosting, and decorate the top. This cake is much nicer when it is a few days old, which is the case with all layer cakes. Being very rich this cake is cut into fine slices when sent to the table. Remnants of the cake can be kept for some time by taking care of them as directed under Cakes, General directions (1904).

Bride's Cake (1913)

1/2 cup Cottolene
2 cups fine granulated sugar
1/2 cup milk
2-1/2 cups pastry flour

3 teaspoons baking powder
1/2 teaspoon salt
1 teaspoon orange extract
Whites of 8 eggs

Process: Cream Cottolene, add sugar gradually, beating constantly. Mix and sift flour with baking powder and salt; add alternately to first mixture with milk, continue beating. Add extract, and cut and fold in the whites of eggs beaten until stiff and dry. Fill a tube cake pan well-greased with Cottolene, two-thirds full, and bake fifty minutes in a moderate oven. When slightly cool,

Bride's Cake (1911)

One and one-half cupfuls of sugar
One-half cupful of butter
One-half cupful of sweet milk
Two cupfuls of flour

One-quarter cupful corn-starch
Six egg whites
One and one-half teaspoonfuls baking powder
One teaspoonful vanilla

Cream the sugar and butter, add milk, flour and corn-starch into which the baking powder has been thoroughly sifted, stir in the whites of eggs quickly with the flavouring.

Bride's Cake 1 (1894)

One-half cup butter
Two cups sugar
Whites five eggs
One cup cold water
Three cups flour

One teaspoon soda
Two of cream tartar
Sift last two into the flour
Flavour with almond

Make one sheet.

Bride's Cake 2 (1894)

Whites of four eggs
One cup sugar
Half-cup butter
One-half cup milk

Two cups flour
Two teaspoons cream tartar
Half teaspoon soda
Flavour with almond

Bridgeport Cake (1876)

One cup of butter
Two cups of sugar
Three and a fourth cup of flour
Four eggs

One cup of milk or cream
Juice and rind of one lemon
Two teaspoons of baking powder
Two cups of currants

Bridgewater Cake (1894)

Two cups sugar
Two-thirds cup butter
Three eggs
Three and a half cups flour

One cup sweet milk
Half teaspoon soda
One teaspoon cream tartar

Brioche, or Propheten Kuchen (1873)
(Brioche)

Weigh a pound and a half of flour. Mix two ounces of yeast with a cup of warm milk and stir it into a quarter of the flour; there must be milk enough to make this a soft dough. Set it to rise. Put the rest of the flour on a pasteboard, make a hollow in the middle, slice a pound of butter in small pieces, throwing them into the flour. Break ten eggs into the hollow of the flour. Sprinkle over an ounce of sifted sugar and half an ounce of salt. Add about a teacupful of milk, sufficient to work the whole into a fine smooth dough. Knead it well, and when the yeast sponge is risen, add this to the other dough, and knead the whole together until it has a fine smoothness. Put it into a pan and set it in a cold place for twelve hours; then turn it out on a floured pasteboard, and quickly mould it into a round mass; return it to the pan and set it by again for two or three hours. When it rises, flour the pasteboard and turn it out as before. Cut off one-fourth of it. Mould the three-fourths into a round loaf; put it on a buttered tin and press a hollow in the middle. Egg it over with the paste-brush, mould the smaller piece of dough pear-shaped; put its point into the hollow of the larger loaf, brush it all over with egg, and set it at once in a moderate oven, to bake an hour or an hour and a quarter.
The brioche is nicer baked in a large round tin of suitable shape, which must be buttered.

Brioche Cake (1920)

¾ pound sifted flour
½ pound butter
4 eggs
2 tablespoonfuls sugar
1 yeast cake dissolved in ½ cup warm milk
½ teaspoonful salt

Mix ½ cup flour with the salt, yeast and milk into a batter and set it in a warm place to rise until very light; then stir the butter to a cream and add the sugar, the eggs, 1 at a time, stirring a few minutes between each addition; as soon as the batter is light add it gradually to the butter and egg mixture, add the flour and work it with your hands on a floured board into a soft dough; cover and let it rise to double its height; work it thoroughly and let it rise again; when the dough has attained double its size butter a deep, round cake mould and cover the bottom with a round piece of buttered paper; take one-sixth of the dough off and lay it aside; shape the remaining dough into a round loaf and put it into the buttered pan; make a hollow in centre; form the small piece of dough into the shape of a pear and put the pointed end into the centre of cake; set it to rise to double its size; brush over with the yolk of 1 egg mixed with 1 tablespoonful water and bake in a medium hot oven.

Brod Kuchen (1912)

Stir two whole eggs and yolks of six eggs
Three fourths cup of sugar
One cup of almonds
One and one-half teaspoons cinnamon
One-fourth teaspoon of cloves
One ounce of citron

Stir until very light, add:

Juice of one-fourth of lemon
One-half glass of sherry wine

Beat the whites of six eggs stiff and mix alternately with mixture with one-half cup of rye bread crumbs ground fine.

Brod Torte (No. 1) (1873)
(Brown Bread Cake)

Half a pound of blanched and a quarter of a pound of unpeeled almonds must be well pounded together. Mix with them, by degrees, a pound of sifted sugar, the yolks of twenty eggs, a spoonful of mixed spice, a quarter of a pound of grated chocolate, half a stick of vanilla pounded, and half a pound of stale brown bread grated and moistened with wine. Mix all thoroughly. Have the whites of ten eggs whisked to a snow and stir this in lightly at last. Butter a large brioche or other mould, sprinkle it with raspings, pour in the mass, and bake it an hour in a moderate oven.
This torte is much improved by an icing of the following;
Chocolate Icing: Three ounces of sifted sugar, two ounces of grated vanilla chocolate, and the whites of two small eggs whisked well for half an hour, spread on the cake, and dried.

Brod Torte (No. 2) (1873)
(Brown Bread Cake)

Pound in a mortar half a pound of sweet almonds in their peels, and with them half an ounce of bitter ones blanched; using white of egg to keep them from clogging. Mix these in a pan with three-quarters of a pound of sifted sugar, the yolks of sixteen eggs, the grated peel of a lemon, two ounces of candied peel, sliced thin, a quarter of an ounce of powdered cinnamon, and half a nutmeg. Stir these for half an hour. Then add a quarter of a pound of brown bread, grated and sifted, and slightly moistened with wine or arrack, stir this well into the rest, and then stir in lightly the whites of the eggs, whisked to a stiff snow. Butter well and strew with crumbs of toasted bread a large cake mould. Put in the mass and bake it about an hour and a half in a moderate oven.

Brod Torte mit Chocolade (1873)
(Bread Cake with Chocolate)

Ingredients:

The yolks of twelve eggs
Half a pound of sifted sugar
Four ounces of chocolate, grated fine
A quarter of an ounce of powdered cinnamon

Half a pound of stale brown bread, grated and sifted
Two inches of vanilla, pounded with sugar
The egg-whites whisked to a snow

Proceed as directed in the above recipe.

Brown Nut Cake (N.D.)

2 cups sugar
¾ cup butter
4 eggs
1 cup unblanched almonds, chopped

1 cup grated sweet chocolate
1 cup milk
2 cups flour
2 teaspoons baking powder

Brown Sugar Cake (1893)

Two and a half cups brown sugar
3 eggs
1 cup butter
½ cup milk

3 cups flour
1 cup raisins (chopped and stoned)
⅓ teaspoon soda in 1 teaspoon molasses
⅓ of a nutmeg

Bublanina Cherry Cake (1920)

Cream:

¼ lb. butter

½ cup sugar

Add: 3 egg yolks

Beat: Add alternately, beating after each addition:

½ cup milk

1½ cups flour

Fold in:

3 beaten egg whites
1 tsp. lemon extract

1 tsp. salt

Pour into greased pan (9 by 13 inches.) Sprinkle about 1 or 1½ cups pitted cherries over the batter. Bake at 375 degrees until brown. Sprinkle powdered sugar over the top and cut into squares to serve.

Buckwheat Cakes (No. 1) (1904)

To every cupful of flour take a cupful of hot water, a large tablespoonful of thick sour cream, or if you have no cream, take melted butter or lard, yeast and a little salt. Currants can also be added. After all is stirred together take a spoon and beat the dough well, set it aside to raise and make into small or large cakes like the above.

Buckwheat Cakes (No, 2) (1904)

Two cupfuls of buckwheat flour, 3 cupfuls of hot water, 1 cupful of thick sour cream and salt are stirred well together and baked immediately in hot butter to a golden-brown colour.
The cream can be omitted and instead use 1 cupful of cold grated potatoes. Buttermilk can be substituted for the water if desired.

Buckwheat Cakes (1922)

3½ cups buckwheat flour
1-quart water
½ cup white flour
1 teaspoon salt

½ ounce compressed yeast
1 teaspoon sugar
2 tablespoons molasses

Dissolve the yeast in a little tepid water. Add the sugar and the rest of the water, also tepid. Mix with the buckwheat and white flours and salt to make a light batter.
Raise overnight, add the molasses and bake on a greased, heated iron griddle browning well on both sides. Serve steaming hot with butter and syrup or sugar.

Buckwheat Cakes (1864)

Do, dear James, mix up the cakes: Just one quart of meal it takes; Pour the water on the pot; Be careful it is not too hot; Sift the meal well through your hand: Thicken well - don't let it stand; Stir it quick, - clash, clatter, clatter! O what light, delicious batter! Now listen to the next command: On the dresser let it stand Just three quarters of an hour, to feel the gently rising power of powders, melted into yeast: To lighten well this precious feast. See, now it rises to the brim! Quick, take the ladle, dip it in; So, let it rest, until the fire the griddle heats as you desire. Be careful that the coals are glowing, no smoke around its white curls throwing; Apply the suet, softly, lightly; The griddle's black face shines more brightly. Now pour the batter on; delicious! Don't, dear James, think me officious, but lift the tender edges lightly; Now turn it over quickly, sprightly. 'Tis done! Now on the white plate lay it: Smoking hot, with butter spread, 'Tis quite enough to turn our head!

Buckwheat Cakes (1913)

Stir together one and one-half cupfuls of buckwheat flour and half a cupful of graham flour, add half an even teaspoonful of salt. Scald a cupful of milk and add a cupful of hot water. Add a third of a yeast cake that has been dissolved in warm water, and a tablespoonful of dark molasses. Beat all together and let it rise overnight. A few minutes before baking dissolve half an even teaspoonful of saleratus in a little warm water, mix it thoroughly in the batter. Take a large spoonful of batter for each cake and have the griddle hot.
(Half a cupful of the batter may be used to raise the pancakes instead of the yeast. Fill up the cup with water and set it in the refrigerator until wanted. Then pour off the water.)

Buckwheat Cakes (1840)

Take a quart of buckwheat meal, mix with it a tea-spoonful of salt, and add a handful of Indian meal. Pour a large table-spoonful of the best brewer's yeast into the centre of the meal. Then mix it gradually with cold water till it becomes a batter. Cover it, put it in a warm place and set it to rise; it will take about three hours. When it is quite light, and covered with bubbles, it is fit to bake. Put your griddle over the fire, and let it get quite hot before you begin. Grease it well with a piece of butter tied in a rag. Then dip out a large ladle full of the batter and bake it on the griddle; turning it with a broad wooden paddle. Let the cakes be of large size, and even at the edges. Ragged edges to batter cakes look very badly. Butter them as you take them off the griddle. Put several on a plate and cut them across in six pieces.

Grease the griddle anew, between baking each cake.

If your batter has been mixed overnight and is found to be sour in the morning, melt in warm water a piece of pearl-ash the size of a grain of corn, or a little larger; stir it into the batter; let it set half an hour, and then bake it. The pearl-ash will remove the sour taste and increase the lightness of the cakes.

Buckwheat Cakes (1869)

Take quart of buckwheat flour, half a pint of wheat flour, and a spoonful of salt; make them into a thick batter, with milk-warm water, put in a half tea-cup of yeast, and beat it well, set it by the fire to rise, and if it should be light before you are ready to bake, put a tea-cup of cold water on the top, to prevent it from running over, if it should get sour, pour in a tea-spoonful of salaeratus, dissolved in hot water, just before you bake.

It is best to make them up quite thick, and thin them with a little warm water before you bake; butter them just as you send them to table. If you can get brewers' yeast, it is much better for buckwheat cakes. In very cold weather, they may be kept made up for several days, and baked as required.

Buckwheat Cakes (1894)

Two cups buckwheat
One of white flour

One-half cup yeast

In the morning add two teaspoons sugar, and one teaspoon soda.

Buckwheat Cakes with Baking Powder (1920)
(Galettes de Sarrasin à la Levure en Poudre)

This paste should be made just when ready to use, in the same proportions and in the same manner as the buckwheat cakes with yeast, only suppressing the yeast. When ready divide it into two parts and incorporate into one of these two tablespoonfuls of baking powder; mix thoroughly and cook at once, proceeding exactly as for the others. As soon as the first part is exhausted put the same quantity of baking powder into the second part and proceed precisely as for the first.

Buckwheat Cakes with Sour Milk (1876)

One quart of sour milk
And flour enough to make a batter, not too stiff
One even tablespoon of salt

One teaspoon of soda (if the milk is very sour, add more)

Bake in small cakes. They are very nice.

Buckwheat Cakes with Yeast (1920)
(Galettes de Sarrasin à la Levure)

Put a pound of buckwheat flour in a bowl with four ounces of corn flour, two ounces of sugar and a coffeespoonful of salt; dilute all these ingredients with a quart of water, beat the mixture well to have it smooth, then add three-quarters of an ounce of yeast dissolved in a little tepid water; when all has been well stirred together cover the vessel with a cloth and keep it in a temperate place until the dough has risen to double its volume, which will take at least four hours or even more; stir with a spoon and work into it two tablespoonfuls of molasses; the paste is now ready. Heat a griddle, and as soon as it is sufficiently hot, and smokes rub it over with a cloth and butter with clarified butter or lard; pour on enough preparation to form small cakes three and a half to four inches in diameter, and a quarter of an inch thick; in order to have them round and of equal thickness iron rings levelled on the outside are used. When the cakes are firm enough, which will take about two or three minutes, lift up the rings and turn the cakes over to finish cooking for two or three minutes longer. Dress them on a very hot covered dish and serve at once.

Butter Cakes (1920)

1 yeast cake
1-quart sifted flour

1½ pints warm milk or water
1 teaspoonful salt

Dissolve the yeast in a little warm water; sift the flour and salt into a mixing bowl, make a hollow in centre, pour in the yeast and water, mix into a batter and let it stand overnight (this is called setting a sponge); next morning stir 1 cup sugar with ½ cup lard and ½ cup butter to a cream and add 2 eggs, 1 at a time, stirring a few minutes between each addition; then add the grated rind of 1 lemon and a very little powdered cardamon; mix this thoroughly with the sponge, add sufficient sifted flour to make a soft dough, cover it with a clean cloth and set in a warm place to rise to double its height; then butter 4 long, shallow tin pans (12 inches long, 8 inches wide and 1 inch deep) and dust each one with flour; when the dough has attained the desired lightness divide it into 4 equal parts; roll each part out on the pastry board, put it into the pan, press evenly all over and again set it to rise to top of pan; when ready to bake brush each cake over with melted butter, sprinkle over 2 tablespoonfuls granulated sugar mixed with a little cinnamon and bake in a quick oven to a light brown; as soon as done remove the cakes from the pans and lay them on a long platter, one over the other, with the sugared sides together; when cold serve with coffee.

Butter Cakes (1920)
(With Baking Powder)

2 cups sifted flour
2 eggs
1½ teaspoonfuls baking powder
1 tablespoonful melted butter

1 cup milk
½ teaspoonful salt
the grated rind of 1 lemon
½ cup well washed currants

Sift flour, salt and baking powder into a mixing bowl, make a hollow in centre, put in the 2 whites and 1 yolk of eggs well beaten, add the lemon, the melted butter and mix it with the milk into a thick batter; lastly stir in the currants; spread the mixture into 2 well-greased, shallow tin pans; first brush them over with the remaining yolk, then with 2 tablespoonfuls melted butter; mix 3 tablespoonfuls granulated sugar, 2 tablespoonfuls finely cut citron, ½ cup finely chopped almonds together, sprinkle this over the 2 cakes and bake immediately in a quick oven till done and a light brown. Prepared flour may be substituted for baking powder.

Butterkuchen (1910)

Prepare the dough as in recipe "Blechkuchen" (1910). Let it rise well after being spread on the tin, press the surface in a little and put ½ lb. butter in little lumps all over it. Strew with ¼ lb. castor sugar and bake a good brown in a quick oven.

Butterless-Milkless-Eggless Cake (1922)

2 cupfuls brown sugar
1 teaspoonful powdered cloves
⅔ cupful Crisco
½ teaspoonful powdered mace

2 cupfuls water
½ teaspoonful grated nutmeg
2 cupfuls sultana raisins
2 teaspoonfuls baking soda

2 cupfuls seeded raisins
4 cupfuls flour
1 teaspoonful salt
1 teaspoonful baking powder

2 teaspoonfuls powdered cinnamon
1½ cupfuls chopped nut meats
3 tablespoonfuls warm water

Put Crisco into saucepan, add sugar, water, raisins, salt, and spices, and boil three minutes. Cool, and when cold add flour, baking powder, soda dissolved in warm water and nut meats. Mix and turn into Criscoed and floured cake tin and bake in slow oven one and a half hours.
Sufficient for one medium-sized cake.

Butter-Mandel-Torte (1910)
(Almond Spongecake)

1 lb. butter
⅓ lb. sweet almonds
8 bitter almonds
1 lb. sugar
½ oz. baking powder

Grated rind of 1 lemon
1 lb. flour
½ gill rum
8 eggs

Cream the butter, add the beaten-up eggs and sugar and stir for ¾ hour. Then add the grated lemon peel and almonds, the rum, half of the flour, mixed with baking powder, and half of the whites of eggs, whisked stiffly. When well mixed, add the remaining flour and whisked whites. Fill a well-buttered tin and bake 1 to 1¼ hour. The substitution of hazelnuts for almonds is a great improvement.

Butter-milk Batter Cakes (1869)

Soak pieces of dry stale bread in a quart of butter-milk, until soft, break in two eggs, add a little butter or lard, and salt and flour enough to make it stick together, beat it well, add a tea-spoonful of salaeratus, dissolved in warm water; thin it with a little sweet milk, and bake as other batter cakes. They may be prepared in a short time.

Butter-milk Cake (1911)

Cream three tablespoons of butter with one cup of sugar
Add one cup of buttermilk
One well beaten egg

Two cups of flour sifted with four teaspoons of baking powder
One-half cup of seeded raisins cut in pieces and rolled in flour

Butter-milk Cakes (1869)

You may make a very good batter cake without eggs. To a quart of butter-milk, put a piece of lard, the size of an egg; warm them together, and stir in a tea-spoonful of salaeratus; make it in a thin batter with flour; beat it a few minutes, and bake it as other cakes.

Butter-milk Cakes (1869)

One pound of sugar
A quarter of a pound of butter
Three eggs
A tea-cup of butter-milk

Nutmeg or cinnamon to taste
Add as much flour as will make a dough that will roll out

Cut in round cakes and bake with a quick heat.

Buttermilk Muffins (1911)

Sift four cups of flour
One quarter cup of cornmeal
One level teaspoon each of salt and soda three times

Beat two eggs well
Add a level tablespoon of sugar
Four cups of buttermilk

The dry ingredients and beat hard for two minutes. Bake in muffin rings or hot greased gem pans. One-half the recipe will be enough for a small family.

Butter Sponge Cake (No. 1) (1922)

One pound of sugar
Sixteen eggs
One pound of flour

Four ounces of butter
Vanilla flavour

Beat the sugar and eggs on a slow fire till light and foamy; but do not let it get hot, not more than blood warm. Take off the fire and beat till cold; add the flavour and mix in the well sifted flour. When the flour is in, add the melted butter Hot. Fill into moulds and bake.
These cakes are best baked in wooden frames, as generally used for large square cakes, or in rings. Take the frames and rub lightly with butter or lard and dust with powdered sugar. Put a sheet of paper on the pan, dust also and set on the frame. Fill in the mixture and bake in a medium heat.

Butter Sponge Cake (No.2) (1922)

Sixteen eggs
Ten yolks
One pound of flour

One pound of sugar
Four ounces of butter
Vanilla

Mix the same as Butter Sponge Cake (No. 1) (1922)

Butter Sponge Cake (No.3) (1922)

One pound of sugar
Sixteen eggs
One pound of flour

Eight ounces of butter
Vanilla

Separate the eggs, beat the whites firm, then add the sugar gradually, beating all the time. Add the flavour and stir in the yolks. Add the flour; mix it in half and add the melted butter hot, and finish mixing. Bake the same as Butter Sponge Cake (No. 1) (1922) in layers or in one loaf.

Butter-Zopf (1910)
(Butter Twist)

1½ lb. flour
3 oz. sugar
2 oz. yeast
½ pint milk
2 eggs

4 oz. butter
8 bitter almonds
Grated rind of a lemon
Salt

Prepare the yeast with the milk as in recipe " Napfkuchen" and allow to rise. Sift the flour, melt the butter and mix both with the beaten-up eggs, the sugar, risen yeast, grated almonds, lemon peel and a little salt. Knead well. Cut into long strips and loosely plait to a twist, broader in the middle than at the ends, which should be pinched together to a point. Allow to rise a little more and then brush over with butter and bake in a medium oven. On taking out of the oven, brush over again with butter and sprinkle thickly with sugar.

Part 4: C

Cake (1898)
(A Plain)
Cake (1893)
(An excellent receipt)
Cake (1898)
(Birthday)
Cake, Pound (1898)
(Rich)
Cake for Jelly Roll or Charlotte Russe (1917)
Cake Made with Cream (1893)
Cake Shortcake (1905)
Cakes Stuffed with Apricot (1920)
(Gâteaux Fourrés à l'Abricot)
Cakes with Fat (1820)
Cakes with Fat (1820)
(Variations)
Cakes without Fat (1820)
Cakes without Fat (1820)
(Suggested Variations)
California Cake (1920)
(Made with Yolks)
California Cake (1897)
(Kalifornia-kaka)
Callas (1893)
Callas (1893)
(A Creole Cake Eaten Hot with Coffee)
Cambridge Muffins (1917)
Canada War Cake (1917)
(without Butter, Eggs, or Milk)
Candy Cake (1820)
Can't Fail Breakfast Muffins (N.D.)
Caramel Cake (1922)
Caramel Cake (1922)
Caramel Cake (1893)
Caramel Cake (1894)
Caramel Pineapple Cake (1922)
(Skillet Cake)
Caraway Cake (1878)
Carmelite Cake (1904)
Carolina Cakes (1876)
Carolina Muffins (1876)
Carrot Cake (1904)
Casinos (1920)
(Casinos)
Cerealine Muffins (1893)
Chamouinx Cake (1920)
(Gâteau Chamounix)
Chaperone Sponge Cake (1893)
Cheap Cake (1893)
Cheap Fruit Cake (1876)
Cheap Fruit Cake (1911)

Cheap Raisin and Currant Cakes (1922)
Cheap Sponge Cake (1893)
Cheese Cake (1920)
Cheesecakes (1864)
Cherry Cake (1898)
Cherry Torte (1922)
Cherry Valley Cake (1876)
Chess Cake (1893)
Chicken Short-cake (1902)
Chocolate Cake (1897)
(Chokolad-kaka)
Chocolate Cake (1904)
Chocolate Cake 1 (1876)
Chocolate Cake 2 (1876)
Chocolate Cake (1911)
Chocolate Cake (N.D.)
Chocolate Cake (1922)
Chocolate Cake (1905)
Chocolate Cake (1909)
Chocolate Cake (1913)
Chocolate Cake (1893)
Chocolate Cake (1893)
Chocolate Cake 1 (1911)
Chocolate Cake 2 (1911)
Chocolate Cake 3 (1911)
Chocolate Cake 1 (1894)
Chocolate Cake 2 (1894)
Chocolate Cake 3 (1894)
Chocolatc Cakc No. 1 (1913)
Chocolate Cake No. 2 (1913)
Chocolate Cake (1909)
(Or Devil's Food)
Chocolate Cake (1890)
Chocolate Cake (1912)
Chocolate Cake (1904)
Chocolate Caramel Cake (1912)
Chocolate Cocoanut Cake (1894)
Chocolate Cocoanut Cakes (1909)
Chocolate Cream Cake (1920)
Chocolate Fudge Cake (1912)
Chocolate Fudge Cake (1922)
Chocolate Gingerbread (1909)
Chocolate Glacé Cake (1909)
Chocolate Ice Box Cake (N.D.)
Chocolate Layer Cake (1909)
Chocolate Layer Cake (1920)
Chocolate Layer Cake (1911)
Chocolate Layer Cake (1913)
Chocolate Loaf Cake (N.D.)
Chocolate Loaf Cakes (1911)
Chocolate Marble Cake 1 (1909)

Chocolate Marble Cake 2 (1909)
Chocolate Nut Cake (1913)
Chocolate Sponge Cake (1913)
Chocolate Surprise Cakes (N.D.)
Chocolade Torte (No. 1) (1893)
(Chocolate Cake)
Chocolade Torte (No. 2) (1893)
(Chocolate Cake)
Christmas Cake (1922)
(Black Cake)
Christmas Cake (1913)
Christmas Pecan Cake (N.D.)
Chrysanthemum Cake (1920)
Cider Cake (1840)
Cider Cake (1869)
Cinderella Cakes (1909)
Cinderella's (1840)
(Or German Puffs)
Citron Cake (1920)
Citron Cake (1894)
Citron or Almond Cake (1876)
Clove Cake (1876)
Clove Cake (1894)
Clove Cake (1893)
Clove Cake (1876)
Cocoa Cake (1909)
Cocoa Cake (1911)
Cocoa Marble Cake 1 (1909)
Cocoa Marble Cake 2 (1909)
Cocoa Sponge Cake 1 (1909)
Cocoa Sponge Cake 2 (1909)
Cocoanut Cake (1889)
Coconut Cake (1912)
Cocoanut Cake (1876)
Cocoanut Cake (1922)
Cocoanut Cake Icing (1922)
Cocoa-nut Cake (1840)
Cocoanut Cake (1913)
Cocoanut Cake 1 (1876)
Cocoanut Cake 2 (1876)
Cocoanut Cake 3 (1876)
Cocoanut Cake 4 (1876)
Cocoanut Cake 1 (1894)
Cocoanut Cake 2 (1894)
Cocoanut Cake 3 (1894)
Cocoanut Cake 4 (1894)
Cocoanut Cake 5 (1894)
Cocoanut Cake 6 (1894)
(One, Two, Three, Four)
Cocoanut Cake (1893)
Cocoanut Cakes (1876)
Cocoanut Cakes (1876)
Cocoanut Cakes (1876)

Cocoanut Cheese Cakes (1898)
Cocoanut Cream Cake (1894)
Cocoa-nut Jumbles (1840)
Cocoanut Layer Cake (1922)
Cocoanut Layer Cake (1920)
Cocoanut Layer Cake (1922)
Coffee Cake (1922)
Coffee Cake (1864)
(Old recipe)
Coffee Cake 1 (1876)
Coffee Cake 2 (1876)
Coffee Cake 3 (1876)
Coffee Cake (1913)
Coffee Cake (1893)
Coffee Cake (1890)
Coffee Cake No. 1 (1913)
Coffee Cake No. 2 (1913)
Coffee Cake No. 3 (1913)
Coffee Cream Cakes and Filling (1911)
Coffee Layer Cake (1922)
Cold Water Cake (1894)
Cold Water Pone (1869)
Columbia Muffins (1922)
Columbian Ginger Cake (1893)
Common Cheese Cake (1840)
Common Gingerbread (1840)
Common Jumbles (1840)
Common Wheat Cakes (No. 1) (1904)
Common Wheat Cakes (No. 2) (1904)
Compiègne Cake (1920)
(Gâteau Compiègne)
Composition Cake (1876)
Composition Cake (1894)
Conde Cakes (1920)
(Gâteaux Condé)
Connecticut Election Cake (1893)
Cooking-school Muffins (1905)
Corn and Rice Muffins (1917)
Corn Bannock (1860)
Corn Batter Cakes (1869)
Corn Bread or Johnny-Cake (1894)
Corn Cake (1893)
Corn Cake (1893)
Corn Cake 1 (1894)
Corn Cake 2 (1894)
Corn Cake 3 (1894)
Corn Cakes (1922)
Corn Cakes (1913)
Corn Griddle Cakes (1876)
Corn Griddle Cakes (1893)
(Old Virginia Slap Jacks)
Corn Griddle Cakes with Water (1876)
Corn-Meal Batter Cakes (1899)

Corn Meal Griddle Cakes (1917)
Cornmeal Muffins (1922)
Corn Muffins (1922)
Corn Muffins 1 (1876)
Corn Muffins 2 (1876)
Corn Muffins (1917)
Corn Starch Cake (1894)
Corn Starch Cake 1 (1876)
Corn Starch Cake 2 (1876)
Corn Starch Cake 3 (1876)
Corn Starch Cake (1893)
Corn Starch Cake (1893)
Corn-starch Cake (1902)
Cornstarch Cake (1899)
Corn Starch Loaf Cake (1913)
Cornelia Cake (1909)
Cream Almond Cake (1893)
Cream Cake (1894)
Cream Cake (1876)
Cream Cake (1899)
Cream Cake (1913)
Cream Cake (1893)
Cream Cake 1 (1876)
Cream Cake 2 (1876)
Cream Cake 3 (1876)
Cream Cake 4 (1876)
Cream Cake or Pie (1911)
Cream Cake Paste (1920)
(Pâte à Chou)
Cream Cakes (1840)
Cream Cakes (1911)
Cream Cakes 1 (1894)
Cream Cakes 2 (1894)
Cream Cakes Glassé (1920)
Cream Cakes Iced with Chocolate, Vanilla or
Coffee (1920)
(Choux à la Crème Glacés an Chocolat, à la
Vanille ou au Café)
Cream Cakes with Burnt Almonds and Glazed
Cream Cakes (1920)
(Choux Pralinés et Choux Glacés)
Cream Cakes with Whipped Cream or St. Honore
Cream (1920)
(Choux à la Crème Fouettée on à la Crème St.
Honoré)

Cream Koch (1920)
(with Sponge Cake)
Cream Layer Cake (1913)
Cream Layer Cake (1911)
Cream Puffs (1922)
Cream Puffs (1911)
Cream Puff Balls (1922)
Cream Sponge Cake (1876)
Cream Sponge Cake (1913)
Cream Sponge Cake (1893)
Cream Sponge Cake 1 (1876)
Cream Sponge Cake 2 (1876)
Crisco Batter Cakes (1922)
Crisco Fruit Cake (1922)
Crisco Sponge Cake (1922)
Crisp Ginger-cake (1869)
Crisp White Corncake (1911)
Crown of Brioche (1920)
(Couronne de Brioche)
Crumb Coffee Cake (N.D.)
Crumb Griddle Cakes (1902)
Crumb Griddle Cakes (1911)
Crumbled Paste Cakes (1920)
(Gâteaux en Pâte Fondante) (1920)
Cup Cake (1904)
Cup Cake 1 (1876)
Cup Cake 2 (1876)
Cup Cake (1869)
Cup Cake (1912)
Cup Cakes (1922)
Currant Cake, Citron Cake, or Raisin Cake (1922)
Currant Cake (1904)
Currant Cake (1913)
Currant Cake (1898)
Currant Cake (1894)
Currant Cake (1893)
Currant Cake (1904)
Currant Cake (1904)
Cushion Cake (1922)
Custard Cake (1876)
Custard Cakes (1840)
Custard Corn Cake (1917)
Custard Pie (Cake Crumbs) (1917)

Cake (1898)
(A Plain)

Ingredients:

1¼ lbs. flour
1 tea-spoonful baking powder
6 oz. butter, or clarified dripping
½ lb. currants

6 oz. sugar
½ pint milk
A pinch salt

Method: Wash and pick the currants and dry them thoroughly. Mix the baking powder and salt with the flour, and rub in the butter or dripping, add the currants and sugar, and mix well. Make the milk warm but not hot, moisten the cake with it, and beat it for a few minutes. Then half fill a buttered cake tin with the mixture and bake in a moderately quick oven. When cooked turn the cake out of the tin and stand it on its side to cool.
Time: 1½ hours.
Sufficient for: 1 large cake.

Cake (1893)
(An excellent receipt)

Two eggs
1 cup sugar
1½ cups flour
½ cup milk
¼ cup butter

1 teaspoon cream tartar
½ soda
Crystaline salt
Flavour as you like

Beat the eggs, rub the butter and sugar together, add the eggs and beat, dissolve soda in the milk, put cream tartar in flour, sift twice to make it right, add milk and beat, add flour.

Cake (1898)
(Birthday)

Ingredients:

1 lb. flour
1 tea-spoonful baking powder
1 pinch salt
½ lb. butter
6 oz. currants
6 oz. sultanas

4 oz. candied peel
4 oz. sugar
2 oz. ground sweet almonds
3 eggs
¼ pint milk
1 tablespoonful brandy

Icing made with whites of 3 eggs and sugar in proportion

Method: Wash, pick, and dry the currants, pick the sultanas and finely shred the candied peel. Mix the baking-powder and salt with the flour, and lightly rub in the butter; add the fruit, peel, sugar, and almonds, and mix all well together. Beat and strain the eggs, add the milk and brandy to them, moisten the cake with these, and beat well for a few minutes. Line a cake tin with buttered paper, and half fill it with the mixture. Bake it carefully in a good oven, and when done take the cake out of the tin and stand it upon its side to cool.
As soon as it is cold make an icing as directed above, and cover the cake with it, using the blade of a knife to spread the icing. Keep about a table-spoonful of the icing, and colour it with 2 or 3 drops of cochineal; twist a cornet of stiff writing-paper, fill it with the coloured icing, and write the date of the birthday on top of the

cake. Set it in a very cool oven for the icing to harden and put it away to become firm. This cake should be made at least 2 days before it is needed.
Time To bake cake: 1¾ to 2 hours.
To set the icing: 30 minutes.
Sufficient for: 1 large cake.

Cake, Pound (1898)
(Rich)

Ingredients:

½ lb. flour
½ lb. butter
½ lb. pounded sugar
½ lb. currants
2 oz. candied peel
4 eggs
1 table-spoonful brandy

Method: Wash, pick, and dry the currants, and finely shred the candied peel. Beat the butter to a cream, dredge in the flour, sugar, currants, and peel. Beat and strain the eggs, add the brandy to them, and moisten the cake with these. Beat thoroughly for a few minutes, then half fill a cake tin which has been lined with buttered paper and bake in a good oven. When cooked turn the cake out of the tin and stand it on its side to cool.
Time: 1½ hours.
Sufficient for: 1 cake, moderate size.

Cake for Jelly Roll or Charlotte Russe (1917)

2 eggs
1 cup flour
1 cup powdered sugar
1-1/2 teaspoons baking powder
1/3 cup hot water
1/4 teaspoon salt

Beat the eggs very light, add sugar gradually, and continue beating; add water, flour, baking powder, and salt. Pour into a greased, paper-lined dripping pan and bake in a moderate oven about fifteen minutes. The cake should be about half an inch thick when baked. Trim off the edges, spread with jam or jelly, and roll firmly; wrap in a paper napkin to keep in shape. For Charlotte Russe cut cake into pieces to fit paper cases and fill with Charlotte Russe Mixture.

Cake Made with Cream (1893)

Break two eggs in a cup and fill with cream, and one cup sugar, one teaspoonful cream tartar, one-half teaspoonful soda and one and one- half cup of flour, with a little salt.

Cake Shortcake (1905)

1 small cup sugar
1/2 cup butter
1 cup cold water
1 egg
2 cups flour
3 teaspoonfuls baking-powder

Rub the butter and sugar to a cream; sift the flour and baking-powder together; beat the egg stiff without separating; put the egg with the sugar and butter, add the water and flour in turn, a little at a time, stirring steadily; bake in two layer-tins. Put crushed berries between, and whole berries on top.
Tiny field strawberries make the most delicious shortcake of all.

Cakes Stuffed with Apricot (1920)
(Gâteaux Fourrés à l'Abricot)

Roll out some puff paste parings to an eighth of an inch in thickness; cut it into rounds with a channelled pastry cutter two and a quarter inches in diameter. Place half these rounds on a moistened baking sheet, fill the centres with well-reduced apricot marmalade, wet over the borders and cover with the remaining rounds, fastening them together; egg over twice, mark a rosette on top and push into a brisk oven to bake. When the cakes are almost done sift powdered sugar over and finish cooking, allowing the sugar to melt well.

Cakes with Fat (1820)

Two methods may be employed in mixing:

Cake method of mixing:
1. Cream fat and sugar.
2. Add egg yolk well beaten.
3. Mix and sift dry ingredients and add alternately with liquid.
4. Fold in beaten whites.

Quick or Muffin method of mixing:
1. Soften fat and add to liquids.
2. Mix and sift dry ingredients.
3. Combine 1 and 2.

Both methods are satisfactory for plain cakes. Most butter cakes are a reduction or slight variation of the One, Two, Three, Four Cake, which consists of:

1/2 to 1 c. fat	4 eggs
3 c. flour	1 tsp. vanilla
2 c. sugar	1 c. milk
4 tsp. baking powder	

This makes a satisfactory loaf or layer cake.
Bakes to perfection as a loaf in fireless cooker in 1¼ hours with stones at 350 F.

Standard Proportions:

6 tbsp. fat	2 eggs
1½ c. flour	1 tsp. vanilla
1 c. sugar	1/2 c. milk
2 tsp. baking powder	

Mix either method.

Cakes with Fat (1820)
(Variations)

Boston Cream Pie: Bake in a thick layer in a round pan. Cut horizontally.
Spread cream filling between and dust top with powdered sugar or flute it with meringue or whipped cream.

Chocolate Cake: Add two squares or 6 tablespoons of ground chocolate plus one tablespoon molasses.

Caramel Cake: Add 1/2 cup caramel syrup instead of milk.
(Caramel syrup: Over a low fire melt ¼ cup sugar in small pan, stirring constantly. When sugar has turned to a light brown syrup, remove from fire. Add 1 cup boiling water and cook to a syrup consistency.)

Date Cake: Add 1/2 cup chopped dates, mixed with dry ingredients.

Marble Cake: Make part plain and part chocolate and alternate by spoonfuls when putting into pan, drawing tip of spoon back and forth through each colour.

Mocha Cake: Flavour with coffee extract and use mocha filling.

Nut Cake: Add ⅓ cup chopped nuts.

Orange Cake: Bake in layers, using orange filling and frosting.

Raisin Cake: Add ⅓ cup raisins.

Spice Cake: Add coffee extract in place of milk and spices as desired.

Cakes without Fat (1820)

Sponge Cake:

True sponge cakes are leavened only with air incorporated into the beaten eggs.
The yolks are beaten well with a Dover type of beater.
The sugar is gradually beaten with a wooden spoon into the yolks. Add flavouring.
The whites are beaten only till stiff and folded carefully into the yolks and sugar.
Sift the flour once and measure it. Sift it several times and fold it into the mixture, taking great care not to beat.
Bake in a Turk's Head cake pan in a slow oven. Invert and leave till cold. The pan for sponge cake is not greased.

Standard Sponge Cake:

6 eggs
1 c. sugar sifted 5 times

1 c. pastry flour sifted 5 times
Grated rind and juice of one-half lemon

Cakes without Fat (1820)
(Suggested Variations)

Jelly Roll: Bake in a thin sheet. Spread with jam or jelly and roll while hot.

Crescents: Cut with crescent cutter and ice with powdered sugar icing.

Lady Fingers: Shape with pastry tube.

California Cake (1920)
(Made with Yolks)

¼ c. fat
1 c. flour
½ c. sugar
1½ tsp. baking powder

5 egg yolks
1 tsp. orange extract
¼ c. milk

Cream fat and sugar. Add yolks beaten well and extract. Mix and sift flour and baking powder and add alternately with milk to first mixture.

California Cake (1897)
(Kalifornia-kaka)

Two cups sugar
1 cup butter
1 cup milk
2 whole eggs

3 teaspoons baking powder
3 cups sifted flour
Also, fruit and flavours to suit

This recipe is enough is enough for 2 cakes.

Callas (1893)

Three eggs
1 cup of sugar
1 cup flour
3 tablespoons of water

2 teaspoons Congress Yeast Powder
A little Crystaline salt
And any flavour liked

These need a quick oven. One tablespoon in a saucer. When done, turn on a napkin, and press in the form of a calla lilly. Fill with whipped cream slightly sweetened and flavoured.

Callas (1893)
(A Creole Cake Eaten Hot with Coffee)

One teacup of rice well boiled and mashed
One small coffee cup of sugar
Two tablespoons yeast

Three eggs
Flour sufficient to make a thick batter

Beat the whole well together and fry in hot lard. Be careful not to have the batter too thin, or it will not fry well.

Cambridge Muffins (1917)

1/4 cup shortening
2 cups flour
1/4 cup sugar
4 teaspoons baking powder

1 egg
1/4 teaspoon salt
3/4 cup milk

Cream the shortening; add the sugar and egg well beaten; beat well, add the milk, flour, baking powder, and salt, which have been sifted together; beat again, and bake in hot greased muffin pans twenty minutes in a moderate oven.

Canada War Cake (1917)
(Without Butter, Eggs, or Milk)

1 cup brown sugar
1 teaspoon cinnamon
1/4 cup shortening
1/2 teaspoon mace
1 cup boiling water

1/4 teaspoon clove
2 cups seeded raisins
1 teaspoon soda
1/2 teaspoon salt
2 cups flour

Mix sugar, shortening, water, raisins, and salt; boil five minutes; cool, and add spices, soda, and flour sifted together; beat well; pour into a greased, paper-lined bread pan, and bake in a slow oven one hour.

Candy Cake (1820)

1 c. light brown sugar
1 lb. walnuts weighed
1 c. dark brown sugar in shell
½ c. flour
1 tsp. baking powder
⅓ tsp. salt
2 eggs
1 c. raisins

Mix well. Line a cake pan with heavy paper. Grease and flour this. Pour in the cake batter and bake very slowly, since it burns easily. Cut in squares. This is a good candy substitute for an afternoon or evening party.

Can't Fail Breakfast Muffins (N.D.)

1 egg well beaten
1 teaspoon sugar
1 rounded tablespoon butter
1 teaspoon salt

Beat these ingredients together until light, then add one cup milk, two cups flour, sifted, with two teaspoons of baking powder. Drop in well-greased muffin rings and bake twenty minutes in quick oven. Serve with butter and syrup.

Caramel Cake (1922)

½ cupful butter
¼ teaspoon salt
¾ cupful sugar
1 cup milk
4 egg yolks, beaten light
1 teaspoon vanilla
Second ¾ cupful sugar
4 egg whites, stiffly beaten
4 teaspoons baking powder
4 cups flour

Cream shortening with ¾ cup sugar. Beat egg yolks until light and add second ¾ cup sugar, beating well. Add the egg and sugar mixture to that of the shortening and sugar, mixing well. Sift the flour, add the baking powder and salt and sift three times. Add this flour mixture and the milk alternately to the first mixture. Then add vanilla extract. Fold in the egg whites and bake in two-layer cake pans in a moderate oven, 350° F. Put the layers together and cover cake with a caramel frosting.

Caramel Cake (1922)

For Cake:

1¼ cupfuls sifted sugar
2 teaspoonfuls baking powder
2 eggs
1 teaspoonful vanilla extract
½ cupful Crisco
½ cupful granulated sugar
1 cupful cold water
½ teaspoonful salt
3 cupfuls flour
¼ cupful boiling water

For Filling:

1 teaspoonful Crisco
½ cupful brown sugar
1-ounce chocolate
½ cupful granulated sugar
1 teaspoonful vanilla extract
Pinch salt

½ cupful hot water

For cake: Put granulated sugar into small pan and melt over fire till brown, remove from fire, add boiling water, stir quickly, return to stove, and stir until thick syrup; set aside to cool. Beat Crisco and sugar to a cream, add eggs well beaten, flour, baking powder, salt, vanilla, three tablespoonfuls of the syrup and water. Mix and beat two minutes, then divide into two Criscoed and floured layer tins and bake in moderate oven twenty minutes.
For filling: Melt granulated sugar in small pan and stir until it becomes a light brown syrup, add the water gradually, then brown sugar, Crisco, salt, and chocolate, stirring all the time. Cook until it forms a soft ball when tried in cold water, or 240° F. Remove from fire, add vanilla, beat until creamy, then spread between cakes.
Sufficient for: one layer cake.

Caramel Cake (1893)

One even cup butter
Two even cups sugar
Three even cups flour
Whites of eight eggs

Two even teaspoonfuls baking powder
One teaspoonful vanilla
One cup milk

Stir butter and sugar to a cream, add milk slowly, then flour in which the baking powder has been mixed, and lastly the well beaten whites of eggs and vanilla. Bake in three layers and to prevent sticking use white paper cut the size of the tin and well-greased with lard.

Caramel Filling:

Two cups of brown sugar
One cup of cream or milk

Three tablespoonfuls butter
One teaspoonful vanilla

Boil until the mixture will hold together in water; then spread between the layers and on the outside. If it curdles when boiling, strain through coarse sieve and put on the stove again. When done, put in vanilla.

Caramel Cake (1894)

Two cups sugar
Three-fourths cup butter
Not quite a cup milk
Whites of eight eggs

Three cups flour
Two teaspoons baking powder
Flavour to taste

Bake in three layers.

Icing:

Two cups sugar
Butter size of a walnut

Not quite a cup of milk

Boil ten minutes, cool, then beat until stiff enough to spread on the cake.

Caramel Pineapple Cake (1922)
(Skillet Cake)

Put three tablespoonsful of butter and a cupful of brown sugar in an iron frying pan. Let it simmer for a few minutes. Then add sliced canned pineapple just to fit pan. A medium pan requires about seven slices around

and one in the middle. Then make a batter of three eggs, one and a half cups of sugar, one-half cup water, one teaspoon vanilla, a pinch of salt, one and a half teaspoons baking powder, one and a half cups flour.
Pour this batter over the pineapple; put frying pan into oven, leaving it in a hot oven for ten minutes; reduce heat and bake about fifty minutes. Turn out of the pan on a large plate.
Serve with whipped cream,

Caraway Cake (1878)

Beat to a cream, four ounces each of butter and sugar (cost twelve cents)
Stir in two eggs (cost two cents)

One gill of milk (cost one cent)
One pound of sifted flour (cost four cents)
Five cents' worth of caraway seed

Bake the cake for two hours in a deep earthen dish, testing it with a clean broom splint to be sure it is done before you take it from the oven. It will cost about twenty-four cents.

Carmelite Cake (1904)

9 Whole and the yolks of 2 eggs
¾ pound of sifted sugar
½ pound of almonds coarsely pounded with rose-water

8 tablespoonfuls of cherry cordial
The grated rind of a lemon
A little cinnamon
1 nutmeg

The whole eggs and the egg yolks are whipped together, adding the other ingredients. Then stir all together for ½ hour, ½ pound of flour is added and the cake baked in a moderate oven.

Carolina Cakes (1876)

Four eggs
Two cups of sugar
A half-cup of butter
One cup of cream

Thicken with flour
Two teaspoons of cream tartar in flour
Add one teaspoon of soda the last thing

Flavour with lemon and drop from the spoon.

Carolina Muffins (1876)

Melt in a quart of milk a piece of butter the size of an egg, stir in one quart of meal, one-half gill of yeast, one tablespoon of molasses. Let them rise five hours and bake in muffin rings.

Carrot Cake (1904)

10 ounces of carrots
14 eggs
11 ounces of sifted sugar

10 ounces of sweet and 2 ounces of bitter, grated, almonds
2 heaping tablespoonfuls of sifted potato flour or cornstarch

Wash the carrots, cook them in water until about half done and then grate them; the heart is not used. Then stir the yolks of eggs with the sugar, the juice of a lemon and part of the grated rind of a lemon and the almonds, add the carrots, stir for half an hour as directed under general directions (1904), mix the beaten whites of 9 eggs with the potato flour and bake like almond cake for 1½ hours.

Casinos (1920)

(Casinos)

For these cakes take puff paste made at six turns, having it an eighth of an inch thick; cut half of the rolled-out layer in two-inch in diameter rounds with a channeled pastry cutter, and range them on a slightly dampened baking sheet, then egg over. Divide the other half of the layer into the same number of rounds, but only an inch and a half in diameter; empty the centres of these with a pastry cutter an inch in diameter so as to form into rings, then lay them on top of the rounds; egg over lightly and decorate the surface of each one with a rosette of fine halved almonds burnt with egg-white and sugar, and then bake the cakes in a hot oven. When done fill the center holes with orange or quince jelly.

Cerealine Muffins (1893)

Two cups Cerealine Flakes
2¼ cups milk
2 cups flour
2 teaspoon baking powder
½ teaspoon Crystaline salt
1 egg
2 teaspoon melted butter
1 tablespoon of sugar

Put Cerealine in a bowl and pour milk over it. Sift flour, salt, sugar and Baking Powder into mixing dish, and mix thoroughly, then add contents of bowl melted butter and egg well beaten. Stir vigorously until batter is smooth and bake in greased gem tins.

Chamouinx Cake (1920)
(Gâteau Chamounix)

Bake in a slack oven a small Genoese preparation placed in a border mould, it having a round-shaped bottom buttered and bestrewn with chopped almonds. After it is taken from the oven, cold and pared, brush the surface over with apricot marmalade and lay it on a pastry grate, then cover entirely with kirsch icing, and when this is dry dress on a dish. Suppress the shells from about a hundred chestnuts, without touching the skins; boil them slowly in plenty of water in a covered vessel, then drain off the water, leaving them covered with a hot cloth; now quickly remove the skins; pound and rub the chestnuts through a sieve into a saucepan with three-quarters of their weight of powdered sugar added, also a small bit of vanilla; stir this well over a moderate fire until it detaches from the bottom and leave it till nearly cold, then dilute with a little light syrup and kirsch; incorporate into the mixture a few spoonfuls of well-drained whipped cream, but without weakening it, keeping it quite consistent, then stir on ice for ten minutes to harden, adding a salpicon of vari-coloured fruits after it is removed. With this preparation fill up the hollow of the cake and smooth it to a dome-shape, then decorate through a cornet with whipped cream slightly sweetened and flavoured with vanilla.

Chaperone Sponge Cake (1893)

Mix one and one-half cups pulverized sugar; one teacup flour; a little salt; one teaspoon baking powder; beat the whites of eleven eggs to a stiff froth; flavour with lemon or vanilla; mix all together and bake. Use yolks for custard or gold cake

Cheap Cake (1893)

One cup sugar
¼ cup butter
½ cup milk
1½ cups flour
2 eggs
1 teaspoon cream tartar
½ of soda
¾ cup raisins

Cheap Fruit Cake (1876)

One egg
One cup of sugar
One and a half cups of flour
A half-cup of butter
Two-thirds of a cup of currants
One cup of raisins

A half teaspoon of soda
Three tablespoons of sour milk
Two tablespoons of yeast
One teaspoon each of cinnamon, cloves and nutmeg

Cheap Fruit Cake (1911)

2 cups of sugar
½ cup of molasses
½ cup milk
1 cup of butter
4 cups of flour
1 teaspoon soda

3 eggs
Spice of all kinds
1 cup raisins
1 cup currants
½ cup citron

Will make two loaves.

Cheap Raisin and Currant Cakes (1922)

Two pounds of sugar
One and one quarter pounds of butter
One and one-half pints of eggs
One and one-half pints of milk

Three pounds of flour
Three quarters of an ounce of baking powder
Flavour mace and lemon

Mix like New York Pound Cake (No.2) (1922). Add the fruit when the flour is half mixed in and finish mixing. Bake about 350 degrees Fahrenheit, in small pound tins, or in large slab cake.

Cheap Sponge Cake (1893)

Three eggs beaten separately
1 cup sugar
1 cup flour
1 teaspoon Rumford Baking Powder

¼ teaspoon Crystaline salt
3 tablespoons lukewarm water
1 tablespoon vinegar

Beat the yolks of the eggs until thick, add gradually the sugar, water, and flour mixed and sifted with the baking powder and Crystaline salt. Add the whites of the eggs beaten until stiff, and the vinegar. Bake in a buttered angel-cake pan 45 minutes.

Cheese Cake (1920)

Dissolve ½ yeast cake in ½ pint warm milk and add 1-pound sifted flour, 2 eggs, ½ teaspoonful salt, 2 tablespoonfuls butter and ½ tablespoonful sugar; work this into a soft dough and set it in a warm place to rise to double its height; then roll it out ⅛ of an inch in thickness; butter 2 large cheese or pie plates, cover them with the dough, ornament the edge and let it rise again until light; mix 1-pound fresh pot cheese with 1½ cups thick sweet or sour cream, ¾ cup sugar (or sweeten to taste), 3 eggs and ½ cup currants; when this is well mixed together brush the dough over with melted butter and fill the plate with the cheese mixture; bake in a medium hot oven.

Cheesecakes (1864)

Treat here, ye shepherds blithe! your damsels sweet, For pies and cheesecakes are for damsels meet.

GAY.

Put two quarts of new milk into a stewpan; set it near the fire, and stir in two tablespoonfuls of rennet; let it stand till it is set (this will take about an hour); break it well with your hand, and let it remain half an hour longer; then pour off the whey, and put the curd into a cullender to drain; when quite dry, put it in a mortar, and pound it quite smooth; then add four ounces of powdered sugar, and three ounces of fresh butter; oil it first by putting it in a little potting pot, and setting it near the fire; stir it all well together; beat the yolks of four eggs in a basin with a little nutmeg grated, lemon-peel, and a glass of brandy; add this to the curd, with two ounces of currants washed and picked; stir it all well together; have your tins ready lined with puff paste, about a quarter of an inch thick; notch them all round the edge, and fill each with the curd.
Bake them twenty minutes.

Cherry Cake (1898)

Ingredients:

6 oz. flour
6 oz. sugar
6 oz. glacé cherries

4 oz. butter
4 eggs

Method: Beat and strain the eggs, add the sugar gradually, and dredge in the flour, beating all the time, then add the butter which must be melted but not hot, a tea-spoonful at a time, and lastly, the cherries; beat the cake well, pour it into a cake-tin lined with buttered paper, and bake for an hour in a moderate oven, covering the top with a buttered paper when half cooked.
Time: 1 hour.
Sufficient for: 1 cake of moderate size.

Cherry Torte (1922)

¼ cup butter
2 egg yolks
¼ cup lard
½ cup flour

4 tablespoons sugar
½ teaspoon baking powder
2 teaspoons cinnamon

Line a form with this dough.
Strain the juice from one quart of cherries.
Make a custard:

4 eggs, yolks and whites beaten (separately)
¾ cup sugar

½ cup sour cream

Put chopped almonds on dough, then cherries, and then pour custard over all. Bake 45 minutes in slow oven.

Cherry Valley Cake (1876)

Three-fourths of a cup of butter
One cup of milk
Two cups of sugar
Three fresh eggs

Three cups of flour
Two teaspoons of cream tartar
One teaspoon of soda
Flavour with vanilla

Chess Cake (1893)

Four eggs beaten separately and added to one cup of butter and one cup of sugar thoroughly creamed, flavour with nutmeg; line small patty pans with puff paste; place in the bottom a teaspoonful of jelly and pour over it a tablespoonful of the egg, butter and sugar mixture; bake in a rather slow oven. This is a nice tart for lunch or picnics as it keeps well and never gets dry

Chicken Short-cake (1902)

Mix 2 teaspoonfuls of baking powder with 1 pt. of flour. Rub it into a half cup of butter, add 1 cup of sweet milk. Bake quickly. Have prepared nice pieces of cold chicken, heat with gravy or a little soup stock, season well. Add some chopped parsley, pour over the short-cake and serve at once.

Chocolate Cake (1897)
(Chokolad-kaka)

One cup butter
2 of sugar
5 eggs, leaving out 2 of the whites

1 scant cup of milk
2 teaspoons of baking powder; mix well with 3 cups of flour

Bake in 2 long shallow tins.

Dressing: Beat the whites of 2 eggs to a stiff froth, add a scant cup and half of sugar; flavour with vanilla, add 6 tablespoons of grated chocolate; add the dressing when the cake is cold and cut in diamond shapes.

Chocolate Cake (1904)

Stir ½ pound of butter to a cream
Add 6 ounces of sugar
The yolks of 8 eggs
6 ounces of dissolved chocolate

1 spoonful of vanilla
1 spoonful of lemon sugar
¼ pound of flour

Constantly stirring and beat the dough for ¼ hour. Then stir through it the beaten whites of 6 eggs, pour into a buttered mould and bake in a moderately hot oven for 1 hour. Spread with an icing made of 2 ounces of chocolate, 4 spoonfuls of water and 3 ounces of sugar, and before serving spread over all some whipped cream.

Chocolate Cake 1 (1876)

One good cup of butter
Two cups of sugar
Three and a fourth cup of flour

Five eggs leaving out two of the whites for icing
One small cup of milk
One and a half teaspoons of baking powder

Bake in a dripping-pan and leave it in until used, as it is too light and soft to be removed.

Chocolate for filling: To the whites of two eggs beaten to a froth, add sufficient powdered sugar and grated chocolate to make a light, delicate icing, and two teaspoons of vanilla. Ice the cake while hot.

Chocolate Cake 2 (1876)

One cup of butter
Two cups of sugar
Whites of eight eggs

A half-cup of sweet milk
One teaspoon of baking powder in three cups of flour

Icing: A fourth of a pound of German chocolate and a half cup of milk; grate the chocolate and mix with the milk, thicken with sugar; boil the mixture till it candies, then spread between the layers.

Chocolate Cake (1911)

1 cup brown sugar
¼ cup sour milk
¼ cup butter
2 squares chocolate, dissolved in ½ cup hot water

1 teaspoon soda
1 cup flour, before sifting
Vanilla

This makes a thin mixture, but do not be alarmed, as it is quite right.

Frosting for Chocolate Cake:

1 cup granulated sugar

3 tablespoons hot water

Boil until it makes a soft ball in water. Turn this over white of one egg, well beaten. Beat all together until stiff, then turn over the cake.

Chocolate Cake (N.D.)

Part I.

½ cup strong coffee
¾ cup grated chocolate

½ cup brown sugar

Put in sauce pan and cook until thick. Set aside to cool.

Part II.

1 teaspoon baking soda
1 cup brown sugar
1 teaspoon baking powder
½ cup butter

½ cup strong coffee
1¾ cups flour
2 eggs
1 teaspoon vanilla

Cream butter and sugar, add coffee, eggs, and Part I. Add flour, sifted with soda and baking powder. Bake in layers and use Mocha frosting.

Chocolate Cake (1922)

For Cake:

1 cupful sugar
2 cupfuls flour
¾ teaspoonful salt
1 teaspoonful baking powder
¼ cupful grated chocolate

½ cupful sultana raisins
¾ cupful Crisco
½ cupful candied chopped citron peel
5 eggs

For Chocolate Frosting:

2 tablespoonfuls Crisco
2 cupfuls powdered sugar
2 squares melted bitter chocolate

6 tablespoonfuls coffee
¼ teaspoonful salt
½ teaspoonful vanilla extract

For cake: Cream Crisco; add sugar gradually, yolks of eggs well beaten, milk, flour, salt, baking powder, grated chocolate, citron, and raisins. Mix and beat two minutes, then fold in stiffly beaten whites of eggs. Turn into Criscoed and floured tin and bake for one and a quarter hour in a moderate oven. When cold cover with frosting

For chocolate frosting: Knead Crisco into sugar. Melt chocolate, add coffee, sugar, salt, and Crisco, and stir until thick, then add vanilla and put away to cool. When cold spread on cake. This frosting may be used any time. It is just as good made one day and used the next by adding a little more hot coffee. It is always soft, creamy and delicious.

Sufficient for: one cake.

Chocolate Cake (1905)

Material:

1/4 cup butter
1/2 cup sugar
1 egg
1/2 cup milk

1 scant cup Pillsbury's Best Flour
2 teaspoons baking powder
1 square melted chocolate
1/4 teaspoon vanilla

Way of preparing: Stir butter, egg and sugar until creamy. Add milk little at a time, stirring in gradually flour, sifted with baking powder. Now stir in melted chocolate, add vanilla and beat hard. Bake twenty minutes in a greased shallow pan.

Chocolate Cake (1909)

For two sheets of cake:

Use three ounces of Walter Baker & Co.'s Premium No. 1 Chocolate
Three eggs
One cupful and three-fourths of sifted pastry flour
One cupful and three-fourths of sugar

Half a cupful of butter
Half a cupful of milk
Half a teaspoonful of vanilla extract
One teaspoonful and a half of baking powder

Grate the chocolate. Beat the butter to a cream, and gradually beat in the sugar. Beat in the milk and vanilla, then the eggs (already well beaten), next the chocolate, and finally the flour, in which the baking powder should be mixed. Pour into two well-buttered shallow cake pans. Bake for twenty-five minutes in a moderate oven. Frost or not, as you like.

Chocolate Cake (1913)

Sift together two cups flour, one cup corn starch, and two teaspoonfuls baking powder, add to a cup of butter, creamed light with two cups sugar and one cup sweet cream. Add the stiffly beaten whites of seven eggs, flavour with vanilla, and bake in layers. For the filling boil together to a thick syrup, three cups sugar, one cup water, and half a cake of grated chocolate. Pour upon three egg-whites beaten very stiff, flavour with vanilla or bitter almond, and spread between layers

Chocolate Cake (1893)

Have ready one-half pound sweet chocolate grated; one-fourth pound chopped citron; one-fourth pound almonds blanched and chopped; five soda crackers browned and rolled very fine; wineglass of brandy and the juice and grated rind of two lemons; separate the yolks of eggs from the whites; beat yolks well, mix with other ingredients and lastly add the whites whipped to a stiff froth; bake two hours in a slow oven; cover with frosting and ornament with candied fruit.

Chocolate Cake (1893)

One cup sugar
½ cup butter
½ cup milk

1½ cups flour
2 eggs
1 teaspoon baking powder

Cream butter and sugar together, add eggs well beaten, then the milk, beat, add flour with baking powder, Crystaline salt, flavour to taste.
Frosting: One fourth cake of chocolate, put in a little water in a bowl over teakettle, add 1 cup confectioners' sugar, add water enough to make it the right thickness - vanilla.

Chocolate Cake 1 (1911)

Beat one cup of butter to a cream with two cups of sugar, add the yolks of five eggs, beaten until light-coloured, and one cup of milk. Sift three and one-half cups of flour with five level teaspoons of baking powder and add to the first mixture. Stir well and fold in the beaten whites of two eggs. Beat in layer cake tins and spread the following mixture between when the cakes are nearly cold. Beat one and one-half cups of powdered sugar, three level tablespoons of cocoa, one teaspoon of vanilla, and the whites of three eggs together until a smooth mixture is made that will spread easily. The exact amount of sugar varies a little on account of size of eggs.

Chocolate Cake 2 (1911)

Cook one cup of sugar, one-half cup of milk, one-half cup of grated chocolate and the beaten yolk of one egg together until smooth. When done add a teaspoon of vanilla and cool. Beat one-half cup of butter to a cream, add one cup of sugar slowly, and beat smooth. Add two beaten eggs, one-half cup of milk, two cups of flour in which two-thirds teaspoon of soda has been sifted and when well beaten add the cool chocolate mixture. Bake in four layers and put together with a white boiled icing.

Chocolate Cake 3 (1911)

Cook one cup of sugar, one-half cup of milk, one cup of grated chocolate and the beaten yolk of one egg together until smooth. When done add a teaspoon of vanilla and cool. Beat one-half cup of butter to a cream, add one cup of sugar slowly and beat smooth. Add two beaten eggs, one-half cup of milk, two cups of flour in which two-thirds teaspoon of soda has been sifted, and when well beaten add the cool chocolate mixture. Bake in four layers and put together with a white boiled icing.

Chocolate Cake 1 (1894)

One cup butter
Two cups sugar
Three and a half cups flour
Five eggs, leaving out whites of two

One cup milk
Teaspoon cream tartar
One-half teaspoon soda

Frosting: While hot, frost with the following: Whites of two eggs, one and a half cups sugar, six tablespoons grated chocolate.

Chocolate Cake 2 (1894)

One cup sugar
Half cup butter
Two cups milk
Two cups flour
Two eggs

Teaspoon soda
Grate two squares chocolate, mix with another half-cup milk
Add yolk of one egg
One teaspoon vanilla and sweeten to taste

Boil the mixture until soft, add to the other, bake three-quarters of an hour.

Chocolate Cake 3 (1894)

One cup sugar
One-fourth cup butter
One-fourth cup milk
One-half cup grated chocolate, dissolved in one-fourth cup boiling water

Two eggs
One cup bread flour
One teaspoon cream tartar
One-half teaspoon soda

Flavour with vanilla and frost with boiled chocolate frosting.

Chocolate Cake No. 1 (1913)

Cook together one-half cupful each of grated chocolate, milk and sugar with the yolk of an egg. Boil until thick and flavour with vanilla. Let it cool.
Cream together half a cupful each of butter and sugar, add a gill of sour milk, two cupfuls of flour, two beaten eggs and an even teaspoonful of saleratus dissolved in a little hot water. Stir the boiled mixture into the batter and bake in layers. Put the cake together with a white filling.

Chocolate Cake No. 2 (1913)

Cream together a cupful of sugar and a piece of butter the size of an egg. Add three well beaten eggs, a heaping tablespoonful of grated chocolate and a cupful of milk. Beat thoroughly and stir in a cupful of flour that has been sifted with a rounding teaspoonful of baking powder, a pinch of salt, and flavouring. Add flour if necessary and beat until very smooth. Bake in a medium oven.

Chocolate Cake (1909)
(Or Devil's Food)

5 level tablespoonfuls of butter
1-1/4 cups of sugar
3-1/2 squares of Baker's Chocolate, (melted)
3 eggs

1 teaspoonful of vanilla
3/4 a cup of milk
3-1/2 level teaspoonfuls of baking powder
1-1/2 cups of sifted pastry flour

Cream the butter, add sugar and chocolate, then the unbeaten eggs and vanilla, and beat together until very smooth. Sift the baking powder with one-half a cup of the flour, and use first; then alternate the milk and the remaining flour, and make the mixture stiff enough to drop from the spoon. Beat until very smooth and bake in loaf in moderate oven.

Chocolate Cake (1890)

One cupful of sugar
One-half cupful of butter

One half-cupful of sour milk
Two eggs

2 cupfuls of flour   1 small teaspoonful of soda

Grate one-half cake of chocolate, mix with one-half cupful of sweet milk and the yolk of one egg, sweeten to taste, add one teaspoonful of vanilla, and cook until stiff. Cool, and add to cake mixture. Bake in a moderate oven and frost with confectioner's sugar. This makes a nice layer cake, using frosting for filling. Sweet milk and baking powder may be used instead of sour milk and soda.

Chocolate Cake (1912)

One-half cup of butter
Two cups of brown sugar
Three-fourths cup of butter or sour milk
One-half cup of boiling water
One full teaspoon of soda

Three cups of flour
Three eggs
One-half cake of chocolate
One teaspoon of vanilla

Mix soda with grated chocolate and pour over the boiling water, let stand while mixing cake; bake in a mould, pan with stem. Remove when cold, cover over with white icing. When this cools, cover with a caramel or chocolate icing. Fill the center with whipped cream, sweetened and flavoured with chopped almonds enfolded, or it can be cooked in layer pans and filled with a layer each of white and chocolate icing. Fruits and nuts can be added to the cake batter. Bake in a loaf pan and serve without icing.

Chocolate Cake (1904)

14 eggs
½ pound of sifted sugar
½ pound of grated almonds

6 ounces of finely grated and sifted sweet chocolate
⅛ ounce of cinnamon
A teaspoonful of baking powder

The yolks of 12 eggs and 2 whole eggs are whipped with sugar, almonds and chocolate for ¼ hour, or stirred for ½ hour, then lightly stir through it the beaten whites of the eggs, quickly stirring in the baking powder and bake the cakes for 1 hour as directed for almond cake.

Chocolate Caramel Cake (1912)

One-half cup of butter
One cup of sugar
One-half cup of sweet milk
Three cups of flour

Two eggs
One teaspoon of soda dissolved in one-third cup of boiling water

Put on the stove one cup of sweet milk and one-half cup of chocolate, stir until dissolved and then stir into it one cup of sugar and the yolk of one egg. Boil all together and when cool flavour with vanilla. While this is cooling, beat up the first part of cake, add the chocolate custard, bake in layer cake pans and fill with caramel, chocolate or plain white icing.

Chocolate Cocoanut Cake (1894)

One-half cup butter
One cup sugar
One egg and yolks of two
One cup sweet milk
Two cups flour

One tablespoon baking powder
Two small cakes of chocolate
One-fourth cup cocoanut
Salt

Beat sugar and butter together, add the beaten eggs, flour, powder and milk; put cocoanut in milk to soften and add melted chocolate last. Bake in three layers. Fill with one cup sugar, boil until it hairs; beat the whites of the two eggs to a stiff froth, add one-fourth cake chocolate, one-fourth cup cocoanut. Flavour with vanilla. Improves by keeping a little while.

Chocolate Cocoanut Cakes (1909)

2/3 a cup of granulated sugar
1/4 a cup scant measure of water
One cup, less one tablespoonful, of glucose

1/2 a pound of desiccated cocoanut
1/2 a pound or Baker's "Dot" Chocolate

Heat the sugar, water and glucose to the boiling point, add the cocoanut and stir constantly while cooking to the soft ball degree, or, until a little of the candy dropped on a cold marble may be rolled into a ball. Drop, by small teaspoonfuls, onto a marble or waxed paper, to make small, thick, rather uneven rounds. When cold coat with "Dot" Chocolate melted over hot water and cooled properly. These cakes are very easily coated.

Chocolate Cream Cake (1920)

1 cup sugar
½ cup milk
1½ cups prepared flour

1 tablespoonful butter
2 eggs

Mix the same as in foregoing recipe; bake in 2 layers in jelly tins;

For the cream:

Boil ¾ cup milk
add ½ tablespoonful butter
2 tablespoonfuls grated chocolate

½ cup sugar
1 tablespoonful corn-starch wet with a little cold water

Stir and boil for a few minutes; remove from fire and mix with 1 beaten egg and ½ teaspoonful vanilla extract; when cold lay one of the cake layers on a flat dish and spread half the chocolate mixture over it; put on the other layer, spread over the top the remaining chocolate cream and decorate the top with shelled walnuts

Chocolate Fudge Cake (1912)

One-half cup of butter
One cup of sugar
Three fourths cups of flour

Two squares of unsweetened chocolate
Two eggs beaten until light
One teaspoon of vanilla

Bake in shallow pans twenty minutes.

Chocolate Fudge Cake (1922)

1 cup butter
5 teaspoons baking powder
2 cups sugar
¼ teaspoon salt

4 eggs
1 cup milk
3 cups flour
4 squares chocolate

Cream the butter and sugar. Separate the eggs and beat the yolks well and the whites stiff. Add the yolks to the butter and sugar. Sift the flour, baking powder and salt and add alternating with the milk.
Melt the chocolate and add. Fold in the beaten whites and bake in three layers m. a moderate oven (350 degrees F.). Frost with a thick fudge frosting. This makes a very rich cake.

Chocolate Gingerbread (1909)

Mix in a large bowl one cupful of molasses, half a cupful of sour milk or cream, one teaspoonful of ginger, one of cinnamon, half a teaspoonful of salt. Dissolve one teaspoonful of soda in a teaspoonful of cold water; add this and two tablespoonfuls of melted butter to the mixture. Now stir in two cupfuls of sifted flour, and finally add two ounces of Walter Baker & Co.'s Chocolate and one tablespoonful of butter, melted together. Pour the mixture into three well-buttered, deep tin plates, and bake in a moderately hot oven for about twenty minutes.
Vanilla Icing: Break the white of one large egg into a bowl, and gradually beat into it one cupful of confectioners' sugar. Beat for three minutes, add half a teaspoonful of vanilla extract, and spread thinly on the cakes.
Chocolate Icing: Make a vanilla icing and add one tablespoonful of cold water to it. Scrape fine one ounce of Walter Baker & Co.'s Premium No. 1 Chocolate and put it in a small iron or granite-ware saucepan, with two tablespoonfuls of confectioners' sugar and one tablespoonful of hot water. Stir over a hot fire until smooth and glossy, then add another tablespoonful of hot water. Stir the dissolved chocolate into the vanilla icing.

Chocolate Glacé Cake (1909)

Beat to a cream a generous half cupful of butter, and gradually beat into this one cupful of sugar. Add one ounce of Walter Baker & Co.'s Premium No. 1 Chocolate, melted; also, two unbeaten eggs. Beat vigorously for five minutes; then stir in half a cupful of milk, and lastly, one cupful and a half of flour, with which has been mixed one generous teaspoonful of baking powder. Flavour with one teaspoonful of vanilla. Pour into a buttered, shallow cake pan, and bake for half an hour in a moderate oven. When cool, spread with glacé frosting.
Glacé Frosting: Put half a cupful of sugar and three tablespoonfuls of water in a small saucepan. Stir over the fire until the sugar is nearly melted. Take the spoon from the pan before the sugar really begins to boil, because it would spoil the icing if the syrup were stirred after it begins to boil. After boiling gently for four minutes, add half a teaspoonful of vanilla extract, but do not stir; then set away to cool. When the syrup is about blood warm, beat it with a wooden spoon until thick and white. Now put the saucepan in another with boiling water and stir until the icing is thin enough to pour. Spread quickly on the cake.
Chocolate Glacé: After making a glacé frosting, dissolve one ounce of Walter Baker & Co.'s Premium No. 1 Chocolate in a cup, and put it with the frosting, adding also a tablespoonful of boiling water.

Chocolate Ice Box Cake (N.D.)

30 lady fingers	3 tablespoons sugar
3 tablespoons water	½ pound sweet chocolate
4 eggs separated	Small piece butter

Line a spring pan with lady fingers, side and bottom. Melt the chocolate in a double boiler, add sugar and water with yolks beaten well, cook slowly until thick and smooth, stirring constantly, beat the whites stiff, and when chocolate is cold add to the whites. Pour it on the lady fingers and place more lady fingers on the top of the filling and set in ice box for 24 hours. When ready to serve add the whipping cream, over top place nuts or cherries.

Chocolate Layer Cake (1909)

Beat half a cupful of butter to a cream, and gradually beat into it one cupful of sugar. When this is light, beat in half a cupful of milk, a little at a time, and one teaspoonful of vanilla. Beat the whites of six eggs to a stiff froth. Mix half a teaspoonful of baking powder with two scant cupfuls of sifted flour. Stir the flour and whites of eggs alternately into the mixture. Have three deep tin plates well-buttered and spread two-thirds of the batter in two of them.

Into the remaining batter stir one ounce of Walter Baker & Co.'s Premium No. 1 Chocolate, melted, and spread this batter in the third plate. Bake the cakes in a moderate oven for about twenty minutes. Put a layer of white cake on a large plate and spread with white icing. Put the dark cake on this, and also spread with white icing. On this put the third cake. Spread with chocolate icing.

To Make the Icing: Put into a granite-ware saucepan two gills of sugar and one of water and boil gently until bubbles begin to come from the bottom--say, about five minutes. Take from the fire instantly. Do not stir or shake the sugar while it is cooking. Pour the hot syrup in a thin stream into the whites of two eggs that have been beaten to a stiff froth, beating the mixture all the time. Continue to beat until the icing is thick. Flavour with one teaspoonful of vanilla. Use two-thirds of this as a white icing, and to the remaining third add one ounce of melted chocolate. To melt the chocolate, shave it fine and put in a cup, which is then to be placed in a pan of boiling water.

Chocolate Layer Cake (1920)

4 eggs
1 cup butter
2 cups sugar
1 cup milk
3 cups prepared flour
1 teaspoonful vanilla

Stir butter and sugar to a light white cream and add the eggs, 1 at a time, stirring a few minutes between each addition; next add vanilla, the sifted flour and milk alternately; bake in paper lined jelly tins in a quick oven; make 4 layers; in the meantime prepare the following filling: - Beat the whites of 3 eggs to a stiff froth and add 1½ cups powdered sugar, 4 tablespoonfuls Baker's grated chocolate and 1 teaspoonful vanilla; mix all well together and put it between the layers and on top; or put boiled chocolate glaze between the layers and over the top. The top of cake may be ornamented with blanched almonds laid in a circle around the top and some in the centre.

Chocolate Layer Cake (1911)

Beat a half cupful butter to a cream, adding gradually one cupful sugar. When light beat in a little at a time, a half cupful milk and a teaspoonful vanilla. Beat the whites of six eggs to a stiff froth and sift a teaspoonful and a half with two cupfuls flour. Add the sifted flour to the mixture. Then fold in the whipped whites. Have three buttered layer cake tins ready and put two-thirds of the mixture into two of them, into the third tin put the remainder of the batter, having first added to it two tablespoons melted chocolate. Bake the cakes in a rather quick oven for twenty minutes. Put a layer of the white cake on a large plate and cover with white icing, on this lay a dark layer and cover with more of the white icing. On this put the third cake and cover with the chocolate icing. Put into a graniteware pan one cupful and a half cupful water and cook gently until bubbles begin to rise from bottom. Do not stir or shake while cooking. Take at once from the stove and pour in a thin stream over the stiffly whipped whites of two eggs. Beat it until thick, flavour with vanilla, and use two-thirds of this for the white icing. Into the remainder put a tablespoon and a half-melted chocolate and a suspicion of cinnamon extract and frost the top and sides of the cake.

Chocolate Layer Cake (1913)

4 squares chocolate
3 tablespoons boiling water
1/3 cup Cottolene
1-1/2 cups sugar
1/2 cup milk
2 cups pastry flour
2 teaspoons baking powder
1/4 teaspoon salt
3 eggs
1/2 teaspoon Vanilla

Process: Melt chocolate over hot water, add boiling water and cook over hot water until smooth, stirring constantly. Cream Cottolene, add sugar gradually, stirring constantly; add chocolate mixture. Add yolks of eggs well beaten. Mix and sift flour, baking powder and salt, add alternately to first mixture with milk. Add flavouring and cut and fold in the stiffly beaten whites of eggs. Turn into buttered layer cake pans and bake fifteen minutes in a hot oven. Spread with Boiled Frosting and sprinkle with shredded toasted almonds before frosting sets.

Chocolate Loaf Cake (N.D.)

½ cup butter
½ teaspoon salt
½ cup sugar
1 teaspoon vanilla
Yolks of four eggs

2 squares of chocolate melted in five tablespoons of hot water
½ cup milk
1¾ cups flour
2 teaspoons baking powder

Cream butter and sugar, add egg yolks and beat well. Add chocolate, then vanilla, flour and baking powder. Lastly fold in the whites of the eggs, beaten stiff, and bake in a loaf pan for one hour.

Chocolate Loaf Cakes (1911)

Cream one cup of butter, add two and one-half cups of sugar and beat to a cream. Beat the yolks of five eggs light, add to the butter and sugar, with one cup of milk and three cups of flour in which four level teaspoons of baking powder have been sifted, the stiffly beaten whites of five eggs and two teaspoons of vanilla flavouring and two squares of chocolate melted. Bake in a moderate oven.

Chocolate Marble Cake 1 (1909)

Put one ounce of Walter Baker & Co.'s Chocolate and one tablespoonful of butter in a cup, and set this in a pan of boiling water. Beat to a cream half a cupful of butter and one cupful of sugar. Gradually beat in half a cupful of milk. Now add the whites of six eggs beaten to a stiff froth, one teaspoonful of vanilla, and a cupful and a half of sifted flour, in which is mixed one teaspoonful of baking powder. Put about one-third of this mixture into another bowl and stir the melted butter and chocolate into it. Drop the white-and-brown mixture in spoonfuls into a well-buttered deep cake pan and bake in a moderate oven for about forty-five minutes; or, the cake can be baked in a sheet and iced with a chocolate or white icing.

Chocolate Marble Cake 2 (1909)

This is the same as the Cocoa Marble Cake. Add to one-third of the mixture one and one-half squares of Baker's Chocolate in place of the cocoa, and one cup of chopped walnuts to the other part in place of the shredded cocoanut.

Chocolate Nut Cake (1913)

1/3 cup Cottolene
2 cups sugar
4 eggs
1 cup milk
2-1/3 cups flour

4 teaspoons baking powder
1/4 teaspoon salt
2 squares chocolate melted
3/4 cup English walnut meats broken in pieces
1/2 teaspoon vanilla

Process: Cream Cottolene, add gradually one cup sugar, stirring constantly. Beat egg yolks thick and light, add gradually remaining cup of sugar; combine mixtures. Add melted chocolate. Mix and sift flour, baking powder and salt; add to first mixture alternately with milk. Add nut meats and vanilla, then cut and fold in the whites of eggs beaten stiff. Turn into a well-greased tube pan and bake forty-five minutes a moderate oven. Cool and spread with boiled frosting.

Chocolate Sponge Cake (1913)

Sift together a large cupful of flour and a teaspoonful of baking powder with half an even teaspoonful of salt, an even teaspoonful of grated nutmeg and a teaspoonful of orange juice. Add a square of chocolate, melted, and two well beaten eggs. Stir thoroughly and pour in half a cupful of boiling water. Beat all together until smooth.

Chocolate Surprise Cakes (N.D.)

1½ cups flour, sifted
1½ squares chocolate
¾ cup sugar

1 tablespoon melted shortening
1 teaspoon soda
1 cup thick cream or milk

Beat until smooth. Bake for twenty minutes in muffin tins. Cut out center of each, fill with whipped cream, replace crust and cover with chocolate icing.

Chocolade Torte (No. 1) (1893)
(Chocolate Cake)

Half a pound of blanched almonds, well pounded, half a pound of sifted sugar, the yolks of nine eggs, added by degrees, must be beaten to a cream. Then mix in a quarter of a pound of grated chocolate, half a stick of vanilla pounded, two ounces of fine breadcrumbs, and, lastly, the whites of five eggs whipped to a snow. Butter a mould and strew it with crumbs. Bake it in a moderate oven.

Chocolade Torte (No. 2) (1893)
(Chocolate Cake)

Half a pound of sifted sugar, with five eggs, and the yolks of five others, must be beaten half an hour. Then add two ounces and a half of grated chocolate, four ounces of fine flour, a little lemon-peel, and the whites of the five eggs beaten to a snow. Mix the whole well and bake it in a thickly buttered mould.

Christmas Cake (1922)
(Black Cake)

1 lb. sugar
1 lb. butter
1 lb. flour
10 eggs
½ pt. brandy
4 lbs. currants
2½ lbs. raisins, seeded

1 lbs. citron
½ lbs. orange peel
¼ pt. black molasses
½ oz. cloves
½ oz. ginger
1 oz. cinnamon
Lemon and almond flavour

Mix like the fruit cake, American Fruit Cake (1922)

Christmas Cake (1913)

Prepare fruit first. Cut small half a pound of homemade citron drained from syrup, wash and seed one-pound raisins, pick, wash and dry one-pound currants, mince a teacup of any firm preserve - quince, peach or pear, or use a cupful of preserved cherries whole. Shred fine four ounces of homemade candied peel, also four ounces of preserved ginger, add a cupful of nutmeats - pecans or English walnuts, or even scalybarks, cutting them in bits, mix all well together, then pour upon them the strained juice of three oranges, and three lemons, also add the grated yellow peel. Next pour on half a pint of whiskey, a gill of rum, and a tumbler of cordial - peach or blackberry, and homemade if possible. Let stand overnight, in a warm place – the fruit should take up the most part of the liquor. A glass of tart jelly is held an improvement by some. I do not put it in - the preserves suit my palate better. Cream a full pound of butter with four cups sifted sugar, beat into it one at a time, ten large fresh eggs. After them put in four cups dried and sifted flour, mix smooth, then put in the fruit, drained from the liquor and lightly dredged with hot, sifted flour. Mix well, then add the liquor drained from the fruit, along with a tablespoonful of lemon essence, and as much vanilla or rose water. If the batter is too stiff to stir well, thin with either a little sweet cream or boiling water, or cordial. Pour into pans buttered and lined with five thicknesses of buttered paper, set the pans in other pans of hot water inside a warm but not brisk oven, shield the tops with double paper, and let rise half an hour. Increase heat then, but the baking must be slow. Four to five hours is required, according to the size of pans. Keep covered until the last half hour - then the heat may be sensibly increased. Test with straws - when they come out clean, take up, set pans on racks, cover with thick cloth and let cool thoroughly. Frost next day, with either plain or boiled frosting. By baking the cake in rather small square moulds, set close in a larger pan, the squares can be cut without waste and frosted to make individual cakes.

Christmas Pecan Cake (N.D.)

1-pound sugar
½ pound butter
6 eggs
1-pound white raisins
1-pound flour
1 teaspoon baking powder

1-pound pecan meats
2 teaspoons grated nutmeg, dissolved in wine glass of brandy or cider
½ pound candied cherries and pineapple may be added to half the amount of raisins

Bake slowly for three hours in a tube pan lined with seven of heavy brown paper. Slice thin.

Chrysanthemum Cake (1920)

½ pint butter
1-pint sugar
1½ pints flour sifted with 1½ teaspoonfuls baking powder

The grated rind of 1 orange
½ pint milk
The whites of 8 eggs

Stir butter and sugar with your right hand to a light white cream; beat the whites to a stiff froth, add them to the creamed butter and mix well together with a spoon; add alternately the flour and milk; then add the grated orange peel and a few drops of cochineal, to colour the mixture a delicate pink; butter 3 large jelly tins, dust them with fine bread crumbs, fill in the mixture in equal parts and bake in a medium hot oven; when done remove the cakes from the pans and lay them aside to cool; mix ½ cup powdered sugar with the beaten whites of 2 eggs; spread this icing over the layers and sprinkle them thickly with freshly grated cocoanut; lay the layers over one another, cover the top with pink icing and sprinkle over some cocoanut.

Cider Cake (1840)

Pick, wash, and dry a pound of currants, and sprinkle them well with flour; and prepare two nutmegs, and a large table-spoonful of powdered cinnamon. Sift half a pound and two ounces of flour. Stir together till very light, six ounces of fresh butter, and half a pound of powdered white sugar; and add gradually the spice, with two wine glasses of brandy, (or one of brandy and one of white wine.) Beat four eggs very light and stir them into the mixture alternately with the flour. Add by degrees half a pint of brisk cider; and then stir in the currants, a few at a time. Lastly, a small tea-spoonful of pearl-ash or salaeratus dissolved in a little warm water. Having stirred the whole very hard, put it into a buttered tin pan, and let it stand before the fire half an hour previous to baking. Bake it in a brisk oven an hour or more according to its thickness. Or you may bake it as little cakes, putting it into small tins; in which case use but half a pound of flour in raising the batter.

Cider Cake (1869)

Take a pound and a half of flour
Three-quarters of sugar

A quarter of a pound of butter

Dissolve a tea-spoonful of salaeratus in as much cider as will make it a soft dough, and bake it in shallow pans; season it with spice to your taste

Cinderella Cakes (1909)

Use two eggs
One cupful of sugar
One cupful and a quarter of flour
One gill of cold water
One tablespoonful of lemon juice

One teaspoonful of baking powder
One ounce of Walter Baker & Co.'s Premium No. 1 Chocolate
Half a tumbler of any kind of jelly
Chocolate icing the same as for éclairs

Separate the eggs and beat the yolks and sugar together until light. Beat the whites until light, and then beat them with yolks and sugar and grated chocolate. Next beat in the lemon juice and water, and finally the flour, in which the baking powder should be mixed. Beat for three minutes, and then pour the batter into two pans, and bake in a moderate oven for about eighteen minutes. When done, spread one sheet of cake with the jelly, and press the other sheet over it; and when cold, cut into little squares and triangular pieces. Stick a wooden toothpick into each of these pieces and dip each one into the hot icing, afterwards removing the toothpick, of course.

Cinderella's (1840)
(Or German Puffs)

Sift eight table-spoonfuls of the finest flour. Cut up in a quart of rich milk, half a pound of fresh butter, and set it on the stove, or near the fire, till it has melted. Beat eight eggs very light, and stir them gradually into the milk and butter, alternately with the flour. Add a powdered nutmeg, and a tea-spoonful of powdered cinnamon. Mix the whole very well to a fine smooth batter, in which there must be no lumps. Butter some large common tea-cups and divide the mixture among them till they are half full or a little more. Set them immediately in a quick oven and bake them about a quarter of an hour. When done, turn them out into a dish and grate white sugar over them. Serve them up hot, with a sauce of sweetened cream flavoured with wine and nutmeg; or you may eat them with molasses and butter; or with sugar and wine. Send them round whole, for they will fall almost as soon as cut.

Citron Cake (1920)

Cut ½ pound citron into fine slices and prepare a cake batter the same as for Plain Cake; butter a large, round pan and line it with buttered paper; pour in a layer of cake batter; then a layer of sliced citron; then batter and citron again; continue until all is used; bake in a medium hot oven till done, which will take about 1¼ hours; if the oven should be too hot cover the cake with buttered paper.

Citron Cake (1894)

One-pound sugar
Three-quarters pound butter
One-pound flour
Eight eggs

Half cup sour milk
One- half teaspoon cream tartar
One teaspoon soda
One-pound citron

Citron or Almond Cake (1876)

Whites of ten eggs well beaten
A half-cup of butter
A half-cup of milk
One cup of sugar
Two small teaspoons of baking powder
Two cups of flour

Put citron or almond in layers of about one-half pound (scant weight).

Clove Cake (1876)

One pound of flour
One pound of sugar
A half-pound of butter
Four eggs
One cup of sweet milk
One teaspoon of baking powder
One teaspoon of cloves
One nutmeg
One teaspoon of strong cinnamon

Clove Cake (1894)

Two cups sugar
One cup butter
Two cups stoned raisins, chopped fine
One teaspoon cloves
Two of nutmeg
One and one-half of cinnamon
One cup milk, two eggs
One-half teaspoon soda
One teaspoon cream tartar
Two and one-half cups flour

This cake is better when a week old than when first baked.

Clove Cake (1893)

One cup butter
1 cup sugar
1 cup milk
1 cup molasses
2 eggs
1 teaspoon soda
Tablespoon cloves
Cup currants
1½ cups flour

Clove Cake (1876)

One cup of molasses
A half-cup of sour milk
Two cups of flour
One egg
One teaspoon of soda
One tablespoon of ground cloves

Cocoa Cake (1909)

1/2 a cup of butter
3/4 a cup of milk
1 cup of sugar
6 level tablespoonfuls of Baker's Cocoa
3 eggs
2 level teaspoonfuls of baking powder
1 teaspoonful of vanilla
1-1/2 or 2 cups of sifted pastry flour

Cream the butter, stir in the sugar gradually, add the unbeaten eggs, and beat all together until very creamy. Sift together one-half cup of the flour, the cocoa and baking powder; use this flour first, then alternate the milk and remaining flour, using enough to make mixture stiff enough to drop from the spoon; add vanilla and beat until very smooth; then bake in loaf in moderately hot oven thirty-five or forty minutes.

Tests for baking cake. It is baked enough when:
1. It shrinks from the pan.
2. Touching it on the top, springs back.
3. No singing sound.

Cocoa Cake (1911)

Cream one-half cup of butter, add one cup of sugar, and beat again. Add the beaten yolks of three eggs and a teaspoon of vanilla. Sift two cups of pastry flour twice with one-quarter cup of cocoa and four level teaspoons of baking powder. Add to the first mixture alternately with three-quarters cup of milk, beat hard, and fold in the stiffly beaten whites of three eggs. Bake in a loaf and cover with white icing.

Cocoa Marble Cake 1 (1909)

6 level tablespoonfuls of butter
1 cup of granulated sugar
3 eggs

1 teaspoonful of vanilla
3/4 a cup of milk

Three level teaspoonfuls of baking powder, about one and three-quarter cups of sifted flour, or flour enough to make mixture stiff enough to drop from the spoon. Mix in the order given. Reserve one-third of this mixture and add to it four level tablespoonfuls of Baker's Cocoa and to the other one cup of shredded cocoanut. Bake thirty-five or forty minutes according to size and shape of pan.

Cocoa Marble Cake 2 (1909)

1/3 a cup of butter
1 cup of sugar
1 egg
1/2 a cup of milk

1 teaspoonful of vanilla
2 cups of flour
2 teaspoonfuls of baking powder
3 tablespoonfuls of Baker's Cocoa

Cream the butter, add sugar, vanilla and egg; beat thoroughly, then add flour (in which is mixed the baking powder) and milk, alternately, until all added. To one-third of the mixture add the cocoa and drop the white and brown mixture in spoonfuls into small, deep pans, and bake about forty minutes in moderate oven.

Cocoa Sponge Cake 1 (1909)

4 eggs
1/4 a cup of sugar
Pinch of salt

4 tablespoonfuls of Baker's Cocoa
1/2 a cup of sifted pastry flour
1 teaspoonful of vanilla

Separate yolks from whites of eggs; beat yolks in a small bowl with the Dover egg-beater until very thick; add sugar, salt and vanilla, and beat again until very thick. Sift cocoa and the flour together and stir very lightly into the mixture; fold in the stiffly beaten whites of the eggs and bake in a loaf in a moderate oven until done.
Do not butter the pan, but when cake is baked, invert the pan; and when cool, remove the cake.

Cocoa Sponge Cake 2 (1909)

3 eggs
1-1/2 cups of sugar
1/2 a cup of cold water
1 teaspoonful of vanilla

1-3/4 cups of flour
1/4 a cup of Baker's Cocoa
2 teaspoonfuls of baking powder
1 teaspoonful of cinnamon

Beat yolks of eggs light, add water, vanilla and sugar; beat again thoroughly; then add the flour, with which the baking powder, cocoa and cinnamon have been sifted. Fold in the stiffly beaten whites of the eggs. Bake in a rather quick oven for twenty-five or thirty minutes.

Cocoanut Cake (1889)

One cup of butter
Two cups of sugar
Two-thirds cup of milk
Whites of six eggs

Yolks of four eggs
Two and a half cups of flour
Two teaspoonfuls baking powder
Flavour with a tablespoonful of vanilla

Bake in four layers.

Filling:

Three eggs, with the yolks of the two remaining from the cake, well beaten

One cup of sugar
The juice of two lemons

Cook in vessel set in hot water, on the stove, until it thickens. Stir constantly.
When cold, stir into it a third part of two grated cocoanuts. Spread upon three of the cakes.
Frosting: Make a thick, stiff, soft frosting, using a heaping cup of sugar to the white of one egg, and only a half teaspoonful of lemon juice, to whiten it. Flavour with half a teaspoonful of vanilla extract; mix with it a third part of two grated cocoanuts that is, half of what is left. Spread over the top and sides of the loaf, and, while soft, shower over it the remainder of the cocoanut, insuring its adhering to the cake.
This is the most delicious of all cocoanut cakes. It is a dessert dish properly, to be eaten with a fork.

Coconut Cake (1912)

One-half cup of butter
Two cups of sugar
Three and one-half cups of flour
One cup of milk
Two teaspoons of baking powder

Whites of five eggs
One full cup of grated cocoanut
One-half pound of blanched shredded almonds
One-fourth pound of shredded citron

Mix and bake according to rules for mixing and baking loaf cake. Cook one and one-half hours.

Cocoanut Cake (1876)

One pound of sugar
A half-pound of butter
Six eggs

Three fourths of a pound of flour
One pound of grated cocoanut, put in just before baking

Cocoanut Cake (1922)

2 cups flour
1 cup sugar
1 cup milk

2 eggs
½ cup butter
2 teaspoons baking powder

Cream sugar and butter, add slightly beaten eggs. Stir thoroughly. Add milk and beat together. Add sifted flour and baking powder mixed. Pour into buttered pans and bake in moderate oven twenty-five to thirty minutes.

Cocoanut Cake Icing (1922)

2 cups confectioners' sugar
2 tablespoons butter

½ cup cream or milk

Beat together, add few drops vanilla extract. Spread icing on cake and sprinkle cocoanut on top.

Cocoa-nut Cake (1840)

Cut up and wash a cocoa-nut, and grate as much of it as will weigh a pound. Powder a pound of loaf-sugar. Beat fifteen eggs very light; and then beat into them, gradually, the sugar. Then add by degrees the cocoa-nut; and lastly, a handful of sifted flour. Stir the whole very hard, and bake it either in a large tin pan, or in little tins. The oven should be rather quick.

Cocoanut Cake (1913)

2/3 cup Cottolene
2 cups sugar
3 eggs. 3 cups flour
5 teaspoons baking powder

1/4 teaspoon salt
1 cup milk
1/2 teaspoon each lemon and vanilla

Process: Cream Cottolene, add one cup sugar gradually, stirring constantly. Beat yolks thick and light, add remaining cup sugar gradually, continue beating. Combine mixtures. Mix and sift flour, baking powder and salt. Add to first mixture alternately with milk. Add vanilla and fold in the whites of eggs beaten stiff and dry. Turn into two well-greased, square cake pans and bake fifteen minutes in a moderate oven. Spread one layer thickly with Boiled Frosting, sprinkle heavily with fresh grated cocoanut, cover with remaining layer. Spread top and sides with frosting, and sprinkle with cocoanut before frosting glazes.

Cocoanut Cake 1 (1876)

Three cups of sugar
One cup of butter
Four cups of flour

One cup of water
Whites of eight eggs
Three teaspoons of baking powder

Before mixing the cake, make the frosting, as follows:
Pour over one and a half cups of cocoanut sufficient good, sour cream to thoroughly mix it, add sugar to sweeten it, let it stand until the cake is cool, then put it between the layers. The cream must be free from any bitter taste and very thick. Blanched almonds chopped fine are excellent instead of cocoanut.

Cocoanut Cake 2 (1876)

Two cups of sugar
A half-cup of butter
One cup of milk

Three cups of flour
Whites of ten eggs
Three teaspoons of yeast powder

Icing:

Twelve teaspoons of pulverized sugar
One egg beaten to a stiff froth

One large, fresh cocoanut grated and sprinkled
between the layers on the icing

Cocoanut Cake 3 (1876)

Whites of six eggs
One and a half cups of sugar
A half-cup of butter
A half-cup of cold water

One and a half cups of flour
A half-cup of corn starch
One teaspoon of baking powder to each cup of flour

Frosting:

Whites of three eggs
Six tablespoons of pulverized sugar

One cup of cocoanut

Bake in four round tins.

Cocoanut Cake 4 (1876)

One cup of sugar
Two cups of flour
Three- fourths of a cup of butter

One-fourth cup of sweet milk
Two teaspoons of baking powder
The yolks of eight eggs

Bake in three cakes; then take the whites of four eggs beaten to a stiff froth with pulverized sugar, add one cocoanut (grated) and spread between the layers; frost the top.

Cocoanut Cake 1 (1894)

One cup sugar
Two cups flour
Two cups cocoanut
Two tablespoons butter

Two eggs
Teaspoon cream tartar
Half teaspoon soda

Soak the cocoanut in a cup of milk.

Cocoanut Cake 2 (1894)

Two cups sugar
One cup butter
One cup milk
Four cups flour

Teaspoon soda
Two of cream tartar
Whites of seven eggs
One cup grated cocoanut

Frosting:

Whites of three eggs
One cup grated cocoanut

Sugar as for other frosting

Cocoanut Cake 3 (1894)

Four cups flour
Three cups sugar
One cup butter
One cup milk
One teaspoon cream tartar

One-half teaspoon soda
Five eggs
One cocoanut grated
Juice of a lemon

Cocoanut Cake 4 (1894)

One-pound sugar
One-half pound butter
Threequarters pound flour

Five eggs
One cocoanut grated

Cocoanut Cake 5 (1894)

One cup butter
Two cups sugar
Whites of ten eggs
Four cups flour

One cup milk
One cup prepared cocoanut soaked in the milk
Two teaspoons baking powder

Bake in sheets in a rather quick oven. If you use the fresh cocoanut use two cups of it.

Cocoanut Cake 6 (1894)
(One, Two, Three, Four)

One cup butter
Two cups sugar
Three cups flour
Four eggs (using the whites only)
One cup milk

One teaspoon cream tartar sifted into the flour
One-half teaspoon soda in the milk
One-half of a cocoanut, grated, and stirred in at the last

Cocoanut Cake (1893)

Two cups sugar
1 cup butter, cream together
4 eggs beaten very light

1 cup milk
3 cups of flour
3 teaspoons baking powder

Bake in 3 layers.

Filling:

1 cup sugar
1 egg
Juice and rind of 1 lemon

1 tablespoon butter
1 cup grated cocoanut

Boil all together.

Frosting: 1 cup powdered sugar wet with teaspoon milk, spread on top and sprinkle over cocoanut.

Cocoanut Cakes (1876)

Take equal parts of grated cocoanut and powdered white sugar; add whites of eggs beaten to a stiff froth, six to a pound, or enough to wet the whole; drop the mixture on buttered tins in cakes the size of a cent, and several inches apart. Bake immediately in a moderate oven.

Cocoanut Cakes (1876)

Grate fine one cocoanut and add two cups of sugar and the white of one egg beaten to a froth. Drop on flat buttered tins and bake slowly.

Cocoanut Cakes (1876)

One pound of sugar
One pound of grated cocoanut

Whites of six eggs beaten to a stiff froth

Cocoanut Cheese Cakes (1898)

Ingredients:

3 oz. dessicated cocoanut
3 oz. sugar
3 eggs

1 dessertspoonful brandy
Crust made with 8 oz. flour, and other ingredients in proportion

Method: Beat and strain the eggs, mix with them the cocoanut and sugar, and stir in the brandy. Beat well together for 2 or 3 minutes. Butter some pattypans and line them with crust, fill them with the cocoanut mixture, and bake in a moderate oven.
Time: 15 to 20 minutes.
Sufficient for: 12 cheesecakes.

Cocoanut Cream Cake (1894)

Three eggs
One cup sugar
One cup flour
Two tablespoons melted butter

Three tablespoons milk
One teaspoon cream tartar
One-half teaspoon soda

Filling:

One-half pint milk
One tablespoon flour
Small pinch salt

Three tablespoons sugar
Yolk of one egg; the white for frosting

Use shredded cocoanut in both frosting and filling, and flavour with vanilla.

Cocoa-nut Jumbles (1840)

Grate a large cocoa-nut. Rub half a pound of butter into a pound of sifted flour, and wet it with, three beaten eggs, and a little rose water. Add by degrees the cocoa-nut, so as to form a stiff dough. Flour your hands and your paste-hoard, and dividing the dough into equal portions, make the jumbles with your hands into long rolls, and then curl them round and join the ends so as to form rings. Grate loaf-sugar over them, lay them in buttered pans, (not so near as to run into each other,) and bake them in a quick oven from five to ten minutes.

Cocoanut Layer Cake (1922)

Beat ¼ cup Crisco with 1 cup sugar till creamy
Add 2 well beaten eggs
¼ teaspoon salt

2½ cups flour sifted with 2 teaspoons baking powder
1 cup water
½ teaspoon almond extract

Mix and divide into Criscoed and floured layer tins. Bake 20 minutes in moderate oven. Use boiled frosting

Cocoanut Layer Cake (1920)

¾ cup sugar
½ cup butter
1½ cups prepared flour

The grated rind and juice of ½ lemon,
The whites of 3 eggs
½ cup milk

Stir butter and sugar to a light white cream; beat the whites to a stiff froth and add them by degrees alternately with the sifted flour and milk to the creamed butter and sugar; butter 2 good sized jelly cake tins and line them with buttered paper; put an equal portion in each tin, spread it evenly with a broad-bladed knife dipped in water and bake them in a medium hot oven to a delicate brown colour; when done remove them from oven and let them stand for a few minutes; then turn the cakes onto buttered paper to cool; in the meantime grate 1 cocoanut and beat the white of 1 egg to a stiff froth; add ¾ cup powdered sugar and the juice of ½ lemon; lay one cake layer, bottom side up, on a jelly cake dish, spread over half the white icing and sprinkle over a thick layer of the freshly grated cocoanut; put on the remaining layer, right side up, spread over the rest of icing, cover with a thick layer of the cocoanut and sift over some powdered sugar. This cake may be served as a dessert with vanilla sauce.

Cocoanut Layer Cake (1922)

For Cake:

1 cupful sugar
½ cupful Crisco
3 cupfuls flour
1 cupful milk

½ teaspoonful salt
2 teaspoonfuls vanilla extract
4 eggs
3 teaspoonfuls baking powder

For Filling:

1 teaspoonful Crisco
1 teaspoonful vanilla extract
1 cupful sugar
1 white of egg

1 cupful water
½ cupful chopped cocoanut
Pinch cream of tartar
¼ teaspoonful salt

For cake: Cream Crisco and sugar together, sift the flour, baking powder, and salt, and add alternately with the beaten yolks of eggs and milk. Beat thoroughly, then add stiffly beaten whites of eggs and flavouring and mix gently. Grease layer tins with Crisco, then flour them and divide mixture into three portions. Bake in a moderate oven twenty minutes.
For filling: Boil water and sugar together, add Crisco and cream of tartar, and boil until it forms a soft ball when tried in cold water, or 240° F. Beat white of egg to stiff froth, add salt, then pour in syrup gradually, add vanilla and beat until thick and cold. Spread on cake and sprinkle over with cocoanut.
Sufficient for three layers.

Coffee Cake (1922)

Enough for 2 Cakes.

3½ - 4 cups of flour
¼ lb. of sugar
1 pt. of milk
3 eggs

¼ lb. of butter
1 cent yeast
½ grated lemon rind

Preparation: The milk is made lukewarm and stirred to a smooth batter with 3 1/4 cups of flour, then the yeast dissolved in 1/4 cup of lukewarm, milk is mixed in quickly and put in a warm place to rise. After the sponge has risen well, mix in the melted butter, sugar, grated lemon rind, the eggs and the rest of the flour, stir the dough thoroughly with a spoon. Butter 3 tins and put in the dough about 1 inch thick, then set to rise; after this strew on sugar, cinnamon and put on small pieces of butter and some chopped almonds. Bake in medium hot oven

Coffee Cake (1864)
(Old recipe)

1 cup sugar
1 teaspoon cloves
1 cup molasses
1 teaspoon soda
4 cups flour

2 teaspoons cream of tartar
1 cup strong coffee
1 egg
1 teaspoon nutmeg
1-pound raisins

Coffee Cake 1 (1876)

Four eggs
Two coffeecups of sugar
Two coffeecups of molasses
One coffeecup of butter
One coffeecup of strong coffee
Five coffeecups of flour

Two teaspoons of cloves
Two teaspoons of nutmeg
Two teaspoons of cinnamon
Two teaspoons of baking powder
Three-quarters of a pound of raisins
Three-quarters of a pound of currants

Coffee Cake 2 (1876)

One cup of sugar
One cup of butter
One cup of molasses
One cup of cold coffee
Five cups of flour
One egg

One teaspoon of cloves
One teaspoon of nutmeg
One teaspoon of cinnamon
One teaspoon of soda
One pint of raisins

Coffee Cake 3 (1876)

One coffeecup of molasses
One coffeecup of coffee
One and a half coffeecups of brown sugar
One coffeecup of butter
Five eggs
Four cups of flour
One teaspoon of soda

One pound of raisins
One pound of currants
One pound of citron
Three tablespoons of cinnamon
One teaspoon of cloves
One nutmeg

Coffee Cake (1913)

Beat together until light, one egg, one cup sugar, butter the size of a large egg. Add alternately one cup milk, and two cups flour with two teaspoonfuls baking powder sifted in it. Put in pan, and sprinkle thickly all over top with sugar and powdered cinnamon. Bake rather quickly but do not scorch.

Coffee Cake (1893)

One-fourth cup butter   ½ cup sugar

½ cup molasses
½ cup coffee
2 eggs
2½ cups flour
2½ teaspoons Rumford Baking Powder

½ teaspoon Crystaline salt
½ teaspoon cinnamon
½ teaspoon allspice
½ nutmeg grated
½ pound raisins stoned and cut into pieces

Cream the butter add gradually the sugar. Add the molasses, well-beaten eggs, the fruit and the coffee. Mix and sift the dry ingredients and add to the mixture. Bake in a cake-pan 50 minutes.

Coffee Cake (1890)

Two cupfuls of sugar
Three-fourths of a cupful of butter
3 eggs
1¼ cupfuls of cold coffee
3 cupfuls of flour

1 teaspoonful each of nutmeg, cinnamon, cloves, allspice and essence of vanilla
Raisins, currants, citron
3 teaspoonfuls of baking powder

Coffee Cake No. 1 (1913)

Cream together two-thirds of a cupful of sugar and a heaping tablespoonful of shortening. Two well beaten eggs, half a cupful of strong liquid coffee. Sift two scant cupfuls of flour with two rounding teaspoonfuls of baking powder and an even teaspoonful of ground cinnamon, a pinch of ground cloves, and a pinch of salt. Mix all the ingredients thoroughly and add half a cupful each of currants, chopped seeded raisins and chopped nuts, that have been dredged in flour. Bake in greased cake pan.

Coffee Cake No. 2 (1913)

One cupful of flour, two-thirds of a cupful of sugar creamed, with the same amount of mixed shortening (suet, butter, lard or drippings), a cupful of molasses, one of strong liquid coffee, an even teaspoonful of saleratus dissolved in a little water, a pinch of salt, an even teaspoonful or more of mixed spices, and half a cupful of chopped raisins. Bake in a greased cake pan. This will keep like fruit cake.

Coffee Cake No. 3 (1913)

Cream together two-thirds of a cupful of sugar and half a cupful of any shortening. Mix half a yeast cake with a little water, and a pint of milk, and flavour with nutmeg and lemon. Beat all together, with enough flour for a dough, not quite as stiff as bread dough. Let it rise, put in a pan and let it rise again. Dot the top with little lumps of butter, sugar, cinnamon and crushed peanuts.

Coffee Cream Cakes and Filling (1911)

Roll good plain paste three-eighths of an inch thick and cut in rounds and through a pastry tube force a cream cake mixture to make a border come out even with the edge of the round, and bake in a hot oven. Fill and frost. For the cream cake mixture put one cup of boiling water, one-half cup of butter and one level tablespoon of sugar together in a saucepan and boil one minute, then add one and three-quarters cups of flour all at once. Stir rapidly and when the cooked mixture cleaves from the pan add five eggs one at a time, beating well between each addition. Do not beat the eggs before adding.

Coffee Layer Cake (1922)

Dark Part:

1 cupful dark brown sugar

2 cupfuls flour

⅔ cupful cold strong coffee
2 teaspoonfuls baking powder
3 yolks of eggs
½ teaspoonful powdered cinnamon
½ cupful Crisco

1 tablespoonful molasses
½ teaspoonful powdered cloves
¼ cupful raisins
½ teaspoonful grated nutmeg
½ teaspoonful salt

White Part:

½ cupful Crisco
2 cupfuls flour
1 cupful granulated sugar
2 teaspoonfuls baking powder

3 whites of eggs
1 teaspoonful vanilla extract
⅔ cupful milk
½ teaspoonful salt

For dark part: Cream Crisco and sugar, add yolks well beaten, coffee, molasses, flour, salt, baking powder, spices and raisins. Mix and divide into two Criscoed and floured layer tins and bake in moderately hot oven twenty minutes.

For white part: Cream Crisco and sugar, add milk, vanilla, flour, salt, baking powder, then fold in stiffly beaten whites of eggs. Bake in two layers. Put layers together and ice with following frosting.

Put 2 cupfuls dark brown sugar and ¾ cupful water into saucepan, add 1 tablespoonful Crisco and 1 teaspoonful vanilla extract. Boil till mixture forms soft ball when tried in cold water, or 240° F., remove from stove, beat till it begins to cream, then add 1 cupful chopped raisins. Spread on cake and allow to dry.
Sufficient for: one large layer cake.

Cold Water Cake (1894)

Two cups sugar
One cup butter
One cup cold water
Four cups flour
One cup each raisins and currants

Three eggs
Teaspoon soda
Half teaspoon cream tartar
Salt
Teaspoon each of all kinds spice

Put all together and stir well with the hand until smooth.

Cold Water Pone (1869)

Make a stiff batter with a quart of Indian meal, cold water and a little salt; work it well with the hand; grease a pan or oven and bake it three-quarters of an hour. Eat it hot at dinner, or with milk at supper.

Columbia Muffins (1922)

3 tablespoonfuls sugar
1½ cupfuls milk
3 tablespoonfuls Crisco
1 teaspoonful salt

1 egg
3½ teaspoonfuls baking powder
3½ cupfuls sifted flour

Sift flour, salt, and baking powder together. Cream Crisco and sugar, add egg well beaten, then milk and flour mixture. Divide into Criscoed and floured gem pans and bake twenty-five minutes in hot oven.
Sufficient for: twenty muffins.

Columbian Ginger Cake (1893)

One cup molasses
One cup sugar

One-half cup water
One-half cup lard

One teaspoonful soda	Season with ginger or cinnamon

Put flour in until stiff enough to roll out thin and cut into small cakes

Common Cheese Cake (1840)

Boil a quart of rich milk. Beat eight eggs, put them to the milk, and let the milk and eggs boil together till they become a curd. Then drain it through a very clean sieve, till all the whey is out. Put the curd into a deep dish, and mix with it half a pound of butter, working them well together. When it is cold, add to it the beaten yolks of four eggs, and four large table-spoonfuls of powdered white sugar; also, a grated nutmeg. Lastly, stir in, by degrees, half a pound of currants that have been previously picked, washed, dried, and dredged with flour. Lay. puff paste round the rim of the dish and bake the cheese cake half an hour. Send it to table cold.

Common Gingerbread (1840)

Cut up a pound of butter in a quart of West India molasses, which must be perfectly sweet; if it is in the least sour, use sugar house molasses instead. Warm it slightly, just enough to melt the butter. Crush with the rolling-pin, on the paste-board, half a pound of brown sugar, and add it by degrees to the molasses and butter; then stir in a tea-cup full of powdered ginger, a large tea-spoonful of powdered cloves, and a table-spoonful of powdered cinnamon. Add gradually sufficient flour to make a dough stiff enough to roll out easily; and lastly, a small tea-spoonful of pearl-ash melted in a little warm water. Mix and stir the dough very hard with a spaddle, or a wooden spoon; but do not knead it. Then divide it with a knife into equal portions; and, having floured your hands, roll it out on the paste-board into long even strips. Place them in shallow tin pans, that have been buttered; either laying the strips side by side in straight round sticks, (uniting them at both ends,) or coil them into rings one within another, as you see them at the cake shops. Bake them in a brisk oven, taking care that they do not burn; gingerbread scorching sooner than any other cake.
To save time and trouble, you may roll out the dough into a sheet near an inch thick and cut it into round flat cakes with a tin cutter, or with the edge of a tumbler.
Ground ginger loses much of its strength by keeping. Therefore, it will be frequently found necessary to put in more than the quantity given in the receipt.

Common Jumbles (1840)

Sift a pound of flour into a large pan. Cut up a pound of butter into a pound of powdered white sugar and stir them to a cream. Beat six eggs till very light, and then pour them all at once into the pan of flour; next add the butter and sugar, with a large table-spoonful of mixed mace and cinnamon, two grated nutmegs, and a tea-spoonful of essence of lemon or a wine glass of rose water. When all the ingredients are in, stir the mixture very hard with a broad knife. Having floured your hands and spread some flour on the paste-board, make the dough into long rolls, (all of equal size,) and form them into rings by joining the two ends very nicely. Lay them on buttered tins and bake them in a quick oven from five to ten minutes. Grate sugar over them when cool.

Common Wheat Cakes (No. 1) (1904)

1⅓ pounds of flour	3 eggs
1 quart of lukewarm milk	Yeast
¼ cupful of melted butter or lard	A little salt

Are made into a dough as in the above receipt and are then baked in butter, making 2 large cakes.

Common Wheat Cakes (No. 2) (1904)

Take 2 pounds of flour
Yeast
1 cupful of melted butter
¼ pound of currants

3 - 5 eggs
If wished some lemon peel
About 1 pint of milk

And bake in an oblong pan. Serve warm or cold with butter.

Compiègne Cake (1920)
(Gâteau Compiègne)

Dilute three-quarters of an ounce of compressed yeast in a vessel with one gill of warm milk; strain, return it to the vessel and incorporate five ounces of flour to make a soft leaven; put this on a floured table, mold and replace it in the vessel after cleaning it out well; cover over with a cloth and leave in a mild temperature to rise to double its size. In another vessel place threequarters of a pound of flour, form a hole in the center and in it lay an ounce of sugar and a heavy pinch of salt (according to the saltiness of the butter), two eggs, eight yolks and six ounces of butter. Mix all well together to form into a paste, working it forcibly for a few moments in order to give it body, then add slowly one gill of rich cream; continue to work the paste until it has plenty of body, then mix in the leaven very lightly, also one pint of well-drained whipped cream. Butter a large plain cylindrical mold seven inches in diameter by seven inches high; fill it up three-quarters with the above paste and leave it in a mild temperature until quite full; stand it on a pie plate and push it carefully into a very slack oven. It should take an hour and a half to an hour and three-quarters to bake; take it out as soon as done, invert it on a grate and let cool off. Dress on a folded napkin to serve.

Composition Cake (1876)

Two cups of sugar
One cup of butter
Five eggs

Three cups of flour
Lemon
A little soda

Composition Cake (1894)

Two cups butter
Three cups sugar
One cup milk
Five cups flour

Five eggs
One-pound raisins
One nutmeg
Teaspoon soda

Conde Cakes (1920)
(Gâteaux Condé)

Mix in a vessel four or five spoonfuls of chopped almonds with an equal quantity of powdered sugar; wet slowly with egg-whites so as to obtain a thin but not too flowing paste. Roll out some fragments of puff paste into long strips, three and a half inches wide; cover the tops with the almond preparation and cut the sides straight, then cut them across in one-inch wide pieces; take them up one at a time on the blade of a palette knife and range in straight rows on a baking sheet, slightly apart from each other. Besprinkle the cakes with tine sugar and cook in a slack oven; remove when nicely done by passing a knife under to detach from the pan.

Connecticut Election Cake (1893)

Two pounds best pastry flour
One-pound shortening (half butter and half lard)
One pound and two ounces sugar

Whites of two eggs
One nutmeg
Half a pound of raisins (loose Muscatels)

Quarter teaspoon of mace
One tablespoon of lemon juice
One tablespoon extract of orange

Half-teaspoon salt
Half a compressed yeast cake
Two ounces of citron

Work the shortening and sugar to a cream; then rub half of it into the flour; dissolve the yeast cake in a little warm water; mix the flour and yeast with sufficient milk (about one and a half pints that has been scalded and cooled) to make a batter about like graham bread; work with the hands for at least twenty minutes; make at night and set in a moderately warm room to rise; in the morning add the remainder of the shortening and sugar; work again with the hands, as when first made, for fifteen or twenty minutes, and set to rise again. Seed and cut the raisins, grate the nutmeg and sprinkle that and the mace over the raisins. When the cake is light, add first the lemon juice, then extract of orange and whites of eggs, well beaten; stir in fruit well-floured: dip into three pans, buttered and lined with paper. Let it stand until it begins to rise - it will come up very quickly in the oven if it has been twice well raised. Have oven hot enough to check the rising after it has reached the top of the pans; after it begins to brown, check the fire and let it bake rather slowly the remainder of the time. Whole time, one hour and a quarter

Cooking-school Muffins (1905)

2 cups sifted flour
2 teaspoonfuls baking-powder
1/2 teaspoonful of salt

1 cup of milk
2 eggs
1 large teaspoonful of melted butter

Mix the flour, salt, and baking-powder, and sift. Beat the yolks of the eggs, put in the butter with them and the milk, then the flour, and last the stiff whites of the eggs. Have the muffin-tins hot, pour in the batter and bake fifteen or twenty minutes. These must be eaten at once or they will fall.

Corn and Rice Muffins (1917)

1 cup cooked rice
1 tablespoon sugar
2/3 cup hot milk
1 egg
1/2 cup corn meal

1/2 cup flour
2 tablespoons bacon fat
3 teaspoons baking powder
1/2 teaspoon salt

Pour hot milk over rice, and work with a fork to separate grains; add corn meal, bacon fat, salt, and sugar; when cool add egg well beaten, flour, and baking powder; beat well; bake in well-greased muffin pans in hot oven twenty minutes.

Corn Bannock (1860)

To one quart of sour milk, put a tea-spoonful of salaeratus, dissolved in water; warm the milk slightly, beat up an egg, and put in corn meal enough to make it as thick as pudding batter, and some salt; grease a pan and bake it, or you may put it in six or eight saucers.

Corn Batter Cakes (1869)

Take a quart of good milk, three eggs, a little salt, and as much sifted corn meal as will make a thin batter; beat all well together, with a spoonful of wheat flour to keep them from breaking, bake in small cakes, keep them hot, and butter just as you send to table. Another way to make corn batter cakes, is to take a quart of corn meal, two eggs, a small lump of butter or lard, and mix it up with milk, or half water, if milk is scarce, and bake them either thin or thick.

Corn Bread or Johnny-Cake (1894)

One pint of buttermilk or sour milk
One-pint corn meal
One egg

One teaspoon soda
One teaspoon salt
Two teaspoons sugar or molasses

Dissolve the soda in a little warm water and add it the last thing. Bake half an hour in a quick oven.

Corn Cake (1893)

One pint of milk
Half a pint of Indian meal
Four eggs

A scant tablespoonful of butter
Salt
One teaspoonful of sugar

Pour the milk boiling on the sifted meal. When cold, add the butter (melted), the salt, the sugar, the yolks of the eggs, and, lastly, the whites, well beaten. Bake half an hour in a hot oven. It is very nice baked in iron or tin gem pans, the cups an inch and a half deep

Corn Cake (1893)

1 cup flour
½ sugar
½ meal
1 egg

⅔ cup sweet milk
1 tablespoon melted butter
1 teaspoon cream tartar
¾ soda

Mix ingredients, then add the milk and egg well beaten, add hot melted butter. Bake quick in shallow pan.

Corn Cake 1 (1894)

One-pint sour milk
One-pint Indian meal
One-pint flour
Two tablespoons sugar

Salt
One egg
A small piece of butter
One teaspoon soda

Corn Cake 2 (1894)

One cup meal
One cup flour
One cup sugar
Butter size of an egg

One cup milk
One-half teaspoon soda dissolved in milk
Two teaspoons cream tartar sifted in with flour

Corn Cake 3 (1894)

One cup Indian meal
One cup flour
One-half teaspoon soda
One teaspoon cream tartar sifted in with meal

Teaspoon salt
One egg, without beating
One cup milk

All beaten very thoroughly together for fifteen minutes and bake in round pans twenty minutes.

Corn Cakes (1922)

Make a custard from 2 eggs well beaten, ½ cup milk, ½ tablespoon Crisco, and ½ tablespoon sugar; beat into this ¾ of cup of canned corn. Sift together twice, ⅞ cup of flour, 1 tablespoon baking powder, and ½ teaspoon salt; beat into other mixture, and drop in Criscoed muffin rings by the tablespoon; set in a Criscoed dripping pan, and baked in a moderate oven until done.

Corn Cakes (1913)

Pour boiling water on half a cupful of cornmeal and let it stand for twenty minutes. Add an even teaspoonful of salt, a rounding teaspoonful of sugar, a beaten egg and a cupful of flour sifted with a rounding teaspoonful of baking powder. Pour in enough sweet milk to make a smooth batter.

Corn Griddle Cakes (1876)

One pint of sour milk
Three eggs
Meal enough to make a thin batter
One teaspoon of salt
One small teaspoon of soda, or less, according to the sourness of the milk

Corn Griddle Cakes (1893)
(Old Virginia Slap Jacks)

One or two eggs, whites beaten to a froth
One quart of sweet milk
Pinch of salt
Meal enough to make a thin batter

Bake very thin on hot griddle and serve at once. Meal must not be too finely ground or bolted.

Corn Griddle Cakes with Water (1876)

One pint of corn meal, one tablespoon of lard. Pour boiling water (be sure the water is boiling), to make a stiff mush, then thin with cold water, add two well-beaten eggs, and a large pinch of salt; also, tablespoon of syrup.

Corn-Meal Batter Cakes (1899)

To two cups of cold corn-meal mush, add one cup of sifted flour, and a pinch of salt; beat well the yolks of two eggs, to which add two-thirds of a cup of milk, and stir into the mush; beat thoroughly until light and smooth, adding a little more milk if necessary, to make the batter of proper consistency. Then gently stir in the whites of the eggs beaten to a stiff froth and bake in small cakes on both sides on a hot frying-pan or on a griddle, slightly buttered. Serve hot. Very nice. Try them.

Corn Meal Griddle Cakes (1917)

1-1/2 cups corn meal
1 egg well beaten
1/2 cup flour
3/4 cup milk
4 teaspoons baking powder
3/4 cup water
3/4 teaspoon salt
1 tablespoon melted shortening
1 tablespoon molasses

Mix in order given, beat well, and cook on a hot, greased griddle. If all of the batter is not needed at once, cover what is left, and keep in a cold place; add one-half teaspoon of baking powder, and beat vigorously before using; or half of the recipe may be used and the extra half egg used in some other way.

Cornmeal Muffins (1922)

1 cup cornmeal
2 cups white flour
4 teaspoons baking powder
1/3 cup butter
2 eggs
½ cup sugar
1 cup milk
½ teaspoon salt

Sift the baking powder, flour, cornmeal, salt. Cream the butter with the sugar and add the beaten eggs whole. Beat all thoroughly and then add to the dry ingredients. Add the milk gradually. Bake in greased muffin tins for fifteen minutes in a hot oven.

Corn Muffins (1922)

2 cups corn meal
1 cup sour milk
1 cup flour
¼ teaspoon soda
2 tablespoons sugar
3 tablespoons melted shortening
1 teaspoon salt
2 tablespoons sugar
2 teaspoons baking powder

Pour ½ cup scalding water over corn meal. Let stand until cool. Mix all other ingredients with corn meal except flour and baking powder and beat well. Add flour and baking powder. Bake in hot oven until brown.

Corn Muffins 1 (1876)

One pint of corn meal scalded with three pints of boiling water (if possible scald night before); when cold, add two-thirds of a cup of melted butter and six eggs. Bake in rings.

Corn Muffins 2 (1876)

One quart of sour milk
One small teaspoon of soda
One small teaspoon of salt
Four tablespoons of lard
Six eggs, yolks and whites beaten separately
Corn meal to make just thick enough to run

Bake in a hot oven.

Corn Muffins (1917)

1 cup corn meal
2 tablespoons sugar
1 cup flour
1 beaten egg
4 teaspoons baking powder
1 cup milk and water mixed
1/2 teaspoon salt
4 tablespoons melted shortening

Mix in order given, beat well, and bake in greased gem pans in hot oven twenty minutes.

Corn Starch Cake (1894)

One cup butter
Two cups sugar
One cup sweet milk
One cup corn starch
Two cups flour
Whites of seven eggs
Teaspoon soda
Two teaspoons cream tartar
Flavour with lemon or almond
Frosting will improve it

Very nice.

Corn Starch Cake 1 (1876)

One cup of sugar and a half cup of butter beaten to a cream
A half-cup of corn starch
A half-cup of sweet milk with one-half teaspoon of soda

Whites of four eggs beaten to a stiff froth
One cup of flour with one teaspoon of cream tartar
Flavour to the taste

Corn Starch Cake 2 (1876)

One cup of butter
Two cups of sugar
One cup of sweet milk
One cup of corn starch
Two cups of flour

Whites of six eggs beaten to a stiff froth
Two teaspoons of cream tartar
One teaspoon of soda
Flavour with lemon

Corn Starch Cake 3 (1876)

Two cups of sugar
Two cups of sifted flour
One cup of corn starch sifted in flour
One cup of butter beaten to a cream with sugar
One cup of sweet milk

Two even teaspoons of baking powder sifted in flour
The whites of eight eggs beaten to a stiff froth and added the last thing
Flavour to the taste

Bake in a slow oven three-quarters of an hour.

Corn Starch Cake (1893)

One cup butter
Two cups sugar
One teaspoon cream tartar
One-half teaspoon soda

Two cups flour
One cup corn starch
Four eggs
One cup milk

Corn Starch Cake (1893)

One and half cups sugar
½ cup butter, cream together
Whites of 6 eggs well beaten
Mix with butter and sugar
½ cup cornstarch

1½ cups flour
½ cup milk
1 teaspoon cream tartar
½ soda

Sift cornstarch and flour, cream tartar and soda into beaten sugar.

Corn-starch Cake (1902)

Beat well the whites of 4 eggs, beat the yolks, then beat them together. Cream a 1/4 of a lb. of butter. Add to it gradually 1/2 a lb. of granulated sugar and beat until light, then add the eggs and beat again. Mix 2 ozs. Of corn-starch with a quarter of a lb. of wheat flour; add a teaspoonful of baking powder and sift, stir this into the cake. Add the grated rind of 1/2 a lemon, bake in greased gem pans in a moderate oven 15 minutes.

Cornstarch Cake (1899)

Take the whites of three eggs
One-half cup of cornstarch
One-half cup of butter
One cup of sugar

One-half cup of sweet milk
One cup of flour
One teaspoonful of baking-powder

Mix the butter and sugar to a cream; dissolve the cornstarch with the milk and add to the butter and sugar; sift the baking-powder into the flour, and stir into the mixture, and lastly fold in the whites of the eggs which have been beaten stiff. Bake at once in a moderate oven.

Corn Starch Loaf Cake (1913)

2/3 cup Cottolene
2 cups fine sugar
1 cup milk
1 cup corn starch
2 cups flour

1-1/2 tablespoons baking powder
Whites 5 eggs beaten stiff
1/2 teaspoon salt
1 teaspoon vanilla

Process: Cream Cottolene, add sugar gradually, stirring constantly. Mix and sift flour, corn starch, baking powder and salt; add alternately to first mixture with milk, add vanilla, then cut and fold in whites of eggs. Turn mixture into two well-greased, brick-shaped bread pans and bake forty-five minutes in a moderate oven. Spread with Maple Frosting and stick with blanched and shredded almonds slightly toasted.

Cornelia Cake (1909)

Weigh 3 eggs and take an equal weight of sugar, butter and flour. Cream the butter and sugar, add 2 eggs and beat well, add the juice and the grated rind of ½ an orange and half the flour. Beat until smooth, then add the third egg and the rest of the flour sifted with a level teaspoonful of baking-powder.
Bake in a loaf and ice with orange icing.

Cream Almond Cake (1893)

One cup butter
2 cups sugar
1 cup milk
1 cup cornstarch

2 cups flour
2 teaspoons Rumford Baking Powder
5 egg whites
½ teaspoon almond extract

Cream the butter, add gradually the sugar, add the almond. Mix and sift the flour, cornstarch and baking powder. Add alternately with the milk to the first mixture. Beat the whites until stiff; add and beat vigorously. This makes two loaves.

Cream Cake (1894)

Two cups sugar, one cup sour cream, rubbed together; two well beaten eggs, teaspoon saleratus dissolved in milk, flour enough to make it a little stiffer than common cake; flavour to taste; bake from half to three-quarters of an hour.

Cream Cake (1876)

One cup of sugar
One cup of sour cream
1 egg

Two cups of flour
Piece of butter the size of a walnut
A half teaspoon of soda

Flavour to the taste

Cream Cake (1899)

One cupful each of sugar and sweet milk
One egg
One tablespoonful of butter

Two cupfuls of flour
Two teaspoonfuls of baking-powder

Bake in three shallow tins. Make a filling to put between the layers as follows: Heat one cupful of milk to boiling, then add one-fourth of a cup of sugar, one dessertspoonful of flour rubbed smooth in a little of the cold milk, and one beaten egg. Boil until thickened, and place between the layers.

Cream Cake (1913)

Cream together very light two cups butter, three cups sugar, one cup sweet cream. Add gradually four cups flour sifted with one teaspoonful baking powder, then fold in the whites of fourteen eggs beaten very stiff with a pinch of salt. Flavour with bitter almonds, bake in loaves or layers, and frost with pink icing, flavoured with rose water

Cream Cake (1893)

Half-pint water and 1 cup butter melted together. Stir in till smooth 2 cups flour. Cool and add 5 well-beaten eggs. Drop small spoonful 3 inches apart on well-buttered pans. Bake 20 minutes.

Cream for inside:

1-pint milk
2 eggs

1 cup sugar
¾ cup flour

Boil milk, add sugar, flour and eggs after beating together. This makes 20 cakes.

Cream Cake 1 (1876)

Three eggs
One cup of sugar
One and a half cups of flour

Two tablespoons of cold water
Two teaspoons of baking powder

Cream:

One pint of sweet milk
Two eggs
Two-thirds of a cup of sugar

Two large tablespoons of corn starch
A half-cup of butter
Flavour with lemon

Cook the cream well and let it cool before putting in the cake.

Cream Cake 2 (1876)

One cup of sugar
Three eggs
One cup of flour

One teaspoon of baking powder
One tablespoon of butter

Bake in layers.

Cream: Scald a half pint of sweet milk; add one egg beaten with a heaping teaspoon of sugar and one teaspoon of corn starch, and boil until quite thick. Let the cream cool before putting together.

Cream Cake 3 (1876)

Four eggs
One cup of sugar
One cup of flour
One teaspoon of baking powder mixed in the flour
One tablespoon of water

Bake the cake in two pie-tins; while hot split the cake, and put in this:

Cream:

Boil one cup of milk or cream
Add three tablespoons of sugar
One egg
One large tablespoon of corn starch mixed in a little milk
When nearly done one tablespoon of butter
Flavour to the taste

Cream Cake 4 (1876)

One cup of sugar
One cup of flour
Four eggs
Butter the size of an egg
One teaspoon of baking powder

Bake in jelly-cake pans.

Cream: Scald one goblet of milk and add the whites of two eggs, one tablespoon of corn starch, a half-cup of sugar and flavour to the taste.

Cream Cake or Pie (1911)

This recipe makes a simple layer cake to be filled in various ways. Cream one-quarter cup of butter with one cup of sugar, add the beaten yolks of two eggs and one teaspoon of vanilla. Now beat hard, then mix in one-half cup of milk alternately with one and one-half cups of flour sifted twice with two level teaspoons of baking powder. Beat just enough to make smooth, then fold in lightly the stiffly beaten whites of two eggs and pour into an oblong shallow pan that is buttered, floured and rapped to shake out all that is superfluous. Bake about twenty minutes, take from pan and cool. Just before serving split the cake and fill with a cooked cream filling or with sweet thick cream beaten, sweetened with powdered sugar and flavoured to the taste.

Cream Cake Paste (1920)
(Pâte à Chou)

Put into a saucepan half a pint of water, a grain of salt, one ounce of sugar and two ounces of butter; set the saucepan on the fire and when the butter floats, remove the pan from off the range, and incorporate into it a quarter of a pound of fine flour, stir vigorously not to have it the least lumpy, and put it back on to a slow fire to dry until it detaches easily from the bottom, then take it off once more, and mix in a tablespoonful of orange flower-water; four or five minutes later stir in four or five eggs, adding them one at the time; it must now be more consistent than otherwise, and if a little of it should be dropped from the spoon, it must retain its shape and not spread.

Cream Cakes (1840)

Having beaten three eggs very light, stir them into a quart of cream alternately with a quart of sifted flour; and add one wine glass of strong yeast, and a salt-spoon of salt. Cover the batter and set it near the fire to rise. When it is quite light, stir in a large table-spoonful of butter that has been warmed by the fire. Bake the cakes in muffin rings, and send them to table hot, split with your fingers, and buttered.

Cream Cakes (1911)

1 cup hot water
⅓ cup butter

3 eggs
1 heaping cup flour

Melt the butter in the hot water; while it boils slowly stir in flour till a smooth paste. Let cool while beating 3 eggs, then stir eggs into paste. Bake in hot oven 25 minutes.
Makes thirteen.

Filling:

½ cup sugar
3 spoonfuls flour

1 egg
1 cup boiling milk

Beat eggs, add sugar and flour mixed. Stir in boiling milk and cook till creamy.

Cream Cakes 1 (1894)

One-pint hot water
Half-pound butter
Three-quarters pound flour

Ten eggs
One teaspoon soda, dry

Boil the water and butter together and stir in the flour while boiling; let it cool, then stir in the eggs one at a time, without beating. Drop on buttered tins and bake in a hot oven.

Inside:

One cup flour
Two cups sugar
One-quart milk

Four eggs,
Pinch of salt

Boil the milk, beat the flour, sugar and eggs together, and stir into the milk while boiling. Flavour.

Cream Cakes 2 (1894)

Let one cupful of hot water and one-half cupful of butter come to a boil; while boiling stir in one cup flour; when cold, stir in three eggs, not beaten. Drop by spoonfuls into a buttered tin and bake in a quick oven.
Filling: One cup milk, one-half cup sugar, bring to a boil and add two tablespoons flour, or one tablespoon corn starch, beaten smooth, with a spoonful milk, one egg, well beaten. When the cream cakes are cold, split, but not wholly; lay round and fill.

Cream Cakes Glassé (1920)

Boil ½ pint milk with 2 ounces butter, add 4 ounces flour, stir until it forms into a smooth paste and loosens itself from the bottom and sides of the saucepan, transfer the paste to a dish, and when nearly cold add the yolks of 4 eggs, and last the beaten whites; drop this mixture (by tablespoonfuls) on to buttered tins, not too close together, brush them over with the beaten egg, and bake to a fine golden colour and well done. When done and cold, cut the cakes open on the side and fill them with vanilla cream, half the quantity of cream will be sufficient. Place the cakes on a sieve, boil 1 cup of sugar with ½ cup water till the sugar begins to turn light brown (caramel), instantly remove, and pour it over the cakes.

Cream Cakes Iced with Chocolate, Vanilla or Coffee (1920)
(Choux à la Crème Glacés an Chocolat, à la Vanille ou au Café)

On a lightly buttered baking sheet lay some small round cream cakes made of cream cake paste pushed through a pocket; egg over and set into a medium oven to cook; detach them from the pan as soon as done, and when cold split through the sides and fill with vanilla pastry cream and ice over with chocolate, vanilla or coffee fondant, the same as eclairs.

Cream Cakes with Burnt Almonds and Glazed Cream Cakes (1920)
(Choux Pralinés et Choux Glacés)

Lay on a baking sheet about twelve small cream cakes; egg over and lay on each a small pinch of shredded or chopped almonds, and cover these with a pinch of powdered sugar; cook the cakes in a slack oven and when they become cold open and fill them either with apricot marmalade, currant, quince or apple jelly, or else with Chantilly cream or St. Honore cream.
To Glaze the Cream Cakes: Take them up one by one and dip the upper parts into sugar cooked to "crack", then lay them at once on a wire grate to drain off the surplus sugar. These can also be filled with pastry cream flavoured with vanilla, orange or orange flower water.

Cream Cakes with Whipped Cream or St. Honore Cream (1920)
(Choux à la Crème Fouettée on à la Crème St. Honoré)

With some cream cake paste pushed through a socket pocket dress on a lightly buttered baking sheet some small round cakes, an inch and a half in diameter; cover over with powdered sugar and leave stand for a few moments, then remove all the sugar that has failed to adhere to the paste; push into a very slack oven to cook. Detach them from the pan as soon as done and split open the side to fill with pastry cream, or whipped cream flavoured with vanilla. They can also be filled through the top by making an opening and placing the cover on upside down. Push a small string of royal icing around the edge all around the opening. Dredge over some fine pink coloured sugar and fill the insides with St. Honore cream pushed in through a pocket.

Cream Koch (1920)
(With Sponge Cake)

Spread 8 small slices of sponge cake with quince, apple or currant jelly, put 2 together, cut them through the centre and lay into a buttered dish; pour over a little cherry, Madeira or fruit syrup; pour over it a cream koch the same as in foregoing recipe, sprinkle with sugar and bake about 10 minutes. Or dip the cake into the syrup of preserved fruit--either peaches or cherries - and lay some fruit over it; then cover with same cream and bake 15 minutes.

Cream Layer Cake (1913)

Cream together a rounding tablespoonful of butter with one and one-half cupfuls of sugar, add a cupful of sweet cream, two well beaten eggs and two cupfuls of flour sifted with two teaspoonfuls of baking powder. Bake in three layers.

Cream Layer Cake (1911)

Cream one-quarter cup of butter well with one cup of sugar, add the yolks of three eggs beaten light, one-half cup of milk, then one and one-half cups of flour sifted twice with three level teaspoons of baking powder. Stir in lightly last of all the whites of three eggs beaten stiff. Bake in a pan large enough to make one thin cake and bake. Cool and split, then spread on one-half pint of cream beaten light, sweetened, and flavoured with a few drops of vanilla. Put on the top cake and dust with powdered sugar.

Cream Puffs (1922)

1 cupful water
5 tablespoonfuls Crisco
1 cupful flour

4 eggs
¼ teaspoonful salt

Put Crisco into small saucepan, add water, bring to boiling point, add quickly flour and salt, stir well with wooden spoon until mixture leaves sides of pan, remove pan from fire, allow mixture to become cool, but not cold, add eggs, one at a time, and beat each one thoroughly in. Set in cool place one hour. Put mixture into forcing bag with tube and force it on to a tin greased with Crisco into small rounds; bake in hot oven forty minutes. When cold split them open on one side and fill with whipped cream sweetened and flavoured to taste.
To make eclairs with this mixture press it on to tins in strips three and a half inches long, and a little distance apart. Brush over tops with beaten egg and bake in moderate oven thirty minutes. Cut open one side, then fill and dip top into chocolate icing.
Sufficient for: fifteen cream puffs.

Cream Puffs (1911)

½ cup butter, melted in 1 cup boiling water. Stir in 1 cup flour while boiling; take from stove, cool; 3 eggs, one after the other without beating, drop on buttered tins, far enough apart; bake in quick oven 30 minutes.

Filling:

1 cup milk

½ cup sugar

Thicken with cornstarch. Flavour with vanilla.

Cream Puff Balls (1922)

1 cupful flour
½ cupful water
½ cupful Crisco

4 eggs
½ teaspoonful salt

Put Crisco and water into small saucepan, bring to boil, add quickly flour and salt, stir well with wooden spoon until mixture leaves sides of pan, remove from fire, allow to cool, but not become cold, add eggs, beating each one thoroughly in. Turn mixture on to well Criscoed plate and divide into small puffs or cakes. Put on Criscoed tins and bake a golden brown in hot oven, thirty minutes. These puffs may be filled with preserves, custard, or savory mixtures.
Sufficient for: thirty puffs.

Cream Sponge Cake (1876)

One cup of sugar
One cup of flour

A half-cup of cream
Two eggs, whites and yolks beaten separately

Flavour with vanilla and beat well before the flour is put in.

Cream Sponge Cake (1913)

Beat thoroughly the yolks of two eggs and add a cupful of sugar and a pinch of salt. Sift together a cupful of flower with a rounding teaspoonful of baking powder. Mix all the ingredients, pour in half a cupful of sweet cream and stir in lightly the well beaten whites of the eggs. Add a little flour if necessary.

Cream Sponge Cake (1893)

Two eggs well beaten, put into a cup, fill cup with sweet cream, put in mixing dish, add 1 cup sugar, 1½ cups flour, 1 teaspoon baking powder, pinch of Crystaline salt. Stir well together. Bake in moderately hot oven.

Cream Sponge Cake 1 (1876)

Four eggs
One coffeecup of flour
One cup of sugar
One tablespoon of water

Cream: Put one pint of cream or sweet milk on the stove and let it scald; mix thoroughly together one egg, one tablespoon of flour, a half-cup of sugar and a half cup of butter and add to the scalding milk or cream; stir until the custard is quite thick; flavour to the taste. Bake the cake in layers in mountain-cake pans and spread the cream between.

Cream Sponge Cake 2 (1876)

Make a sponge cake, bake it in three or four layers, and have ready the following cream for filling: Boil one pint of milk, beat two eggs, add one cup of sugar and one-half cup of flour; stir all into the milk and let it boil till it thickens, then flavour. Put this between the cakes; ice the top.

Crisco Batter Cakes (1922)

3 eggs
1 cupful buttermilk
½ cupful melted Crisco
½ teaspoonful baking soda
1 cupful flour
1 teaspoonful baking powder
½ teaspoonful salt

Beat up yolks of eggs, add milk, Crisco, and flour mixed with salt, soda, and baking powder and beat till smooth. Fold in whites beaten to a stiff froth. Drop in large spoonfuls on ungreased skillet or griddle. Serve hot with butter or maple syrup.
Sufficient for: fifteen cakes.

Crisco Fruit Cake (1922)

1½ cupfuls Crisco
1 lb. seeded raisins
2 cupfuls sugar
1 lb. glace cherries
4 cupfuls flour
1 teaspoonful baking soda
6 eggs
1 teaspoonful salt
1 wineglassful brandy
½ cupful New Orleans molasses
½ lb. blanched and chopped almonds
½ cupful cold black coffee
½ lb. English walnut meats (broken in small pieces)
1 teaspoonful grated nutmeg
2 teaspoonfuls powdered cinnamon
½ lb. stoned and chopped dates
1 lb. currants
1 teaspoonful powdered cloves

Cream Crisco and sugar together, add eggs well beaten, beat five minutes, then add coffee, soda mixed with molasses, brandy, flour sifted with salt and spices. Now add raisins, currants, dates, cherries cut in halves, and nuts. Mix carefully and turn into Criscoed and papered tin and bake in moderate oven two and a half hours. Brandy may be omitted.
Sufficient for: one large cake.

Crisco Sponge Cake (1922)

3 eggs
1¼ cupfuls flour
1 cupful sugar
2 teaspoonfuls baking powder

½ cupful Crisco
½ teaspoonful orange extract
½ teaspoonful salt
½ cupful cold water

Cream Crisco; add salt, yolks of eggs well beaten, and sugar, and beat for five minutes, add orange extract and cold water. Beat up whites of eggs to a stiff froth and add alternately with the flour sifted with the baking powder. Divide into Criscoed and floured gem pans and bake in a moderate oven for fifteen minutes.
Sufficient for: twelve cakes.

Crisp Ginger-cake (1869)

Take three pounds of flour, one of sugar, and one of butter; mix these together with three table-spoonsful of ginger, some cloves and anise seed, and wet it with molasses; roll it thin; cut it in shapes and bake with a quick heat.

Crisp White Corncake (1911)

Two cups scalded milk, one cup white cornmeal, two level teaspoons salt. Mix the salt and cornmeal and add gradually the hot milk. When well mixed, pour into a buttered dripping pan and bake in a moderate oven until crisp. Serve cut in squares. The mixture should not be more than one-fourth inch deep when poured into pan.

Crown of Brioche (1920)
(Couronne de Brioche)

Put two pounds of brioche paste that has been sufficiently raised and hardened on ice on a floured table, form it into a ball and lay it on a round baking sheet covered with paper; flatten it slightly with the hands and make a hole in the center, spreading out the paste so that it forms into a large ring; place it on a baking dish, equalize, egg and gash around inside of the crown with the tip of a knife, raising the dough; push into a well-heated oven and bake for thirty-five minutes. These crowns can be made of a smaller size, two ounces each, to be served for breakfast.

Crumb Coffee Cake (N.D.)

3 cups flour
Pinch of salt

1 cup sugar
½ cup shortening

Crumb together and save ¾ cup of the mixture for the top of the cake. Add one egg, one teaspoon cinnamon, ½ teaspoon cloves, and 1 teaspoon soda in a cup of sour milk. Before putting in oven sprinkle top with the ¾ cup crumbs. Bake in moderate oven. Will make two cakes 8 by 10 inches. Good hot or cold.

Crumb Griddle Cakes (1902)

Put a large cup of bread crumbs to soak in a qt. of sour milk overnight; in the morning rub through a sieve. Add the yolks of 4 eggs, well beaten, 2 teaspoonfuls of soda dissolved in a little water, 1 tablespoonful melted butter, and enough corn-meal to make it the consistency of ordinary griddle cakes. Add the whites of the eggs just before frying.

Crumb Griddle Cakes (1911)

Soak one pint of bread crumbs in one pint of sour milk for an hour, then add a level teaspoon of soda dissolved in one cup of sweet milk, and one well beaten egg, half a teaspoon of salt and flour enough to make a drop batter as thick as griddle cakes are usually made.

Crumbled Paste Cakes (1920)
(Gâteaux en Pâte Fondante) (1920)

Mix slowly with the hands twelve ounces of butter and a pound of flour in such a way as to have it crumbling like semolina, then lay it on a table in the shape of a ring and in the center place twelve ounces of sugar, six egg-yolks, three eggs, some grated lemon peel and a grain of salt. Mingle the whole simply with the blade of a knife and incorporate this liquid into the crumbled flour; work together quickly and roll it into a ball; wrap up in a cloth and leave stand for two hours in a very cool place. Lay the paste on a floured table and divide it into small parts; roll out each of these pieces into strings four and one-half inches long; curl both extremities of each string in two spirals, bring these spirals together so as to form a sort of eye-glass imitation, arrange them gradually on a baking-sheet and let them dry for two hours. Then bake in a slack oven.

Cup Cake (1904)

4 eggs	1 cupful of milk
1½ cupfuls of butter	3 cupfuls of raisins, currants
2 cupfuls of sifted sugar	Cloves
3 cupfuls of flour	The grated peel of a lemon

Stir the butter to a cream, add spices and eggs, then milk and flour and at last raisins and currants. To this cake take 1 teaspoonful of baking powder, mixing it with the flour.
Bake the cake for 2 hours in a moderately hot oven.

Cup Cake 1 (1876)

One and a half cups of butter	One cup of sweet milk
Three cups of sugar	One teaspoon of soda
Five cups of flour	Two teaspoons of cream tartar
Five eggs	

Cup Cake 2 (1876)

One cup of butter	One cup of cold water
Two cups of sugar	Lemon flavour
Three and a half cups of flour	One teaspoon of baking powder mixed well in the
Four eggs	half cup of flour and put in the last thing

Excellent for layer cakes.

Cup Cake (1869)

Take four cups of flour	One of melted butter
Three of sugar	

One of sour cream, with a tea-spoonful of salaeratus dissolved in it

Three eggs
Season it with brandy and nutmeg

Mix and bake it as pound cake.

Cup Cake (1912)

Cream one cup of butter with two cups of sugar
Add one-half cup of milk
The yolks of four eggs beaten

Three cups of flour
Two full teaspoons of baking powder
The whites of four eggs beaten stiff

Bake in gem pans or in layer pans or in a mould.

Cup Cakes (1922)

1 cup sugar
1 cup milk
¼ cup shortening
1 egg

3 teaspoons baking powder
1 teaspoon vanilla
¼ teaspoon salt
2 cups flour

Sift and mix the dry ingredients.
Melt the shortening, add the milk, beaten egg and vanilla. Mix the dry and wet ingredients and stir well. Bake in muffin tins for fifteen to twenty minutes in a moderate oven.

Currant Cake, Citron Cake or Raisin Cake (1922)

One pound of sugar
One pound of butter

Ten eggs
Four ounces of flour

Mix like Pound Cake and add from one to two pounds of the above named fruits. Flavour lemon and mace.

Currant Cake (1904)

For this use a good omelette batter, taking a little sugar and salt, 1 small soup plateful of ripe currants, ¼ pound of sugar and ¼ pound of grated wheat bread. Heat the butter in the pan until quite hot, put in the batter, lay the currants on this, and before turning sprinkle over it a little finely grated bread. After the omelette is baked on both sides, put on a plate and strew a little sugar over it.

Currant Cake (1913)

Sift together two cupfuls of flour and a heaping teaspoonful of baking powder, with a pinch of salt.
Cream together half a cupful of sugar and the same amount of shortening. Take a small cupful of currants that have been washed and dried, stir them in the flour, then stir all the ingredients together with two well beaten eggs and half a cupful of sweet milk (or more, if too stiff). Bake in greased tart shell pans rather than muffin pans.

Currant Cake (1898)

Ingredients:

1 lb. flour
6 oz. butter

6 oz. sugar
6 oz. currants

¼ pint milk
2 eggs

1 tea-spoonful baking-powder

Method: Mix the baking-powder with the flour and rub the butter into them; add the currants, which must be washed, picked, and dried, and the sugar. Beat and strain the eggs, mix the milk with them, and moisten the cake with these, beat well for a few minutes, put the mixture in a cake tin lined with buttered paper, and bake for 1½ hours.
Time: 1½ hours.
Sufficient for: 1 moderate sized cake.

Currant Cake (1894)

Three-quarters of a cup of butter
Two cups sugar
Three cups flour
One cup milk

One and one-half cups currants
Four eggs
One teaspoon soda
Two teaspoons cream tartar

Currant Cake (1893)

One cup sugar
⅔ cup butter
1 cup flour before sifting
3 eggs

1 tablespoon milk
A piece of soda the size of a pea
1 cup of currants

Currant Cake (1904)

A cream or puff paste
1½ pounds of currants

1 pound of sifted sugar
A few tablespoonfuls of grated wheat bread

Roll out the dough, strew over it plenty of grated bread and on thin lay the currants. In forming the edge and in baking proceed as directed for gooseberry cake.

Currant Cake (1904)

1 pound of melted butter, poured from the settlings
1 pound of cornstarch
¾ -1 pound of sifted sugar
¼ pound of washed and dried currants

The grated peel of a lemon
1 grated nutmeg or a teaspoonful of mace
12 eggs
½ glassful of arracorrum

Cream the butter and stir in the sugar and spices, yolks of eggs one by one; then stir briskly for ½ hour longer. Add the currants, after these the beaten whites of the eggs, then the cornstarch and at last the arrac.

Cushion Cake (1922)

Cream 1 cup Crisco with ½ cup sugar, add 2 well beaten eggs, and ½ cup milk. Sift 2 cups flour, 2 teaspoons baking powder, and ½ teaspoon salt, and add to Crisco mixture, with 1 teaspoon vanilla extract. Divide into 2 parts, add to 1 part 2 tablespoons molasses, 1 cup seeded raisins, ½ teaspoon cloves, 1 teaspoon cinnamon, and ¼ teaspoon grated nutmeg. Bake in Criscoed and floured cake tin for 20 minutes. Take out of oven, spread white part on top, return to oven and bake until done.

Custard Cake (1876)

Two cups of sugar
Four eggs
One tablespoon of butter
A half-cup of water
Two and one-half cups of flour
Two teaspoons of baking powder
Flavour with lemon

Custard: Two eggs, one cup of sugar, one cup of sweet milk and two teaspoons of corn starch; flavour.

Custard Cakes (1840)

Mix together a pound of sifted flour and a quarter of a pound of powdered loaf-sugar. Divide into four a pound of fresh butter; mix one-fourth of it with the flour and make it into a dough. Then roll it out and put in the three remaining divisions of the butter at three more rollings. Set the paste in a cool place till the custard is ready. For the custard, beat very light the yolk only of eight eggs, and then stir them gradually into a pint of rich cream, adding three ounces of powdered white sugar, a grated nutmeg, and ratafia, peach-water, or essence of lemon, to your taste. Put the mixture into a deep dish; set it in an iron baking pan or a Dutch oven half full of boiling water and bake it a quarter of an hour. Then put it to cool.

In the meantime, roll out the paste into a thin sheet; cut it into little round cakes about the size of a dollar, and bake them on flat tins. When they are done, spread some of the cakes thickly with the custard, and lay others on the top of them, making them fit closely in the manner of lids.

You may bake the paste in patty-pans like shells and put in the custard after they come out of the oven. If the custard is baked in the paste, it will be clammy and heavy at the bottom.

They are sometimes called cream cakes or cream tarts.

Custard Corn Cake (1917)

1/2 cup corn meal
1 cup sour milk
1/2 cup flour
1 egg
2 tablespoons sugar
2 tablespoons melted shortening
1/2 teaspoon salt
1/2 cup sweet milk
1/2 teaspoon soda

Mix and sift dry ingredients; add sour milk and egg well beaten and beat thoroughly; melt shortening in an earthen baking dish, pour in batter, pour the sweet milk over it, and bake in a hot oven twenty-five minutes. Cut in wedge-shaped pieces for serving.

Custard Pie (1917)
(Cake Crumbs)

2 cups hot milk
1 egg slightly beaten
1/2 cup dry cake crumbs
1/8 teaspoon salt
2 tablespoons sugar
Nutmeg

Mix crumbs and milk, let stand for five minutes, and press through a sieve; add sugar, egg, and salt; line a deep plate with paste rolled thin; build up a firm edge of crust, fill with custard, and dust with nutmeg. Bake about forty minutes. The oven should be hot for the first ten minutes, and then the heat should be reduced.

Part 5: D

Dansk Lagkage (N.D.)
(Danish Layer Cake)
Dark Fruit Cake (N.D.)
Dark Fruit Cake (1820)
D'Artois Cake with Apricot Marmalade or
Almond Cream (1920)
(Gâteau D'Artois à la Marmelade d'Abricots ou à
la Crème d'Amandes)
Date and Walnut Torte (1922)
Date Cake (1904)
(Arabian Receipt)
Date Cake (1917)
Date Cake (1911)
Date Cake (1912)
Date Loaf (1912)
Davis Cake (1890)
Dayton Cake (1894)
Delicate Cake (1889)
Delicate Cake (1922)
Delicate Cake (1893)
Delicate Cake 1 (1876)
Delicate Cake 2 (1876)
Delicate Cake 3 (1876)
Delicate Cake 4 (1876)
Delicate Cake 5 (1876)
Delicate Cake 6 (1876)
Delicate Cake 1 (1893)
Delicate Cake 2 (1893)
Delicate cake 1 (1894)
Delicate cake 2 (1894)
Delicate Cake 1 (1893)
Delicate Cake 2 (1893)
Delicious Cake (1911)
Delicious Cake (1893)
Delicious Cake 1 (1894)
Delicious Cake 2 (1894)
Denmark Cake (1920)
Delicate Sponge Cake (1920)
Derby Cake (1864)
Dessertbiskuit (1910)
Devil's Cake in Layers (1913)
Devil's Food (1820)
Devil's Food Cake (N.D.)
Devil's Food Cake (1922)
Devil's Food Nut Cake (1922)
Dicker Pfefferkuchen mit Honig (1910)
(Ginger Cake with Honey)
Dominion Apple Cake (1922)
Domino Cake (1905)
Domino Cakes (1922)
Dorbas Torte (1922)
Dorothy Cake (1820)
Dough Cake (1876)
Dover Cake (1876)
Dover Cake (1869)
Dream Cakes (1913)
Dried Apple Cake (1902)
Dried Crumb Griddle Cakes (1917)
Dried Prune Cake (1904)
Drop Ginger Cakes (1876)
Dutch Apple Cake (N.D.)
Dutch Apple Cake (1917)
Dutch Apple Cake 1 (1893)
Dutch Apple Cake 2 (1893)
Dutchess Cake (1920)

Dansk Lagkage (N.D.)
(Danish Layer Cake)

1 cup Butter	Pinch of Salt
2 cups Flour	1 teaspoon Vanilla
1/2 cup Sugar	2 Eggs
2 teasp. Baking Powder	1/2 cup Milk

Cream sugar and butter together until it has the consistency of whipped cream. Beat eggs and add vanilla and milk to them. Sift flour, baking powder and salt together 3 times. Add to the creamed butter-sugar mixture alternately with the milk-egg mixture. Bake in 5 layers at 375° until brown. Fill layers alternately with jelly and custard; top with whipped cream.

Dark Fruit Cake (N.D.)

1-pound granulated sugar	4 apples
1-pound butter or substitute	1 tablespoon molasses
8 eggs	1 cup sour milk
2 pounds raisins	1 cup grape juice
½ pound currants	1 teaspoon soda
½ pound citron	2 teaspoons each cinnamon, cloves and nutmeg
½ pound figs	1¼ pounds Swan's Down cake flour
1-pound shelled nuts	2 teaspoons baking powder

Bake slowly.

Dark Fruit Cake (1820)

(Makes 10 lbs. keeps for years)

1 lb. butter substitute	1 lb. citron
4 lbs. seeded raisins	1¼ lb. flour
1¼ lbs. sugar	1 tsp. cinnamon
2 lbs. currants or seedless raisins	1 tsp. soda
10 eggs	1 tsp. mace
½ c. brandy or grape juice	

Cream butter and sugar. Add egg yolks, spices and liquor. Mix flour and soda with fruit and add. Fold in stiffly beaten egg whites. Bake in slow oven about three hours.

D'Artois Cake with Apricot Marmalade or Almond Cream (1920)
(Gâteau D'Artois à la Marmelade d'Abricots ou à la Crème d'Amandes)

Roll some puff paste parings into a layer three-sixteenths of an inch in thickness and cut this into two bands, each three inches wide - Lay one of these bands on a baking sheet and cover the center with apricot marmalade or almond cream; moisten the edges of the paste with a brush dipped in water, then cover with the second band; pare them straight, scallop the edges and mark the band across one and a quarter inches apart with a knife; within this space place leaves formed with the tip of the blade of a small knife. Bake in a quick oven and when the cake is nearly done dredge with sugar and finish cooking and glazing. Cut it through the divided sections with a large sharp knife.

Date and Walnut Torte (1922)

6 eggs
½ pound dates (cut fine)
½ pound powdered sugar
2 tablespoons flour
1 cup walnuts (chopped)
1 teaspoon baking powder

Beat eggs very light and add sugar, nuts and dates. Lastly add the flour mixed with baking powder. Bake in a slow oven, one hour. Serve with whipped cream.

Date Cake (1904)
(Arabian Receipt)

6 ounces of flour
3 ounces of creamed butter
3 ounces of sugar
The yolks of 3 eggs
The beaten whites of the eggs
Finely cut lemon peel

Are made into a light dough which is put into a dish and baked until about half done.

In the meantime:

Stir the whites of 8 eggs to a froth
Add 10 ounces of sugar
10 ounces of grated almonds
10 ounces of nicely sliced dates
1 glassful of Madeira

Pour this over the cake and bake until done. At last cover the cake with a three-coloured icing seasoned with plenty of lemon juice, so that it will have an acidulous taste, and lay over this dates and preserved fruits.

Date Cake (1917)

1/3 cup melted shortening
1-3/4 cups flour
1-1/4 cups brown sugar
3-1/2 teaspoons baking powder
1 egg unbeaten
1/2 teaspoon mace
1/2 cup milk
1 cup dates stoned and chopped

Mix in order given and beat vigorously for three or four minutes; bake in two layer-cake pans in a moderate oven for twenty-five minutes; when partly cool spread with tart jelly and sprinkle top layer with powdered sugar.

Date Cake (1911)

Sift two cups of flour with four level teaspoons of baking powder, one-half level teaspoon of salt and one-quarter cup of butter. Beat one egg, add three-quarters cup of milk and mix into the ingredients. Add last one and one-half cups of dates stoned and cut into small pieces and rolled in flour. Bake in a sheet in a moderate oven and serve warm or with a liquid sauce as a pudding.

Date Cake (1912)

Cream one-third of a cup of butter until soft and add one and one-third cups of brown sugar, two eggs, one-half cup of milk, one and three-fourths cups of flour, one tablespoon of cinnamon, a little nutmeg and one-half pound of dates, stoned and chopped, one teaspoon of baking powder. Beat all the ingredients together until light, line and grease a shallow pan, bake forty or forty-five minutes. Remove from pan, cut in squares and sprinkle over with pulverized sugar. One-half cup of nuts can be added to this receipt if desired.

Date Loaf (1912)

One pound of seeded dates
One pound of English Walnuts
One cup of sugar
One cup of flour

One teaspoon of vanilla
Two teaspoons of baking powder
One fourth teaspoon of salt
Four eggs

Seed the dates and press into shape, add nuts; sift the flour, sugar, salt and baking powder together and mix with the dates and nuts, beat eggs separately and work the yolk with the cake mixture, stir in the whites. Bake in a greased and floured shallow pan one hour. When cold remove from pan and cut in slender, oblong pieces. Stack on plate, log cabin style.

Davis Cake (1890)

One cupful, (or 5 ounces), of butter
2 cups, not quite full, of sugar
3 cups even full of flour
1 cup, not quite full, of sweet milk

2 teaspoonfuls of baking powder
5 eggs (whites only)
2 teaspoonfuls of vanilla

Dayton Cake (1894)

One cup butter
Two cups sugar
Three cups flour
Five eggs

One-half cup milk
Teaspoon cream tartar
One-half teaspoon soda

This cake is very nice spiced a good deal, with raisins and other fruit added.

Delicate Cake (1889)

Half-pound butter
Three-fourths pound flour

One-pound sugar
Whites of fourteen eggs

Rub together the butter and flour. Add the sugar, which has been stirred lightly into the well-beaten whites of the eggs. Stir well. Flavour with bitter almond. Bake in oblong sponge-cake pans, with buttered paper.

Delicate Cake (1922)

½ cup butter
½ cup milk
1½ cups sugar

4 egg whites
2 cups flour
2 teaspoons baking powder

Mix and sift the dry ingredients. Cream the shortening and sugar and add flour and milk alternately. Fold in the well beaten egg whites and bake in a thin sheet in a moderate oven 25 minutes.

Delicate Cake (1893)

Beat to a cream:

½ cup butter
1 cup sugar

½ cup milk
2 scant cups flour

1 teaspoon soda
2 teaspoons cream tartar

3 eggs
1 cup currants

Delicate Cake 1 (1876)

Whites of nine eggs
Two cups of powdered white sugar
A half-cup of butter

Three cups of flour
One teaspoon of baking powder
Flavour with almond or rose

Delicate Cake 2 (1876)

One cup of sugar
A half-cup of butter
A half-cup of sweet milk
Two cups of flour

Whites of six eggs
One teaspoon of baking powder
Flavour to the taste

This is always good.

Delicate Cake 3 (1876)

A scant half cup of butter
One and a half cups of pulverized sugar
A half-cup of water
Whites of six eggs

Two cups of flour
One teaspoon of baking powder
Flavour with bitter almonds

Delicate Cake 4 (1876)

A half-cup of butter
One and a half cups of white sugar
A half-cup of sweet milk
One and a half cups of flour

A half-cup of corn starch
One teaspoon of baking powder
Whites of six eggs well beaten together

Beat the sugar and butter to a cream, add the whites of the eggs, after which the milk, and lastly the flour. Mix the corn starch and baking powder well in the flour. Flavour with vanilla or lemon.

Delicate Cake 5 (1876)

One cup of butter
One cup of sweet milk
Three cups of pulverized sugar
Five cups of flour

One teaspoon of soda
Two teaspoons of cream tartar
The whites of twelve eggs

Delicate Cake 6 (1876)

Whites of eighteen eggs
One pound of sugar
Nine ounces of butter
A half-cup of sweet milk

A half teaspoon of soda
One teaspoon of cream tartar
Add flour enough with two eggs to weigh one pound

Mix butter and sugar till very light, add flour, then milk, and the whites the last thing.

Delicate Cake 1 (1893)

Four ounces butter
Fourteen ounces sugar
Whites of six eggs

Twelve ounces of flour
Two teaspoons of baking powder
One cup of milk

Rub the butter and sugar together until they form a cream, stir the baking powder through the flour, then add it, a cupful at a time, to the butter and sugar, then stir in the milk, putting in the whites of the eggs after being beaten to a froth, a large spoonful at a time. Bake in a brisk oven.

Delicate Cake 2 (1893)

Use the same size cup for all ingredients.

Two cups (coffee) sugar
One-half cup butter
Stir to a cream
Whites of eight eggs beaten stiff

Three-fourths cup sweet milk
Two and one-half cups flour
Two teaspoons baking powder stirred into flour
Put whites of eggs in last and stir gently

Delicate cake 1 (1894)

Two cups sugar
One-half cup butter
Whites of six eggs
Three-quarters cup sweet milk

Nearly three cups flour
Half teaspoon soda
One teaspoon cream tartar
Lemon for flavouring

Delicate Cake 2 (1894)

One and one-half cups sugar
One-half cup butter
One-half cup milk

Half teaspoon soda
Two cups flour, into which rub one teaspoon cream tartar

Add last the whites of four eggs beaten to a stiff froth. Flavour with lemon.

Delicate Cake 1 (1893)

One cup sugar
½ cup butter
Whites of 3 eggs
½ cup milk

2 cups flour
1½ teaspoons baking powder
Crystaline salt and vanilla

Cream, butter and sugar; add 3 eggs well beaten, then milk, beat together with egg beater 10 minutes; fold in flour.

Delicate Cake 2 (1893)

Two cups sugar
Half-cup butter
¾ cup milk
White of 6 eggs

½ teaspoon soda
1 spoon cream tartar
3 cups of flour

Cream the butter and sugar, add the whites of eggs beaten to a stiff froth, beat thoroughly, add milk with soda, last add flour and cream tartar.

Delicate Sponge Cake (1920)

9 eggs
1½ small cups granulated sugar
1½ small cups flour (sifted 3 times)
The grated rind and juice of 1 lemon

Put the 9 yolks in a bowl and the whites into a deep dish; add to the yolks ½ the sugar and stir them to a cream; beat the whites to a stiff froth and add the remaining sugar, beating constantly; then add slowly, in small portions, the creamed yolks; next the lemon; continue the beating with an egg beater until all is well mixed; then stir in lightly the sifted flour; butter a long, shallow pan and line it with buttered paper; pour in the mixture and bake in a slow oven ¾ hour to a delicate brown; when done carefully remove the cake from oven and let it stand for a few minutes before taking out of the pan. This cake may be iced either with clear icing or wine or fruit glaze.

Delicious Cake (1911)

2 cups sugar
1 cup butter
1 cup milk
3 cups flour
3 eggs
½ teaspoon soda
1 teaspoon cream tartar

Cream butter and sugar together; add the yolks of the eggs, then the beaten whites. Dissolve the soda in the milk, rub the cream of tartar in the flour and add last.

Delicious Cake (1893)

One cup of butter
2 cups sugar beaten to a cream
Yolks of 3 eggs
1 cup of milk
3 cups flour
2 teaspoons Rumford Baking Powder
Whites of 3 eggs beaten, stiff
Flavour to taste
½ cup of melted butter added last

Bake in quick oven.

Delicious Cake 1 (1894)

Two cups sugar
One cup butter
One cup milk
Three cups flour
Three eggs
Half teaspoon soda
Scant teaspoon cream tartar

Stir the butter and sugar together, add beaten yolks, then the beaten whites. Dissolve the soda in the milk, rub cream tartar in the flour and add the last thing. Very nice.

Delicious Cake 2 (1894)

One-pound sugar
One-half pound butter
Yolks of fourteen eggs
One-pound flour
Two teaspoons cream of tartar sifted in flour
One cup sweet cream
One teaspoon soda dissolved in a little water

Bake in a quick oven.

Denmark Cake (1920)

Two pounds flour
2 teaspoonfuls baking powder
1¾ pound sugar
1-pound butter
2 pounds raisins
8 eggs

1-pint sweet milk
½ pint wine
3 tablespoonfuls allspice
3 tablespoonfuls cinnamon
4 nutmegs

Sift flour and baking powder together, stir butter and sugar to a cream, add gradually the yolks and spice, then alternately milk, flour, and wine, last the fruit. Bake in a large well-buttered pan in medium-hot oven.

Derby Cake (1864)

Some bring a capon, some Derby cake, some nuts, some apples, some that think they make the better cheesecakes, bring them.

Rub in with the hand one pound of butter into two pounds of sifted flour; put one pound of currants, one pound of good moist sugar, and one egg; mix all together with half pint of milk; roll it out thin and cut it into round cakes with a cutter; lay them on a clean baking plate, and put them into a middling heated oven for about ten minutes.

Dessertbiskuit (1910)

The weight of 4 eggs in sugar
The weight of 2 eggs in flour

2 yolks of eggs
4 whites of eggs

Whisk the whites of eggs stiffly, then stir in lightly the beaten-up yolks, and with a wooden spoon mix with the sugar, and lastly the flour. As in last recipe, sprinkle the paste through the end of a paper funnel into the shape of rings or fingers on to a buttered sheet of paper laid on a sheet of tin. Dust over with castor sugar and bake a pale golden colour.

Devil's Cake in Layers (1913)

Mix one-quarter of a cupful each of grated chocolate, brown sugar and milk; put in a saucepan and boil until like thick cream. Cream together a cupful of brown sugar and a rounding teaspoonful of butter. Add a small cupful of milk and one or two well beaten eggs. Flavour with lemon or vanilla. Now stir in the cold boiled ingredients and beat all thoroughly. Take half a pint of flour and sift it with a heaping teaspoonful of baking powder; add a little milk if the batter is too stiff. It should be quite stiff and beaten until very smooth.
Bake in thin layers and when cool put together with chocolate or other dark filling.

Devil's Food (1820)

½ c. shortening
2 eggs
2 c. sugar
2½ c. flour

2 sq. chocolate in 1 c. boiling water; let simmer 2 minutes
1 tsp. soda in 1/2 c. of very sour milk

Devil's Food Cake (N.D.)

2 cups sugar
½ cup sour milk
⅔ cup butter
2½ cups flour
3 eggs

1 teaspoon soda
1 cup coffee
1 teaspoon vanilla
½ cup cocoa (dry)

Devil's Food Cake (1922)

1½ cupfuls sugar
2 cupfuls flour
1½ cupfuls milk
½ cupful Crisco
½ cake chocolate
1 teaspoonful baking soda

2 teaspoonfuls vanilla extract
3 tablespoonfuls boiling water
2 eggs
Boiled frosting
½ teaspoonful salt

Put ½ cupful of sugar into small saucepan, add chocolate and 1 cupful milk. Put on stove and stir till it boils five minutes, stirring now and then. Remove from fire, add vanilla and set aside to cool. Beat Crisco and remainder of sugar to light cream, then add eggs well beaten and beat two minutes. Now add remainder of milk, soda dissolved in boiling water, flour, salt, and chocolate mixture. Mix carefully and divide into two large greased and floured layer tins and bake in moderate oven twenty-five minutes. Turn to cool and put together with boiled frosting.
Sufficient for: two large layers.

Devil's Food Nut Cake (1922)

2 squares bitter chocolate
2 cups brown sugar
½ cup water
1 egg yolk
1 cup chopped nuts
2 whole eggs

¼ cup shortening
½ cup sour milk
2 cups pastry flour
¼ teaspoon salt
1 teaspoon soda
1 teaspoon vanilla

Cook the chocolate, one-half cup brown sugar, cold water, and the egg yolk in a double boiler, stirring constantly until the mixture thickens. Add the nuts and stand aside to cool.
Cream the shortening and the remaining one and one-half cups sugar; add the well beaten eggs.
Sift the flour, salt and soda and add to the sugar mixture, alternating with the sour milk.
Stir together well and add vanilla. Last add the chocolate nut mixture and pour into a greased and floured cake pan. Bake for three-quarters hour in a moderate oven (350 degrees F.).

Dicker Pfefferkuchen mit Honig (1910)
(Ginger Cake with Honey)

3 lbs. honey
½ lb. sugar
Grated rind of 1 lemon
½ oz. ground cardamom
½ oz. ground cloves
1½ oz. potash
Candied peel to taste

2 teaspoonsful rosewater
3 lbs. flour
½ lb. chopped almonds
¼ lb. butter
½ oz. ground ginger
½ oz. cinnamon

Boil up the sugar and honey and pour into a basin. When a little cool, mix in the flour, the remaining ingredients and the potash dissolved in 2 teaspoonsful rosewater. Work up into a firm dough and leave in a cool place for 3 weeks.

Roll out about an inch thick, place on sheets of buttered tin, brush over with white of egg, whisked with rosewater, and bake a nice brown. Cut up while warm.

Dominion Apple Cake (1922)

2 cups flour
1 teaspoon salt
3 teaspoons baking powder

1 cup milk
2 eggs
3 tablespoons melted Crisco

Mix and sift dry ingredients. Add beaten yolks, Crisco and milk. Beat well; cut and fold in stiffly beaten whites. Spread mixture ½ inch thick on Criscoed pans. Lay apples cut into eighths in 2 rows on top of dough. Sprinkle with sugar; bake in hot oven 30 minutes. Serve with lemon sauce.

Domino Cake (1905)

Make this feather cake and pour it into two pans, so that the bottom shall be just covered, and bake it quickly. When it is done, take it out of the pans and frost it, and while the frosting is still a little soft, mark it off into dominoes. When it is entirely cold, cut these out, and with a clean paint-brush paint little round spots on them with a little melted chocolate, to exactly represent the real dominoes. It is fun to play a game with these at a tea-party and eat them up afterwards.

Domino Cakes (1922)

Bake two sheets of cake of any suitable mixture and fill with jelly, jam or cream.
Prepare two icings – a white and a chocolate.
Ice one part white, one part chocolate.
Cut the iced cake in long strips about two inches wide, while the icing is soft. Draw a line along the center of each strip in reverse colour, then cut the strip in one-inch slices and make the dots to imitate dominoes.

Dorbas Torte (1922)

5 eggs
5 tablespoons flour

4 tablespoons powdered sugar
Pinch of salt

Beat the yolks with the sugar for half an hour, using a wood spoon. Beat the whites stiff and add. Then the flour and salt sifted together.
Mix all thoroughly.
Grease the outside bottom of a cake tin and bake the dough in very thin layers, as many layers as possible, for ten minutes or less in a moderate oven. The length of time for baking depends on the thickness of the layer.
Cream one and one-half pounds unsalted butter with one and one-half cups confectioners' sugar. Add the beaten yolks of two eggs and one quarter pound grated sweet chocolate. Stir into a smooth paste. Spread between the thin layers until it is all used.
Cover with a glaze made by cooking one cup brown sugar with one-quarter cup boiling water until it forms a brittle string when tested in cold water. Spread over the top and sides with a knife dipped in cold water.
Keep the torte cold until ready to serve.

Dorothy Cake (1820)

½ c. fat
2 tsp. baking powder
1½ c. sugar
Flavouring

3 eggs
Nuts, raisins, or cocoa-nut may be added
1 c. milk
2½ c. flour

Mix as butter cake. Bake in layers in moderately hot oven. Use 2 tbsp. less milk and bake as loaf. A very fine-grained cake.

Dough Cake (1876)

One cup of butter
Two cups of sugar
Three cups of light dough
A half teaspoon of soda dissolved in a little water
Raisins, currants and spices to the taste

Dover Cake (1876)

One pound of brown sugar
A half-pound of butter
Six eggs
One teaspoon of cinnamon
One nutmeg
A half wine-glass of rose water
One wine-glass of molasses
One pound of flour (and fruit)

Dover Cake (1869)

One pound of flour
One of sugar
Half a pound of butter
Six eggs
Half a nutmeg
A spoonful of rose brandy

Beat the butter and sugar together, adding the other ingredients, the whites of the eggs beaten separately; bake as pound cake.

Dream Cakes (1913)

Cream well half a cup butter
Add a cup and a half of sugar
Half a cup cold water
Two cups flour sifted twice with two teaspoonfuls baking powder
A teaspoonful lemon extract
the stiffly beaten whites of six eggs

Bake in small shapes, frost, with boiled frosting, and ornament with tiny pink candies.

Dried Apple Cake (1902)

Soak 3 cups of dried apples overnight; drain the water off and cut them up a little and put them over the fire with 2 cups of molasses; boil until thick; take off the fire and put into a bowl. Add a cup of shortening, a tablespoonful of cinnamon, dessertspoonful of cloves, the same of allspice, a cup of sweet milk; when cold a tablespoonful of soda, dissolved in hot water, 4 cups of flour, added by degrees, 3 eggs well beaten, added last. Grease 3 pans well and bake.

Dried Crumb Griddle Cakes (1917)

1 cup dried and sifted bread crumbs
2 tablespoons sugar
1 cup flour
1 egg
1/2 teaspoon salt
1-1/4 cups milk
4 teaspoons baking powder

Dried Prune Cake (1904)

Make a dough as directed, cut some of the dough into long strips, lay them over the fruit, or make the cake as given in the Plum Cake (1904); then take 1 pound of prunes, ½ bottle of white wine, 7 ounces of sugar, ¼ pound of currants, 1 lemon and grated bread. The prunes are scalded (as directed for compotes) and slowly boiled in a little water until the stones will come out. They are then put into an earthenware dish with the broth, wine, sugar, juice and half of the peel of a lemon; cover the dish and boil slowly until tender., ¼ hour before tender put in the washed currants and let them boil until there is but little broth. After this is cold spread it over the dough and bake the cake for 1¼ hours with one degree of heat to a dark yellow colour.

Drop Ginger Cakes (1876)

One pint of molasses
A half pint of buttermilk
One teacup of butter and lard
Four eggs

Two tablespoons of ginger
One tablespoon of soda
Flour sufficient to make a stiff batter

Drop into a shallow pan.

Dutch Apple Cake (N.D.)

1½ tablespoons butter
1 teaspoon baking powder
2½ tablespoons sugar

¼ teaspoon salt
Water to make soft dough

Sift dry ingredients. Work butter in with knife. Add beaten egg and water. Handle very lightly. Put in square shallow pan and fill with sliced apples. On top put the following mixture:

¾ cup sugar
½ teaspoon cinnamon

2 tablespoons flour

Bake until apples are soft.

Dutch Apple Cake (1917)

1-1/2 cups flour
1/2 cup milk
3 teaspoons baking powder
2 tablespoons melted shortening
1/2 teaspoon salt

3 apples
3 tablespoons sugar
2 tablespoons sugar
1 egg
1/4 teaspoon cinnamon

Sift together flour, baking powder, salt, and sugar; add egg well beaten, milk, and shortening; beat well, and spread in a greased pan, having mixture about an inch deep; core, pare, and quarter apples, cut in thick slices, and arrange in rows on top of cake; sprinkle with sugar and cinnamon, and bake.

Dutch Apple Cake 1 (1893)

One-pint flour
½ teaspoon Crystaline salt
2 teaspoons baking powder
¼ cup butter

1 egg
1 scant cup milk
4 sour apples
2 tablespoons sugar

Cut apples into eighths and press into cake after it is in the pan, then sprinkle sugar on top; bake in hot oven 20 or 30, minutes.

Dutch Apple Cake 2 (1893)

One tablespoon butter
1 tablespoon sugar
1 egg

1 cup milk
2 cups flour
1 heaping teaspoon baking powder

Put in pan, spread apples on top sprinkle with sugar, add spice, served with boiled sauce.

Dutchess Cake (1920)

1 cup butter
1 cup milk
2 cups sugar

3 cups prepared flour
The yolks of 8 eggs
2 teaspoonfuls peach extract

Stir butter and sugar with the right hand to a light white cream; then stir with a spoon and add the yolks, 2 at a time, stirring a few minutes between each addition; next add the flavouring, the sifted flour and milk alternately; butter a large, round cake pan and line it with buttered paper; pour in the cake mixture and bake in a medium hot oven 1 hour.

NOTE: 1-pint shelled walnuts broken into pieces may be stirred into this cake mixture or Brazil nuts may be used; also, peanuts broken into pieces

Part 6: E

Easy Fruit-cake (1905)
Economy Cake (1820)
Economy Cake 1 (1876)
Economy Cake 2 (1876)
Economy Cakes 3 (1876)
Economy Cake (1913)
Economical Cake (1897)
(Ekonomisk kaka)
Eggless Cake (1913)
Eggless Cake (1911)
Eggless Chocolate Cake (1922)
Eggless Spice Cake 1 (1922)
Eggless Spice Cake 2 (1922)
Eier Kuchen or Eierwähen (1873)
(A Custard Cake)
Eierplätzchen (1910)
Elberfeld Krengel (1873)
(An Elberfeld Cake)
Eleanor's Cakes (1905)
Election Cake No. 1 (1889)
Election Cake No. 2 (1889)
Election Cake No. 3 (1889)
Election Cake No. 4 (1889)
Election Cake No. 5 (1889)
Election Cake No. 6 (1889)
Election Cake No. 7 (1889)
Election Cake No. 8 (1889)
Election Cake No. 9 (1889)
Election Cake No. 10 (1889)
Election Cake No. 11 (1889)

Election Cake 1 (1876)
Election Cake 2 (1876)
Election Cake (1920)
Election Cake (1840)
Election Cake (1893)
(One Hundred Years Old)
Emmy's Cake (1897)
(Emmys kaka)
English Christmas Cake (1922)
English Fruit Cake (1922)
English Fruit Cake (1893)
English Layer Cake (1908)
English Fruit Cake (1820)
English Muffins (1922)
English Muffins (1908)
English Muffins (1902)
English Muffins (1911)
English Muffins (1890)
English Plum Cake (1904)
English Seed Pound Cake (1922)
English Tea Cake (1820)
English Tea Cakes (1908)
English Walnut Cake (1894)
Engracia Cake (1909)
Entire Wheat Muffins (1911)
Esmé Shortcake (1909)
Esther's Molasses Cake for Lunch (1890)
Excellent Cake (1893)
Exposition Orange Cake (1893)
Exposition Orange Cake Filling (1893)

Easy Fruit-cake (1905)

1 cup butter	1 cup raisins
1 cup sugar	1 egg
1 cup molasses	1 teaspoonful soda
1 cup milk	2 teaspoonfuls mixed spices
1 cup currants	3 cups flour

Wash and dry the currants. Buy the seeded raisins and wash these, too, and then chop them. Cream the butter and sugar, add the egg beaten well without separating, then the molasses with the soda stirred in it, then the milk, then the cinnamon and cloves. Measure the flour, and then take out a half-cup of it, and stir in the raisins and currants, to keep them from going to the bottom of the cake when it is baked. Stir these in, add the rest of the flour, and beat well. Bake in two buttered bread-pans.

Economy Cake (1820)

1 c. brown sugar	1 c. raisins
1 tsp. ginger	1 tsp. soda
1 c. water	1/2 c. fat
2 tsp. cinnamon	2 c. flour

Bring sugar and water to boil. Add raisins and cook 5 minutes. Add fat and spice. Cool and add sifted soda and flour. Bake in a moderate oven. More fruit and nuts may be added.

Economy Cake 1 (1876)

Make a sponge with one pint of water and one cup of yeast; when light, add one cup of butter, two cups of sugar, three eggs, spices, and flour until it is as thick as you can well stir it.

Economy Cake 2 (1876)

One teacup of sugar	One tablespoon of butter
One teacup of milk	A half teaspoon of soda
Three teacups of flour	One teaspoon of cream tartar
One egg	Flavour to the taste

Bake immediately.

Economy Cakes 3 (1876)

Bread that is sour can be made into good breakfast cakes. Cut it in small pieces, and, if not wanted for immediate use, it can be kept a number of weeks by drying the pieces in a moderately hot oven; care must be taken that it does not burn. When you wish to make cakes for breakfast, soak the bread overnight in cold water; in the morning, drain off all the water, mash the bread fine, and to every three pints put one teaspoon of salt, three eggs, one teaspoon of soda dissolved in milk, one pint of wheat or rye flour; add sufficient milk to enable you to fry them as you would buckwheat cakes. If the flour which is used is mixed overnight with a large spoon of yeast, the eggs may be omitted.

Economy Cake (1913)

Cream together a cupful of sugar and half a cupful of shortening composed of bacon drippings and dried-out suet. Add the well beaten yolk of an egg and a pinch of salt. Sift a cupful of flour with two rounding

teaspoonfuls of baking powder. Stir all together and pour in a small cupful of milk, or milk and water, adding any preferred flavouring, and flour enough to make a good batter. Stir until very smooth.
Beat the egg white until very stiff, add sugar and flavouring, and use it to frost the cold cake.

Economical Cake (1897)
(Ekonomisk kaka)

One-pound flour
¼ pound sugar
¼ pound butter or lard
Half-pound currants

1 teaspoon soda
4 whites of eggs
And a half pint milk

To be real economical you can make a very good cake even if you leave the eggs and currants. Beat he batter to a cream and stir in all the ingredients but soda which add lastly when all is well worked. Put the cake into a buttered mould and bake in a moderate oven one hour and a half.

Eggless Cake (1913)

Cream together a cupful of granulated sugar and half a cupful of butter. Add a cupful of sour milk, half a cupful of cocoa (dry), an even teaspoonful of saleratus dissolved in hot water, a pinch of salt, and flavouring. Mix with enough sifted flour to make a stiff batter.

Eggless Cake (1911)

One and one-half cups sugar
One cup sour milk
Three cups sifted flour
One-half cup shortening
One teaspoon soda

One-half teaspoon cinnamon
One-half teaspoon nutmeg
One cup chopped raisins
Salt

Eggless Chocolate Cake (1922)

2 squares chocolate
1 cup milk
1 cup sugar
1½ cups flour

1 tablespoon melted shortening
1 teaspoon vanilla
⅓ teaspoon salt
1 teaspoon soda

Dissolve the soda in a half cup of milk. Grate the chocolate and melt in the remainder of the milk. Mix together the sugar and shortening, add vanilla, salt, the soda dissolved in the milk, and the flour; beat thoroughly. Then beat in the milk, still hot, in which the chocolate has been melted. Bake in a loaf about fifty minutes in a moderate oven. This cake will keep moist for several days.

Eggless Spice Cake 1 (1922)

3 cups pastry flour
1 teaspoon mace
1 cup sugar
1 teaspoon cloves
3 teaspoons baking powder
½ cup liquid fat

½ teaspoon salt
1¼ cups water
1 teaspoon cinnamon
1 teaspoon vanilla
½ teaspoon allspice

Sift together all dry ingredients. Add liquid fat with water and vanilla and stir until well mixed. Bake in layers in a moderately hot oven 20 minutes; in a loaf in a moderate oven 45 minutes.

Eggless Spice Cake 2 (1922)

3 cups pastry flour
1 cup sugar
3 teaspoons baking powder
½ teaspoon salt
1 teaspoon cinnamon
½ teaspoon allspice

1 teaspoon mace
1 teaspoon cloves
½ cup melted shortening
1¼ cups water
1 teaspoon vanilla

Sift together all dry ingredients. Add shortening with water and vanilla and stir until well mixed. Bake in layers in a moderately hot oven (375 degrees) 20 minutes; in a loaf in a moderate oven (350 degrees) 45 minutes. When cool spread with maple icing:

1 tablespoon hot coffee
Few drops of vanilla

3 tablespoons maple syrup
Confectioners' sugar

Mix together coffee, syrup and vanilla and beat in confectioners' sugar until stiff enough to spread.

Eier Kuchen or Eierwähen (1873)
(A Custard Cake)

Three well-beaten eggs, three tablespoonfuls of flour, a little salt, and a pint of milk; to be thoroughly stirred. Butter a flat tin that has an edge all round; cover it with a thin bread-dough raised at the edges; pour over it the butter, which must he of the thickness of cream only. Cut little pieces of butter over and bake a nice yellow colour.

Eierplätzchen (1910)

2 hard-boiled eggs
4 oz. butter
10 oz. flour

2 raw yolks
4 oz. sugar

Beat the raw yolks well and stir into them the rubbed hard-boiled yolks. Then add the butter, sugar and lastly the flour. Mix well, roll out and cut with a cutter into various shapes. Brush over with yolk of egg, sprinkle with sugar and cinnamon and bake on a well-buttered tin.

Elberfeld Krengel (1873)
(An Elberfeld Cake)

Mix half a pint of warm milk with two ounces of yeast and five or six eggs; stir in a pound of flour and set it to rise. When it has risen, add a quarter of a pound of sugar, three-quarters of a pound of warmed butter, and beat in by degrees nearly another pound of flour. It must be of the consistency of bread dough. Roll it out about half an inch thick, and twice as long as it is broad. Spread over it threequarters of a pound of currants, previously plumped in warm water, and over these, sprinkle a quarter of a pound of sugar mixed with a large teaspoonful of powdered cinnamon. Or, instead of the currants, &c., spread over a layer of fine preserve. Roll the dough up carefully lengthways, then form it into a ring on a tin. Leave it to rise, and when it appears to lighten brush it over with warmed butter and bake it in a good moderate oven from half to three-quarters of an hour.

Eleanor's Cakes (1905)

1/4 cup of butter
1/2 cup of sugar
1/4 cup of milk
1 egg

1 cup flour
1 teaspoonful baking-powder
1/2 teaspoonful of vanilla

Rub the butter and sugar to a cream, beat the egg light without separating, and put it in next; then the milk, a little at a time; mix the baking-powder with the flour and stir in, and last the vanilla. Bake in small scalloped tins and fill each one only half-full.

Election Cake No. 1 (1889)

Eight pounds flour
Four and a quarter pounds butter
Four and a quarter pounds sugar
Five eggs
One-quart home-made yeast
Four pounds raisins

One-pound citron
One-ounce mace
One-ounce nutmeg
New milk to make the batter sufficiently thin
One tumbler mixed wine and brandy

Beat to a cream the butter and sugar.
Mix half of it with the flour at two o'clock in the afternoon, wet with the new milk, slightly warm. The batter should be thinner than biscuit dough. Add the yeast; a little salt. Let it rise. When light, at night, add all other ingredients, with balance of butter and sugar. Let it rise again; then put in pans, making ten medium-sized loaves. Let it rise an hour.

Election Cake No. 2 (1889)

Eight quarts flour
Three and a half pounds sugar
Three pounds butter
Five eggs
One-quart home-made yeast

Three quarts milk
Six pounds raisins
Half-ounce mace
Half-ounce nutmeg
Half pint wine

Election Cake No. 3 (1889)

Four and a half pounds of flour
Two and a half pounds of sugar
Two and a quarter pounds of butter
Four eggs
Half-ounce nutmeg

Half-ounce mace
One tumblerful brandy and wine
Two pounds raisins
Half-pound citron

At noon, or early in the afternoon, begin making this cake. Rub together the butter and flour; wet it with one quart of milk, lukewarm, and either a half pint distillers' yeast or one cake and a half of compressed yeast. Beat well, cover the pan with a cloth and set in a warm place to rise. At night, when very light, add the sugar, spice, and eggs. Set the pan in a moderately warm place. Early next morning, add the fruit and wine, the grated peel of a lemon, half a teaspoonful extract of rose. Put into pans covered with buttered paper. Let them stand an hour, then put in as many as the oven will hold, selecting the smallest pans to bake first. A half teaspoonful of soda, dissolved in a little warm water, will be safe. This receipt makes seven loaves, which require to bake an hour or more.

Election Cake No. 4 (1889)

Twelve quarts of flour
Six pounds of sugar
Six pounds of butter
Twelve eggs
One-pint wine and brandy

One-quart hop yeast
Six pounds raisins
One-ounce mace
three ounces nutmeg

This cake is put together as directed in the preceding receipt, except that half only of the butter is mixed with the flour, in making the sponge. The remaining butter is added with the sugar, when worked over at night. The receipt makes twelve loaves.

Election Cake No. 5 (1889)

Four and a half pounds sugar
Four and a quarter pounds butter
One-peck sifted flour
Two quarts of milk
Six eggs

Four and a half pounds raisins
Half pint wine
Half pint brandy
Nutmeg, and mace

The yeast for this cake is preferably homemade, for which the receipt has already been given. The quantity is three-fourths of a quart, and the cake is mixed as in Receipt Election Cake 3.

Election Cake No. 6 (1889)

Two quarts flour
One and a half pounds sugar
One-pound butter and lard
One-pint home-made yeast
One pint or more new milk

One egg
One wineglass (sherry) of brandy and wine, mixed
Two nutmegs
One-pound raisins

Mix at 2 P.M., adding half the butter and sugar, worked to a cream, with yeast, milk, a little salt, and all the flour. When light, at evening, work in the rest of the materials. Beat well. Let it rise over night, and, in the morning, work over, put in pans, and let it rise an hour. Bake in moderate oven. Frost the loaves.

Election Cake No. 7 (1889)

Six pounds flour
Three and a half pounds sugar
Nutmeg, mace
Half a pint of St. Croix rum
One and a half pounds of raisins

One orange
A pound of citron
Two and a half pounds butter and lard, beaten to a cream

Take the flour and half the shortening, with one and a half cups of good yeast and milk enough to make a stiff batter. Let it rise over night, then add the rest of the shortening, and let it rise again. When light, add nutmeg, mace, half a pint of St. Croix rum, one and a half pounds of raisins, one orange, a pound of citron. Add the well-beaten whites of two eggs, two teaspoonfuls of baking powder. Put the batter in the pans; allow it to rise an hour.

Election Cake No. 8 (1889)

It is essential for this cake that the yeast should be made expressly for it.

Boil one potato in a pint of water; ten minutes before it is soft, add a teaspoonful of hops. The water should be reduced one-half. Rub the potato through a hair sieve, and, when cool, add to the hop water one sixth of a Fleischman yeast cake and four tablespoonfuls of flour, taken from that weighed out for the cake. Rub smooth, stir into the liquid, and let the whole rise, adding a half teaspoonful of salt.

The Cake: The receipt, in full, makes fourteen loaves, and is usually divided.

Eight pounds pastry flour	Half-ounce mace
Four and a half pounds sugar	Eight eggs
Four and a half pounds butter (part Deerfoot or Strawberry Hill lard can be used)	One and a half gills of brandy
	One and a half gills of wine
Six pounds raisins	Three pints milk
Two pounds citron	The juice of one or two oranges and a little grated peel
Two pounds currants or Sultana raisins	
One-ounce nutmeg	

At noon, rub well together the butter and sugar, until like pudding sauce.

Mix well half of this with the flour; add the milk, which must be lukewarm; a teaspoonful of salt; the eggs, and lastly, the yeast. Beat it half an hour. Set in warm place. By ten o'clock it will be light. Add the remaining butter and sugar, wine, brandy, spices, and orange juice. Beat half an hour. Set it in a warm place until morning. Stir into it, very lightly, the fruit, well dredged with flour, which must be taken from that measured for the cake.

Let it stand in the pans, which must be lined with buttered paper, an hour and a half before baking. It must not be stirred in the oven, nor the place of the pans changed.

Frost the loaves. The pans must be filled two thirds full. The batter must be very thin; if too stiff, warm with a little warm milk.

Election Cake No. 9 (1889)

Four pounds flour	Four eggs
Two pounds sugar	One quart of new milk
One-pound lard	Two heaping teaspoonfuls mace
One-pound butter	Four nutmegs
Two pounds raisins	A tumblerful of wine and brandy
One-pound citron	One-pint home-made yeast

In the morning, cream the butter and lard, and, when very light, add the sugar, mixing well. Take a little less than half the butter and rub well into the flour, which should be well warmed; add the milk, slightly warmed, and the yeast. Mix thoroughly, and let it stand where it will keep warm until it becomes very light, which should be about nine or ten o'clock at night. Do not disturb it while rising.

Beat the eggs separately and mix with the remainder of the shortening, adding the spice and wine, etc. Mix well, and let it rise a second time. In the morning, when light, fill the pans two-thirds full, putting in a little at a time and dropping the fruit in thickly in layers. Bake in a slow oven.

The Yeast: Boil a small handful of hops in one quart of water, strain through a sieve; pour, boiling hot, over the flour, to make a thin batter. When cool, add a half pint of distillery yeast; strain again, and let it stand until very light and foaming. Make the yeast the day before it is to be used.

Election Cake No. 10 (1889)
(Plain)

Three cups of new milk, warm	One cup home-made yeast
One cup sugar	

At two o'clock P.M. make a stiff batter, and let it rise. Beat well, and add, about bed time, three cups of sugar; two cups of butter; half cup sweet lard; one egg; one-pound raisins; half pound citron, sliced thin; three nutmegs; four teaspoonfuls mace, powdered; half wineglass brandy; half wineglass wine.

Election Cake No. 11 (1889)

Ten cups of flour
Four cups milk
Two cups sugar

One cup home-made yeast, or two thirds of a cup of distillers' yeast, omitting a little to add in the morning

Beat the batter well. Let it rise over night.
Take two cups of sugar; three cups butter; two eggs.
Add the balance of yeast and these ingredients to the batter; beat very hard, and, when well mixed, let it rise again. When very light, add half ounce of nutmeg and a quarter ounce of mace; two pounds raisins; one-pound citron; one teaspoonful of soda; two teaspoonfuls of cream tartar; one wineglass of brandy.
Let the cake rise again, in the pans, before putting it in the oven.

Election Cake 1 (1876)

Four pounds of flour and enough warm milk to make a stiff batter, one and a half pounds of butter and two and a half pounds of sugar. Stir butter and sugar well together; take half the mixture and beat into the batter and one pint of good yeast; beat thoroughly and let it stand one night; in the morning add the remainder of the butter and sugar and six eggs, beaten very light, then a half-pound of flour, two pounds of raisins, one pound of currants, grated lemon peel, cinnamon, mace and a small teaspoon of cloves. Let it rise twice before putting it into pans. The more this cake is beaten it is.

Election Cake 2 (1876)

One cup of yeast
One cup of sweet milk
One cup of lard

One cup of sugar
One egg and flour enough to make a stiff batter

Mix these at night and in the morning:

Add two cups of sugar
Two eggs
One cup of butter
One teaspoon of mace

One tablespoon of cinnamon
Flour enough to make it as stiff as other cake
Raisins and currants

This makes three good sized cakes. Let it rise in the pans an hour or more; bake in a moderate oven and ice when done.

Election Cake (1920)

One-and-a-half-pint lukewarm milk
1-pound sugar
½ pound lard
½ pound butter
2 pounds flour
The whites of 4 eggs

1-pound citron
1-pound seeded raisins
1 teaspoonful mace
½ cupful rum
3 yeast cakes

Break the yeast into a cup of lukewarm milk, add 1 teaspoonful sugar, set the cup in a warm place till the yeast rises to the surface, put 1 cupful flour into a bowl, add the yeast, mix into a stiff batter, cover, and set in a warm place to rise till the sponge is very light. In the meantime stir butter, lard, and sugar to a cream, add the mace, then alternately milk and flour, then the fruit and rum, and last the 4 whites beaten to a stiff froth; beat the whole with the hand 10 minutes, then add the sponge; continue to beat a few minutes longer, cover, and set it in a warm place to rise till double its size; butter and dust with flour a large round cake pan, pour in the cake mixture, and bake in a medium-hot oven till done. When cold, ice the cake with rum icing.

Election Cake (1840)

Make a sponge (as it is called) in the following manner: - Sift into a pan two pounds and a half of flour; and into a deep plate another pound. Take a second pan and stir a large table-spoonful of the best West India molasses into five gills or two tumblers and a half of strong fresh yeast; adding a Jill of water, warm, but not hot. Then stir gradually into the yeast, &c. the pound of flour that you have sifted separately. Cover it, and let it set by the fire three hours to rise. While it is rising, prepare the other ingredients, by stirring in a deep pan two pounds of fresh butter and two pounds of powdered sugar, till they are quite light and creamy; adding to them a table-spoonful of powdered cinnamon; a tea-spoonful of powdered mace; and two powdered nutmegs. Stir in also half a pint of rich milk. Beat fourteen eggs till very smooth and thick, and stir them gradually into the mixture, alternately with the two pounds and a half of flour which you sifted first. When the sponge is quite light, mix the whole together, and bake it in buttered tin pans in a moderate oven. It should be eaten fresh, as no sweet cake made with yeast is so good after the first day. If it is not probable that the whole will come into use on the day it is baked, mix but half the above quantity.

Election Cake (1893)
(One Hundred Years Old)

Four pounds flour
Two pounds butter
Two and one-half pounds sugar
Two and one-half pounds raisins
One-half pound citron

One-half ounce mace
Tumbler of brandy
One-pint yeast
One and one-half pint milk
Eight eggs

Add to the yeast one pint of milk; then beat in smoothly three pints of flour. Take all the flour and half the sugar and butter (when beaten to a cream); add the milk and yeast and make a dough a little softer than bread. When raised very light, add remainder of ingredients and let it rise again. When very light put into pans. Bake in moderate oven one hour.

Emmy's Cake (1897)
(Emmys kaka)

Pare and cut in 2, a number of apples, scald some plums, and remove their kernel stones and then boil both parts together in strongly sugared water. A big piece of sugar, quickly dipped in water must now be put in a wrought iron pan over the fire to be browned, but carefully guarded against burning. Place the sugar in a previously heated mould and put on top the boiled apples and plums, which cover with beaten eggs. Bake in oven, tip over plate when ready, and serve with vanilla sauce.

English Christmas Cake (1922)

2 lbs. butter
2¼ lbs. sugar
2¼ lbs. flour
1 qt. eggs
½ lbs. blanched and chopped almonds

¼ pt. rum or brandy
2½ lbs. sultanas
1½ lbs. currants
1½ lbs. mixed peel
½ oz. ground mace

Mix like other fruit cakes.

Many of the English FRUIT, BRIDES and CHRISTMAS CAKES are iced with the almond paste while warm, right after they are baked; and when the paste is dry, a coat of Royal or Fondant Icing is put over the almond icing and then decorated.

Another way is to put the Almond Paste on with a bag and star tube, put it back in the oven and brown it lightly in a quick heat, instead of using two coats, and decorate with French Fruit.

English Fruit Cake (1922)

2 lbs. sugar
2½ lbs. butter
2½ lbs. flour
1 qt. eggs
1 lbs. chopped almonds
½ pt. brandy or rum

3 lbs. currants
2 lbs. sultana raisins
1½ lbs. citron
1 lbs. orange and lemon peel
1 grated nutmeg
1 oz. mixed spice

Prepare just like American Fruit Cake (1922).

Both mixtures may be used for WEDDING CAKES. For this purpose, they should be baked in tin hoops of a convenient size.

Pans generally used for the fruit cake have slanting sides. If baked in straight sided hoops less trimming is required, and the decorated cake look better.

English Fruit Cake (1893)

Four cups brown sugar
Two cups butter
Twelve eggs
One lemon, grated
Two nutmegs, grated
One-half tablespoonful cloves
One tablespoonful cinnamon
One tablespoonful allspice

One-half pint cream
One cup pure brandy
Eight cups flour, sifted
One-half cup molasses
Two and one-half pounds raisins, seeded, whole
Two and one- half pounds currants
Six teaspoonfuls baking powder
One level teaspoonful soda

The success of this cake depends very largely upon having every ingredient prepared before commencing to use them. Begin by thoroughly mixing sugar and butter, then yolks of eggs well beaten; put the soda into the molasses and cream, add this to the above; next add spices and stir up thoroughly; now add the brandy (good whisky will do); take a portion of the flour and thoroughly flour the fruit with it; put the baking powder in the flour that remains and sift part of it into the mixture; now add the beaten whites of eggs and stir gently; stir in the fruit, bake from two to two and one-half hours in a moderate oven

English Layer Cake (1908)

Bake 3 layers of sponge-cake; then mix some jelly with wine and spread between the layers and over the top and sides. Cover with a rich chocolate icing, flavoured with vanilla

English Fruit Cake (1820)

1½ lbs. flour
1 lb. mixed candied fruit
1 lb. butter
1 lb. blanched and sliced almonds
1½ lbs. brown sugar
1 c. brandy or substitute

4 tbsp. nutmeg
2 tbsp. lemon juice
Grated rind of 2 lemons
1 c. molasses
3 lbs. raisins
2 tbsp. mace

7 eggs
4 lbs. currants
2 tbsp. cloves
1 lb. figs
¾ lb. citron
1 tbsp. soda

Bake 3 to 4 hours in slow oven (200 to 250).

English Muffins (1922)

4 cups flour
3 tablespoons butter
1 cake compressed yeast
1 teaspoon salt
2 cups hot milk

Dissolve the yeast in a little warm milk.
Cool milk and when lukewarm, add butter and salt. Mix with yeast paste. Mix the flour with this liquid and let stand for several hours in a warm place.
Grease a dozen muffin rings. Fill the rings half full of the batter. As dough starts to rise place muffins with rings on heated, greased griddle. Let bake slowly.
When golden brown, turn with a pancake turner and bake slowly on other side until done. Do not bake too well. When cool, split in two, toast on the cut side, butter generously and serve with marmalade or honey or maple syrup.

English Muffins (1908)

Take 1 quart of warm milk, 1/2 cup of yeast, 1 teaspoonful of salt and flour enough to make a stiff batter; let stand to raise until light. Then add 1/2 cup of melted butter, 1 teaspoonful of soda dissolved in a little water; add enough flour to make a very stiff batter and let raise half an hour. Then fill well-greased muffin-rings half full with the batter and bake in a quick oven until done. Serve with butter.

English Muffins (1902)

Scald 1 pt. of milk and add 1 oz. of butter and let cool; when cool add 1/4 of a yeast cake, a teaspoonful of salt and three cups of flour, beat well, cover and let rise about two hours. When light, add sufficient flour to make a soft dough; work lightly and divide into small balls; put each one into a well-greased muffin ring and let rise again. Then bake on a hot griddle. When ready to eat tear them open and butter.

English Muffins (1911)

One-pint milk, two level tablespoons shortening (butter or lard), two level teaspoons sugar, one level teaspoon salt, one yeast cake dissolved in one-fourth cup lukewarm water, flour. Scald the milk and add the shortening, sugar, and salt. When lukewarm add the yeast and sufficient flour to make a good batter. Here one's judgment must be used. Beat well and let rise until double in bulk. Warm and butter a griddle and place on it buttered muffin rings. Fill not quite half full of the batter, cover and cook slowly until double, then heat the griddle quickly and cook for about ten minutes, browning nicely underneath. Then turn them and brown the other side. When cool split, toast and butter.

English Muffins (1890)

One pint of warm water, dissolve one-half cake of compressed yeast; 1 pint of milk. No salt. The beaten whites of 4 eggs; flour enough to make a stiff batter. Set it to rise over night and bake in rings on buttered griddle. Toast cold ones' next morning.

English Plum Cake (1904)

Melt 1 pound of nice butter, clarify and let it cool again, take:

1 pound of sifted sugar	2 ounces of finely cut citron
1 pound of cornstarch	¼ ounce of cinnamon
1 pound of nicely washed and dried currants	½ ounce of cloves, both ground
12 eggs	A wineglassful of Madeira or arrac

Stir the butter to a cream, add, one by one, the yolks of the eggs, spices, sugar, currants and stir all for half an hour as directed under (General Directions (1904). Lightly stir through it the beaten whites of the eggs, then the starch and finally the Madeira, put the cake into a moderate oven and bake for 1¼ hours. If baking powder is added to the flour it will greatly improve the cake.

English Seed Pound Cake (1922)

One pound and four ounces of sugar	One pound and six ounces of flour
One pound of butter	One eighth of an ounce of baking powder
Twelve eggs	The grated rind of one lemon
A half-ounce of carraway seed	

Mix the same as Pound Cake. Add one more egg, or a little milk, if the mixture requires it.
(Oil of carraway may be used with very little of the seed if too much seed is objectable).

English Tea Cake (1820)

½ lb. butter	½ lb. sugar
¾ lb. flour	Grated rind of 1 lemon
2 tsp. baking powder	½lb. currants, or ⅓ lb. seedless white raisins
4 eggs	

Cream butter and work in the flour, then the sugar and currants. Beat eggs well and add to mixture with lemon rind. Bake slowly 1¼ hours. Blanched almonds or candied cherries may be added. This is excellent sliced thin and served with ice cream or with tea. It keeps well.

English Tea Cakes (1908)

Beat 1/4 pound of butter with 1/4 pound of sugar to a cream. Add 1 egg and 1 teaspoonful each of cinnamon and mace. Mix with 6 ounces of sifted flour, a pinch of salt and milk enough to make a stiff dough; then roll out very thin. Cut into round cakes and bake in a quick oven until done.

English Walnut Cake (1894)

One scant cup butter	Four eggs
Two cups sugar	One-pound English walnuts
Three cups flour	One teaspoon cream tartar
One cup milk	Half teaspoon soda

Bake in sheets.

Engracia Cake (1909)

Beat the yolks of 10 eggs with 1 pound of powdered sugar and the juice of ½ an orange; add alternately 1 pound of flour and the beaten whites of lo eggs; use no baking powder. Bake in small triangular moulds in a moderate oven and when cold join 5 of these cakes with thick orange marmalade. Dip in fondant icing coloured orange, drain on a wire broiler and redip if necessary.

Entire Wheat Muffins (1911)

2 cups entire wheat flour
1 teaspoon soda
1 teaspoon salt
2 teaspoons cream tartar

¼ cup sugar or molasses
1 egg beaten until light and added to
1 cup milk
1 tablespoon melted butter

Mix in order given and bake 20 minutes in hot oven.

Esmé Shortcake (1909)

Rub ¾ cupful of lard, or lard and butter, into 1 quart of flour which has been sifted with 2 teaspoonfuls of baking-powder; beat 2 eggs, stir in 2 cupfuls of sweet milk and add to the flour; knead well and roll out in two portions one-half inch thick. Place one layer in a buttered tin, cover with diced orange pulp, sprinkle with sugar and moisten the edge all around; put the second sheet of dough on top and press the edges well together; bake twenty-five minutes in a quick oven.

Esther's Molasses Cake for Lunch (1890)

One cupful of molasses
1 teaspoonful of soda
1 cupful of boiling water

1 tablespoonful of melted butter
Flour enough to make a soft batter
One-half teaspoonful of ginger

To be eaten warm. If used as a dessert, serve it with a lemon sauce.

Excellent Cake (1893)

Three cups sugar
4 cups flour
1 cup milk
1 cup butter
2 cups currents
½ cup citron

5 eggs
1 teaspoon cream tartar
One-half soda
Crystaline salt
Spices

Exposition Orange Cake (1893)

Two cups sugar
Two cups of sifted flour
One-half cup of water
Two teaspoonfuls yeast powder mixed with the flour

The yolks of five eggs and the whites of three beaten separately
The grating and juice of one orange

Bake in layers like jelly cake.

Filling: One cup sugar, grating and juice one orange, whites of two eggs beaten into a froth.

Exposition Orange Cake Filling (1893)

One cup sugar, grating and juice one orange, whites of two eggs beaten into a froth

Part 7: F

Fairy Gingerbread (1820)
Fancy Cakes-Soft (1920)
(Petits Fours Moelleux)
Farina Cake (1904)
Farina Cakes (1876)
Favart Cake (1920)
(Gâteau Favart)
Feather Cake 1 (1876)
Feather Cake 2 (1876)
Feather Cake 3 (1876)
Feather Cake (1922)
Feather Cake (1911)
Feather Cake (1894)
Feather Cake (1893)
Feather Sponge (1820)
(Made with Potato Flour)
Federal Cakes (1840)
Field's Potato Flour Muffins (N.D.)
Fig Cake (1876)
Fig Cake (1922)
Fig Cake (1922)
Fig Cake (1899)
Fig Cake (1911)
Fig Cake (1894)
Fig Layer Cake (1911)
Filbert Cakes with Rum Small (1920)
(Petits Gâteaux d'Avelines au Rhum)
Filled Sand Cake (1904)
Fine Ginger Dessert Cakes (1889)
Fine Sponge Cake (1920)
Five O'Clocks (1889)
Flag Cake (1922)
Flammen Torte (1873)
(Flame Cake)
Flannel Cakes (1905)
Flannel Cakes (1913)
Flannel Cakes (1840)
Flannel Cakes (1869)
Flannel Cakes (1920)
(Galettes Légères)
Flannel Cakes (1894)
Fleury Cake (1920)
(Gâteau Fleury)
Florida Corn Cake (1902)
Francillon Cakes (1920)
(Gâteaux Francillon)
Franklin Cake (1840)
French Cake (1876)
French Cake (1894)
French Fruit Cake (No. 1) (1922)
French Fruit Cake (No. 2) (1922)
French Loaf Cake (1876)
French Loaf Cake (1893)
French Loaf Cake (1894)
French Pastry Cake (N.D.)
French Tourte a la Crème (1922)
Fried Cakes 1 (1876)
Fried Cakes 2 (1876)
Fried Cakes 3 (1876)
Fried Cakes with Apple Sauce (1922)
Fried Cornmeal Nut Cakes (1922)
Fritters, Cake (1898)
Fruit Cake (1897)
(Frukt-kaka)
Fruit Cake (1889)
Fruit Cake (1904)
Fruit Cake 1 (1876)
Fruit Cake 2 (1876)
Fruit Cake 3 (1876)
Fruit Cake 4 (1876)
Fruit Cake 5 (1876)
Fruit Cake (1890)
Fruit Cake (1913)
Fruit Cake (1920)
Fruit Cake (1920)
(Gâteau aux Fruits)
Fruit Cake (1911)
Fruit Cake 1 (1893)
Fruit Cake 2 (1893)
Fruit Cake 3 (1893)
Fruit Cake 1 (1893)
Fruit Cake 2 (1893)
Fruit Cake 3 (1893)
Fruit Cake 1 (1894)
Fruit Cake 2 (1894)
Fruit Cake 3 (1894)
Fruit Cake (1912)
Fruit Cake from Bread Dough (1913)
Fruit Drop Cakes (1876)
Fruit Drop Cakes (1922)
Fruit Drop Cakes (1922)
Fruit Layer Cake (1912)
Fruit or Plum Cake (1869)
Fruit Queen Cakes (1840)
Fruit-Nut Loaf Cake (1922)
Fruit Gems (1876)
Fryeburg Sponge Cake (1911)
Fudge Cake (1911)
Fudge Cake (1922)
Fudge Cake (1917)

Fairy Gingerbread (1820)

¾ c. brown sugar
2 tsp. soda
2 eggs
1c. boiling water
¾ c. light molasses

1 tbsp. ginger
¾ c. melted fat
2 tsp. cinnamon
2½ c. flour
Other spice if desired

Sift dry ingredients, beat eggs, add molasses, softened fat, and lastly boiling water with soda in it. Makes a thin batter but is very tender. Bake in gem pans.

Fancy Cakes-Soft (1920)
(Petits Fours Moelleux)

Crush one pound of almonds with a pound and a half of sugar and five egg-whites; let this paste be very fine; lay it on a table and add a tablespoonful of strawberry essence and three more whites and beat until it is very smooth and has attained body. Put a part of it in a channelled socket pocket and push it on a paper-covered baking sheet into small cakes shaped like an S, commas, knobs, etc. Decorate each one with a fancifully cut candied fruit or very white almonds and leave to dry in a cool place for four or five hours. Then bake in a hot oven and gum as soon as removed.

Farina Cake (1904)

Farina biscuits are easy to make and are nice for the sick, but the finest farina is required. To ½ pound of farina take 8 - 10 eggs, ¾ pound of sugar, 1 lemon and almonds if liked. Stir the yolks of the eggs to a cream with the sifted sugar, beat the whites of the eggs to a stiff froth, stir into the farina a little at a time, then season with lemon peel grated on sugar and the juice of 1 lemon.
Bake the cake in a buttered mould dusted with grated wheat bread, for 1 hour in a moderately hot oven.

Farina Cakes (1876)

Take one pint of sweet milk and let it come to a boil; stir in enough farina to make a stiff batter and let it cool, then stir in eight eggs, well beaten, small piece of butter, salt to season well. A little chopped parsley improves the taste. Cook as batter cakes.

Favart Cake (1920)
(Gâteau Favart)

Whip sixteen eggs in a basin with one pound of powdered sugar and two ounces of vanilla sugar; beat till very light while heating slightly, then stir in with a spoon one pound of sifted flour and later three-quarters of a pound of melted butter. Butter a hexagonal mold with clarified butter, flour it over and fill it three-quarters full with the preparation. Bake in a slow oven; when done, unmould on a grate and when thoroughly cold cover with peach marmalade, ice with kirsch icing, dredging the top with chopped burnt almonds and some small one-eighth inch squares of angelica and citron.

Feather Cake 1 (1876)

Two cups of sugar
Three cups of flour
A half-cup of butter

Two thirds of a cup of milk
Two eggs
Two teaspoons of baking powder

Feather Cake 2 (1876)

One cup of sugar
Two cups of flour
Two-thirds of a cup of milk
One teaspoon of butter

One egg
One teaspoon of cream tartar
A half teaspoon of soda

Feather Cake 3 (1876)

Whites of three eggs
One cup of sugar
A half-cup of butter
A half-cup of sweet milk

Two cups of flour
One and a half teaspoons of baking powder
Flavour to the taste

Feather Cake (1922)

Cream ½ cup Crisco with ½ cup sugar, and ½ teaspoon salt, and 2 eggs beaten with ½ cup sugar, 1 teaspoon lemon extract, 1 cup milk, 2½ cups flour, and 2½ teaspoons baking powder. Beat 2 minutes and turn into Criscoed and floured cake tin. Bake in moderate oven for ¾ of an hour.

Feather Cake (1911)

Sift one cup of sugar, two cups of sifted flour, three level teaspoons of baking powder and a few grains of salt. Add one cup of milk, one well beaten egg, three tablespoons of melted butter and a teaspoon of vanilla or lemon flavouring or a level teaspoon of mixed spices. Beat hard and bake in a loaf in a moderate oven about half an hour.

Feather Cake (1894)

One and a half cups sugar
Three cups flour
One-quarter cup butter
Three-quarters cup milk
Two eggs

Two teaspoons cream tartar
One teaspoon soda
Salt
Flavour with lemon

Feather Cake (1893)

Beat to a cream ½ cup of butter, add to this 2 cups sugar, beat well; add 1 cup milk with 1 teaspoon soda dissolved in it; beat well; add 1 cup flour with 2 teaspoons cream tartar previously rubbed into it; add the well-beaten yolks of 3 eggs, beat the whites stiff; add them with 2 cups of flour. Beat well between each addition.

Feather Sponge (1820)
(Made with Potato Flour)

4 eggs
2/3 c. potato flour (good only with the best grade potato flour) or a prepared cake
1 c. sugar

1 tsp. baking powder
1 tsp. flavouring
Flour

Beat yolks and whites separately. Beat one-half of the sugar into yolks and one-half into the whites. Pour yolks and sugar over sifted flour and baking powder. Mix well. Add the whites and sugar and flavouring.

Bake in a loaf or in two layers. This is a very tender sponge cake and makes an excellent dessert served with sliced bananas and whipped cream or strawberries and whipped cream.

Federal Cakes (1840)

Sift two pounds of flour into a deep pan and cut up in it a pound of fresh butter; rub the butter into the flour with your hands, adding by degrees, half a pound of powdered white sugar; a tea-spoonful of powdered cinnamon; a beaten nutmeg; a glass of wine or brandy, and two glasses of rose water. Beat four eggs very light; and add them to the mixture with a salt-spoonful of pearl-ash melted in a little lukewarm water. Mix all well together; add, if necessary, sufficient cold water to make it into a dough just stiff enough to roll out; knead it slightly, and then roll it out into a sheet about half an inch thick. Cut it out into small cakes with a tin cutter, or with the edge of a tumbler; dipping the cutter frequently into flour, to prevent its sticking. Lay the cakes in shallow pans buttered, or on flat sheets of tin, (taking care not to let them touch, lest they should run into each other,) and bake them of a light brown in a brisk oven. They are best the second day.

Field's Potato Flour Muffins (N.D.)

4 eggs
1 teaspoon baking powder
¼ teaspoon salt
½ cup white potato flour
2 tablespoons ice water
1 tablespoon sugar

Beat whites of eggs very stiff and dry. Add salt and sugar to beaten yolks and fold into whites. Sift flour and baking powder twice and beat thoroughly into egg mixture. Add ice water last. Bake in moderate oven from fifteen to twenty minutes.

Fig Cake (1876)

Whites of eight eggs
One and a half cups of sugar
One cup of butter
One cup of sweet milk
Two and a half cups of flour
Three teaspoons of baking powder
Two pounds of chopped figs

Fig Cake (1922)

1 cup sugar
½ pound figs
½ cup butter
1 teaspoon soda
2 eggs
1 cup of boiling water
1 cup raisins
2 cups flour

Cream butter and sugar, add eggs. Put figs and raisins through food chopper and add to boiling water; add soda; add pinch of nutmeg and cinnamon. Add flour. Bake in two layers in moderate oven.

Fig Cake (1922)

1 cupful sugar
½ cupful Crisco
3 eggs
3 teaspoonfuls baking powder
1 cupful milk
½ teaspoonful salt
2 teaspoonfuls powdered cinnamon
1 teaspoonful vanilla extract
½ teaspoonful grated nutmeg
3 cupfuls flour
1 cupful shredded figs

Wash and dry figs then shred them. Cream Crisco and sugar together, add eggs well beaten, and beat five

minutes. Sift dry ingredients and add to first mixture alternately with milk. Add figs and flavourings and turn into Criscoed and floured cake tin. Bake one hour in moderate oven.
Sufficient for one small cake.

Fig Cake (1899)

Take one cupful of sugar,
Two-thirds of a cupful of sweet milk
Two tablespoonfuls of butter

Two cupfuls of flour
Two teaspoonfuls of baking-powder
The whites of four eggs

Sift the flour before measuring. Rub the sugar and butter to a cream, add the milk, the flour, and baking-powder, and, lastly, the whites of the eggs beaten to a stiff froth. Add any flavouring desired and bake in three layers. Cook together for ten minutes one-half pound of figs chopped fine, one small cupful of water and one-half cupful of sugar and spread between the layers.

Fig Cake (1911)

Two cupfuls of sugar
Two-thirds of a cup of butter
One cupful of milk
Four even cupfuls of flour

Five eggs
Two teaspoonfuls of cream of tartar
One of soda, sifted with the flour

Mix the butter and sugar until creamed, add the unbeaten yolks of the eggs, add the milk and the flour slowly, beating all the time, lastly the whites of the eggs. Flavour two cupfuls of chopped figs and mix in. Bake quickly.

Fig Cake (1894)

Two cups sugar
One-half cup butter
One cup milk
Whites five eggs, beaten stiff

Three cups flour
Two teaspoons baking powder
About one cup figs cut up quite fine and sifted over with flour

Soaking them overnight in wine or brandy improves them. Nice.

Fig Layer Cake (1911)

Cream one-quarter cup of butter with one cup of sugar, add one beaten egg, one cup of milk, two cups of flour sifted twice with four teaspoons of baking powder. Bake in layer tins.
For the filling-chop one-half pound of figs fine, add one-half cup of sugar and one-quarter cup of cold water. Cook in a double boiler until soft, let cool, and spread between the cakes.

Filbert Cakes with Rum Small (1920)
(Petits Gâteaux d'Avelines au Rhum)

Roast half a pound of filberts; clean them well by removing their outer reddish skins, then pound with three-quarters of a pound of sugar, two eggs and half a gill of rum, making it into quite a fine paste; lay this in a vessel and soften it gradually with eight egg-yolks, continuing to beat until it is frothy, then add two ounces of finely shredded citron, four ounces of potato fecula, four ounces of melted butter and lastly six firmly beaten egg-whites. Pour this paste on a buttered sheet covered with paper, spread it out to half an inch in thickness and cook in a slow oven. Turn the cake over on a grate when done and leave to cool and set until the following day. Pare and cut it either in lozenges, oblongs or other shapes; steep each one slightly in Jamaica rum and ice over, dipping them into Jamaica rum fondant; bestrew the cakes with chopped-up roasted filberts.

Filled Sand Cake (1904)

A puff paste made of ½ pound of flour, also 6 ounces of sugar, 6 ounces of butter, ¼ pound of powdered sugar, 12 eggs, and apricot marmalade for filling. Cream the butter and stir it for ¼ hour with the yolks of the eggs and sugar, then lightly mix through it the beaten whites of the eggs and the powdered sugar. This is made into; a thin round cake, baked and spread with the marmalade. The puff paste is perforated so that it will not blister, lay it on the baked cake, spread with the beaten egg and bake. Puff paste must bake quickly.

Fine Ginger Dessert Cakes (1889)

Rub half a pound of fresh butter into three quarters of a pound of flour; beat three eggs with three quarters of a pound of powdered sugar and half a glass of rosewater, the grated peel of a lemon, and a teaspoonful of the best powdered ginger--use the ginger carefully, trying a level spoonful first. Then mix all into a paste. If the flavour of ginger is not strong enough, add more; they should taste well of it, without being hot in the mouth. Roll the paste a quarter of an inch thick, and cut into small oval or round cakes, sift powdered sugar over them, and bake rather slowly a very pale brown

Fine Sponge Cake (1920)

| 1-pound powdered sugar | not quite 1 pound (about 2 tablespoonfuls less) of flour |
| 12 eggs | then add the grated rind and juice of 1 lemon |

Put the flour into a tin pan and set it in front of oven to get warm; put the eggs, sugar and lemon into a deep stone mixing bowl; set the bowl into a large dishpan of hot water in such a way that the bowl is half covered with water; beat the contents of bowl with an egg beater for ¾ hour; then slowly add the flour, continue the beating for a few minutes longer and pour the mixture into a large round pan or 2 medium sized ones; the pan should be previously well buttered and lined with fine brown buttered or waxed paper; bake 1 hour in a slow oven. Sponge cake made according to this recipe is elegant, but care must be taken to follow the instructions exactly. Half these quantities will make a good-sized cake. If the oven should be rather hot at the bottom put in a large pie plate with salt, set the pan with cake onto it and bake.

Five O'Clocks (1889)

One cup of butter	Half a nutmeg
Two cups of sugar	Ten drops rosewater
Three cups of sifted flour	Grated peel of one lemon
Four eggs, beaten separately	One dessertspoonful vanilla
Half cup milk or sour cream if cream is used, add	One glass sherry or half glass brandy
A quarter teaspoonful of soda	Half a pound of citron, cut fine

Stir butter and sugar together, add the wine, flavouring, and lemon peel. Stir in the milk, alternately, with half the flour. Add two level teaspoonfuls baking powder in a little of the flour. Stir in the beaten eggs, alternately, with the remaining flour, reserving a very little to dredge the citron.
Lastly, add the fruit. Half a pound of raisins may be used, if desired. Bake in small block-tin pattypans. This receipt makes sixty cakes. Frost with the Asquam frosting. Two eggs will frost all.

Asquam Frosting: To the white of one egg, take one and a quarter cups of pulverized sugar. Stir in the sugar without beating the egg. Add three drops rose water, ten of vanilla, and the juice of half a lemon. It will at once become very white, and will harden in a very few moments, which is its chief claim to distinction.

Flag Cake (1922)

⅔ cup sugar
½ cup Crisco
⅔ cup milk
1⅔ cups flour
2 teaspoons baking powder
½ teaspoon salt
Whites of 4 eggs,
1 teaspoon vanilla

Cream Crisco and sugar together, add flour, salt, baking powder, milk, vanilla and whites of eggs beaten to a stiff froth. Mix carefully, turn into Criscoed and floured tin and bake in moderate oven

Flammen Torte (1873)
(Flame Cake)

This is a supper dish. Choose a flat sponge cake or cut a deep one into three or four slices and arrange them closely together. Soak it with arrack or brandy and set fire to it as it is being carried to table.

Flannel Cakes (1905)

1 tablespoonful of butter
1 tablespoonful of sugar
2 eggs
2 cupfuls of flour
1 teaspoonful of baking-powder
Milk enough to make a smooth, rather thin batter

Rub the butter and sugar to a cream, add the eggs, beaten together lightly, then the flour, in which you have mixed the baking-powder, and then the milk. It is easy to know when you have the batter just right, for you can put a tiny bit on the griddle and make a little cake; if it rises high and is thick, put more milk in the batter; if it is too thin, it will run about on the griddle, and you must add more flour; but it is better not to thin it too much, but to add more milk if the batter is too thick.

Flannel Cakes (1913)

Cream together a rounding tablespoonful each of butter and sugar, add two well-beaten eggs, one and one-half cupfuls of flour into which has been sifted a rounding teaspoonful of baking powder.

Flannel Cakes (1840)

Put a table-spoonful of butter into a quart of milk, and warm them together till the butter has melted; then stir it well and set it away to cool. Beat five eggs as light as possible and stir them into the milk in turn with three pints of sifted flour; add a small tea-spoonful of salt, and a large table-spoonful and a half of the best fresh yeast. Set the pan of batter near the fire to rise; and if the yeast is good, it will be light in three hours. Then bake it on a griddle in the manner of buckwheat cakes. Send them to table hot and cut across into four pieces. This batter may be baked in waffle-irons. If so, send to table with the cakes powdered white sugar and cinnamon.

Flannel Cakes (1869)

Warm a quart of milk, put in a spoonful of butter, a little salt, and two eggs well beaten, stir in flour till it is a thin batter, and two spoonsful of yeast; beat all well together, adding the eggs at the last; allow it five hours to rise, and bake it on the griddle in cakes, the size of a breakfast plate. Do not butter them till you send them to the table.

Flannel Cakes (1920)

(Galettes Légères)

Place in a bowl, four ounces of butter and two ounces of sugar; work well together to obtain a creamy preparation, then add four whole eggs one by one, and after the eggs are well incorporated put in eight ounces of flour and two gills of milk. Have the paste nice and smooth, and just when ready to use add a tablespoonful of baking powder mingled with an equal quantity of flour, then finish cooking and serve exactly the same as the buckwheat cakes.

Flannel Cakes (1894)

To two ounces of butter add a pint of hot milk to melt the butter, a pint of cold milk, five eggs, flour enough to make a stiff batter, teaspoon salt, two tablespoons yeast; set it to rise in a warm place about three hours; butter the griddle and pour on the batter in small cakes.

Fleury Cake (1920)
(Gâteau Fleury)

Make a biscuit preparation with a pound of sugar, having two ounces of it flavoured with vanilla, eight ounces of flour and four ounces of fecula sifted together; three-quarters of a pound of roasted and pounded filberts, twenty-two egg-yolks, six beaten whites and a grain of salt. Bake in a slack oven on a baking sheet covered with paper, having it at least half an inch thick, and when done put aside to cool for twelve hours. With seven or eight egg-yolks, some sugar, six gills of milk and a piece of vanilla, prepare an English cream; as soon as it thickens remove and mix in a quarter of a pound of roasted chopped filberts, and pour it at once into a glazed vessel, working till cold; then strain through a tammy and return it to the saucepan to beat oil a slow fire for two minutes to have it lukewarm; remove once more and incorporate into it, without ceasing to stir, one-half pound of fresh butter divided in small pats; the cream should now be quite consistent and slightly frothy; divide it into two parts, and colour one with carmine mixed with a little syrup so that it acquires a pinkish hue, leaving the other half white. Have a hexagon (six-sided) shaped cardboard pattern and with it cut three or four pieces from the prepared biscuit; split them through their thickness, mask them over with apricot marmalade, and reconstruct them as before; fasten these pieces on a thin Genoese bottom a third of an inch wider than the biscuit, and on this, with the remainder of the biscuit cut thin and also masked with apricot, raise an even pyramid, cut hexagonally; cover it as well as its base with a thin layer of the butter cream. Roast in the oven half a pound of filberts cut up small; when removed besprinkle with fine sugar, and when nearly cold apply them in smooth layers against the thickness of the base on which the pyramid stands, pressing them down with the blade of a knife to equalize the surface, leaving no open space whatever between. Introduce a part of the white cream into a small fancy socket pocket, and push on the surfaces of the pyramid small, plain, close flowers, strictly following the divisions of the hexagon; next to these push some pink flowers, alternating the shades, in the different compartments. When the pyramid is entirely covered push a large rose on top, having the two colours mixed, then with a smaller socket surround the base of the cake with small roses made of the two colours. Keep the cake for a quarter of an hour on ice to have the cream harden superficially, and on removing slip it carefully on a napkin, and serve at once, for the buttered cream must remain hard.

Florida Corn Cake (1902)

One egg
1 cup of milk
1 tablespoonful salt fat pork
1 teaspoonful salt

1 of sugar
2 cups white corn-meal
1 tablespoonful baking powder

Mix all thoroughly and bake in 2 thin cakes.

Francillon Cakes (1920)

(Gâteaux Francillon)

These are prepared with one pound of peeled sweet almonds, fourteen ounces of clarified butter kneaded with twenty ounces of vanilla sugar, also four and a half ounces of flour, two ounces of fecula, ten or twelve egg-yolks, seven or eight beaten whites, and a grain of salt. Pound the almonds with one egg-white, dilute with a glassful of good milk, and pass through a sieve; put the butter into a vessel, and with a spoon beat in the eggs, one at a time. When the whole is creamy mix in the sugar, the almonds, the beaten whites, and the sifted flour and fecula. Line a thin raised-edge baking sheet with sweet paste, pour in the preparation, smooth nicely and bake in a slack oven; when unmoulded and cold brush apricot marmalade over the top, and cut it into small cakes without separating the pieces; ice the surface with kirsch icing, and detach from each other only when this becomes dry, then dress.

Franklin Cake (1840)

Mix together a pint of molasses, and half a pint of milk, and cut up in it half a pound of butter. Warm them just enough to melt the butter, and then stir in six ounces of brown sugar; adding three table-spoonfuls of ginger, a table-spoonful of powdered cinnamon, a tea-spoonful of powdered cloves, and a grated nutmeg. Beat seven eggs very light, and stir them gradually into the mixture, in turn with a pound and two ounces of flour. Add, at the last, the grated peel and juice of two large lemons or oranges; or twelve drops of essence of lemon, there being no pearl-ash in this gingerbread. Stir the mixture very hard; put it into little queen cake tins, well-buttered; and bake it in a moderate oven. It is best the second day and will keep soft a week.

French Cake (1876)

Two cups of sugar
Three cups of flour
One cup of milk
A half-cup of butter
Three eggs

Two teaspoons of cream tartar
One teaspoon of soda
One cup of raisins
Two teaspoons of cinnamon
One of cloves

French Cake (1894)

Two cups sugar
One-half cup butter
One cup milk

Three cups flour
Two teaspoons cream tartar
One teaspoon soda dissolved in milk

Beat the sugar, butter, cream tartar and yolks together, whites separately, four eggs.

French Fruit Cake (No. 1) (1922)

1 lbs. Butter
A pinch of baking powder
1¼ lbs. flour

10 eggs
1 lbs. sugar
Orange flavour

One and one-half pounds of French fruits glacés, cut into dice, consisting of cherries, apricots, angelica, orange, or pomegranate.
Mix like other fruit cakes

French Fruit Cake (No. 2) (1922)

1½ lbs. sugar
1 lbs. butter

1¾ pts. Whites of eggs
1¾ lbs. flour

¼ oz. baking powder
1 lb. French fruit, mixed
½ lb. blanched and sliced almonds
½ lb. sultanas

4 oz. soft preserved orange peel
¼ oz. cream of tartar
Flavour orange

Ice both cakes with almond or fondant, the fondant coloured pink and flavoured with maraschino. Decorate the centre with a basket of French fruits and a border of angelica and cherries.

French Loaf Cake (1876)

One pound of sugar
A half-pound of butter
One pound of flour
One cup of new milk

Five eggs
One pound of raisins
Spice to the taste

French Loaf Cake (1893)

Two and one-half cups sugar
One cup butter
One cup milk
Four cups flour
Three eggs
One wine glass sherry
One wine glass brandy

One- half teaspoon soda
one-pound raisins (stoned)
One-half pound citron
One teaspoon cloves
Two teaspoons cinnamon
One nutmeg

Bake one hour

French Loaf Cake (1894)

One-pound sugar
Half-pound butter
Two eggs
Half-pint milk
One-pound flour
One tea-spoon soda

One-pound raisins
One cup currants
One nutmeg
Citron
Wine-glass of brandy

French Pastry Cake (N.D.)

2 cups sugar
½ cup cocoa, dissolved in ¾ cup boiling coffee
½ cup butter

3 egg yolks
½ teaspoon baking soda, dissolved in ½ cup milk or cream

Let cool, add 3 cups flour and 3 beaten egg whites, flavour if desired.

Filling:

3 cups powdered sugar
6 tablespoons butter

6 tablespoons cocoa
6 tablespoons hot coffee

French Tourte a la Crème (1922)

Roll out a bottom from Puff Paste (1922) or Quick Puff Paste (1922). Put on a border from the same paste. Fill the center with almond paste cream. Wash over the rim with egg wash and bake to a nice colour. Serve plain, dusted with sugar, or decorate with meringue.

Fried Cakes 1 (1876)

Two cups of sour milk
Two cups of sugar
Two-thirds of a cup of lard
Two eggs

One teaspoon of ginger
Salt
One teaspoon of soda
Flour sufficient to roll

Fry in hot lard.

Fried Cakes 2 (1876)

Two cups of sugar
Two cups of sour milk
One egg
One tablespoon of lard

Two teaspoons of soda
A little allspice
Flour to roll nicely

Fry in hot lard.

Fried Cakes 3 (1876)

One cup of sugar
Three eggs
Six tablespoons of melted lard
A half pint of sweet milk

Three teaspoons of baking powder
One teaspoon of mace
One teaspoon of salt
Flour to mix soft

Fried Cakes with Apple Sauce (1922)

1 cupful sugar
1 teaspoonful baking soda
4 tablespoonfuls Crisco
1 teaspoonful baking powder
3 cupfuls sour milk

½ teaspoonful salt
¼ teaspoonful grated nutmeg
Flour
1 teaspoonful lemon extract
Apple sauce

Cream Crisco, gradually add sugar, then add salt, nutmeg, lemon, soda, baking powder, sour milk and sufficient flour to make stiffish dough. Roll out on floured baking board, cut with large round cutter, and fry in hot Crisco until well cooked and nicely browned on both sides. Drain and serve with hot apple sauce.
Sufficient for: twenty cakes.

Fried Cornmeal Nut Cakes (1922)

2 cupfuls yellow cornmeal
1 teaspoonful salt
2 tablespoonfuls melted Crisco

1 egg
3 cupfuls boiling water
½ cupful chopped nut meats

Bring water and salt to boil, stir in cornmeal, add nut meats, and stir and cook ten minutes. Remove from fire and add egg well beaten, and melted Crisco. Turn into Criscoed tin and cool. When cold, slice and fry in hot Crisco. Serve with honey or maple syrup.
Sufficient for six or eight slices.

Fritters, Cake (1898)

Ingredients:

½ lb. plum cake   frying batter

Method: Cut the cake into small, neat pieces, about 2\ inches in length, 1 inch wide, and | inch thick, dip them in the batter, and fry them in plenty of boiling lard a light golden colour. Turn them on to kitchen paper to drain, sift pounded sugar over, and serve very hot.
Time: 6 or 7 minutes.
Sufficient for: 3 or 4 persons.

Fruit Cake (1897)
(Frukt-kaka)

One cup butter	1 teaspoon soda
1 cup brown sugar	1 pound flour
Half pint sirup	One and a half pounds currants
2 eggs	Same of raisins
1 cup sour milk	Cinnamon and spices to suit

Fruit Cake (1889)

One-pound flour	Half-pound citron
One-pound sugar	Mace, nutmeg, cinnamon, and cloves, one-half ounce each
One-pound butter	
One-pound eggs	One glass of brandy
Two pounds raisins	Half teaspoonful soda
Two pounds currants	

Fruit Cake (1904)

1 quart of milk	2 ounces of finely sliced citron
2 pounds of freshened butter	The grated peel of a lemon
1 pound of stoned raisins sprinkled with a little rum	A little mace,
1 pound of cleaned currants	The yolks of 6 eggs,
Yeast	1 teaspoonful of salt,
3 ounces of sweet, and ½ ounce of bitter chopped almonds	Flour enough to make a thick dough

Take 1 large or 2 small forms, butter them and sprinkle with sweet almonds, put in the dough, and set aside in a warm place. When the dough is raised, put it into a medium hot oven, spread with butter, strew sugar and cinnamon over it and bake.

Fruit Cake 1 (1876)

Two and a half pounds of flour	Six pounds of currants
Two and a half pounds of sugar	One pound of citron
Two and a half pounds of butter	One and a half ounces of nutmeg
Twenty-five eggs	Three-fourths of an ounce of mace
Three pounds of raisins	

Mix like pound-cake; rub the fruit into flour.

Fruit Cake 2 (1876)

Two cups of brown sugar
One cup of butter
One cup of lard
One cup of sweet milk
Four eggs
Four cups of flour
Two teaspoons of cream tartar

One teaspoon of soda
One cup of molasses
One pound of raisins
A half-pound of citron
One tablespoon of cinnamon
A half teaspoon of cloves
One nutmeg

Fruit Cake 3 (1876)

One pound of butter
One pound of flour
One pound of sugar
Ten eggs
Three pounds of raisins
Three pounds of currants
One pound of citron

One pound of sliced figs
One pound of blanched almonds sliced
Three tablespoons of cinnamon
One teaspoon of cloves
One nutmeg
One teaspoon of mace
Three large teaspoons of baking powder

Fruit Cake 4 (1876)

Twelve eggs well beaten
One pound of butter
One pound of brown sugar
One pound of sifted flour
A half-cup of molasses
Three pounds of stoned raisins
Three pounds of currants

One pound of citron
Two tablespoons of cinnamon
A small teaspoon of cloves
Grated peel of one lemon,
A half nutmeg
Rose essence.

Beat the yolks of the eggs, butter and sugar together until light; whip the whites to a stiff froth and stir in alternately with the flour; add the spices, currants and raisins; put a layer of dough into the pan, next a layer of citron sliced thin, and so alternately until all is in. Bake four hours.

Fruit Cake 5 (1876)

One pound of butter
One pound of brown sugar
Twelve eggs
Two pounds of raisins,
Two pounds of currants

One pound of citron
A tablespoon of mace and cinnamon
A teaspoon of cloves and nutmeg
Extract of lemon or rose
One pound of flour

Dredge the fruit in one-half the flour and brown the remainder.

Fruit Cake (1890)

Eleven eggs
1 and a quarter pounds of flour
1 and a quarter pounds of sugar
1 and a quarter pounds of butter
1 pound of currants

2 pounds of raisins
1 pound of citron
6 teaspoonfuls of mace
2 teaspoonfuls of cloves
2 teaspoonfuls of cinnamon

2 teaspoonfuls of allspice
One quarter teaspoonful of soda
2 tablespoonfuls of cream

2 nutmegs
1 gill of molasses
1 gill of brandy

Butter must be beaten to a cream and whites of the egg beaten separately and added slowly with the flour. Fruit well chopped and well dredged. Spices must be mixed with the brandy and molasses. To be baked in two loaves for about two hours. It will keep two years.

Fruit Cake (1913)

Cream together a cupful of sugar and half a cupful of butter. Add the well beaten yolks of three eggs. Mix together a quarter of a pound each of chopped seeded raisins, finely chopped citron and dried currants (well washed). Sift a half pint of flour with a heaping teaspoonful of baking powder. Dredge the fruit in this and season with half an even teaspoonful of ground nutmeg, an even teaspoonful of ground cinnamon and a pinch of salt. Now stir all together and add the well beaten whites of the eggs. Bake in a moderate oven.

Fruit Cake (1920)

Prepare a cake batter the same as for Plain Cake; remove the stones from ½ pound raisins; cut ¼ pound citron into fine slices and mix the raisins and citron with ½ pound well washed and dried currants; dust the fruit with flour, stir it into the cake mixture and finish the same as Plain Cake.

Fruit Cake (1920)
(Gâteau aux Fruits)

Proportions:

One pound and a half of butter
A pound and a half of sugar
A pound and a half of flour
Twenty eggs
Four pounds of seeded Malaga raisins
Four pounds of Smyrna raisins
Four pounds of citron
Ten pounds of currants

Two gills of rum
Two gills of brandy
Four gills of molasses
One ounce of cinnamon
Half an ounce of allspice
A quarter of an ounce of mace
A quarter of an ounce of nutmeg

Beat the butter and sugar together in a tinned basin until creamy and white; adding the eggs one by one add the flour and mix perfectly, then put in the Malaga and Smyrna raisins, the currants, the finely cut-up citron and the spices; afterward the liquors and molasses; work until thoroughly mixed. For this quantity have two very strong tin molds twelve inches long at the bottom and five inches wide, with a quarter of an inch splay on each side, the depth to be six and a quarter inches. These molds must be furnished with covers closing on the outside. Butter and line them with buttered paper. Divide the preparation into two equal parts, one into each mold; cover the tops with buttered paper, put on the covers, then set both molds on a baking sheet and push into a slack oven. They take from six and a half to seven hours to bake. When partly done turn the molds upside down and finish cooking; remove from the oven, lift off the covers and arrange them one beside the other; lay blocks of wood on top, two and a quarter inches thick and of the same dimensions as the opening of the mold, or even slightly narrower, so they can enter the mold with facility. On each block lay a board and on this a sufficiently heavy weight to allow these blocks to enter entirely inside the mold, leaving it in this position for twelve hours in a cool place. Unmould the cakes carefully, wrap them in paper, and range in a hermetically closed tin box. These cakes require to be made two months beforehand and be left tightly closed so they acquire the mellowness and flavour characteristic of their kind. When needed for use remove from the boxes, take off the paper adhering to the cakes, and cut each one into even eight crosswise slices; divide all of these on the widest side into five equal-sized pieces, therefore obtaining forty pieces from each mold; wrap each one of these small pieces in a separate piece of waxed paper, then in tin foil, and after all are prepared put them into small cardboard boxes manufactured expressly for this purpose, they to be four and three-quarter inches long by an inch and a half wide and an inch and an eighth deep; these are the inside measurements; place on the covers, tie with a white ribbon once around their length and then around their width, forming it into a pretty bow, which must come exactly in the center of the top of the box. For the machine for cutting these cakes see. These machines greatly facilitate the cutting. To have them very regular, according to the above proportions, put the whole cake in machine, cut it in transversal slices one after the other, pressing the cake forward on the machine for each slice that is cut. Machine is used for dividing the first slices and to cut them very even, passing the blade of the knife between the vertical guides of the machine. If instead of small cakes in boxes a large one be desired, then put the preparation into one large round mold sixteen inches in diameter at the bottom and eighteen inches at the top or opening; it must be five and a half inches deep and furnished with a tube in the center five and a half inches at the bottom and five at the top. Cover the insides with bands of buttered paper, overlapping each other, and cook the cake the same as the preceding ones in a slack oven, leaving it in from seven to seven and a half hours. Let it get perfectly cold by placing on top a board seventeen inches in diameter, having a hole in the center five and a half inches in diameter, then press down lightly. These cakes ought to be made two months before they are needed and kept in a cool place. When required for use unmould, remove the paper and ice over with several layers of royal icing; slide on a board covered with lace paper, and after the icing is perfectly dry decorate with more royal icing. A fine gum-paste vase can be placed in the center, filled with flowers or other ornaments.

Fruit Cake (1911)

One cup dark sugar
One-half cup butter
One cup molasses
One cup coffee (cold liquid)
Three eggs
Three tablespoons mixed spices

One-pound currants
Two pounds raisins
Three cups flour
Three teaspoons baking powder
One-fourth pound citron

Fruit Cake 1 (1893)

One-half pound of butter
½ pound sugar
4 eggs
½ cup molasses
½ cup of jam
1-pound raisins

1-pound currents
½ pound citron
1 teaspoon soda
1 cup milk or water
Flour and spices

Fruit Cake 2 (1893)

Two and one-half cups brown sugar
½ cup molasses
1 cup butter
5 eggs, saving whites of 2 for frosting
3½ cups flour
½ teaspoon soda
1 of baking powder
1 teaspoon cinnamon

1 of mace
½ of cloves
A little nutmeg and allspice
Crystaline salt
1-pound raisins
1-pound currants
½ pound citron
½ cup milk

Bake in a moderate oven from 2 to 3 hours. Grows better the longer it is kept.

Fruit Cake 3 (1893)

One and one-half cups butter
3 cups brown sugar
1 cup molasses
1 cup milk
5 eggs
1-pound raisins

1-pound currants
½ pound citron
Spices
½ teaspoon soda
6 cups flour

Fruit Cake 1 (1893)

One and one-half pound of flour
One and one-half pound of sugar
One and one-fourth pound of butter
Two pounds of raisins
Two pounds of currants
Three-fourths pound candied lemon

Four nutmegs
One teaspoonful soda
One teaspoonful cinnamon
One teaspoonful cloves
One cup brandy or wine

Bake slowly.

Fruit Cake 2 (1893)

Yolks of one dozen eggs
One-pound dried currants
One-pound seeded raisins
One-pound butter
One-half pound citron
One-pound brown sugar

One cup sorghum molasses
One-pound blanched almonds
One-half pound Brazil nuts
One-half cup sour milk
Two teaspoonfuls soda
Six cups flour, with cinnamon, allspice and cloves

The flour should be browned in slow oven in order to make the cake look dark and rich. This recipe will make a very large cake, the same to be baked for three hours in slow oven

---

Fruit Cake 3 (1893)

One-pound butter
One-pound brown sugar
One-pound flour
Twelve eggs
Four pounds currants
Four pounds raisins
One-pound citron
Two pounds figs
Two pounds blanched almonds

Two oranges
One tablespoonful cinnamon
One tablespoonful allspice
One-half tablespoonful mace
One-half tablespoonful cloves
One nutmeg
One lemon peel (chopped fine)
One gill wine
One gill brandy

Chop orange peel and pulp (removing seeds), then work in all the sugar you can (this is extra sugar), slice the almonds thin, also citron, chop figs quite fine. Fruit should he weighed after seeding and currants washed. Beat whites and yolks of eggs separately and roll fruit in flour before putting together. This makes a ten quart pan full. One tablespoonful baking powder; five pounds raisins, four pounds seeded; four and one-fourth pounds currants, four pounds washed; six pounds almonds, two pounds blanched

---

Fruit Cake 1 (1894)

One-pound citron
Two pounds currants
Two pounds raisins
One-pound flour
One-pound butter
One-pound sugar

Nine eggs
Half teaspoon soda
Half cup molasses
Teaspoon each, cloves, nutmeg, mace, cinnamon and allspice
Two of lemon

Fruit Cake 2 (1894)

Five eggs
Two cups brown sugar
One-half cup molasses
One and a half cups butter

Three and a half cups flour
Three-quarters pound citron
One and a half pounds currants, same of raisins
Spice of all kinds

Bake three or four hours very slowly.

Fruit Cake 3 (1894)

One and one-half pounds brown sugar
One-pound butter (or two cups melted)
One-pound flour (or one quart)
Four pounds raisins chopped
Three pounds currants
One-pound citron, chopped or sliced
One half pound chopped almonds
Ten eggs

Three tablespoons cassia
Three tablespoons cloves
Two tablespoons mace
Three nutmegs
Two ounces vanilla or part rose extract
Teaspoon soda dissolved in one-half cup coffee, brandy or butter

Add the beaten whites of the eggs the last thing. Steam four hours and dry in the oven for twenty-minutes. It will keep perfectly for an indefinite time if not eaten.

Fruit Cake (1912)

One pound of butter
One pound of sugar
One pound of browned flour
One tablespoon each of allspice and cinnamon
One teaspoon each of nutmeg and cloves
Twelve eggs
Four pounds of raisins
One-half pound of citron

One-fourth pound each of candied orange and lemon peel
One-half pound each of crystallized cherries and pineapple
One pound of almonds cut fine and soaked overnight in one-half cup of rose water
One pound of pecans
One glass of grape jelly
One-half glass of blackberry cordial

Cut fruit in small pieces and soak overnight in one cup of good whiskey or brandy. Follow directions for mixing fruit cake and stir into the batter just before putting in the fruit, one square of melted chocolate (about two teaspoonsful), bake four hours.

Fruit Cake from Bread Dough (1913)

Rub together until creamy one-half cup of butter or Glendale Butterine, one half cup of Armour's Simon Pure Leaf Lard and two cups of granulated sugar. Add three eggs well beaten, one cup of raisins, one teaspoon of cinnamon, one teaspoon of nutmeg, one half teaspoon of soda dissolved in a little water. Add this mixture to three cups of very light sponge and beat well, adding a little more flour if needed. Should be as thick as ordinary loaf cake batter. Fill greased bread pans half full and let rise one hour. Bake in a moderate oven forty-five minutes.

Fruit Drop Cakes (1876)

Two pounds of flour
One pound of butter
One pound of sugar

One pound of currants
Three eggs
Flavour with lemon

Strew tin sheets with flour and powdered sugar and drop in small cakes. Bake in a quick oven.

Fruit Drop Cakes (1922)

1 egg
⅛ teaspoon salt
⅔ cups of sugar
¼ teaspoon vanilla
⅔ cups of water
¼ teaspoon cinnamon
1¾ cups of flour

¼ cup of chopped figs
2 teaspoons baking powder
½ cup of chopped nuts
⅓ cup of milk
¼ cup of chopped dates
2½ tablespoons of butter

Cream the butter; add the sugar, then the well beaten egg. Mix and sift the flour, baking powder, cinnamon and salt and add alternately with milk diluted with water to the first mixture. Add the vanilla, nuts, dates and figs. Mix well and drop from spoon onto a baking sheet and bake in a moderately hot oven. This recipe makes about twenty-eight cakes.

Fruit Drop Cakes (1922)

1 cupful sugar
4 tablespoonfuls chopped nut meats
½ cupful Crisco
2 cupfuls flour
2 tablespoonfuls chopped candied citron peel
2 teaspoonfuls baking powder

1 teaspoonful salt
3 eggs
4 tablespoonfuls currants
⅔ cupful milk
1 teaspoonful vanilla extract

Cream Crisco and sugar together, add yolks of eggs well beaten. Beat whites stiffly and add alternately with milk. Add sifted flour, baking powder and salt, then fruits, nuts and extract. Divide mixture into Criscoed and floured gem pans and bake twenty minutes in moderate oven.
Sufficient for eighteen drop cakes

Fruit Layer Cake (1912)

Three-fourths cup of butter
Two cups of sugar
Three cups of flour
Two teaspoons of baking powder

One-half cup of milk
Whites of six eggs
Two cups of seeded chopped raisins and dates mixed

Fruit or Plum Cake (1869)

Dry and sift a pound of flour, roll a pound of sugar, and beat it with a pound of butter, and the yolks of ten eggs well beaten; wash and dry a pound of currants and rub them in flour; stone and cut half a pound of raisins, and mix in with a glass of rose brandy, and a grated nutmeg, or mace; when all the rest are well mixed together, beat up the whites of the eggs, and add them; bake it an hour and a half

Fruit Queen Cakes (1840)

Make them in the Queen Cake manner, with the addition of a pound of currants, (picked, washed, dried, and floured,) and the juice and grated peel of two large lemons, stirred in gradually at the last. Instead of currants, you may put in sultana or seedless raisins, cut in half and floured.
You may make a fruit pound cake in this manner.

Fruit-Nut Loaf Cake (1922)

Add ¼ cup chopped blanched almonds, ¼ cup dried currants, ¼ cup chopped candied citron to the recipe for Pound Cake. Trim the top with whole blanched almonds arranged in a pattern and bake with a paper cover for the last half hour of the baking.

Fruit Gems (1876)

Take gem batter and add chopped raisins, dates and figs, together or separate; roll the fruit in dry flour. Suit your taste as to proportions of fruit. If a little sweet cream is used in mixing dough, the cakes will be nice enough for dessert or a lunch for traveling.

Fryeburg Sponge Cake (1911)

1 cup of sugar
3 eggs
3 tablespoonfuls of milk
½ teaspoonful of soda
1 teaspoonful of cream tartar

A little salt
1 cup of flour, rounded up
1 tablespoonful of cornstarch
Flavour

Fudge Cake (1911)

1 cup sugar
2 tablespoons cocoa
¼ cup butter
1 egg
1 teaspoon salt

1 teaspoon soda dissolved in ½ cup sour milk
1½ cups flour
¼ cup boiling water
Add a little vanilla

To be put together in above order. Bake in a shallow tin. When cool, split open and fill.

Filling:

1 cup hot water
1 tablespoonful cocoa
⅔ cup sugar
1 tablespoon butter

1 tablespoon cornstarch, mixed with ½ cup cold water
Add a little vanilla

Cook until thick and spread when cool.

Fudge Cake (1922)

1 cup butter

1 teaspoon vanilla

2 cups of granulated sugar
1 cup of pecan nuts (cut fine)
4 eggs

3 squares of Baker's chocolate
2 cups of flour

Mix in order given and bake in sheet pan on wax paper. Cut in squares while hot, pieces to be about two inches square and one and one-half inches thick.

Fudge Cake (1917)

1/4 cup shortening
1/2 cup milk
1 cup brown sugar
1-1/2 cups flour

1 square chocolate
3 teaspoons baking powder
1 egg well beaten
1/4 teaspoon salt

Cream shortening, add sugar, and beat well; add chocolate melted and egg; beat again; add milk; add flour, baking powder, and salt sifted together; beat for two minutes. Pour into two greased layer-cake pans and bake in a moderate oven about eighteen minutes. Fill, and spread top with Fudge Filling.

Part 8: G

Gâteau à la Weckesser (1920)
Gem Cake (1899)
Geneva Cake (1904)
Gennoise Cake (1922)
Genoa Cake (1922)
Genoa Cake (1909)
Genoa Pound Cake (1922)
Genoese Cake (1920)
(Gâteau Génoise)
Genoese Cake-Light (1920)
(Génoise Légère)
Genoeses with Cream Meringued (1920)
(Génoises à la Crème Meringues)
Genoise Sponge Cake (1922)
Génoises (1898)
Georgie's Cake (1893)
German Apple Cake (1908)
German Brod Tourte (1922)
German Cake (1894)
German Cakes (1876)
German Coffee Cake 1 (1913)
German Coffee Cake 2 (1913)
German Plum Cake (1873)
(Plum Cake)
German Prune Cake (1902)
German Short Paste (1922)
Ginger Apple Cake (1917)
Ginger Bread (1893)
Ginger Bread (1893)
Ginger Bread (N.D.)
Ginger Bread (1893)
Gingerbread (1920)
Gingerbread (1893)
Gingerbread (1905)
Gingerbread (1864)
Ginger Bread (1905)
Gingerbread (1922)
Ginger Bread, (1876)
(Plain)
Ginger Bread (1876)
Ginger-Bread (1898)
Ginger-Bread (1898)
(Another Recipe)
Gingerbread 1 (1894)
(Sugar)
Gingerbread 2 (1894)
(Hard Sugar)
Gingerbread 3 (1894)
(Maggie's)
Gingerbread 4 (1894)
(Molasses)

Gingerbread 5 (1894)
Gingerbread 6 (1894)
(Simplest and Best)
Ginger Cake (1876)
Ginger Cake (1922)
Ginger Cake (1894)
Ginger Cup-cake (1869)
Ginger Plum Cake (1840)
Ginger Sponge Cake (1876)
Glasgow Cakes (1909)
Gold and Silver Cake (1897)
(Guld-och Silfver-kaka)
Gold and Silver Cake (1893)
Gold Bar Cake (1909)
Gold Cake 1 (1876)
Gold Cake 2 (1876)
Gold Cake (1911)
Gold Cake (1922)
Gold Cake (1911)
Gold Cake (1893)
Gold Cake 1 (1894)
Gold Cake 2 (1894)
Gold Thread Cake (1909)
Golden Cake (1894)
Goldenrod Cake (1909)
Golden Corn Muffins (1922)
Golden Orange Cake (1922)
Good Batter for large Cakes (1904)
Gooseberry Cake (1904)
Gooseberry Cakes and Tarts (1920)
(Gâteaux et Tartes aux Groseilles Vertes)
Graham Cake (1894)
Graham Cakes (1876)
Graham Cracker Cake (1922)
Graham Flour Muffins (1922)
Graham Gems 1 (1876)
Graham Gems 2 (1876)
Graham Muffins (1911)
Graham Muffins (1890)
Graham Muffins (1876)
Graham Muffins (1876)
Grandmother's Bread Cake (1893)
Grandmother's Little Feather Cake (1905)
Grange Cake (1911)
Granose Fruit-Cake (1899)
Grape Cake (1904)
Greek Cakes (1908)
Green Corn Cakes (1876)
Griddle Cakes (N.D.)
Griddle-cakes (1905)
Gries-Torte (1910)

(Ground Rice Spongecake)
Gugelhopfen (No. 1) (1873)
(Savoy Cake, or German Brioche)
Gugelhopfen (No. 2) (1873)
(Savoy Cake)
Gugelhopfen (1920)

(Cougloff)
Gum Lu (1914)
(Golden Cakes)
Guss Torte or Kuchen (1873)
(A Fruit Cake) (Guss - a creamy mixture)

Gâteau à la Weckesser (1920)

Half-pound of granulated sugar
13 yolks
9 whites

½ pound flour
The rind and juice of 1 lemon

Stir sugar and yolks for 25 minutes by the clock, then beat the whites to a stiff froth; add the yolks and sugar slowly to the white while beating constantly, add the lemon, continue the beating 5 minutes, then add the sifted flour, stir in lightly; butter a large round pan and dust it with flour, pour in the batter, place the cake on a pan of salt, and bake in a slow oven. When done, turn it on to a board, which should be dusted with powdered sugar; let it lie till cold, then spread a layer of pineapple marmalade over the cake, ice it with white sugar glaze, and decorate the cake with candied fruit, of plums, apricots, and cherries. The fruit must be cut into small slices and the cherries in small dice.

Gem Cake (1899)

Beat to a foam the yolk of one egg, one cup of sugar, and one cup of cold sweet cream; a little grated lemon rind may be added for flavouring. Stir in slowly, beating thoroughly, two cupfuls of flour into which a heaping tablespoonful of cornstarch has been sifted. Beat until light and smooth; then add the well-beaten whites of two eggs, stirring just enough to mix them in. Turn into heated gem irons, previously buttered, and bake in a rather quick oven.

Geneva Cake (1904)

1 pound of sifted flour
1 pound of melted butter
1 pound of powdered sugar

¼ pound of grated almonds
The grated peel of a lemon
26 eggs

12 of the eggs are boiled until hard, grate the yolks, and mix them with the almonds; after the butter becomes hard it is creamed and then gradually add 6 whole eggs, constantly stirring, also the yolks of 8 eggs, sugar, lemon peel, almonds and at last the flour. This dough will make 6 cakes; bake them to a dark yellow colour, spread with jelly, marmalade or fruit or with lemon cream as given under Brides Cake (1904), and lay one on the other. After trimming the edges pour a frosting over the top.

Gennoise Cake (1922)

¾ cupful flour
1 teaspoonful baking powder
6 tablespoonfuls sugar
½ teaspoonful almond extract
6 tablespoonfuls melted Crisco

Boiled frosting
4 eggs
Preserved cherries or cocoanut
¼ teaspoonful salt

Break eggs into bowl, add sugar and beat for ten minutes over a pan of boiling water. Remove from water and beat till mixture is thick and cold; remove beater, sift in flour, salt, and baking powder; mix carefully, add melted Crisco and almond extract. Turn at once into small square greased and papered tin and bake in a moderate oven twenty minutes. Turn out and remove paper. Cool and cut in eight square pieces. Cover with boiled frosting and decorate with cherries or cocoanut.
Sufficient for: eight small cakes.

Genoa Cake (1922)

¼ pound Crisco, and ¼ pound butter. Mix to a cream with ½ pound sugar, add little mace, stir in gradually yolk of 6 eggs and ½ beaten whites, 10 ounces flour. Beat well for 1 minute, add 1-pound raisins, ¼ pound citron, cut very fine, grated rind of 1 lemon, and 2 ounces chopped almonds. Mix well, add remainder of beaten whites last. Mix well, put in pan lined with paper, sprinkle top with chopped almonds and bake in slow oven.

Genoa Cake (1909)

Beat the yolks of 5 eggs with 2 cupfuls of sugar; add the juice of 2 oranges and water, if necessary, to make 1 cupful, the grated rind of 2 oranges, 2 cupfuls of flour sifted with 1 teaspoonful of baking-powder and the beaten whites of 5 eggs. Bake in layers and spread with the following jelly: Dissolve 1 heaping teaspoonful of granulated gelatine in a little cold water, add to the juice and grated rind of 2 oranges and ½ cupful of sugar; boil together for ten minutes and use while warm.

Genoa Pound Cake (1922)

One pound of sugar
One pound of butter
Fifteen eggs
One and one-half pounds of flour

The grated rind of one lemon
The juice of half a lemon
Flavour of mace
A pinch of soda

Sift the soda well in the flour. Cream same as for other pound cake, adding the lemon juice and flavour, and mix in the flour. A little milk may be added if needed. Bake like pound cakes; or in small pans, dusted with sugar and with a strip of lemon peel on top.

Genoese Cake (1920)
(Gâteau Génoise)

Butter a pound cake mould and line it with paper. Have one pound of sugar, part of it being flavoured with vanilla, in a basin with sixteen whole eggs; whip this till light, warming the preparation over a slow fire. To have this attain a proper degree of lightness it will be necessary to whip for at least forty minutes, then mix in one pound of sifted flour, and lastly half a pound of melted butter. Fill the mold three-quarters full with this and bake in a slack oven for an hour and a quarter. Remove, unmould on a grate and cool thoroughly. Then pare it very straight and cover with a layer of apricot marmalade; ice with vanilla fondant. After the icing has dried thoroughly slip the cake on a dish and decorate either with royal icing or fanciful cuts of fruits; surround with a circle of preserved plums and cherries.

Genoese Cake-Light (1920)
(Génoise Légère)

Put twelve whole eggs and eight yolks into a basin with one pound of sugar, a part of it being flavoured with vanilla; beat together vigorously for twenty minutes on a slow fire, barely heating the preparation, and when well beaten and very light mix in lightly one pound of sifted flour, using a small skimmer or spoon, then half a pound of melted fresh butter added a little at a time. Butter lightly a pan twelve inches long by seven and a half wide and two inches deep; glaze it with flour and sugar, half and half, well mixed together and sifted through a sieve. Fill the pan three-quarters full with the preparation, lay it in a baking pan and place it in a slack oven to bake for forty-five to fifty minutes. As soon as the cake is done, remove and unmould it on a wire grate to get cold; afterward cover it lightly with well-reduced peach or apricot jam and ice over with water icing flavoured with vanilla; place for an instant at the entrance of the oven to dry the icing; allow to cool; cut the Genoese cake into oblong pieces and serve.
This cake can also be made in a round mold and iced exactly the same, decorating the top with candied fruits; dress on a round plate ornamented with lace paper.

Genoeses with Cream Meringued (1920)
(Génoises à la Crème Meringues)

Butter and flour some tartlet molds, fill them with Genoese preparation and cook in a slack oven; unmould as soon as done and when cold hollow out the centres. Fill the cakes with a St. Honore cream preparation flavoured with orange; colour it lightly with a little green; cover this with meringue laid on in beads pushed through a pocket; spread fine sugar over this and place in the oven to colour the meringue.

Genoise Sponge Cake (1922)

Sixteen whole eggs
Six yolks
One pound of sugar
Twelve ounces of flour

Four ounces of cornstarch
Eight ounces of butter
The grated rind of one lemon

Make the same as Butter Sponge Cake (No. 1) (1922)

Génoises (1898)

Ingredients:

3 eggs
3 oz. flour
1 oz. ground almonds

1 oz. sugar
1 tablespoonful cream
½ oz. butter

Method: Beat and strain the eggs. Dredge in the flour, almonds, and sugar, beating all the time. Add the butter, melted, but not hot, and the cream, which must be whipped. Beat well for 3 minutes and pour the mixture into a shallow buttered tin. Bake in a moderate oven, testing it with a skewer in the usual way. Turn it out when cooked and put it in a cool place. Serve the génoise cold, cut into small rounds or squares.
Time: About 25 minutes.
Sufficient for: 12 little cakes.

Georgie's Cake (1893)

Three teaspoonfuls of soda
One cup butter
One cup molasses
Two cups brown sugar
Two cups sour milk

Four eggs
Four and one-half cups flour
One tablespoonful mixed spices
Two pounds dates seeded and chopped fine

Rub the butter and sugar to a cream, add the molasses, then the sour milk, break one egg in at a time and beat well; sift the soda in the flour and add, saving a little to dust the dates; add the spices and last of all add the dates; bake slowly like a fruit cake.

German Apple Cake (1908)

Make a biscuit dough; roll out very thin and put on a well-buttered cake-pan. Have ready some apples. Cut in quarters; lay closely on the cake; sprinkle thick with brown sugar; add some cinnamon and a handful of currants. Pour some fresh melted butter over the cake; set in the oven to bake until done. Serve with coffee.

German Brod Tourte (1922)

Pound three quarters of a pound of dried and browned almonds with six eggs and add one pound of powdered sugar; work in to it gradually twelve more yolks and add six ounces of dried and browned rye bread crumbs moistened with one half of a gill of rum; add four ounces of cocoa powder and one ounce of ground cinnamon, cloves and all spice mixed together; add four ounces of orange peel and four ounces of citron cut very fine. Beat the whites of the eggs firm and add to it the mixture with four ounces of flour. Bake in one large ring form in a slow oven. When baked and cool ice with a nice liquor - flavoured icing and decorate with fruit.

German Cake (1894)

One cup butter
Two cups sugar
Three and a half cups flour
Half teaspoon soda

One of cream tartar
Half cup milk
Four eggs

Drop into buttered tins, sprinkle with sugar and cinnamon.

German Cakes (1876)

Two pounds of flour
One pound of sugar
One pound of butter

Three eggs
One teaspoon of cinnamon
One wine glass of rose water

Roll the dough thin; cut into cakes and cover with almonds, blanched and cut in halves.

German Coffee Cake 1 (1913)

Beat six fresh eggs very light with one pound of sugar, and one-pound flour. Add the peel of a lemon grated, and one yeast cake dissolved in a little hot milk or water. Let stand till very light, then roll into sheets one inch thick, spread them thickly with melted butter - half a pound will be required, sprinkle with two ounces bitter almonds blanched and shredded fine, mixed with four ounces sugar, and a teaspoonful powdered cinnamon. Let rise again and bake in a moderate oven. Good hot or cold.

German Coffee Cake 2 (1913)

1 cup scalded milk
3 tablespoons Cottolene
1/3 cup sugar
1/2 teaspoon salt

1 compressed yeast cake dissolved in 1/4 cup lukewarm water
1 egg well beaten
1/2 cup seeded and shredded raisins
Flour

Process: Put Cottolene, sugar and salt in mixing bowl; add scalded milk. When lukewarm add dissolved yeast cake, beaten egg and sufficient flour to make a very thick batter. Beat thoroughly until mixture is smooth. Add raisins, cover closely and set to rise. When light, spread dough in buttered dripping pan one inch in thickness; cover and let rise again. Before placing in the oven, brush over with beaten egg and cover with the following mixture:
Melt one-third cup butter in a sauce-pan, add one-half cup sugar, mix with one and one-half teaspoons cinnamon. When sugar is partially melted add one and one-half tablespoons flour. Mix well and spread on cake, strew top with blanched and shredded almonds, bake twenty-five minutes in a moderate oven.

German Plum Cake (1873)
(Plum Cake)

Beat a pound of warmed butter to a cream. Stir in by degrees the yolks of twelve eggs, a pound of sifted sugar, the grated rind of a lemon, a quarter of a pound of candied peel cut thin, a small nutmeg grated, eight cloves pounded fine, a little salt, a pound of fine flour, a pound of sultana raisins, and a pound of currants, both carefully washed, dried, and picked. When all is thoroughly well beaten, add the whites of the eggs whisked to a stiff snow, and a glass of arrack, rum, or Madeira wine. Line one large or two smaller cake-tins with buttered paper. Bake in a very moderate oven from an hour and a half to two hours. Set it back when it begins to colour yellow. Sprinkle the cake while warm with fine rum or arrack It is better kept a few days before cutting and will keep good several weeks.

German Prune Cake (1902)

For this use a recipe for short cake adding more milk to make it into a thick batter. Turn into a shallow, oblong pan and over the top press lightly into the mixture a close layer of partly cooked prunes. Sprinkle thickly with granulated sugar and bake in a quick oven. Serve hot.

German Short Paste (1922)

Take eight ounces of almond paste
Eight ounces of flour
Eight of cake crumbs
Six ounces of sugar
Four ounces of butter

Four eggs
The grated rind of one lemon
Half a teaspoon of ground cloves and cinnamon
A pinch of powdered ammonia

Rub the butter into the flour and mix with the sugar and the spices; soften the almond paste with the eggs; add the lemon rind and ammonia and mix all together into a smooth paste. Put away in a jar well covered in a cold place.

Ginger Apple Cake (1917)

Follow any recipe for gingerbread, bake in two layers, and put Apple Filling between layers and on top.

Ginger Bread (1893)

Half cup molasses
Half cup of sugar
½ cup of sour milk
Butter size of an egg

Crystaline salt
½ teaspoon soda
1½ cups flour
1 egg, spice

Ginger Bread (1893)

One cup molasses (boil and cool)
½ cup sugar
½ shortening
1 teaspoon soda

1 cup hot water
Sweet or sour milk, as preferred
1 teaspoon each of ginger and cinnamon
Crystaline salt

Ginger Bread (N.D.)

1 cup granulated sugar
2 tablespoons molasses
4 tablespoons melted butter
1 level teaspoon salt

1 teaspoon mixed spice
1 tablespoon cinnamon
1 cup sour milk
2 cups well sifted flour

1 teaspoon baking soda

Stir well together sugar, molasses, butter, salt and spices, then add egg and sour milk and soda. Pour in flour, beat until smooth. Bake in moderate oven 40 to 60 minutes.

Ginger Bread (1893)

½ cup butter and ½ cup sugar beaten together
½ cup molasses
½ cup sour milk

2 scant cups flour
1 even teaspoon soda

Serve warm with whipped cream.
Very nice.

Gingerbread (1920)

One cup brown sugar
1 cup molasses
½ cup butter or lard
2 eggs
1 tablespoonful ginger

½ teaspoonful ground mace
½ cup cold coffee
½ teaspoonful salt
1 heaping teaspoonful baking powder sifted with
3 cups of flour

Stir butter or lard with the sugar to a cream, add the eggs one at a time, stirring a few minutes between each addition; then add the spice and syrup, last the flour and coffee alternately; pour the mixture into a square or long pan previously well buttered and dusted with flour; bake in a medium-hot oven.

Gingerbread (1893)

One-half cup of molasses
One-half cup of sugar
One-half cup of butter
One-half cup of sour milk
One and one-half cup of flour

Two small eggs
One-half teaspoon of soda
Teaspoonful of cinnamon, ginger
and one-half teaspoon of cloves
A little nutmeg

Gingerbread (1905)

1 cup molasses
1 egg
1 teaspoonful of soda
1 teaspoonful of ginger

1 tablespoonful melted butter
1/2 cup of milk
2 cups of flour

Beat the eggs without separating, but very light; put the soda into the molasses, put them in the milk, with the ginger and butter, then one cup of flour, measure in a medium-sized cup and only level, then the egg, and last the rest of the flour. Bake in a buttered biscuit-tin. For a change, sometimes add a teaspoonful of cloves and cinnamon, mixed, to this, and a cup of chopped almonds. Or, when the gingerbread is ready for the oven drop over halves of almonds.

Gingerbread (1864)

Whence oft with sugared cates she doth 'em greet, And gingerbread, if rare, now certes doubly sweet.
SHENSTONE.

To three quarters of a pound of treacle, beat one egg strained; mix four ounces of brown sugar, half an ounce of ginger sifted, of cloves, mace, allspice, and nutmeg, a quarter of an ounce; beat all as fine as possible; melt one pound of butter, and mix with the above: add as much flour as will knead it into a pretty stiff paste; roll it out, and cut it in cakes.

Ginger Bread (1905)

Material:

1/2 cup molasses
1 cup sugar
5 tablespoons melted butter
1/2 teaspoon cinnamon
1/2 teaspoon ginger

1 teaspoon salt
1 teaspoon soda
1 egg
2-1/2 cups Pillsbury's Best
1 cup hot water

Way of Preparing: Put molasses in a bowl. Add sugar, melted butter, cinnamon and ginger. Put soda and salt in a cup and fill with hot water. Stir into first mixture. Add flour, then well beaten egg. Beat hard. Bake for thirty minutes in a well-greased pan. Watch oven closely, as ginger bread burns easily. This makes a good-sized cake.

Gingerbread (1922)

½ cupful sugar
2 teaspoonfuls powdered ginger
1 egg
1 teaspoonful powdered cinnamon
½ cupful molasses
½ cupful milk

½ teaspoonful powdered cloves
1⅓ cupfuls flour
½ teaspoonful baking soda or 2 teaspoonfuls baking powder
¼ cupful Crisco
1 teaspoonful salt

Sauce:

1 teaspoonful Crisco
1 tablespoonful flour
1 cupful (½ lb.) maple sugar

1 egg
1 cupful boiling water

For cake: Cream Crisco and sugar together, add egg well beaten, molasses, milk, soda, flour, salt, and spices. Mix and turn into Criscoed tin and bake in moderate oven forty minutes.
For sauce: Dissolve maple sugar in boiling water. Rub together Crisco and flour. Add gradually boiling syrup; and lastly the beaten egg. Then return to fire and stir briskly until thickened.
Sufficient for one small gingerbread.

Ginger Bread (1876)
(Plain)

One cup of molasses
One heaping tablespoon of butter
One egg
One teaspoon of ginger

A little salt
A half-cup of sweet cream
Half a teaspoon of soda
Flour enough to mix soft

Roll in sheets, score with a knife in squares or diamonds, and bake.

Ginger Bread (1876)

Three eggs
One cup of molasses
One cup of brown sugar
One cup of sour milk

One cup of butter
Four cups of flour
One tablespoon of soda
One teaspoon of cream tartar

Bake half an hour.

Ginger-Bread (1898)

Ingredients:

½ lb. flour
10 oz. golden syrup
2 oz. butter
2 oz. candied orange peel

2 oz. brown sugar
½ oz. ground ginger
2 eggs

Method: Beat and strain the eggs. Mix the syrup with them and sift in the flour. Cut the orange peel into small pieces, and add it together with the sugar and ginger, beating all the time. Then add the butter, which must be melted, but not hot, and beat the mixture thoroughly. Pour it into a buttered tin, and bake in a moderately quick oven, covering the top with a buttered paper when half done. When cooked, let it cool partly before turning out of the tin.
Time: 1 hour.
Sufficient for: 1 good sized cake.

Ginger-Bread (1898)
(Another Recipe)

Ingredients:

½ lb. flour
½ lb. golden syrup
¼ lb. ginger preserved in syrup
2 oz. butter

2 oz. sugar
¼ oz. ground ginger
3 eggs

Method: Beat and strain the eggs. Mix the syrup with them and sift in the flour and ground ginger. Add the preserved ginger cut into very small pieces, and the sugar, and beat well. Then add the butter, which must be melted, but not hot, and beat the mixture thoroughly. Pour it into a buttered cake-tin and bake it carefully in a moderately quick oven.
Time: 1 hour.
Sufficient for: 1 good sized cake.

Gingerbread 1 (1894)
(Sugar)

Six cups flour
Two cups sugar
One cup butter

One cup milk
Teaspoon soda

Roll thin.

Gingerbread 2 (1894)
(Hard Sugar)

Three quarters pound sugar
Same of butter
One and a half pounds flour
Four eggs
Ginger
Small teaspoon soda

Roll very thin and bake on tin sheets.

Gingerbread 3 (1894)
(Maggie's)

One cup molasses
One-half cup butter and lard mixed
Two-thirds cup sour milk
Teaspoon soda
Teaspoon ginger
Five coffee cups flour

Mix as soft as you can roll.

Gingerbread 4 (1894)
(Molasses)

One cup molasses
One large tablespoon lard
Teaspoon salt
Teaspoon ginger
Teaspoon soda dissolved in one-half cup of cold water
Three scant cups flour

Gingerbread 5 (1894)

One cup molasses
Butter size of an egg
One egg
One-half cup sour milk
One and one-half cups flour
One teaspoon soda
Cloves
Ginger

Beat molasses, egg and butter together, add flour gradually, alternating with the milk.

Gingerbread 6 (1894)
(Simplest and Best)

One cup molasses
One heaping tablespoon of shortening (butter and lard)
One teaspoon salt
A little of all kinds spices
One teaspoon soda in one-half cup hot coffee
Flour for a soft batter

Ginger Cake (1876)

Beat one and a half cups of sugar and a half cup of butter to a cream and add two eggs, one small tablespoon of ginger, one heaping tablespoon of cinnamon, one cup of sour milk, one heaping teaspoon of soda and flour enough to make it as stiff as cupcake.

Ginger Cake (1922)

½ cup sugar
1 scant teaspoon soda
½ cup dark molasses
1 scant teaspoon ginger
Lard, size of an egg

1 large cup of flour
1 egg
¾ cup boiling water
⅛ teaspoon salt

Add melted lard to sugar, then molasses and soda and beaten egg. Sift flour, salt and ginger and add the boiling water last. Bake in moderate oven about 25 or 30 minutes. (The mixture before baking is very thin.)

Ginger Cake (1894)

One cup molasses
One cup brown sugar
Three-fourths cup lard or butter
Three cups flour

One cup boiling water
Two teaspoons soda
Two eggs
Spice to taste

Boil molasses, sugar, flour and butter together, then add hot water and soda, lastly the eggs. Bake in a cool oven.

Ginger Cup-cake (1869)

Three cups of flour
One of sugar
One of molasses
One of butter

A table-spoonful of ginger
One tea-spoonful of salaeratus
Three eggs

Bake in pans.
A pound of stoned and chopped raisins is an improvement

Ginger Plum Cake (1840)

Stone a pound and a half of raisins and cut them in two. Wash and dry half a pound of currants. Sift into a pan two pounds of flour. Put into another pan a pound of brown sugar, (rolled fine,) and cut up in it a pound of fresh butter. Stir the butter and sugar to a cream and add to it two table-spoonfuls of the best ginger; one table-spoonful of powdered cinnamon; and one of powdered cloves. Then beat six eggs very light, and add them gradually to the butter and sugar, in turn with the flour and a quart of molasses. Lastly, stir in a tea-spoonful of pearl-ash dissolved in a little vinegar, and add by degrees the fruit, which must be well dredged with flour. Stir all very hard; put the mixture into a buttered pan and bake it in a moderate oven. Take care not to let it burn.

Ginger Sponge Cake (1876)

Two-thirds of a cup of sugar
A half-cup of molasses
A half-cup of butter
A half-cup of sweet milk

Two cups of flour
Two eggs
Two teaspoons of ginger
One teaspoon of soda

Glasgow Cakes (1909)

Cream 1 tablespoonful of butter with 1 tablespoonful of powdered sugar
Add the beaten yolks of 6 eggs

The juice of 3 oranges, and the grated rind of ½ an orange

1 cupful of flour sifted with ½ teaspoonful of baking powder

Bake in small tins and cover with fondant icing. Decorate with tiny rounds cut out of candied orange peel, and young orange shoots or strips of angelica.

Gold and Silver Cake (1897)
(Guld-och Silfver-kaka)

Gold Part:

8 yolks of eggs
1 cup of butter
2 cups sugar
4 cups flour

1 cup sour milk
1 teaspoon soda
1 teaspoon corn starch
Some lemon or vanilla

Silver Part:

2 cups sugar
1 of butter
4 of flour
One of milk

1 teaspoon soda
1 teaspoon corn starch
8 whites of eggs
Some almonds

Put in 1 spoon of each part alternately.

Gold and Silver Cake (1893)

One cup of white sugar
½ cup of butter
⅔ cup sweet milk
2 cups flour

2 teaspoons baking powder
Flavour,
Add last the whites of 4 eggs well beaten

Gold cake the same, adding 1 whole egg to the 4 yolks.

Gold Bar Cake (1909)

Bake a brick-shaped sponge cake, when cold remove the center leaving the bottom and sides 1 inch thick. Make icing by beating the white of 1 egg with 1 tablespoonful of orange juice, 1 teaspoonful of grated orange rind and confectioner's sugar to make very stiff. Spread this on the outside of the cake and allow it to harden. Just before serving fill with the following cream. Beat the yolks of 6 eggs and the whites of 3 with ¾ cupful of sugar; add ¾ cupful of white wine, the juice of 1 lemon, the juice of 2 oranges and the grated rind, 1½ cupfuls of water in which 2 level teaspoonfuls of corn-starch have been mixed. Cook in a double boiler until thick, add the beaten whites of 3 eggs, mix thoroughly and allow it to become very cold.

Gold Cake 1 (1876)

Beat the yolks of eight eggs with one cup of sugar and three fourths of a cup of butter, previously beaten to a cream; add two cups of sifted flour, a half teaspoon of soda dissolved in one-half cup of sweet milk, and, when well mixed, bake in shallow pans.

Gold Cake 2 (1876)

Yolks of twelve eggs
Five cups of flour
Three cups of white sugar
One cup of butter

One and a half cups of cream or milk
A half teaspoon of soda
One teaspoon of cream tartar

Beat the eggs with the sugar, then stir in the butter, softened by the fire; dissolve the soda, and sift the cream tartar with one cup of the flour; mix all together, then sift and stir in the rest of the flour. Bake in a deep loaf pan. These, baked as " Marbled Cake," give another variety.

Gold Cake (1911)

2 cups, not quite full, of flour
1 cup sugar
½ cup sweet milk
½ teaspoonful soda

1 teaspoonful cream tartar
Yolks of 4 eggs
Flavour to taste

Gold Cake (1922)

¾ cupful sugar
1½ cupfuls flour
5 tablespoonfuls Crisco
½ teaspoonful salt

½ cupful milk
3 teaspoonfuls baking powder
4 yolks of eggs
½ teaspoonful lemon extract

Cream Crisco and sugar together. Beat egg yolks very light and add to creamed mixture. Add dry ingredients, milk, and lemon extract and mix well. Turn into a small Criscoed and floured cake tin and bake in moderate oven forty-five minutes.
Sufficient for one small cake.

Gold Cake (1911)

Mix the yolks of four eggs
One cup of sugar
One-half cup of sweet milk
One-half cup of butter

Three cups of flour sifted three times
One teaspoonful of cream of tartar
One-half teaspoon of soda

Beat very thoroughly. Use a moderate cake oven.

Gold Cake (1893)

One cup of sugar
½ cup butter
2 yolks and 1 whole egg

½ cup milk
½ teaspoon baking powder
1½ cups flour

Gold Cake 1 (1894)

Yolks of eight eggs
One tablespoon butter
Four cups flour
One cup sweet milk

Two cups sugar
Teaspoon soda
Two of cream tartar
Flavour with lemon

Gold Cake 2 (1894)

One cup butter
Two cups sugar
Three cups flour
One cup sweet milk

One teaspoon cream tartar
One half teaspoon soda
Yolks six eggs and one whole egg
Flavour with lemon

Use whites of two eggs for frosting.

Gold Thread Cake (1909)

Beat the yolks of 6 eggs and the white of 1 egg with 1½ cupfuls of sugar; add 4 tablespoonfuls of melted butter, 1 cupful of milk and 2 cupfuls of flour sifted with 2 teaspoonfuls of baking-powder.

Bake in layers and spread with any preferred orange icing.

Golden Cake (1894)

Yolks of eight eggs
One cup sugar
Two cups flour
One-half cup butter

One-half cup milk
One teaspoon cream tartar
Half teaspoon soda

Flavour with vanilla.

Goldenrod Cake (1909)

Cream 1 pound of butter with 1¼ pounds of sugar, add the yolks of 10 eggs and the whites of 3; beat until smooth and light and add the juice and grated rind of 1 large orange, 1 pint of milk, 2 pounds of flour sifted with 1½ ounces of baking-powder and stir until smooth. Bake in goldenrod pans and when cold ice with the following:
Icing: Grate the rind of 1 small orange, add the yolk of 1 egg and stir in confectioner's sugar until stiff; add 2 tablespoonfuls of boiling water, the juice of 1 small orange and ½ lemon and sugar to make as thick as fondant. Colour a delicate orange, ice the tops and sides of the cakes and leave them in a warm place to dry.

Golden Corn Muffins (1922)

1 cupful flour
1 cupful milk
2 tablespoonfuls Crisco
2 eggs

1 cupful yellow cornmeal
1 teaspoonful salt
3 tablespoonfuls sugar
3 teaspoonfuls baking powder

Cream Crisco and sugar thoroughly together, add eggs well beaten and milk. Then stir in slowly dry ingredients which have been sifted together three times. Divide into greased gem pans and bake in moderately hot oven twenty-five minutes.
Sufficient for: twelve muffins.

Golden Orange Cake (1922)

2 cupfuls sugar
S eggs or yolks of 10 eggs
1 teaspoonful salt
4 cupfuls flour
1 teaspoonful orange extract

1 cupful Crisco
1 cupful milk
4 teaspoonfuls baking powder
Orange icing

For cake: Cream Crisco and sugar together, add salt, eggs well beaten, orange extract, and flour and baking powder alternately with milk. Mix carefully and turn into Criscoed and floured cake tin and bake in moderate oven about one hour. This mixture may be baked in layers.
For icing: Boil 1 cupful water with 2 cupfuls sugar till it forms soft ball when tried in cold water, or 240° F., then pour over well beaten yolks of four eggs, beat until smooth and thick, add 1½ teaspoonfuls orange extract and spread at once on cake.
Sufficient for: one large cake.

Good Batter for large Cakes (1904)

To 1⅛ pounds of flour take 1 pound of freshened butter, 2 ounces, of sugar and ½ wineglassful of cold water. This is all worked together, but not kneaded. Then set the dough aside in a cool place, roll and bake in a moderately hot oven.

Gooseberry Cake (1904)

Make either a puff or a cream paste - the latter is preferable. 1½ pounds of cleaned and washed green gooseberries, or the same quantity of ripe gooseberries, for which less sugar is necessary, about 1 pound of sifted sugar and a little cinnamon.
Roll the dough evenly about ⅛ inch thick, spread to the thickness of about ½ inch with cooked gooseberry compote, putting strips of dough over the top, and bake for ¼ - ½ hour. After the dough is rolled lay a round cover over it and trim with a knife. Then lay it on the cake dish, around the top put an edge of the crust of the remaining dough cutting into small strips and twisting them. Boll out the remainder of the dough quite thin, cut into strips about ½ inch wide and lay them on the fruit.

Gooseberry Cakes and Tarts (1920)
(Gâteaux et Tartes aux Groseilles Vertes)

Prepare a tart paste with one pound of flour, three-quarters of a pound of butter, five ounces of powdered sugar, two whole eggs, three yolks, salt and lemon flavouring. Divide this paste into two parts and roll them out separately into oblong layers not too thin; roll one of these on the pin to unroll on a large baking sheet, cutting off the four sides evenly, and edge it with a small band of the paste laid on higher, forming a border of half an inch; prick the paste. Cook this flat till it is half done in a very slack oven, not allowing it to brown, then take it out and let get cold. Fill the hollow as high up as the border with blanched gooseberries without boiling, so that they remain whole; smooth them evenly and egg over the raised border. Roll the second flat on the rolling-pin and unroll it on top of the other; press down the edges, fastening them together, and egg the surface. Lay the baking sheet on top of another and push the two into a slack oven (the second one is to prevent the half-cooked paste from burning). When the top paste is well dried remove from the fire and glaze over with a thin layer of fondant flavoured with lemon; let get cold, then cut the cake into three and a half inch wide strips and these across in such a way as to obtain oblong pieces. Round tarts may be prepared in the same way.

Graham Cake (1894)

One half cup butter
One and one-half cups sugar
One cup milk
Three and a half cups pastry flour

One and one-half cups raisins stoned and chopped
One egg
One teaspoon soda, nutmeg

Sift sugar over the top and bake an hour and a half in a moderate oven.

Graham Cakes (1876)

One cup sweet milk, with a large spoon of sour milk
Small lump of butter
One egg
One fourth spoon of soda
Teaspoon of sugar
Flour enough to make a batter

Graham Cracker Cake (1922)

½ pound graham crackers crush to powder form
½ cup butter
½ cup sugar
1½ teaspoons baking powder
Pinch soda
2 eggs
¾ cup sour milk
2 teaspoons vanilla

Cream butter, add crushed crackers, baking powder and soda, sugar; add egg yolks, stir; add sour milk. Stir constantly; add beaten egg whites, and vanilla. Pour in buttered cake tin; place in oven; bake.

Graham Flour Muffins (1922)

1 cup graham flour
1 cup milk
½ cup white flour
1 egg
3½ teaspoons baking powder
¼ teaspoon salt

Beat the egg well. Sift the flour to remove any coarse bran flakes. Mix with salt and the baking powder. Add the egg and pour in enough milk to make a stiff batter, beat well and bake in buttered muffin tins for fifteen minutes in a hot oven.

Graham Gems 1 (1876)

Four small tea-cups of sour milk
Three tablespoons of shortening
Three tablespoons of molasses
Salt
Two teaspoons of soda
Graham flour to make it just thick enough to drop from a spoon

This will fill two sets of gem pans.

Graham Gems 2 (1876)

One tea-cup of milk
One even cup of Graham flour
A little salt
One egg

Bake in gem pans.

Graham Muffins (1911)

Heat to the boiling point two cups of milk, add a tablespoon of butter and stir until melted. Sift two cups of whole wheat flour, one-half cup of white flour, two teaspoons of baking powder. Pour on the milk and butter, beat, add the yolks of two eggs well beaten, then the stiffly beaten whites. Bake in hot greased gem pan.

Graham Muffins (1890)

One pint of Graham flour
1 pint of wheat flour

2 eggs, beaten light
1 tablespoonful of melted butter
1 teaspoonful of sugar

A pinch of salt
2 teaspoonfuls of baking powder
Milk enough to make a thick batter

Graham Muffins (1876)

One quart of sweet milk, warm
One-half tea-cup of yeast and a little salt
Stir in flour and let rise; when light

Add four well beaten eggs
One-half cup of sugar
One-half cup of butter or lard

Let rise again, and then bake in muffin rings.

Graham Muffins (1876)

Two eggs
One teaspoon of soda
One tablespoon of molasses or sugar

One pint of sour milk
Or one-half pint of milk and one-half pint of cream

Grandmother's Bread Cake (1893)

Three cups sugar
One cup butter
Three eggs
One bowlful stoned raisins, floured

One teaspoonful allspice, ground
One teaspoonful cloves, ground
One tablespoonful cinnamon, ground

When well mixed add three cups of bread sponge before the flour is added for kneading; stir well and then add flour until as stiff as can be easily stirred; half fill two medium-sized pans and stand in a warm place till light and bake in a moderate oven.

Grandmother's Little Feather Cake (1905)

1 cup of sugar
2 tablespoonfuls soft butter
1 egg

1/2 cup milk and water mixed
1 1/2 cups sifted flour
1 teaspoonful baking-powder

Rub the butter and sugar to a cream. Beat the yolk of the egg stiff and put that in; then add part of the milk and water, and part of the flour and baking-powder, which has been sifted together; next the vanilla, and last the stiff whites of the eggs, not stirred in, but just lightly folded in. If you put them in heavily and roughly, cake will always be heavy. Bake this in a buttered biscuit-tin and cut in squares when cold. It is nice covered with caramel or chocolate frosting.

Grange Cake (1911)

3 cups of sugar
1 cup of butter
5 cups of flour
1½ cups of milk or water
1½ cups of chopped raisins

2 eggs
2 tablespoonfuls of molasses
1 teaspoonful soda, dissolved in a little water
Spice

Granose Fruit-Cake (1899)

Take a shallow pudding dish, cover the bottom with raspberries, strawberries, or other small fruits, then add a layer of granose, thus alternating until the dish is full. Let stand in a cool place for an hour, then cut into slices, and serve with milk or cream.

Grape Cake (1904)

Take 1 pound of flour
¾ pound of butter
1 cupful of sugar
Cinnamon
Salt
The yolks of 5 eggs
Knead quickly

Roll out the dough, lay it into a buttered pan and sprinkle over it finely pounded almonds; then beat the whites of 12 eggs, mix with 1½ pounds of pounded sugar and 3 pounds of white grapes, fill into the pan and bake. This will make 2 medium-sized cakes.

Greek Cakes (1908)

Mix 1/2 pound of butter and 1 cup of sugar to a cream; add 4 well-beaten eggs and the grated rind and juice of 1/2 lemon. Then stir in 1/2 pound of flour and work into a smooth dough. Lay on a well-floured baking-board and roll out thin. Cut into fancy shapes and bake in a moderate oven until done. Cover with a white icing, flavoured with vanilla

Green Corn Cakes (1876)

Mix a pint of grated sweet corn with three tablespoonfuls of milk, a teacup of flour, a large spoonful of salt, a little pepper and one egg. Drop this mixture by the large spoonful into a frying-pan, and fry till brown; use butter for frying. These are nice served with meat for dinner.

Griddle Cakes (N.D.)

1 cup sour milk (thick)
Flour enough to make thin batter
1 teaspoon baking powder
½ teaspoon soda
½ teaspoon salt
1 tablespoon (heaping) corn meal

Griddle-cakes (1905)

2 eggs
1 cup of milk
1 1/2 cups flour
2 teaspoonfuls of baking-powder
1/2 teaspoonful of salt

Put the eggs in a bowl without separating them and beat them with a spoon till light. Put in the milk, then the flour mixed with the salt, and last the baking-powder all alone. Bake on a hot, buttered griddle. This seems a queer rule, but it makes delicious cakes, especially if eaten with sugar and thick cream.

Gries-Torte (1910)
(Ground Rice Spongecake)

10 oz. ground rice
10 bitter almonds
4 oz. sweet almonds
10 eggs
1 lb. sugar
Grated peel and the juice of ½ lemon

Beat the yolks and sugar to a froth and add the grated almonds and sugar. Stir all for ½ hour and then add alternately the ground rice and the whites of eggs, whisked stiffly. Fill a well-buttered cake tin and bake 1 hour. The cake may be cut through when cold and a layer of jam spread on the under half, the top then being placed on it again.

Gugelhopfen (No. 1) (1873)
(Savoy Cake, or German Brioche)

Beat a pound of butter to a cream. Stir in, by degrees, a quarter of a pound of sifted sugar, sixteen well-beaten eggs, a pound and a half of fine flour, and a pint of good milk. Stir all nearly an hour. Then add two tablespoonfuls of good yeast, a little salt, and a quarter of a pound of sultana raisins. Some throw in a handful of currants, but these are not necessary. Butter thickly a large Turk's-cap or brioche mould, strew it with chopped almonds, and dredge it with sugar. Fill the mould three parts full, and set it in a warm place to rise, which will take from two to three hours. When risen, set it at once in a moderate oven. About an hour will bake it. Do not let it get more than pale brown. Turn it out of the mould warm, and when cold, sift a little sugar over it.

Gugelhopfen (No. 2) (1873)
(Savoy Cake)

Three-quarters of a pound of flour
Half a pound of butter
The yolks of nine eggs

Two tablespoonfuls of yeast
A teacupful of milk
Three ounces of sifted sugar

Stir it above half an hour one way, then add the whites of six eggs whisked to a snow. Butter a form as above, and sprinkle in as many chopped almonds as will hang on the butter. Fill rather more than half full, set it to rise, bake it in a moderate oven, and dredge sugar over when turned out.

Gugelhopfen (1920)
(Cougloff)

Butter well the inside of a baba mold having fluted sides; decorate the interior with halved almonds and keep it cool. Form a hollow in the center of four ounces of sifted flour; in it lay half an ounce of yeast, diluting it little by little with a small quantity of tepid milk; mix both flour and liquid slowly together to obtain a soft paste; gather it all up, lay it on the table and form into a ball, cutting a cross on top; place in a basin, cover with a cloth and leave in a mild temperature to have it rise to double its volume. In another vessel work ten ounces of butter with a spatula to a light cream. Lay three-quarters of a pound of flour in a circle on the table; in the center put one ounce of sugar and a little salt; dissolve these with a little water, then add four whole eggs and four separate yolks; mix the whole well and knead the paste vigorously to have it smooth with plenty of body, proceeding the same as for a baba paste; add slowly a gill and a half of good cream; continue to knead the paste until it is quite glossy, then add the butter slowly, knead once more for a few moments, put in the leaven and mingle all well together, then add four ounce of seeded Malaga raisins. As soon as all the ingredients are perfectly combined lay the paste in the mold to reach to two-thirds of its height and set it in a mild temperature until it raises to the top. Place the mold on a baking pan and bake in a slack oven for two hours; unmould on a wire grate.

Gum Lu (1914)
(Golden Cakes)

One and one half cupfuls of rice flour
One cupful of honey
One quarter cupful of mixed nuts, chopped

Three teaspoonfuls of clarified goose fat
Yolks of two eggs
Pinch of salt

Take one and one half cupfuls of rice flour and a pinch of salt and into this work three teaspoonfuls of clarified goose fat. Then chop very fine about quarter of a cup of minced nuts. Beat the yolks of two eggs and mix all together. Now pour in one cup of raw, dark honey. If too moist, add more flour. Stir thoroughly for fifteen or twenty minutes, and pour into small cake pans, well oiled, and bake slowly for two hours.

Guss Torte or Kuchen (1873)
(A Fruit Cake) (Guss - a creamy mixture)

Line a tin with thin tart-paste; spread on it any kind of preserved or fresh fruit that has been stewed with sugar and cooled. Then pour over it the following "guss: two ounces of sifted sugar, two ounces of pounded almonds, two eggs, and a drachm of cinnamon, thoroughly beaten, with as much sour cream as will make the mixture flow smoothly. Bake it a pale-yellow colour.

Part 9: H

Ham Cakes (1893)
Hamilton Chocolate Cake (1820)
Harlequin Cake (1893)
Harrison Cake 1 (1876)
Harrison Cake 2 (1876)
Harrison Cake (1894)
Hartford Election Cake (1894)
Hartford Election Cake (1889)
(Yeast)
Hasty Cake (1897)
(Kaka i hast)
Hasty Cake (1922)
Hazel-Nut Cake (1920)
(Gâteau aux Noisettes)
Hazel Nut Cake (1912)
Hazel Nut Torte (1820)
Hefen Teig (1873)
(Yeast Dough)
Hefen-Waffeln (1910)
(Yeast Wafers)
Henry Cake (1894)
Hickory Nut Cake (1911)
Hickory-Nut Cake 1 (1876)
Hickory-Nut Cake 2 (1876)
Hickory-Nut Cake 3 (1876)
Hickory-Nut Cake (1894)
Himbeer Kuchen (1873)
(Raspberry Cake)

Hoe Cake (1902)
Hoe Cake (1913)
Hoe Cake (1840)
Hominy Cakes (1911)
Hominy Muffins (1911)
Honey Cake (1820)
Honey Cake Special (1820)
Honey Cakes (1840)
Honey Ginger Cake (1840)
Honey-Cake (1864)
Honey Tea Cakes (1912)
Honigkuchen – I (1910)
(Honey Cakes - I)
Honigkuchen – II (1910)
(Honey Cakes - II)
Horseshoe Cakes (1902)
Hot Lemonade Cake (1820)
Hot Water Gingerbread (1917)
(without Egg)
Hot Water Gingerbread (1917)
(with Egg)
Hot Water Sponge Cake (1893)
Hot Water Sponge Cake (1912)
Huckleberry Cake (1840)
Huckleberry Cakes (1911)
Hungarian Spice Cakes (1908)
Hurry Up Cake (1922)

Ham Cakes (1893)

Chop fine 1 cup ham, beat light 4 eggs, mix together, drop by tablespoonful in hot buttered frying pan. Very nice for breakfast.

Hamilton Chocolate Cake (1820)

1 c. brown sugar
1 tsp vanilla
1/2, c. fat
2 eggs beaten separately
⅔ c. milk

2 c. flour
1/2 c. ground chocolate, dissolved in 2 tbsp. hot water
2 tsp. baking powder
1/2 tsp. soda

Use cake method of mixing. Bake one hour in a loaf pan.

Harlequin Cake (1893)

One cup butter creamed with 2 cups sugar
3 eggs
3 cups flour
1 cup milk

1 teaspoon cream tartar
½ soda
Whites of eggs beaten stiff

Mix in the order given, then divide the dough into four equal parts, have two parts plain dough, and colour the third part with two squares of chocolate melted, and the fourth part with red gelatine dissolved in a little water. Bake each on Washington pie tins; when all are done, put first light, then chocolate, then light then pink, and frost the top with white frosting; between each layer put the following to stick them together: Beat 1 egg, and add 1 cup sugar mixed with two tablespoons flour, grated rind and juice of 1 lemon, add to this slowly 1 cup boiling water, and cook in double boiler until smooth.

Harrison Cake 1 (1876)

One coffeecup of molasses
One and a half cups of butter
One and a half cups of milk
Two teaspoons of soda
Four eggs
Two cups of sugar

A fourth of a pound of citron
A half-pound of raisins
One spoon of cloves
One teaspoon of nutmeg
One teaspoon of cinnamon
Six coffeecups of flour

This will make two large loaves. Bake two hours. It will keep a year.

Harrison Cake 2 (1876)

Two cups of sugar
One cup of molasses
One cup of butter
One cup of sweet milk
Five cups of flour

Four eggs
One teaspoon of soda
Spice
All kinds of fruit

Harrison Cake (1894)

Two cups molasses

Two cups butter

One cup milk	Two pounds chopped raisins
Five cups flour	Teaspoon soda
Four eggs	Spice to taste

Hartford Election Cake (1894)

Two and a half pounds butter	Four eggs
Three pounds sugar	One-pint yeast
Four and a half pounds flour	One-quart milk
Three pounds raisins	

Mix the butter and sugar as for pound cake; take one-half thus beaten and mix with flour, milk and yeast, and set it to rise over night. In the morning add the other half of sugar and butter, eggs, raisins and spices and let it rise again. Put in pans and let stand an hour before baking.

Hartford Election Cake (1889)
(Yeast)

Three pints of water; eight good-sized potatoes, peeled and cut in slices.
Boil in the water with a small handful of hops, until tender. Rub through a sieve. Pour the boiling water in which the potatoes were cooked upon the strained potatoes, through a sieve.
Stir in enough flour to make a stiff batter.
Make the batter very sweet with brown sugar.
Add a coffee cup of distiller's yeast.
Let it rise twenty-four hours before using.
Where the use of domestic yeast is impracticable, that obtained from the distillery can be substituted.
It has been claimed that the compressed yeast of modern use, is worthless for making election cake. This is incorrect, for although it is undoubtedly less successful, as a rule, still excellent loaf cake has been made of it. It requires a cake and a half of Fleischman's yeast to raise seven loaves of cake.

Hasty Cake (1897)
(Kaka i hast)

Two yolks and 2 whole eggs you beat with 3 tablespoons of sugar until it whitens. Then stir in a little grated lemon rind and a few pounded bitter almonds and a heaping spoonful of corn starch. Bake in moulds buttered and breaded.

Hasty Cake (1922)

1 cup sugar	2 teaspoons baking powder
2 eggs	½ teaspoon vanilla
1½ cups flour	¼ teaspoon salt
Milk	¼ cup melted butter or shortening

Mix sugar, flour, baking powder and salt together. Put butter in measuring cup, add the eggs and fill cup with milk. Add liquid to the dry ingredients and mix well. Pour into an oblong pan. Bake in a hot oven (400° Fahrenheit) 20 minutes. Cool and cover with any quick frosting.

Hazel-Nut Cake (1920)
(Gâteau aux Noisettes)

Prepare a fine paste with two eggs, four ounces of almonds and four ounces of hazel-nuts, both well pounded. Put into a basin a pound and a quarter of sugar with twenty egg-yolks, beat till quite frothy, then stir in the almond and nut paste, continuing to beat for a few moments longer, mix in lightly three-quarters of a pound of flour and twenty egg-whites whipped to a stiff froth. Divide this preparation in three rings eight inches in diameter lined with paper; bake the cakes in a slow oven; turn them out as soon as done and leave cool off entirely, then mask each with a thick layer of pastry cream highly flavoured with vanilla, adding to it a few roasted hazelnuts pounded with a little cream. Lay one round on top of the other to form into one large cake; pare it well rounded and very uniform with a knife and cover it entirely with reduced apricot marmalade; ice the cake with vanilla icing. As soon as this is hard and dry slide the cake on a dish covered with lace paper and decorate the top with a fine display of royal icing ornamentation. Surround the bottom of the cake with small

Hazel Nut Cake (1912)

One-half pound of hazel nut kernels
One cup of ground or chopped almonds
One and one-half cups of sugar

Eight eggs
Two heaping teaspoons of crumbs
Flavour

Cook slowly.

Hazel Nut Torte (1820)

1 ½ c. sugar
1 ½ c- hazel nuts chopped fine (Walnuts may be used)
9 eggs
½ tsp. cinnamon

½ tsp. mace
1 c. cracker crumbs, rolled very fine
½ tsp. nutmeg
1 tsp. vanilla

Separate eggs. Beat the yolks with the sugar for thirty minutes, using wooden spoon. This continued beating and stirring dissolves the sugar and incorporates the needed air. Add cracker crumbs and spices. Beat egg whites stiff with whisk or whip type of beater. Fold in whites and vanilla. Butter a deep, square cake pan and pour in the batter. Bake in a slow oven for thirty minutes. Increase the heat to moderate for about twenty-five minutes more. Should be light and delicate in texture. Requires no icing, though melted sweet chocolate is sometimes spread over top.

Hefen Teig (1873)
(Yeast Dough)

To a pound of flour use an ounce of dry yeast, or two tablespoonfuls of brewer's yeast. Stir it into a cup of lukewarm milk, and with it mix a batter of a quarter of the flour in the middle of the rest. Cut up on the top of the flour from a quarter to half a pound of butter and set it to rise in a warm place. Then sprinkle over it a little salt and a couple of ounces of powdered sugar. Mix the whole well together and let it rise a second time, when it is ready to roll out for use. Bread dough from the bakers, with or without butter rolled in, is also used for common kuchen.

Hefen-Waffeln (1910)
(Yeast Wafers)

¾ lb. flour
1 oz. yeast
6 oz. butter

2 eggs
1-pint milk
A little grated lemon peel

Crumble the yeast, pour half of the milk, lukewarm, over it and stir in ¼ lb. of the flour. Stand on one side for at least 10 minutes to rise. Mix the remaining flour, milk, beaten-up eggs, butter and sugar and a little grated lemon peel and then add the risen yeast. Knead well and stand in a warm place to rise. When well risen, fill the greased and heated Waffeleisen with spoonsful and proceed as in previous recipes.

Henry Cake (1894)

One-half cup of butter
Two cups sugar
One cup milk
Three and a half cups flour
Three eggs

One teaspoon cream tartar
One-half teaspoon soda
One cup chopped walnuts
One cup currants

Flavour with lemon.

Hickory Nut Cake (1911)

Cream one cup of butter with two cups of sugar, add the well beaten yolks of four eggs, and one-half cup of milk. Sift three level teaspoons of baking powder twice with two and one-half cups of pastry flour. Reserve one-half cup of the flour and add the remainder to the first mixture. Now fold in the whites of four eggs beaten stiff, one teaspoon of lemon juice, half a dozen gratings of the yellow rind of lemon and one cup each of seeded and chopped raisins and of chopped hickory nuts mixed with the reserved half cup of flour. Bake in a moderate oven, cover with a white icing and garnish without meats

Hickory-Nut Cake 1 (1876)

Whites of eight eggs
Three cups of sugar
One cup of butter
One cup of sweet milk
Two and a half cups of flour

One cup of corn starch
Two teaspoons of baking powder in a little milk
A large pint of hickory- nut meats stirred in the last thing

Hickory-Nut Cake 2 (1876)

Whites of twelve eggs
Three large coffeecups of white sugar
One coffeecup of butter
One coffeecup of milk

Five and a half coffeecups of flour
Two teaspoons of baking powder
A pint of nut meats

Bake in layers as for jelly cake, with icing between, or in a large cake. If baked in a loaf, the cake will be much improved by adding a pound of raisins.

Hickory-Nut Cake 3 (1876)

One and a half cups of sugar
One cup of butter
Two cups of flour
Three-fourths of a cup of sweet milk

Whites of four eggs
One heaping teaspoon of baking powder
One large cup of nut meats.

Hickory-Nut Cake (1894)

One cup butter

Four cups flour

Three cups sugar
One cup sweet milk
Four eggs, teaspoon soda

One-pint hickory nut meat
Half pint raisins

Himbeer Kuchen (1873)
(Raspberry Cake)

Set a quart of raspberries over the fire, with three ounces of sugar sprinkled over. Do not stir but shake them now and then. Before they fall, take out the fruit with a perforated spoon, and boil down the syrup. Meanwhile, stir three ounces of butter to a cream, add two ounces of blanched almonds pounded, an ounce of sugar, an ounce of grated bread, and the yolks of four eggs; mix these well, and then stir in the whites of the eggs whisked to a snow. Cover a shallow tin with tart-paste, spread on this the fruit and syrup; then spread over the mass, and bake the kuchen in a brisk oven.

Hoe Cake (1902)

Make a thin batter of corn-meal and milk, add a little melted butter, and a little salt. If sweet milk is used, add a teaspoonful of baking powder; if sour milk 1/2 a teaspoonful of soda. Put a little fat in a frying pan; when hot pour in the batter till 1/2 an inch in thickness; when brown on one side turn. Serve hot.

Hoe Cake (1913)

Sift a pint of cornmeal with a teaspoonful of salt. Make a dough with a little water, shape into cakes and bake in greased pans in a hot oven.

Hoe Cake (1840)

Beat the whites of three eggs to a stiff froth and sift into a pan a quart of wheat flour, adding a salt-spoon of salt. Make a hole in the middle and mix in the white of egg so as to form a thick batter, and then add two table-spoonfuls of the best fresh yeast. Cover it, and let it stand all night. In the morning, take a hoe-iron (such as are made purposely for cakes) and prop it before the fire till, it is well heated. Then flour a tea-saucer, and filling it with batter, shake it about, and clap it to the hoe, (which must be previously greased,) and the batter will adhere, till it is baked. Repeat this with each cake. Keep them hot and eat them with butter.

Hominy Cakes (1911)

To two cups of boiled hominy add two tablespoons of melted butter. Break the whole very fine with spoon or fork. Add two well beaten eggs, one-third teaspoon of salt, and a saltspoon of pepper. Form into little cakes, after adding enough milk to make it of the right consistency to handle. Set cakes on buttered dish and dust with a little finely grated cheese. Bake in hot oven and serve at once.

Hominy Muffins (1911)

Sift twice together one and one-half cups of flour, three level teaspoons of baking powder, one level tablespoon of sugar, and a saltspoon of salt; To one cup of boiled hominy add two tablespoons of melted butter and one cup of milk. Add to the dry ingredients and beat, then add two well beaten eggs. Pour the batter into hot greased gem pans and bake.

Honey Cake (1820)

1 c. sugar
1 tsp. cinnamon and allspice

1 c. chopped citron
1 c. chopped nut meats

2 tbsp. honey
4 eggs
2 c. flour

¾ c. chocolate
1 tsp. baking powder

Mix in order given. Bake in thin sheet. Cut in small rectangles when done. May be frosted with a white icing if desired.

Honey Cake Special (1820)

3 eggs
½ tsp. allspice
1 c. light brown sugar
1 tsp. cinnamon
1½ c. honey

1¾ c. flour
½ c. ground chocolate
3 tsp. baking powder
½ tsp. cloves
¾ c. chopped nuts

Beat eggs and sugar together. Add honey, chocolate and spices, then flour and baking powder and lastly the nuts. Grease and flour a piece of heavy paper. Line bottom of a pan about 9 in. x 13 in. by 2 in. deep. Pour in the cake batter. Brush cream over top and place on it walnut halves at intervals. Bake in a slow oven till done, about 40 minutes. Honey mixtures burn easily, so the utmost care must be taken in baking.

Honey Cakes (1840)

Take a quart of strained honey, half a pound of fresh butter, and a small tea-spoonful of pearl-ash dissolved in a wine glass of water. Add by degrees as much sifted flour as will make a stiff paste. Work the whole well together. Roll it out about half an inch thick. Cut it into cakes with the edge of a tumbler or with a tin-cake cutter. Lay them on buttered tins and bake them with rather a brisk fire but see that they do not burn.

Honey Ginger Cake (1840)

Rub together a pound of sifted flour and three-quarters of a pound of fresh butter. Mix in, a tea-cup of fine brown sugar, two large table-spoonfuls of strong ginger, and (If you like them) two table-spoonfuls of carraway seeds. Having beaten five eggs, add them to the mixture alternately with a pint of strained honey; stirring in towards the last a small tea-spoonful of pearl-ash, that has been melted in a very little water.
Having beaten or stirred the mixture long enough to make it perfectly light, transfer it to a square iron or block-tin pan, (which must be well buttered,) put it into a moderate oven, and bake it an hour or more, in proportion to its thickness.
When cool, cut it into squares. It is best if eaten fresh, but it will keep very well a week.

Honey-Cake (1864)

In vain the circled loaves attempt to lie Concealed in flaskets from my curious eye; In vain the cheeses, offspring of the pail, Or honeyed cakes, which gods themselves regale. PARNELL.

One pound and a half of dried sifted flour, three quarters of a pound of honey, half a pound of finely powdered loaf sugar, a quarter of a pound of citron, and half an ounce of orange-peel cut small, of powdered ginger and cinnamon, three quarters of an ounce. Melt the sugar with the honey and mix in the other ingredients; roll out the paste and cut it into small cakes of any form.

Honey Tea Cakes (1912)

Four cups of flour, two tablespoons of softened butter, mix together, make into a dough with one-fourth cup of molasses, one cup of strained honey, one-fourth cup of water and one-fourth teaspoon of soda, bake on greased baking sheets.

Honigkuchen – I (1910)
(Honey Cakes - I)

1 lb. honey
2 lbs. flour
½ lb. sugar
3 whole eggs
2 oz. butter
1 tablespoonful rum

1 teaspoonful ground cinnamon
1 teaspoonful potash
A little ground ginger
A little ground mace
2 oz. chopped candied peel
A little grated lemon peel

Warm the honey sufficiently for the butter to melt in it. Dissolve the potash in the rum and add it also to the honey. Shake the flour into a basin, make a hollow in the middle, pour into it the beaten-up eggs, the lukewarm honey and the remaining ingredients. Mix well and knead to a firm paste. Roll out very thinly, cut into various shapes with a cutter, place on a buttered tin and bake a light brown. The cakes may also be brushed over with white of egg and sprinkled with chopped almonds.

Honigkuchen – II (1910)
(Honey Cake - II)

1 lb. honey
½ lb. sugar
½ gill rosewater
½ oz. potash
1½ lb. flour
3 eggs

½ lb. chopped hazelnut kernels
5 ground cloves
½ oz. cinnamon, ground
½ tablespoonful grated lemon peel
16 grated bitter almonds

Mix the flour, chopped hazelnuts, cinnamon, cloves, lemon peel and almonds. Boil up the honey with the sugar and when cool, pour into the flour and spice, with the potash dissolved in ½ gill rosewater and beaten up with the 3 eggs. Mix well and knead with the hands. Immediately the paste begins to stiffen, roll it out about ½ inch thick and bake in a moderate oven on a buttered tin with a turned-up edge. Cut up and ornament with a thin sugar icing. Before baking the cake, sliced almonds and strips of candied peel may be arranged on it.

Horseshoe Cakes (1902)

Beat together very light 3/4 of a lb. of sugar and the same of butter, add 4 eggs and mix in 1-1/4 lbs. of flour. Mix 1/4 of a lb. of sugar and flour together and lay in on the bread board. Take a small spoonful of the mixture and roll it with a broad-blade knife in the flour and sugar. When rolled to the right length lay on tin sheet in the form of a horseshoe and bake.

Hot Lemonade Cake (1820)

1½ c. sugar
½ c. almonds or walnuts, ground fine
6 eggs
Rind of 1 lemon
¼ tsp. cinnamon

¼ tsp. baking powder
1½ c. sifted bread crumbs
½ tsp. bitter almond
Flavouring

Beat yolks, add sugar gradually; bread crumbs, baking powder, grated lemon rind and flavouring. Fold the whites in last. Bake in a square pan in a slow oven one hour. When cake is removed from pan, pour over it one cup of very strong boiling lemonade.

Hot Water Gingerbread (1917) (without Egg)

1/4 cup shortening
1 teaspoon soda
1 cup dark molasses
1/2 teaspoon salt

1/2 cup boiling water
1-1/2 teaspoons ginger
2 cups bread flour
1/2 teaspoon cinnamon

Mix shortening, molasses, and water; add dry ingredients sifted together, and beat well. Pour into greased muffin pans and bake in a moderate oven twenty minutes; or pour into a greased shallow pan and bake twenty-five minutes.

Hot Water Gingerbread (1917) (with Egg)

1/3 cup beef drippings
2-3/4 cups flour
2/3 cup boiling water
1 teaspoon soda

1 cup dark molasses
½ teaspoon salt
1 egg well beaten
1-1/2 teaspoons ginger

Pour boiling water over shortening, add molasses and egg; mix and sift dry ingredients, add to first mixture, and beat well. Pour into a shallow, greased cake pan, and bake in a moderate oven twenty-five minutes.

Hot Water Sponge Cake (1893)

Two eggs
1 cup sugar
1 cup flour

1 teaspoon baking powder
The last thing: add ½ cup boiling water

Hot Water Sponge Cake (1912)

Four eggs beaten separately
One cup of boiling water
Two cups of sugar

Three cups of flour
One teaspoon of lemon juice
Two rounding teaspoons of baking powder

Beat the sugar and yolks together, until light, pour on boiling water, add the flour and baking powder, fold in the whites beaten stiff. Bake in ungreased pans lined with paper, either in layers or mould.

Huckleberry Cake (1840)

Spread a quart of ripe huckleberries on a large dish and dredge them thickly with flour. Mix together half a pint of milk; half a pint of molasses; half a pint of powdered sugar; and half a pound of butter. Warm them by the fire till the butter is quite soft; then stir them all together and set them away till cold. Prepare a large tablespoonful of powdered cloves and cinnamon mixed. Beat five eggs very light and stir them gradually into the other ingredients; adding, by degrees, sufficient gifted flour to make a thick batter. Then stir in a small teaspoonful of pearl-ash or dissolved salaeratus. Lastly, add by degrees the huckleberries. Put the mixture into a buttered pan, or into little tins and bake it in a moderate oven. It is best the second day.

Huckleberry Cakes (1911)

Mix together one quart of flour, one teaspoon salt, four teaspoons baking powder and one-half cup of sugar. Mix one-third cup butter, melted with one cup of milk. Add it to the flour and then add enough more milk to make a dough stiff enough to keep in shape when dropped from a spoon. Flour one pint of berries, stir in quickly, and drop by the large spoonful on a buttered pan or in muffin rings. Bake twenty minutes.

Hungarian Spice Cakes (1908)

Sift 1 pound of flour
Beat the yolks of 4 eggs with 1 pound of sugar
Add 1/2-ounce cinnamon
1/2 ounce of ginger
1/4 teaspoonful of cloves
Some grated lemon peel
A pinch of salt

Make all into a dough and roll into small cakes about an inch in diameter. Put on well-buttered baking-plates, sprinkled with flour, and bake in a moderate oven until a rich brown. Serve with wine

---

Hurry Up Cake (1922)

¾ cupful sugar
½ teaspoonful lemon extract
1½ cupfuls flour
2 whites of eggs
4 tablespoonfuls Crisco
¼ teaspoonful salt
½ teaspoonful almond extract
2 teaspoonfuls baking powder
Milk

Sift flour, baking powder, salt and sugar into bowl. Put whites of eggs into measuring cup, add Crisco, and fill cup with milk. Add to dry mixture with extracts and beat vigorously six minutes. Pour into small Criscoed and floured cake tin and bake in moderate oven forty-five minutes. Cake may be frosted if liked. Sufficient for one small cake.

Part 10: I

Ice Box Cake (1922)
Ice Box Cake 1 (N.D.)
Ice Box Cake 2 (N.D.)
Ice Cream Cake (1876)
Ice Cream Cake (1911)
Ice Cream Cake (1894)
Ice-Water Sponge Cake (1876)
Icing Cake (1876)
Imperial Cake (1897)
(Kejsarkaka)
Imperial Cake (1889)
Imperial Cake (1894)
Imperial Muffins (1922)
Indian Batter Cakes (1840)
Indian Breakfast Cake (1894)
Indian Cake (1894)

Indian Cakes (1920)
(Galettes Indiennes)
Indian Cakes (1878)
Indian Drop Cake (1894)
Indian Loaf Cake (1840)
Indian Meal Griddle Cakes (1911)
Indian Mush Cakes (1840)
Indian Pound Cake (1840)
Indian Pound Cake (1869)
Indio Cake (1820)
Individual Shortcakes (1911)
Inexpensive Devil's Food (1820)
Irish Batter Cakes (1908)
Italian Batter Cakes (1908)
Italian Sugar Cakes (1908)

Ice Box Cake (1922)

Line the bottom of a melon or spring form with lady fingers, separated and with the curved sides toward the pan.
Place the filling on the layer of lady fingers and arrange in layers until the form is full or the material used up. Finish the top with a few lady fingers laid in spokes from the center.
Stand in the icebox for twenty-four hours. When ready to serve, remove the band of the form and serve on the metal bottom on the platter. Cover with sweetened whipped cream and chopped nuts or candied cherries, etc.
Filling: Melt one-half pound sweet chocolate in a double boiler, add three tablespoons sugar. Beat yolks of four eggs and stir in three tablespoons water. Cook slowly with the chocolate in the double boiler until the sauce is smooth and thick; stir all the while to make smooth. Cool and add the white beaten stiff. Use this filling as directed above.
Such a filling will require two and a half dozen lady fingers.

Ice Box Cake 1 (N.D.)

2 bars German sweet chocolate
2 tablespoons boiling water
2 tablespoons powdered sugar
4 eggs
18 lady fingers

Dissolve chocolate in water in double boiler. Add sugar, beat until cold, add yolks one at a time, then the beaten whites. Line dish with paraffin paper and put in a layer of split lady fingers, then a layer of the chocolate mixture and alternate lady fingers and chocolate with a top layer of lady fingers. Let stand in refrigerator for 24 hours and serve with whipped cream.

Ice Box Cake 2 (N.D.)

1-pound sweet butter
1 teaspoon lemon juice
1-pound 4x sugar
1 tablespoon vanilla
6 eggs
2 dozen lady fingers
½ pound blanched almonds

Cream butter and sugar, put one egg in at a time, beat well add flavouring and then almonds.
Place lady fingers upright around side of the pan and line bottom of it, put in the mixture and place in ice-box overnight. When ready to serve add two bottles of whipped cream on top.

Ice Cream Cake (1876)

One cup of butter
Two cups of sugar
One cup of sweet milk
Three and a half cups of flour
Yolks of nine eggs
Three teaspoons of baking powder

Cream for cake: Whites of three eggs and two and a half cups of pulverized sugar, put the sugar on the stove with a few drops of water, let it come to a boil and get a little candied; then remove from the fire and stir in the whites beaten to a stiff froth; beat thoroughly and flavour with vanilla.

Ice Cream Cake (1911)

Cream three-quarters cup of butter with two cups of fine granulated sugar. Add one cup of milk with two cups of flour and three-quarters cup of corn-starch sifted twice with five level teaspoons of baking powder. Fold in slowly the whites of seven eggs and bake in layers

Ice Cream Cake (1894)

Two coffee cups A sugar
One scant cup butter (melted just enough to make it soft)
One cup milk
Whites of eight eggs
Three cups flour
Three heaping teaspoons baking powder

Sift your flour, roll your sugar; cream the sugar and butter, then add milk; then add one-third of eggs and one cup flour, then another one-third of eggs and cup flour, then last one third eggs and last cup flour, then add baking powder last of all. After the dough is thoroughly mixed, if it runs off the spoon add another one-half cup flour. Grease your pans well, put two layers of paper in the bottom of the pans. Rake in three layers. When nearly cold trim all the brown part off, then ice.

Icing:

Whites of three eggs, well beaten
Nearly three cups powdered sugar (or one pound)
Three-fourths cup water

Mix sugar and water, boil until the syrup will collect in the bottom of a cup of cold water; have the eggs in a dish and pour the hot syrup upon them slowly; stir constantly until nearly cold then add a teaspoon of vanilla. If the icing seems too hard add a little hot water, and if it sticks to the knife dip the knife in hot water. Very nice.

Ice-Water Sponge Cake (1876)

One and a half cups of sugar
One and a half cups of flour
Three eggs
One ~~and a~~ half cups of ice-water
One and a half teaspoons of baking powder

Beat yolks and sugar with one tablespoon of water, thoroughly. Better than any ten-egg cake I ever ate.

Icing Cake (1876)

Ten eggs
One pound of sifted sugar
A half-pound of flour
Flavour with the grated rind and half the juice of one lemon

Make into sponge cake batter, bake in jelly pans.

Icing:

Whites of three eggs
One and a half pounds of pulverized sugar
Grated rind and juice of a sour orange
The juice of the half lemon left from cake

Make into icing and spread between the layers of cake.

Imperial Cake (1897)
(Kejsarkaka)

One pound of flour
Half a pound of butter
12 ounces of sugar
4 eggs
Half a pound of currants (well washed)
Half a teaspoon of soda dissolved in hot water

Grated rind and juice of half a lemon

1 teaspoonful of cinnamon

Drop from a spoon upon a well buttered paper, lining a baking pan.
Bake quickly.

Imperial Cake (1889)

One-pound butter
One-pound sugar
One-pound flour
One-pound raisins
Three-fourths pound almonds, blanched and slit

Three-fourths pound citron
One-pound currants, if desired
One wineglass of brandy and rose water (not extract of rose)
The juice and rind of a lemon

Rub the butter and sugar to a cream, with a little rose water. One small teaspoonful mace improves the flavour. Beat the eggs separately.
This makes three loaves.
Bake, in a bread oven, about an hour. A third of a teaspoonful of soda, or less, improves it, as there is so much fruit in it.

Imperial Cake (1894)

One-pound butter
One-pound sugar
One-pound chopped raisins
One-quarter pound citron
One-pound flour

Half-pound blanched almonds put in whole
Eight eggs
Mace
One glass of wine

Imperial Muffins (1922)

½ cupful scalded milk
⅓ yeast cake
¼ cupful sugar
¾ cupful lukewarm water

¼ cupful Crisco
1¾ cupfuls flour
1 teaspoonful salt
1 cupful cornmeal

Add sugar and salt to milk; when lukewarm add yeast cake dissolved in ¼ cupful of the water, and 1¼ cupfuls flour, cover, and let rise until light, then add Crisco, cornmeal, remaining flour and water. Let rise over night, in morning fill Criscoed muffin rings, two-thirds full; let rise until rings are full and bake thirty minutes in hot oven.

Indian Batter Cakes (1840)

Mix together a quart of sifted Indian meal, (the yellow meal is best for all purposes,) and a handful of wheat flour. Warm a quart of milk and stir into it a small tea-spoonful of salt, and two large table-spoonfuls of the best fresh yeast. Beat three eggs very light and stir them gradually into the milk in turn with the meal. Cover it and set it to rise for three or four hours. When quite light, bake it on a griddle in the manner of buckwheat cakes. Butter them, cut them across, and send them to table hot, with molasses in a sauce-boat.
If the batter should chance to become sour before it is baked, stir in about a salt-spoonful of pearl-ash dissolved in a little lukewarm water; and let it set half an hour longer before it is baked.

Indian Breakfast Cake (1894)

Two cups Indian meal

One third cup flour

Two and a half cups sour milk
One egg

Soda to sweeten the milk

Indian Cake (1894)

Two cups meal
One cup flour
One cup cream
One cup milk

Two-thirds cup sugar
Three eggs
One teaspoon soda
One of salt

Indian Cakes (1920)
(Galettes Indiennes)

Have in a vessel six ounces of wheat flour and four ounces of corn flour sifted together; add one ounce of powdered sugar, a pinch of salt and one gill of milk. Mix well in order to obtain a smooth-running paste, then pour in an ounce and a half of melted butter. Just when ready to cook the cakes add to the mixture a teaspoonful of baking powder, already mingled with a teaspoonful of flour, and finish exactly the same as for the buckwheat cakes. When cooked dish and set a cover on top, serving them immediately.

Indian Cakes (1878)

These are prepared in the same way as Johnny Cake, except that the batter is made about as thin as buckwheat cakes and baked upon a greased griddle over the fire instead of in the oven. The most economical way of greasing the griddle is to put a small piece of fat salt pork upon a fork and rub it over the surface of the griddle after it is well heated.

Indian Drop Cake (1894)

Three cups meal
One cup flour
One-pint sour milk
Two eggs

Two large spoons butter
One cup sugar
Soda enough to sweeten the milk

Indian Loaf Cake (1840)

Mix a tea-cup full of powdered white sugar with a quart of rich milk and cut up in the milk two ounces of butter, adding a salt-spoonful of salt. Put this mixture into a covered pan or skillet and set it on coals till it is scalding hot. Then take it off, and scald with it as much yellow Indian meal (previously sifted) as will make it of the consistence of thick boiled mush. Beat the whole very hard for a quarter of an hour, and then set it away to cool.
While it is cooling, beat three eggs very light, and stir them gradually into the mixture when it is about as warm as new milk. Add a tea-cup full of good strong yeast and beat the whole another quarter of an hour – for much of the goodness of this cake depends on its being long and well beaten. Then have ready a turban mould or earthen pan with a pipe in the centre, (to diffuse the heat through the middle of the cake.) The pan must be very well buttered, as Indian meal is apt to stick. Put in the mixture, cover it, and set it in a warm place to rise. It should be light in about four hours. Then bake it two hours in a moderate oven. When done, turn it oat with the broad surface downwards, and send it to table hot and whole. Cut it into slices and eat it with butter.
This will be found an excellent cake. If wanted for breakfast, mix it, and set it to rise the night before. If properly made, standing all night will not injure it. Like all Indian cakes, (of which this is one of the best,) it should be eaten warm.

It will be much improved by adding to the mixture, a salt-spoon of pearl-ash, or salaeratus, dissolved in a little water.

Indian Meal Griddle Cakes (1911)

1-pint sour milk
1 egg
1 teaspoon salt
1/2 teaspoon soda
1 tablespoon soda
1 tablespoon molasses
½ tablespoon melted lard
1/4 cup of flour

Meal enough to make a good frying batter.

Indian Mush Cakes (1840)

Pour into a pan, three pints of cold water, and stir gradually into it a quart of sifted Indian meal which has been mixed with half a pint of wheat flour, and a small tea-spoonful of salt. Give it a hard stirring at the last. Have ready a hot griddle, and bake the batter immediately, in cakes about the size of a saucer. Send them to table piled evenly, but not cut. Eat them with butter or molasses.
This is the most economical and expeditious way of making soft Indian cakes; but it cannot be recommended as the best. It will be some improvement to mix the meal with milk rather than water.

Indian Pound Cake (1840)

Sift a pint of fine yellow Indian meal, and half a pint of wheat flour, and mix them well together. Prepare a nutmeg beaten and mixed with a table-spoonful of powdered cinnamon. Stir together till very light, half a pound of powdered white sugar; and half a pound of fresh butter; adding the spice, with a glass of white wine, and a glass of brandy. Having beaten eight eggs as light as possible, stir them into the butter and sugar, a little at a time in turn with the meal. Give the whole a hard stirring at the last; put it into a well-buttered tin pan and bake it about an hour and a half.
This cake (like everything else in which Indian meal is an ingredient) should be eaten quite fresh; it is then very nice. When stale, (even a day old,) it becomes dry and rough as if made with saw-dust.

Indian Pound Cake (1869)

Take three-quarters of a pound of Indian meal sifted, and one-quarter of wheat flour; roll a pound of sugar, work into it three-quarters of a pound of butter; season with nutmeg and rose brandy; add four eggs beaten light; mix and bake as other pound cake

Indio Cake (1820)

1 c. stoned and chopped dates
3 tbsp. butter
1 egg
1 c. sugar
1 c. boiling water
1 c. nut meats
¼ tsp. salt
3 tsp. baking powder
1½ c. flour
1 tsp maple flavouring

Sprinkle the ½ tsp. soda over the chopped dates and add the boiling water. Let stand until cool. Cream the butter, sugar and mapleine and mix with dates. Beat the egg, add the salt and stir into mixture. Then add the flour and baking powder, which should be sifted three times. Mix thoroughly and bake in a moderate oven for about 25 minutes.

Individual Shortcakes (1911)

Sift two cups of flour, three teaspoons of baking powder, and one-half level teaspoon of salt together. Add two well beaten eggs and one-half cup of melted butter. Beat and pour into greased muffin pans until they are two-thirds full. Bake in a hot oven, then split and butter. Crush a quart box of any kind of berries, sprinkle with one-half of cup of sugar and use as a filling for the little shortcakes.

Inexpensive Devil's Food (1820)

1 c. sugar
½ tsp. soda
4 tbsp. fat
1 tsp. baking powder
1 c. boiling water

1½ c. flour
1 egg
¼ tsp. salt
6 tbsp. ground chocolate

Boil chocolate and ½ cup water together until creamy about 2 minutes. Cool. Cream fat and sugar. Beat egg and add to above. Add chocolate mixture. Add flour sifted with baking powder and salt. Add soda to ½ cup boiling water. Stir into mixture and beat well. Bake in 2 layers. (A thin batter.)

Irish Batter Cakes (1908)

Beat the yolks of 4 eggs; add a pinch of salt, 1 tablespoonful of melted butter, 1 small cup of milk and sifted flour enough to make a smooth batter. Beat well. Add the whites of eggs, beaten stiff and let fry a golden colour; then spread with jam and serve hot

Italian Batter Cakes (1908)

Beat 3 yolks of eggs with 1 cup of milk, a Salt-spoonful of salt, 1 tablespoonful of olive-oil and 1 tablespoonful of sugar. Mix with 1/2 cup of flour and the beaten whites of the eggs. Fry until light brown. Serve with cooked fruit

Italian Sugar Cakes (1908)

Beat 1-1/2 pounds of sugar and 1/2 pound of butter to a cream; add 4 yolks of eggs, a pinch of salt and nutmeg. Stir in 1/2 pound of flour, 4 ounces of currants, 2 ounces of chopped almonds, 1 tablespoonful of citron and candied orange peel chopped fine. Add the whites beaten stiff and bake in small well-buttered cake-tins until done; then cover with a thin icing

Part 11: J

Jam Cake (1922)
Jam Fruit Cake (1912)
Jamaica Cake (1920)
(Gâteau à la Jamaïque)
Japanese Cakes (1920)
(Gâteaux Japonais)
Javaneses (1920)
(Javanais)
Jelly Cake 1 (1876)
Jelly Cake 2 (1876)
Jelly Cake (1840)
Jelly Cake (1894)
Jelly Cake (1869)
Jelly Cake Meringued (1920)
(Gâteau à la Gelée Meringué)
Jelly Cake, No. 1 (1920)
Jelly Cake, No. 2 (1920)
Jelly Cake, No. 3 (1920)
Jelly Roll (1913)
Jelly Roll (1920)
Jelly Roll (1922)
Jenny Lind Cake (1893)

Jewish Purim Cakes (1908)
Johnny Cake (1911)
Johnny Cake (1899)
Johnny Cake (1905)
Johnny Cake (1913)
Johnny Cake (1840)
Johnny Cake (1893)
Johnny Cake (1878)
Johnny Cakes (1864)
Journey Cake (1869)
Julia Cake (1894)
Jumbles 1 (1876)
Jumbles 2 (1876)
Jumbles 3 (1876)
Jumbles 4 (1876)
Jumbles (1920)
(Jumbles)
Jumbles 1 (1894)
Jumbles 2 (1894)
(Soft)
Jumbles (1911)

Jam Cake (1922)

Cream ⅔ cup Crisco with 1 cup sugar
Add 3 well beaten eggs
½ cup sour cream
1 teaspoon soda
2 cups flour

½ glass strawberry preserves
1 teaspoon cinnamon
½ teaspoon each cloves
½ teaspoon nutmeg
½ teaspoon salt

Mix and bake in layers. Put strawberry preserves between

Jam Fruit Cake (1912)

One cup of butter
Two cups of brown or white sugar
Four cups of flour
Two cups of jam
Two cups of raisins, if desired
One teaspoon of soda

One-fourth teaspoon of cream of tartar in last cup of flour
One cup of cream
One tablespoon each of cinnamon and allspice
A little nutmeg
Six eggs beaten separately

Jamaica Cake (1920)
(Gâteau à la Jamaïque)

Beat up a pound of sugar with fourteen egg-yolks, so as to have it frothy, then add slowly twelve beaten-up whites and at the same time one pound of sifted rice flour, then a pound of melted butter, also pouring it in slowly with some grated lemon peel, a grain of salt, six ounces of candied orange peels cut in small pieces and six ounces of small raisins. Bake this preparation in a slack oven after placing it in a buttered and floured spiral mold; when the cake is unmoulded and cold apricot the surface and glaze with rum icing. Dress on a napkin and decorate with whipped cream.

Japanese Cakes (1920)
(Gâteaux Japonais)

Pound half a pound of unpeeled almonds with half a pound of sugar; pass it through a sieve, add half a pound of flour and mix the whole together. Dress this flour in a crown shape and in the center place four ounces of kneaded butter and three or four egg-whites; work the whole to obtain a fine smooth paste, then leave it rest for one hour in a very cold place; roll it out to an eighth of an inch in thickness and cut this into three-inch wide bands; egg these over and strew with chopped-up almonds. Range the bands two by two, one on top of the other, pressing them down lightly so they adhere together, then cut them across in small sticks three-quarters of an inch wide; lay them on buttered and floured sheets and bake in a hot oven; after removing ice over with a brush wet with rum icing.

Javaneses (1920)
(Javanais)

Cook a little Genoese preparation on a baking sheet, having it a quarter of an inch thick. Then divide it into two even parts; cover one of these with a layer of Quillet coffee cream a quarter of an inch thick and lay the other half on top, pressing it down lightly so it will adhere to the cream; cover over with apricot marmalade and place the cake in the ice-box to harden the cream. Then cut it out with an oval pastry cutter two and a quarter inches long by one inch wide. Glaze these separate cakes with coffee fondant and in the center of each lay a pinch of lightly burnt chopped almonds.

Jelly Cake 1 (1876)

Yolks of eight eggs
A half-cup of butter
A half-cup of milk
One cup of sugar

Two cups of flour
One teaspoon of cream tartar
A half teaspoon of soda

Bake in layers and spread jelly between.

Jelly Cake 2 (1876)

Three eggs
One cup of sugar
One heaping cup of flour

One tablespoon of melted butter
Two tablespoons of sweet milk
One and a half teaspoons of baking powder

Bake in two tins with buttered paper on the bottom; turn out when done, spread jelly on the bottom and roll.

Jelly Cake (1840)

Sift three quarters of a pound of flour. Stir to a cream a pound of butter and a pound of powdered white sugar and mix in half a tea-cup of rose water, and a grated nutmeg, with a tea-spoonful of powdered cinnamon. Beat ten eggs very light, and add them gradually to the mixture, alternately with the flour; stirring the whole very hard. Put your griddle into the oven of a stove; and when it is quite hot, grease it with fresh butter tied in a clean rag, and set on it a tin cake-ring, (about the size of a large dinner plate,) greased also. Dip out two large table-spoonfuls and a half of the cake batter; put it within the tin ring and bake it about five minutes (or a little longer) without turning it. When it is done, take it carefully off; place it on a large dish to cool; wipe the griddle, grease it afresh, and put on another cake. Proceed thus till all the batter is baked. When the cakes are cool, spread every one thickly over with grape jelly, peach marmalade, or any other sweetmeat that is smooth and thick; currant jelly will be found too thin, and is liable to run off. Lay the cakes smoothly one on another, (each having a layer of jelly or marmalade between,) and either grate loaf-sugar over the top one, or ice it smoothly; marking the icing with cross lines of coloured sugar-sand, all the lines meeting at the centre so as to divide the cake, when cut, into triangular or wedge-shaped slices. If you ice it, add a few drops of essence of lemon to the icing.
Jelly cake should be eaten fresh. It is best the day it is baked.
You may bake small jelly cakes in muffin rings.

Jelly Cake (1894)

Two and one-half cups sugar
One cup butter
One cup milk
Four cups flour

Three eggs
One teaspoon cream tartar
Half teaspoon soda

Jelly Cake (1869)

This cake can be made by the sponge, cup, or Dover cake recipe; have shallow tin pans or plates of the same size, butter them, and pour in the batter so as to be about half an inch thick when baked; they take but a few minutes to bake of a light-brown; and as you take them from the oven, put them on a china plate, with a layer of jelly between each cake, till you have four or five layers; cut the cake in slices before handing it. Currant jelly is to be preferred, but quince will answer, or peach marmalade

Jelly Cake Meringued (1920)

(Gâteau à la Gelée Meringué)

Have eight egg-yolks in a vessel with half a pound of sugar and the peel of one lemon; beat with a spatula until it becomes light and creamy, then add half a pound of flour, four ounces of melted butter and lastly eight firmly whipped egg-whites. Take some jelly cake molds eight inches in diameter and half an inch deep; butter and flour their insides and fill them to the top with the mixture, then bake in a hot oven. As soon as done unmould on grates and leave stand to cool. Place three of these cakes one on top of the other with a layer of currant jelly spread between each, pare the cake round, decorate the surface with a handsome rosette of Italian meringue in the center, it having six to eight leaves, with an empty space in the middle; around the edges dress a continuous wreath of these rosettes, also hollow in the center. Stand the cake for two or three minutes in the oven to dry the meringue decorations, then take out and fill the cavities with apple, currant and quince jellies and apricot marmalade, alternating the different colours; set it on a lace-paper covered dish. Instead of covering the jelly cake with meringue, a piece of cardboard the same diameter as the cake, having a design of any kind cut out to form a stencil, may be used; lay it over the cake, sprinkle it entirely with finely powdered sugar, remove the cardboard carefully and the design will be found imprinted on the cake.

Jelly Cake, No. 1 (1920)

3 eggs
1 cup powdered sugar
1 cup sifted flour mixed with 1 teaspoonful baking powder
2 tablespoonfuls water
The grated rind of ½ lemon

Stir sugar and eggs to a cream and add alternately the sifted flour, water and lemon; butter 3 medium sized jelly tins and dust them with finely sifted bread crumbs; put an equal portion of the cake mixture into each tin, spread it evenly and bake in a medium hot oven to a delicate brown; when done remove the cakes from oven.

Jelly Cake, No. 2 (1920)

¾ cup butter
2 cups sugar
1 cup milk
3 cups flour
1½ teaspoonfuls baking powder
4 eggs
1 teaspoonful essence of lemon

Stir butter and sugar with the right hand to a light white cream; then stir with a spoon and add the eggs, 1 at a time, stirring a few minutes between each addition; next add the lemon and then alternately the milk and flour; bake in 3 jelly cake tins in a medium hot oven to a delicate brown colour; the tins should be lined with buttered paper; when cold lay the layers over one another with jelly between and dust the top with powdered sugar or ice it with fruit icing

Jelly Cake, No. 3 (1920)

Stir ¼ pound butter with ½ pound powdered sugar to a light cream and add alternately 1½ cups prepared flour (sifted), the whites of 4 eggs beaten to a stiff froth and 10 drops extract of bitter almonds; butter 2 good sized jelly cake tins and line them with buttered paper; put an equal portion of the cake mixture into each one, spread it evenly with a knife dipped in water and bake to a delicate brown colour; when cold arrange in layers with jelly between and sift fine sugar over the top.

Jelly Roll (1913)

Sift together a cupful of flour and a rounding teaspoonful of baking powder. Take a cupful of sugar and cream it with a rounding teaspoonful of butter. Add two well beaten eggs (the whites beaten separately and added last), a pinch of salt, an even teaspoonful of lemon juice and a spoonful or two of water.
Beat thoroughly and when smooth bake in a thin layer in a long square-cornered pan. Grease the pan and sprinkle it with a little flour. Turn out the cake on a napkin, spread it with jelly while still warm, and roll.

Jelly Roll (1920)

One half pound sugar
9 ounces flour
1 teaspoonful baking powder

1 gill of milk (½ cupful)
3 eggs
½ teaspoonful lemon extract

Sift flour, sugar, and powder into a bowl and make a hollow in the center; put in milk, eggs, and lemon extract, mix all together; butter a large shallow tin pan, cover with paper, spread on the mixture thin and evenly, bake in slow oven. When done, remove the pan, let it stand a few minutes to cool off a little, then turn it upside down on a clean piece of paper, remove the paper carefully from the cake which has laid in the pan, spread some currant jelly over the surface, roll the cake up like a music roll, let it lie rolled in the paper till cold. This preparation is also nice for lady fingers.

Jelly Roll (1922)

4 eggs
1 teaspoonful baking powder
1 cupful sugar
¼ teaspoonful salt
2 tablespoonfuls melted Crisco

4 tablespoonfuls milk
2 cupfuls flour
Jelly or preserves
1 teaspoonful lemon extract

Beat eggs and sugar together twenty minutes, remove beater, sift in flour, salt, and baking powder, add milk, extract, and melted Crisco. Grease large flat tin with Crisco, dust over with flour, pour in mixture and spread out evenly. Bake twelve minutes in moderately hot oven. Turn out on sugared paper, spread quickly with jelly or preserve and roll up at once. The cake will crack if spreading and rolling are not quickly done. Sliced jelly roll is delicious with custard.
Sufficient for one jelly roll.

Jenny Lind Cake (1893)

Two cups sugar
1 cup butter
3½ cups flour
1 cup milk

4 eggs, leaving out white of one for frosting
2 teaspoons cream tartar
1 soda, vanilla

Bake in three sheets, in the third put all kinds of spices, 2 tablespoons molasses, 1 cup of fruit, raisins, currants, citron, place the dark sheet in middle, put jelly between, frost top.

Jewish Purim Cakes (1908)

Beat 1 cup of sugar with 1/2 cup of butter to a cream; add 2 beaten eggs, a pinch of salt, 1/2 cup of milk and the grated peel of 1/2 lemon. Add enough sifted flour with 1 teaspoonful of baking-powder to make a soft biscuit dough. Put on a well-floured baking-board. Roll out a half inch thick. Cut into triangles and drop in a kettle of hot rendered butter; fry until a golden brown. Then mix some powdered sugar with a little milk and flavour with vanilla. Spread on the top

Johnny Cake (1911)

1 cup meal
1/2 cup flour
1 teaspoon soda
Salt

2 tablespoons molasses
1 tablespoon sugar
Sour milk to mix

Johnny Cake (1899)

Take one quart of sour milk
Three eggs
Three tablespoonfuls of melted butter
One of sugar

A teaspoonful of salt
One cupful of white flour
Enough corn-meal to make a rather thin batter
One teaspoonful of soda

Beat the whites and yolks of the eggs separately. Dissolve the soda in a little hot water and add to the milk, stirring gently; then add the sugar, beaten yolks, and melted butter, stirring all well together; then add the flour and meal, and beat thoroughly; lastly, add the beaten whites; a little more meal may be used if the batter is found to be too thin. Bake in a long pan or gem irons in a hot oven and serve hot.

Johnny Cake (1905)

Material:

3/4 cup corn meal
3/4 cup Pillsbury's Best Flour
3 teaspoons baking powder
1/2 teaspoon salt

2 tablespoons sugar
1 egg
1 cup milk
1 tablespoon melted butter

Way of preparing: Sift cornmeal, flour, baking powder, sugar and salt together. Add milk gradually, well beaten egg and melted butter. Grease shallow pan, heat slightly, pour in mixture and bake twenty minutes in hot oven.

Johnny Cake (1913)

One cupful of buttermilk or sour milk
One and one-half cupfuls of yellow cornmeal
One cupful of flour

A teaspoonful of saleratus dissolved in a little water
A scant teaspoonful of salt

Add a heaping tablespoonful of shortening, melted. Beat into a smooth batter.

Johnny Cake (1840)

Sift a quart of Indian meal into a pan; make a hole in the middle and pour in a pint of warm water. Mix the meal and water gradually into a batter, adding a small tea-spoonful of salt. Beat it very hard, and for a long time, till it becomes quite light. Then spread it thick and even on a stout piece of smooth board. Place it upright on the hearth before a clear fire, with a flat iron or something of the sort to support the board behind and bake it well. Cut it into squares and split and butter them hot.

Johnny Cake (1893)

One and one-half cups Cerealine
1 cup boiled yellow corn meal

½ cup sugar
2 cups flour

2 tablespoons baking powder
2 tablespoons melted butter, or lard
2 cups milk, or milk and water

2 eggs
1 teaspoon Crystaline salt

Put Cerealine and milk in a bowl. Sift flour, salt, baking powder, sugar and cornmeal into mixing dish, and mix well, then add Cerealine and milk, butter and eggs well beaten. Mix until smooth and bake in a sheet. Can also be baked in muffin tins.

Johnny Cake (1878)

Mix one pound of Indian meal, (cost four cents,)
One ounce of lard, (cost one cent,)

One teaspoonful of salt, with sufficient boiling water to make a stiff batter.

Put it by the tablespoonful into a greased baking pan and bake it thoroughly.
Five cents' worth makes a hearty meal, with a little butter or molasses.

Johnny Cakes (1864)

Some talk of hoecake, fair Virginia's pride! Rich Johnny cake this mouth has often tried; Both please me well, their virtues much the same; Alike their fabric, as allied their fame. BARLOW.

A quart of sifted Indian meal, and a handful of wheat flour sifted; mix them; three eggs, well beaten; two tablespoonfuls of fresh brewer's yeast, or flour of home-made yeast, a teaspoonful of salt, and a quart of milk.

Journey Cake (1869)

Pour boiling water on a quart of meal, put in a little lard and salt, and mix it well, have an oak board with a rim of iron at the bottom, and an iron handle fastened to it that will prop it up to the fire; put some of the dough, on it, dip your hand in cold water and smooth it over; score it with a knife, and set it before coals to bake.

Julia Cake (1894)

One cup sugar
One-half cup butter
One-half cup sweet milk
Two eggs

Two cups flour
Teaspoon cream tartar
Half teaspoon soda
Vanilla

Jumbles 1 (1876)

Five cups of flour
Two cups of sugar
One cup of butter
Two eggs

A half-cup of sweet milk
Two teaspoons of baking powder
Flavour with caraway seed, lemon or nutmeg

Mix the ingredients together and work in flour till it will roll nicely. Very fine.

Jumbles 2 (1876)

Two cups of pulverized sugar
One and a third cup of butter
Four eggs, yolks and whites beaten separately

One teaspoon of soda dissolved in two tablespoons of sweet milk
Flour sufficient to roll out soft

Sprinkle white sugar over them before putting them into the oven.

Jumbles 3 (1876)

One cup of butter
Three-fourths of a cup of sweet milk
Three cups of sugar
Four eggs
Three teaspoons of baking powder

Mix very soft, roll and cut out; have a plate of coffee sugar ready and drop each cake bottom side up on the sugar, and immediately transfer to the baking-pan. Bake in a moderately quick oven.

Jumbles 4 (1876)

Three-fourths of a pound of butter
Three-fourths of a pound of sugar
Four eggs
One nutmeg
A fourth of a pound of flour

Roll in fine sugar and flour mixed and bake in a quick oven.

Jumbles (1920)
(Jumbles)

Work to a cream one pound of butter with one pound of sugar, add a little grated nutmeg and five eggs, one at a time, then a pound and a quarter of flour. Place this preparation in a pocket furnished with a channeled socket five-sixteenths of an inch in diameter and dress on a buttered sheet in the shape of one and a halt inch rounds, keeping them an Inch and a quarter apart, then bake in a hot oven. As soon as done remove them from the oven and when cool detach at once from the sheet.

Jumbles 1 (1894)

Three cups butter
Three cups sugar
Six eggs
One-third cup milk
Half teaspoon soda
Flour to roll easily

Scatter on sugar, cut in fancy shapes. This makes many and will keep well. Nice.

Jumbles 2 (1894)
(Soft)

Two cups sugar
One cup butter
Three eggs
Two-thirds cup sour milk
Half teaspoon soda
Four heaping cupfuls flour

Drop them on a tin with a spoon some distance apart; if too thin add a little more flour.

Jumbles (1911)

1½ cups sugar
2 eggs
½ cup butter
½ cup milk
1 teaspoon soda
2 teaspoons cream tartar
Lemon to tast

Mix as soft as can be handled; cut with small cutter, and sprinkle top with cocoanut.

Part 12: K

Kaffeekringel (1910)
Kaffeekuchen (1910)
Kaiser Kuchen (1873)
(Imperial Cake)
Kartoffel Torte (1873)
(Potato Cake)
Käsekuchen (No.1) (1873)
(Cheese Cake)
Käsekuchen (No.2) (1873)
(Cheese Cake)
Käsekuchen (1910)
(Cheese Cake)
King's Cake (1904)
Kirschkuchen (1910)
(Cherry Cake)
Kirschen Kuchen (No.1) (1873)
(Cherry Cake)
Kirschen Kuchen (No.2) (1873)
(Cherry Cake)
Kirschen Kuchen (No.3) (1873)
(Cherry Cake)
Kirschen Kuchen (No.4) (1873)
(Plainer Cherry Cake)
Kirsch-Torte (1910)
(Cherry Cake)
Kleine Biskuittörtchen (1910)
Kleine Kirschtörtchen (1910)
(Cherry Tartlets)
Kleine Sandkuchen (1910)
Königskuchen (1910)
(King Cake)
Krack Torte (1873)
(Crack Tart)
Kuchen Michel (1873)
(A Savoury Cake)
Kugelhupf (1920)
Kümmel-Kakes (1910)
(Carraway Biscuits)
Kümmelstangen (1910)
(Carraway Sticks)

Kaffeekringel (1910)

2 oz. butter
3 oz. sugar
¾ lb. flour
2 eggs
½ teaspoonful baking powder

Beat the eggs well with the butter and sugar, then stir in the flour, sifted and mixed with the baking powder and mix thoroughly to a firm dough. Form into rings and other shapes and throw into steaming hot fat. When a light brown, take out and drain on blotting paper over a sieve.

Kaffeekuchen (1910)

2 lbs. flour
1-pint milk
1 lb. butter
¾ lb. currants
14 oz. sugar
3 oz. yeast
3 eggs
Grated rind of 1 lemon
10 bitter almonds

Prepare the yeast with ½ pint milk and a little of the flour, as in recipe "Napfkuchen." Allow to rise for 10 minutes. Mix with the remaining flour, 4 oz. sugar, the grated almonds and lemon peel, 10 oz. butter, the beaten-up eggs, milk, and lastly the risen yeast. Knead the dough well, then roll out, about ½ inch high, place on a buttered tin and stand on one side to rise further. When about twice as high, brush over with the remaining 6 oz. butter (melted) and sprinkle over with the rest of the sugar. Bake 30 minutes in a hot oven and then cut up into pieces the desired size.

Kaiser Kuchen (1873)
(Imperial Cake)

Soak the crumb of three French rolls in cold milk and press it out dry; beat this bread well with a quarter of a pound of warmed butter and the yolks of six eggs. Add two ounces each of powdered sugar, sultana raisins, currants, candied peel, almonds blanched and pounded, and a little grated lemon-peel; whisk the egg-whites to a stiff snow, and mix it with the rest. Butter a shallow cake-tin well, strew it with fine crumbs, and bake it in a moderate oven; turn it out, and sift sugar plentifully over.

Kartoffel Torte (1873)
(Potato Cake)

Stir the yolks of ten eggs and six ounces of sifted sugar twenty minutes
Then add two ounces of sweet and half an ounce of bitter almonds blanched and pounded together
Half a pound of cold mealy potatoes grated
Two ounces of arrowroot or corn-flour
The grated rind of half a lemon

When these are well mixed, stir in the whites of the ten eggs beaten to a snow. Butter the cake-mould well and strew it with raspings or grated toast. Bake it in a well-heated oven.

Käsekuchen (No.1) (1873)
(Cheese Cake)

Stir together the yolks of six eggs, two ounces of sugar, a pint of milk, and either a little sour milk or a squeeze of lemon-juice. Set it over the fire and stir till it curdles. Turn it out on a napkin spread over a sieve, and let the whey drain through. Beat a quarter of a pound of butter to a cream; add two ounces of potato-flour or cold mealy potatoes grated, an ounce and a half each of currants and sultana raisins, three well-beaten eggs, and three-quarters of a pint of good milk. Stir all well; rub the curd smooth and stir it into the rest. Spread a shallow dish or tin with good tart-paste, cover it with the mass, strew over some finely cut blanched almonds and coarsely powdered sugar. Bake it a deep yellow colour, not brown. This mixture is also nice for small tins or pattypans.

Käsekuchen (No. 2) (1873)
(Cheese Cake)

Put milk alone over the fire to curdle, with either prepared rennet, sour milk, or a little lemon-juice. If you have a soup plate full of curds, beat them up with three ounces of butter warmed, two or three eggs, a quarter of a pound of currants well washed and plumped in hot water, and some grated lemon-peel or powdered cinnamon. Line a flat dish or pattypans with thin paste and cover it with sufficient of the mass.

Käsekuchen (1910)
(Cheese Cake)

4 lbs. white milk cheese
3 oz. butter
4 oz. sugar

2 eggs
4 oz. currants
A few bitter almonds

Prepare the dough according to recipe " Blechkuchen," and arrange on a buttered tin with shallow turned-up edge. Allow to rise to twice its height, then mix all the above ingredients well and spread over the risen dough. Bake in a quick oven.

King's Cake (1904)

¾ pound of butter stirred to a cream
Gradually add the yolks of 10 eggs
¾ pound of sugar
A little salt

Lemon extract
2 ounces of sweet and ⅓ ounce of bitter almonds
1 spoonful of French brandy

Stirring well together.
Then mix:

¾ pound of flour
3 ounces of currants
3 ounces of chopped citron

2 teaspoonfuls of baking powder
Stir the whites of 8 eggs through the dough

Put into a mould and bake slowly for 2 hours.

Kirschkuchen (1910)
(Cherry Cake)

Prepare as Pflaumenkuchen, allowing 2 lbs. of stoned cherries, which should first have some of their juice pressed out of them.

Kirschen Kuchen (No.1) (1873)
(Cherry Cake)

Soak half a pound of sliced bread in as much cold milk as it will absorb; press it out; add six eggs well beaten, two ounces of almonds pounded, a quarter of a pound of sugar, a quarter of a pound of butter warmed, and a small teaspoonful of powdered cinnamon; when these are well mixed, stir in a pound and a half of cherries.

An inch-deep tin must be buttered well; fill it with the mass, and strew sugar and cinnamon over the top, with a few sliced almonds. Bake slowly in a moderate oven.

Kirschen Kuchen (No. 2) (1873)
(Cherry Cake)

Cover an inch-deep tin with a mürberteig; the paste must always come up the sides of these tins to the edge. Lay in about two pounds of cherries, two deep nearly; put it in a well-heated oven for a quarter of an hour. During the time, mix five or six well-beaten eggs with half a pint of sour cream or fresh milk, six ounces of sugar, and a teaspoonful of powdered cinnamon. Draw the cake out of the oven, quickly pour the custard over, and return it to bake sufficiently.

Kirschen Kuchen (No. 3) (1873)
(Cherry Cake)

Lay cherries closely on a good thin paste and strew over them a handful of sugar; mix four eggs, a pint of milk, two ounces of pounded almonds, three or four ounces of sugar, and half a teaspoonful of powdered cinnamon. Stir all thoroughly and pour it over the cherries; bake in a moderate oven.

Kirschen Kuchen (No. 4) (1873)
(Plainer Cherry Cake)

Spread a tin with any plain paste, cover it with cherries, and pour over the following mass: two tablespoonfuls of flour, the same of sugar, and two beaten eggs, thinned with milk to the consistency of thick cream.

Kirsch-Torte (1910)
(Cherry Cake)

½ lb. flour
¼ lb. potato flour
½ lb. butter
1½ lb. cherries, stoned and some of the juice pressed out

½ oz. baking powder
½ lb. sugar
5 tablespoonsful dry breadcrumbs
6 eggs
Grated rind of a lemon

Cream the butter, then add the sugar, beaten-up eggs, grated lemon peel and finally the flour mixed with the baking powder. Stir well together. Fill a well-buttered cake tin with half this quantity, strew in 3 tablespoonsful dry breadcrumbs, lay the cherries on this, sprinkle another 2 tablespoonsful breadcrumbs over them, and then cover with the remainder of the paste. Bake about 1 hour.
Stoned, skinned plums may be substituted for the cherries.

Kleine Biskuittörtchen (1910)

3 eggs
7 oz. castor sugar

2 oz. grated sweet almonds
4 oz. potato flour

Beat the eggs and sugar to a froth and stir in the grated almonds and potato flour. Fill little patty pans, buttered and dusted over with potato flour and bake in a moderate oven.

Kleine Kirschtörtchen (1910)
(Cherry Tartlets)

½ lb. flour
2 lbs. stoned sour cherries
3 oz. butter

1 tablespoonful dry breadcrumbs
2 tablespoonsful milk
1 egg

Mix the butter, sugar and flour well, make a hollow in the middle and pour in the egg, beaten up with the milk. Mix thoroughly and let the paste stand 15 minutes in a cool place. Then roll out about ⅓ inch thick and cut into rounds. Place a little edging of the paste on each round to form a rim. Sprinkle with dry grated breadcrumbs, fill with cherries, dusted over with sugar, and bake in a hot oven. Sprinkle well with sugar before eating.

Gooseberry tartlets are prepared in the same manner, the gooseberries being first just brought to the boil and then drained.

Kleine Sandkuchen (1910)

1 lb. butter
1 lb. sugar
1 lb. wheaten flour

½ lb. potato flour
8 eggs
Lemon or vanilla flavouring

Cream the butter, add the sugar and beaten-up eggs and stir all together ½ hour. Add the flavouring and lastly the flour, gradually. Put into little heaps on a buttered sheet of tin and bake at once in a hot oven to a golden colour.

Königskuchen (1910)
(King Cake)

1 lb. butter
1 lb. sugar
¾ lb. flour
¼ lb. potato flour
½ oz. baking powder
Grated rind of a lemon

8 eggs
½ lb. currants
2 oz. sweet almonds
8 bitter almonds
2 oz. candied peel
1 tablespoonful rum

Cream the butter, then add the sugar and yolks and stir all ¾ hour. Next add the grated lemon peel, almonds, chopped candied peel and rum and stir in alternately the sifted flour, mixed with baking powder and the whisked whites of eggs. Stir in lightly, last of all, the currants well washed and dried, fill a long, square tin (tin-loaf shape) and bake 1 to 1¼ hour.

Krack Torte (1873)
(Crack Tart)

Half a pound of blanched almonds pounded
Quarter of a pound of sugar
Quarter of a pound of butter

Quarter of a pound of flour
One egg

Mix these into a paste; roll it out into a thin round cake; bake it on a flat buttered tin in a moderate oven. When served, spread any fine preserve over, and ornament it with small ratafias, of which you may arrange a border round. Or, having baked small ornamental cut-out cakes of the paste, lay them on as ornament.

Kuchen Michel (1873)
(A Savoury Cake)

Mix two large tablespoonfuls of fine flour smooth with four eggs, and milk enough to make the mixture as thin as cream. Stir it well, add salt and some finely minced chives. Butter a shallow tin or dish and bake the michel a rich yellow.

Kugelhupf (1920)

Also called Bunt Kuchen

One-pound flour
10 ounces butter
2 yeast cakes
6 whole eggs and 6 yolks
¾ cup of sugar
½ teaspoonful salt
1 cupful seeded raisins

Break the yeast into a small bowl, add ½ cupful lukewarm milk and 1 teaspoonful sugar; let it stand till the yeast rises to the surface, then add ½ cupful of flour, mix to a stiff batter; cover and let stand till it is a light sponge. In the meantime stir butter and sugar to a cream; add the yolks one at a time, then alternately a little flour and 1 whole egg, till all are used; beat this with the right hand 10 minutes; add the raisins, and last the sponge; continue to beat 5 minutes; butter a large ribbed form with tube in the center; dust with powdered sugar, pour in the cake mixture; set the form in a warm place till the contents has risen to double its size; then place the form on a tin with salt and bake in a medium-hot oven about 45 minutes. When done, take it out of the oven, let it stand a few minutes, then turn the cake out of the form, dust it with sugar, and serve when cold.

Kümmel-Kakes (1910)
(Carraway Biscuits)

1 lb. flour
½ oz. baking powder
½ oz. ground carraway seed
1 oz. salt
½ pint milk
½ lb. cornflour
½ lb. butter

Cream the butter and stir in the flour, salt and ground carraway. Then add the milk and mix thoroughly. Roll out ½ inch thick, cut into various shapes with a cutter, sprinkle over with salt and carraway and bake in a hot oven.
To be eaten buttered, with slices of cheese or cold meat laid on.

Kümmelstangen (1910)
(Carraway Sticks)

½ lb. flour
1 teaspoonful Parmesan cheese
3 oz. butter
1 teaspoonful salt
1 egg
1 tablespoonful milk
1 extra yolk
A pinch of white pepper
Ground carraway
½ oz. baking powder

Cream the butter, stir in the yolks, salt, pepper, milk, cheese, (which may also be omitted, if preferred), and lastly the flour, sifted with the baking powder. Form into little rolls, about 2 inches long and ½ inch thick, brush over with the beaten-up egg, sprinkle thickly with carraway and bake in a cool oven.

Part 13: L

Ladies' Cake (1893)
Lady Baltimore Cake (1922)
Lady Baltimore Cake Filling and Frosting (1922)
Lady Baltimore Cake (1922)
Lady Baltimore (1912)
Lady Cake 1 (1876)
Lady Cake 2 (1876)
Lady Cake 1 (1920)
Lady Cake 2 (1920)
Lady Cake (1920)
(Gâteau des Dames)
Lady Cake (1894)
Lady Cake (1893)
Lady Cake (1840)
Lady Cake (No. 1) (1922)
Lady Cake (No. 2) (1922)
Lady Cake (No. 3) (1922)
Lady Cake (No. 4) (1922)
Lady Finger Cake (1912)
Lady Fingers (1876)
Lady Fingers (1920)
(Biscuits à la Cuiller)
Lafayette Gingerbread (1864)
Lagen-Torte (1910)
Lapland Cakes (1876)
Laplander Cakes (1902)
Large Brioche with Head (1920)
(Grosse Brioche à Tête)
Layer Cake (1904)
Layer Cake (1905)
Layer Cake (1911)
Layer Cake No. 1 (1912)
Layer Cake No. 2 (1912)
Layer Cake, Yellow (No. 1) (1922)
Layer Cake, Yellow (No. 2) (1922)
Layer Cake, Yellow (No. 3) (1922)
Layer Cake, Yellow (No. 4) (1922)
Layer Cake, Yellow (No. 5) (1922)
Layer Cake, White (No.1) (1922)
Layer Cake, White (No.2) (1922)
Layer Fruit-Cake (1876)
Lemon Cake 1 (1876)
Lemon Cake 2 (1876)
Lemon Cake 3 (1876)
Lemon Cake (1913)
Lemon Cake (1893)
Lemon Cake (1898)
Lemon Cake with Icing (1904)

Lemon Cheese – Cake Mixture (1898)
Lemon Cheese-Cakes (1898)
Lemon Cream Cake (1920)
Lemon Currant Cake (1876)
Lemon Ice Box Cake (N.D.)
Lemon Jelly Cake 1 (1876)
Lemon Jelly Cake 2 (1876)
Lemon Jelly Cake 3 (1876)
Lemon Layer Cake (1922)
Lemon Layer Cake (1899)
Lemon Layer Cake (1920)
Lemon or Orange Cake (1876)
Lemon Snaps (1876)
Lemon Snaps (1894)
Lemon Sponge Cake (1899)
Lemon Sponge Cake (1869)
Lightened Pone (1869)
Lightning Cake (1820)
Lightnings (1897)
(Blixtar)
Lily Cake (1876)
Lily Cake (1893)
Lincoln Cake (1876)
Lincoln Cake (1893)
Linzer Cake (1904)
Linzer Torte (1910)
Linzer Torte (1873)
Linzer Cake, (No. 1)
Linzer Torte (1873)
Linzer Cake, (No. 2)
Linzer Torte (1873)
Linzer Cake, (No. 3)
Linzer Torteletten (1873)
(Linzer Tartlets)
Linzer Tourte (1922)
Lise's Sponge Cake (N.D)
Little Indian Cakes (1869)
Little Plum Cakes (1876)
Loaf Cake (1869)
Loaf Ginger Cake (1893)
Löffelbiskuit (1910)
Lord Baltimore Cake (1922)
Love Cake (1904)
Lubec Marzapan (1904)
Lucile Shortcake (1909)
Lunch Cakes (1922)
Luncheon Cake (1913)

Ladies' Cake (1893)

Yolks of three eggs
1½ cups of sugar, beat together
Add ⅔ of a cup cold water, mix well
Add 2 cups flour

2 teaspoons Royal Baking Powder
Whites of 3 eggs beaten stiff
Flavour to taste
½ cup of melted butter added last

Bake in quick oven.

Lady Baltimore Cake (1922)

3 cups cake flour
3 teaspoons baking powder
Whites of three eggs
¼ teaspoon salt

½ cup butter
½ cup milk
½ cup water
1½ cups sugar

Sift baking powder, salt and flour three times. Cream butter and gradually add sugar until thoroughly mixed. Add the flour and milk alternately, stirring until smooth. Stir in one teaspoon vanilla and one-quarter teaspoon almond flavouring. Beat the whites stiff and fold in. Bake in layers in a moderate oven (350 degrees F.).

Lady Baltimore Cake Filling and Frosting (1922)

Make a syrup of two cups sugar and three-quarters cup water; cook to the soft ball stage. Pour over the whites of two eggs beaten stiff; beat until the mixture stands. Retain one-third for cake icing.
Grind one-quarter pound figs or dates with one-half pound raisins and one-half pound nut meats. Add the ground fruits and nuts to remaining two-thirds of mixture.
Spread between layers and on top of cake. Frost entire cake with plain icing.

Lady Baltimore Cake (1922)

(White Cake)

1 cupful sugar
2½ cupfuls flour
¾ cupful Crisco
2½ teaspoonfuls baking powder

½ cupful cold water
½ teaspoonful salt
1 teaspoonful vanilla extract
6 whites of eggs

For the Filling:

1 cupful sugar
Pinch cream of tartar
½ cupful boiling water
½ cupful chopped candied cherries

2 whites of eggs
½ cupful chopped candied pineapple
1 teaspoonful vanilla extract

For cake: Cream Crisco and sugar together. Sift together three times dry ingredients and add alternately with water. Add vanilla, beat mixture well then fold in stiffly beaten whites of eggs. Divide into two Criscoed and floured layer cake tins and bake in moderate oven twenty-five minutes.
For filling: Put sugar and water into saucepan, stir till boiling, add cream of tartar, then boil until it forms a soft ball when tried in cold water, or 240° F.; pour on to the stiffly beaten whites of eggs, pouring in a steady stream and very slowly, adding while beating vanilla, cherries and pineapple, beat till thick and divide between and on top of cake.
Sufficient for: one large layer cake.

Lady Baltimore (1912)

Three-fourths cup butter
One and one-half cup of sugar
One-half cup of milk
Three cups of flour

Two teaspoons of baking powder
Whites of six eggs
One teaspoon of almond extract

Follow directions for mixing, bake in layers and fill with the following icing:
Soak one-half pound of seeded chopped raisins and one-half pound of chopped English walnut meats in one cup of sherry for one hour. Make a plain white icing and flavour with rose water or vanilla. Mix the raisins and nuts with a small portion of icing and spread between cakes. Spread top and sides with plain icing or reserve some of the raisins and nuts and mix in with icing and spread.

Lady Cake 1 (1876)

Whites of sixteen eggs
One pound of sugar
Three-fourths of a pound of butter

One pound of flour
One teaspoon of extract of bitter almonds or vanilla

Beat the butter and sugar to a cream, mix in flour till very stiff, then add the other ingredients, and frost.

Lady Cake 2 (1876)

One cup of butter
Three cups of sugar
One cup of sweet milk

Whites of eight eggs
Four cups of flour
Two heaping teaspoons of baking powder

Lady Cake 1 (1920)

1 cup butter
2 cups sugar
1 cup milk

3 cups prepared flour
The whites of 8 eggs
The grated rind and juice of 1 lemon

Stir butter and sugar with your hand to a light white cream and beat the whites to a stiff froth; take a silver spoon and stir the whites, the lemon, sifted flour and milk alternately into the creamed butter and sugar; butter a large mould and line it with buttered paper; pour in the mixture and bake 1 hour.
NOTE: ½ pound blanched almonds cut into strips may be stirred into the cake mixture and flavoured with vanilla; or 1-pint shelled walnuts broken into pieces or ½ pound finely cut citron can be stirred into the batter and flavoured with essence of almonds; ice with clear icing.

Lady Cake 2 (1920)

Six ounces butter
½ pound sugar
1-pound flour
10 whites of eggs

½ pint whipped cream
1 teaspoonful baking powder
1 teaspoonful vanilla sugar

Stir butter and sugar to a cream until white and frothy, add the vanilla sugar, sift flour and baking powder together, beat ½ pint cream until stiff; beat also the 10 whites to a stiff froth, then add alternately the three ingredients to the creamed butter and sugar; butter and dust with flour a large round pan, pour in the mixture, and bake in a medium-hot oven. When done and cold, ice it with clear icing.

Lady Cake (1920)
(Gâteau des Dames)

Put fourteen ounces of butter and twenty ounces of sugar in a metal bowl and work together with the hands for fifteen or twenty minutes to have it quite frothy, then add four ounces of almonds, including a few bitter ones, pounded with a little water, and work again for a few moments. Now put in one gill of brandy or rum, twenty ounces of flour and finally twenty very stiffly whipped egg-whites. Butter a pound-cake mold, line it throughout with paper and fill it three-quarters full with the preparation; bake in a very slow oven. (Once the cake is in the oven it must not be touched until baked.) Take it out, unmould and leave to get thoroughly cold. Then ice with royal icing and stand it at once on a lace-paper covered board. After the icing has dried decorate the cake with more royal icing.

Lady Cake (1894)

One-half cup butter creamed, add gradually one cup sugar, one-half cup milk, one-half cup cornstarch, one cup flour, one even teaspoon baking powder, whites of four eggs. Flavour with almond and a drop of lemon.

Lady Cake (1893)

One cup sugar
½ cup butter
½ cup milk
2 cups flour, with 1 teaspoon baking powder sifted with it

Whites of 4 eggs beaten to a stiff froth and added the last thing
Flavour to taste

Lady Cake (1840)

Take a quarter of a pound of shelled bitter almonds, or peach-kernels. Put them into a bowl of boiling water, (renewing the water as it cools) and let them lie in it till the skin peels off easily; then throw them, as they, are blanched, into a bowl of cold water, which will much improve their whiteness. Pound them, one at a time, in a mortar; pouring in frequently a few drops of rose water to prevent them from oiling and being heavy. Cut up three quarters of a pound of fresh butter into a whole pound of powdered loaf-sugar. Having warmed it, stir it to a light cream, and then add very gradually the pounded almonds, beating them in very hard. Sift into a separate pan half a pound and two ounces of flour, and beat in another pan to a stiff froth, the, whites only of seventeen eggs. Stir the flour and the white of egg alternately into the pan of butter, sugar and almonds, a very little at a time of each. Having beaten the whole as hard as possible, put it into a buttered tin pan, (a square one is best,) and set it immediately into a moderate oven. Bake it about an hour, more or less, according to its thickness. When cool, ice it, flavouring the icing, with oil of lemon. It is best the day after it is baked, but it may be eaten fresh. When you put it away wrap it in a thick cloth.
If you bake it in little tins, use two ounces less of flour.

Lady Cake (No. 1) (1922)

Three pounds and four ounces of powdered sugar (or very fine granulated)
Three pounds of white butter
Three pints of whites of eggs

One pound of strong flour
Three pounds of cake flour
One ounce of baking powder
Flavour of vanilla and mace, or rose

Cream butter, two pounds of the sugar with one pint of whites; beat the other two pints to a firm froth and add the remaining sugar as for meringue; mix both parts together, add the flour with baking powder, mix lightly but fully and bake like Pound Cake.

This makes a very rich birthday or brides cake mixture.

Lady Cake (No. 2) (1922)

Two pounds of butter
Two and one-half pounds of sugar
Two and three-quarter pints of whites of eggs
Two and one-half pounds of flour
One eighth of an ounce of cream of tartar
One eighth of an ounce of soda

Sift the soda and cream of tartar in the flour (use a strong cake flour, or half spring and half winter). Mix and bake the same as Lady Cake (No. 1) (1922).

Lady Cake (No. 3) (1922)

One pound and eight ounces of sugar
One pound and two ounces of butter
One and one-half pints whites of eggs
One and one-half pounds of flour
One eighth of an ounce of soda
One quarter of an ounce of cream of tartar
Flavour rose and almond

Bake the same as Pound Cake

Lady Cake (No. 4) (1922)

Two pounds of sugar
One and half pounds of white butter
Two pounds of flour
Four ounces of cornstarch
One quart of whites of eggs
Half a teaspoon of baking powder
Flavour rose and almond

Cream the sugar and butter with half of the whites and mix with the flour; then draw in the other whites beaten to a firm froth. Mix them well. Bake in medium heat of 250 to 300 degrees Fahrenheit.

Lady Finger Cake (1912)

Six eggs
One cup of sugar
Juice of one-half lemon and grated peel of one,
Six lady fingers

Beat yolks and sugar together until light, add lemon juice and peel, add lady fingers crumbled or grated fine, fold in the whites, bake slowly in shallow round mould.

Lady Fingers (1876)

Four eggs
Two cups of butter
Three cups of flour
Two cups of sugar
Flavour to the taste

If made into a paste for fingers, add just enough flour to bring it into a roll the size of a finger. They are nice dipped in icing.

Lady Fingers (Biscuits à la Cuiller) (1920)

Separate the whites from twenty eggs and pour them into a basin; leave the yolks in another vessel; to these yolks add a pound of powdered sugar, part of it being flavoured with vanilla and beat up to make a very light preparation; then put in one pound of sifted flour and the twenty whites beaten to a stiff froth, stirring the whole lightly together. Pour a part of this preparation into a pocket furnished with a half-inch diameter socket and through it push biscuits four and a half inches in length, keeping them slightly apart and laying them on sheets of paper; bestrew with powdered sugar; put on a baking sheet and leave stand a moment until the sugar begins to dissolve, then push it into a moderate oven. As soon as they are of a light golden colour and the crust begins to harden remove at once from the oven and from the baking sheet, then range them on a table till cold.

Another Recipe is: one pound of sugar, twelve eggs, half a pound of flour, a grain of salt, grated zest or a spoonful of orange flower water.

Lafayette Gingerbread (1864)

Must see Rheims, much famed, 'tis said, For making kings and gingerbread.
MOORE.

Five eggs	Four tablespoonfuls of ginger
Half-pound of brown sugar	Two large sticks of cinnamon
Half-pound fresh butter	Three dozen grains of allspice
A pint of sugarhouse molasses	Three dozen of cloves
A pound and a half of flour	Juice and grated peel of two lemons

Stir the butter and sugar to a cream; beat the eggs very well; pour the molasses at once into the butter and sugar. Add the ginger and other spice and stir all well together. Put in the eggs and flour alternately, stirring all the time. Stir the whole very hard and put in the lemon at the last. When the whole is mixed, stir it till very light. Butter an earthen pan, or a thick tin or iron one, and put the gingerbread in it. Bake it in a moderate oven an hour or more, according to its thickness, or you may bake it in small cakes or little tins.

Lagen-Torte (1910)

1 lb. flour	6 raw yolks
¾ lb. firm butter	4 boiled yolks
¼ lb. sugar	

Sift the flour, pull the butter into small pieces, add to the flour, stir in the sugar and the rubbed hard-boiled yolks, the 6 well-beaten raw yolks, and mix thoroughly and quickly to a paste. Roll out into four pieces, bake on buttered sheets of tin, spread three of them each with a different jam and spread an icing of any kind over the top.

Lapland Cakes (1876)

Beat very light five eggs with a pint of sweet cream, then beat in well one and one-half pints flour; bake in tins or cups in quick oven.

Laplander Cakes (1902)

One pt. of milk	A tablespoonful of butter
1 pt. of flour	A pinch of salt
2 eggs well beaten	A tablespoonful of sugar

Have the pans very hot before filling.

Large Brioche with Head (1920)

(Grosse Brioche à Tête)

Have a brioche paste prepared the same as described; put this in a vessel in a cool place and let it rise to half its size again. Then work it once more and set it in the ice-box for two hours to have it harden. Butter a tin mold six and a half inches in diameter and eight inches deep; line it with paper and butter this over. Mold a four-pound round-shaped piece of the paste, put it in the mold, then mold another pound piece and roll it on the table on one side to give it a long pear-form appearance; with dampened fingers make a hole in the center of the first paste and in it insert the pointed end of the pear; leave the mold in a moderately heated place to have the paste rise to the level of the top, then egg it over twice and put in a slack oven to cook for two hours. Unmould as soon as done, allow to cool and dress on a folded napkin. In case there be no mold at hand use a cylinder of strong paper the same diameter as the mold.

Layer Cake (1904)

A layer cake that will keep fresh for a long time is made of 8 eggs, the weight of the eggs in sugar, butter and flour.
The butter is melted, poured from the settlings and then allowed to cool again, add the sugar by degrees, and stir until all is melted. Then gradually put in the eggs and stir the whole for ½ hour as given under (General Directions (1904) mix the flour through this, and then bake three cakes to a dark yellow colour, spread two with jelly and lay the third on this. The next day cut the edge smoothly and dust sugar over the top. Lemon peel and lemon juice can also be added to this cake making one cake and spreading it with jelly and then with the beaten whites of 3 eggs, seasoning with a little vanilla, and set it in the oven a few moments to dry.

Layer Cake (1905)

1 cup sugar
1/2 cup water
2 eggs
2 teaspoonfuls baking-powder

1/2 cup butter
2 1/2 cups flour
Teaspoonful vanilla

Rub the butter to a cream in a deep bowl and put in the sugar a little at a time, and rub this till it, too, creams. Then put in the beaten yolks of the eggs, and then the water. Beat the egg-whites well, and fold in half, then add the flour, in which you have mixed and sifted the baking-powder, and then put in the vanilla and the rest of the eggs.
Divide in two layers, or in three if the tins are small, and bake till a light brown.

Layer Cake (1911)

One and one-half cups of sugar
Two-thirds of a cup of butter
The whites of six eggs
One cup of sweet milk

Two and one-half cups of pastry flour
Two teaspoonfuls of baking powder
Flavour with lemon

Put two-thirds of the mixture into jelly tins.
To the rest add:

Two tablespoonfuls of molasses
One-half cup of raisins (seeded)
Three figs (chopped)

One teaspoonful cinnamon
One-half teaspoonful allspice
Two tablespoonfuls of flour

Bake, when cool, together with jelly, having the dark layer in the centre

Layer Cake No. 1 (1912)

One cup of butter
Two cups of sugar
Three and one-half cups of flour
One cup of sweet milk or water

Two teaspoons of baking powder
Whites of eight eggs
One teaspoon vanilla

Cream butter add sugar and cream well together, alternate milk and flour, adding the baking powder to the last cup of flour. Add the stiffly beaten whites of eggs last. Bake in layer cake pans, twenty-five or thirty minutes.

Layer Cake No. 2 (1912)

One-half cup of butter
Two cups of sugar
Two and one-half cups of flour
One cup of milk

Two teaspoons of baking powder
Whites of five eggs
One teaspoon of vanilla or one-half teaspoon of almond extract

Layer Cake, Yellow (No. 1) (1922)

1 qt. of eggs
1 qt. of milk
2 ozs. of cream
3 lbs. of sugar

4½ lbs. of flour
2½ lbs. of butter
1 oz. of soda
Lemon or vanilla flavour

Layer Cake, Yellow (No. 2) (1922)

2 lbs. of sugar
1 pt. of milk
2 oz. of baking powder
1 lbs. of butter

3 lbs. of flour
20 eggs
Lemon and mace flavour

Layer Cake, Yellow (No. 3) (1922)

2 lbs. of sugar
½ pt. of eggs
1½ ozs. of baking powder
1 lbs. of butter and lard

1 qt. of milk
3 lbs. of flour
Flavour

Layer Cake, Yellow (No. 4) (1922)

1 lb. of sugar
½ pt. of eggs
1½ ozs. of baking powder
1 lb. of butter and lard

1½ pt. of milk
2 lbs. of flour
Flavour

Layer Cake, Yellow (No.5) (1922)

2½ lbs. of sugar
1½ pts. of milk
1½ ozs of baking powder
½ lbs. of butter

2½ lbs. of flour
8 eggs
Flavour

Layer Cake, White (No.1) (1922)

1 lb. of sugar
1½ lbs. of flour
1 oz. of baking powder
¾ lbs. of butter
¾ pts. whites of eggs
¾ pts. milk
Vanilla flavour

Layer Cake, White (No.2) (1922)

½ lbs. of sugar
1¾ lbs. of butter and lard
1½ ozs of baking powder
1 pt. of milk
2 lbs. of flour
¾ pts whites of eggs
Vanilla flavour

Layer Fruit-Cake (1876)

Whites of eight eggs
Three cups of sugar
One cup of butter
One cup of sweet milk
Three full cups of flour
Two teaspoons of baking powder

Icing: One pint of sugar and the whites of three eggs beaten to a stiff froth; add sufficient water to the sugar to melt it, boil to a thick syrup, pour a little at a time boiling hot into the whites, stirring rapidly, and beat until smooth. Take a pound of raisins and a half pound of dates, stone the raisins, cut the dates into small pieces and mix together; spread one layer of the cake with icing rather thick, cover the icing with fruit, add a little more icing, then another layer of cake and ice the cake all over.
This makes two large cakes.

Lemon Cake 1 (1876)

Stir to a cream one teacup of butter and three cups of pulverized sugar; add the yolks of five eggs well beaten, one teacup of sweet milk, one lemon grated, whites of five eggs, four and one-half cups of flour and one teaspoon of soda. Bake in two tins half an hour.

Lemon Cake 2 (1876)

Three cups of sugar
One cup of milk
One cup of butter
Five eggs
Four cups of flour
One-half teaspoon of soda
The juice and grated peel of one lemon

Lemon Cake 3 (1876)

One cup of butter
One cup of milk
Three cups of pulverized sugar
Four cups of flour
Whites of ten eggs
Two teaspoons of cream tartar in the flour
Grated rind and juice of one lemon
One teaspoon of soda the last thing

Lemon Cake (1913)

Cream together a cupful of sugar and half a cupful of shortening. Sift a large cupful of flour, add an even teaspoonful of saleratus that has been dissolved, and a dash of salt. Stir all together and pour in half a cupful of sour milk, a tablespoonful of lemon juice and a bit of grated rind. Beat the yolks of two eggs and the white of one; stir all together thoroughly, adding flour if necessary. Bake slowly. The top may be frosted with the remaining white of the eggs.

Lemon Cake (1893)

Two eggs
1 cup sugar
4 tablespoons milk (real tablespoons remember)
¼ teaspoon Crystaline salt
1 teaspoon baking powder, sifted, with 1 heaping cup flour

Beat yolks of eggs and sugar together, add whites well beaten, add milk in which Crystaline salt has been dissolved, then add flour. Bake in two pie tins.

Lemon batter filling:

Grated rind and juice of 1 lemon
⅔ cup sugar
1 egg
Scant teaspoon butter

Put lemon juice and rind into dish, set in boiling water, stir in sugar. When melted and hot, stir in beaten egg, and stir until mixture thickens, stir in butter and cooly stirring once in a while; put between pies. This cake is better second or third day.

Lemon Cake (1898)

Ingredients:

The rind and juice of 1 lemon
4 oz. flour
8 oz. sifted sugar
4 eggs

Method: Break the eggs, carefully separating the whites from the yolks. Beat and strain the yolks, and mix with them gradually the sugar, flour, and grated lemon rind; beat the whites of eggs to a stiff froth, mix them in well, add the lemon juice, and beat thoroughly. Pour the mixture into a buttered mould, and bake in a moderate oven, covering the top with a buttered paper when half cooked.
Time: 40 minutes.
Sufficient for: 1 cake of moderate size.

Lemon Cake with Icing (1904)

Make a puff paste, take a few fresh lemons, sugar, biscuit and for the icing 4 eggs, 1 pint of sweetened thick cream. Bake a cake, sprinkle sugar over it, cover, with lemon slices freed from peel and seeds, sweeten with plenty of sugar, lay biscuit slices over this and then pour over it the eggs; cream and sugar whipped with a beater, and set in the oven until the icing is thick.

Lemon Cheese – Cake Mixture (1898)

Ingredients:

6 oz. pounded sugar
2 oz. butter
Strained juice of 2 small or 1½ large lemons
Finely-chopped rind of 1 lemon
3 eggs

Method: Put the sugar, butter, lemon juice, and finely-chopped rind into a small lined saucepan. Beat the eggs, strain them, and add them to the other ingredients. Set the saucepan over a moderate fire and stir

constantly. The mixture will become thin and syrupy as the butter and sugar melt, and then will begin to thicken like custard. Watch it carefully, and stir it unceasingly, as it will curdle if cooked too fast. When of the consistency of honey remove it from the fire, continue stirring for a few minutes until the mixture has somewhat cooled, and then set it aside for use. It may be poured into a jar, which should be tied down with parchment paper whilst hot and will keep good for 2 or 3 months.
Time: About 20 minutes.
Sufficient for: 12 cheese-cakes.

Lemon Cheese-Cakes (1898)

Ingredients:

Puff crust or short crust made with 8 oz. flour and other ingredients in proportion

Lemon cheese-cake mixture

Method: Make the crust as directed, roll it out thinly, and line some buttered patty-pans with it. Ornament the edges neatly, fill the centre of each with cheese-cake mixture, and bake in a moderate oven.
Time: 15 to 20 minutes.
Sufficient for: 12 cheese-cakes.

Lemon Cream Cake (1920)

½ cup butter
1 cup sugar
The whites of 3 eggs

½ cup milk
1½ cups prepared flour
The grated rind and juice of ½ lemon

Stir butter and sugar to a cream; beat the whites to a stiff froth and add them alternately with the sifted flour and milk to the creamed butter and sugar; add lastly the lemon; butter 2 jelly tins and dust them with cracker dust; put in the mixture, spread it evenly with a knife and bake a light brown; when done put a napkin or clean cloth on the kitchen table and dust with powdered sugar; turn the cakes upside down onto the napkin and let them lay till cold; cream for filling: - Boil ¾ cup milk with 2 tablespoonfuls sugar; dissolve 1 tablespoonful corn-starch in ¼ cup cold milk, stir it into the boiling milk and boil a few minutes; add 1 teaspoonful butter, a pinch of salt and remove it from fire; beat up the yolks of 3 eggs with 1 tablespoonful cold milk, stir them into the corn-starch and add 1 teaspoonful essence of lemon; when cold put 1 layer of cake, upside down, onto a plate and spread over the cream; put the other layer over it, right side up, and dust the top with powdered sugar.

Lemon Currant Cake (1876)

One pound of sugar
One pound of butter
One pound of flour

Nine eggs leaving out two yolks
The juice of one lemon and the grated peel of two
two cups of currants

Rub the butter and sugar together till very light, then add the yolks of the eggs well beaten, and a part of the flour; beat the whites to a stiff froth and add them with the remainder of the flour; beat well together; cover the bottom of the pan with white paper and butter; bake in a rather slow oven.

Lemon Ice Box Cake (N.D.)

2½ dozen lady fingers
½ pound butter
4 eggs, beaten separately

1 lemon
1 large cup sugar

Cream butter and sugar, add beaten yolks, grated rind and juice of lemon and beaten egg whites. Line tin with lady fingers, add mixture. Dot with bits of pineapple and Maraschino cherries, and alternate mixture cherries and pineapple with lady fingers until all are used.

Let stand on ice 24 hours and serve with whipped cream.

Lemon Jelly Cake 1 (1876)

A half-cup of butter
Two cups of sugar
One cup of sweet milk

Three and a half cups of flour
Four eggs
Two teaspoons of baking powder

Jelly:

Grated rind and juice of one lemon,
Two-thirds of a cup of sugar,

One egg
One tablespoon of cold water.

Set on the stove and stir till it boils; when cool, put between the layers of cake.

Lemon Jelly Cake 2 (1876)

One cup of butter
Two cups of sugar
Three and one-half cups of flour

Whites of eight eggs beaten to a stiff froth
Two-thirds of a cup of cold water
One teaspoon of yeast powder

Beat butter and sugar together till very light; pour in the water, add the flour and whites of eggs alternately, reserving the half cup of flour to mix thoroughly with the yeast powder, and stir in the last thing.

Lemon Jelly:

Grate two lemons
One cup of white sugar
One tablespoon of corn starch

Two eggs
A lump of butter the size of a walnut

Separate the eggs - beat the whites to a stiff froth, the yolks till very light, add the sugar and the lemons to the yolks, mix the corn starch with a little cold water, pour in a half pint of boiling water, mix all together, let it scald, and stir in the whites just before taking it from the stove. Let it cool before putting it between the layers. This jelly is very good between layers of sponge cake, leaving out the eggs.

Lemon Jelly Cake 3 (1876)

One and a half cups of sugar
Two tablespoons of butter
A half-cup of sweet milk

One and a half teaspoons of baking powder
Five eggs, saving two of the whites for jelly
~~Three~~ (2½) cups of flour

Jelly: Whites of two eggs well beaten, one cup of sugar and one lemon.

Lemon Layer Cake (1922)

For Cake:

6 tablespoonfuls sugar
¼ teaspoonful salt
3 tablespoonfuls Crisco

1 teaspoonful baking powder
3 eggs
12 tablespoonfuls flour

Grated rind 1 lemon

For Lemon Filling:

4 tablespoonfuls Crisco
4 yolks of eggs
2 lemons

1 white of egg
¾ cupful sugar
¼ teaspoonful salt

For cake: Put the eggs, sugar, and lemon rind into basin, stand it over pan of boiling water, and beat until warm; then remove from hot water, and continue beating until mixture is stiff and cold; then add flour mixed with baking powder and salt, and pass through sieve, add Crisco melted but cool, taking care to stir very gently, but on no account, beat it. Divide mixture into two small Criscoed and floured layer cake tins and bake ten minutes in moderately hot oven. Turn out and cool, then put together with lemon Filling.
For filling: Beat up eggs in saucepan, add Crisco, salt, grated rinds and strained lemon juice. Stir with wooden spoon over gentle heat until mixture just comes to boiling point. When cold use.
Sufficient for one layer cake.

Lemon Layer Cake (1899)

Take one cupful of sugar
Two eggs
Two tablespoonfuls of butter

Three-fourths of a cup of cold water
Two cupfuls of flour
Two teaspoonfuls of baking-powder

Bake in three shallow tins, and put together in layers, with a jelly made of three-fourths of a cupful of sugar, one egg, and the juice and grated rind of a lemon, stirred thoroughly, and cooked over steam.

Lemon Layer Cake (1920)

1 cup butter
1 cup milk
2 cups sugar

3 cups prepared flour
The whites of 6 eggs

Stir butter and sugar with the right hand to a light white cream, then stir it with a spoon; beat the whites to a stiff froth; add by degrees the sifted flour, the beaten whites and milk alternately to the above mixture; butter 4 good sized jelly tins and line them with buttered paper; then fill in a thin layer of the cake mixture, spread it smooth with a knife and bake in a medium hot oven to a light brown and well done; in the meantime prepare a filling as follows: - Put in a small saucepan the grated rind and juice of 1 lemon, the yolks of 6 eggs, 1 tablespoonful butter and 2 tablespoonfuls water; set the saucepan in a vessel of boiling water and stir till contents thicken; remove from fire when cold, add 1 cup sugar; when cake is done remove it from oven, lay a clean cloth on a table, dust over some powdered sugar and turn the cake out of pan onto the cloth; when cold put 1 layer on a jelly cake dish, bottom side up, and spread over ⅓ of the lemon mixture; put on another layer, upside down, and spread it with the mixture; then treat the third layer the same way; then put on the last layer, right side up, and cover the top with a lemon glaze or dust it with powdered sugar.
NOTE: If this cake is not wanted so large it may be divided into 2 cakes, taking 2 layers for each cake; or use half the quantities. Cream or jelly may be used instead of lemon filling.

Lemon or Orange Cake (1876)

Eight eggs
Two cups of sugar
One cup of butter

A half-cup of milk
Two teaspoons of baking powder
Four cups of flour

Use only the yolks. Bake in layers.

Icing: Beat the whites to a stiff froth and put into a coffee cup of dry powdered sugar, the juice of three lemons and the grated rind of two. For orange cake, make the icing with oranges.

Lemon Snaps (1876)

One cup of butter
Two cups of sugar
Four teaspoons of water
2 eggs

One and a half teaspoons of baking powder
Rind and juice of one lemon
Flour sufficient to roll

After they are cut out put on the white of an egg and sprinkle with sugar.

Lemon Snaps (1894)

One cup butter
Two cups sugar
One third cup milk

Three eggs
Teaspoon soda
Two teaspoons lemon

Lemon Sponge Cake (1899)

Take four eggs
One cup of sugar

One tablespoonful of lemon juice with a little of the grated rind
One cupful of flour

Beat the yolks of the eggs to a foam, then beat in the sugar, adding a little at a time; add the lemon juice and grated rind; beat the whites of the eggs until very stiff, then lightly fold and chop them into the mixture. Sift the flour slowly into the mixture, and carefully fold it in. Do not beat after the flour has been added. Bake in a rather shallow pan in a moderately quick oven.

Lemon Sponge Cake (1869)

Take ten eggs, separate them
A pound of loaf-sugar

Half a pound of flour
The grated peel of two lemons and the juice of one

Beat the yolks with the sugar, the whites alone, when add them and sift in the flour by degrees; beat well, have your pan buttered, and bake with a quick heat either in a stove or Dutch-oven, or a brick oven, the heat should not be quite so great as for light bread - it will bake in about an hour.

Lightened Pone (1869)

Take half a gallon of corn meal, and pour boiling water on one-third of it; mix it together with warm water till it is a thick batter; put in two table-spoonsful of lively yeast, and one of salt; stir it well and set it by the fire to rise; when it begins to open on the top, grease the Dutch-oven and put it to bake, or bake it in a pan in a stove.

Lightning Cake (1820)

1¼ c. flour
⅓ c. fat or oil
¾ c. sugar
2 eggs

3 tsp. baking powder
milk
½ tsp. salt

Sift dry ingredients. Put fat into a cup. Add eggs unbeaten. Fill up cup with milk. Beat 3 minutes. Vary with chocolate, cocoanut, nuts or spices.

Lightnings (1897)
(Blixtar)

Stir a pound of butter together with half a pound sugar until it rises and forms small bladders. Then add 2 whole eggs, beaten with 2 whites, a little pounded cinnamon and bitter almonds, a spoonful gelatine and a pound of flour. Pour out the mixture on flat pans, bake, and cut in squares. This cake can be dried and preserved for some time.

Lily Cake (1876)

Two cups of sugar
One cup of butter
One cup of water
One cup of corn starch

Two cups of flour
Whites of six eggs
One and a half teaspoons of baking powder

Beat the water, starch and baking powder together, and flavour to the taste.

Lily Cake (1893)

One-third cup butter
1 cup sugar
½ cup milk
1¾ cups flour

2½ teaspoons Rumford Baking Powder
3 egg whites
⅓ teaspoon lemon extract
⅔ teaspoon vanilla

Mix as Snow Cake. Cover with chocolate frosting.

Lincoln Cake (1876)

Two cups of sugar
Two eggs
A half-cup of butter
One cup of sweet milk

Four cups of flour
Two teaspoons of baking powder
Flavour to the taste

Lincoln Cake (1893)

One teacup of sugar, ½ cup butter, stir to a cream, then add ½ cup milk and 1 cup flour, stir well, then add a grated lemon and 2 eggs, beat to a froth, then add another cup flour, lastly add one-half teaspoon soda.

Linzer Cake (1904)

½ pound of grated almonds mixed with 1 ounce of bitter ones
½ pound of flour
½ pound of sugar
6 ounces of butter

The yolks of 2 raw eggs
The finely grated yolks of 3 hard-boiled eggs
The thin peel of 1 lemon
2 tablespoonfuls of arrac or rum

Made into a dough and rolled out. Put a border of the crust around the edge and then bake. Spread with any kind of preserved fruit.

Linzer Torte (1910)

1 lb. flour	10 oz. sugar
10 oz. butter	5 eggs
½ lb. blanched, grated sweet almonds	Jam
2 tablespoonsful rum	10 bitter almonds

Cream the butter, then add the beaten-up eggs, sugar, almonds, rum and flour. Stir well, working the paste with the hands finally. Leave in a cool place for an hour, then roll out, place on two buttered sheets of tin and bake a light brown. Allow to cool, spread jam on one portion, cover with the other, and spread over the top layer any icing desired.

Linzer Torte (No. 1) (1873)
(Linzer Cake)

There are many ways of compounding linzer torten, of nearly the same ingredients.
Firstly:

Take three-quarters of a pound of flour	Half a pound of sweet almonds and half an ounce
Half a pound of butter	of bitter ones, blanched and pounded with white of
Six ounces of sugar	egg to keep them from caking together hard
The grated rind of half a lemon	The yolks of eight hard-boiled eggs rubbed smooth

Put the flour on the paste-board; slice the butter on it in little pieces and mix it in with the knife; add the other ingredients, and a few spoonfuls of milk, enough to form a smooth mass, as you would mix a short paste for tarts. Roll out, with dredging, a round cake, not more than a third of an inch thick. A large plate will assist you to cut it quite round. Lay it on a buttered paper on a flat tin; spread over it a thick layer of apricot, raspberry, or other preserve, to within a good half-inch of the edge. Spin out, with rolling. little strings of paste, or cut very narrow strips of it, and crossbar the cake to the edge of the paste. The bars must be the size of a quill-pen in width, and twice that width apart. Begin across the middle of the cake each way, and by laying the bars alternately on each side they will interlace prettily. When the cake is thus covered, moisten round the edge, and lay round on it a band of paste about three-quarters of an inch wide. Notch it round the edge; egg the paste over and dredge it with sugar. Pin a paper round to prevent scorching and bake it in a moderate oven a deep yellow. Remove the paper from the border when cold and place it carefully on a cake-dish or salver.

Linzer Torte (No. 2) (1873)
(Linzer Cake)

Half a pound of almonds blanched and pounded	Three well beaten eggs
Half a pound of sifted sugar	Three-quarters of a pound of flour
Half a pound of butter	

Must be mixed lightly in the manner of tart paste, rolled out thin, and spread on a flat buttered tin. Preserve to be spread over, and either a thin cover of the paste, or narrow strips of the same laid across to form a network; then a thin border of paste laid round the edge. When drawn from the oven, brush the cake over with egg, and dredge with sugar.
It must be baked a pale colour, in a moderate oven.

Linzer Torte (No. 3) (1873)
(Linzer Cake)

A quarter of a pound of almonds powdered rough,
Half a pound of sifted sugar,
Half a pound of butter,
One large or two small eggs,
A drachm of powdered cinnamon,
Threequarters of a pound of flour.

Proceed as in previous recipes.

Another mass:

Three-quarters of a pound of flour
Half a pound of butter
Six ounces of almonds
Six ounces of sugar
The yolks of six eggs

Linzer Torteletten (1873)
(Linzer Tartlets)

Roll out the linzer paste very thin, and, with a round cutter, stamp out the sizes required to line small patty-pans, which must be buttered. Put any sort of preserve in these, and spin across a network of the paste. Brush them over with egg and bake in a slow oven.

Linzer Tourte (1922)

Roll out a bottom from paste German Short Paste. Put on a large raised edge from a strip of the same paste. Fill with a cherry fruit jam, or a compote of pitted cherries. From the same paste form a lattice of strips and cover the cherries. Bake in a medium heat, dust with sugar and serve.

Lise's Sponge Cake (N.D)

2 Eggs
2 teasp. Baking Powder
1 cup Sugar
1/2 cup hot Milk
1 cup sifted Cake Flour
Butter, the size of a walnut

Beat the eggs light with a rotary egg beater. Add sugar slowly, beating continuously. Sift flour and baking powder together and stir into the egg mixture. Melt the butter in the hot milk and pour over the first mixture. Beat well. Bake in 3 layers at 375. Fill with custard and jelly. Cover top with whipped cream.

Little Indian Cakes (1869)

Put a spoonful of lard in a quart of meal, and two tea-spoonsful of salt, pour boiling water on half the meal, stir it; then add as much cold water as will enable you to make it out in cakes of a convenient size, bake on the bake-iron over the fire.

Little Plum Cakes (1876)

Make a dough as for pound cake, then add raisins and currants.
Bake in patty pans.

Loaf Cake (1869)

Take about a pound of risen bread dough, work into it a tea-cup of butter, three eggs beaten, a pound of sugar, a nutmeg grated and a glass of brandy or wine; a pound of raisins, stoned and chopped, should be added after it is well beaten; half a pint of cream slightly warmed, with a table-spoonful of vinegar, and a tea-spoonful of dissolved salaeratus should be stirred in just as you are ready to bake it; also sifted flour enough to make it the proper consistence; bake in a large pan, in a brick oven or stove, and it will require an hour and a quarter.

Loaf Ginger Cake (1893)

Two eggs
One-half cup molasses
Two-thirds cup sugar
Half cup lard or butter
One-half cup milk

Three cups flour
One tablespoon ginger
One teaspoonful cinnamon
One-half tablespoonful soda dissolved in boiling water

Stir in quickly and put in the oven at once.

Löffelbiskuit (1910)

3 eggs

The weight of 3 eggs in flour and in sugar

Beat the yolks with the sugar to a froth and stir in alternately the flour and the whites of eggs, whisked stiffly. Place a piece of well-buttered white paper on a sheet of tin. Twist a sheet of white paper into the shape of a funnel, cut off the tip, fill with the batter and sprinkle on to the buttered paper in little strips about 4 inches long. Dust over with castor sugar and bake a golden colour.

Lord Baltimore Cake (1922)

1 cupful sugar
2½ cupfuls flour
¾ cupful Crisco
2½ teaspoonfuls baking powder

½ cupful cold water
½ teaspoonful salt
1 teaspoonful vanilla extract
6 yolks of eggs

Filling or Frosting:

1 cupful sugar
1 teaspoonful vanilla extract
½ cupful boiling water
½ cupful chopped raisins

2 whites of eggs
½ cupful chopped nut meats
Pinch cream of tartar
5 chopped figs

For cake: Cream Crisco and sugar together. Sift together three times dry ingredients and add alternately with water. Add vanilla, beat mixture well, then fold in beaten yolks of eggs. Divide into two Criscoed and floured layer cake tins and bake in moderate oven twenty-five minutes.
For filling: Put sugar and water into saucepan, stir till boiling, add cream of tartar, then boil until it forms soft ball when tried in cold water, or 240° F.; pour on to stiffly beaten whites of eggs, pouring in steady stream and very slowly, adding while beating vanilla, raisins, nuts, and figs, beat until thick and divide between and on top of cake.
Sufficient for one large layer cake.

Love Cake (1904)

Take 1½ pounds of flour for a puff paste or cream paste, of this make 3 cakes, spread with butter, sugar, cinnamon and bake, to a golden brown. After they are cold spread over the first cake a thick wine cream, over the second a raspberry or currant jelly, and then put one on the other, and on the following day trim the outer edge Smooth with a sharp knife, cover the cake with any icing desired, such as chocolate or sugar and lemon juice, and decorate with preserved fruits.

Lubec Marzapan (1904)

1 pound of fresh, sweet almonds
1 pound of powdered sugar
Orange flower water
Some sugar for dusting

Blanch the almonds and dry them in a cloth, grate and then put. them into a stewpan on a slow fire with orange flower water and stir until they no longer adhere to the hands, but they must not be any dryer. Then put on a bread board dusted with sugar, roll, dusting enough sugar underneath and over the almond paste to prevent sticking, form into cakes with a nice edge or stamp out small figures and bake in a slow oven, not allowing the marzapan to become hard, but keeping it white and soft.

Lucile Shortcake (1909)

Bake flat circles of puff-paste the size of a pie tin; just before serving cover each circle with diced and drained orange pulp and put together like layer cake. Ice the top and serve with the drained orange juice sweetened to taste.

Lunch Cakes (1922)

1 scant cupful sugar
2 cupfuls flour
6 tablespoonfuls Crisco
3 teaspoonfuls baking powder
1 cupful milk
1 teaspoonful salt
2 eggs
1 teaspoonful vanilla extract

Cream Crisco and sugar together, then add well beaten eggs. Sift dry ingredients and add to first mixture alternately with milk. Divide into Criscoed and floured gem pans and bake in moderately hot oven fifteen minutes.
Sufficient for: fifteen cakes.

Luncheon Cake (1913)

Dissolve half an even teaspoonful of saleratus in a little hot water, stir it in a cupful of molasses with a rounding teaspoonful of ground cinnamon, a tablespoonful of melted butter, a pinch of salt and a spoonful of tart fruit juice. Pour in half a cupful of water and stir in a well beaten egg. Add sifted flour enough for a soft batter and bake slowly. Serve warm.

Part 14: M

Macaroon Cake (1904)
Macaroon Cream Cake (1904)
Madeira Cakes (No. 1) (1922)
Madeira Cakes (No. 2) (1922)
Madeira Cakes (No. 3) (1922)
Madeira Cake (1898)
Madison Cake (1876)
Madison Cake (1869)
Madison Fruit Cake (1922)
Magdalenen Torte (1873)
(Magdalen Cake)
Magic Cake (1894)
Mahogany Cake (1820)
Makovy Dort Poppy Seed Cake (1920)
Malted Milk Cake (1922)
Mammy's Ginger Cakes (1913)
Mandarin Cake (1920)
(Gâteau Mandarin)
Mandel or Sudel Torte (1873)
(Almond Cake)
Mandel Kuchen (1873)
Almond Cake (No.1)
Mandel Kuchen (1873)
Almond Cake (No.2)
Mandelbrötchen (1910)
(Almond Cakes)
Mandelkuchen (1910)
(Almond Cake)
Madelines No.1 (1889)
Madelines No.2 (1889)
Mandelringe (1910)
(Almond Rings)
Mandelspäne (1910)
(Almond Chips)
Mandel-Torte (1910)
(Almond Cake)
Mandel Torte (1893)
Almond Cake (No.1)
Mandel Torte (1893)
Almond Cake (No.2)
Mannheim Apple Cake (1904)
Marble Cake 1 (1876)
Marble Cake 2 (1876)
Marble Cake (1911)
Marble Cake (1922)
Marble Cake (1922)
Marble Cake (1913)
Marble Cake (1920)
Marble Cake (1913)
Marble Cake (1913)
Marble Cake (1894)

Marble Cake 1 (1893)
Marble Cake 2 (1893)
Marble Cakes (1922)
Marbled Chocolate Cake (1894)
Margaret's Own Cake (1905)
Margarettes (1911)
Marillan Cakes (1920)
(Gâteaux Marillan)
Marly Cake (1920)
(Gâteau Marly)
Marmalade Cake (1922)
Marmalade Cake (1840)
Mars Cakes (1920)
(Gâteaux Mars)
Marshall Cake (1894)
Maryland Corn Cakes (1869)
Marzipan (1910)
(Marchpane)
Measure Pound Cake (1913)
Meat Short Cake (1893)
Meringue Cake (N.D.)
Meringue Tourte (1922)
Milan Apple Cake (1904)
Milfoil Cake, Pompadour (1920)
(Gâteau Mille-Feuilles, Pompadour)
Milfoil with Preserves (1920)
(Gâteau Mille-Feuilles aux Confitures)
Millionaire Cake (1920)
Miss Farmer's Chocolate Nougat Cake (1909)
Mocha Cake (1911)
Mocha Cake (1922)
Mocha Cake (1920)
(Gâteau Moka)
Mohn-Striezel (1910)
Mohn-Torte (1910)
(Poppy Cake)
Molasses Cake (1913)
Molasses Cake (1920)
Molasses Cake 1 (1894)
Molasses Cake 2 (1894)
Molasses Cake 3 (1894)
(Drop)
Molasses Cake 4 (1894)
(Mrs. Clark's)
Molasses Drop Cake (1894)
Mor's Sur Fløde Kage (N.D.)
(Mother's Sour Cream Cake)
Moravian Sugar Cake (1840)
Mosaic Cake (1820)
Mother Hubbard Cake (1894)
Mother's Cake (1913)

Mountain Cake 1 (1876)
Mountain Cake (1893)
Mousseline Biscuit (1920)
(Biscuit Mousseline)
Mrs. Black's Orange Cake (1909)
Mrs. Carpenter's Wedding Cake (1876)
Mrs. Dodge's Wedding Cake (1876)
Mrs. Harmon's Fruit Cake (1876)
Mrs. Madison's Whim (1893)
Mrs. Mason's Cake (1876)
Mrs. Rorer's Chocolate Cake (1909)
Mrs. Sherman's Almond Cake (1876)
Mrs. Sibley's Raised Cake (1876)
Mrs. Speed's Layer Cake (1876)
Muffins (1905)
Muffins (1911)
Muffins (1911)
Muffins (1890)
Muffins 1 (1894)
Muffins 2 (1894)
Muffins 3 (1894)
(English)
Muffins 4 (1894)
(Graham)
Muffins 5 (1894)
(Graham)
Muffins 6 (1894)
(Indian Meal)
Muffins 7 (1894)
(Raised)
Muffins 8 (1894)
(Raised)

Muffins 9 (1894)
(Rye)
Muffins 10 (1894)
(White)
Muffins 1 (1876)
Muffins 2 (1876)
Muffins 3 (1876)
Muffins 4 (1876)
Muffins 5 (1876)
Muffins 6 (1876)
Muffins (1864)
Muffins 1 (N.D.)
Muffins 2 (N.D.)
Muffins (1922)
Muffins (1893)
Muffins (1893)
Mürbekuchen – I (1910)
Mürbekuchen – II (1910)
Mürber Teig (No. 1) (1873)
(Short Crust for Savoury Pasties)
Mürber Teig (No. 2) (1873)
(Short Crust)
Mürber Teig (No. 3) (1873)
(Short Crust)
Mürber Teig (No. 4) (1873)
(Common Short Crust)
Mush (1876)
Mush Batter Cakes (1913)
(For Invalids)
Mush Flannel Cakes (1869)
Mush, Mush Cakes, and Fried Mush (1869)
Muster Gingerbread (1911)

Macaroon Cake (1904)

¾ pound of sweet and a few bitter almonds are coarsely pounded with a little white of an egg
½ pound of sifted sugar, (sugar and almonds both warmed)
The whites of 5 eggs
Juice and part of the lemon peel or some orange peel grated on sugar

Mix the almonds with the sugar and the whites of the eggs, add the juice and peel of a lemon, spread this on the wafers laid together in the form of a cake. Bake the cake in a moderate oven and spread with jelly.

Macaroon Cream Cake (1904)

Bake a macaroon cake as directed under Almond Cake (No.2) (1904); marmalade, the whites of 6 eggs, ¼ pound of sifted sugar and a little vanilla.
After the cake has cooled it is spread with the preserves, the whites of eggs are beaten to a stiff froth, then mix them with the vanilla and spread over it the preserved fruit. Strew sugar over the frosting and set in the oven until dry.

Madeira Cakes (No. 1) (1922)

One pound four ounces of sugar
One pound one ounce of butter
One pound four ounces of flour
A pinch of baking powder
Nine eggs
A half pint of whites of eggs

Mix same as for pound cakes. Bake in small square tins, with a strip of citron on top.
This mixture is well suited for a light fruit cake.

Madeira Cakes (No.2) (1922)

One pound eight ounces of butter
One pound twelve ounces of sugar
Sixteen eggs
Eight ounces of cornstarch
One pound four ounces of flour
An eighth of an ounce of baking powder
A little milk
The grated rind of one lemon
A little mace

Sift flour, starch and baking powder well together. Mix same as for pound cake, adding the milk when the flour is nearly all mixed in. Bake in 250 degrees Fahrenheit.

Madeira Cakes (No. 3) (1922)

One pound eight ounces of sugar
One pound of butter
Sixteen eggs
One and one-half pounds of flour
Four ounces of cornstarch
The grated rind of one lemon

Mix the same as Madeira Cakes (No.2) (1922). Bake in small pans and dust with sugar before baking.

Madeira Cake (1898)

Ingredients:

6 oz. flour
4 oz. sugar
4 oz. butter
4 eggs

Grated rind of 1 lemon

Method: Beat and strain the eggs, then add gradually the sugar, and dredge in the flour, beating all the time. Add the butter, which must be melted, but not hot, a tea-spoonful at a time, beating thoroughly as each portion is added. Add the lemon rind, beat well, turn the mixture into a cake-tin lined with buttered paper, and bake in a moderate oven, covering the top with paper if it is inclined to burn.
Time: 1 hour.
Sufficient for: 1 cake of moderate size.

Madison Cake (1876)

A half-pound of butter
Three-fourths of a pound of sugar
One pound of flour

Three-fourths of a pound of raisins
Three fourths of a pound of currants
Eight eggs and one gill of cream

Madison Cake (1869)

Take a pound and a quarter of flour
The same of sugar and butter
Five eggs
A pound of raisins, and one of currants
Two glasses of wine or brandy

Mace
Nutmeg
A tea-spoonful of salaeratus, dissolved in a pint of new milk

Bake it as pound cake.

Madison Fruit Cake (1922)

One and one-half pounds of sugar
One of butter
Twelve eggs
A half pint of cream
Two pounds of flour

One grated nutmeg
One pound of currants
One pound of seeded raisins
A half-pound of citron

Mix like other fruit cakes.

Magdalenen Torte (1873)
Magdalen Cake

Stir six ounces of butter to a cream. Add by degrees ten eggs, half a pound of sifted sugar, then half a pound of fine flour. Stir all briskly for half an hour; then stir in an ounce and a half of candied orange-peel sliced very thin. Butter a cake-mould, strew it with sliced almonds, fill in the mass, strew sliced almonds on the top, and bake it at once.

Magic Cake (1894)

One cup sugar
Half-cup butter
One and a half cups flour
Three eggs

Three tablespoons milk
Half teaspoon soda
Teaspoon cream tartar
Flavour with vanilla or nutmeg

Mahogany Cake (1820)

1.

4 sq. bitter chocolate
1 egg
½ c milk
1 c. brown sugar

Cook in double boiler till thick and creamy.

2.

1 c. brown sugar
½ c. milk or water
2 c. prepared cake or pastry flour sifted 3 times before measuring
2 eggs
1 tsp. soda
2 tsp. baking powder
1 tsp. vanilla
½ c. fat

Mix by cake method, adding first mixture when cool.
Bake in two large or three medium layers. Put into very moderate oven, 200 to 250, and increase gradually to 300 up to 350 until done.
Use mocha filling or any other filling and icing.

Makovy Dort Poppy Seed Cake (1920)

½ cup poppy seed (ground)
1 cup milk
¾ cup butter
1½ cups sugar
2 cups sifted flour
1½ tsp. baking powder
4 egg whites (well beaten)
1 tsp. vanilla

Soak poppy seed in milk for 2 hours. Cream butter and add sugar. Add poppy seed and milk. Add dry ingredients slowly. Fold in beaten egg whites. Bake in layers or loaf pan. Bake at 350 degrees.

Filling for Layers or Frosting for Loaf:

1 tbsp. corn starch
1½ cups milk
¾ cup sugar
4 egg yolks
½ cup chopped nuts
1 tsp. vanilla

Dissolve corn starch in a little of the milk and cook over double boiler with milk until mixture thickens. Add sugar, beaten egg yolks and chopped nuts. (½ recipe is sufficient to ice loaf cake.)

Malted Milk Cake (1922)

Cream one-half cup butter, add one cup sugar gradually. Beat in one egg; then add three heaping teaspoons chocolate malted milk, one-half teaspoon vanilla, one-fourth teaspoon salt. Add one teaspoon soda to one cup sour milk and then add alternately with two cups sifted flour to the first mixture. Bake in buttered layer-cake pans. Put together and cover with white icing.

Mammy's Ginger Cakes (1913)

Beat four eggs very light with a good pinch of salt and a cup of coffee sugar. Add three cups of rich molasses, and a cup of boiling water with two teaspoonfuls soda dissolved in it. Mix well in two tablespoonfuls pounded ginger. Sift five pints of flour with a teaspoonful of salt, rub into it lightly two cups sweet lard, then add the molasses mixture and knead to a firm dough, adding more flour if needed or, if too stiff, a little sweet milk. Roll out half an inch thick, cut into big squares, bake in a quick oven, and brush over the tops while blazing hot a little butter, molasses and boiling water. Let stand in a warm place until dry. These might properly be called First Monday Ginger Cakes, since our Mammy made them to sell upon that day to the crowds which came to court, thereby turning many an honest fip or picayune

Mandarin Cake (1920)
(Gâteau Mandarin)

Fasten on a dish a wooden bottom about an inch thick and cover it with white paper. Heat a medium-sized biscuit mold, grease it over with melted veal kidney suet mixed with melted butter, and turn it over to drain out all the fat, then glaze with sugar mixed with fecula. Beat up vigorously in a basin twelve egg-yolks with three-quarters of a pound of powdered sugar, having one quarter of it grated on two mandarins, and add a grain of salt. When this preparation becomes creamy, incorporate into it ten or eleven beaten whites, and at the same time let fall into it through a sieve a pound of fine flour and fecula mixed together; carefully work without breaking, and with it fill the mold nearly to the top; surround the exterior of the top with a band of buttered paper, then lay it on a small baking sheet covered with a thick layer of hot cinders, and push it into a moderate oven to bake for one hour, carefully turning the baking sheet around at frequent intervals. On removing the biscuit from the oven detach it from the top, inserting a small knife around the edges, and unmould on a grate, and when perfectly cold cut the bottom off straight, then let it get stale for seven or eight hours. Should the surface of the biscuit not be smooth, or else too brown, stand it upright on the grate and brush over entirely with apricot marmalade, then cover with raw vanilla icing; when this is dry, cut a round piece from the cut side, about a quarter of an inch from the edge, remove this piece and empty out the biscuit as neatly as possible, not approaching the edges too closely. Cut across through the center about twelve small, fresh and sound mandarins; remove the insides neatly from the peel, keeping these as whole as possible, and lay them on one side; suppress the white pith and seeds from the fruit, and crush the pulp to rub it through a sieve; put this into a vessel and mix with it a few spoonfuls of champagne, some syrup, a small bunch of lemon peel and a few spoonfuls of calf's foot jelly, sweetened and clarified; let infuse together for fifteen minutes. With a vegetable spoon scoop out all the white part from the halved mandarin peels, and incrust them in a thick layer of pounded, slightly salted ice, suppressing the lemon peel from the preparation; thicken it lightly while stirring on ice, and with it fill the empty peels; brush them over with jelly and keep on ice for a quarter of an hour. Open five or six oranges from the stalk end; with a tin tube empty them out entirely, suppressing all the white pith; incrust them in pounded, unsalted ice, and then fill them with clear jelly flavoured with orange, alternated with layers of blanc-mange, also flavoured with orange; harden both of these preparations on ice. Now fill the empty biscuit with well-drained and sweetened whipped cream flavoured with Curacoa and orange peel. Close the opening with the removed piece and dress on the center of the wooden bottom. Surround with the filled halved mandarins, and the base of the dish with the oranges cut in six, then cut off straight on one end so as to maintain them upright.

Mandel or Sudel Torte (1873)
(Almond Cake)

Stir half a pound of butter to a cream. Add half a pound of sifted sugar and two well-beaten eggs, then half a pound of almonds blanched and pounded, and, by degrees, half a pound of flour. Stir the whole briskly. Put it in a well buttered mould and bake it in a quick oven.

Mandel Kuchen (No.1) (1873)
(Almond Cake)

Blanch and pound half a pound of almonds; beat them well with a quarter of a pound of sifted sugar and the yolks of eight eggs. Soak the crumb of two rolls in cold milk, press it out, and add it with two ounces of thinly-cut candied peel to the almond mixture. Stir all briskly, then add the whites of six eggs whipped to a snow and well stirred in. Bake it in a shallow mould well buttered and sprinkled with raspings and crumbs. When the cake is done turn it out, stick it all over with blanched almonds cut in slices, half the length showing; sift plenty of sugar over when cold.

Mandel Kuchen (No. 2) (1873)
(Almond Cake)

Blanch half a pound of almonds and cut each one lengthways into four or five shreds; peel a lemon thin and cut the peel into thread-like strips. Boil this and the almonds with the juice of the lemon and a quarter of a pound of sugar, until it thickens like a syrup. Meantime, spread a flat tin with good tart-paste, pour the syrup away from the almonds and peel; spread the latter over the paste, and bake in a quick oven. When cold, pour the syrup over the cake.

Mandelbrötchen (1910)
(Almond Cakes)

10 oz. sweet almonds
3 eggs
2 extra yolks
4 oz. sugar
3 ground cloves

½ lb. flour
4 oz. butter
A pinch of cinnamon
A pinch of ground ginger

Cream the butter, add the sugar and the eggs and stir 30 minutes. Then add the spices, almonds and lastly the flour. Place in little heaps on a buttered tin and bake a golden brown.

Mandelkuchen (1910)
(Almond Cake)

¾ lb. butter
3 oz. sweet almonds
6 oz. sugar
6 eggs

1 lb. flour
Grated rind of 1 lemon
½ oz. baking powder

Cream half the butter, then stir it well with the beaten-up yolks, sugar, grated lemon peel and the flour, the latter mixed with the baking powder and sifted. Finally stir in the whisked whites of eggs. Spread about ¼ inch high on a buttered tin, sprinkle over with sugar and coarsely-chopped almonds, scatter the remaining butter in small lumps over it and bake in a moderate oven for 30 minutes.

Madelines No.1 (1889)

These delicious little cakes can be either made of very rich batter, in which case they can be kept much longer, or after a simpler receipt.

Three-quarters pound of butter
One-pound sugar
One-pound flour
Nine eggs

Half-wineglass brandy
Grated peel of one lemon
Half grated nutmeg
Half teaspoonful Royal baking powder

Stir butter to a cream, add sugar, beat well. Add the beaten yolks of eggs alternately, with half the flour, then the beaten whites with the balance of flour. The brandy, spices, and lemon may be added to sugar and butter, when beaten well. Sift the baking powder in the flour before adding eggs. Butter two or three dripping pans well. Pour in the batter half an inch thick. Fill as many pans as the oven will hold. The mixture will bake in ten minutes in a moderate oven.

When it has been out of the oven two minutes, cut it in squares with a warm knife. Spread each square with either strawberry, raspberry, apricot, or green gage jam (the very acid kinds will not do) or chopped crystalized fruits or chopped blanched nuts. On this drop from a spoon a thick layer of soft frosting, taking care that it does not run down the sides. Make the frosting as follows:

To the white of one egg, take a heaping cup of powdered sugar, stir it in without first beating the egg, add three drops of rose water, five of vanilla, and the juice of a quarter of a lemon.

Madelines No. 2 (1889)

One cup butter
Two cups sugar
Two-thirds cup milk
Six eggs
Two small teaspoonfuls baking powder

Two and a half cups flour
Flavour with half a glass brandy
Half a nutmeg
The grated rind of a lemon

Bake as directed in preceding receipt and use the jam and frosting in the same way. These are very delicate and light but will not keep as long as madelines made of richer cake.

Mandelringe (1910)
(Almond Rings)

½ lb. sweet almonds
6 oz. sugar
6 oz. flour
4 ground cloves

15 bitter almonds
4 yolks
1 teaspoonful ground cinnamon
½ teaspoonful ground ginger

Beat the yolks and sugar 15 minutes to a froth and stir in the cinnamon, cloves and ginger and then the grated almonds and the flour. With this paste make little rings, brush them over with yolk of egg and poppyseeds (or chopped almonds, if preferred) and bake on a buttered tin in a moderate oven.

Mandelspäne (1910)
(Almond Chips)

¼ lb. sweet almonds
¼l lb. sugar

1 oz. potato flour
2 whites of eggs

Beat the whites and sugar for 10 minutes, then stir in the flour and grated almonds and mix well. Spread ¼ inch thick on rice paper and bake on a buttered tin in a moderate oven. Remove at once from tin and, while warm, twist round a rolling pin to dry in a curve.

Mandel-Torte (1910)
(Almond Cake)

1 lb. sugar
10 bitter almonds
8 eggs

1 lb. sweet almonds
4 oz. potato flour

Blanch the almonds and grate them finely. Beat the sugar and yolks ½ to ¾ hour to a froth and stir in alternately the potato flour, whisked whites of eggs and grated almonds.
Fill a well-buttered tin and bake 1 hour.

Mandel Torte (No.1) (1893)

(Almond Cake)

Blanch and pound quite fine six ounces of sweet almonds. Stir the yolks of nine eggs, with six ounces of sifted sugar, half an hour. Then add the almonds, and, by degrees, two ounces of fine flour. Add the whites of the nine eggs, whisked to a snow. Stir all briskly together. Butter thickly a rather flat cake-tin, or mould, and bake in a well heated oven.

Mandel Torte (No. 2) (1893)
(Almond Cake)

A pound of blanched almonds must be well pounded with a little white of egg, to keep them from oiling. Then add a pound of sifted sugar, and, by degrees, the yolks of eighteen eggs. Stir briskly for half an hour. Add the whites of nine eggs whipped to a snow. Butter thickly a large mould, strew a lining of bread-crumbs on the butter, pour in the mass, and bake it an hour.
Small tins, or patty-pans, buttered, sprinkled with crumbs, filled with the above mass, and baked in a moderate oven, are very good.

Mannheim Apple Cake (1904)

3 ounces of creamed butter
6 ounces of sugar
5 whole eggs

The peel of ¼ of a lemon
½ pound of flour

Are stirred to a light dough, which is put into a buttered pan, sprinkled with grated roll, covered thickly with apple slices.
Pour over this an icing made of 1 cupful of sour cream, 3 eggs, sugar and vanilla. Bake in a moderate oven.

Marble Cake 1 (1876)

Spice Part:

A half-cup of butter
A half-cup of molasses
One cup of brown sugar
Yolks of four eggs
A half-cup of sweet milk

Two cups of flour
One teaspoon of baking powder
One teaspoon each of allspice, cinnamon and nutmeg
A half teaspoon of cloves

White Part:

One and a half cups of white sugar
A half-cup of butter
Whites of four eggs beaten light

A half-cup of sweet milk
Two cups of flour
One large teaspoon of baking powder

Marble Cake 2 (1876)

White Part:

One cup of butter
Three cups of sugar
One cup of milk

Two teaspoons of baking powder
Five cups of flour
The whites of eight eggs

Spice Part:

One cup of butter
Two cups of brown sugar
One cup of molasses
Yolks of three eggs

White of one egg
One teaspoon of each kind of spice
Three teaspoons of baking powder

Put them into the pan alternately; a white layer on the bottom and top.

Marble Cake (1911)

1 cup sugar
½ cup butter
1 cup milk
2½ cups flour

1 egg
1 teaspoon soda
2 teaspoons cream tartar

Take ⅓ of mixture and add to it ½ teaspoon each of cinnamon, cloves, nutmeg, and allspice, with ½ cup raisins. Put in pan in alternate spoonfuls.

Marble Cake (1922)

2 cupfuls sugar
2 tablespoonfuls melted chocolate
1 cupful Crisco
3½ cupfuls flour
1 teaspoonful powdered cinnamon
4 eggs

1 cupful milk
½ teaspoonful grated nutmeg
3 teaspoonfuls baking powder
½ teaspoonful powdered allspice
2 tablespoonfuls molasses
1 teaspoonful salt

Cream Crisco, add gradually the sugar, yolks of eggs beaten until thick, flour, salt, baking powder, milk, and egg whites beaten to stiff froth. Mix carefully and to one-third the mixture add spices, molasses, and melted chocolate. Drop in Criscoed cake pan alternately a spoonful of each mixture and draw spoon through once or twice to make colours lie in lines. Bake in moderately hot oven one hour.
Sufficient for: one medium-sized cake

Marble Cake (1913)

Light Part:

Cream together half a cupful of sugar and a heaping teaspoonful of butter. Add half a cupful of milk and the beaten whites of two eggs. Sift a rounding teaspoonful of baking powder with a large cupful of flour. Stir all well, adding flour or milk if necessary.

Dark Part:

Cream together half a cupful of brown sugar and a rounding teaspoonful of butter. Add one quarter of a cupful each of molasses and milk, an even teaspoonful each of ground cinnamon and grated nutmeg, and half an even teaspoonful of allspice.
Prepare the flour as for the light part, adding half an even teaspoonful of saleratus dissolved in the beaten yolks of the eggs. Stir well together.
Grease a cake pan and put in spoonfuls of each colour alternately. Bake in a moderate oven, covering for about ten minutes, that it may not brown too quickly.

Marble Cake (1920)

Take the same mixture as for Plain Cake and divide it into 3 equal parts; add to one part some red sugar or a little prepared cochineal, to give it a fine pink tint; stir into another part 3 tablespoonfuls grated chocolate and leave the third part plain; butter a large cake pan and line it with buttered paper; fill the pan about ½ inch deep with the plain batter and drop upon this in 3 or 4 places 1 spoonful of the dark and pink batters; pour in more plain batter; then drop in the pink and brown the same way; continue until all is used; the pink may be omitted if the colouring is not handy; bake the same as Plain Cake; when done ice the cake with boiled chocolate glaze.

Marble Cake (1913)

Make up egg-yolks into spice cake, beat the whites very light, and add them to three cups of sifted sugar, beaten smooth in a large cup of creamed butter. Put in a wineglass of whiskey or brandy, then add three cups and a half flour sifted three times with a heaping teaspoonful baking powder. Put the light and dark batter by alternate spoonfuls in pans well-buttered and papered, let rise and bake the same as spice cake.
Else bake the light and dark batter in layers, put together with any good filling, and frost with caramel frosting.

Marble Cake (1913)

1/3 cup Cottolene
1 cup sugar
2 eggs
1/2 cup milk
1/2 teaspoon cinnamon

1/2 teaspoon nutmeg
1/4 teaspoon salt
1-3/4 cups flour
3 teaspoons baking powder
1 tablespoon molasses

Process: Cream Cottolene, add sugar gradually, yolks of eggs beaten until thick and light, flour sifted with baking powder, alternately with milk. Fold in whites of eggs beaten until stiff. Turn one-third of this batter into a bowl and add to it molasses and spices. Pour into well-greased pan, alternating light and dark mixtures to give it the "marbled" appearance. Bake forty to forty-five

Marble Cake (1894)

One-half cup butter
One cup sugar
One-half cup milk
One and three-fourths cups pastry flour

Whites of four eggs
One-half teaspoon cream tartar
One-fourth teaspoon soda

In another dish mix:

One-half cup molasses
One cup sugar
One-half cup butter
Two and one-half cups flour
One-fourth cup milk
Yolks of four eggs

One teaspoon cinnamon
Three-fourths teaspoon cloves
One teaspoon nutmeg
Little mace
One-half teaspoon cream tartar
One-fourth teaspoon soda

Put spices and cream tartar and soda in the flour; put a layer of dark mixture into the pan, then one of the light and alternate until all is used. Draw a fork through the sides and middle of the whole once.

Marble Cake 1 (1893)

Three eggs
1 cup butter
1 cup sugar
½ cup milk

1 teaspoon soda
2 of cream tartar
4 cups flour

Take part of the batter and flavour with spices and add 1 cup of molasses.

Marble Cake 2 (1893)

(White part)

Whites 4 eggs
1 cup of sugar
½ cup butter
½ cup milk

2 teaspoons baking powder
2½ cups flour
Lemon

(Dark part)

Yolks 4 eggs
1 cup of brown sugar
½ cup molasses
½ butter

½ cup sour milk
Spices,
1 teaspoonful soda
1½ cup flour

Put in pan alternately.

Marble Cakes (1922)

Take white cake mixtures Silver Cake (No. 1) (1922) or Silver Cake (No. 2) (1922); colour one fourth part pink, and one fourth part chocolate; put a thin layer of the white mixture on the bottom, put the other colours in turns in the center; finish the top with a thin layer of white cake and bake.
Ice with a soft water icing; colour a little of the icing pink and chocolate, put each in a paper cornet and draw straight lines in alternate colours across the soft white icing, then draw the knife in straight lines or in zig zag across the coloured strips while the icing is soft.

Marbled Chocolate Cake (1894)

One cup butter
Two cups powdered sugar
Three cups flour
Four eggs

One cup sweet milk
Half teaspoon soda
One teaspoon cream tartar

After this is well mixed take out one and one-half cups of it and mix with it enough chocolate previously melted in a few drops of hot water to give a dark colour, then put in pans in separate layers and bake half an hour.

Margaret's Own Cake (1905)

5 eggs
1 cup granulated sugar
1 cup of flour

1 pinch of salt
1/2 teaspoonful of lemon-juice, or vanilla

Separate the eggs and beat the yolks very light and foamy; then put in the sugar which you have sifted, a little at a time, and the flour in the same way, but put them in in turn, first sugar, then flour, and so on. Then put in the flavouring, and last fold in the whites of the eggs, beaten very stiff. Bake in a buttered pan.

Margarettes (1911)

One-half pound of peanuts
One pound of dates chopped fine

One Cup of milk

One cup of milk in the dates, and boil, add peanuts.
Make a boiled icing. Take the long branch crackers, spread the filling between the crackers, put on the icing, and put in the oven to brown.

Marillan Cakes (1920)
(Gâteaux Marillan)

Bake a baba in a flat mold having a cover, or else in a tin mold covered with another. Moisten the crust lightly with baba syrup and cut it two-thirds across without detaching it at the further end; empty the crumbs out partly and fill this double crust with flavoured whipped cream or else with smooth cooked Italian cream. The top and around the base of the cake should be covered with liquid apricot marmalade laid on with a brush.

Marly Cake (1920)
(Gâteau Marly)

Butter and glaze two dome-shaped pointed molds, seven inches high by six inches in diameter; fill them almost to the top with a lemon-flavored biscuit preparation, the same as for mandarin cakes, and surround the opening with a band of buttered paper; stand them upright on a raised-edge baking sheet and bake the biscuits in a slow oven for one hour. Remove and unmould on a pastry grate, and when cold cut the bottoms off straight and let get stale for the next twelve hours. Now lay the cakes on a grate, placing them on the cut end and brush them over lightly with apricot marmalade, then cover one of them entirely with pink icing and the other with white. Two minutes after, without letting it get dry, divide each biscuit into eight pieces from top to bottom, pointed on the tops, and when the icing is thoroughly dry take up the pieces one by one and reconstruct them into one biscuit, only being careful to alternate the colours, having first a pink piece and then a white one; empty the inside of the biscuit as neatly as possible and fill the center with St. Honore cream, to which pounded almonds and a little kirsch have been added, dressing it in layers alternated with cut-up macaroons soaked in rum. Invert the biscuit on a cold dish covered over with a folded napkin.

Marmalade Cake (1922)

½ cupful sugar
½ teaspoonful salt
½ cupful Crisco
1 egg

1 cupful marmalade
2 cupfuls flour
1½ teaspoonfuls baking powder
½ teaspoonful powdered ginger

Sift salt, flour, and baking powder into basin, rub in Crisco with finger tips, add ginger and egg well beaten. Knead lightly to smooth paste and divide into two pieces. Roll out pieces and line Criscoed dinner plate with one of them. Spread over with marmalade, cover with remaining piece of paste, pinch neatly round the edges and bake in moderate oven half an hour. Cut like pie and serve hot or cold.
Sufficient for: eight pieces.

Marmalade Cake (1840)

Make a batter as for queen-cake and bake it in small tin rings on a griddle. Beat white of egg, and powdered loaf-sugar according to the preceding receipt, flavouring it with lemon. When the batter is baked into cakes, and they are quite cool, spread over each a thick layer of marmalade, and then heap on with a spoon tire icing or white of egg and sugar. Pile it high and set the cakes in a moderate oven till the icing is coloured of a very pale brown.
Instead of small ones you may bake the whole in one large cake

Mars Cakes (1920)
(Gâteaux Mars)

Roll out some foundation paste to an eighth of an inch in thickness; cut this into three-inch wide bands and cover these with a layer of almond cream mixed with as much vanilla pastry cream; bake in a slow oven, and when done and cold mask over with a layer of meringue, having it three-quarters of an inch thick; smooth the sides and tops well. Slit these bands across one inch and a quarter apart with the tip of a small knife and decorate each section with halved almonds or thin slices of almonds cut lengthwise and laid on symmetrically in imitation of branches, having a dry currant between each one. Cut the cakes where they have been slit, place them on a baking sheet, dredge with sugar and set into a slack oven to colour the meringue; the bands may be left whole and divided where they were slit while yet hot.

Marshall Cake (1894)

Two and a half cups sugar
One cup butter
One cup milk

Four cups flour
Four eggs
Teaspoon soda and one of cream tartar

Bake in two sheets plain; for the third sheet, add two tablespoons molasses, one cup raisins, one cup currants, one-quarter pound citron, all kinds spices. Wet this sheet with the white of an egg and place between the light ones.

Maryland Corn Cakes (1869)

Mix a pint of corn meal with rich milk, a little salt, and an egg, it should be well beaten with a spoon, and made thin enough to pour on the iron; take in cakes the size of a breakfast plate; butter and send them hot to table.

Marzipan (1910)
(Marchpane)

1 lb. sweet almonds
1 lb. castor sugar

1 oz. bitter almonds
4 tablespoonsful rosewater

Blanch the almonds and grate them finely. Then mix them well with the sugar and rosewater, kneading well, so that the paste can be easily rolled out. Form into a ball and leave for some hours, before working up into various shapes or spreading, thinly rolled out, on Torten or Pfefferkuchen.

Measure Pound Cake (1913)

Cream well together, one cup butter, one and three-quarter cups sugar, when very light, drop in an egg-yolk unbeaten, beat hard, put in another yolk, beat again hard, then another, and repeat the hard beating. When very light add alternately two and one-half cups flour, and one cup milk, mix well, then add half a cup flour sifted three times with three even teaspoonfuls baking powder. Follow this with the egg-whites beaten stiff.

Flavour with brandy - a tablespoonful and a half. Bake in a moderate oven about an hour. Serve with any approved pudding sauce or use as other cake. Nearly as good as the pound cake of our grandmothers.

Meat Short Cake (1893)

Make a crust like biscuit, using a little more butter: divide in halves, roll about half an inch thick; put in a biscuit pan spread with butter, roll other half and lay over it, bake in hot oven. Chop pieces of cold meat coarsely, put in stew pan with cold gravy, if you have it, if not, use water; season with butter and Crystaline salt and thicken with a little flour; simmer until ready to use. Split the cake when done and pour in the warm meat and gravy; put on top crust and send to the table immediately. Cold turkey or chicken are nice used in this way.

Meringue Cake (N.D.)

½ cup butter and ½ cup sugar creamed together
1 cup flour
¼ teaspoon salt

1 teaspoon baking powder
3 egg yolks
5 tablespoons milk

Meringue:

3 egg whites beaten stiff with pinch of salt
½ cup blanched almonds or walnuts

1 cup sugar added slowly

Spread batter in layer pan, spread meringue over batter and bake slowly one-half hour.

Custard:

1 beaten egg
1 cup sugar mixed with two scant tablespoons corn starch

1 teaspoon vanilla
1 cup milk

Cook in double boiler until thick. When cake is cold cut in half, spread custard between halves to make layer cake. Serve as dessert with whipped cream.

Meringue Tourte (1922)

Bake a bottom with raised edge from Bottom Paste for Large Cakes and Layers (1922) or German Short Paste (1922). Spread with raspberry jam. Take Meringue Paste (No.1) (1922) and with bag and tube put on a border and network, dust with sugar and colour nicely in the oven.

Milan Apple Cake (1904)

Bake a cake as given under Linzer Cake (1904). In the meantime, stew some nice cooking apples in wine with sugar and lemon peel until tender, but they must not fall to pieces. Also scald 6 ounces of rice and boil with cream, sugar and vanilla until tender and thick and stir until cold. The apples must be cold before putting them on the cake, which must also be cold. Spread the cake with apricot marmalade, mix a glassful of Marascino through the rice and spread evenly on the cake, lay the apple slices on this, cover with thinned apple jelly and dot the cake with preserved cherries.

Milfoil Cake, Pompadour (1920)
(Gâteau Mille-Feuilles, Pompadour)

Prepare some rounds of puff paste the same way and size as the milfoil with preserves; cover each of these with vanilla-flavoured English cream, dredging the top with a salpicon of candied fruits cut in one-eighth inch squares and macerated in kirsch. After the cake is formed, pare it round and cover with firmly beaten and well-drained whipped cream sweetened with fine vanilla sugar. Dress this in a dome-form on top, and decorate through a cornet with whipped cream tinted a pale pink; strew with thin green fillets of pistachios. Slip the cake on a flat two inches wider than itself and covered with strawberry icing, sprinkled with red sugar; surround the base of the cake with small lady bouchées iced with strawberry.

Milfoil with Preserves (1920)
(Gâteau Mille-Feuilles aux Confitures)

This requires some puff paste of twelve turns; divide it into six-ounce pieces, roll them out to three-sixteenths of an inch in thickness and cut into rounds seven inches in diameter; lay these on baking sheets slightly moistened with cold water applied with a brush; from the center of each piece remove a two-inch diameter round and leave these to rest in a cold place for half an hour; bestrew lightly with sugar, prick and bake in a slack oven. After taking them out detach from the sheets and lay them at once on grates to get cold, then stand one on top of the other intercalated with a layer either of currant jelly, apricot marmalade or peach marmalade; pare the cake neatly into a perfect round and cover with Italian meringue on the edges. Sprinkle over it a mixture made of equal parts of Mocha sugar, half of which is coloured with carmine with a little syrup, chopped almonds, chopped pistachios and currants. Lay the cake on a tart dish and push into a moderate oven for a few moments to dry the meringue without colouring it, then place it on a round made of a three-eighths of an inch thickness of frolle paste, and iced over with pink icing, strewn with pink sugar, it having a border of gum paste or English paste. Dress the milfoil either on a napkin or on a socle, and garnish around with small bouchées filled with currant jelly, these being called Wells of Love.

Millionaire Cake (1920)

Cream the yolks of three eggs with one-half cup powdered sugar for ten minutes, add one-half teaspoonful vanilla and three quarters of a cup of flour sifted with one-fourth of a teaspoonful of baking powder and the beaten whites of the three eggs, butter six small layer cake tins and put in the mixture. Bake in a quick oven ten minutes.
Filling: Put two tablespoonfuls of chocolate and three tablespoonfuls sugar with one-half cup strong coffee and boil for ten minutes, when almost cold add one-half cup well-washed butter, teaspoon vanilla in small portions; when thick and creamy spread between layers and on top and decorate with candied cherries.

Miss Farmer's Chocolate Nougat Cake (1909)

1/4 a cup of butter	3 teaspoonfuls of baking powder
1-1/2 cups of powdered sugar	1/2 teaspoonful of vanilla
1 egg	2 squares of chocolate, melted
1 cup of milk	1/2 a cup of powdered sugar
2 cups of bread flour	2/3 a cup of almonds blanched and shredded

Cream the butter, add gradually one and one-half cups of sugar, and egg unbeaten; when well mixed, add two-thirds milk, flour mixed and sifted with baking powder, and vanilla. To melted chocolate, add one-third a cup of powdered sugar, place on range, add gradually remaining milk, and cook until smooth. Cool slightly and add to cake mixture. Bake fifteen to twenty minutes in round layer-cake pans. Put between layers and on top of cake White Mountain Cream sprinkled with almonds

Mocha Cake (1911)

1 cup sugar	1 cup flour

1 teaspoon cream of tartar
½ teaspoon soda
1 large teaspoon melted butter

½ cup boiling milk
2 eggs, not beaten

Sift flour, sugar, cream of tartar, soda together twice. Add butter, then break in eggs, stir. Add milk last. Stir briskly. Bake in moderate oven 20 minutes.

Frosting:

1 cup powdered sugar
Small piece of butter
2 tablespoons coffee

2 teaspoons cocoa
½ teaspoon vanilla

Cream butter and sugar. Add cocoa, then coffee and vanilla. Add more sugar, if necessary. Spread with knife dipped in hot water.

Mocha Cake (1922)

Sift 6 cups flour with 1 teaspoon baking powder into a basin
Add 1 teaspoon each of powdered cinnamon, nutmeg, and cloves

1 cup brown sugar
½ teaspoonful salt
1 cup Crisco

Rub well together

Add ½ a cup golden syrup
1 cup strong cold coffee
2 well beaten eggs

1 cup currants
1 cup sultana raisins

Mix well together.
Pour into Criscoed and papered tin and bake in moderate

Mocha Cake (1920)
(Gâteau Moka)

Deposit in a vessel half a pound of sugar, six egg-yolks and one whole egg; beat for fifteen minutes to have it light, then add six ounces of flour and two ounces of fecula sifted together, also two tablespoonfuls of brandy, six ounces of melted butter, and lastly six well-whipped egg whites. Bake this in a buttered and paper-lined pound-cake mold; as soon as done remove, unmould on a grate and leave it there until perfectly cold. Now pare the cake very straight and cut it across in two even parts; fill it with a three-eighths of an inch-thick layer of Mocha cream; cover the top and sides with the same and decorate the surface through a channeled socket pocket, using more of the cream; dredge with Mocha sugar. Leave the cake in a cool place until required for serving.
Mocha Sugar: Is made by pounding loaf sugar in a mortar and passing it through a six-mesh sieve cloth.

Mohn-Striezel (1910)

For the dough:

1½ lb. flour
2 oz. sugar
½ pint milk

2 oz. yeast
3 oz. butter
2 eggs

In addition:

1 lb. blue poppy seeds	6 oz. sugar
2 oz. sweet almonds	2 oz. currants
3 oz. butter	3 tablespoonsful milk

Prepare the yeast as in " Napfkuchen" recipe with ½ lb. flour, the milk, flour, a little sugar and allow to rise. Then mix it well with the remaining flour, sugar and the butter (melted) and stand the dough to rise.

When well risen, roll out thinly, brush over with butter and spread on it a paste, made of the poppy seeds and other ingredients stated. Roll together and place on a sheet of tin, well buttered and sprinkled with flour, to rise still further. Then brush over with egg and bake in a medium oven. When taken out of the oven, brush over again with hot butter and sprinkle thickly with sugar.

The poppy must be soaked for an hour, then boiled for 10 minutes in 1-pint milk, shaken on to a sieve to drain and pounded in a mortar before mixing with the other ingredients.

Mohn-Torte (1910)
(Poppy Cake)

½ lb. white poppy seeds	¾ lb. sugar
¾ pint milk	8 eggs
¼ lb. sweet almonds	

Scald the poppy seeds, boil in the milk and drain on a sieve. Then pound in a mortar. Beat the sugar and yolks to a froth, add the poppy seeds and grated almonds and, lastly, stir in the stiffly-whisked whites of eggs. Fill a well-buttered shallow tin (with movable bottom) lined with breadcrumbs and bake in a moderate oven for 1 hour.

Molasses Cake (1913)

Stir a tablespoonful of melted butter into two thirds of a cupful of molasses with half a cupful of sugar and a well beaten egg. Dissolve half an even teaspoonful of saleratus in a tablespoonful of hot water. Stir the ingredients thoroughly and pour in two-thirds of a cupful of (liquid) coffee and add about one and one-half cupfuls of flour. Bake in a loaf tin.

Molasses Cake (1920)

One cup molasses	½ tablespoonful ginger
½ cup butter	2 cups flour sifted with 1 teaspoonful baking powder
2 eggs	
½ cup milk	

Mix and bake the same as above.

Molasses Cake 1 (1894)

One cup molasses	Teaspoon soda
Two cups sugar	One cup boiling water
One-half cup butter or lard	Salt and ginger

To be made soft and dropped from the spoon.

Molasses Cake 2 (1894)

One-pint molasses
Six ounces butter
Three well beaten eggs
One-half pint milk
One teaspoon soda

Warm molasses enough to melt butter, dissolve soda in milk, mix, add eggs, thicken with flour to the consistency of pound cake. Flavour with lemon.

Molasses Cake 3 (1894)
(Drop)

One cup molasses
One cup sugar
One cup warm water
Teaspoon soda
Flour enough to drop from a spoon
One tablespoon butter

Molasses Cake 4 (1894)
(Mrs. Clark's)

One cup sugar
One-half cup butter
Two eggs
Teaspoon cream tartar
Half teaspoon soda
Two cups flour
Half-cup milk

Molasses Drop Cake (1894)

One cup sugar
One cup molasses
One-half cup butter or lard
One cup cold water
One egg
One large teaspoon soda
Five cups flour
Flavour with cloves and cinnamon

Mor's Sur Fløde Kage (N.D.)
(Mother's Sour Cream Cake)

2 Eggs
1½ cups Sifted Flour
1 cup Sugar
1 teaspoon each, Cinnamon, nutmeg and soda
1 cup thick Sour Cream
2 tablespoons molasses
1/2 teaspoon Cloves

Beat the eggs until thick and light coloured. Beat in the sugar. Add sour cream and molasses and mix well. Sift dry ingredients together and add to first mixture. Bake in four layers. Put together with raisin filling.

Raisin Filling:

2 cups Sugar
1 cup Seeded Raisins
1 cup Water
2 Egg Whites

Boil water, sugar and chopped raisins until a little dropped into cold water will form a soft ball. Pour over the stiffly beaten egg whites and stir until cool enough to spread. Some cooks like to alternate this filling with layers of plum jam. Use the raisin filling for the top and sides of the cake, or whipped cream may be used for the top.

Moravian Sugar Cake (1840)

Cut up a quarter of a pound of butter into a pint of rich milk, and warm it till the butter becomes soft; then stir it about in the milk so as to mix them well. Sift three quarters of a pound of flour (or a pint and a half) into a deep pan, and making a hole in the middle of it, stir in a large table-spoonful of the best brewer's yeast in which a salt-spoonful of salt has been dissolved; and then thin it with the milk and butter. Cover it and set it near the fire to rise. If the yeast is sufficiently strong, it will most probably be light in two hours. When it is quite light, mix with the dough a well-beaten egg and three quarters of a pound more of sifted flour; adding a table-spoonful of powdered cinnamon, and stirring it very hard. Butter a deep square baking pan and put the mixture into it. Set it to rise again, as before. Mix together five ounces or a large coffee-cup of fine brown sugar; two ounces of butter; and two table-spoonfuls of powdered cinnamon. When the dough is thoroughly light, make deep incisions all over it, at equal distances, and fill them with the mixture of butter, sugar and cinnamon; pressing it hard down into the bottom of the holes, and closing the dough a little at the top to prevent the seasoning from running out. Strew some sugar over the top of the cake; set it immediately into the oven and bake it from twenty minutes to half an hour, or more, in a brisk oven, in proportion to its thickness. When cool, cut it into squares. This is a very good plain cake; but do not attempt it unless you have excellent yeast.

Mosaic Cake (1820)

1 c. sugar	¼ tsp. nutmeg
1 tbsp., melted unsweetened chocolate	¾ c. milk
½ c. fat	¼ tsp. allspice
1¾ c. flour	1½ tsp. baking powder
¼ tsp. cinnamon	½ tsp. salt
2 eggs	1 tbsp. molasses

Mix first six ingredients according to cake method number one. Separate into three parts.
To one add spices, molasses and melted chocolate. To the second add pink colouring and ½ tsp. rose flavouring. To the third add ½ tsp. vanilla. Into a round cake pan put an outer ring of the white, then a ring of pink, and the innermost ring of the black. On top of that put three more rings reversing the order and so on till all batter is used. This makes Mosaic Cake.
For marbled effect drop into a loaf cake pan alternately a spoonful of each mixture, drawing the spoon through each colour two or three times to make the colours lie in patterns. Bake in a moderate oven about ¾ hour.

Mother Hubbard Cake (1894)

One and one-half cups sugar	Five eggs
One cup butter	One-half teaspoon baking powder
Two cups flour	

Cream butter and add flour a little at a time, cream together; beat eggs and sugar very lightly; put baking powder in the flour, one teaspoon vanilla. It is nice with a little mace.

Mother's Cake (1913)

Two cups of sugar	Three cups of flour
Three eggs	Three teaspoons of baking powder
One half cup of Armour's Simon-Pure Leaf Lard	One half teaspoon of vanilla extract

Icing: One generous cup of XXX sugar, softened with a glass of pineapple marmalade and a few drops of vanilla.

Mountain Cake 1 (1876)

One cup of sugar
A half-cup of butter
A half-cup of milk
Two cups of flour

Whites of two eggs
One teaspoon of baking powder
Flavour to the taste

This makes one loaf.

Mountain Cake 2 (1876)

Three cups of sugar
One cup of butter
A half-cup of milk
The whites of ten eggs

Four and a half cups of flour
A half teaspoon of soda
One teaspoon of cream tartar sifted with the flour
Flavour to the taste

Mountain Cake (1893)

One cup sugar
½ cup butter
½ cup milk
2 eggs

2 cups flour
1 teaspoon lemon
2 teaspoons of baking powder

Mousseline Biscuit (1920)
(Biscuit Mousseline)

Mix and work eight egg-yolks and two whole eggs in a basin with one pound of sugar; when quite light add two ounces of orange sugar and continue to stir the preparation for a few moments longer; add four ounces of flour and four ounces of fecula and finally eight stiffly beaten egg-whites. Butter a cylindrical timbale mold, glaze it with icing sugar and fecula, half of each, then fill the mold three-quarters full with the above composition; set it in a very slack oven and let bake for an hour and a half. As soon as the biscuit is done unmould on a grate, leave to cool and afterward pare it very straight; ice over with strawberry icing and dress the cake on a dish. Put into a copper pan five spoonfuls of strawberry pulp and mix into it sufficient orange sugar to form a flowing paste. Heat and when quite hot pour it over five stiffly beaten egg-whites. Just when serving fill the hollow in the cylindrical mold with this preparation, dressing it in the shape of a dome; surround the base of this cream with a circle of preserved cherries and small lozenges of angelica. Arrange around the bottom of the cake some small Genoese cakes iced with strawberry and cut into rectangulars.

Mrs. Black's Orange Cake (1909)

Cream 1 cupful of butter with 3 cupfuls of sugar; add the yolks of 5 eggs, 1 cupful of milk, 4 cupfuls of flour sifted with 2 teaspoonfuls of baking-powder and the beaten whites of 5 eggs. Bake in layers and when done spread with the following jelly: Bring the juice and grated rind of 2 oranges to boil with 1 cupful of sugar; place in a double boiler, add 2 beaten eggs and stir until thick as custard.

Mrs. Carpenter's Wedding Cake (1876)

Fifteen eggs
Whites and yolks beaten separately
One and a half pounds of butter
One and a half pounds of sugar
One and a half pounds of flour

Three pounds of seeded raisins
Three pounds of currants
One and a half pounds of citron
A half pint of molasses
One ounce of ground mace

One ounce of cinnamon

Very fine.

Mrs. Dodge's Wedding Cake (1876)

Four pounds of flour
Three pounds of brown sugar
Twenty-seven eggs
Five pounds of stoned raisins
Five pounds of currants

One pound of citron
A half-pound of preserved orange peel
Allspice, cloves, cinnamon, nutmeg, mace
Three teaspoons of soda

Mrs. Harmon's Fruit Cake (1876)

One coffeecup of sugar
Two-thirds of a teacup of butter
Two thirds of a teacup of molasses
One teacup of buttermilk

Spice and fruit of all kind
One egg and the white of another
One teaspoon of soda
Flour to make a stiff batter

Mrs. Madison's Whim (1893)

Two pounds flour
2 pounds sugar
2 pounds butter
12 eggs
2 nutmegs

2 wine glasses rose water, in which lemon rind has been steeped
2 pounds raisins
1 teaspoon soda

Mrs. Mason's Cake (1876)

Four cups of flour
Two cups of sugar
One and a half cups of sweet milk

Put in one cup of butter and, while boiling
Add one teaspoon of soda
Spice and fruit to taste

Mrs. Rorer's Chocolate Cake (1909)

2 ounces of chocolate
4 eggs
1/2 a cup of milk
1 teaspoonful of vanilla

1/2 a cup of butter
1-1/2 cups of sugar
1 heaping teaspoonful of baking powder
1-3/4 cups of flour

Dissolve the chocolate in five tablespoonfuls of boiling water. Beat the butter to a cream, add the yolks, beat again, then the milk, then the melted chocolate and flour. Give the whole a vigorous beating. Now beat the whites of the eggs to a stiff froth and stir them carefully into the mixture; add the vanilla and baking powder. Mix quickly and lightly, turn into well-greased cake pan and bake in a moderate oven forty-five minutes.

Mrs. Sherman's Almond Cake (1876)

Two cups of sugar
One cup of butter
Two cups of flour

Six eggs
One cup of milk
Three teaspoons of baking powder

Bake in layers.
Icing:

One coffee-cup of thick sour cream
Two eggs
One pound of almonds blanched and chopped

Sugar to taste (make rather sweet)
Flavour with vanilla

Spread between the layers.

Mrs. Sibley's Raised Cake (1876)

One pint of new milk
A half-cup of good yeast
One cup of shortening

Three eggs
Two cups of brown sugar
Spices of all kinds and fruit

Stir stiff with flour; let it rise; and bake slowly for one hour.

Mrs. Speed's Layer Cake (1876)

Four eggs
Two cups of sugar
Two cups of flour

Two teaspoons of baking powder
Three-fourths of a cup of boiling water

Beat the yolks and sugar till very light, add flour and whites alternately and, just before putting in the oven, stir in the boiling water. Bake in a large bread pan; have the cake one inch thick when done; then cut into pieces.
Icing. - White of one egg, large cup of sugar, and the grated rind and juice of one lemon. Spread between the layers and ice over the top. This is excellent.

Muffins (1905)

Material:

1/3 cup butter
1/4 cup sugar
1/4 teaspoon salt
1 egg

2 cups Pillsbury's Best
4 teaspoons baking powder
1 cup milk

Way of Preparing: Beat butter, sugar and egg until creamy. Add milk little at a time, stirring in gradually flour sifted with salt and baking powder. Grease muffin pan, heat slightly, put in mixture and bake in quick oven.

Muffins (1911)

Sift a saltspoon of salt, two level teaspoons baking powder; and two cups of flour together. Beat the yolks of two eggs, add one cup of milk, two tablespoons of melted butter, and the dry ingredients. Beat, add lightly the stiffly beaten whites of two eggs, fill hot buttered gem pans two-thirds full, and bake in a hot oven.

Muffins (1911)

1 pt. sour cream
2 eggs

1 teaspoon soda
A little salt

Add flour to make a batter and drop in hot tins.

Muffins (1890)

One-half cup of sugar	2 tablespoonfuls butter
One-half cup of milk	2 heaping teaspoonfuls of baking powder
2 eggs	Flour enough to make like cake

Muffins 1 (1894)

One cup sweet milk and an iron spoonful extra	One of soda
Three cups flour	Butter size of small egg
One egg	Tablespoon sugar
Two teaspoons cream tartar	

Beat egg, sugar, butter and cream tartar together; stir in part of milk while putting in the flour, dissolve soda in remainder of the milk and stir in after it is well mixed.

Muffins 2 (1894)

One egg	Teaspoon butter rubbed into the flour
Pint of flour	Teaspoon cream tartar
One and a half pints milk	Half teaspoon soda

Muffins 3 (1894)
(English)

Two quarts flour	One teaspoon salt
One-third of a yeast cake	Cold water to moisten

Make the dough as stiff as for bread and rise overnight; roll out until one-half inch thick; cut with large biscuit cutter; put them on a griddle on the back of the stove till they rise; then move forward to cook, turning over when done one side; remove from the fire when done; cover and allow to stand long enough to be made tender by the steam; split open, butter and serve; or when cold, split, toast and butter.

Muffins 4 (1894)
(Graham)

One cup flour	Teaspoon salt
Two cups wheat meal	Half cup yeast, well mixed
Two tablespoons sugar	

Add half teaspoon soda dissolved in a little milk; not too stiff, almost thin as a batter.

Muffins 5 (1894)
(Graham)

One egg	One cup wheat flour
Half-cup sugar	One and a half cups graham flour
Butter size of an egg	Half a teaspoon soda
One and a half cups sour milk	

Bake in hot roll pans.

Muffins 6 (1894)
(Indian Meal)

One cup meal scalded in one-pint milk
Butter size of an egg
Tablespoon sugar
Salt

One egg
Half-cup yeast
Flour enough for rather a stiff batter

Bake in a quick oven.

Muffins 7 (1894)
(Raised)

One-pint sweet milk
Half-cup yeast
Two tablespoons sugar

Flour enough to make batter a little thicker than for fritters

Rise over night; add in the morning two eggs and bake in a quick oven.

Muffins 8 (1894)
(Raised)

One-quart flour
Half a teacup yeast
Two well beaten eggs

One and a half pints warm milk
Half a gill melted butter

Let rise, and when light bake in rings well buttered.

Muffins 9 (1894)
(Rye)

One-pint sour milk
One-pint rye meal
Half cup molasses

One egg
One teaspoon saleratus
Cup flour

Bake one-half hour.

Muffins 10 (1894)
(White)

One cup milk
One and a half cups flour
One heaping teaspoon baking powder

Whites of two eggs
One-fourth cup butter
A little salt

Bake in a quick oven.

Muffins 1 (1876)

One quart of sour milk
One dessert spoon of salt
One teaspoon of soda

Three tablespoons of melted butter or lard
Five eggs, whites and yolks beaten separately

Make a thin batter and put the whites in last. Butter the rings or pans and have hot before putting into the oven.

Muffins 2 (1876)

One quart of sweet milk
Two eggs
One tablespoon of butter

One teacup of yeast
Flour to make a stiff batter
A little salt

When light bake quickly.

Muffins 3 (1876)

Rub a piece of butter the size of an egg in two quarts of flour, add three eggs well beaten, a little salt, one teacup of yeast, one pint of milk, one pint of water. Beat the eggs and milk together, then add the water, stir in the flour and butter, add the yeast and let it stand until morning. Place rings in dripping-pan, fill and bake in slow oven.

Muffins 4 (1876)

One quart of flour
One and one-half pints of warm milk
One-half tea-cup of yeast

Two tablespoons of melted butter
Two eggs
One teaspoon of saleratus

Set the batter in a warm place; when light, bake in rings.

Muffins 5 (1876)

One egg, well beaten
One large spoon of sugar
One and one fourth cups of flour

One cup of milk
One teaspoon melted butter
A little salt

Put two teaspoons baking powder into the flour. Bake in rings.

Muffins 6 (1876)

Melt one ounce of butter in a pint of milk; add a little yeast and two eggs, well beaten; stir in flour enough to make a stiff batter. Set it to rise and, when quite light, add a little salt. Bake in rings on a hot griddle, filling the rings half full of the batter.

Muffins (1864)

Friend, I am a shrewd observer, and will guess What cakes you doat on for your favourite mess.
ARMSTRONG.

Take a pint of warm milk, and a quarter pint of thick small-beer yeast; strain them into a pan, and add sufficient flour to make it like a batter; cover it over, and let it stand in a warm place until it has risen; then add a quarter of a pint of warm milk, and an ounce of butter rubbed in some flour quite fine; mix them well together; add sufficient flour to make it into a dough; cover it over. Let it stand half an hour; work it up again; break it into small pieces, roll them up quite round, and cover them over for a quarter of an hour, then bake them.

Muffins 1 (N.D.)

2 cups flour
4 teaspoons baking powder
1 teaspoon salt
4 tablespoons sugar

2 eggs (separate eggs)
1 cup sweet milk
¼ cup butter (melt)

Muffins 2 (N.D.)

1½ cups flour
½ teaspoon salt
3 teaspoons baking powder
1 tablespoon sugar

1 egg
2 level tablespoons butter
1 cup milk

Mix dry ingredients, adding beaten egg, milk and butter. Bake in moderate oven.

Muffins (1922)

1 cupful scalded milk
1½ teaspoonfuls salt
2 tablespoonfuls Crisco
½ yeast cake

1 cupful boiling water
1 egg
¼ cupful sugar
4 cupfuls flour

Add Crisco, salt, and half of sugar to milk and water; when lukewarm add yeast mixed with remaining sugar, egg well beaten, and flour. Beat thoroughly, cover, and let rise until light. Put greased muffin rings on hot griddle greased with Crisco. Fill half full with raised muffin mixture and cook slowly until well risen and browned underneath. Turn muffins and rings and brown other side. When muffins are cold, split open, toast, and serve with marmalade.
Sufficient for sixteen muffins.

Muffins (1893)

1 cup milk
3 cups flour
½ cup sugar

Piece of butter size of an egg
1 teaspoon baking powder

Bake in muffin tins.

Muffins (1893)

One egg
1 cup milk
2 tablespoons of sugar
Butter the size of an egg

3 cups flour
2 teaspoons cream tartar
1 teaspoon soda
A bit of Crystaline salt

Mürbekuchen – I (1910)

½ lb. butter
4 tablespoonsful sweet cream

¾ lb. flour
2 oz. sugar

Cream the butter, and mix well with the cream, sugar and flour. Roll out, cut into various shapes with a cutter, brush over with egg, sprinkle with sugar and bake a pale yellow on a buttered tin.

Mürbekuchen – II (1910)

½ lb. butter
½ lb. sugar
1 lb. flour
3 eggs
½ oz. baking powder
Vanilla or lemon flavouring

Cream the butter, and then stir in the sugar, beaten-up eggs, flavouring and the flour, sifted and mixed with baking powder. Stand the paste on one side for a time, then roll out and proceed as in previous recipe.

Mürber Teig (No. 1) (1873)
(Short Crust for Savoury Pasties)

To a pound of fine flour, on the pasteboard, slice in a pound of butter. Chop and mix it well with a knife, then add a little salt, the yolks of four eggs, and milk or water enough to bind lightly. Roll it out. Fold, and roll it three times.

Mürber Teig (No. 2) (1873)
(Short Crust)

Mix, on a pasteboard or marble slab, a pound of flour and two ounces of sifted sugar. Rub into this half a pound of butter. Stir the yolks of two eggs in a little milk or water, with which mix the paste smooth. Roll it out thin, fold it together, heat it well with the rolling-pin, fold, and roll it out twice.

Mürber Teig (No. 3) (1873)
(Short Crust)

Mix a pound of flour with a quarter of a pound of sifted sugar. Slice on it ten ounces of butter. Chop all together with a knife, then add the yolks of six eggs and a glass of brandy. Proceed as in the preceding recipe.

Mürber Teig (No. 4) (1873)
(Common Short Crust)

Three-quarters of a pound of flour, a quarter of a pound of butter, two ounces of sugar, a well-beaten egg, and a little salt. Rub the butter and sugar into the flour; beat up the egg in a little water to mix the paste, which must be lightly done, and as lightly rolled out and moulded. Lard or clarified drippings may be used for economy, either with or without butter.

Mush (1876)

Mix corn meal with cold water and stir into a pot of boiling water till stiff enough to let the paddle or spoon stand in it. Salt to your taste, and boil one or two hours, being careful not to let it burn. Pour it into a dripping-pan, and when cold, slice thin and fry brown on griddles with a little lard.

Mush Batter Cakes (1913)
(For Invalids)

Bring half a pint of water to a bubbling boil in something open, add to it a pinch of salt, then by littles, strew in a cup of sifted meal, stirring it well to avoid lumps. Let cool partly, then cook by small spoonfuls on a hot griddle very lightly greased. Make the spoonfuls brown on both sides and serve very hot.

Mush Flannel Cakes (1869)

Mix a pint of corn mush with two of wheat flour, a spoonful of butter or lard, two eggs and half a tea-cup of yeast; make it in a batter with water or milk and bake like buckwheat cakes.

Mush, Mush Cakes, and Fried Mush (1869)

Mush will keep for several days in cool weather; the best way of making it is to have a pot of boiling water, and stir in corn meal, mixed with water, and salt enough to season the whole; let it boil, and if it is not thick enough you can add more meal; keep stirring all the time to prevent it from being lumpy. It should boil an hour.
To make the cakes, take a quart of cold mush, mix in it half a pint of wheat flour, and a little butter or lard, make it out in little cakes with your hands, flour them and bake them on a griddle or in a dripping pan. Fried mush is a good plain dessert, eaten with sugar and cream. Cut the cold mush in slices, half an inch thick, or make them into small cakes, dip them in flour, and fry them in hot lard.

Muster Gingerbread (1911)

½ cup sugar
¼ cup butter
1 egg
½ cup molasses
½ cup sour milk

1 even teaspoonful soda dissolved in the milk
1 teaspoonful ginger
A little salt
1½ cups flour

Part 15: N

Napfkuchen mit Hefe (1910)
(Plain Yeast Cake)
Neapolitan Cake (1876)
Neapolitan Cake (1920)
Neapolitan Cake (1920)
(Gâteau Napolitain)
Never Fail Devil's Food Cake (N.D.)
New England Election Cake (1913)
New England Raised Loaf Cake (1893)
New Year Cake (1869)
New York Pound Cake (No.1) (1922)
New York Pound Cake (No.2) (1922)
Newport Tea Cakes (1902)
Nice Breakfast Cakes (1876)
Nice Cake (1894)
Nice Griddle Cakes (1876)
Nice Johnny-Cake (1876)
Nice Rice Cake (1904)
North Dakota Sponge Cake (1893)
Nougatine Cake (1920)
(Gâteau Nougatine)
Novelty Cake (1820)
Nugget Cake (1909)
Number Cake (1876)
Nun's Cake (N.D.)
Nuss-Torte (1910)
(Nut Cake)
Nut and Raisin Cake (1913)
Nut Cake (1912)
Nut Cake (1899)
Nut Cake (1920)
Nut Cake 1 (1893)
(Very old French recipe)
Nut Cake 2 (1893)
Nut Cake 3 (1893)
Nut Cake 1 (1893)
Nut Cake 2 (1893)
Nut Cake 1 (1894)
Nut Cake 2 (1894)
(Cream)
Nut Cake 3 (1894)
(Golden)
Nut Layer Cake (1912)

Napfkuchen mit Hefe (1910)
(Plain Yeast Cake)

1¼ lb. sifted flour
1½ oz. yeast
½ pint milk
3 eggs
5 oz. sugar

5 oz. butter
4 oz. currants
12 bitter almonds
4 oz. raisins
Lemon peel to taste

Crumble up the yeast in a basin, sprinkle ½ teaspoonful of sugar over it and allow it to stand for 10 minutes. Then pour a gill of lukewarm milk on it, mix well and stir in sufficient of the sifted flour to make a paste. Stand in a warm place - not on the stove – to rise.

Beat the eggs and sugar to a froth, add the grated almonds and lemon peel and the butter (melted), then the risen prepared yeast and the remainder of the milk. Mix well, gradually add the flour, and then stir in the currants and raisins.

Beat this dough well with the rolling-pin till it no longer sticks to it. Well butter a fireproof earthenware mould (Napfkuchenform) or special cake tin made with a projection running up the middle allowing the heat to penetrate better. Line it with breadcrumbs and fill it half full with the dough. Stand in a warm place, covered over with a cloth, till it has risen to the top of the mould. Then put into the oven and bake 1 hour.

Neapolitan Cake (1876)

First make the dark cake after the following recipe:

One cup of butter
Two cups of brown sugar
One cup of molasses
One cup of strong coffee
Four and a half teacups of flour
Four eggs
Two teaspoons of soda
Two teaspoons of cinnamon

One teaspoon of cloves
One teaspoon of mace
One pound of raisins
One pound of currants
A fourth of a pound of citron
(more fruit makes the cake handsomer, but this quantity will do)

Bake the cake in round pans with straight sides. The loaves should be one and a half inches in thickness after baking.

The white cake is made as follows:

One cup of butter
Four cups of powdered white sugar
Two cups of sweet milk
Two cups of corn starch mixed with the flour

Four and a half cups of sifted flour
Whites of eight eggs
Six teaspoons of baking powder
Flavour slightly with bitter almonds

Bake in the pans used for the black cake, making the light and dark loaves of the same thickness. After the cake is all cold, each black loaf should be spread with a thick frosting: made as follows:

White of one egg beaten light
Glacéd rind of two and the juice of three lemons

Powdered sugar enough to make a thick frosting

Lay the white and black loaves alternately; frost all over as you would any other loaf; be particular to use no other flavouring than lemon in the frosting. This makes an elegant cake, equally tempting to the eye and the palate.

Neapolitan Cake (1920)

Roll out some puff paste to ⅛ inch in thickness, cut it into 3 strips 5 inches wide and about 10 inches long; moisten a large shallow tin pan with cold water, put in the strips, dust them with powdered sugar, and bake in a medium-hot oven. When done and cold, cover 1 strip with boiled vanilla cream, put over this the second strip, and spread over some currant jelly; lay on the third strip. Mix ½ cup powdered sugar with 1 tablespoonful boiling water and a few drops of lemon juice, pour it over the cake, and set aside till firm.

Neapolitan Cake (1920)
(Gâteau Napolitain)

Crush one pound and ten ounces of almonds with a pound and a quarter of sugar; reduce to a fine powder; pass this through a sieve. Sift on the table two pounds of flour, make a hollow in the center and in it lay the almond and sugar powder, a pound and a half of butter, a pinch of salt and four whole eggs; work the whole together just enough to form a smooth, firm paste, for if worked too much it is liable to crumble. Lay it in a vessel and leave in a cool place to rest; one hour later divide this paste into sixteen or twenty even parts and roll them to a quarter of an inch thick by six and a quarter inches in diameter; empty out the centres with a two-inch pastry cutter. Have two of the flats a little thicker and two inches wider in diameter than the others; bake on a buttered and floured baking sheet in a hot oven, and as soon as done take them out and leave to cool under the pressure of a weight; pare the large rounds eight inches in diameter and put them once more under a weight; when cold ice either with white or pink icing; mask the small flats with well-strained and reduced apricot marmalade; now lay them one over the other; pare them evenly to have the cake six inches in diameter, and cover the whole with well reduced and well-cooked apricot marmalade; place the cake on one of the large flats and over lay the second large one. Decorate around with fanciful cuts of almond gum paste and the top with a cupola of royal icing or gum paste. Ornament around the edge of the large flat with a double border of the same paste and arrange the cake on a richly decorated stand. This cake is intended for a sideboard. It can also be made with almond biscuit.

Never Fail Devil's Food Cake (N.D.)

2 tablespoons butter
2 eggs, separated
1½ cups Swansdown flour
¼ teaspoon salt
1 cup sugar

2 teaspoons vanilla
1 cup sour milk or cream
2 squares chocolate
1 teaspoon baking soda

Cream butter and sugar, add yolks then flour and milk alternately. The soda should be beaten into the milk before using. Then add chocolate, vanilla, and fold in whites.

New England Election Cake (1913)

1 cup bread dough slightly rounded
1/3 cup Cottolene
2 eggs
1 cup soft brown sugar
1/2 cup sour milk
2/3 cup seeded and shredded raisins
6 large figs chopped fine

1-1/4 cups flour
1/2 teaspoon soda
1/4 teaspoon cloves
1/2 teaspoon nutmeg
1/2 teaspoon cinnamon
1 teaspoon salt

Process: Cream Cottolene and work it in the dough with the hand. Add eggs well beaten, sugar, soda dissolved in milk, fruit dredged with one-fourth cup flour, remainder flour mixed and sifted with spices and salt. Beat thoroughly with the hand. Turn mixture into a well-buttered, brick-shaped bread pan, cover and let rise for one and a quarter hours in a warm place. Bake one hour in a moderate oven. Spread with Milk Frosting.

New England Raised Loaf Cake (1893)

One pound of sugar
Two pounds of flour
Three eggs
One-fourth pound citron
One pound of butter
One pint of milk
One pound of raisins
One good-sized wine glass rum or brandy
One-half nutmeg
One cup yeast

Cream one-half butter and sugar; mix this with all the flour, yeast and milk; let this mixture stand in a warm place until quite light, then add the remaining half of butter and sugar creamed and the eggs beaten very light; then let the mixture stand in a warm place until again very light; then add rum, raisins, citron and nutmegs then put into pans for baking, letting it remain out of oven until very light again. This makes three loaves. Bake about one hour.

New Year Cake (1869)

Mix together three pounds of flour, a pound and a half of sugar, and three-quarters of a pound of butter: dissolve a tea-spoonful of salaeratus in enough new milk to wet the flour; mix them together; grate in a nutmeg, or the peel of a lemon; roll them out, cut them in shapes, and bake.

New York Pound Cake (No.1) (1922)

Two pounds of powdered sugar
One and one quarter pounds of butter (or use half butter and half lard)
One and one-half pints of eggs
One and one-half pints of milk
Two and three-quarter pounds of flour
One and one-half ounces of baking powder
Vanilla flavour

New York Pound Cake (No.2) (1922)

One pound and eight ounces of sugar
One pound of butter
Ten eggs
One-pint milk
Two and one quarter pounds of flour
One and one quarter ounces of baking powder
Flavour

Cream butter and sugar; gradually work in the eggs and add the milk, (leave out a little of the milk; add it after the flour is drawn in), and finish mixing.
This mixture, like Plain Genoa Pound Cake (1922), may be for a stock mixture for other cakes (see New Receipts and Points on Cake Making).
For light fruit cakes add four ounces more of flour and add one and one-half pounds of fruit – sultanas, citron or currants, etc. Bake in about 300 degrees Fahrenheit.

Newport Tea Cakes (1902)

Sift together 3 cups of sifted flour and a teaspoonful of salt. Beat the yolks of three eggs until very light, add 1 pt. of milk and stir into the dry ingredients. Then beat the whites of three eggs, beaten dry. Bake in small buttered tins in a very hot oven.

Nice Breakfast Cakes (1876)

Three tablespoons of melted butter	Three tablespoons of hot water

Put these into a coffee-cup and fill to overflowing with molasses; add two teaspoons soda, one tablespoon ginger, and a little cinnamon. Mix soft and roll out.

Nice Cake (1894)

One and one-half cups butter
One cup sugar
Half-cup milk
Two cups flour

Three eggs
Teaspoon cream tartar
Half teaspoon soda

Beat the whites separately and add just before going into the oven. Bake thirty minutes.

Nice Griddle Cakes (1876)

One-pint sour cream
One pint of sour milk
One teaspoon of salt

Four eggs
Flour enough to make a thin batter
One teaspoon or more of soda

Bake on griddles well-greased.

Nice Johnny Cake (1876)

Three teacups corn meal
One teacup of flour
Two teacups sweet milk
One teacup sour cream

One egg
One teaspoon soda
One teaspoon salt

Nice Rice Cake (1904)

Boil ¼ pound of rice in sweet cream with salt and 2 ounces of sugar, flavoured with vanilla, until thick. By the addition of a variety of ingredients a number of different kinds of the rice cake can be prepared. After stirring through the rice, the yolks of 6 eggs and 2 ounces of grated roll, stir in 2 ounces of sliced citron or 3 ounces of scalded raisins or 3 ounces of any kind of scalded candied fruit, also almonds, spices or grated nuts. In the meantime, bake a puff paste, two crusts of the same size, spread first with fruit marmalade or a thick wine-cream, then with the rice, put on the top crust and serve immediately.

North Dakota Sponge Cake (1893)

One cup of sugar
One cup of flour

Four eggs

Beat yolks of eggs to a light creamy mixture, pour over the sugar and beat two minutes; add whites beaten to a foam, and stir hard for two minutes; now add one cup of flour which has been sifted three times, and to which was added a pinch of salt; stir very lightly, usually four whisks of the spoon is sufficient; now pour into a shallow pan; let stand one minute; raise the pan several inches from the table and let it drop suddenly, striking flat on the bottom; this will cause air bubbles to break and make the cake fine grained; put into a very moderate oven and in five minutes heat quickly; twelve to fifteen minutes will suffice. Have ready a lemon frosting, and the result will be a most beautiful cake, fit to grace any occasion.

Nougatine Cake (1920)

(Gâteau Nougatine)

Make a biscuit preparation with a pound of powdered sugar, a pound of flour, six whole eggs, eighteen yolks, six beaten whites, vanilla and a grain of salt. Bake this in a slack oven in three or four smooth fruit pie circles, six or seven inches in diameter by an inch to an inch and a half high. These circles should be buttered with clarified butter and glazed with fecula. After taking them from the oven remove from the circles and leave to get thoroughly cold for twelve hours. Prepare a buttered orange cream the same as for the Fleury cake. Mince half a pound of sweet peeled almonds, previously dried on a sheet of paper then roasted in a pan to brown nicely. Cut the biscuits into transversal slices three-eighths of an inch thick, and taking up seven or eight of these, one by one, cover one side with a layer of the prepared cream, then put one on top of the other so as to form into a regular-shaped cake, and cover the top and sides at once with another layer of cream; now spread over the whole a layer of the roasted almonds, fastening them on with the blade of a knife, so as to equalize its thickness; besprinkle lightly with fine vanilla sugar, and push the cake for one minute in a hot oven, simply to have the sugar adhere to the almonds, then take out at once and when cold dress on a napkin.

Novelty Cake (1820)

¼ c. fat
2 tsp. baking powder
1 c. sugar
½ c. milk

2 eggs
1 tsp. vanilla
1½ c. flour

Filling:

½ c. brown sugar
1 tbsp. melted butter
1 tsp. cinnamon

2 tbsp. flour
½ c. chopped nuts

Mix well

Put half of the cake batter in the pan and cover with some of the filling. Then spread over the rest of the batter and then the filling. Bake in an oblong shallow pan 7x11 inches for twenty-five minutes.

Nugget Cake (1909)

Cream ½ cupful of butter with 2 cupfuls of sugar; add 4 eggs beaten without separating, 1 cupful of lukewarm water and 3 cupfuls of flour sifted with 2 teaspoonfuls of baking-powder; beat well, add the grated rind and the diced pulp of 1 orange and bake in a moderate oven for three-quarters of an hour.

Number Cake (1876)

One cup of butter
Two cups of sugar
Three cups of flour

Four eggs, or whites of seven
A half-cup of sweet milk
Two teaspoons of baking powder

Beat the whites to a stiff froth and flavour to the taste.

Nun's Cake (N.D.)

1 cup butter
2½ teaspoons baking powder
1½ cups powdered sugar

¼ teaspoon salt
Yolks of 5 eggs
3 teaspoons caraway seed

Whites of 2 eggs
¾ cup milk
2 teaspoons rose water
½ teaspoon cinnamon
3 cups flour extract

Beat butter until creamy, add sugar and egg yolks, stir in unbeaten egg whites and beat for one minute. Add flour, milk and flavourings. Bake in a moderate oven.

Nuss-Torte (1910)
(Nut Cake)

¾ lb. nuts
10 eggs
¾ lb. sugar
A few bitter almonds

Beat the sugar and yolks to a froth, then stir in alternately the grated nuts and whisked whites of eggs. Bake 1 hour in well-buttered tin. Spread with sugar or chocolate icing, and ornament with candied walnuts or hazelnuts.
½ lb. hazelnuts and ¼ lb. sweet almonds may be taken instead of the whole quantity of hazelnuts.

Nut and Raisin Cake (1913)

1/3 cup Cottolene
1 cup fine sugar
3 eggs unbeaten
1 cup pecan nut meats
2/3 cup raisins
2 cups pastry flour
4 teaspoons baking powder
3/4 cup milk
Grated rind of half an orange
1/2 teaspoon cinnamon
1/4 teaspoon mace
1/4 teaspoon salt

Process: Cream Cottolene, add sugar gradually, stirring constantly, add eggs, one at a time and beating each in thoroughly before adding another. Pass nuts and raisins through meat chopper, then mix with flour sifted with baking powder, salt and spices; add alternately to first mixture with milk, beating constantly. Turn mixture into a well-greased tube pan and bake thirty-five to forty minutes in a moderate oven. Spread with Caramel Frosting with Nuts

Nut Cake (1912)

Seven eggs beaten separately
One cup of butter
Two cups of sugar
Four cups of flour
One and one-half pounds of raisins
Two nutmegs
One tablespoon of cinnamon
Two teaspoons of baking powder
Two cups of mixed nuts chopped
One wine glass of whiskey

Bake two hours.

Nut Cake (1899)

Mix one and one-half cups of sugar and two tablespoonfuls of butter to a cream; then add two well-beaten eggs and one cup of milk; sift two tablespoonfuls of baking-powder with two cups of flour and stir into the mixture. Lastly stir in one cupful of nuts crushed with a rolling-pin or chopped very fine. Stir well and bake in a moderate oven. Walnuts, hickory nuts, and butternuts are best for this cake, but other nuts will do.

Nut Cake (1920)

Prepare a cake batter the same as for Plain Cake, stir in 1-pint shelled walnuts broken into pieces and finish the same as Plain Cake; or stir 3 cups freshly grated cocoanut into the plain cake batter; or stir 1-pint shelled hickory nuts into the plain cake batter; or almonds cut into strips; Brazil nuts may also be used.

Nut Cake 1 (1893)
(Very old French recipe)

Four tablespoons of flour
Four tablespoons of brown sugar
One tablespoon of butter

One egg
One teacup of chopped nuts
A pinch of salt and black pepper

Grease and heat a long biscuit pan, mix all ingredients well and spread thinly on heated pan. Bakes in a few moments. When done and while warm, run a knife through centre of pan lengthwise, then crosswise in strips. Turn pan over, and when cool cakes should be quite crisp.

Nut Cake 2 (1893)

One-half cup butter
Two cups sugar
One cup milk
Three cups flour

Four eggs
One-pint nut meats
Two teaspoons baking powder

Cream butter and sugar. Add eggs well whipped, milk, flour with baking powder, and nut meats chopped fine. Bake in loaf. English walnuts best.

Nut Cake 3 (1893)

One and one-half cup sugar
One-half cup butter
Whites of six eggs, beaten stiff
One-half cup milk
One and two-thirds cup flour

One-third cup corn starch
One teaspoon baking powder
One and one-half pound English walnuts, chopped fine and floured

Bake slowly in moderate oven.

Nut Cake 1 (1893)

Cream ½ cup butter
1 cup sugar
2 eggs
⅓ cup milk

2 cups flour (scant)
Add 1-pound nuts or ½ pound figs

Nut Cake 2 (1893)

Three eggs
1½ cups sugar
⅔ cup butter
2½ cups flour

1-pound English walnuts
1 cup chopped raisins
½ cup of milk
1 heaping teaspoon baking powder

Nut Cake 1 (1894)

One cup butter

Two cups sugar

One cup milk
Three and one-half cups flour
Three eggs
One-half teaspoon soda

One teaspoon cream tartar
One-pound English walnuts
One-pound stoned raisins

Nut Cake 2 (1894)
(Cream)

Three-fourths cup butter
Two cups sugar
Three and one-fourth cups flour

Three even teaspoons baking powder
One cup milk
Five eggs

Bake in jelly cake tins.
Make the filling as follows:

Whites of two eggs

One and one-half cups powdered sugar

Put the eggs in a bowl, sprinkle in one tablespoon sugar; beat with a wire whisk five minutes, add the rest of the sugar gradually, a tablespoon at a time; when all is added, and it is smooth and creamy, flavour and stir in three-fourths cup nuts chopped fine. Spread this icing between the layers; sprinkle each layer with nuts. Ice the top with plain icing and lay on whole or half nuts over all.

Nut Cake 3 (1894)
(Golden)

Cream three-fourths cup butter and one and one-half cups sugar together
Add yolks of eight eggs
One whole egg beaten till thick
One-half cup milk

Two cups of flour sifted with one and one-half teaspoons cream tartar
One-half teaspoon soda
Two teaspoons brandy
One cup chopped nuts slightly floured

Bake in individual pans; frost with golden frosting made as follows: - One yolk beaten slightly, one teaspoon wine; confectioners' sugar to make it stiff enough to spread.

Nut Layer Cake (1912)

One-half cup of butter
Two cups of sugar
One cup of milk
Three and one-half cups of flour

One cup of chopped nuts
Two teaspoons of baking powder
The whites of seven eggs

Fill with seafoam icing with nuts added.

Part 16: O

Oatcakes (1898)
Oat Cakes (1922)
Oat Meal Cakes No. 1 (1912)
Oat Meal Cakes No. 1 (1912)
Oat Meal Cakes (1893)
Oatmeal Cake (1911)
Oat Meal Gems 1 (1876)
Oat Meal Gems 2 (1876)
Occidental Fudge Cake (1820)
Old Fashioned Hickorynut Cake (1922)
Old-Fashioned Pork Cake (1917)
Old Fashioned Raisin Cake (1922)
Old Fashioned Seed Cake (1922)
Old Time Pound Cakes (No. 1) (1922)
Old Time Pound Cakes (No. 2) (1922)
Old Virginia Bread Cake (1893)
One-Egg Cake (1917)
One-Egg Cake (1920)
Orange Cake (1904)
Orange Cake (1912)
Orange Cake 1 (1876)
Orange Cake 2 (1876)
Orange Cake 3 (1876)
Orange Cake (1917)
Orange Cake (1913)
Orange Cake (1893)
Orange Cake (1894)
Orange Cake 1 (1893)
Orange Cake 2 (1893)
Orange Cake 3 (1893)
Orange Cake 4 (1893)
Orange Cake (1890)
Orange Cake (1904)
Orange Cake with Milk Icing (1909)
Orange Cheesecakes (1909)
Orange Cheesecakes (1898)
Orange Fruit Cake (1909)
Orange Gingerbread (1909)
Orange Lady Cake (1909)
Orange Layer Cake (1922)
Orange Layer Cake (1920)
Orange Shortcake (1913)
Orange Short Cake (1893)
Orange Sponge (1909)
Orange Sunshine Cake (1893)
Orange Tourte (1922)
Orange Washington Cake (1909)
Ormond Cake (1909)
Oyster Shortcake (1922)
Oyster Shortcake (1912)

Oatcakes (1898)

Ingredients:

½ lb. medium oatmeal
1 oz. flour
1 oz. butter
1 small tea-spoonful salt
4 or 5 table-spoonfuls water

Method: Mix the oatmeal, flour. and salt together and rub in the butter. Mix the meal to a smooth paste, with just sufficient water to moisten it, using a wooden spoon to mix it with. Flour the pastry-board well, turn the paste on to it, knead it up with a little flour until it is firm enough to roll out, then roll it very thin. Cut it in 4-inch squares and divide each square cross-wise to make triangles. Lay them on a floured baking-sheet and bake 20 to 30 minutes in a moderate oven until crisp.
Time: 20 to 30 minutes.
Sufficient for: 18 oatcakes.

Oat Cakes (1922)

Mix 1 tablespoon butter, ½ teaspoon salt and ¼ teaspoon baking soda with 1 cup boiling water. Stir in enough oatmeal to make a stiff dough. Knead well and roll out thin, cut into squares and bake on a frying pan or griddle. Dry out in a warm oven.

Oat Meal Cakes No. 1 (1912)

One and one-half cups of sugar
Two tablespoons of melted butter
Two eggs
Two teaspoons of bitter almond
Three and one-half cups of Quaker oats
Two teaspoons of baking powder

Bake on greased baking sheet and remove while hot.

Oat Meal Cakes No. 2 (1912)

One cupful of sugar
One cupful of lard
One-half cupful of sweet milk
One-half teaspoonful of soda
One package of oatmeal
One nutmeg, grated
One level teaspoonful of ginger
Same of cinnamon and half as much of cloves

Flour to make as soft a dough as can be handled, as the less flour used the crisper they will be when baked. Make a ball about as large as a walnut, roll in the hands, then flatten as thin as possible. Bake in a slow oven until a rich golden brown. A cupful of raisins or half a cupful of chopped nut meats or both, are an improvement.

Oat Meal Cakes (1893)

One cup of cream
2 cups of sour milk
2 teaspoons of soda,
Oat meal sufficient to make a thick batter

Bake in roll pan.

Oatmeal Cake (1911)

Mix fine oatmeal into a stiff dough with milk-warm water, roll it to the thinness almost of a wafer, bake on a griddle or iron plate placed over a slow fire for three or four minutes, then place it on edge before the fire to harden. This will be good for months, if kept in a dry place.

Oat Meal Gems 1 (1876)

Two cups of sour milk or buttermilk; stir in three cups of oat meal; then add one teaspoon of salt, and one teaspoon of soda dissolved in a little cold water. Bake in gem pans or in a sheet. The oven should be hot enough to bake in fifteen minutes.

Oat Meal Gems 2 (1876)

Soak two cups of oat meal in two cups of cold water and a little salt, overnight; in the morning add two cups of sour milk or one cup of milk and one of cream, one-half cup sugar, two teaspoons soda, flour enough to make a stiff batter. Have gem pans hot and bake in a quick oven.

Occidental Fudge Cake (1820)

¼ c. fat
1¼ c. flour
1 c. sugar
2½ tsp. baking powder

2 eggs
½ c. milk
2 sq. bitter chocolate
1 tsp. vanilla

Cream one-half of the sugar with the fat and one-half with the yolks. Combine, mix and sift dry ingredients. Add alternately to first mixture with milk. Fold in the beaten whites and then add the chocolate. Bake in a shallow pan 7 x 11 in. in a moderate oven for forty minutes. Cover with Reliable Frosting and when cold pour over this melted bitter chocolate.

Old Fashioned Hickorynut Cake (1922)

Cream together three-fourths of a cupful of butter and two cupfuls of light "C" sugar; add to this mixture one cupful of cold water, the well beaten yolks of four eggs, half a teaspoonful each of ground cinnamon and mace, and three cupfuls of flour into which has been sifted three teaspoonfuls of baking powder, and one-half teaspoonful of salt. Now add the stiffly beaten whites of the eggs, folding them in very carefully. Take two cupfuls of blanched hickorynut meats, chop them very fine, roll them in flour, and add gradually to the mixture, stirring well all the time. Pour into a loaf cake tin, cover with browned flour for the first half hour it is in the oven, or better still, with a piece of oiled paper - this merely to prevent its becoming too brown, before well done. Let bake for an hour. When cool turn out of the tin, cover with boiled icing, and decorate with whole nut kernels.
Would advise the using of oiled paper, rather than the flour, for preventing its becoming brown too soon. There is danger of the flour sinking into the batter and spoiling the delicacy of the cake.

Old-Fashioned Pork Cake (1917)

1/2-pound fat salt pork
1/4-pound citron shredded
1 cup boiling water
1 nutmeg grated
1 cup molasses
2 teaspoons cinnamon
1 cup sugar

1/2 teaspoon cloves
2 eggs beaten
1/2 teaspoon allspice
1/2-pound raisins
1 teaspoon soda
1/2-pound currants
4 cups flour

Put pork through meat chopper, using finest cutter; add boiling water and let stand fifteen minutes; add molasses, sugar, eggs, and fruit, and mix well; add dry ingredients, which have been sifted together; beat well; pour into two deep greased and paper-lined pans; and bake in a slow oven, two hours. This cake keeps well if stored in a covered stone crock. It may be reheated in the top of double boiler, and served hot with pudding sauce.

Old Fashioned Raisin Cake (1922)

½ cup butter
1 cup raisins
1 heaping cup sugar
½ teaspoon vanilla
⅓ cup sour cream or milk
¼ teaspoon mace

2 eggs
¼ teaspoon cinnamon
2 cups flour
¼ teaspoon ginger
2 level teaspoons baking powder
¼ teaspoon soda in milk

Bake in square pan, in moderate oven, one hour.

Old Fashioned Seed Cake (1922)

2 cupfuls sugar
1 teaspoonful salt
1½ cupfuls Crisco

2 tablespoonfuls carraway seeds
4 cupfuls flour
12 eggs

Cream Crisco and sugar thoroughly together, then drop in eggs one by one, beating each one in well before next is added, sift in flour and salt, add carraway seeds. Turn into Criscoed and papered loaf tin and bake in moderately hot oven one and a half hours.
Sufficient for: one large cake.

Old Time Pound Cakes (No. 1) (1922)

One pound of Sugar
One pound of Butter
One pound of Flour

One pint of eggs, a little nutmeg grated
And the grated rind of one Lemon

Old Time Pound Cakes (No. 2) (1922)

One pound of Sugar
One pound of Butter

One pound of Flour
Twelve Eggs Mace and Lemon

Grate the lemon rind on the sugar, add the nutmeg and rub butter and sugar to a light cream; add the eggs two at a time, beat them in well, then add the flour; mix in lightly but fully. Put the mixture in paper lined pans. A pound cake should be about two and one-half inches thick when baked; it bakes best in this thickness and has a nice appearance when cut. A baking heat of 200 to 250 degrees Fahrenheit is the most suitable for this cake.

Old Virginia Bread Cake (1893)

One and one-half pounds flour
One-pound white sugar
Ten ounces of butter
One-half teacup sweet milk
One-half teacup good yeast

Four eggs
One cup of currants and seed-less raisins, chopped and mixed together
One teaspoonful each mace and cinnamon and a little allspice

Work butter and sugar together; sift flour into a bowl; stir in milk and yeast with one-half the creamed butter and sugar; beat hard and long until very light; set to rise in a moderately warm place overnight. In the morning, if it be well risen, work in the remainder of the butter and sugar and the eggs; dredge the fruit with flour and beat in a little at a time with the spice; beat for fully five minutes; divide and put into two pans to rise. The second rising generally requires about three hours. When the dough is very light bake in a moderate oven. When carefully made this cake is very fine

One-Egg Cake (1917)

2 tablespoons butter
1-1/2 cups flour
1/2 cup sugar
2-1/2 teaspoons baking powder

1 egg
Grated rind of 1 lemon
1/2 cup milk

Cream the butter, add the sugar and the well-beaten egg; beat thoroughly, add the other ingredients

One-Egg Cake (1920)

One cup sugar
1 egg
A piece of butter the size of a walnut

2 scant cups of flour sifted with 1 heaping teaspoonful baking powder
½ teaspoonful extract of lemon or vanilla
1 cup of milk

Rub butter and flour together, add the sugar, milk, and egg; mix into a batter, butter a square pan, dust with flour, put in the mixture, and bake in a medium-hot oven till done. This mixture may be baked in 3 small jelly tins, and when done lay them over one another with jelly marmalade or cream between them; or bake it in a pan 12 inches long and 8 inches wide and 1½ inch deep. When done, cut the cake in half, lay them over one another with jelly or cream between, then mix 1 cup sifted powdered sugar with 1 teaspoonful lemon juice and 2 tablespoonfuls boiling water, stir until smooth, pour the icing over the cake, and let stand till firm.
For a chocolate cake: bake the cake the same way, then mix 1 cup of powdered sugar with the white of 1 egg; melt 4 ounces Baker's chocolate, add it to the sugar, mix all together, put half of it between the cake, and spread the remaining over the top of the cake.
For a strawberry shortcake: bake the mixture in 2 small well-buttered and floured jelly tins, wash and mash 1 quart of strawberries, mix with ½ cup sugar, put half of them between the 2 layers, and the remainder on top; serve with cream or vanilla sauce, or put some whipped cream over the strawberries.

Orange Cake (1904)

Make an almond dough of 6 ounces of grated almonds
½ pound of sifted sugar
12 eggs (the whites beaten to a froth)

A little more than 2 ounces of flour
2 tablespoonfuls of arrac
Or else half of the puff paste as given under Saarbruck Puff Paste

And out of this bake two layers.
Then on the stove beat to a thick cream:

2 whole and the yolks of 4 eggs
½ pound of sifted sugar
The juice of 4 oranges

The juice of 2 lemons
The rind of an orange grated on some sugar

Spread over one layer, put the other layer on this and frost the latter with the following:

The juice of 1 orange is stirred with ¼ pound of sifted sugar and 1 tablespoonful of water; then follow the directions as given by taking 1 - 2 teaspoonfuls of raspberry juice the frosting will be of a pretty red colour; when using this omit the water so that the frosting will not be too thin. Decorate the top layer with candied orange slices.

Orange Cake (1912)

Two whole eggs
The yolks of six
Three-fourths cup of butter
Two cups of sugar
One cup of sweet milk

Four cups of flour
Two teaspoons of baking powder
One teaspoon of orange juice
The grated rind of one-half orange

Follow the rules for mixing and baking.

Filling for Orange Cake:

Beat the yolks of two eggs
Beat into it three-fourths cup of powdered sugar

Two tablespoons of melted butter

Dissolve two heaping teaspoons of corn starch in one-half cup of cold water. Add one cup of boiling water and cook until it thickens. Then add the above mixture and cook a few minutes. Flavour with one third cup of orange juice and one tablespoon of lemon juice. Spread between cakes when cold.

Orange Cake 1 (1876)

Two and a half cups of sugar
One and a half cups of butter
One cup of milk

Five cups of flour
Seven eggs, omitting the yolks of three
Two teaspoons of baking powder

Bake in four layers.
Frosting: Beat the whites of two eggs stiff, add sugar for a very stiff frosting and the grated rind and juice of four oranges; beat thoroughly and spread between the layers.

Orange Cake 2 (1876)

One half cup of butter
One and a half cups of sugar
A half-cup of water
Two heaping cups of flour

Whites of four eggs
Yolks of three
Grated rind and juice of one orange
Two teaspoons of baking powder

Frosting: Whites of two eggs, sugar sufficient to stiffen and the grated rind and juice of one orange.

Orange Cake 3 (1876)

Two cups of sugar
Two cups of flour
A half-cup of cold water
A pinch of salt
Two teaspoons of baking powder

Four eggs, reserving the white of one for frosting
And two oranges
The whole of one chopped fine and stirred in the cake
The juice of the other put into the frosting

Bake in three layers. This is just as good with lemons.

Orange Cake (1917)

1/4 cup shortening
1-1/2 cups flour
1 cup sugar
2-1/2 teaspoons baking powder
1 egg Grated rind
1/2 orange
1/2 cup milk

Cream the shortening, add sugar and egg well beaten; add milk, flour, baking powder, and rind; beat well, and bake in two layer pans about twenty minutes in a moderate oven. Fill and cover top with Orange Icing.

Orange Cake (1913)

Cream a cup of butter with two cups sugar, beat into it a cup of cold water, then add four cups flour thrice sifted with two teaspoonfuls baking powder, alternate the flour with three well-beaten eggs. Flavour to taste, bake in layers, and put together with orange frosting made thus. Cook together till it threads the strained juice and grated yellow peel of a large sweet orange with one cup sugar, then beat the hot syrup into two egg-whites whipped as stiff as possible. Beat smooth and spread while hot

Orange Cake (1893)

One coffee cup sugar
One-half coffee cup butter
Two coffee cups flour
One-half coffee cup milk
Yolks of four eggs
Whites of two eggs
Two teaspoons of baking powder

Bake in four layer tins. For the filling, grate the yellow part of the rind of two oranges and mix it with the juice and one coffee cup of powdered sugar; spread, this mixture between the cakes; frost the cake, using the two remaining whites of eggs beaten thoroughly, adding two small cups of powdered sugar

Orange Cake (1894)

Cream three-fourths cup butter, add slowly two cups sugar, and cream together. Into three cups sifted pastry flour mix two teaspoons baking powder, add one tablespoon of the prepared flour to the butter and sugar. Then add four eggs, one at a time without first beating, with a tablespoon of the flour before breaking in each egg; then add the remainder of the flour alternating with one cupful of milk. Flavour with orange. Bake about forty minutes in a moderate oven.
Orange Frosting: Yolk of one egg, extract of orange, enough confectioners' sugar to make it thick enough to spread.

Orange Cake 1 (1893)

Four eggs
2 cups sugar
1 cup butter
1 cup milk
3 cups flour
2 teaspoons baking powder

Cream butter and sugar.
Frosting: Juice and rind of one orange, thickened with powdered sugar.

Orange Cake 2 (1893)

One cup sugar
⅓ cup butter

1½ cups flour
½ cup milk
2 eggs
1½ teaspoons baking powder

Bake in two sheets.
Filling:

Juice of 1 orange
Juice of ½ lemon
⅔ teaspoon grated orange peel
Fill up the cup of liquid to ¾ full of cold water

Put in double boiler, add ½ cup sugar, 1 tablespoon corn starch, boil till thickened, add yolk of egg, stir in and take off fire.
Frosting: White of 1 egg, 5 ounces confectioners' sugar, ⅓ teaspoon grated orange peel,

Orange Cake 3 (1893)

One orange grated
1 cup sugar
3 tablespoons butter
3 eggs, saving out the whites of one
1⅓ cups flour
1 teaspoon cream tartar
½ teaspoon soda dissolved in a little milk

Frosting:

Juice of 1 orange
White of 1 egg
One-pound confectioners' sugar
2 teaspoons corn starch

Cut the cake in three layers, or, better, bake in two thin sheets and spread frosting between the layers and on top.

Orange Cake 4 (1893)

One cup sugar
⅓ cup butter
½ cup milk
2 cups flour
1 teaspoon baking powder
Grated rind and juice of one orange

Orange Cake (1890)

One and a half cupfuls of sugar
½ cupful of butter
Whites of four eggs
1 cupful of milk
2 cupfuls of flour

Filling:

1 apple, stewed and sifted
2 oranges, grated
Yolks of 3 eggs, well beaten
Sugar

Cook until the consistency of thick cream. Yolk of one egg for frosting.

Orange Cake (1904)

½ pound of sugar
6 ounces of grated almonds
12 eggs
2 ounces of flour
2 tablespoonfuls of arrac

After stirring this together as directed in the receipt for almond cake, bake 2 cakes.

Then take 2 whole and the yolks of 4 eggs
The juice of 4 oranges
The grated rind of an orange

The juice of 2 lemons
¼ pound of sugar

Put on the fire and whip with a beater until it is quite thick. This cream is spread on one of the cakes, put the other on this, and pour the following icing over the top: Mix the juice of 1 orange with ¼ pound of sifted sugar and 1 tablespoonful of water for ¼ hour and spread smoothly.

Orange Cake with Milk Icing (1909)

Cream ½ cupful of butter with 1½ cupfuls of sugar
Add ¾ cupful of sweet milk
The beaten yolks of 4 eggs

2 cupfuls of flour sifted with 1 teaspoonful of baking-powder
And the beaten whites of 4 eggs

Bake in layers and put together with the following:
Orange Milk Icing: Boil 2 cupfuls of sugar with 1 cupful of milk for ten minutes, pour into a bowl 1and stir until cool; have ½ an orange grated, pulp and peel together, and the juice of 1 orange; add this to the sugar and beat until cold.

Orange Cheesecakes (1909)

Blanch ½ pound of almonds and beat in a mortar with orange- flower water, ½, pound of powdered sugar and 1 pound of butter. Beat the yolks of 10 eggs and the whites of 4; pound in a mortar, 2 candied oranges and 1 fresh one with the bitterness boiled out. When these are soft mix all the ingredients and bake in small moulds.

Orange Cheese-Cakes (1898)

Ingredients:

3 table-spoonfuls orange marmalade
2 eggs

Paste made with 8 oz. flour, and other ingredients in proportion

Method: Beat and strain the eggs, and add them to the marmalade, mixing very thoroughly. Butter some patty-pans, line them with the paste, rolled out thin; put some of the mixture in each, and bake in a moderately quick oven.
Time: 15 to 20 minutes.
Sufficient for: 12 cheese-cakes.

Orange Fruit Cake (1909)

Cream 1 pound of butter and 1 pound of sugar
Add ten beaten eggs

1 pound of flour
The juice of 2 oranges and the grated peel of 1

Beat all until very light.

Flour 2 pounds of seeded raisins
¾ pound of citron

½ pound of candied orange peel chopped or cut in bits

Add this to the batter and bake in two pans for four hours.

Orange Gingerbread (1909)

Heat 1¾ pounds of molasses and ¾ pound of butter over a slow fire; beat well and add ¾ pound of brown sugar, 2¼ pounds of flour, ½ pound of preserved orange peel, 1 ounce of ground ginger, 1 grated nutmeg, ½ cupful of orange juice and 1 level teaspoonful of soda. Work the dough well and leave in a cool place overnight. Next day turn out on a well-floured board and roll very thin, cut in small squares, lay these one inch apart on waxed tins and brush over with the beaten yolk of 1 egg mixed with ½ cupful of milk. Bake in a moderate oven, and when done brush again with the egg and milk.

Orange Lady Cake (1909)

Cream ½ cupful of butter with 1½ cupfuls of sugar; add the juice and grated rind of 1 orange with warm water to make 1 cupful, 2½ cupfuls of flour sifted twice before measuring and then sifted with 2 level teaspoonfuls of baking-powder; mix thoroughly and add the beaten whites of 4 eggs. Bake forty-five minutes in a moderate oven and when cool ice the top and sides.

Orange Layer Cake (1922)

1½ cups sugar
2 teaspoons baking powder
½ cup butter or shortening
3 cups pastry flour
2 eggs

½ teaspoon salt
Juice and grated rind of one orange
¼ teaspoon soda
1 cup water

Cream the butter with the sugar; add the beaten eggs. Add one teaspoon grated rind of orange.
Add to the foregoing, the sifted flour, salt and baking powder. Dissolve the soda in the cup of boiling water and alternating with the orange juice add to the mixture. Stir until creamy. Bake in greased layer pans for twenty minutes in a moderate oven.
Top and Filling for Cake: Beat stiff the whites of two eggs and add two cups confectioners' sugar. Add the juice of two large oranges and the grated peel of one. Stir together well and spread thick over top and layers.

Orange Layer Cake (1920)

½ cup butter
1 cup sugar
½ cup milk

The whites of 3 eggs
1½ cups prepared flour
The grated rind of ½ orange

Stir butter and sugar with your right hand to a light white cream and add the grated orange rind; beat the whites to a stiff froth; then add them alternately with the sifted flour and milk to the above mixture; butter 2 large jelly cake tins and line them with buttered tissue paper; put an equal portion of the cake batter into each pan; spread it evenly with a broad-bladed knife dipped in water and bake the cakes in a medium hot oven till a light brown and done, which will take from 15 to 20 minutes; to ascertain when cakes are done thrust a knitting needle into the centre of them; if it comes out clean the cakes are done; if any dough adheres to it the baking must be continued; as soon as the cakes are done remove them from the oven; lay a clean cloth or paper on the kitchen table and dust over it some powdered sugar; turn the cakes out of pans upside down onto the cloth and let them lay till cold; in the meantime prepare the filling, as follows: Put in a small saucepan the juice of 1 orange, 1 teaspoonful lemon juice, a little grated orange peel, 1 teaspoonful butter and the yolks of 3 eggs; set the saucepan in a vessel of boiling water and stir the contents till they thicken; remove from the fire and when cold add ½ cup sugar; lay one layer of cake, bottom side up, on a jelly cake dish and spread over it the orange mixture; lay over the remaining layer, right side up, and dust with powdered sugar; or ice the cake with clear icing; or cover the top of cake with an orange glaze

Orange Shortcake (1913)

Sift together a large cupful of flour, a rounding teaspoonful of baking powder and a pinch of salt.
Mix with a piece of butter the size of a walnut. (Cut it into the flour.) Add milk enough to make a dough that will roll out. Bake in one piece and split it open, spread it with butter, then with small pieces of orange, sweetened to taste. Cover with a meringue or soft custard. Other fruit may be used.

Orange Short Cake (1893)

Orange shortcake is very nice. The only difficulty to overcome in making this toothsome dish is to get rid of the white fibres which intersect the pulp of the orange, and this is, after all, a very easy matter. To prepare the oranges, simply cut them in half, without peeling, and take out the lobes precisely as when eating an orange with a spoon. The shortcake is made like very short, soft biscuit and baked in a round tin in a quick oven. When it is done, split it, sprinkle sugar over the prepared oranges, put a layer on the under crust, replace the upper part, upon which put more of the prepared oranges and serve at once with cream

Orange Sponge (1909)

Steep 1 box of gelatine for one hour in 1 cupful of cold water, then dissolve in 1 cupful of boiling water. When cool, add the juice of 6 oranges and 1 lemon and 1 cupful of sugar; strain and let cool. When it begins to stiffen, add the whites of 3 eggs beaten with 3 tablespoonfuls of sugar, stir until it will not separate then pour into a mould to harden. Serve with boiled custard.

Orange Sunshine Cake (1893)

Whites of 6 eggs well beaten with half teaspoon cream tartar, add small cup sifted sugar, add the yolks of 3 eggs well beaten, juice and rind ½ orange, fold in ½ cup flour sifted 4 times. Bake in angel cake tin, have oven quite hot at first, bake 40 minutes if possible.

Orange Tourte (1922)

Bake from the Genoise Sponge Cake (1922), three even layers in large rings and let cool. Make the Orange filling, and when cool spread on two of the layers. On top of each layer of cream put a layer of thin slices of oranges from which the seeds and the white pith has been removed. Place together with the third layer on top. Ice with orange fondant icing and decorate with slices of orange which have been split in its natural quarters and dipped in caramel sugar; or decorate with fruit glace, or with both oranges and fruits.

Orange Washington Cake (1909)

Cream ½ cupful of butter with 2 cupfuls of sugar, add the yolks of 4 eggs, the juice of 2 oranges and the grated rind of 1, 3 cupfuls of flour, in which 1 heaping teaspoonful of baking-powder has been sifted, and the beaten whites of 4 eggs. Bake quickly in two thick layers and when done spread them with the following:
Filling: Dissolve 3 tablespoonfuls of corn-starch in ½ cupful of cold water and stir into 1½ cupfuls of boiling water; add 1 cupful of sugar, 1 tablespoonful of butter, the juice of 3 oranges and the grated rind of 2, and the beaten yolks of 3 eggs. Cook until thick and put on the cake while warm.

Ormond Cake (1909)

Beat the yolks of 5 eggs with 2 cupfuls of sugar; add ½ cupful of water, the juice of 2 oranges, the grated rind of 1 orange, 2 cupfuls of flour sifted with 2 teaspoonfuls of baking-powder, and the beaten whites of 4 eggs. Bake in layers and spread with the following filling: Melt ½ cupful of butter with 1 cupful of sugar; add the juice of 2 oranges and the grated rind of 1 orange, the yolks of 3 eggs and the beaten white of 1; cook to a thick cream. Cover the top and sides of the cake with icing made with the whites of 2 eggs beaten with powdered sugar until thick, and flavour with orange juice and a little grated rind.

Oyster Shortcake (1922)

2 cupfuls flour
1-quart oysters
2 teaspoonfuls baking powder
½ cupful Crisco
½ teaspoonful salt

2 tablespoonfuls cornstarch
¾ cupful milk
¼ cupful cream
Salt and pepper to taste

Mix flour, baking powder and ½ teaspoonful salt, then sift twice, work in Crisco with tips of fingers, add milk gradually. The dough should be just soft enough to handle. Toss on floured baking board, divide into two parts, pat lightly and roll out. Place in two shallow Criscoed cake tins and bake in quick oven fifteen minutes. Spread them with butter. Moisten cornstarch with cream, put into pan with oysters and seasonings and make very hot. Allow to cook a few minutes then pour half over one crust, place other crust on top and pour over rest of oysters. Serve at once.
Sufficient for: one large shortcake.

Oyster Shortcake (1912)

Boll plain paste quite thin, fit over an inverted baking dish and bake. Cut a plain piece for the top and bake on a sheet. Prepare oysters a-la-France. Remove the pastry from the inverted dish and put on a flat platter. Fill with oyster mixture, put pastry top on and serve as ordinary meat pie. The top can be made very ornamental by cutting leaves or fancy shapes from pastry, moisten with cold water around the edge of top crust and lay the leaves on, overlapping each other and bake together.
Individual shortcakes can be made the same way by the use of small tin moulds, cooking the shells on inverted moulds, the tops separately on baking sheets, and filling the shells with oyster mixture and placing the tops over just before serving.

Part 17: P

Pan Cakes (1869)
Parisian Cake (1904)
Parisian Cakes (1920)
(Gâteaux Parisiens)
Peach Cake with Sweetened Cream (1913)
Peach Shortcake (1922)
Peach Shortcake (1920)
Pearl Grit Gems (1876)
Pecan Cake (1893)
Pensacola Cake (1909)
Pfefferkuchen (1910)
(Gingerbread)
Pflaumenkuchen (1910)
Piccolomini Cake (1894)
Pineapple Cake (1913)
Pineapple Cake (1920)
Pineapple Cake (1920)
(Gâteau Ananas)
Pine-apple Sponge (1898)
Pineapple Upside Down Cake (1922)
Pink Cake (1876)
Plain Apple Cake (1904)
Plain Cake (1922)
Plain Cake (1917)
Plain Cake (1920)
Plain Cake (1911)
Plain Cake with Fruit Jelly (1904)
Plain Cider Cake (1840)
Plain Genoa Pound Cake (1922)
Plain Ginger Cakes (1913)
Plain Griddle Cakes (1917)
Plain Jelly Cake (1913)
Plain Layer Cake (1913)
Plain Muffins (1917)
Plain Orange Cake (1909)
Plain Pound Cake (1922)
Plain Pound Cake (1893)
Plain Raisin Cake (1894)
Plain Sponge Cake (No. 1) (1922)
Plain Sponge Cake (No. 2) (1922)
Plain Strawberry Shortcake (1920)
Plain Tea Cake (1911)
Plain White Cake No, 1 (1912)
Plain White Cake No, 1 (1912)
Pleasant Point Eggless Cake (1911)
Plum Cake (1898)
(Plain)
Plum Cake (1898)
(Good)
Plum Cake (1920)
(Gâteau aux Raisins de Corinthe)
Plum Cake (1904)
Plum-Cake (1864)
Plunderbretzel – Kranzkuchen (1910)
Polnischer Krengel (1910)
Pome-de-Terres (1912)
Pomme de Terre Cake (1820)
Poppy Seed Cakes (1922)
Poppyseed Cake (1922)
Pork Cake (1913)
Pork Cake No. 1 (1876)
Pork Cake No. 2 (1876)
(Fruit)
Portuguese Coffee Cake (1904)
Potato Cake (1904)
Potato Cake No. 1 (1912)
Potato Cake No. 2 (1912)
Potato Cake (1909)
Potato Cake (1836)
Potato Cakes (1876)
Potato Cakes (1922)
Potato Cakes (1899)
Potato Cakes (1905)
Potato Cakes (1913)
Potato Cakes (1920)
(Gâteaux de Pommes de Terre)
Potato Cakes (1894)
Potato Cakes with Ham (1920)
(Galettes de Pommes de Terre au Jambon)
Potato Chocolate Cake (1820)
Potato Flour Cake (1911)
Potato Flour Muffins (1922)
Potato Torte (1820)
Pound Cake No. 1 (1889)
Pound Cake No. 2 (1889)
Pound Cake 1 (1876)
Pound Cake 2 (1876)
Pound Cake (1922)
Pound Cake (N.D.)
Pound Cake (1922)
Pound Cake (1913)
(Aunt Polly Rives)
Pound Cake (1840)
Pound Cake (1869)
Pound Cake (1920)
(Pound Cake)
Pound Cake (1894)
Pound Cake (No.1) (1922)
Pound Cake (No.2) (1922)
Poverty Cake (1911)
Princess Cake (1922)
Prune Cake (1820)

Puff Cake (1913)
Pumpernickel-Torte (1910)
(Pumpernickel Spongecake)
Punch Cake, Punch Biscuit, Imitation of Boar's Head, a Book or a Ham (1920)
(Gâteau Punch, Punch Biscuit, Imitation de Hure de Sanglier, d'un Livre ou d'un Jambon)

Punch Layer Cake (1904)
Punsch Torte (1893)
Punch Cake (1922)
Punch Tourte
Pyramid Birthday Cake (1921)

Pan Cakes (1869)

Take five eggs to a quart of milk, make a thin batter with flour, have a little hot lard in the frying-pan, and pour in enough batter to cover the bottom; turn and fry the other side; if eggs are scarce, a tea-spoonful of salaeratus will supply the place of two. Eat them with wine and sugar.

Parisian Cake (1904)

Dissolve some yeast in a cupful of milk.
Then stir 1 pound of butter to a cream

Add 3 whole eggs
The yolks of 3 eggs
5 ounces of sugar
¼ pound each of currants and raisins
½ teaspoonful of salt
2 ounces of citron
½ ounce of grated bitter almonds

1 spoonful of vanilla
Grated lemon peel
Mace
3 spoonfuls of Cognac
The dissolved yeast,
Last add 1¼ pounds of sifted flour

Whip the dough hard until light, put it into a large buttered pan, set aside to raise and then bake in a moderate oven to a light brown colour. Turn the cake out of the pan, sift over it some powdered sugar and then hold a red-hot shovel over it to glaze it.

Parisian Cakes (1920)
(Gâteaux Parisiens)

Lay a band of puff paste parings three and a half inches wide by twelve inches long on a baking sheet; on the edges place small narrow bands of the same or else twist the edge to form a border; fill it with vanilla pastry cream; prick the bottom and push into a hot oven. As soon as done remove the band and allow to cool. Then cover with a preparation made of very lightly beaten royal icing into which shredded almonds have been mixed; dredge over with sugar; cut into crosswise slices an inch and a quarter in size; place these on a baking sheet, then in the oven to colour; remove and stand on a wire grate to get perfectly cold.

Peach Cake with Sweetened Cream (1913)

2 cups flour
4 teaspoons baking powder
1/2 teaspoon salt
3 tablespoons Cottolene

3/4 cup rich milk
5 peaches
Sultana raisins
Mace and sugar

Process: Mix and sift the first three ingredients. Rub in Cottolene with tips of fingers, add milk, mixing it in with a knife. This dough must be soft enough to spread in a shallow, well-buttered pan to the depth of one inch. (Add more milk if necessary.) Pare ripe, juicy peaches; cut in halves lengthwise, remove stones and press halves into dough (cut side up) in parallel rows, leaving a little space between rows. Brush peaches over with melted butter, sprinkle with raisins, granulated sugar

Peach Shortcake (1922)

2 cupfuls sugar
¾ cupful Crisco
1 cupful milk
1 teaspoonful baking powder

5 eggs
½ teaspoonful salt
3 cupfuls flour
1 teaspoonful almond extract

Quartered peaches

Cream Crisco and sugar together, then add milk, eggs one by one, always beating well between each one, flour sifted with baking powder and salt, then add extract. Mix and divide into two layer tins that have been greased with Crisco and bake twenty minutes in moderate oven. Turn out and spread with butter. Put together with quartered and sweetened peaches and pile some peaches on top.
Sufficient for: one cake.

Peach Shortcake (1920)

Peach Shortcake is made the same as Strawberry Shortcake. In place of berries take peaches pared and cut into slices. Or this cake may be made of all kinds of preserved fruit and served either with sweet cream or vanilla sauce.

Pearl Grit Gems (1876)

Stir the grits into hot water and boil half an hour. When cold, take three cups of grits, and the same of either white or Graham flour, one pint of milk or water, and a little salt. Put into hot gem pans, and bake half an hour, or until brown. Baking powder can be used, though it is unnecessary.

Pecan Cake (1893)

One cup of butter
Two and a half cups of flour
Two cups of sugar

One-half cup of sweet milk
Whites of eight eggs
Two teaspoonfuls baking powder

Beat together butter and sugar; add a little of the beaten egg; then put in a cup of flour, then some milk, then again flour and milk; put all the milk in with the second cup of flour; then add the rest of the egg.
Icing to fill and put over top of Pecan Cake: Whites of six eggs, beaten stiff with powdered sugar; one small can of grated pineapple and two cups of pecans, chopped fine. The nuts should soak awhile in the pineapple before mixing them into the egg and sugar. Put whole pecan kernels over the top of the cake while the icing is still soft.

Pensacola Cake (1909)

Cream ½ pound of butter with 1 pound of sugar; add 2 tablespoonfuls of brandy and beat in the yolks of 8 eggs; add 1 pound of seeded raisins, 1 pound of sifted flour, the beaten whites of 8 eggs and the juice and the grated rind of ½ a large orange. Add no baking-powder or soda.

Pfefferkuchen (1910)
(Gingerbread)

5 eggs
6 powdered cloves
½ grated nutmeg
¼ oz. ground ginger
9 oz. castor sugar

6 oz. mixed peel
¼ lb. sweet almonds
¼ oz. carbonate of soda
¼ teaspoonful ground cinnamon
2 tablespoonsful milk

Whisk the eggs in a basin and add to them the cloves, nutmeg, cinnamon and castor sugar. Beat these well for about 10 minutes.
Next add the peel, cut into thin but rather large pieces, the flour well dried, the almonds, blanched and cut into halves, and carbonate of soda mixed in 2 tablespoonsful of milk.

Stir quickly and pour into a deep baking tin lined with butter, or, which is much better, wafer papers. Shake some more almonds on the top and bake in a moderate oven, three-quarters of an hour. When nearly done, sprinkle a little icing sugar on the top.

This will keep well in a dry tin.

Pflaumenkuchen (1910)

Prepare the dough as in recipe "Blechkuchen." Let it rise to about ½ inch or more on the sheet of tin, then brush over with 3 oz. butter (melted) and sprinkle with the same quantity of grated roll or dry breadcrumbs. Take 5 lbs. of plums, stone them, cut into quarters lengthwise and place them closely side by side on the dough. Bake ½ to ¾ hour, and sprinkle thickly with sugar immediately on taking out of the oven.

Piccolomini Cake (1894)

Three cups sugar, one cup butter, rub to a cream; beat five eggs very light, and stir gradually into the mixture together with four full cups flour and one of sweet milk. Dissolve in a little warm water half teaspoon soda, one teaspoon cream tartar, add nutmeg and wine glass rose water.

Pineapple Cake (1913)

Cream half a cupful of butter and a large cupful of confectioners' sugar, add a cupful of minced pineapple and two well beaten eggs. Sift together a cupful of flour and a rounding teaspoonful of baking powder. Mix all the ingredients and pour in half a cupful of milk. Make a thick batter, adding the necessary flour.

Pineapple Cake (1920)

½ pound butter
1-pound powdered sugar
¾ pound flour
1 heaping teaspoonful baking powder

½ pint pineapple syrup
2 whole eggs, the yolks of 4
1 teaspoonful essence of vanilla

Wash the butter several times in cold water and dry it in a napkin; put butter and sugar in a mixing bowl and stir with the right hand to a light white cream; then stir with a spoon and add the 2 whole eggs, 1 at a time, stirring a few minutes between each addition; next add the yolks, 1 at a time; sift flour and baking powder together; add the flour and pineapple syrup alternately to the above mixture; butter 3 large, deep jelly cake tins and dust them with flour; put an equal portion of the cake batter into each pan, spread it evenly with a broad-bladed knife dipped in water and bake the cakes in a medium hot oven to a delicate brown; when done remove the cakes from the oven; lay a napkin on a pastry board and dust over some powdered sugar; turn the cake out, upside down, onto the napkin; when cold put one cake, bottom side up, on a cake dish and spread over a layer of pineapple marmalade; put on the last layer, right side up, and cover the top with pineapple glaze made as follows: - Stir ½ pound powdered sugar with 3 or 4 tablespoonfuls pineapple syrup and a few drops of prepared saffron to a stiff sauce; set it for a few minutes over the fire, stirring constantly until lukewarm; then pour it by spoonfuls over the cake and lay some preserved pineapple slices in a circle around the cake; or use candied pineapple.

Pineapple Cake (1920)
(Gâteau Ananas)

Prepare a Savoy biscuit composition in the following proportions:

One pound of sugar
Fourteen yolks

Two whole eggs

Three-quarters of a pound of fecula and flour, half of each	Fourteen whipped whites
Some pineapple extract

Bake a part of this in a Savarin mold seven and a quarter inches in diameter, buttered and glazed with sugar and fecula, and the remainder in a charlotte mold six inches wide by seven high. As soon as both are cooked unmould the cakes and allow to cool. Cover the one baked in the Savarin mold with apricot marmalade, and ice with pink fondant flavoured with kirsch; as soon as this is dry slip it on a sweet paste foundation, sprinkled over with green granulated sugar; put a pad of biscuit in the center, and range it on a dish or board covered with lace paper. Pare the cake baked in the charlotte mold to the shape of a sugar loaf, then cut it into transversal slices three-eighths of an inch thick; cover all of these with a light layer of apricot marmalade, and reconstruct the cake as before; cover its entire surface with Italian meringue flavoured with orange and slightly tinted with vegetable yellow; pour some of the same meringue in a pocket with a channeled socket and push it through to imitate the rough skin of a pineapple, forming points on the entire surface of the cake; stand it on a tart plate and push it into a slack oven to barely dry the meringue; remove it at once and allow to cool thoroughly; place it on a grate and ice over with yellow orange icing, and when this is dry detach the pineapple cautiously from the grate and place it on top of the biscuit. Over the points of the rough pineapple form the tips with chocolate icing pushed through a cornet. Decorate the top with stalks cut from angelica dipped in sugar cooked to "crack" having the base of the pineapple surrounded by leaves of the same.

Pine-apple Sponge (1898)

Ingredients:

¾ lb. preserved pine-apple	1 dessertspoonful lemon juice
¼ pint syrup from the tin	4 lumps of sugar
¾ pint water	Whites of 2 eggs
½ oz. isinglass	

Method: Cut the pine-apple into dice, put it in a lined saucepan with the syrup, water, isinglass, lemon juice, and sugar, and let them simmer gently for ¼ hour. Strain all through a fine sieve, pressing the pine-apple strongly to extract as much of its juice as possible. Set aside in a cool place. When the jelly is cool and just beginning to set, whisk the whites of the eggs to as firm a froth as possible, add the half-liquid jelly, a spoonful at a time, and continue beating until the whole becomes of the consistency of a sponge. Pour the mixture into a well-wetted mould and set it aside to become firm. This should be made some hours before it is required for use. In summer, the beating should be done over ice.
Time: ¼ hour to make jelly.
20 minutes to beat sponge.
Sufficient for: 1½ pint mould.

Pineapple Upside Down Cake (1922)

¼ pound butter	1 cup brown sugar
1 medium can pineapple	

Melt butter slightly in heavy frying pan. Spread over this the brown sugar and then lay on pineapple.

Batter:

3 eggs	1 teaspoon baking powder
1 cup flour	5 tablespoons pineapple juice
1 cup sugar	

Beat egg yolks, add sugar, pineapple juice, flour sifted with baking powder. Fold in beaten egg whites. Pour over first mixture and bake in moderate oven. When done place cake plate on top of pan and reverse. Serve with whipped cream. (Pan should be eleven inches in diameter - and three inches deep.)

Pink Cake (1876)

One cup of sugar
A half-cup of butter
Two cups of flour

Whites of five eggs
Two teaspoons of baking powder
Analine the size of two grains of wheat

Tie the last in a thin cloth and pour over it a half teaspoon of hot water. The analine can be put in one half the mixture and dropped into the pan with alternate spoons of the white, making a marbled cake which is very ornamental. The effect is better to have the mixtures put together in small quantities.

Plain Apple Cake (1904)

Butter a pan, sprinkle over it some grated wheat bread and fill with alternate layers of grated roll (or brown bread) and apple slices. Over each layer put sugar, pieces of butter and a little fruit jelly. Then bake the cake, having grated bread for the top layer, for 1 hour. Half an hour before the cake is done make a cream for it, using 1 cupful of sour cream, the yolks of 4 eggs, 3 ounces of sugar and 1⅔ ounces of grated almonds, pour this over the cake and then bake until done.

Plain Cake (1922)

⅓ cup butter or shortening
1¾ teaspoons baking powder
1 cup sugar

½ cup milk
2 eggs
1 teaspoon vanilla

Cream the butter and the sugar. Add the eggs, well beaten. Sift the dry ingredients together and add alternating with the milk. Add the vanilla and bake in layers for twenty minutes in a moderate oven (375 degrees F.).
Fill and frost as desired. This recipe may be modified by adding nuts, cocoanut, spices, etc., and by frosting in an attractive way

Plain Cake (1917)

1/3 cup shortening
1-2/3 cups flour
1 cup sugar
3 teaspoons baking powder

2 eggs
Few grains salt
1/2 cup milk
1/2 teaspoon lemon extract

Beat shortening and sugar until light and creamy; add eggs well beaten, flour, baking powder, salt, and extract; beat well, pour into a greased and papered cake pan, and bake about half an hour in a moderate oven, or in two layer-cake pans about twenty minutes. This is an excellent foundation cake for use with various flavourings, icings, and fillings.

Plain Cake (1920)

1 cup butter
1 cup milk
2 cups sugar

3 cups prepared flour
4 eggs
the grated rind of 1 lemon

Stir butter and sugar to a light white cream with your right hand; then stir with a silver spoon, add the eggs, 1 at a time, stirring a few minutes between each addition; next add the sifted flour and milk alternately; butter a large, round cake pan and line it with buttered paper; pour in the cake mixture and bake in a medium hot oven for 1 hour; to ascertain if cake is done thrust a knitting needle into centre of cake; if it comes out clean the cake is done; if not, the baking must be continued; when done remove the cake from oven and let it stand 10 minutes; then turn it out of pan, remove the paper and set the cake in a cool place or put it when cold in a tin cake box. If plain flour is used take 1½ teaspoonfuls baking powder and sift it with the flour. Measure with a cup which holds half a pint.

Plain Cake (1911)

Beat together one-half cup of butter and two cups of sugar until light and creamy, add the well beaten yolks of three eggs, one-half cup of milk, three cups of flour in which three teaspoons of baking powder have been sifted, and last the stiffly beaten whites of three eggs. Add any flavouring preferred and bake in a moderate oven.

Plain Cake with Fruit Jelly (1904)

Cream ½ pound of butter, ½ pound of sugar and stir into it the yolks of 6 eggs. Beat for ½ hour, then mix with the flour and the beaten whites of the eggs and bake to a light brown colour. After it is cool pieces of jelly are laid over the cake.

Plain Cider Cake (1840)

Sift into a large pan a pound and a half of flour and rub into it half a pound of butter. Mix in three-quarters of a pound of powdered white sugar and melt a small teaspoonful of salaratus or pearl-ash in a pint of the best cider. Pour the cider into the other ingredients while it is foaming and stir the whole very hard. Have ready a buttered square pan, put in the mixture, and set It immediately in a rather brisk oven. Bake it an hour or more, according to its thickness. This is a tea cake and should be eaten fresh. Cut it into squares, split and butter them.

Plain Genoa Pound Cake (1922)

One and one-half pounds of sugar
One pound of butter
Ten eggs
Two pounds of flour

One and one-half ounces of baking powder
Lemon flavour
Milk to mix

Mix the same as Pound Cake (No.2) (1922)
This mixture may be used for a stock mixture to make a variety of other cakes, making the mixture rather slack at the start and changing the ingredients, adding more eggs or flour, as suggested in New Receipts and Points on Cake Making (1922).

Plain Ginger Cakes (1913)

1 cup N. O. molasses
2 teaspoons soda
1/2 cup Cottolene
1/2 cup boiling water
4 cups flour

1 teaspoon salt
1 tablespoon ginger
1 teaspoon cinnamon
1/4 teaspoon cloves

Process: Add soda to molasses. Melt Cottolene in boiling water; combine in mixing bowl. Mix and sift flour, salt and spices, add to first mixture and beat thoroughly. Chill dough and roll a small portion at a time to one-half inch thickness, shape with a round cutter. Press a seeded raisin in top of each, sprinkle with coarse granulated sugar. Bake in a moderate oven. It may be necessary to add to add more flour.

Plain Griddle Cakes (1917)

1-1/2 cups flour
1 egg well beaten
3 teaspoons baking powder
1 tablespoon melted shortening
1/2 teaspoon salt

1/2 cup milk
1 tablespoon sugar
3/4 cup water

Mix and sift dry ingredients; add egg well beaten, shortening, and liquid; beat well, and cook on a hot griddle. The cakes should be small and should be served very hot with butter and sirup.

Plain Jelly Cake (1913)

Cream together a heaping cupful of powdered sugar and half a cupful of butter. Sift a heaping cupful of flour with a rounding teaspoonful of baking powder and a dash of salt. Add the well beaten yolks of three eggs and beat all the ingredients together until very smooth. Beat the whites of the eggs until very stiff and stir them in lightly the last thing before baking. Bake in greased layer tins and when cold put together with jelly.

Plain Layer Cake (1913)

Cream together a cupful of sugar and half a cupful of butter. Add the beaten yolks of two eggs, a small cupful of sweet milk, or water, and one and one-half cupfuls of flour sifted with a rounding teaspoonful of baking powder and a pinch of salt. Stir well and put in the beaten whites last. Bake slowly in layer pans.

Plain Muffins (1917)

2 cups flour
1 egg
4 teaspoons baking powder
1 cup milk

1/2 teaspoon salt
2 tablespoons melted shortening
2 tablespoons sugar

Mix and sift dry ingredients; add egg well beaten, milk, and shortening; beat well, and bake in greased muffin pans in moderate oven twenty minutes. For fruit muffins add one cup of figs, dates, or cooked prunes cut in pieces.

Plain Orange Cake (1909)

Beat 2 eggs with 1 cupful of sugar, add 1 tablespoonful of melted butter, ½ cupful of milk and 1½ cupfuls of flour sifted with 2 level teaspoonfuls of baking-powder. Beat until smooth, stir in the juice and the grated rind of ½ an orange and bake in a loaf in a moderate oven.

Plain Pound Cake (1922)

1-pound butter
10 eggs
1-pound sugar

1 cup milk
1-pound flour
½ teaspoon salt

Cream the butter and the sugar thoroughly together. Add the well-beaten eggs. Sift the dry ingredients together and add with the milk. Pour into buttered bread pan and bake in a slow oven (320 degrees F.) for an hour and a quarter.

Plain Pound Cake (1893)

One cup butter
2 cups sugar

4 cups flour
5 eggs

Sprinkle sugar over top. Makes 2 tins.

Plain Raisin Cake (1894)

One-half cup molasses
one cup sugar
one half cup butter
one-half cup sour milk

teaspoon soda
two eggs
three cups flour
Raisins and spice

Plain Sponge Cake (No. 1) (1922)

One pound of sugar
One pound of flour

Twelve eggs
Flavour

Beat sugar and eggs together slightly warm and then cold.
Mix and bake the same as Butter Sponge Cake (No. 1) (1922)

Plain Sponge Cake (No. 2) (1922)

One pound of sugar
One pound of flour
One pint of eggs

A half pint of yolks
Lemon or vanilla flavour

Mix the same as Butter Sponge Cake (No. 1) (1922). Bake in medium heat 300 to 350 degrees Fahrenheit.

Plain Strawberry Shortcake (1920)

1-quart flour
½ teaspoonful salt
½ cup butter

2 cups milk
2 teaspoonfuls baking powder

Sift flour, powder and salt into a bowl, add the butter and chop it very fine with a chopper in the flour; then mix it with the milk into a soft dough; divide it into two equal parts and roll them out to the size of a jelly plate; butter a deep jelly tin, put in 1 layer and brush it over with melted butter, put on the other layer and bake in a quick oven; when done remove it from oven, separate the 2 layers with a broad-bladed knife and spread them with butter; mash some fresh strawberries with a silver spoon, cover the bottom layer with the mashed strawberries and sprinkle thickly with powdered sugar; lay on the other layer with the crust side downward, cover with a thick layer of strawberries, sprinkle with sugar and serve with vanilla sauce, sweet cream or the following sauce: - Beat 2 eggs until they foam, add 2 small cups milk, stirring constantly, sweeten to taste and flavour with vanilla extract.

Plain Tea Cake (1911)

Cream two level tablespoons of butter and one cup of sugar together, add one beaten egg, one cup of milk and two cups of flour in which three level teaspoons of baking powder have been sifted. Bake in a sheet and serve while fresh.

Plain White Cake No, 1 (1912)

One cup of butter
Three cups of sugar
One cup of milk or water
Five cups of flour
Two full teaspoons of baking powder
Whites of twelve eggs

Cream the butter and add the flour, alternating with milk. Put baking powder in the last cup of flour. Beat the whites very stiff, add sugar gradually. Combine the two mixtures, adding a little at a time. Bake in a mould or in layer cake pans. This is a delicious, fine grained cake and is especially good for baking in large sheets to cut into small cakes. Have a pan made twelve by fourteen inches and one and three-fourths inches deep; line the pan with greased paper and cook forty to fifty minutes in a slow oven at first, then increase the heat. Turn out at once when done on a folded cloth, let stand until cold. Trim and cut into shape.

Plain White Cake No, 2 (1912)

One and one-fourth cups of butter
Two and one-half cups of sugar
Four cups of flour
One-fourth teaspoon of soda
One level teaspoon of cream of tartar

Dissolve in one tablespoon of hot water or one tablespoon whiskey or sherry wine. Mix as above recipe. Bake in a mould with stem. Line with paper and grease well. Bake one and one-half to two hours, in a very slow oven at first. Cover over the top of mould with greased paper, put a pan of water on upper grate, leave the cover on until the cake has risen to the top of the pan; remove the greased paper and continue to bake it until it begins to brown, then take the pan of water from upper grate and finish the cooking, always observing the rule of increasing heat. The whites of fourteen eggs.

Pleasant Point Eggless Cake (1911)

1 cup sugar
½ cup butter or lard
2 cups flour
½ teaspoonful soda
½ cup sour milk
1 cup raisins
½ teaspoonful each of cloves, cinnamon, nutmeg
A little salt

Bake in a slow oven ¾ of an hour.

Plum Cake (1898)
(Plain)

Ingredients:

1¼ lbs. flour
½ lb. raisins
6 oz. butter or good beef dripping
6 oz. sugar
A pinch of salt
1 teaspoonful baking-powder
½ pint milk

Method: Mix the flour, salt and baking powder together. Stone and divide the raisins. Rub the butter or dripping into the flour, add the raisins and sugar, and moisten the mixture with the milk, beating it well with

a wooden spoon. Beat the cake for five minutes, then put it into a well-buttered cake tin and bake it in a moderate oven, covering the top with a buttered paper when half done.
Time: 1½ hours.
Sufficient for: 1 moderate-sized cake.

Plum Cake (1898)
(Good)

Ingredients:

1 lb. flour	½ lb. currants
a pinch of salt	2 oz. mixed candied peel
½ lb. butter	¼ pint milk
½ lb. raisins	2 eggs
½ lb. sugar	1 table-spoonful brandy

Method: Mix the flour and salt together and rub in the butter. Stone and divide the raisins, wash and pick the currants, and cut the candied peel into small pieces, mix these with the flour, and add the sugar. Beat and strain the eggs, add the milk and brandy, and moisten the cake with these. Beat the cake for a few minutes, then put it into a well-buttered cake tin, and bake it in a good oven for about if to 2 hours, covering the top with a buttered paper when half done.
Time: 1½ to 2 hours.
Sufficient for: 1 moderate-sized cake.

Plum Cake (1920)
(Gâteau aux Raisins de Corinthe)

Butter a charlotte mold five and a half inches in diameter by five inches high; at the bottom lay a round piece of paper and line the sides with a band of the same. This should reach threequarters of an inch beyond the edge and should be serrated all around. Place three-quarters of a pound of butter in a vessel with the same weight of sugar and beat together to have it creamy, then add six whole eggs, one at a time, one gill of rum, six ounces of currants cleaned and softened in hot water, three ounces of preserved cherries cut in four, three ounces of citron cut up finely, a pinch of powdered carbonate of ammonia, and lastly fourteen ounces of sifted flour. Fill the mold threequarters full with this and stand it on a baking plate; push it into a slack oven to bake, and when done unmould on a grate to cool thoroughly without removing the paper, then place it on a dish covered with a folded napkin and serve.

Plum Cake (1904)

Make a dough as given; take fresh plums, sifted sugar, cinnamon and grated bread.
Lay the plums on a sieve and then put them into boiling water until the skin can be easily taken off with a knife and after this is done, stone and lay them into a dish. Then make the dough, which can be moulded immediately without being first set aside. To do this put it into the mould in pieces and press it with the hands (which should be dusted with flour) uniformly all around, a little thicker at the sides, however, so as to make the edge about 1½ inches high; all thin spots should be covered with pieces of dough. The projecting edge should be scolloped with the fingers and then bent upwards, all scollops pointing in the same direction. Dust the dough plentifully with rolled crackers, turn each plum in powdered sugar and arrange them in circular form, beginning at the edge and working towards the center, putting them in closely together. Sprinkle with cinnamon and then bake the cake for 1¼ hours with 1 degree of heat (see General Directions (1904)). The juice of the plums is put on a soup plate with some sugar, set on the back part of the stove until thick and pour it over the cake when the latter is to be served.

The above given quantities are for a large cake. This is very nice when warm and also very good when a few days old, first putting it into a hot oven for ¼ hour. When plums cannot be obtained use prune sauce and then bake for ¼ hour.

Plum-Cake (1864)

First in place, Plum-cake is seen o'er smaller pastry ware, And ice on that. SWIFT.

Pick two pounds of currants very clean, and wash them, draining them through a cullender. Wipe them in a towel, spread them out in a large dish, and set them near the fire or in the hot sun to dry, placing the dish in a slanting position. Having stoned two pounds of best raisins, cut them in half, and when all are done, sprinkle them well with sifted flour, to prevent their sinking to the bottom of the cake. When the currants are dry, sprinkle them also with flour.

Pound the spice, two tablespoonfuls of cinnamon, two nutmegs, powdered; sift and mix the cinnamon and nutmeg together. Mix also a large glass of wine and brandy, half a glass of rose-water in a tumbler or cup. Cut a pound of citron in slips; sift a pound of flour in a broad dish, sift a pound of powdered white sugar into a deep earthen pan, and cut a pound of butter into it. Warm it near the fire, if the weather is too cold for it to mix easily. Stir the butter and sugar to a cream; beat twelve eggs as light as possible; stir them into the butter and sugar alternately with the flour; stir very hard; add gradually the spice and liquor. Stir the raisins and currants alternately in the mixture, taking care that they are well floured. Stir the whole as hard as possible, for ten minutes after the ingredients are in.

Cover the bottom and sides of a large tin or earthen pan with sheets of white paper well-buttered and put into it some of the mixture. Then spread some citron on it, which must not be cut too small; next put a layer of the mixture, and then a layer of citron, and so on till all is in, having a layer of mixture at the top.

This cake will require four or five hours baking, in proportion to its thickness.

Ice it next day.

Plunderbretzel – Kranzkuchen (1910)

1½ lb. flour	1 egg
¾ lb. butter	3 extra yolks
2 oz. yeast	8 oz. sugar
½ pint milk	4 oz. sweet almonds
½ lb. sultanas	Grated rind of ½ lemon

Mix the flour, lukewarm milk, yeast, 1 egg, and the 3 extra yolks, ¼ lb. butter and ¼ lb. sugar well and stand, covered over, in a warm place to rise. Then place the dough on a floured pasteboard and roll out about ½ inch thick. Press the rest of the butter to a firm square lump, place in the middle of the rolled-out paste and fold the latter over it. Roll out well, then turn the corners to the centre again, press together and roll out once more. Repeat this process several times and then stand in a cool place for ½ hour. Then roll out again to about ¼ inch thick and 18 inches long, and sprinkle over with the remaining ¼ lb. sugar, grated lemon peel and the sultanas and chopped almonds. Roll together, form into a looped twist (Bretzel) or circle (Kranz), and place on a buttered sheet of tin. When risen, bake in a brisk oven. On taking out, brush over with butter and sprinkle with sugar and cinnamon.

Polnischer Krengel (1910)

4 eggs	1½ lb. flour
½ pint milk	1 gill creamed butter
1 teaspoonful salt	1 oz. yeast

In addition:

¾ lb. butter
¼ lb. sugar

Grated rind of 1 lemon
½ lb. currants or ¼ lb. grated almonds

Dissolve the yeast in the lukewarm milk, sift the flour and stir it in with the creamed butter and beaten-up eggs. Mix very thoroughly. Make a serviette very wet in cold water, wring it out and well butter the centre of it. Place the dough on this and then tie firmly together, allowing plenty of room for the dough to rise. Then put into a pail of cold water overnight. Next day remove the cloth and roll out very thinly. Sprinkle over with currants or ½ lb. sultanas, or ¼ lb. grated almonds, with ¾ lb. butter, in little lumps, ¼ lb. sugar and the grated rind of a lemon. Roll together and form into a twisted Bretzel, or looped twist. Stand to rise for 2 hours in a warm pan, then brush over with egg, sprinkle with sugar, and bake in a moderate oven for 30 minutes.

Pome-de-Terres (1912)

Cook angel food cake in square pans two inches deep, break in irregular pieces, dip in plain white icing, sprinkle over with cinnamon. Angel food baked in loaf pans can be used the same way, but layer pans make a larger yield and are easier to break into the size pieces desired.

Pomme de Terre Cake (1820)

2 c. sugar
½ tsp. soda
¾ c. fat
2 tsp. vanilla
4 eggs
2 squares bitter chocolate (melted)

2½ c. flour
½ tsp. salt
1 c. nuts
½ c. sour cream or milk
1 c. raw grated potato
2 tsp. baking powder

Cream fat and sugar. Add sour cream and grated potato. Add flour sifted with baking powder and soda. Add nuts and melted chocolate. Fold in the whites. Do not grate potato until ready to add to batter. Bake in a loaf. Cakes of this type are better after "ripening" twenty-four hours in a bread box.

Poppy Seed Cakes (1922)

Cream ⅓ cup butter scant, 1 cup of sugar, 2 whites of eggs well beaten. Put ⅓ cup poppy seed in bowl and pour over ⅔ cup of milk Let stand while mixing the other part of cake. Add milk and 1½ cups of flour in which 2 teaspoons of baking powder is sifted. Beat well each operation.
Bake in a square shallow pan in a moderate oven. Cover with any desired icing and cut into squares.

Poppyseed Cake (1922)

1 cup poppyseed
2 cups flour
1½ cups milk
2 teaspoons baking powder

1½ cups sugar
4 whites of eggs, beaten
½ cup butter
1 teaspoon vanilla

Grind poppyseed. Heat ½ of the milk; pour over poppyseed and let stand overnight. Cream butter and sugar and add the poppyseed mixture. Add flour and baking powder mixed alternately with milk. Add the beaten whites and flavour. Turn in a well-greased spring, form and bake in moderate oven forty-five minutes.

Pork Cake (1913)

Mince half a pound of fat salt pork, pour over it half a cupful of boiling water, add half a pint each of brown sugar and New Orleans molasses. Stir in half a pound each of chopped seeded raisins and chopped stoned dates, a heaping teaspoonful of finely shaved citron, an even teaspoonful of ground cinnamon, half an even teaspoonful of grated nutmeg, allspice and cloves. Sift a large cupful of flour, add half an even teaspoonful of saleratus that has been dissolved in a little water, and a pinch of salt. Stir until smooth, adding sifted flour to make a stiff batter. Bake in a loaf.

Pork Cake No. 1 (1876)

Pour over one pound of pork chopped fine, one cup of boiling water, and add two cups of molasses, one cup of sugar, two teaspoons of soda, spices to the taste, one and a half or two pounds of raisins, one pound of citron, two eggs and flour to make as stiff as pound cake.

Pork Cake 2 (1876)
(Fruit)

Pour over one pound of fat pork cut fine, one pint of boiling water, and add two and a half cups of molasses and one cup of brown sugar or three cups of molasses, raisins, currants and citron, one tablespoon of ground cinnamon, one tablespoon of ground cloves, one small teaspoon of soda and, if you use the cake immediately, two eggs.

Portuguese Coffee Cake (1904)

Rub ½ pound of butter to a cream, add the yolks of 6 eggs, ½ pound of sugar, 1 glassful of Madeira, 1 spoonful of orange-flower water, a little salt, ¼ pound of cleaned raisins, 10 ounces of rice or wheat flour, 1 teaspoonful of baking powder, stir through it the beaten whites of the eggs, put into a buttered mould and bake for 1½ hours. Spread over it any kind of an icing.

Potato Cake (1904)

1¼ pounds of grated potatoes	5 ounces of sweet and 1 ounce of bitter almonds
16 eggs	1 lemon
¾ pound of sifted sugar	2 heaping tablespoonfuls of sifted potato flour

Boil the potatoes in their jackets the day before, but not too tender, peel when cold, grate and then weigh them. Of this take 1¼ pounds, spread on a flat dish and set aside until the next day. Then stir the yolks of the eggs, and the sugar with the lemon peel grated over it, with the juice and the almonds for half an hour, gradually add the potatoes and then lightly stir through the mass the beaten whites of the eggs and the potato flour. The cake is immediately filled into a buttered form, put into the oven and baked the same as almond cake, very mealy potatoes are necessary.

Potato Cake No. 1 (1912)

Two-thirds of a cup of butter	One and one-half cups of chopped nuts
Two cups of granulated sugar	Four eggs
One-half cup of milk	Two heaping teaspoons of baking powder
One and one-half cup of mashed Irish potatoes	One teaspoon of cinnamon
One and one-half cups of flour	One nutmeg
One-half cup of grated chocolate	

Potato Cake No. 2 (1912)

One cup of butter	One cup of potato
Two cups of sugar	One cup of chopped nuts

One-half teaspoon of cinnamon
One-fourth teaspoon of cloves and nutmeg
One-half cup of sweet milk
Two and one-half cups of flour

Two teaspoons baking powder
One heaping teaspoon of cocoa dissolved in three teaspoons of hot water
Four eggs

Potato Cake (1909)

Two cups of white sugar
One cup of butter
One cup of hot mashed potatoes
One cup of chopped walnuts
Half a cup of sweet milk
Two cups of flour

Four eggs well beaten
Five teaspoonfuls of melted chocolate
One tablespoonful each of cloves, cinnamon and nutmeg
Two teaspoonfuls of baking powder

Bake in layers and use marshmallow filling.

Potato Cake (1836)

Roast in the ashes a dozen small or six large potatoes. When done, peel them, and put them into a pan with a little salt, and the rind of a lemon grated. Add a quarter of a pound of butter, or half a pint of cream, and a quarter of a pound of sugar. Having mashed the potatoes with this mixture, rub it through a cullender, and stir it very hard. Then set it away to cool.
Beat eight eggs and stir them gradually into the mixture. Season it with a tea-spoonful of mixed spice, and half a glass of rose-water.
Butter a mould or a deep dish and spread the inside all over with grated bread. Put in the mixture and bake it for three quarters of an hour.

Potato Cakes (1876)

Take enough good-sized potatoes for a meal, peel and grate on a coarse grater and stir in from three to five eggs, then add a little flour and season to taste. Beat well and fry in hot lard. One good sized spoonful makes a cake.

Potato Cakes (1922)

Season cold or hot potatoes highly and add enough beaten egg to moisten. Mold into cakes and roll in flour. Sauté a golden brown.

Potato Cakes (1899)

To two cups of well-mashed cold potatoes, add the well-beaten yolk of one egg; work well together, and form into small, round cakes about half an inch thick; place on buttered tins, brush over with the beaten white of an egg, and brown in a hot oven.

Potato Cakes (1905)

Take two cups of mashed potato and mix well with the beaten yolk of one egg and make into small flat cakes; dip each into flour. Heat two tablespoonfuls of nice dripping, and when it is hot lay in the cakes and brown, turning each with the cake-turner as it gets crusty on the bottom.

Potato Cakes (1913)

Take two cupfuls of mashed potatoes and mix them with a cupful of canned salmon broken into small pieces, and a tablespoonful of cooked cornmeal. Stir well, shape into little flat cakes and fry.

Potato Cakes (1920)
(Gâteaux de Pommes de Terre)

Bake eight potatoes in the oven, and when done cut them lengthwise in two, empty out entirely, and place this in a saucepan with two finely chopped shallots fried in butter, and a pound of lean meat, either of veal or lamb or dark poultry meat, chives, salt, pepper, nutmeg, two ounces of butter, six egg-yolks, and two gills of veloute sauce. With this preparation make inch and a half diameter balls flattening them down to five-eighths of an inch in thickness; roll in beaten egg-white, then in flour,

Potato Cakes (1894)

Half a dozen common sized potatoes, boiled and mashed smooth, a spoonful flour, two eggs, salt and pepper; stir until quite soft; fry like fritters.

Potato Cakes with Ham (1920)
(Galettes de Pommes de Terre au Jambon)

Lay in a saucepan one pint of mashed potatoes, rubbed through a sieve; mix in with it a lump of butter, a pinch of sugar, nutmeg, a handful of grated parmesan, six raw egg-yolks, two beaten whites, a little salt and four ounces of cooked and finely chopped lean ham. Heat a griddle or frying-pan, butter well the surface, take the preparation up with a spoon, and let it fall on it in rounds three inches each, keeping them slightly apart; cook them on a slow fire, turning over; when nicely coloured and hardened drain and serve hot. The preparation may be let fall into three-inch diameter rings, five- sixteenths of an inch thick, filling them to the top; in this way the cakes will be more uniform than when cooked as above.

Potato Chocolate Cake (1820)

2 c. sugar
2 tsp. baking powder
⅔ c. fat
2 sq. chocolate
1 c. hot mashed potatoes (unseasoned)
1 c. chopped nuts
1 tsp. cinnamon
½ c. sweet milk or cold water or coffee
1 tsp. cloves
½ tsp. nutmeg
2 c. flour
4 eggs

Cream butter and sugar, add well beaten egg yolks. Add hot mashed potatoes, then alternately the flour, sifted with baking powder, cinnamon, cloves and nutmeg and milk. Add melted chocolate.
Stir in nut meats and fold in stiffly beaten whites. Bake in two layers.

Potato Flour Cake (1911)

4 eggs, beaten separate and then together

Add:

1 cup of sugar
Pinch of salt
1 tablespoon cold water
1 teaspoon vanilla
A good half cup of potato flour with 1 rounding teaspoon of baking powder in it

Potato Flour Muffins (1922)

½ cup white potato flour
1 tablespoon sugar
3 teaspoons baking powder
¼ teaspoon salt
2 eggs
3 tablespoons ice water

Sift the flour and baking powder twice.
Beat the yolks, add the sugar and salt. Beat the whites until very stiff. Add the beaten whites to the beaten yolks and add the dry ingredients.
Beat all together thoroughly and add the ice water last. Bake in greased muffin tins in a hot oven for fifteen minutes. Serve hot with butter.

Potato Torte (1820)

1 c. fat creamed
Gradually beat in 1½ c. sugar
Add 3 beaten egg yolks
1 c. cold riced potato (unseasoned)
¾ c. ground chocolate
1 c. finely chopped walnuts
Grated rind of 1 lemon
2 c. flour sifted with 3 tsp. baking powder
lastly 3 egg whites beaten light

Bake in loaf about 45 minutes or in 2 layers about 20 minutes. Excellent baked in Turk's Head pan and frosted with seven-minute Icing.

Pound Cake No. 1 (1889)

One pound two ounces of butter
One-pound sugar
Fourteen ounces flour
Ten eggs, beaten separately
Half teaspoonful mace
One wineglass brandy

Pound Cake No. 2 (1889)

One-pound sugar
Three-fourths pound butter
One-pound flour
Ten eggs, beaten separately
One-pound raisins, or half pound citron
Three-fourths wineglass brandy
Ten drops extract of rose
Half a nutmeg
Grated peel of one lemon

Stir, till very light, the butter and sugar together. Mix the yolks, whites, and flour, alternately. Lastly, add the flavouring and the raisins, dredged with a little of the flour.

Pound Cake 1 (1876)

One pound of butter
One pound of sugar
One pound of flour
Nine eggs leaving out two yolks
Grated peel of one lemon

Beat the whites to a stiff froth and the butter to a cream; add the sugar and the yolks and beat till very light; then the flour and whites of eggs, alternately. Bake in a moderate oven.

Pound Cake 2 (1876)

Rub one pound of sugar and three-fourths of a pound of butter to a cream; add the well beaten yolks often eggs, then the whites beaten to a froth. Stir in gradually one pound of flour.

Pound Cake (1922)

1 cup butter   1¼ cups sugar

Cream butter and add sugar gradually, creaming mixture well. Add the yolks of four eggs, then the whites to which has been added 1 level teaspoon cream tartar; then add ½ cup of milk; then 2½ cups pastry flour; sift it three times with ½ level teaspoon baking soda. 1 teaspoon vanilla.
Bake in a slow oven about one hour.

Pound Cake (N.D.)

Cream 1 cup butter; add gradually 1½ cups sugar. Cream well. Break into this 5 eggs, one at a time, beating well after each egg. Then add 2 cups well sifted flour. Flavouring. May add citron. For flavouring, a combination of almond, lemon and vanilla extracts is delicious.

Pound Cake (1922)

2 cupfuls sugar   2 teaspoonfuls salt
12 eggs   ½ teaspoonful powdered mace
2 cupfuls Crisco   3 tablespoonfuls brandy
4 cupfuls flour

Cream Crisco and sugar thoroughly together, add yolks of eggs well beaten, fold in whites of eggs beaten to a stiff froth, add brandy, flour, salt and mace, and mix lightly and quickly. Turn into a papered cake pan and bake in a slow oven for one hour and twenty minutes.
Sufficient for: one large cake.

Pound Cake (1913)
(Aunt Polly Rives)

Take ten fresh eggs, their weight in fresh butter, white sugar, and thrice sifted flour. Separate the eggs, beat yolks to a cream-yellow, add the sugar, cupful at a time, beat hard, then the butter creamed to a froth, then half the flour, then two wineglasses of whiskey or brandy or good sherry or rose water, beat hard five minutes, then add the rest of the flour, taking care not to pack it in the handling. Beat fifteen minutes longer, then fold in with long strokes, the egg-whites beaten with a good pinch of salt until they stick to the dish. Barely mix them through the batter, then pour it into deep pans, or ovens, lined with double greased papers. The vessels also must be well buttered. Bake with quick heat, letting the cake rise well before browning. Slack heat when it is a very light brown and cook until a straw thrust to the bottom comes out clean. Turn out upon a thick, folded cloth, cover with another thinner cloth, and let cool. Frost when cool, either with the boiled frosting directed for cheesecakes or with plain frosting made thus. Beat three egg-whites well chilled to the stiffest possible froth with a pinch of salt, and a very little cold water. Add to them gradually when thus beaten a pound of sugar sifted with a teaspoonful of cream of tartar. Mix very smooth, and apply with a broad-bladed knife, dipping it now and then in cold water to keep the frosting smooth. It should dry a quarter-inch thick and be delicious eating. Frosted cake keeps fresh three times as long as that left naked.

Pound Cake (1840)

Prepare a table-spoonful of powdered cinnamon, a tea-spoonful of powdered mace, and two nutmegs grated or powdered. Mix together in a tumbler, a glass of white - wine, a glass of brandy, and a glass of rose water.

Sift a pound of the finest flour into a broad pan and powder a pound of loaf-sugar. Put the sugar into a deep pan and cut up in it a pound of fresh butter. Warm them by the fire till soft; and then stir them to a cream. When they are perfectly light, add gradually the spice and liquor, a little at a time. Beat ten eggs as light as possible, and stir them by degrees into the mixture, alternately with the flour. Then add twelve drops of oil of lemon; or more, if it is not strong. Stir the whole very hard; put it into a deep tin pan with straight or upright sides and bake it in a moderate oven from two to three hours. If baked in a Dutch oven, take off the lid when you have ascertained that the cake is quite done, and let it remain in the oven to cool gradually. If any part is burnt, scrape it off as soon as cold.

It may be iced either warm or cool; first dredging the cake with flour and then wiping it off. It will be best to put on two coats of icing; the second coat not till the first is entirely dry. Flavour the icing with essence of lemon, or with extract of roses.

This cake will be very delicate if made with a pound of rice flour instead of wheat.

Pound Cake (1869)

Wash the salt from a pound of butter, and beat it with a pound of loaf sugar till it is as soft as cream; have a pound of flour sifted, and beat ten eggs, the whites and yolks separately; put alternately into the butter and sugar the flour and eggs, continue to beat till they are all in, and the cake looks light; add some grated lemon peel, a nutmeg, and half a wine-glass of brandy; butter the pan, and bake it an hour; when it is nearly cold, ice it. If you want a very large cake, double the quantity. You can tell when a cake is done by running in a broom-straw, or the blade of a bright knife; if it comes out without sticking, it is done, but if not, set it back. You can keep a cake a great while in a stone pan that has a lid to fit tight

Pound Cake (1920)
(Pound Cake)

Put twelve eggs and four ounces of sugar in a basin and whip until they become quite light, warming them slightly over the fire. In a large metal vessel lay one pound of butter and threequarters of a pound of sugar; work with the hands until creamy and light, then add gradually the prepared eggs, beating continuously, and a gill of brandy or rum, and lastly one pound of sifted flour. Butter a pound cake mold, line it with paper and pour in the preparation, having it threequarters full, then place it in a slow oven to bake for an hour and three-quarters to two hours. Remove from the oven, unmould, and leave stand till cold, then ice it with icing flavoured with rum. After this is dry slip the cake on a board or dish and decorate with royal icing.

Pound Cake (1894)

Rub one-pound sugar and three-quarters pound butter to a cream, add the well beaten yolks of ten eggs, then the whites, and stir in gradually a pound of sifted flour.

Pound Cake (No.1) (1922)

Three pounds of sugar
Two and one-half pounds of butter
Three pounds of flour

Thirty-six eggs
One-eighth of an ounce of baking powder
Vanilla flavour

Sift the powder in the flour and mix the same as Old Time Pound Cake (No.1) (1922).

Pound Cake (No.2) (1922)

One and three-quarters pounds of sugar
One and one-half pounds of butter
Twenty-four eggs

Two and one-quarter pounds of flour
One-half of a teaspoonful of baking powder
One-eighth of a pint of milk

Lemon and mace, or vanilla flavour

Cream butter and sugar as in the other mixture; sift the flour and baking powder together, then add half of the flour. Mix in well, add milk; mix again, add the rest of the flour and finish mixing. A little more or less of the milk may be required to make smooth, which may be added after the flour is in, beating the mixture smooth again.

Poverty Cake (1911)

½ cup sugar
½ cup molasses
½ cup sour milk
2 cups flour

1 cup chopped raisins
All kinds of spices
1 good teaspoon soda
4 large tablespoons melted butter

Princess Cake (1922)

Line small square cake tin with plain Crisco pastry. Sprinkle in ½ cup cleaned currants. Cream ½ cup Crisco with 1 cup sugar, then add 3 well beaten eggs, 3 cups flour, 1½ teaspoons baking powder, and ½ teaspoon salt. Divide mixture into 2 portions. Add 1 tablespoon grated chocolate and 4 tablespoons milk to 1 portion. Put cake mixtures in spoonfuls on top of currants and bake in a moderate oven for 35 minutes. Serve in square pieces.

Prune Cake (1820)

1 c. sugar
½ to ⅔ c. sour milk
⅓ c. fat
¼ tsp salt
2 eggs
1 c. cooked prunes, cut into pieces

1½ c. flour
½ tsp. nutmeg
1 tsp. soda
⅛ tsp. cloves
¾ tsp. baking powder
½ tsp. cinnamon

Bake in a loaf or two layers.

Puff Cake (1913)

Cream together half a cupful of butter and a cupful of sugar. Sift together a cupful of flour, a heaping teaspoonful of baking powder and a third of a cupful of cornstarch, adding flavouring and a pinch of salt. Stir all the ingredients together and add the stiffly beaten whites of five eggs. Bake in a slow oven.
Do not open the oven for fifteen minutes, and then carefully, without jarring the cake.

Pumpernickel-Torte (1910)
(Pumpernickel Spongecake)

4 oz. grated Pumpernickel
4 oz. sweet almonds
10 bitter almonds
10 eggs

Grated rind of 1 lemon
1 lb. sugar
2 ground cloves

Beat the sugar with the eggs for ½ hour to a thick cream. Then add the grated almonds and spice, and finally the grated Pumpernickel which must be very dry. Glaze with sugar or chocolate icing.

Punch Cake, Punch Biscuit, Imitation of Boar's Head, a Book or a Ham (1920)

(Gâteau Punch, Punch Biscuit, Imitation de Hure de Sanglier, d'un Livre ou d'un Jambon)

Put eight ounces of fine white apple marmalade and eight ounces of sugar in a copper pan; stand this on the fire and cook for a few moments to reduce the marmalade, then remove and add a quarter of a gill of rum, a quarter of a gill of Curacoa and eight well-beaten egg-whites. Bake a Savoy biscuit in a buttered timbale mold, glazed with sugar and fecula; as soon as done, unmould, cool and cut it straight, then empty it from the bottom, leaving an inch-thick crust all around. Fill the empty cake with the above apples, lay over a round of frolle paste the same dimensions as the cake and invert it on a grate; ice with orange fondant flavoured with rum and Curacoa. After the icing has dried slide the cake on a dish, decorate with fanciful cuts of candied fruits and surround the base with a circle of greengages.

Punch Biscuit Paste:

One pound of sugar	Eleven yolks
Half a pound of flour	Four whipped whites
Half a pound of fecula	A small glassful of rum
Nine ounces of melted butter	Chopped lemon and orange peel
Three whole eggs	A grain of salt

Place the sugar in a vessel; add the yolks slowly, creaming together with a spoon, and when very light put in the butter, the rum, the whipped whites, the fecula, the sifted flour, and lastly the peels and salt.

Boar's Head Imitation (Hure de Sanglier): Bake thoroughly a punch biscuit in an oval mold the same size as a natural boar's head, fourteen by nine inches on the top and six inches deep, the splay to be half an inch. The next day cut the biscuit the shape of a boar's head; hollow it out underneath and replace the biscuit that is removed by the same soaked in maraschino so as to make a paste, into which mix plenty of candied fruits. Lay the cake on an oval foundation the size of the head, and cover with well-cooked apricot marmalade, then coat the whole with cooked chocolate icing. As soon as the icing is dry cut out the snout, leaving it partly opened, hollow out the cavities for the eyes, and on each side of the snout place two large fangs made of almond paste and dipped in clear dissolved gelatine. Imitate the eyes by two rounded balls of almond paste, placing a black spot in the center; mold these in a teaspoon with clarified gelatine; unmould and when cold fasten them in the cavities made to hold the eyes. Dress the cake on a foundation glazed with green fondant. Decorate the head with fruits and transparent hatelets, ornamented with large fruits; the base should be surrounded with chopped jelly and jelly croûtons.

A Book Imitation (Un Livre): To be prepared the same as the boar's head with punch biscuit, the two covers and the back of the binding made of almond paste. Empty out the center, leaving the top cover stationary. Glaze the sides of the book with orange icing, the cover with coffee icing and decorate the whole with royal icing. Fill the inside with tutti-frutti ice cream. This book can be laid on a socle or a cushion glazed with pink icing.

Ham Imitation (Jambon): As for the boar's head, prepare a punch biscuit fourteen inches long, nine inches wide and four and a half inches thick; after being cooked and thoroughly cold, trim it to the shape of a ham, then cut it through its thickness; empty it out and fill the center with a Bengalian charlotte preparation. Fasten the two parts together again with apricot marmalade and coat it over with the same. Glaze the handle end one-third of the length of the ham with chocolate icing to imitate the rind and the other two-thirds with white prunelle icing. Stand the ham on a foundation bottom made of frolle paste, and on the chocolate end stick a piece of pointed wood three-quarters of an inch in diameter by five inches in length; trim the end of this with a large paper rosette. Decorate the white part of the ham with almond paste flavoured with chocolate or pistachio. Leave it to cool perfectly, then coat with jelly. Lay the ham on a small low socle (for this see ham à la Gatti) and decorate around with chopped jelly and croûtons. These cakes can also be made to imitate a salmon, a swan, Foies-gras patty, boned turkey or any other design.

Punch Layer Cake (1904)

¾ pound of butter	¾ pound of sugar

¾ pound of cornstarch
9 eggs

1 lemon
½ cupful of arrac

The butter is freshened, creamed and stirred with the yolks of the eggs, sugar, lemon peel and lemon juice for ½ hour, as given under General Directions (1904). Then add the starch, lightly stir through it the beaten whites of the eggs, and after the arrac is stirred through the cake it is baked the same as sand cakes, Cover the cakes with punch frosting.

Punsch Torte (1893)
(Punch Cake)

Three round shallow cake-tins, the size of the largest dinner-plate, must be lined with buttered paper. Make the "biscuit torte" mass. Divide this into the three tins, equally, so that each cake shall be, when baked, a good inch thick. Bake these a day before you want them.
Rasp off the yellow of a lemon with lumps of sugar. Squeeze its juice on them and put them in a pint of arrack or fine rum. Soak the cakes with this and let them dry again. Cover one cake with a layer of any fine preserve; lay another cake on it evenly; spread on this a layer of different jam, or marmalade, and put the third cake on it. Make an icing of the white of one egg whisked to a snow, a quarter of a pound of finest sifted sugar, and a large tablespoonful of arrack.
Spread on the icing and leave it to dry in a warm place.

Punch Tourte (1922)

Bake four thin layers from Mixture Genoise Sponge Cake (1922). Take some firm apple marmalade and mix with some good rum, the juice and grated rind one lemon or orange, and spread it between the layers. Ice with a punch flavoured fondant and decorate with royal icing and fruit.

Pyramid Birthday Cake (1921)

Bake any good layer cake or other simple cake mixture in one or two thin sheets, in a large pan. When done cut into as many graduated circles as the child is years old. Ice each circle, top and sides, with any good cake icing, either white or tinted, and lay one above the other with layers of jelly or preserves between slices. Around each layer arrange a decoration of fresh or candied fruits of bright colours, glacéed nuts, candied rose petals or violets, bits of angelica, or any other effective decoration. Let the cake stand on a handsomely decorated dish, and small flags be inserted in the topmost layer.

Part 18: Q

Queen Cake (1897)
(Drottning-kaka)
Queen Cake (1840)
Queen Cake (1869)
Queen Cake (1920)
(Gâteau Reine)
Queen Cakes (1922)
Queen Cakes (1913)

Quick Cake (1911)
Quick Coffee Cake (1922)
Quick Coffee Cake (1917)
Quick Loaf Cake (1889)
Quick Muffins (1922)
Quick Muffins in Rings (1911)
Quince Cakes (1878)

Queen Cake (1897)
(Drottning-kaka)

Beat a pound of butter to cream and mix with a tablespoonful rosewater; add a pound fine white sugar, 10 beaten eggs and a pound and a quarter sifted flour. Mix well and beat, and then add half a pound of shelled almonds, blanched and beaten to a paste. Butter tin basins, line them with white paper, fill in the mixture one inch and a half deep, and bake for 1 hour in a quick oven.

Queen Cake (1840)

Sift fourteen ounces of the finest flour, being two ounces less than a pound. Cakes baked in little tins, should have a smaller proportion of flour than those that are done in large loaves. Prepare a table-spoonful of beaten cinnamon, a tea-spoonful of mace, and two beaten nutmegs; and mix them all together when powdered. Mix in a tumbler, half a glass of white wine, half a glass of brandy, and half a glass of rose water. Powder a pound of loaf-sugar and sift it into a deep pan; cut up in it a pound of fresh butter; warm them by the fire and stir them to a cream. Add gradually the spice and the liquor. Beat ten eggs very light and stir them into the mixture in turn with the flour. Stir in twelve drops of essence of lemon and beat the whole very hard. Butter some little tins; half fill them with the mixture; set them into a brisk oven, and cake them about a quarter of an hour. When done, they will shrink from the sides of the tins. After you turn them out, spread them on an inverted sieve to cool. If you have occasion to fill your tins a second time, scrape and wipe them well before they are used again.
Make an icing flavoured with oil of lemon, or with extract of roses; and spread two coats of it on the queen cakes. Set them to dry in a warm place, but not near enough the fire to discolour the icing and cause it to crack.
Queen cakes are best the day they are baked.

Queen Cake (1869)

Mix a pound of dried flour, the same of sifted sugar, and currants; wash a pound of butter, add rose water - beat it well - a tea-cup of cream; then mix with it eight eggs, yolks and whites beaten separately; add the dry ingredients by degrees; beat the whole an hour, bake in little tins, or saucers, filling only half.

Queen Cake (1920)
(Gâteau Reine)

Beat up a pound of butter with twelve egg-yolks, adding a pound of sugar, a little at a time, half a pound of ground almonds, half a pound of fecula and then seven beaten whites, one quart in volume of drained whipped cream, vanilla or lemon flavoured, a few candied orange flowers and a grain of salt, the cream to be added lastly. Bake in a slack oven in a spiral mold glazed with sugar. After the cake is unmoulded and cold cover with apricot marmalade and ice with maraschino icing. No good results can be expected unless good cream is used.

Queen Cakes (1922)

½ cup sugar
½ cup Crisco
½ teaspoon salt
3 eggs
¼ cup currants
¼ cup glace cherries (cut in dice)

Grate nutmeg
Thin rind ½ lemon (chopped finely)
Juice 1 lemon
1 cup flour
4 tablespoons rice flour
1 teaspoon baking powder

Put Crisco and sugar in basin and work with wooden spoon to cream, add salt and eggs 1 by 1, and beat mixture thoroughly. Mix in separate basin fruit, lemon rind, flours and baking powder. Stir this into other mixture, add nutmeg, and strained lemon juice. Stir mixture several minutes longer. Have ready Criscoed gem tins, three-parts fill them with mixture and bake in fairly hot oven from 20 to 25 minutes. Unmould cakes and place on sieve to cool. Cakes may be coated with chocolate or boiled frosting.

Queen Cakes (1913)

"Take a pound of sugar, beat and sift it, a pound of well dried flour, a pound of butter, eight eggs, and half a pound of currants, washed and picked; grate a nutmeg and an equal quantity of mace and cinnamon, work the butter to a cream, put in the sugar, beat the whites of the eggs twenty minutes and mix them with the butter and sugar. Then beat the yolks for half an hour and put them to the butter. Beat the whole together and when it is ready for the oven, put in the flour, spices and currants, sift a little sugar over them, and bake them in tins."

Quick Cake (1911)

1 cup sugar
1 ½ cups sifted flour
2 teaspoonfuls baking powder, all together
Add ¼ cup butter

Break 2 eggs in a cup, fill with sweet milk, beat all together
1 teaspoonful vanilla

Quick Coffee Cake (1922)

1½ cups sifted flour
6 teaspoons sugar
2 teaspoons baking powder
2 teaspoons shortening

½ teaspoon salt
1 egg
¼ teaspoon mace or nutmeg
½ cup milk or water

Sift dry ingredients, cut in shortening, add unbeaten egg and milk and stir to a smooth dough. Turn in a shallow pan and cover with top mixture.
Mixture to be sprinkled over the top of the dough before baking:

4 tablespoons sugar
1 teaspoon butter

2 tablespoons flour
¼ teaspoon mace or nutmeg

With a fork mix all ingredients thoroughly, scatter over top of coffee cake and bake in a hot oven over 400 degrees twenty-five minutes.

Quick Coffee Cake (1917)

1/4 cup shortening
2-1/2 cups flour
1/4 cup sugar
5 teaspoons baking powder
1 egg

1/2 teaspoon salt
1 cup milk and water mixed
2 tablespoons sugar
1/2 cup seedless raisins
1 teaspoon cinnamon

Cream the shortening and sugar; add egg well beaten, milk, raisins, flour, baking powder, and salt; spread in a greased shallow pan, brush with melted butter, and sprinkle with cinnamon and sugar; bake in hot oven fifteen to twenty minutes.

Quick Loaf Cake (1889)

One and a half pounds flour	One cup of milk
Half-pound butter	Half a nutmeg
Three-fourths pound sugar	Half a teaspoonful cinnamon
Three eggs	Two teaspoonfuls baking powder
One glass of wine	One-pound raisins

Quick Muffins (1922)

8 tablespoons flour	3 teaspoons baking powder
1 egg	3 tablespoons melted butter
1 tablespoon sugar	½ teaspoon salt
1 cup milk	

Sift dry ingredients into mixing bowl; drop egg in center, add milk, a little at time, and beat until smooth. Add melted butter the last thing. Bake in greased muffin tins about fifteen minutes.

Quick Muffins in Rings (1911)

Beat two eggs, yolks; and whites separately. Add to the yolks two cups of milk, one level teaspoon of salt, one tablespoon of melted butter and two cups of flour in which two level teaspoons of baking powder have been sifted and last the stiffly beaten whites of the eggs. When well mixed bake in greased muffin rings on a hot griddle. Turn over when risen and set, as both sides must be browned.

Quince Cakes (1878)

Wash some quinces, boil them in enough water to cover them, until they are tender enough to rub through a sieve; to each quart add a pound and a half of loaf sugar, place the mixture over the fire, and heat to the boiling point, stirring it constantly, but do not let it boil. Oil some plates, spread the quince upon them, and dry it in the mouth of a cool oven. Then cut it in cakes, pack it in a tin box, between layers of white wrapping paper, when it is thoroughly cold, and keep it in a cool, dry place.

Part 19: R

Rahm Kuchen (1873)
(Cream Cake)
Railroad Cake 1 (1876)
Railroad Cake 2 (1876)
Raised Buckwheat Cakes (1917)
Raised Cake 1 (1876)
Raised Cake 2 (1876)
Raised Corn Muffins (1917)
Raised Fruit-Cake (1899)
Raised Loaf Cake (1894)
Raised Muffins (1917)
Raised Oatmeal Muffins (1917)
(Uncooked Oats)
Raised Plum Cake (1869)
Raisin Cake (1820)
Raisin Cake (1876)
Raisin Cake (1911)
Raisin Cakelets (1913)
Raisin Cup Cakes (1914)
Raspberry Muffins (1922)
Raspberry Short Cake (1876)
Real Gold Cake (1913)
Real Silver Cake (1913)
Rehrücken (1910)
(Saddle of Venison - A Viennese Cake)
Rhode Island Cakes (1913)
Rhode Island Corn Cake (1917)
Ribbon Cake (1904)
Ribbon Cake (1911)
Ribbon Cake (1913)
Ribbon Cake 1 (1893)
Ribbon Cake 2 (1893)
Rice and Lemon Cake (1904)
Rice Cake (1904)
Rice Cake (1898)
Rice Cake (1836)
Rice Cakes (1922)
Rice Cakes (1840)
Rice Cakes (1840)
Rice Cakes (1920)
(Galettes au Riz)
Rice Cakes (1920)
(Gâteaux au Riz)
Rice Cakes (1878)
Rice Cakes (1898)
(Small, for Afternoon Tea)
Rice Flour Cake (1894)
Rice Flour Pound Cake (1869)
Rice Gems 1 (1876)
Rice Gems 2 (1876)
Rice Gems 3 (1876)
Rice Griddle Cakes (1876)
Rice Griddle Cakes (1917)
Rice Johnny Cake (1902)
Rice Muffins (1893)
Rice Sponge Cake (1869)
Rice Tea Cake (1876)
Rich Bride Cake (1897)
(Fin brud-kaka)
Rich Cake (1876)
Rich Chocolate Cake (1913)
Rich Coffee Cake (1876)
Rich Fruit Cake (1920)
Rock Cake (1876)
Rock Cake (1840)
Rock Cakes (1878)
Rockland Cake (1894)
Rockland Cake (1911)
Rodonkuchen, or Napfkuchen (No.1) (1873)
(Rodon Cake)
Gerührter Napfkuchen (No. 2) (1873)
(Rodon Cake)
Rodonkuchen (No. 3) (1873)
(Rodon Cake)
Roederer Cake (1920)
(Gâteau Roederer)
Roll Cake (1904)
Roll Jelly Cake (1876)
Roll Jelly Cake (1893)
Rose Leaf Cakes (1922)
Round Coffee Cake No. 1 (1922)
Round Coffee Cake (No. 2) (1922)
(with Raisins)
Royal Sponge Cake (1899)
Runaway Cakes (1893)
(for breakfast)
Russian Torte (N.D.)
(Angel Food Cake)
Rye and Corn Cakes (1913)
Rye Breakfast Cakes (1911)
Rye Drop Cakes (1876)
Rye Drop Cakes (1922)
Rye Muffins (1922)
Rye Muffins (1893)
Rye Muffins (1917)

Rahm Kuchen (1873)
(Cream Cake)

Spread a tin with tart-paste; beat four eggs and stir them into a pint of cream, with a little salt; add a few little lumps of butter. Pour the cream over the paste and bake a rich yellow.

Railroad Cake 1 (1876)

One cup of sugar
One cup of flour
Three eggs
One tablespoon of butter

Two tablespoons of milk
A half teaspoon of soda
One teaspoon of cream tartar
Flavour

Very good.

Railroad Cake 2 (1876)

Beat well one egg with a cup of sugar; add one cup of sweet cream and ~~one~~ nutmeg. Mix two teaspoons of baking powder with two cups, of flour and add to the above. Bake in shallow tins.

Raised Buckwheat Cakes (1917)

1 cup boiling water
1/4 cup lukewarm water
1/2 teaspoon salt
1 cup buckwheat flour

1 tablespoon molasses
1/4 cup white flour
1/2 yeast cake
1/2 teaspoon soda

Mix boiling water, salt, and molasses, and when lukewarm add yeast dissolved in lukewarm water; add gradually to flour, and beat well; let rise over night, add soda, beat well, and cook the same as Plain Griddle Cakcs

Raised Cake 1 (1876)

One coffeecup of sponge
Two eggs
One cup of sugar
A half-cup of butter

A half-cup of cream
One cup of raisins
A half teaspoon soda
Spices to the taste

Mix quite stiff with flour.

Raised Cake 2 (1876)

Five cups of bread dough
Three cups of sugar
One cup of butter

Three eggs
One bowl of raisins
Spice to taste

Raised Corn Muffins (1917)

1 cup scalded milk
1/4 yeast cake
4 tablespoons shortening
1/4 cup lukewarm water

4 tablespoons sugar
1 cup corn meal
1 teaspoon salt
1-1/2 cups flour

Add shortening, sugar, and salt to milk; when lukewarm add yeast dissolved in water, corn meal, and flour; beat well, let rise over night; beat well, half fill greased muffin rings, let rise until nearly double, and bake in hot oven half an hour.

Raised Fruit-Cake (1899)

Make a sponge of one cup of rich milk, previously scalded and cooled to lukewarm, one and. one-half cups of flour, one-half cup of sugar, and three tablespoonfuls of good lively yeast. Beat well together and let rise until light; then add another half-cup of sugar and a half cup of flour. When risen the second time, add two eggs well beaten, one-half cup of currants, one cup of seeded raisins and one-half cup of flour. Place in a bread pan until very light, and bake.

Raised Loaf Cake (1894)

One cup sugar (heaping)
One-half cup butter
One egg
Small piece of soda dissolved in a teaspoon of warm water

Mace
Cinnamon and nutmeg
Two cups raised bread dough
One cup stoned raisins

Let it rise three hours before baking.

Raised Muffins (1917)

1/2 cup boiling water
1 egg
1/2 cup scalded milk
1/4 yeast cake
1 teaspoon salt

1/4 cup lukewarm water
2 tablespoons sugar
2-1/2 cups flour
2 tablespoons shortening

Pour water and milk over salt, sugar, and shortening; when cool add beaten egg, yeast dissolved in water, and flour; beat well and let rise over night; beat again; fill greased muffin pans two-thirds full, let rise, and bake in a hot oven thirty minutes. Or place greased muffin rings on a hot greased griddle, fill two-thirds full, and cook on top of range about twenty minutes, turning when half cooked.

Raised Oatmeal Muffins (1917)
(Uncooked Oats)

1 cup rolled oats
1 egg
1 cup scalded milk
1/4 yeast cake
2 tablespoons shortening

1/4 cup lukewarm water
1 teaspoon salt
2-1/2 cups flour
1/4 cup molasses

Pour hot milk over oats, add shortening; when lukewarm add salt, molasses, egg well beaten, and yeast cake dissolved in lukewarm water; beat well, and add flour; beat well, and let rise over night; beat again, and half fill greased muffin pans; let rise until nearly double, and bake in a hot oven half an hour.

Raised Plum Cake (1869)

Take three pounds of flour, and mix to it as much new milk as will make a thick batter, and a tea-cup of yeast; when it is light, beat together a pound of butter, a pound of sugar, and four eggs; mix this in with a pound of raisins, stoned and cut, half a pound of currants, a grated nutmeg, and a glass of rose brandy; bake it two hours.

Raisin Cake (1820)

1 c. sugar
1 egg
2 c. flour
½ c. fat
½ tsp. soda
½ tsp. cloves

1 c. raisins, cut fine
1 c. sour milk or boiling water
1 c. nuts, chopped fine
1 tsp. baking powder
2 tsp. cinnamon
½ tsp. nutmeg

Mix as butter cake. Very satisfactory plain cake. Bake in moderate oven as loaf.

Raisin Cake (1876)

Three small cups of sugar
One small cup of butter
One small cup of sweet milk
Whites of eight eggs

Two and a half cups of flour
One cup of corn starch
Two teaspoons of baking powder

Bake in four cakes. Make an icing and spread on the top and bottom of each layer; seed and chop one pound of raisins and put them between the layers after icing.

Raisin Cake (1911)

One cup butter
Three eggs
One and one-half cups sugar
One cup sour milk

One teaspoon soda
One cup raisins
Little nutmeg
Three cups flour

One can use two eggs and one-half cup butter; then bake as usual.

Raisin Cakelets (1913)

1/3 cup Cottolene
1 cup fine sugar
2 eggs well beaten
Yolk 1 egg
1/2 cup milk
2 cups flour

3 teaspoons baking powder
1/4 teaspoon salt
1 cup raisins seeded and cut in pieces
1 tablespoon flour
Blanched and shredded almonds

Process: Cream Cottolene, add sugar gradually, stirring constantly. Add beaten egg yolk and eggs. Mix and sift flour, baking powder and salt. Add to first mixture alternately with milk; add raisins dredged with tablespoon flour. Beat thoroughly and fill small, buttered individual tins two-thirds full. Strew tops with almonds, sprinkle with powdered sugar and bake twelve to fifteen minutes in a moderate oven.

Raisin Cup Cakes (1914)

½ cup butter
½ cup milk
1 cup sugar

2 cups flour
2 eggs
3 teaspoons baking powder

Yolk 1 egg
1 cup raisins
1 tablespoon flour
Shredded almonds

Cream the butter, add sugar gradually, and eggs and egg yolks well beaten. Then add milk, flour mixed and sifted with baking powder, and raisins seeded and cut in pieces and dredged with one tablespoon flour. Beat vigorously and turn into buttered individual tins. Sprinkle tops with shredded almonds and powdered sugar and bake in a moderate oven.

Raspberry Muffins (1922)

Three tablespoons of butter
½ teaspoon of salt
¾ cup of sugar
1 teaspoon of cinnamon
1 egg
1 teaspoon baking soda
1½ cups of flour
1 cup raspberries

Cream the shortening and sugar together. Add the beaten egg and milk alternately with the flour, salt, cinnamon and soda sifted together. Flour the raspberries with an additional two tablespoonfuls of flour, add them to the batter, and bake in greased muffin tins, in a hot oven for 25 minutes.
This mixture also makes delicious cakes for tea when baked in patty tins or may be served as a sweet with lemon sauce.

Raspberry Short Cake (1876)

One quart of flour
Three teaspoons of baking powder
A little salt thoroughly mixed in flour
One half cup of butter or lard rubbed in the flour

Mix with water, soft. Roll in cakes and score the top in squares or diamonds. Bake in a quick oven. When done, split the cake open and spread with butter. Mash and sweeten the raspberries, adding one-half cup of water to make more juice. Put the berries between the two parts of the cake and serve with sweetened cream.

Real Gold Cake (1913)

Beat very light the yolks of sixteen eggs, with a full pound of yellow sugar, and a scant pound of creamed butter. Add a cup of rich sour cream with a teaspoonful soda dissolved in it. Or if you like better, put in the cream *solus*, and add the soda dissolved in a teaspoonful of boiling water at the very last. This makes lighter cake so is worth the extra trouble. Flavour to taste - grated lemon rind is good. Add gradually four cups flour sifted three times at least. Beat hard for ten minutes, then bake in well-greased pans, lined with buttered paper, until well done, let cool partly in the pans, then turn out, dust lightly with flour or corn starch and frost.

Real Silver Cake (1913)

Wash and cream to a froth a pound of fresh butter, work into it a pound of sifted sugar, and a pound of flour, sifted thrice with a teaspoonful of baking powder. Add flavouring - vanilla, lemon or rose water, following it with a wineglass of whiskey. Then fold in the whites of sixteen eggs beaten with a pinch of salt to the stiffest possible froth. If the batter looks too thick add half a cup sweet cream - this will depend on the size of the eggs and the dryness of the flour. Bake in deep pans, else in layers. By baking gold and silver batter in layers and alternating them you can have a fine marble cake. Or by colouring half the white batter pink with vegetable colour to be had from any confectioner, you can have rose-marble cake. This should be iced with pink frosting else with plain white, then dotted over with pink. Very decorative for birthday parties or afternoon teas.

Rehrücken (1910)

(Saddle of Venison - A Viennese Cake)

6 oz. butter	2 oz. almonds grated in their skins
6 eggs	2 oz. flour
4 oz. sugar	4 oz. chocolate

Cream the butter, add the sugar and yolks of eggs and stir for ¾ hour. Then add the grated almonds and alternately the flour and whisked whites of eggs. Fill a special, long cake tin (obtainable from Lademann and Söhne, Wallstrasse, Berlin) and bake 1 hour. As soon as cool, cover with chocolate icing and ornament with blanched almonds, cut into strips.

Rhode Island Cakes (1913)

Take cornmeal and make a thin mush, salt it and add stale bread that has been soaked in milk or water. Beat well and pour on a hot griddle, cook slowly and add a little grease from time to time. A beaten egg may be used with the batter if preferred.

Rhode Island Corn Cake (1917)

1 cup white corn meal	1/4 cup melted shortening
2 tablespoons sugar	1/2 teaspoon
1 cup flour	salt
1 egg	1 cup milk
4 teaspoons baking powder	

Mix and sift dry ingredients; add egg yolk well beaten, shortening, and milk; beat well; fold in the stiffly beaten white of egg, and bake in a greased, shallow pan in hot oven about twenty minutes.

Ribbon Cake (1904)

1 pound of freshened butter	1 teaspoonful of mace
1 pound of sifted sugar	2 teaspoonfuls of cinnamon
1 pound of warmed flour	3 ounces of sweet almonds
16 eggs	½ ounce of bitter grated almonds
1 lemon	

The butter is slowly melted, poured from the settlings and stirred with sugar. Add the yolks of the eggs, juice and grated rind of the lemon, mace, cinnamon and almonds, and this is stirred for ½ hour as given under General Directions (1904). Then stir the beaten whites of the eggs, a spoonful at a time, with the flour to the cake. Spread on the pan to the thickness of about ⅛ inch, and bake to a yellow colour, spread dough over this and bake again, and so on until 5 layers are baked, which must be evenly divided. After the first layer is baked the heat should not be quite so strong from the bottom of the oven, baking the cake principally from the top, but keeping up 2 degrees of heat (see General directions (1904)). This mass can also be baked in one cake and then serve fruit jelly with it.

Ribbon Cake (1911)

2½ cups sugar	½ teaspoon soda
1 cup butter	4 cups flour
1 cup sour milk	4 eggs
1 teaspoon cream tartar	

For the dark part, reserve one-third.

1 cup raisins	2 tablespoons of molasses
1 cup currants	1 teaspoon each of all kinds of spices

Ribbon Cake (1913)

Take two cupfuls of sugar, half a cupful of butter and cream them together. Add a small cupful of milk and three beaten eggs. Stir in two cupfuls of flour sifted with two teaspoonfuls of baking powder. Make three portions of the mixture. To one portion add fruit juice (cherry is good for colouring); to another add one tablespoonful of dark molasses, raisins, currants, spices, etc.
Bake in three greased layer tins and put together with any preferred filling.

Ribbon Cake 1 (1893)

One-half cup butter	Spices
2 cups sugar	3 tablespoons Rumford Baking Powder
4 eggs	½ pound figs chopped fine
1 cup milk	½ cup raisins, stoned and cut into pieces
3½ cups flour	1 tablespoon molasses

Cream the butter and add gradually the sugar and the well-beaten egg yolks. Add the milk and the flour, mixed and sifted with the baking powder. Add the egg whites beaten to a stiff froth. Bake one-half of the mixture in a layer cake pan. To the remainder add the fruit, molasses and spices to taste. Bake and put the layers together with White Mountain Cream.

Ribbon Cake 2 (1893)

Two cups sugar	3 cups flour
⅔ cup butter, creamed together	2 heaping teaspoons baking powder
3 eggs	Crystaline salt
1 cup milk	Vanilla

Put half the mixture in 2 long tins and bake.
To the remainder add:

1 large cooking spoon molasses	Spices
1 cup raisins, stoned and chopped	1 egg
¼ pound citron, sliced	1 large spoon flour

Put the sheets together while warm with jelly. The same rule, without fruit and with an extra egg, makes a nice marble cake.

Rice and Lemon Cake (1904)

For this take a puff paste as given, ½ pound of best rice, ½ pound of sifted sugar and 4 fresh lemons. Wash and scald the rice the evening before and let it soak overnight in plenty of water; the next day put it on the fire in the same water, boil until tender and then pour on a sieve to drain. Grate a lemon on the sugar, cut the rind thinly from 3 lemons, cook the rind in water until tender, cut into strips and candy them the same as in the preceding receipt. Stir the juice of 4 lemons with the sugar and mix through the rice with a salad fork. In the meantime, roll out the under crust and make an edge the width of a finger, brushing first with a little water so that the edge will stick. After the cake is baked and is cool, put the rice over it, and over this the candied lemon peel. Instead of this, preserved apricots can be used.

The above quantities are for a large cake. This cake is very refreshing, and nice when fresh fruits cannot be had.

Rice Cake (1904)

¾ pound of rice
Milk for boiling the rice
6 ounces of butter
The yolks of 12 eggs
The whites of 10 eggs

¼ pound of sweet and a few bitter almonds
⅛ ounce of cinnamon
½ pound of sugared
the grated peel of a lemon
or some candied orange peel

The rice is scalded in water and boiled slowly in milk until tender and thick; the kernels must remain whole. Then cream the butter and add, constantly stirring, the sugar, the yolks of the eggs, almonds and spices and at last the beaten whites of the eggs. The whole is put into a buttered mould which has first been sprinkled with grated bread and sugar, and then baked in a moderately hot oven for 1½ hours. If the rice when cooked should not be thick enough, stir through it some finely grated bread before putting in the whites of the eggs. Instead of the almonds ½ pound of stoned raisins can be cooked with the rice for ¼ hour.

Rice Cake (1898)

Ingredients:

¼ lb. rice flour
¼ lb. flour
6 oz. sugar

¼ lb. butter
4 eggs
grated rind of 1 lemon

Method: Beat and strain the eggs, mix in the sugar, and dredge in the flours and grated lemon-rind, beating constantly, Add the butter (which must be melted, but not hot) by degrees, beating each portion thoroughly in before the next is added. Beat the cake for a few minutes, then half fill a cake-tin lined with buttered paper with the mixture, and bake in a moderate oven, protecting the top of the cake with a piece of buttered paper as soon as it is nicely browned.
Time: 1 hour.
Sufficient for: 1 moderate sized cake.

Rice Cake (1836)

Take half a pound of rice and wash it well. Put it into a pint of cream or milk and boil it soft. Let it get cold. Then stir into it alternately a quarter of a pound of sugar, two ounces of butter, eight eggs well beaten (having left out the whites of four), and a wine-glass of rose-water, or else the grated peel of a lemon. Mix all well. Butter a mould or a deep pan with straight sides and spread grated bread crumbs all over its inside. Put in the mixture and bake it three quarters of an hour. Plain Griddle Cakes.
Ground rice is best for this cake.
If any of the cake is left, you may next day cut it in slices and fry them in butter.
Or, instead of baking the mixture in a large cake, you may put flour on your hands, and roll it into round balls. Make a batter of beaten eggs, sugar, and grated bread; dip the balls into it, and fry them in butter.

Rice Cakes (1922)

2 cups hot boiled rice
2 cups flour
2 eggs

3 teaspoons baking powder
1-pint milk
1 teaspoon salt

Mix flour, baking powder and salt. Beat the yolks and add to the milk; add the dry ingredients and beat well. Fold in the stiff whites and prepare as griddle cakes.
Serve hot with butter, sugar or jelly.

Rice Cakes (1840)

Pick and wash half a pint of rice and boil it very soft. Then drain it, and let it get cold. Sift a pint and a half of flour over the pan of rice and mix in a quarter of a pound of butter that has been warmed by the fire, and a salt-spoonful of salt. Beat five eggs very light and stir them gradually into a quart of milk. Beat the whole very hard, and bake it in muffin rings, or in waffle-irons. Send them to table hot, and eat them with butter, honey, or molasses. You may make these cakes of rice flour instead of mixing together whole rice and wheat flour.

Rice Cakes (1869)

Take a pint of soft boiled rice, a pint of milk, a little salt, and as much corn meal as will make a thin batter with two eggs; beat all together, and bake as corn batter cakes, or make it thicker and bake it in a pan

Rice Cakes (1920)
(Galettes au Riz)

Put in a pan four ounces of wheat flour and four ounces of rice flour sifted together; make a hollow in the center and lay in two ounces of sugar, a pinch of salt, four eggs and one gill of milk; work the flour into the liquid and knead it in such a way as to obtain a smooth dough, then add another gill of milk and continue to work it until the paste is well mixed, then finally pour in two ounces of melted butter and also add half a pint of rice, blanched and cooked till quite soft. Just when ready to use work it well with a teaspoonful of baking powder and a teaspoonful of flour, and when sufficiently kneaded and the paste is smooth it will be ready. Finish like buckwheat cakes.

Rice Cakes (1920)
(Gâteaux au Riz)

Line a few oval-shaped timbale molds, the size of the mold shown in, with puff paste parings; cover the bottoms with apricot marmalade and fill up with a mellow rice cooked with cream and flavoured with vanilla, finishing it with a few egg-yolks; on each place a little butter; push the cakes into the oven, and when done unmould and mask them over with a layer of apricot marmalade, or powder with icing-sugar.

Rice Cakes (1878)

Sift together six ounces each of rice and wheat flour, (cost about seven cents,) rub into them four ounces of lard or meat drippings, (cost four cents,) four eggs, (cost four cents,) and sufficient milk to make a thick cake-batter; beat it thoroughly, pour it into a greased cake-pan, and bake it one hour.

Rice Cakes (1898)
(Small, for Afternoon Tea)

Ingredients:

2 oz. rice flour
2 oz. flour
3 oz. sugar

2 oz. butter
Grated rind of ½ a lemon
2 egg

Method: Beat and strain the eggs, mix in the sugar, dredge in the flours, beating constantly, and add the butter, which must be melted but not hot, a tea-spoonful at a time, beating each portion thoroughly in before the next is added, and put in the lemon rind. Butter some patty-pans, half fill them with the mixture, and bake in a moderate oven.
Time: 15 to 20 minutes.
Sufficient for: 1 dozen cakes.

Rice Flour Cake (1894)

One cup butter	Five eggs
One cup sugar	Two cups rice flour

Rice Flour Pound Cake (1869)

Take seven eggs	And half a pound of butter
A pound of rice flour	Season it with rose water and nutmeg
One of sugar	

Mix and bake it as other pound cake, and ice it.

Rice Gems 1 (1876)

One teacup of cold, boiled rice	Pinch of salt
One pint of corn meal, scalded, with sufficient water to make a thin batter	Three eggs well beaten
	Two teaspoons of baking powder
One tablespoon of butter	

Put the rice into the scalded meal, add the butter, salt and the baking powder last. Have the gem-pans hot and bake quickly.

Rice Gems 2 (1876)

One half pint of corn meal	Salt to taste
Scalded, one cup of rice	Enough milk to make a batter the consistency of griddle cakes or gems
Three eggs	

Rice Gems 3 (1876)

Put to soak at night a cup of cold, boiled rice, in a pint and a half of milk or water. In the morning, add Graham flour until a moderately stiff batter is formed. Put into hot gem pans and bake quickly.

Rice Griddle Cakes (1876)

Two cups of rice in three pints of water; boil until perfectly soft; mash fine with a spoon and add a little salt. When cool, add two eggs beaten very light, then one and one-half pints of milk; beat in by degrees six tea cups of flour. Beat all thoroughly together, then stir in one tablespoon of soda. Bake on a griddle in small cakes. Eat with butter and sugar.

Rice Griddle Cakes (1917)

1 cup cooked rice	1 egg well beaten
2 teaspoons baking powder	1 tablespoon sugar

1 cup milk 1 cup flour
1/2 teaspoon salt Few gratings nutmeg

Mix rice and egg thoroughly with a fork, add milk, and dry ingredients mixed and sifted together; beat well, and cook the same as Plain Griddle Cakes

Rice Johnny Cake (1902)

Take 2 cups of boiled rice and mix with a little cold milk, a little salt and flour enough to hold it together. Spread it a quarter of an inch thick on flat tin sheets, and brown it in front of the fire or put it in the oven. When brown butter it and cut in square slices and serve very hot.

Rice Muffins (1893)

Into 1 pint of flour 1 teaspoon cream tartar
Put 1 teaspoon of sugar 4 teaspoon soda

Rub it through a sieve; add 1 well beaten egg, 1 cup of milk, 1 cup boiled rice. Beat well, bake in roll pan.

Rice Sponge Cake (1869)

Take three-quarters of a pound of rice flour, one pound of white sugar, finely powdered, and ten eggs; beat the yolks with the sugar, the whites alone; add them and the flour to the yolks and sugar, a little at a time; season it with rose brandy and nutmeg and bake it in shallow pans.

Rice Tea Cake (1876)

Two cups of rice flour Two tablespoons of butter
Two heaping cups of wheat flour Two tablespoons of sugar
Four teaspoons of cream tartar A little salt
Two teaspoons of soda One and one-half pints of milk

Bake thin and eat while hot.

Rich Bride Cake (1897)
(Fin brud-kaka)

Take 4 pounds sifted flour 1-ounce mace or nutmeg
4 pounds sweet, fresh butter, beaten to a cream A tablespoon of lemon extract or orange flower water
2 pounds powdered sugar
Take 6 eggs for each pound of flour

Rich Cake (1876)

One coffeecup of butter One nutmeg
Three coffeecups of sugar One cup of raisins
Four coffeecups of flour One cup of currants
A half pint of sweet cream two teaspoons of baking powder
Four eggs

Rich Chocolate Cake (1913)

1/2 cup Cottolene
1-1/2 cups sugar
4 eggs
4 squares chocolate
1 teaspoon cinnamon
1/3 cup hot water

1/2 cup milk
2 cups flour
3 teaspoons baking powder
1/4 teaspoon salt
1 teaspoon vanilla

Process: Cream Cottolene, add sugar gradually, stirring constantly. Melt chocolate over hot water, add hot water specified in recipe and beat immediately into creamed butter and sugar; add yolks of eggs beaten until thick and light. Mix and sift flour, cinnamon, baking powder and salt; add to first mixture alternately with milk, add vanilla. Cut and fold in the stiffly-beaten whites of eggs.

Rich Coffee Cake (1876)

One and a half cups of butter
Two cups of sugar
Four cups of flour
One cup of cold coffee
Four eggs
One nutmeg
Two tablespoons of cinnamon

One teaspoon of cloves
One teaspoon of soda mixed in flour
One cup of molasses
One pound of raisins
One pound of currants
One-half pound of citron

Rich Fruit Cake (1920)

2 pounds stoned raisins
2 pounds seedless raisins
2 pounds well washed and dried currants
1-pound finely sliced citron
1-pound butter
½ pint good brandy
1-pint molasses

1-pound brown sugar
2 teaspoonfuls grated nutmeg
2 teaspoonfuls ground cinnamon, cloves and mace
12 eggs
1-pound flour sifted with 2 teaspoonfuls baking powder

Dredge the fruit with flour; stir butter and sugar with the hand to a light white cream; then stir with a wooden spoon and add the eggs, 1 at a time, stirring a few minutes between each addition; next add the molasses, brandy, spice and sifted flour and lastly stir in the fruit; butter 2 large, round cake pans and line them with brown paper; fill in the mixture and bake in a medium hot oven from 3 to 4 hours. Great care must be taken that the oven is just right, as the cake burns very easily

Rock Cake (1876)

Three-fourths of a pound of sweet almonds blanched and cut fine, one pound of pulverized sugar and the whites of five eggs. Beat the whites to a stiff froth, stir in the sugar then the almonds, and drop on white buttered paper in small cakes, making them cone shaped. Place them in a cool oven until they can be removed from the paper without breaking.

Rock Cake (1840)

Blanch three-quarters of a pound of shelled sweet almonds, and bruise them fine in a mortar, but not to a smooth paste as for maccaroons. Add, as you pound them, a little rose-water. Beat to a stiff froth the whites of four eggs, and then beat in gradually a pound of powdered loaf-sugar. Add a few drops of oil of lemon. Then mix in the pounded almonds. Flour your hands and make the mixture into little cones or pointed cakes. Spread sheets of damp, thin, white paper on buttered sheets of tin, and put the rock cakes on it, rather far apart.

Sprinkle each with powdered loaf-sugar. Bake them of a pale brown, in a brisk oven. They will be done in a few minutes.

When cold, take them off the papers.

Rock Cakes (1878)

Mix well together four ounces each of butter and sugar, (cost twelve cents,) add four ounces of well washed currants, (cost three cents,) one pound of flour, (cost four cents,) and three eggs, (cost three cents;) beat all these ingredients thoroughly, roll them into little balls, or rocks, and bake them on a buttered baking pan. A good supply will cost about twenty-two cents.

Rockland Cake (1894)

One cup butter	Half teaspoon soda
Two cups sugar	Teaspoon cream tartar
One cup milk	Four cups flour
Five eggs	

Makes two loaves.

Rockland Cake (1911)

Two cups sugar	Four cups flour
One cup butter beaten to a cream	Two teaspoonfuls baking powder
Five eggs	One teaspoonful essence of lemon
One cup milk	

Rodonkuchen, or Napfkuchen (No.1) (1873)
(Rodon Cake)

Warm two pounds of flour, of which mix half a pound with half a pint of lukewarm milk, and two ounces of lump yeast, or a small teacup of brewer's yeast. Set it to rise. Beat twelve eggs, grate the rind of a lemon, and pound an ounce of bitter almonds. Mix these ingredients, six ounces of sifted sugar, with the other pound and a half of flour, using lukewarm milk enough to form a thin dough. Having set a pound of butter near the fire to warm, mix in this, and then add the sponge-dough, which must he well risen first. Beat all together a quarter of an hour with a batter-spoon; then add half a pound of stoned raisins or sultanas, a quarter of a pound of currants, and two ounces of almonds cut small. Butter well a large turban mould and strew it with as much minced almonds as will hang to the butter. Fill the mould half full, and let the cake rise in a warm place. Then gently set it in a moderate oven, to bake an hour and a half.

Gerührter Napfkuchen (No. 2) (1873)
(Rodon Cake)

Mix an ounce and a half of lump yeast with about half a pint of lukewarm milk; stir this into a pound of flour and set it to rise. Beat half a pound of butter creamy; stir into it by degrees two ounces of sifted sugar, four eggs, and the yolks of four others, a grated lemon-peel, a little salt and nutmeg, and half an ounce of bitter almonds blanched and pounded. When the yeast-dough is well risen, mix it in with the rest, and add then a quarter of a pound of sultana raisins. Put it in a well-buttered form, and bake it about an hour in a moderate oven.

Rodonkuchen (No. 3) (1873)

(Rodon Cake)

A pound of flour
Half a pound of butter
Three ounces of sugar
Nine eggs

A quarter of a pound of sultana raisins
Half a nutmeg
Half a pint of milk
An ounce of yeast

Proceed as directed for the preceding.

Roederer Cake (1920)
(Gâteau Roederer)

Pound six ounces of almonds and six ounces of pistachios with a little milk to make a fine, soft paste. Put one pound of sugar in a basin, slowly add sixteen whole eggs, and beat until very light, heating it slightly on hot embers or oh a very slow fire; put in the almond paste and continue beating for a few moments longer, then mix in with a small skimmer three-quarters of a pound of rice flour and lastly half a pound of melted butter. Butter a pound cake mold, line it with paper and fill it three-quarters full with the preparation; push into a very slack oven to cook for an hour and a quarter. When done remove arid invert it on a grate to cool, then detach the cake from the paper and cut it across in two; fill it with some Bavarian cream, into which mix three ounces of pistachios pounded with a little vanilla syrup; cover the entire cake with hot apricot marmalade; coat it with pistachio fondant and bestrew immediately with finely shredded green pistachios; let the fondant dry, then slide the cake on a lace-paper covered board or dish and surround the base with a row of small cream cakes, glazed with sugar cooked to "crack" and sprinkled with shredded pistachios.

Roll Cake (1904)

For the dough take 1¼ pounds of flour, ¾ pound of butter, according to taste 2 - 3 ounces of sugar, 3 eggs, yeast, 1 cupful of lukewarm milk; 1 teaspoonful of salt; for on the dough ½ pound of currants, ¼ pound of sugar, 1 ounce of finely sliced citron or some candied orange peel, and ¼ ounce of cinnamon.
After all of the ingredients have been warmed and the yeast dissolved with some sugar and milk, put the melted butter into the center of the Hour, stir sugar, eggs, yeast, salt and milk together, first with a knife and then with the hand, beat the dough and set aside to raise. Then roll to a long strip 6 inches wide, sprinkle with currants washed and dried and then warmed in the oven, sugar the finely sliced citron and cinnamon, roll it out and lay the end of the roll into the pan and then keep on rolling, until the cake is formed, but it must lay so that it will have room to raise. Put into a warm place to raise and bake in a moderate oven for - 1¼ hours.

Roll Jelly Cake (1876)

One cup of sugar, three eggs, one cup of flour and one teaspoon of baking powder. Do not beat the eggs separately; mix all together as quickly as possible and bake in a quick oven. While hot, spread on the jelly, which is to be well beaten before putting on the cake. Roll in a napkin.

Roll Jelly Cake (1893)

Five eggs, two cupfuls of sugar, two of flour, one-half cupful of milk, two teaspoonfuls of cream of tartar, one of soda; bake in square tins, spread with jelly and roll while warm. Lemon jelly is very nice. This recipe makes four rolls

Rose Leaf Cakes (1922)

1 cupful rose leaves
3 eggs

3 cupfuls flour
1 cupful milk

1 cupful sugar
2 teaspoonfuls baking powder
½ cupful Crisco

1 lemon
½ teaspoonful salt

Cream Crisco and sugar thoroughly together, then add eggs well beaten, flour, baking powder, salt, milk, grated rind and 1 tablespoonful lemon juice, and fresh rose leaves. Divide into Criscoed and floured gem pans and bake in moderate oven from twelve to fifteen minutes.
Sufficient for: thirty-five cakes.

Round Coffee Cake No. 1 (1922)

1 lb. of flour
½ lemon peel
½ lb. of butter
1½ cents yeast

½ lb. of sugar
3 eggs
1 cup at milk

Preparation: Cream the butter with sugar and eggs. The yeast is dissolved in 1 cup of lukewarm milk and mixed in, also the grated ½ lemon peel; then stir in the flour and beat the dough well for 20 minutes. Butter a round cake pan with tube, fill in the dough to half full and let it rise in a warm place to the top of the pan. Then bake it 1 hour.

Round Coffee Cake (No. 2) (1922) (with Raisins)

4 cups of flour
½ lemon peel
1 pt. of milk
1 cup of sugar

3 eggs
1 cup of raisins
Scant ½ lb. of butter
2 cents yeast

Preparation: Let the milk get lukewarm and stir to a smooth batter with 2 ¼ cups of flour, mix with the yeast dissolved in ¼ cup of lukewarm milk. Set the sponge to rise in a warm place, then stir in the melted butter, eggs, sugar, grated lemon peel, raisins and the rest of the flour, beat this dough well for 10 minutes. Butter a round cake pan with tube, fill it half full and set to rise in a warm place until the pan is full, then bake to a nice colour for ½ to 1 hour.

Royal Sponge Cake (1899)

Beat separately the whites and yolks of three eggs till very stiff. Boil one cup of sugar with four tablespoonfuls of cold water until it strings or thickens. Put whites and yolks together, pour in the hot sirup, and beat till lukewarm; sift in a cup of flour, flavour, and bake in two layers. Put together with jelly, frost, and sprinkle over desiccated coconut. Very nice.

Runaway Cakes (1893) (for breakfast)

1 cup sweet milk
1 cup sour cream
Soda sufficient to sweeten cream

1 egg
flour to roll out

Roll thin as knife blade; have lard boiling, throw the cakes into the lard, turn them over, and take out immediately.

Russian Torte (N.D.)
(Angel Food Cake)

1 cup egg whites	4 tablespoons water
1½ cups sugar	1 teaspoon vanilla or almond extract
¼ teaspoon salt	1 teaspoon cream of tartar
1 cup cake flour	

Boil sugar and water until it threads. Pour over the beaten egg whites. Add flavouring and beat until cold. Mix and sift flour, cream of tartar and salt several times and fold gradually into egg mixture. Bake fifty minutes in moderate oven keeping covered with heavy brown paper for the first fifteen minutes.
Filling: Soak two tablespoons granulated gelatine in one fourth cup of water for five minutes. Let stand over boiling water to dissolve. Add one cup powdered sugar, two tablespoons strong coffee and one eighth teaspoon salt. Let this mixture stand. Then take eight egg yolks, beaten well, and add one pint of heavy cream and a teaspoon of vanilla. Combine the two mixtures and beat thoroughly.
Cut the angel food cake into two unequal layers and spread the mixture between the layers and over the top and sides. Sprinkle with chopped roasted, brown almonds.
A delicious dessert.

Rye and Corn Cakes (1913)

Take half a cupful each of cornmeal, rye meal and flour, one half an even teaspoonful of salt, half a cupful of dark molasses, a cupful of sour milk in which has been dissolved an even teaspoonful of saleratus; and one or two well-beaten eggs. Fry in deep fat as doughnuts, or thin the mixture and cook as pancakes.

Rye Breakfast Cakes (1911)

Beat the egg light, add one-half cup of sugar, two cups of milk, a saltspoon of salt, one and one-half cups of rye meal, one and one-half cups of flour and three level teaspoons of baking powder. Bake in a hot greased gem pan.

Rye Drop Cakes (1876)

Two cups of rye	a little salt
One cup of flour	two tablespoons of sugar
One pint of milk	one teaspoon of soda
Two eggs	one teaspoon of cream tartar in flour

Rye Drop Cakes (1922)

1 egg, well beaten	½ cup milk
½ level teaspoon salt	2½ teaspoons baking powder
⅔ cup rye flour	2 tablespoons molasses

Sift together flour, baking powder and salt. Add gradually, milk, molasses and the egg. Drop by spoonfuls into new hot fat; drain on brown paper and serve hot.

Rye Muffins (1922)

1 cupful flour	1 egg
2 teaspoonfuls baking powder	1 cupful ryemeal
2 tablespoonfuls melted Crisco	½ teaspoonful salt

2 tablespoonfuls brown sugar	1 cupful milk

Sift flour, meal, baking powder, and salt together. Beat egg and sugar together, then add them with milk and melted Crisco. Mix and divide into Criscoed gem pans and bake in moderate oven twelve minutes.
Sufficient for: twelve muffins.

Rye Muffins (1893)

1 cup rye	Dessert spoon sugar
1 cup flour	2 full teaspoons baking powder
1 cup milk	Crystaline salt
1 egg	

Bake in gem pan, will make one dozen.

Rye Muffins (1917)

1 cup rye flour	1/2 teaspoon salt
2 tablespoons molasses	2 tablespoons melted shortening
1 cup white flour	4 teaspoons baking powder
1 egg	1 cup milk

Mix and sift dry ingredients, add molasses, egg well beaten, shortening, and milk; beat well, half fill greased muffin tins, and bake in moderate oven twenty minutes.

Part 20: S

Saarbruck Puff Paste (1904)
Sacher-Torte (1910)
Salaeratus Cake (1869)
Sally Jewett Cake (1894)
Sally Lunn (1917)
Sally Lunn (1902)
Sally Lunn (1876)
Sally Lunn (1869)
Sally Lunn (1893)
Sally Lunn without Yeast (1876)
Sally White Cake (1893)
Sand Cake (1904)
Sand Cake (1922)
Sand Cake (1920)
(Gâteau Sable)
Sand Cakes (1893)
Sand Tarts (1876)
Sand Torte or Kuchen (1873)
Sand Cake (No. 1)
Sand Torte (1873)
Sand Cake (No. 2)
Sand Tourte (1922)
Santa Barbara Cake (1820)
Saratoga Corn Cake (1902)
Savarin Cake (1920)
Savarin à la Valence (1920)
(Savarin à la Valence)
Savoy Biscuit (1920)
(Biscuit de Savoie)
Schaum Torte (1922)
Schnecken (1922)
(Snails)
Schokoladen-Biscuit (1910)
(Chocolate Spongecake)
Schokoladen-Torte (1910)
(Chocolate Cake)
Scotch Cake (1876)
Scotch Cake (1840)
Scotch Chocolate Cake (1922)
Scotch Cream Muffins (1908)
Scotch Loaf Cake (1908)
Scotch Oat Cakes (1911)
Scotch Queen Cake (1840)
Scotch Shortbread (1922)
Scottish Shortbread (1922)
Scripture Cake (1911)
Seed Cakes (1893)
Seed Cakes (1913)
Seed Cake (1898)
(Plain)
Seed Cake (1898)
(Very Good)
Sexton's Cake (1904)
Sheraton Cake (1909)
Shortbread (1898)
Shortcake (1913)
(Fruit)
Short Cake (1876)
Short Cake (1869)
Short Cakes (1840)
Shortcake (1917)
Shrewsbury Cake (1876)
Shrewsbury Cakes (1902)
Shrewsbury Cakes (1864)
Shrewsbury Cakes (1840)
Shrewsbury Cakes (1913)
Silesian Cheese Cake (1904)
Silver Cake (No.1) (1922)
Silver Cake (No.2) (1922)
Silver Cake 1 (1876)
Silver Cake 2 (1876)
Silver Cake (1911)
Silver Cake (1893)
Silver Cake 1 (1894)
Silver Cake 2 (1894)
Silver Cake (1820)
(Made with Whites)
Silver Nut Cake (1922)
Simnel Cake (1922)
Six Egg Cake (1876)
Skladany Dort s Ovocnymi Rosoly (1920)
Layer Jelly Cake
Small Apple Cakes (1904)
Small Fruit Cake (1913)
Small Royal Cakes 1920)
Small Savarins
(Petits Savarins) (1920)
Small Sponge Cake (1920)
Small Wheat Cakes (1904)
Snippodoodles (1911)
Snow Cake 1 (1876)
Snow Cake 2 (1876)
Snow Cake (1911)
Snow Cake (1894)
Snow Cake (1893)
Snow Cake (1898)
Snowball Cake (1911)
Snowflake Cake (1920)
Snow White Cake (1820)
Soda Cake (1898)
Soft Gingerbread (1905)
(To Be Eaten Hot)

Soft Ginger Bread 1 (1876)
Soft Ginger Bread 2 (1876)
Soft Ginger Bread 3 (1876)
Soft Gingerbread 1 (1893)
Soft Gingerbread 2 (1893)
Soft Ginger Bread (N.D.)
Soft Ginger Bread (1893)
Soft Gingerbread (1921)
Solid Chocolate Cake (1913)
(Mrs. R. Heim)
Sour Cream Cake (N.D.)
Sour Milk Gingerbread (1917)
Sour Milk Griddle Cakes (1922)
Sour Milk Griddle Cakes (1922)
Sour Milk Griddle Cakes (1917)
Sour Milk Griddle Cakes (1913)
Sour Milk Muffins (1917)
Sour Milk Tea Cakes (1922)
Southern Corncake (1911)
Southern Fruit Cake (1922)
Spanish Bun Cake (1913)
Spanish Cake (1922)
Spanish Cake (1908)
Spanish Chocolate Cake (1909)
Spanish Layer Cake (1913)
Spanish Pound Cake (No. 1) (1922)
Spanish Pound Cake (No. 2) (1922)
Spanish Pound Cake (No. 3) (1922)
Spanish Pound Cake (No. 4) (1922)
Speck Kuchen (1873)
Bacon Cake (No.1)
Speck Kuchen mit Kummel (1873)
Bacon Cake with Caraways (No. 2)
Spice Cake (1904)
Spice Cake No. 1 (1912)
Spice Cake No. 2 (1912)
Spice Cake (1876)
Spice Cake (1922)
Spice Cake (N.D.)
Spice Cake (1913)
Spice Cake (1920)
Spice Cake (1913)
Spice Cake (1894)
Spice Cake (1917)
(without Eggs)
Spice Cakes (1876)
Spice Cakes (1911)
Spiced Cake (1913)
(Without Eggs)
Spiced Ginger Bread (1876)
Spiced Ginger Cake (1912)
Spider Cake (1902)
Sponge Cake (1836)

(Called in France Biscuit)
Sponge Cake (1897)
Svamp-kaka
Sponge Cake No. 1 (1889)
Sponge Cake No. 2 (1889)
Sponge Cake No. 3 (1889)
Sponge Cake (1898)
Sponge Cake 1 (1876)
Sponge Cake 2 (1876)
Sponge Cake 3 (1876)
Sponge Cake 4 (1876)
Sponge Cake 5 (1876)
Sponge Cake 6 (1876)
Sponge Cake 7 (1876)
Sponge Cake 8 (1876)
Sponge Cake 9 (1876)
Sponge Cake (1911)
Sponge Cake (1922)
Sponge Cake (1890)
Sponge Cake (N.D.)
Sponge Cake (1899)
Sponge Cake (1905)
Sponge Cake (1905)
Sponge Cake (1864)
Sponge Cake (1913)
Sponge Cake (1920)
(Biscuit Leger)
Sponge Cake (1840)
Sponge Cake (1913)
Sponge Cake (1869)
Sponge Cake (1911)
Sponge Cake (1917)
(Hot Water)
Sponge Cake 1 (1893)
Sponge Cake 2 (1893)
Sponge Cake 3 (1893)
Sponge Cake 4 (1893)
Sponge Cake 5 (1893)
Sponge Cake 6 (1893)
Sponge Cake 7 (1893)
Sponge Cake (1914)
Sponge Cake 1 (1893)
Sponge Cake 2 (1893)
Sponge Cake 3 (1893)
Sponge Cake 1 (1894)
Sponge Cake 2 (1894)
Sponge Cake 3 (1894)
Sponge Cake 4 (1894)
Sponge Cake 5 (1894)
Sponge Cake (1893)
Sponge Cake Croquettes (1911)
Sponge Cake in Small Pans (1869)
Sponge Cake (1922)

Ladyfinger Mixture
Sponge Cakes (1898)
(Small)
Sponge Drop Cakes (1876)
Sponge Gingerbread (1890)
Sponge Layer Cake (1899)
Spritzkuchen (1910)
Squash Griddle Cakes (1902)
Squash Griddle Cakes (1894)
St. Honoré and St. Honoré Sultana (1920)
(St. Honoré et St. Honoré Sultane)
St. Nicholas Cake (1876)
Stachelbeer-Torte (1910)
(Gooseberry Cake)
Stale Bread Cakes (1893)
Steamed Shortcake (1913)
Stolle (1910)
Stollen (1922)
Strawberry Cake with Vanilla Cream (1904)
Strawberry Short Cake (1893)
Strawberry Shortcake, No. 1 (1920)
Strawberry Shortcake, No. 2 (1920)
Strawberry Shortcake (1905)
Strawberry Shortcake (1913)
Strawberry Shortcake (1922)
Strawberry Shortcake (1922)
Strawberry Short Cake 1 (1893)
Strawberry Short Cake 2 (1893)
Strawberry Short Cake (1876)
Strawberry Short Cake (1920)
(Gâteau aux Fraises)
Strawberry Shortcake (1914)
Strawberry Shortcake (1899)

Streusel Coffee Cake (1922)
Streusel Kuchen (1873)
Strewed Cake
Streusselkuchen (1910)
Striezel (1910)
Suabian Cake (1904)
Sugar Cakes (1920)
(Gâteaux au Sucre)
Sultana Cake (1898)
Sultana Tea Cakes (1911)
Sunshine Cake (1922)
Sunshine Cake No. 1 (1912)
Sunshine Cake No. 2 (1912)
Sunshine Cake No. 3 (1912)
Sunshine Cake (1922)
Sunshine Cake (1893)
Sunshine Cake (1911)
Sunshine Layer Cake (N.D.)
Superior Muffins (N.D.)
Surprise Muffins (N.D.)
Süste (1910)
Süster (1873)
Süster Cake
Swedish Batter Cakes (1908)
Sweet Cake (1904)
(Rodon Kuchen)
Sweet Corn Griddle-cakes (1905)
Sweet Milk Griddle Cakes (1922)
Swiss Cream Cake (No.1) (1904)
Swiss Cream Cake (No.2) (1904)
Swiss Roll (1898)

Saarbruck Puff Paste (1904)

⅔ pound of butter prepared as directed
⅔ pound of flour
2 tablespoonfuls of arrac
A large half cupful of cold water

Half of the flour is made into a dough with water and the arrac, then the butter and the remaining flour kneaded into the dough, each part rolled separately, then lay one on the other and roll out three times more.

Sacher-Torte (1910)

½ lb. chocolate
½ lb. castor sugar
½ lb. butter
½ lb. sweet almonds
2 oz. potato flour
8 eggs

Cream the butter, add the beaten-up yolks and sugar, and stir for ¾ hour. Then stir in alternately the flour (mixed with the grated almonds) and the whites, whisked stiffly. Fill a well-buttered tin and bake about an hour. Cover with chocolate icing.

Salaeratus Cake (1869)

Warm a pint of butter-milk, put in it a tea-spoonful of powdered salaeratus, and a piece of lard the size of an egg; stir it into flour till it is a soft dough; roll it out, and bake it on the griddle, or in the dripping-pan of a stove. If you have no sour milk, put a table-spoonful of vinegar in sweet milk.

Sally Jewett Cake (1894)

Three-quarters pound sugar
One half pound butter
One cup molasses
One cup milk
Five eggs
One-pound flour
Heaping teaspoon soda
One-pound raisins
Two tablespoons each cloves and cinnamon
One nutmeg
Currants
Citron
Wine glass brand

Sally Lunn (1917)

2 cups flour
2 eggs
4 teaspoons baking powder
1 cup milk
1/2 teaspoon salt
1/4 cup melted shortening
2 tablespoons sugar

Mix and sift dry ingredients; add eggs well beaten, milk, and shortening; beat thoroughly, pour into shallow greased pan, and bake in a moderate oven twenty minutes.

Sally Lunn (1902)

Heat 1 pt. of milk blood warm
add 3 tablespoonfuls of butter, melted
2 well-beaten eggs
1/2 a yeast cake dissolved in 3 tablespoonfuls of cold water

Pour gradually on the flour and beat into a smooth batter; then add 1 teaspoonful of salt and 2 tablespoonfuls of sugar. Butter baking pans and pour half full. Let it rise for 2 hours in a warm place. Bake 1/2 an hour.

Sally Lunn (1876)

Two well beaten eggs
One-half cup of sweet milk
One-half cup of melted butter
One-half cup of yeast

Two tablespoons of white sugar
One pint of flour
Saltspoon of salt

Mix at night; pour into baking-pans and let rise. Bake in quick oven for breakfast.

Sally Lunn (1869)

Warm a quart of milk with a quarter of a pound of butter, and a heaped spoonful of sugar, beat up three eggs, and put in, with a little salt, and flour enough to make it stiffer than pound cake, beat it well, put in a tea cup of yeast, and let it rise, butter a fluted pan and pour it in, bake it in a quick oven, slice and butter it. If you wish tea at six o'clock, set it to rise at ten in the morning. Bake it an hour.

Sally Lunn (1893)

One pint of milk
Three eggs, well beaten
Salt

One large spoon of butter
Half a teacup of yeast
As much flour as will make a thick batter

Pour into a cake pan and place in a warm spot to rise. Bake in moderate oven. When done, cut with sharp knife crosswise twice, pouring over each part drawn butter. Replacing the parts, cut then like cake, serving at once while hot. This is a great favourite with Southerners.

Sally Lunn without Yeast (1876)

One quart of flour
Two eggs
Two cups of new milk
Large spoon of butter

One-half cup of sugar
Pinch of salt
Three teaspoons of baking powder

Mix baking powder well with flour; warm butter and milk together, stir in flour and eggs, beat well and bake half hour in a hot oven.

Sally White Cake (1893)

One pound of butter
Three pounds of citron
One and one-fourth pound of sugar
One pound of flour
Fifteen eggs
Two small cocoanuts grated

One and one-half pound of almonds, blanched and
pounded (weigh after blanching)
One nutmeg
One tablespoonful of mace
One wineglass of best brandy
One of Madeira or sherry

Bake slowly as a fruit cake and frost.

Sand Cake (1904)

1 pound of fresh butter
1 pound of sifted sugar

½ pound of fine flour
½ pound of sifted cornstarch

10 - 12 fresh eggs
The juice of a lemon

2 tablespoonfuls of arrac

All of this, with the exception of the eggs, must be set in a warm place for a few hours.

The butter is melted and freed from settlings; after it is cold rub to a cream, adding the sugar by degrees with a little lemon peel, stirring constantly. Then stir in one by one the yolks of the eggs, the grated lemon peel and the flour, a spoonful at a time. After this has been stirred for ½ hour, stir through it the arrac and lemon juice and the beaten whites of the eggs, together with a teaspoonful of baking powder. Put this into a prepared form and then into the oven and bake with 2 degrees of heat for 1½ hours, and if the cake is very thick, for 2 hours. During this time the form should not be moved.

This cake can also be divided into three parts, one of which is coloured with chocolate, the other with cochineal, leaving the last yellow, putting one layer on the other, covering the top with a three-coloured frosting seasoned with Maraschino.

Sand Cake (1922)

1 cupful Crisco
5 eggs
1 cupful sugar

½ lb. cornstarch
1 teaspoonful salt
1 teaspoonful lemon extract

Cream the Crisco and salt, add sugar by tablespoonfuls, beating all the time, then add the yolks of the eggs each one separately, then add the cornstarch by tablespoonfuls, lemon extract and lastly whites of eggs beaten to a stiff froth. Turn into a papered cake tin and bake in moderate oven for three-quarters of an hour. Sufficient for one cake.

Sand Cake (1920)
(Gâteau Sable)

Mix twelve ounces of powdered sugar and four ounces of vanilla sugar in a basin with sixteen egg-yolks; beat until light, then add half a pound of flour and half a pound of fecula, sifted together, one pound of melted butter, and lastly the sixteen beaten whites; bake this in a slack oven in a pound cake or manqué mold, buttered and lined with paper, and when done to perfection take it out and invert on a grate to cool. Then cover the cake with well-reduced apricot marmalade and ice over with water icing flavoured with rum. Decorate with candied fruits and dress on a dish covered with lace paper.

Sand Cakes (1893)

One cup sugar
½ cup butter
Crystaline salt
2 eggs, saving out the white of one

¼ cup milk
1 teaspoon cream tartar
½ teaspoon soda

Cut with cookie cutter; wet cakes with white of egg, brush over with sugar. Bake in quick oven.

Sand Tarts (1876)

One pound of flour
One pound of sugar

A half-pound of butter
Two eggs, leaving out one of the whites

Work the butter to a cream, add the sugar, flour and eggs; make a stiff paste, roll very thin and cut in forms. Have ready some powdered sugar and cinnamon; wash the tarts with the beaten white of one egg sprinkle the sugar and cinnamon over them, lay a few blanched almonds on the top, and bake.

Sand Torte or Kuchen (1873)
Sand Cake (No. 1)

Half a pound of butter must be stirred to a cream, then the yolks of twelve eggs added, and half a lemon-peel grated. Add by degrees, half a pound of sifted sugar, a quarter of a pound of fine flour, and the same of potato-flour. When these are well mixed, add the egg-whites, whipped to a snow. Thoroughly stir all together and bake it in a moderate oven.
Half a wineglass of rum or brandy, and the whole lemon peel grated, give richness to this torte.

Sand Torte (1873)
Sand Cake (No. 2)

Half a pound of warmed butter
A quarter of a pound of sifted sugar
Six eggs

The rind and juice of a lemon
Half a pound of fine flour
A quarter of a pound of potato-flour

To be all well stirred.

Bake as directed for other torten in a moderate oven. When three-parts done, gently draw it to the mouth of the oven, and quickly strew over the following; - two or three ounces of almonds cut small and mixed with two ounces of powdered sugar, and a teaspoonful of powdered cinnamon. Put it back to finish baking, but do not let the almonds be done too brown on the top.

Sand Tourte (1922)

Eight ounces of butter
Twelve ounces of sugar
Eight ounces of cornstarch
Four ounces of flour

Fourteen yolks and twelve whites of eggs
The grated rind of one lemon
One quarter of a teaspoonful of mace

Cream butter and sugar and add the yolks gradually with a spoonful of starch and flour; and work it into a cream together; add the flavour and last the whites beaten firm. Bake in a slow heat in a large ring form. Ice with maraschino fondant and decorate nicely.

Santa Barbara Cake (1820)

1/2 c. fat
1 tsp. cloves
1 c. sugar
1 tsp. cinnamon
3 eggs
1 c. sour milk

2 c. flour
1/4 c. nuts chopped fine
1 tsp. soda
1 tsp. nutmeg
Nuts and raisins may be omitted

Saratoga Corn Cake (1902)

Sift together 2 cups of pastry flour
1-1/2 cups of granulated yellow corn-meal
1/2 a cup of sugar
1/2 a teaspoonful of salt

1 teaspoonful of soda.
Beat 2 eggs without separating
Add 2 cups of thick sour cream or milk
And three tablespoonfuls of melted butter

And stir into the dry mixture. Beat thoroughly and bake in a large shallow pan for 25 minutes.

Savarin Cake (1920)

1 cup lukewarm cream or milk
2 yeast cake
3 ounces butter
4 eggs
¼ teaspoonful salt
½ gill Cognac
2 tablespoonfuls powdered sugar
10 ounces sifted flour

Dissolve the yeast in half the milk and mix it with half the sifted flour into a smooth batter; cover and set it in a warm place to rise, which will take about ½ hour; in the meantime stir butter and sugar to a cream and add the eggs, 1 at a time, stirring a few minutes between each addition; next add alternately the remaining milk, brandy, flour and lastly the batter which has been set in a warm place to rise; beat the whole with the right hand for 15 minutes; then cover with a napkin and let it rise in a warm place; butter a round mould which holds about 1½ to 2 quarts and dust with flour; turn the mould upside down, so the loose flour may fall out; when the dough is very light mix it with 2 ounces finely cut almonds and carefully fill it into the mould; set again in a warm place to rise to end of a knitting needle into centre of cake; if the needle comes out clean it is done; if any dough adheres to it the cake must be baked a few minutes longer; as soon as the cake is done turn it onto a round wire grate or sieve and prepare the following glaze: - Place a saucepan with 1 cup sugar and ½ pint cold water over the fire and boil 5 minutes; add 1 glass Jamaica rum, Cognac, sherry wine, kirsch or any other kind of liquor; set the cake with the grate or sieve onto a dish and pour the syrup evenly all over it; pour the syrup which drops from the cake onto the dish back to saucepan again, boil it up and pour over the cake; lift the grate on one side and slide the cake onto a dessert dish; the top may be decorated with preserved cherries or other fruit. The savarin is served as dessert, either hot or cold. Small savarins are baked in small, deep forms and dipped in hot syrup when done.

Savarin à la Valence (1920)
(Savarin à la Valence)

Butter a medium-sized Savarin mold, dredge the bottom with cut-up almonds and fill it half full with Savarin paste into which has been incorporated candied orange peel cut in the shape of small dice. Let it rise in a mild temperature until it reaches the edges, then bake in a slack oven. As soon as it is done remove from the oven, pare it even and unmould on a grate; pour some orange syrup over, cover with apricot marmalade and glaze with fondant, flavoured with orange. When the icing is cold slip the Savarin on to a bottom made of office paste covered with green sugar and dress it on a dish. Decorate the top of the cake with a wreath of angelica lozenges and cherries (demi- sucre); fill the center with Chantilly cream flavoured with orange sugar and place on top a light sugar sultana, then serve.

Savoy Biscuit (1920)
(Biscuit de Savoie)

Grease a high biscuit mold with melted prepared veal kidney suet; drain off any surplus fat by reversing the mold, then glaze with sugar icing and fecula, half of each. Pour into a vessel one pound of powdered sugar flavoured with vanilla and a pinch of salt, add fourteen egg-yolks one at a time and beat the whole forcibly to have it get quite frothy; whip fourteen egg-whites to a stiff froth, and put a fourth part into the yolks, also six ounces of potato fecula and six ounces of flour, the two latter to be sifted together- As soon as the whole is thoroughly combined add the remainder of the beaten whites. With this fill the mold three-quarters full and stand it on a baking pan; fix it so that the mold will not fall; place it carefully in the mildest spot in the oven. In order to bake this biscuit properly it is essential that the oven be first thoroughly heated, then allowed to fall to a mild temperature; leave it in for two and a quarter to two and a half hours. When done to perfection unmould on a grate, cool, pare very straight and dress on a dish; surround the base with a circle of lady bouchées iced with vanilla.

Schaum Torte (1922)

Whites of 6 eggs
1 teaspoon vinegar
2 cups sugar
1 teaspoon vanilla

Beat the whites dry and stiff, adding the sugar a little at a time and then the vinegar and vanilla, beating constantly. Use a spring form. Grease and pour in about two-thirds of the mixture. Form a circle of the remaining third around the edge of the tin. Bake three-quarters to one hour in a slow oven.
Serve filled with fresh berries covered with whipped cream; or with fruit ice cream, trimmed with whipped cream.

Schnecken (1922)
(Snails)

Yeast dough like Coffee Cake (1922)

For the Filling:

⅛ lb. of butter
½ cup of blanched, ground
1 cup of sugar almonds
1 cup of currants

Preparation: The preparation is the same as given under Coffee Cake. Stir in 1 cup of flour more than given in Coffee Cake (1922), roll out the dough to 1-inch thickness, strew it with sugar, cinnamon, currants, almonds, sprinkle with melted butter, roll it up carefully and cut slices off to make the snails.
Place these into a buttered tin and set to rise about ½ hour. Then bake them in a medium hot oven, brush them while hot with melted butter and sprinkle with sugar.

Schokoladen-Biscuit (1910)
(Chocolate Spongecake)

5 oz. cornflour
6 oz. sugar
3 oz. grated chocolate
6 eggs

Whisk the whites of eggs stiffly, then stir into them the beaten-up yolks, sugar, grated chocolate and cornflour. Fill a well-buttered cake tin and bake 1 hour.

Schokoladen-Torte (1910)
(Chocolate Cake)

2 oz. almonds, grated in their skins
4 tablespoonsful flour
4 oz. butter
4 eggs
4 oz. chocolate dissolved in
2 tablespoonsful water
Vanilla flavouring

Cream the butter, add the sugar and beaten-up yolks and stir for ½ hour. Then add the flour, chocolate, grated almonds and the vanilla flavouring. Mix well and finally stir in the well-whisked whites of eggs. Fill a well-buttered cake tin and bake in a moderate oven for 1 hour.

Schwäbische Pfefferkuchen (1910)
(Swabian Pepperbread)

1 lb. flour	4 grains of cardamom
½ lb. sugar	½ oz. potash dissolved in
5 eggs	2 tablespoonsful rosewater
½ pint honey	½ gill rum
¼ lb. butter	2 oz. candied peel
5 to 6 peppercorns	A pinch of ground cinnamon
The grated rind of a lemon	10 ground cloves

Beat the eggs and sugar to a froth, stir in all the spices, the chopped candied peel and rum and stir 15 minutes. Then add the honey, in which the butter has been warmed, the potash (dissolved in 2 tablespoonsful rosewater) and lastly the flour, stirred in gradually.

Fill a well-buttered cake tin, lined with buttered paper, and bake for ¾ hour. Ornament the top of the cake with slices of candied peel and of almonds.

Scotch Cake (1876)

Two and a half pounds of butter (salt thoroughly washed out) and one pound of powdered sugar; stir butter and sugar to a cream, add four pounds of sifted flour, roll a fourth of an inch in thickness and cut in squares; caraway with candy mites on the top. Turn your bake-pans upside down, cover with white paper, lay the cakes on with a knife and bake in a moderate oven. They will keep good for months.

Scotch Cake (1840)

Rub three quarters of a pound of butter into a pound of sifted flour; mix in a pound of powdered sugar, and a large table-spoonful of powdered cinnamon. Mix it into a dough with three well beaten eggs. Roll it out into a sheet; cut it into round cakes and bake them in a quick oven; they will require but a few minutes.

Scotch Chocolate Cake (1922)

½ cup butter or shortening	½ cup sour milk
1½ cups sugar	1 teaspoon soda, mixed with
2 eggs	2 cups of flour
1 square chocolate dissolved in ½ cup of boiling water	1 teaspoon vanilla

Bake in sheet or two layers about thirty minutes,

Scotch Cream Muffins (1908)

Sift 1 pint of flour with 1 teaspoonful of baking-powder; beat three yolks of eggs with a pinch of salt; add 1 pint of cream and 1 tablespoonful of melted butter. Stir in the flour; add the whites beaten to a stiff froth. Beat all well together. Fill the muffin-rings 1/2 full and bake in a quick oven for twenty minutes.

Scotch Loaf Cake (1908)

Mix 1/2 pound of butter with 1/4 pound of sugar, 1/2 cup of chopped nuts and 1/2 cup of shredded citron; then work in 1 pound of sifted flour with 2 teaspoonfuls of baking-powder. Make a loaf a half inch thick and bake in a moderate oven until done

Scotch Oat Cakes (1911)

Can be either fried on a griddle or broiled over a fire. The meal for this purpose should be ground fine. Put a quart of the meal in a baking dish with a teaspoonful of salt. Pour in little by little just enough cold water to make a dough and roll out quickly before it hardens into a circular sheet about a quarter of an inch thick. Cut into four cakes and bake slowly for about twenty minutes on an iron griddle. Do not turn but toast after they are cooked.

Scotch Queen Cake (1840)

Melt a pound of butter by putting it into a skillet on hot coals. Then set it away to cool. Sift a quarter of a peck of flour into a deep pan and mix with it a pound of powdered sugar and a table-spoonful of powdered cinnamon and mace. Make a hole in the middle, put in the melted butter, and mix it with a knife till you have formed of the whole a lump of dough. If it is too stiff, moisten it with a little rose water. Do not knead it; but roll it out into a large oval sheet, an inch thick. Cut it down the middle, and then across, so as to divide it into four cakes. Prick them with a fork, and crimp or scallop the edges neatly. Lay them in shallow pans; set them, in a quick oven and bake them of a light brown. This cake will keep a week or two.
You may mix in with the dough half a pound of currants, picked, washed, and dried.

Scotch Shortbread (1922)

4 cupfuls flour
1 cupful Crisco
¾ cupful sugar

1 large egg
1 teaspoonful salt

Sift flour and salt on to baking board. Cream Crisco, sugar and egg in basin and when thoroughly beaten turn out on board and very gradually knead in flour. Make into two smooth rounds, pinch them round the edges, prick over top with fork, lay on papered tin and bake in moderate oven thirty-five minutes. Leave on tin until cold.
Sufficient for: two round cakes.

Scottish Shortbread (1922)

Cream one-half pound butter with one-quarter cup sugar and add one pound of flour and a pinch of salt. Roll to about one-half inch thickness and prick with a fork. Cut into squares six inches long and lay on buttered baking sheets to bake for fifteen minutes in a hot oven.

Scripture Cake (1911)

1 cup butter	Judges 5:25
3½ cups flour	I Kings 4:22
2 cups sugar	Jer. 6:20
2 cups raisins	I Sam. 30:12
2 cups figs	I Sam. 30:12
1 cup water	Gen. 24:17
1 cup almonds	Gen. 43:11
½ doz. eggs	Isa. 10:14
Tablespoon honey	Exod. 16:21
A pinch of salt	Lev. 2:13
Spices to taste	I Kings 10:10
½ teaspoon soda	Matt. 13:33
1 teaspoon cream tartar	Matt. 13:33
Father Solomon's advice for making good boys	Prov. 23:13

Seed Cakes (1893)

1 cup butter
1½ sugar
2 eggs
1 cup milk

1 teaspoon soda
1 cream tartar
Seeds

Seed Cakes (1913)

2/3 cup Cottolene
2 cups sugar
2 eggs well beaten
1 teaspoon soda
1 cup buttermilk

1 teaspoon salt
Flour
1-1/2 tablespoons caraway seeds
Raisins

Process: Cream Cottolene, add sugar gradually, add well beaten egg, soda dissolved in milk, salt, seeds, and flour to make a soft dough. Chill the dough and shape as other cookies. Place a seeded

Seed Cake (1898)
(Plain)

Ingredients:

1¼ lbs. flour
Pinch of salt
1 teaspoonful baking powder
6 oz. butter or clarified dripping

6 oz. sugar
½ oz. carraway seeds
½ pint milk

Method: Mix the baking-powder and salt with the flour and rub in the butter or dripping; add the seeds and sugar and mix well. Make the milk warm, but not hot; moisten the cake with it, and beat the mixture for 3 or 4 minutes with a wooden spoon. Half fill a buttered cake-tin with the mixture, and bake it in a moderately quick oven, covering the top with a buttered paper when the cake is half cooked. When done, turn the cake out of the tin, and stand it on its side to cool.
Time: 1½ hours.
Sufficient for: 1 good sized cake.

Seed Cake (1898)
(Very Good)

Ingredients:

1 lb. flour
½ lb. butter
½ lb. sugar
½ oz. carraway seeds

1 oz. candied, finely-chopped citron rind
4 eggs
¼ pint milk

Method: Rub the butter into the flour, add the sugar, seeds, and candied peel, and mix well. Beat and strain the eggs, add to them the milk, and moisten the cake with these, beat it with a wooden spoon for 3 or 4 minutes, turn it into a well-buttered tin, and bake in a moderately quick oven, covering the top with a buttered paper when the cake is half-cooked.
Time: 1¼ hours.
Sufficient for: 1 good sized cake.

Sexton's Cake (1904)

1 pound of freshened butter	½ pound of grated almonds
1 pound of flour	9 eggs
¾ pound of sifted sugar	Jelly

Cream the butter, add sugar, eggs and almonds, and stir for ½ hour. Then mix through this the flour and put into a pan, so that it will only be about ½ inch thick and bake to a light brown colour. After the cake is cold dot with jelly and sprinkle sugar over it.

Sheraton Cake (1909)

Cream 1 cupful of sugar and ½ cupful of butter, add the yolks of 4 eggs and the white of 1 and beat well; add ¾ cupful of orange juice and 2 cupfuls of flour sifted with 2 teaspoonfuls of baking-powder. Bake in two layers and when done spread with 1 cupful of orange marmalade into which has been beaten the whites of two eggs. If preferred use this only for the filling and ice the top.

Shortbread (1898)

Ingredients:

1 lb. flour	2 oz. candied orange and citron peel
2 oz. sugar	8 oz. butter

Method: Cut up the candied peel finely and mix it with the sugar and flour. Make the butter liquid, but not hot, and beat it into the other ingredients until they form a firm paste. Turn this on to a floured board and roll it out ¾ inch thick. Cut it into cakes about 10 inches long and 6 inches wide, ornament the edges, and prick the cake all over with a fork. Decorate the cake with long strips of candied peel on top, and bake in a good oven, taking great care not to let it become too brown.
Time: 20 to 30 minutes.
Sufficient for: 2 or 3 cakes of shortbread.

Shortcake (1913)
(Fruit)

Cream together half a cupful each of butter and sugar, add a well beaten egg, a cupful of sweet milk and a cupful of flour into which has been sifted a rounding teaspoonful of baking powder and a pinch of salt. Use more or less flour to make a soft batter. Bake in layer tins in a hot oven. Spread mashed and sugared fruit between the layers and whole berries or fruit slices on top.

Short Cake (1876)

One-quart thick sour cream	A little salt
Two teaspoons of soda	Flour enough to make a soft dough

Short Cake (1869)

To three quarts of flour take three-quarters of a pound of lard, and a spoonful of salt; rub the lard in the flour, and put in cold water, sufficient to make a stiff dough; roll it out without working in thin cakes; have the bake-iron hot, flour it, and bake with a quick heat; when one side is brown, turn and bake the other; when baked in the dripping-pan of a stove, they do without turning; - you may cut them in round cakes, if you choose. Some use half milk and half water; in that case, less lard is required.

Short Cakes (1840)

Rub three quarters of a pound of fresh butter into a pound and a half of sifted flour; and make it into a dough with a little cold water. Roll it out into a sheet half an inch thick and cut it into round cakes with the edge of a tumbler. Prick them with a fork; lay them in a shallow iron pan sprinkled with flour and bake them in a moderate oven till they are brown. Send them to table hot; split and butter them.

Shortcake (1917)

1-1/2 cups flour
3 tablespoons shortening
3 teaspoons baking powder

2/3 cup milk
1/3 teaspoon salt

Mix and sift flour, baking powder, and salt; rub in shortening with finger tips; add milk, and mix well with a knife. Spread in two greased layer-cake pans, patting with the back of a tablespoon until pans are evenly filled. Bake in a hot oven twelve minutes. If individual shortcakes are preferred, roll, cut with a biscuit cutter, and bake quickly about fifteen minutes; split, and put filling between and on top.

Shrewsbury Cake (1876)

Two cups of sugar
One cup of butter
A half-cup of milk

Four eggs
One-third of a teaspoon of soda
Three cups of flour

Bake in flat tins and use frosting flavoured with peach water.

Shrewsbury Cakes (1902)

Sift a lb. of sugar, some cinnamon and a nutmeg into 3 lbs. of flour; add a little rose water, and 3 eggs beaten light and mix well with the flour; then pour into it as much melted butter as will make it a good thickness to roll out. Mould it well, roll thin and cut it into shapes. Bake on tin sheets.

Shrewsbury Cakes (1864)

And here each season do those cakes abide, Whose honoured names the inventive city own, Rendering through Britain's isle Salopia's praises known. SHENSTONE.

Sift one pound of sugar, some pounded cinnamon and a nutmeg grated, into three pounds of flour, the finest sort; add a little rose-water to three eggs well beaten; mix these with the flour, &c.; then pour into it as much butter melted as will make it a good thickness to roll out.
Stir it well and roll thin; cut it into such shapes as you like. Bake on tins.

Shrewsbury Cakes (1840)

Rub three quarters of a pound of butter into two pounds of sifted flour, and mix in half a pound of powdered sugar, and half a pound of currants, washed and dried. Wet it to a stiff paste with rich milk. Roll it out and cut it into cakes. Lay them on buttered baking sheets and put them into a moderate oven.

Shrewsbury Cakes (1913)

This receipt with two that follow, comes down from: "The spacious days of great Elizabeth." They are given verbatim, from the original version, as it seems to me the flavour of the language must add to the flavour of the cakes. "Mix half a pound of butter, well beat like cream, with the same weight of flour, one egg, six ounces of beaten and sifted loaf sugar, and half an ounce of caraway seed. Form these into a paste, roll them thin, and lay them in sheets of tin, then bake them in a slow oven."

Silesian Cheese Cake (1904)

A dough is made as given under Westphalian Cake. No. 3 (1904). For the top take a soup plateful of curds stirred with fresh cream but not too thin, 1 cupful of melted butter, sugar, cinnamon to taste, 2 eggs, with ½ pound of currants stirred through it.
Roll the dough quite thin, put on the pan, let it raise, warming the cheese a little and spread it on the cake and bake quickly. According to the size of the cake, the evening before wanted take 3 quarts of thick milk with the cream, put it into a cheese cloth bag and the next morning use for the cake.
This cake is very nice and refreshing when not left in the oven too long so that it will become dry; it should be eaten when still quite fresh.

Silver Cake (No.1) (1922)

One pound and four ounces of sugar
Twelve ounces of butter
Three quarters of a pint of whites of eggs
Three quarters of a pint of milk
One and one-half pounds of flour
One ounce of baking powder

Cream same as for Pound Cake. Sift the powder in the flower and mix like New York Pound Cake (No.2) (1922). Bake in 300 to 350 degrees Fahrenheit.

Silver Cake (No. 2) (1922)

One and one-half pounds of sugar
One pound of butter
Three quarter of a pint of whites of eggs
Three quarters of a pint of milk
Two pounds of flour
A half-ounce of baking powder

Add flavour and mix like Silver Cake (No. 1) (1922).

Silver Cake 1 (1876)

Two cups of fine white sugar
A half-cup of butter
One cup of sweet milk
Three cups of sifted flour
Whites of eight eggs
Two teaspoons of baking powder
Flavour to the taste

Silver Cake 2 (1876)

Whites of twelve eggs
Five cups of flour
Two and a half cups of white sugar
One cup of butter
One cup of cream or sweet milk
One teaspoon of cream of tartar
A half teaspoon of soda

Beat and mix as the Gold Cake.

Silver Cake (1911)

1 cup of sugar
Whites of 4 eggs
½ cup butter
2 cups flour

½ teaspoonful of soda
1 teaspoonful cream tartar
½ cup of milk, put in last
A little salt

Silver Cake (1893)

Half-cup butter
1 cup sugar
½ cup milk

1 teaspoon baking powder mixed thoroughly with
1½ cups flour

Beat well, add the whites of 4 eggs beaten stiff, and stir in lightly.

Silver Cake 1 (1894)

Two cups of sugar
Two and one-half cups flour
One-half cup butter
Three-quarters cup milk
Whites of eight eggs

Teaspoon cream tartar
Half teaspoon soda
Almond essence
Chocolate frosting

Silver Cake 2 (1894)

One and one-half cups sugar
One-half cup butter
Three-fourths cup sweet milk
Two cups flour

One teaspoon cream tartar
One-half teaspoon soda
Whites of four eggs, well beaten
Flavour with vanilla

Bake in a slow oven.

Silver Cake (1820)
(Made with Whites)

2 c. sugar
3 c. flour
½ c. fat
1 tsp. cream tartar with ½ tsp. soda,

Or 2 tsp. baking powder
4 egg whites
1 c. cold water

Cream butter and sugar. Add beaten whites of eggs. Add cold water. Add sifted dry ingredients and beat briskly 5 minutes.

Silver Nut Cake (1922)

1 cupful sugar
½ teaspoonful salt
½ cupful Crisco
3 teaspoonfuls baking powder
4 whites of eggs

1 cupful chopped pecans or English walnut meats
½ teaspoonful vanilla extract
2 cupfuls flour
½ cupful milk

Cream Crisco and sugar. Sift dry ingredients and add to Crisco mixture, alternating with the milk; add nuts

and vanilla extract. Beat egg whites to stiff froth and fold in at last. Turn into Criscoed and floured cake tin and bake in moderate oven thirty-five minutes.
Sufficient for: one small cake.

Simnel Cake (1922)

¾ cupful sugar
½ cupful chopped candied citron peel
¾ cupful Crisco
4 eggs
2 cupfuls flour

2 cupfuls sultana raisins
1 teaspoonful baking powder
¼ cupful seeded raisins
½ teaspoonful almond extract
¾ teaspoonful salt

For Filling and Icing:

¼ lb. ground almonds
2 eggs

2 cupfuls powdered sugar
1 teaspoonful almond extract

For Cake: Cream Crisco and sugar together, add eggs well beaten, flour, baking powder, salt, almond extract, raisins, and peel. Make filling by mixing almonds with powdered sugar, eggs well beaten and almond extract. Line Criscoed cake tin with paper and place in half of cake mixture, then put in layer of filling, then remaining half of cake mixture. Bake in moderate oven. When cake is nearly baked, place remaining almond paste on top and finish baking. Cake takes from one hour to one and a quarter hours.
Sufficient for: medium-sized cake.

Six Egg Cake (1876)

Six eggs
Two cups of sugar
One cup of butter
One-half cup of new milk

Three and one-half cups of flour
Two teaspoons of cream tartar
A half teaspoon of soda
Flavour

This is as good as pound cake.

Skladany Dort s Ovocnymi Rosoly (1920)
Layer Jelly Cake

½ cup butter
1 cup sugar
3 egg yolks
2 cups sifted flour with 2 tsp. baking powder

1 cup sweet milk
1 tsp. vanilla
3 beaten egg whites

Soften the butter in a deep mixing bowl. Add the sugar, a tablespoon at a time, until all is creamed well. Add the 3 beaten egg yolks, one at a time, beating well after each addition.
Now add 1/2 cup milk and 1/2 of the sifted flour and baking powder. Beat well. Then add ½ cup milk and the rest of the flour. Add vanilla, and last, fold in the beaten egg whites. Bake in four greased and floured cake pans (round) in a 350° degree oven for 20 minutes. Cool on rack. When cool, use any jam or jelly between layers. Sift powdered sugar on top.

Small Apple Cakes (1904)

Pare large cooking apples, cut into slices the thickness of a finger and take out the core. Then let them heat through with a little arrac and sugar. Take 1 small cupful of milk, ¼ pound of flour, the yolks of 4 eggs, a little salt and stir through the dough a little mace or cinnamon. Beat well together and just before baking add the whites of the eggs. Mix the apples through the dough and bake with butter on a hot pan on both sides until done and of a golden-brown colour.

Small Fruit Cake (1913)

Cream together a cupful of brown sugar and half a cupful of butter. Add two well beaten eggs, two thirds of a cupful of sour cream, an even teaspoonful of ground cinnamon, half an even teaspoonful each of grated nutmeg and ground cloves (allspice may be used instead of cloves). Put in an even teaspoonful of saleratus that has been dissolved in a little water.
Take a cupful of seeded raisins, cut them in two, and mix them in the flour with half a cupful of broken walnut meats and a teaspoonful of shaved citron. Beat all the ingredients until very smooth and bake slowly in a loaf pan.

Small Royal Cakes 1920)

Prepare a puff paste and roll it out thin about ¼ of an inch in thickness; mix 6 ounces powdered sugar with the beaten whites of 2 eggs; spread this over the rolled-out paste, cut it into strips of 1½ inches wide and 3½ inches long, lay them in shallow tin pans and bake in a slow oven to a delicate brown.

Small Savarins
(Petits Savarins) (1920)

Butter some Savarin molds, dredge shredded almonds on the bottom and fill half full with Savarin paste; let rise in a mild temperature until the molds are full, then place them in a brisk oven to bake; unmould as soon as removed and dip them in a syrup made as follows.
Into five gills of thirty-two-degree cold syrup, add one gill of kirsch, half a gill of maraschino, half a gill of noyau and half a gill of Curacoa; warm this syrup and then dip in the cakes. When they are well soaked place on a wire grate to drain.

Small Sponge Cake (1920)

Three eggs
½ cup granulated sugar
½ cup flour

The grated rind of ½ lemon
A little lemon juice

Stir the 3 yolks with the sugar 15 minutes, then add the lemon; beat the whites to a stiff froth, add them to the yolks, and beat till the sugar is all dissolved, which will take about 10 minutes, then sift in the flour, stir the flour in lightly; butter and dust with flour a small round pan, pour in the mixture, and bake in a slow oven.

Small Wheat Cakes (1904)

One quart of warm milk
2 ounces of melted butter
3 - 4 eggs
1 tablespoonful of sugar, yeast

1 pound of warmed flour
4 - 6 ounces of currants, cinnamon or mace
A little salt

Stir the milk with the flour, add the other ingredients, whip the batter well, mix with it the currants (warmed) and put in a warm place to raise. If after about 1½ - 2 hours the dough is risen bake in an open pan in butter, or butter and lard mixed, in little cakes the size of a saucer, which are turned once, and then only when the dough is set.

Snippodoodles (1911)

One cup of sugar
One tablespoon of butter
One-half cup of milk
One egg
One cup of flour
One teaspoon of cinnamon

Cream the butter, add the sugar, then the eggs well beaten, then the flour, baking powder and cinnamon, sifted together, and the milk. Spread very thin on the tin sheet and bake. When nearly done sprinkle with sugar; when brown remove from the oven, cut into squares and remove quickly with a knife. They should be thin and crispy.

Snow Cake 1 (1876)

Sift flour and sugar before measuring, then take one tumbler of flour, one and a half tumblers of pulverized sugar and one teaspoon of cream tartar. Mix the above thoroughly and sift into a bowl; beat the whites of ten eggs with one spoonful of vanilla to a stiff froth and pour over the flour, mixing as lightly as possible. Bake in a moderate oven.

Snow Cake 2 (1876)

Whites of ten eggs whipped to a very stiff froth, one and a half tumblers of sifted flour, one and a half tumblers of pulverized sugar, a half teaspoon of salt and one even teaspoon of cream tartar; flavour with one teaspoon of almond. Sift the flour, sugar, cream tartar and salt into a bowl, mix thoroughly and add the flavouring. Beat the eggs very light in a large platter, then with one hand sprinkle the above ingredients into the eggs, dipping slowly and lightly with your egg-beater barely enough to mix; avoid stirring more than necessary. Bake as soon as possible.

Snow Cake (1911)

Beat the white of four eggs stiff. Cream one-half cup of milk and one cup of butter and one cup of sugar, add one-half cup of milk and two cups of flour sifted twice with three level teaspoons of baking-powder. Fold in the whites of the eggs last and half a teaspoon or more of lemon or vanilla flavouring

Snow Cake (1894)

One pound of sugar
Three-quarters pound butter
One-pound flour
Whites of sixteen eggs
Lemon or rose water

Snow Cake (1893)

One-fourth cup butter
1 cup sugar
2 egg whites
½ cup milk
1½ cups flour
1½ teaspoons Rumford Baking Powder
½ teaspoon vanilla

Cream the butter, add gradually the sugar and the vanilla. Beat the whites to a stiff froth and add. Mix and sift the flour and baking powder; add to the first mixture alternately with the milk. Bake in a moderate oven 45 minutes. Cover with boiling frosting.

Snow Cake (1898)

Ingredients:

¼ lb. arrowroot
¼ lb. flour
6 oz. sugar
6 oz. butter
The whites of 3 eggs

Method: Beat the butter to a cream with a wooden spoon; dredge in gradually the arrowroot, flour, and sugar, beating all the time. Beat the whites of eggs to as stiff a froth as possible, stir them into the mixture, and beat it for 3 or 4 minutes. Half fill a buttered cake-tin and bake the cake very carefully in a moderate oven, covering the top with a buttered paper.
Time: 1 hour.
Sufficient for: 1 cake of moderate size.

Snowball Cake (1911)

1 cup sugar
½ cup butter
½ cup sweet milk
2 cups flour
½ teaspoonful soda
1 teaspoonful cream tartar
Whites of 4 eggs

Beat butter and sugar thoroughly. Add the whites of eggs beaten to a stiff foam. Milk and soda last. Flavour to taste.

Snowflake Cake (1920)

2 cups sugar
1 cup butter
1 cup milk
3 cups prepared flour
The grated rind of 1 lemon
The whites of 6 eggs

Stir the butter and sugar to a light white cream; beat the whites to a stiff froth, add them to the creamed butter and add the lemon; then add alternately the milk and sifted flour; bake in 3 layers in large jelly tins; when done remove the cakes from the tins and set aside to cool; beat the whites of 2 eggs to a froth and add ½ cup powdered sugar; spread this over each layer and sprinkle them thickly with freshly grated cocoanut; lay the layers over one another, spread the top layer with the icing, cover it thickly with cocoanut and dust over some powdered sugar.

Snow White Cake (1820)

¾ c. fat
2½ c. prepared cake flour
1½ c. sugar
⅛ tsp. salt
1 c. water
1 tsp. vanilla
6 egg whites, beaten
3 tsp. baking powder stiff

Mix by cake method. Bake in layers or a sheet.

Soda Cake (1898)

Ingredients:

1¼ lbs. flour
6 oz. butter
6 oz. sugar
½ lb. currants
½ tea-spoonful grated nutmeg
½ oz. candied peel

1 small tea-spoonful carbonate of soda   ½ pint milk

Method: Rub the butter into the flour, wash, pick, and dry the currants; shred the candied peel finely, and add these with nutmeg, sugar, and soda to the butter and flour. Mix all well and moisten it with the milk, which should be warmed. Beat the cake for 5 minutes, then put it into a well-buttered cake-tin, and bake it in a moderate oven, covering the top with a buttered paper when half done.
Time: 1 hours.
Sufficient for: 1 good sized cake.

Soft Gingerbread (1905)
(To Be Eaten Hot)

1 cup of molasses
1/2 cup boiling water
1/4 cup melted butter
1 1/2 cups flour

3/4 teaspoonful soda
1 teaspoonful ginger
1/2 teaspoonful salt

Put the soda in the molasses and beat it well in a good-sized bowl, then put in the melted butter, ginger, salt, and flour, and beat again, and add last the water, very hot indeed. Have a buttered tin ready and put it at once in the oven; when half-baked, it is well to put a piece of paper over it, as all gingerbread burns easily.
You can add cloves and cinnamon to this rule, and sometimes you can make it and serve it hot as a pudding, with a sauce of sugar and water, thickened and flavoured.

Soft Ginger Bread 1 (1876)

One cup of molasses and one tablespoon of lard, heated together until hot; add half a cup of sour milk, a teaspoon of ginger and flour to make a stiff batter; dissolve one large teaspoon of soda in hot water and mix in the last thing. Bake in rather a slow oven.

Soft Ginger Bread 2 (1876)

Two-thirds of a cup of molasses
Two-thirds of a cup of sugar
A half-cup of sour milk
One egg

A piece of butter the size of an egg
One teaspoon of ginger
Two large cups of flour
One teaspoon of soda

Soft Ginger Bread 3 (1876)

One cup of molasses
One of cream
Two eggs
Two cups of flour

One teaspoon of ginger
Two teaspoons of baking powder mixed with the flour
One teaspoon of soda

Soft Gingerbread 1 (1893)

One teacup sweet milk
One teacup brown sugar
One teacup butter or mixed butter and lard
One teacup molasses
One tablespoonful ginger
One tablespoonful cinnamon

Four cups flour
Two eggs
One pound of raisins, well-floured before being put in
Two teaspoonfuls baking powder

Soft Gingerbread 2 (1893)

One cupful of molasses
One of butter
One of sugar
One of sour cream
One tablespoonful of ginger

Three eggs
One dessertspoonful of soda
Ground spice according to taste
One quart of sifted flour

Mix the butter and sugar to a cream, then add the other ingredients.

Soft Ginger Bread (N.D.)

1 cup molasses
Lard and butter the size of an egg
1 egg

1 teaspoon ginger
Pinch of salt

Stir stiff with flour and add 1 cup of boiling water and one teaspoon of soda.

Soft Ginger Bread (1893)

One cup molasses
½ cup butter
1 cup boiling water poured on the butter and molasses
2 cups flour

1 teaspoon soda
½ teaspoon ginger
1 egg
Pinch of cloves

Soft Gingerbread (1921)

To two beaten eggs in a mixing-bowl add two tablespoonfuls of butter, melted, three-eighths a cup of sour milk, and one cup of molasses. Beat all together; add two cups of flour, sifted with one-half a teaspoonful of salt and one teaspoonful of baking powder, and one tablespoonful of ginger. Lastly, add one teaspoonful of baking soda, dissolved in two teaspoonfuls of water. Bake in a sheet and serve with whipped cream for a simple dessert.

Solid Chocolate Cake (1913)
(Mrs. R. Heim)

Cream together one cup butter, two of sugar, add six egg-yolks beaten light, then add alternately one cup sour milk with teaspoon soda dissolved in it, and three cups sifted flour. Fold in egg-whites stiffly beaten then add half cake Baker's chocolate melted, and three teaspoonfuls vanilla. Stir hard a minute, pour in deep, well-greased pan, and bake in moderate oven.

Sour Cream Cake (N.D.)

2 eggs beaten and added to a cup of sour-cream
1¾ cups flour
1 teaspoon baking powder

½ teaspoon soda
½ teaspoon salt
1 cup sugar

Beat all together and add 1 cup raisins and nutmeats. Sift flour, baking powder and salt together. Then beat together and add 1 cup raisins and nutmeats.

Sour Milk Gingerbread (1917)

2 cups flour
1 cup molasses
1-1/2 teaspoons soda
1 cup thick sour milk

1 teaspoon ginger
1 egg well beaten
1/4 teaspoon salt

Mix and sift dry ingredients, add molasses, milk, and egg, and beat well; pour into a greased pan, and bake in a moderate oven twenty-five minutes.

Sour Milk Griddle Cakes (1922)

Mix 2½ cups of flour, ½ oz. teaspoon salt and 1¼ teaspoons baking soda. Add 2 cups of sour milk, one beaten egg and 1 teaspoon butter. Beat all together to make smooth batter. Spoon off batter onto a heated, greased iron griddle. Brown on one side and when filled with bubbles, turn and brown on other side. Serve with butter and syrup or with butter and sugar.

Sour Milk Griddle Cakes (1922)

2 cupfuls flour
½ teaspoonful salt
1 tablespoonful melted Crisco
1 teaspoonful baking soda

2 cupfuls sour milk
1 egg
1 tablespoonful sugar

Sift dry ingredients, add milk, well beaten egg, and melted Crisco. Drop by spoonfuls on hot griddle, greased with Crisco. Cook until browned; then turn and cook on other side. Serve hot with syrup.
Sufficient for eighteen cakes.

Sour Milk Griddle Cakes (1917)

2 cups flour
2 teaspoons sugar
1/2 teaspoon salt

2 cups thick sour milk
1 teaspoon soda
1 egg well beaten

Sour Milk Griddle Cakes (1913)

2-1/2 cups flour
1 teaspoon salt
1 tablespoon Cottolene

2 cups rich sour milk
1-1/4 teaspoons soda
1 egg lightly beaten

Process: Mix and sift flour, salt and soda. Add sour milk and beat to a smooth batter. Add Cottolene and well-beaten egg; continue beating until ingredients are thoroughly blended. Batter should be smooth and creamy. Drop by spoonful on well-greased, hot griddle; grease griddle with melted Cottolene. Cook on one side and, when light and covered with bubbles, turn and cook on the other side.

Sour Milk Muffins (1917)

1-1/2 cups flour
1 egg
1 tablespoon sugar
1 cup thick sour milk

1/2 teaspoon soda
2 tablespoons melted shortening
1/2 teaspoon salt

Mix and sift dry ingredients; add egg well beaten, sour milk, and shortening; beat quickly, and bake in greased muffin pans in moderate oven twenty minutes.

Sour Milk Tea Cakes (1922)

1 cupful cornmeal
2 cupfuls flour
4 tablespoonfuls Crisco
¾ cupful sugar
2 eggs
1 teaspoonful baking soda
1½ cupfuls sour milk
1 teaspoonful salt
1 teaspoonful lemon extract

Beat up the eggs, add meal and milk and mix well, add flour, sugar, soda, and salt sifted together. Now add extract and Crisco, melted, and beat two minutes. Divide into Criscoed and floured gem pans and bake in moderate oven fifteen minutes.
Sufficient for: sixteen cakes.

Southern Corncake (1911)

Mix two cups of white cornmeal, a rounding tablespoon of sugar and a level teaspoon of salt, then pour enough hot milk or milk and water to moisten the meal well, but not to make it of a soft consistency. Let stand until cool, then add three well beaten eggs and spread on a buttered shallow pan about half an inch thick. Bake in a quick oven, cut in squares, split and butter while hot.

Southern Fruit Cake (1922)

1 cupful sugar
3 eggs
1 cupful Crisco
1 teaspoonful powdered cinnamon
1 cupful molasses
½ cupful sour cream
1 cupful seeded raisins
3 cupfuls flour
½ cupful currants
1 teaspoonful salt
¼ teaspoonful grated nutmeg
½ teaspoonful baking soda
½ teaspoonful powdered cloves
½ teaspoonful powdered allspice

Cream Crisco and sugar thoroughly together, then add molasses, cream, flour, soda, eggs well beaten, salt, spices, and fruit. Mix well and turn into Criscoed and papered cake tin and bake in slow oven one and a half hours.
Sufficient for: one large cake.

Spanish Bun Cake (1913)

One third cup of Armour's Simon Pure Leaf Lard
One third cup of butterine
Two cups of white sugar
The yolks of four eggs
One cup of cold water
Two heaping cups of flour sifted with two teaspoons of baking powder
One cup each of raisins and nuts

Fold in the whites of four eggs beaten to a stiff froth. Add two teaspoons of ground cinnamon.
Ice with caramel icing.

Spanish Cake (1922)

One pound and eight ounces of sugar
Twelve ounces of butter
Ten ounces of flour
Ten ounces of corn starch

Twenty-two eggs   Orange flower flavour

Separate the eggs; sift the flour and cornstarch together. Cream butter, sugar and yolks the same as four Pound Cake; leave out eight ounces of the sugar; beat the whites firm and add the sugar the same way as for meringue. Mix both parts together and add the flour and starch. Bake in a slow heat as for Pound Cakes. When done, let cool and ice with the Almond Icing; let dry and ice with Pink Fondant, flavour with rose or maraschino, and sprinkle with chopped pistachio nuts.

Spanish Cake (1908)

Beat 1 pound of butter with 1 pound of sugar to a cream. Add the yolks of 8 eggs well beaten. Sift 1 pound of flour with 2 teaspoonfuls of baking-powder and stir together with 1 cup of milk. Add the whites of eggs, beaten to a stiff froth with a pinch of salt. Flavour with rose-water. Bake in a moderate oven until done

Spanish Chocolate Cake (1909)

One cup of sugar
One-half a cup of butter
One-half a cup of sweet milk
Three cups of flour
Two eggs
One teaspoonful of soda dissolved in hot water

Put on the stove one cup of milk, one-half a cup of Baker's Chocolate, grated; stir until dissolved; then stir into it one cup of sugar and the yolk of one egg stirred together; when cool flavour with vanilla. While this is cooling beat up the first part of the cake and add the chocolate custard. Bake in layers. Ice on top and between the layers.

Spanish Layer Cake (1913)

1/3 cup Cottolene
1 cup sugar. Yolks
2 eggs
1/2 cup milk
1-7/8 cups pastry flour
3 teaspoons baking powder
1 teaspoon cinnamon
1/4 teaspoon cloves
1/4 teaspoon salt
Whites 2 eggs

Process: Cream Cottolene, add sugar gradually, stirring constantly. Mix and sift flour, baking powder, spices and salt; add to first mixture alternately with milk. Cut and fold in stiffly beaten whites of eggs. Bake in two well-greased, square, layer cake pans. Spread with a thick layer of

Spanish Pound Cake (No. 1) (1922)

Two pounds and four ounces of sugar
Two pounds of butter
Two and one-half pounds of flour
A half-ounce of baking powder
One quart of yolks
A half pint of milk
Vanilla flavour

Mix and finish as for pound cakes.

Spanish Pound Cake (No. 2) (1922)

One pound and eight ounces of sugar
One pound of butter
One pint of whole eggs, or yolks
Three quarters of a pint of milk
Two pounds of flour
Three quarters of an ounce of baking powder
Orange and vanilla flavour

Mix the same as directed in New York Pound Cake (No.2) (1922)

Spanish Pound Cakes (No. 3) (1922)

One pound of sugar
One pound of butter
One pound of flour
Two ounces of cornstarch

Pinch of baking powder
Sixteen eggs
The grated rind of one lemon
Little mace

Sift the powder in the flour and starch; separate the eggs, rub the yolks with butter and sugar; beat the white firm and mix. Add the flour, draw it in lightly but fully, and bake in 300 degrees Fahrenheit.

Spanish Pound Cake (No. 4) (1922)

One pound and four ounces of powdered sugar
One pound and four ounces of butter
Ten whole eggs
Twelve yolks

One pound of flour
Four ounces of cornstarch
The grated rind of one lemon
A half teaspoon of mace

Sift the flour and starch together; put the eggs, yolks and sugar in a basin or kettle, and beat on a slow fire till warm but not hot. Take off and beat till light and foamy, which will take about thirty minutes or more. Add the flavour, mix in the flour and last, the melted butter. Put in the paper lined pans and bake in a medium heat of 300 to 350 degrees Fahrenheit.

Speck Kuchen (1873)
Bacon Cake (No.1)

Lay a thin paste over a flat baking-tin: raise a little edge to the paste. Beat four eggs, add to them half a pint of milk, two tablespoonfuls of flour, or four of potato-flour, six ounces of bacon rashers cut into very small dice, a little green onion or chives minced very small, some salt and white pepper. Mix all well and spread the mass over the paste. Put a few little pieces of butter over and bake it in a brisk oven.

Speck Kuchen mit Kummel (1873)
Bacon Cake with Caraways (No. 2)

Having spread the paste as above, strew over the bacon cut small. Scatter caraway-seeds over. Mix two or three eggs with a cup of milk and pour it over. Leave out the onion and pepper.

Spice Cake (1904)

This is made and baked the same as sand cake but stir the following spices into the batter with the yolks of the eggs:

⅛ ounce of cinnamon
1 teaspoonful of ground cloves

½ teaspoonful of cardamom seeds
The grated peel of a lemon

If liked add, ½ ounce of chopped citron and ½ ounce of candied orange peel. Mix 1 teaspoonful of baking powder with the whites of the eggs (see General directions (1904)).

Spice Cake No. 1 (1912)

One cup of butter, two cups of sugar

Four cups of flour

One cup of milk   Six eggs
Two teaspoons of baking powder   One teaspoon each of mace, cinnamon and allspice

Spice Cake No. 2 (1912)

One-half pound of flour   one-half glass of sherry wine
One-half pound of pulverized sugar   three eggs
Six ounces of butter   One-tablespoon each of cinnamon and allspice
One-half cup of molasses   One-fourth tablespoon of cloves
One-half cup of sour milk   One-half teaspoon of soda

Cream butter with one-half of the sugar, beat yolks with, other one-half and mix the two, add flour into which the spices have been sifted, then the whites well beaten, then the molasses and wine; lastly the buttermilk into which the soda has been dissolved. Bake in layers and fill with white boiled icing with one-half cup of pecans and raisins or cook in loaf pan.

Spice Cake (1876)

One cup of sugar   Cinnamon
One cup of butter   Nutmeg
Four cups of flour   Cloves
One cup of molasses   One teaspoon of soda
Two eggs

Put in the molasses the last thing before baking.

Spice Cake (1922)

½ cup butter   ½ teaspoon ginger
½ teaspoon cinnamon   ½ cup raisins
1 cup sugar   ¼ teaspoon ground nutmeg
1 teaspoon chopped candied citron   ½ cup currants
2 eggs   ¾ cup milk
2½ cups flour   ¼ teaspoon ground cloves
1 teaspoon grated lemon rind   ½ teaspoon soda
¼ teaspoon salt

Cream the sugar with the butter. Add the beaten eggs. Sift a little flour over the fruit and sift the rest with the spices and salt. Add the spices and salt and flour to the egg-sugar mixture and stir well together.
Dissolve the soda in a little milk. Add to the mixture and then add the floured fruit alternating with the milk. Stir all until smooth and bake in a deep cake pan for one hour in a moderate oven.

Spice Cake (N.D.)

1 cup butter   2 cups flour
1 teaspoon cloves   3 eggs
1½ cups sugar   1 small teaspoon soda dissolved in the sour milk
1 teaspoon nutmeg   2 cups currants, raisins or blueberries
1 cup sour milk   3 teaspoons cinnamon

Spice Cake (1913)

Cream together a cupful of brown sugar and a rounding tablespoonful of butter and tried-out suet mixed. Add half an even teaspoonful of salt, an even teaspoonful each of ground cinnamon and grated nutmeg, half an even teaspoonful each of ground cloves, allspice and mace. Pour in half a cupful of black coffee and half a cupful of rich milk. Sift together one and a half cupfuls of flour and two rounding teaspoonfuls of baking powder. Stir into the flour half a cupful of seeded raisins and mix all the ingredients together. (May be made in layers.)

Spice Cake (1920)

Three fourths cup butter
1 cup molasses
1 cup sugar
3 eggs
3 cups flour sifted with 1½ teaspoonful baking powder

1½ teaspoonful cinnamon
1 teaspoonful cloves
½ grated nutmeg
1 cup sour milk or cold coffee

Stir butter and sugar to a cream, add the eggs one at a time, stir a few minutes between each addition, add molasses and spice, then alternately flour and milk. Butter a square cake pan, dust with flour, pour in the cake mixture, and bake in medium-hot oven; or bake small cakes in gem pans and when cold ice them with sugar glaze.

Spice Cake (1913)

Cream a coffee cup of well washed butter, with two cups yellow sugar and one cup black molasses. Add to it one after the other, seven egg-yolks, beating hard between. When all are in, add one tablespoonful whiskey, or brandy, one teaspoonful grated chocolate, teaspoonful each of powdered cloves, allspice, ginger, mace, and cinnamon, a grated nutmeg, and half a saltspoonful of powdered black pepper. Add also a pinch of salt, and the barest dusting of paprika. If whiskey is for any reason disapproved, use strong, clear coffee instead, putting in two spoonfuls, and leaving out the chocolate. Beat all together hard for ten minutes, then add four scant cups flour browned in the oven but not burned. Sift after browning, adding to it two teaspoonfuls baking powder. Beat hard five minutes after the flour is all in, then pour in a deep, well-greased pan, lined with buttered paper, let rise ten minutes with the oven door open, then bake in quick heat until done through.

Spice Cake (1894)

One cup butter
One and a half cups sugar
Two-thirds cup milk,
Three eggs
Three cups flour

One teaspoon each kind of spice
One cup raisins
One teaspoon soda
Citron and currants if you choose

Bake in roll pans.

Spice Cake (1917)
(without Eggs)

1/3 cup shortening
1-1/2 teaspoons cinnamon
1 cup sugar
3/4 teaspoon nutmeg
1 cup sour milk

1/4 teaspoon cloves
2 cups flour
1/4 teaspoon salt
1 teaspoon soda
1 cup raisins seeded and chopped

Cream shortening and sugar, add sour milk; add dry ingredients sifted together; beat well; add raisins, pour into a greased shallow pan, and bake half an hour in a moderate oven. Dust with confectioners' sugar or cover with plain icing.

Spice Cakes (1876)

One cup of molasses
One ~~and a~~ half cups of butter
A salt-spoon of cloves
A salt-spoon of cinnamon

A salt-spoon of allspice
One teaspoon of soda dissolved in sour milk
Flour sufficient to roll

Spice Cakes (1911)

For little spice cakes cream one-half cup of butter with one cup of sugar, add one beaten egg, one-half cup of sour milk, and one-half level teaspoon each of soda, baking powder, and cinnamon, and a few gratings of nutmeg sifted with two and one-half cups of pastry flour. Stir in one-half cup each of chopped walnut meats and seeded and chopped raisins. Roll out thin and cut in shape or put small spoonfuls some distance apart on a buttered pan and press out with the end of a baking powder can until as thin as needed; do not add more flour. Bake slowly.

Spiced Cake (1913)
(Without Eggs)

Cream together a cupful of brown sugar and half a cupful of butter. Sift together a cupful of flour and an even teaspoonful each of ground cinnamon and allspice. Add to the flour half a cupful or more of seeded raisins or currants and a pinch of salt. Mix all of the ingredients together and add a cupful of sour milk. Dissolve an even teaspoonful of saleratus in a tablespoonful of hot water and beat all thoroughly, adding more flour if necessary for a stiff batter. Bake in a loaf.

Spiced Ginger Bread (1876)

Two cups of molasses
One cup of butter
One cup of sweet milk
Four cups of flour
Two eggs
Two teaspoons of soda

One tablespoon of ginger
One tablespoon of cinnamon
One teaspoon of cloves
One cup of currants
One cup of raisins

Spiced Ginger Cake (1912)

One cup each of butter, sugar and molasses
Three cups of flour
One teaspoon of soda dissolved in a cup of sour cream

One-half grated nutmeg
One teaspoon of cloves
One tablespoon of ginger
One teaspoon of cinnamon if desired

Spider Cake (1902)

Beat 2 eggs very light, add 1 cup sour milk and 1 cup of sweet milk; stir into this 2 cups corn-meal and 1/2 cup of flour, 1 tablespoonful of sugar and 1 teaspoonful each of salt and soda. Mix, and heat thoroughly, and then pour it into the spider; pour over it 1 cup of sweet milk, but *do not stir it into the batter*. Bake in a hot oven 1/2 an hour. Slip it carefully onto a platter and serve at once.

Sponge Cake (1836)
(Called in France Biscuit)

Take ten eggs and beat them till very thick and smooth. Add gradually a pound of powdered loaf-sugar. Rub a lump of loaf-sugar all over the rind of a large lemon, to draw the juice to the surface; then grate the peel of the lemon, and stir it into the mixture, together with the lump of sugar. Squeeze in the juice of the lemon and add two table-spoonfuls of rose-water. Beat the mixture very hard; then take half a pound of potato flour (which is best), or else of fine wheat flour, and stir it in very lightly and slowly. It must be baked immediately. Have ready some small square or oblong cases of thick white paper, with an edge turned up all round, and sewed at the corners. They should be about a finger in length, half a finger in breadth, and an inch and a half in depth. Either butter these paper-cases or sift white sugar all over the inside. Put some of the mixture into each case, but do not fill them to the top. Grate loaf-sugar over the top of each and bake them quickly.
These cakes are much better when baked in paper cases; tins being generally too thick for them. No cake requires greater care in baking. If the oven is not hot enough, both at top and bottom, they will fall and be heavy, and lose their shape.

Sponge Cake (1897)
Svamp-kaka

The desirable feature of good sponge cake is its lightness, which is only attained by long continued hard beating; to do this well requires two persons. While one beats the yolk for 15 to 20 minutes, as light and creamy as possible and then beats in ¾ of a pound of sugar with rose water until thick and light, another person should beat the whites until well frothed, then beat slowly into them the remaining ¼ pound of sugar and whisk it until it no longer stiffens, or until the until the former preparation is complete. Now, lightly and steadily add the last mixture and the flour with the first, a little of each alternately, stirring only enough to mix them well, avoiding hard beating which would toughen the whole. The buttered pans should be ready, and whether round, square or patty pans, fill them half full to ⅔ full: sift sugar over them and bake in a moderate oven.

Material:

Ten ounces of sifted pastry flour	12 eggs
A pound powdered sugar	2 tablespoons rose water

Or other flavours may be used, as almonds, using an ounce of blanched bitter almonds; lemon, use the grated rind and juice of 2 large lemons, mixed and strained after standing an hour, vanilla, use a tablespoon of vanilla sugar, beat in with the yolks at first – the 2 others mix with the sugar.

Sponge Cake No. 1 (1889)

Twelve eggs	The weight of five large eggs in flour
The weight of ten eggs in powdered sugar	The grated peel of a large lemon and half the juice

Stir together the yolks of eggs, and sugar till very light. A wooden spoon or a Dover egg beater will do best to beat with. When light, add the lemon peel and juice.
Beat the whites very light, and stir in gently, but thoroughly, with a silver fork.
Sift the flour in, in three instalments, stirring it in as lightly as consistent with thorough mixing. Practice will give the best peculiar movement of the fork or spoon which scatters the flour, while mixing it in. If the eggs are large, this quantity will make a large milk pan loaf and two oblong bread pan loaves. If the eggs are small, the quantity will fill the milk pan, and is much the best way to bake it. Line the pan with stiff white paper, making the sides straight. Bake an hour, in a moderate oven, watching carefully, to avoid burning.
This cake is the handsomest of all sponge rakes.

Sponge Cake No. 2 (1889)

Twelve eggs
The weight of twelve in sugar
And of six in flour
The grated peel and juice of one lemon

Proceed as in the first receipt. The preponderance of sugar makes the cake less handsome than the first receipt, but moister, and with a sugary crust on top. If sponge cake is frosted, the icing should be flavoured with lemon juice.

Sponge Cake No. 3 (1889)

Nine eggs, ten if small
One-pound pulverized sugar
Half-pound flour (pastry)
The juice and peel, grated, of a lemon

Add the sugar to the whites, sifting it in, and beating it in with a fork. Add the yolks next, then the flour, lastly, the lemon juice and peel.
Line the pans with buttered paper. Bake in a moderate oven. When the cake is in the oven, sit down by the oven door, and watch till it is done.

Sponge Cake (1898)

Ingredients:

6 eggs
¾ lb. sugar
6 oz. flour
Grated rind of 1 lemon

Method: Break the eggs, carefully dividing the yolks from the whites. Beat the yolks and strain them into a basin; beat in the sugar, place the basin in another containing very hot water, and beat the mixture until it is a little warm and thick, then dredge in the flour very gradually, beating constantly until all is added. Lift out the basin, whisk the whites to a stiff froth, add them to the mixture, stir in the grated lemon rind, mix well, and turn into a buttered cake-tin. Bake carefully in a moderately quick oven.
Time: 1 hour.
Sufficient for: 1 good sized cake.

Sponge Cake 1 (1876)

Take the weight of ten eggs in fine, white sugar, and the weight of six eggs in sifted flour; break twelve eggs, putting the whites into the cake bowl; beat them to a stiff froth and add the sugar, stirring briskly. Have the yolks beaten very light, and mix the whole thoroughly, adding two tablespoons of fresh cold or ice water, and flavour as desired, and, lastly the flour, working it as lightly as possible. Turn into square cake pans, lined with buttered paper, and bake immediately in a moderately hot oven; if too hot, a crust forms on the top, which crumbles and disfigures the cake.

Sponge Cake 2 (1876)

Four eggs
Two coffeecups of sugar
Two coffeecups of flour
One heaping teaspoon of baking powder

Beat the eggs and sugar well together and stir in all the flour they will take; then add a half cup of boiling water. Put the baking powder into the remainder of the flour and stir in. Bake quickly.

Sponge Cake 3 (1876)

One and a half cups of white sugar
Four eggs, yolks and whites beaten separately
Two cups of flour
Three tablespoons of cold water
The juice of one lemon
Two teaspoons of baking powder sifted into one-half cup of the flour and add the last thing

Sponge Cake 4 (1876)

One cup of sugar
One cup of flour
Five eggs
One teaspoon of cream tartar
A half teaspoon of soda
Flavour with lemon

Sponge Cake 5 (1876)

Two eggs
Two cups of sugar
Two heaping cups of flour
Two-thirds of a cup of boiling water put in the last thing

Sponge Cake 6 (1876)

Eight eggs, yolks and whites beaten separately
Two cups of sugar
Two cups of flour
Two teaspoons of cream tartar
One teaspoon of soda

Mix the cream tartar in the flour; dissolve the soda in a teaspoon of warm water; beat the yolks and sugar together; stir the whites in lightly, then the flour in the same way, adding a little salt. Flavour with lemon and bake immediately in a moderate oven twenty minutes. If made strictly by this receipt, it will be excellent.

Sponge Cake 7 (1876)

Two cups of sugar
A half-cup of water
Six eggs
One and a half cups of flour
One teaspoon of baking powder

Separate the eggs and beat the yolks and sugar to a cream, then put in the water; mix the baking powder with the flour and stir in, a little at a time, until thoroughly mixed; beat the whites to a stiff froth and mix as lightly as possible through the cake, just before placing it in the oven. The oven must not be too hot when the cake is first put in.

Sponge Cake 8 (1876)

Beat three eggs well with one cup of white sugar and one tablespoon of cold water; add one cup of flour, with two teaspoons of baking powder mixed through, and flavour with lemon. Bake in a shallow pan.

Sponge Cake 9 (1876)

Two cups of sugar
Two cups of flour
A half-cup of water
One teaspoon of yeast powder

Beat the whites to a stiff froth, pour the water over the sugar and stir in the whites, put in the yolks lightly, add the flour and yeast powder and mix just enough to make smooth.

Sponge Cake (1911)

3 eggs
1½ cups sugar
½ cup cold water
2 cups flour
1 teaspoonful cream tartar
½ teaspoonful soda
Salt

Sift cream tartar with 1 cup of the flour; dissolve soda in a little hot water. Rind and juice of 1 orange.

Sponge Cake (1922)

4 eggs
1 teaspoon baking powder
1 cup sugar
¾ cup water
1½ cups flour
1 teaspoon vanilla

Sift the sugar. Then sift the baking powder with one-half cup flour.
Sift the sugar and add gradually to the well beaten yolks, beating constantly. Add the flavouring, the water and one cup of the flour.
Sift the baking powder with one-half cup flour and add to the batter. Fold in the stiffly beaten whites. Pour into a special sponge cake pan, ungreased, and bake for thirty to forty-five minutes in a moderate oven. When baked, invert the pan and cool. Remove from the pan and serve top side down, sprinkled with powdered sugar.

Sponge Cake (1890)

A thoroughly tested recipe.

10 eggs, nine to be beaten separately and very thoroughly, the white of one egg to be left with the yolks
2 large coffee cupfuls of sugar, heapingful
2 large coffee cupfuls of flour evenful
Juice and grated rind of one large lemon
Soda, the size of a pea dissolved in the lemon juice, just before using

Sponge Cake (N.D.)

3 eggs
1½ teaspoons baking powder
1 cup sugar
½ cup water
¼ teaspoon salt
1½ cups cake flour
½ teaspoon vanilla

Beat whites of eggs in mixing bowl, then add one yolk at a time and continue beating. Add sugar gradually, then half of the water and half the flour, then remaining water and flour and flavouring. Use only a Dover beater in mixing the cake. Bake in moderate oven. Very good baked in two layers.

Sponge Cake (1899)

Take three eggs, beat one minute
Then add one and one-half cups of sugar and beat five minutes
Then one cup of flour and beat one minute
Add one teaspoonful of baking-powder in one more cup of flour
One-half cup of cold water and beat one minute

Flavour to taste, and bake.

Sponge Cake (1905)

Material:

1 cup sugar
2 eggs
1/2 cup hot water
1-1/4 cups Pillsbury's Best Flour

1-1/2 teaspoons baking powder
Pinch of salt
1/2 teaspoon vanilla

Way of preparing: Separate eggs, beating whites to a stiff froth. Set them aside. Beat yolks until thick. Add sugar gradually, then water, salt, flour and baking powder. Beat thoroughly. Fold in whites and add vanilla. Bake twenty minutes in a buttered and floured shallow pan in moderate oven.
Bake in a greased and floured 9-inch square or 11×7-inch pan at 350°F. for 24 to 29 minutes.

Sponge Cake (1905)

4 eggs
1 cup powdered sugar
1 cup sifted flour

1 level teaspoonful baking-powder
Juice of half a lemon

Separate the yolks and whites of the eggs and beat them both very light. Mix the sugar in the yolks and beat again till they are very foamy; then put in the stiff whites, and last the flour, sifted with baking-powder; then the lemon-juice. Bake in a buttered biscuit-tin. You can frost and put walnut-halves on top.

Sponge Cake (1864)

On cake luxuriously I dine, And drink the fragrance of the vine, Studious of elegance and ease, Myself alone I seek to please. GAY.

Take the juice and grated rind of a lemon, twelve eggs, twelve ounces of finely pounded loaf sugar, the same of dried and sifted flour; then, beat the yolks of ten eggs; add the sugar by degrees, and beat it till it will stand when dropped from the spoon; put in at separate times the two other eggs, yolks, and whites; whisk the ten whites for eight minutes, and mix in the lemon-juice, and when quite stiff, take as much as the whisk will lift, and put it upon the yolks and sugar, which must be beaten all the time; mix in lightly all the flour and grated peel, and pour it gradually over the whites; stir it together, and bake it in a large buttered tin or small ones; do not more than half fill them.

Sponge Cake (1913)

Beat the yolks of two eggs until very light and add a cupful of sugar. Sift a cupful of flour with a teaspoonful of baking powder. Add the stiffly beaten whites of the eggs to the yolks and sugar, stir in the flour with a pinch of salt, and last of all half a cupful of boiling water, stirring at the time.

Sponge Cake (1920)
(Biscuit Leger)

Set into a basin fourteen whole eggs, two separate yolks, one pound of sugar and the peel of a lemon; beat in such a way as to have a very light composition while heating it slightly; in order to obtain the desired lightness, it will be necessary to beat for at least thirty to forty minutes, then carefully mix in one pound of flour. With this fill a pound cake or "manqué" mold three-quarters full, having it buttered and glazed with sugar and fecula, half of each; bake in a slack oven. Invert the cake as soon as done on a grate, let get thoroughly cold, then bestrew with icing sugar and dress on a dish. This cake may be served plain, without icing, simply bestrewing vanilla sugar over it.

Sponge Cake (1840)

Sift three quarters of a pound of flour and powder a pound of the best loaf-sugar. Grate the yellow rind and squeeze into a saucer the juice of three lemons. Beat twelve eggs; and when they are as light as possible, beat into them gradually and very hard the sugar, adding the lemon, and beating the whole for a long time. Then by degrees, stir in the flour slowly and lightly; for if the flour is stirred hard and fast into sponge cake, it will make it porous and tough.
Have ready buttered, a sufficient number of little square tins, (the thinner they are the better,) half fill them with the mixture; grate loaf-sugar over the top of each; put them immediately into a quick oven and bake them about ten minutes; taking out one to try when you think they are done. Spread them on an inverted sieve to cool. When baked in small square cakes, they are generally called Naples biscuits.
If you are willing to take the trouble, they will bake much nicer in little square paper cases, which you must make of a thick letter paper, turning up the sides all round, and pasting together or sewing up the corners.
If you bake the mixture in one large cake, (which is not advisable unless you have had much practice in baking,) put it into a buttered tin pan or mould, and set it directly into a hot Dutch oven, as it will fall and become heavy if allowed to stand. Keep plenty of live coals on the top, and under the bottom till the cake has risen very high and is of a fine colour; then diminish the fire and keep it moderate till the cake is done. It will take about an hour. When cool, ice it; adding a little essence of lemon or extract of roses to the icing. Sponge cake is best the day it is baked.
Diet Bread is another name for Sponge Cake.
[**Footnote:** Sponge cake may be made with rice flour.]

Sponge Cake (1913)

Beat very light the yolks of seven eggs with three cups sifted sugar, and a pinch of salt. Add to them gradually a cup of hot water, then three scant cups flour sifted thrice with two teaspoonfuls baking powder. Fold in last the stiffly beaten white of the eggs, pour into greased pans, and bake in a quick oven. The batter must not be too thin. If the eggs are large only half a cup of water may be requisite. Flavour with vanilla, putting orange or lemon in the frosting.

Sponge Cake (1869)

Balance twelve fresh eggs with sugar, and six with flour; beat the eggs very light, the whites and yolks separately; mix alternately the sugar and eggs and add the grated peel of a lemon; butter a large pan, or several small ones; add the flour just as it is put in the oven, stirring it just sufficiently to mix. Beating it after the flour is added makes it heavy; pour it in and put it to bake as soon as possible. This makes a good pudding, with white sauce. One-half rice flour is an improvement.

Sponge Cake (1911)

Whites of two eggs beaten to a stiff froth, beat the yolks thoroughly, then beat both together, then add one scant cup of granulated sugar (beating again), one scant cup of flour (beat again), and one teaspoon of baking powder. Sift the flour three or four times, stir the baking powder in the flour, and lastly add five tablespoons of hot water.

Sponge Cake (1917)
(Hot Water)

Yolks of 2 eggs   Whites of 2 eggs

1/4 cup hot water
1 cup flour
7/8 cup sugar
2 teaspoons baking powder

Grated rind
1 lemon
1/4 teaspoon salt

Beat the yolks of eggs until thick and light, add the water and sugar, and beat three minutes with the egg beater; add the lemon rind and the whites stiffly beaten; sift flour, baking powder, and salt, and fold in carefully. Pour into a shallow greased pan and bake in a moderate oven twenty-five minutes.

Sponge Cake 1 (1893)

Whites of 5 eggs
yolks of 3
1 cup of sugar

⅔ cup flour, sift 4 times
⅓ teaspoon cream tartar
pinch Crystaline salt

Beat yolks thoroughly, partly beat whites, then add cream tartar last; then beat very stiff, put in sugar, little at a time, then the yolks, then the flour, teaspoon orange juice. Bake 35 or 40 minutes - moderate oven.

Sponge Cake 2 (1893)

Four eggs beaten separately; add ½ cup of sugar to yolk and ½ cup to white; beat ½ salt-spoon saleratus, 1 teaspoon lemon. Cut in gently to the mixture 1 cup of flour, and bake.

Sponge Cake 3 (1893)

Three eggs beaten 2 minutes
Add 1½ cups sugar, beat 2 minutes
1 cup flour, with 1 teaspoon cream tartar, beat 1 minute

½ cup cold water, with ½ teaspoon soda
Add 1 cup flour
Flavour

Beat all 3 minutes.

Sponge Cake 4 (1893)

Three eggs
1½ cups sugar, beaten together
1 cup of flour
½ teaspoon baking powder, mix the flour

Add ½ cup water; when well stirred in add 1 cup flour
1 heaping teaspoon baking powder
Flavour with lemon juice

Sponge Cake 5 (1893)

Separate 5 eggs and whip both parts stiff, mix together again and add 1 cup of flour, 1 cup sugar, ¼ teaspoon cream tartar, Crystaline salt, flavour with lemon.

Sponge Cake 6 (1893)

Four eggs
1 cup sugar

1 cup flour
1 teaspoon baking powder

When ready for the oven add one-half cup cold water.

Sponge Cake 7 (1893)

Four eggs well beaten
1 cup sugar
2 tablespoons cold water

1 cup flour
1 teaspoon baking powder sifted with flour
Beat all together

This cake keeps moist so well I use it more than any other receipt.

Sponge Cake (1914)

Yolks 6 eggs
Whites 6 eggs
1⅔ cups powdered sugar
1 cup flour

Juice of ½ lemon
1 teaspoon baking powder
Grated rind of ½ lemon
¼ teaspoon salt

Beat yolks of eggs until thick and lemon coloured and add sugar gradually, while continuing the beating: then add juice and rind of lemon. Beat whites of eggs until stiff and dry and add to fruit mixture; then cut and fold in flour mixed and sifted with salt and baking powder. Bake in an unbuttered pan in a slow oven, one hour.

Sponge Cake 1 (1893)

Ten eggs
One-half pound flour
One-pound pulverized sugar

One lemon
Small teaspoon salt

Beat yolks separately and very thoroughly; add sugar, salt, lemon juice and grated peel, and beat again. Beat whites to stiffness and add to the yolks, beating well together. Then cut the flour in slowly with large knife and *avoid beating* after this. Bake in two deep, long, narrow tins, in rather slow oven, but hot on the bottom. The secret of success is in cutting in the flour and the baking. But few people will believe this and cannot reach my standard. I have made this cake for forty years with uniform success.

Sponge Cake 2 (1893)

Six eggs

Two cups of sugar

Beat twenty minutes, stir in lightly two cups of flour and a little salt. Flavour to taste.

Sponge Cake 3 (1893)

Four eggs
Two cups of sifted flour
Two cups of granulated sugar

One cup of boiling water
Two level teaspoonfuls of baking powder

Beat the eggs very light, yolks and whites together; add the sugar, then one cup of flour, little by little; put baking powder in the other cup of flour and add in the same way; then pour in the cup of boiling water, a little at a time, stirring constantly. Flavour with vanilla. Bake in dripping pan twenty-five minutes.

Sponge Cake 1 (1894)

One cup sugar
One cup flour

Four eggs
Half teaspoon soda sifted in dry

Sponge Cake 2 (1894)

Three cups sugar
Six eggs
One cup cold water
Little salt

Four cups flour
Teaspoon soda
Two teaspoons cream tartar

Beat the yolks and stir into sugar until smooth; then add the whites beaten light, then cold water with soda, then flour with cream tartar, two teaspoons lemon put in last.

Sponge Cake 3 (1894)

Four eggs
One cup sugar

One cup flour

Beat the whites stiff, then the sugar must be well beaten into the whites, add next the yolks previously well beaten, and just as you are ready to put into the oven, stir the flour in. Very nice.

Sponge Cake 4 (1894)

Eight eggs
Scant two cups flour

One teaspoon mace

Beat whites and yolks separately, then together, then stir in two cups sugar, and then flour. Bake in quick oven. Nice.

Sponge Cake 5 (1894)

Beat eight eggs very light, add one-pound sugar, twelve ounces flour. Flavour with lemon or almond. Drop them on tins with teaspoon, sift sugar over them and bake in a quick oven.

Sponge Cake (1893)

One cup sugar
3 eggs
¼ cup of hot water

1 cup flour
1 heaping teaspoon baking powder
Salt

Sponge Cake Croquettes (1911)

Cut the crusts from a piece of stale sponge cake. Trim in shape of a croquette. Dry the crusts. Roll them fine. Moisten the cake thoroughly with cream, or wine, or fruit juice, or cream flavoured with cream, or wine, or fruit juice, or cream flavoured with wine or fruit juice. Then roll it in the crumbs.
Put in serving dishes and pour around it soft custard.

Sponge Cake in Small Pans (1869)

Take twelve eggs, with the weight of them in sugar, and the weight of six of them in flour; beat the yolks with the sugar, the whites alone; season with nutmeg or grated lemon peel; put all together, adding the flour the last; stir it quickly after the flour is added, as it will make it heavy to beat it much; grease several small pans and pour it in, bake with a quick heat, and they will be done in half an hour, or less, according to the size. They are pretty iced.

Sponge Cake (1922)

Ladyfinger Mixture

One pound of sugar
Eighteen eggs

One pound and one ounce of flour
Vanilla flavour

Separate the eggs; stir the yolks and sugar light. Keep one ounce of the sugar out. Beat the whites firm and beat in the sugar, then stir in the flavour and yolks and mix in the flour lightly but fully.
Other mixture with the same amount of flour and sugar are made from ten to sixteen eggs to the pound. The "ten eggs" mixture is used for cheaper bakery goods; but the more eggs make a better ladyfinger and raise them up high and smooth in baking.
Bake in about 400 degrees Fahrenheit.

Sponge Cakes (1898)
(Small)

Ingredients

4 eggs
½ lb. sugar

¼ lb. flour
Grated rind of ½ a lemon

Method: Proceed exactly as in preceding recipe. When the mixture is ready put a large table-spoonful into each compartment of a well-buttered sponge cake-tin; sprinkle a little sifted sugar over and bake in a moderately quick oven. When cooked, turn them out of the tin and put them in a cool place to become quite cold, then put them away in a tin canister.
Time: 20 minutes.
Sufficient for: 12 sponge cakes.

Sponge Drop Cakes (1876)

One cup of sugar
One cup of flour

Three eggs
One small teaspoon of baking powder in the flour

Beat the yolks of eggs and sugar thoroughly together, then add the whites beaten to a stiff froth, sprinkle in the flour and stir just enough to wet it. Flavour to the taste. Bake in gem-pans or small tins.

Sponge Gingerbread (1890)

Two and a quarter cupfuls of molasses
1½ cupfuls of sour milk
¾ of a cupful of melted butter
3 eggs

3 teaspoonfuls of soda
3 teaspoonfuls of ginger
5½, or perhaps, 6 cupfuls of flour

Sponge Layer Cake (1899)

Take three eggs, six heaping tablespoonfuls of sugar, and one small cup of flour. Beat the yolks of the eggs and add to the sugar; beat the whites to a stiff froth, and carefully stir into the mixture; then sift in the flour slowly, and carefully stir it in. Add flavouring if desired. Bake in three shallow tins, and, when done, put together in layers with fruit jelly.

Spritzkuchen (1910)

2 oz. butter

¾ pint water

A pinch of salt
½ lb. sifted flour
1½ oz. sugar

6 eggs
Some grated lemon peel or grated almonds

Put the water into a saucepan with the butter, and, as soon as it boils, stir in the sugar, lemon peel, salt and flour, and heat, stirring well, till all becomes a firm, dry mass. Remove from the fire and stir in at once 2 beaten up eggs. When nearly cool, add gradually the remaining 4 eggs. Fill a special cake syringe (Kuchenspritze) three-quarters full with this paste.
Bring 2 lbs. of frying fat to the boil. Take small pieces of paper (about 4 inches square), dip them into the boiling fat, and then press out from the syringe a ring of paste on to each paper, joining the ends of the ring together, so that they do not open out again. Slide the papers into the fat, a few at a time. As the paste rings touch the fat, they come away from the paper and swell out. When they begin to show cracks on the upper side and appear a light brown, turn them and let the other side finish browning. On taking out, dip into a mixture of castor sugar and rosewater, so that they receive a glaze on their upper sides. To make this icing, mix 1 gill rosewater with 1 lb. castor sugar.

Squash Griddle Cakes (1902)

Mix 1 pt. of flour, 1 teaspoonful of baking powder, 1 teaspoonful of salt, and 2 tablespoonfuls of sugar together; sift them; add 2 well-beaten eggs, a pint of milk, and 2 cupfuls of boiled squash that has been strained. Beat until light. Bake on the griddle or add a little more flour and bake in muffin rings.

Squash Griddle Cakes (1894)

One cup sifted squash, one cup sweet milk, one egg, flour enough to make them the right consistency.

St. Honoré and St. Honoré Sultana (1920)
(St. Honoré et St. Honoré Sultane)

Roll out some very fine short paste to obtain a flat three-sixteenths of an inch in thickness and eight inches in diameter; lay it on a round baking pan dampened with water, prick it all over and with a pocket furnished with a half-inch diameter socket push flat on the edges of this a heavy string of cream cake paste. Egg over twice and bake in a slack oven for ten to fifteen minutes. Dress on another tart plate sixteen small round cream cakes, three-quarters of an inch in diameter; egg over and bake them in a moderate oven, then detach from the plate by slipping a knife underneath. Peel two oranges, divide them in sections, leaving on only the fine skin covering the pulp, being careful not to break it, and range them on a grate to dry, either in the air or in a heater. Wash in hot water some candied fruits, such as cherries, apricots, angelica and pears; wipe dry and cut the apricots in four, the angelica in lozenges, the pears in four and leave the cherries whole; have also some loose green grapes, eight pieces of each kind of fruit. Cook some sugar to "crack"; first dip in the cream cakes and arrange them on an oiled baking tin, then drain; proceed the same with the oranges, grapes, apricots, angelica, cherries, pears, etc. On the band fasten the cream cakes with sugar cooked to "crack;" on top of these place a row of quartered oranges, on each quartered orange a glazed cherry, and between each one of the sections place an angelica lozenge or one of the grapes; slip on a dish covered with lace paper. Fill the St. Honoré with St. Honoré cream and serve.

St. Honoré Sultana: Replace the St. Honore cream by a vanilla bavarois cream with plenty of whipped cream, and over the fruits place a spun sugar sultana the shape of an ogive, and around quarters of apricots and pears, both glazed.

St. Nicholas Cake (1876)

One cup of sugar
Two-thirds of a cup of butter
A half-cup of sweet milk
Two eggs

Not quite two cups of flour
A half teaspoon of cream tartar
A fourth of a teaspoon of soda

Stachelbeer-Torte (1910)
(Gooseberry Cake)

Prepare the paste as for Apfel-Torte. When baked, spread almond paste over it and dry grated breadcrumbs. Then put on it 2 lbs. gooseberries, which have just been brought to the boil, but remain whole, drained well and rolled in sugar. Cover the fruit with the whites of eggs, stiffly whisked with 2 oz. castor sugar, and bake a further 5 minutes.

Stale Bread Cakes (1893)

Soak the bread overnight in cold water, add flour enough to make a stiff batter, 3 or 4 well beaten eggs, a little Crystaline salt, 1 teaspoon baking powder. Bake on very hot griddle.

Steamed Shortcake (1913)

Take a large cupful of flour and sift with a rounding teaspoonful of baking powder. Cut into it a piece of butter the size of a walnut, a pinch of salt and enough sweet milk to make a dough to roll out. Line a small round pudding dish, sprinkle on this a thick layer of blueberries, and sugar to taste. Put on the second crust and more berries, then the top. Steam nearly two hours and serve with hard sauce.

Stolle (1910)

2½ lbs. flour
1-pint milk
1 teaspoonful salt
¼ lb. raisins
2 oz. candied peel

2½ oz. yeast
½ lb. butter
7 oz. sugar
¼ lb. currants
A little grated lemon peel

Prepare the yeast as in recipe " Napfkuchen " with a gill of milk and ½ lb. flour and allow to rise. Stir the sugar and salt into the rest of the flour. Make a hole in the centre of it and pour in the milk, the butter (melted) and the risen yeast. Mix thoroughly and knead well. Add the currants, stoned raisins, and chopped candied peel and place in a pan to rise, covered over. When well risen, roll out to a long strip 2 to 3 inches thick, on a sheet of tin that has been well buttered and then sprinkled with flour. Brush over with butter and fold the two edges together to the middle. Allow to rise still further, then bake i hour in a hot oven. When taken out, brush at once with butter and sprinkle thickly with castor sugar.
4 oz. grated sweet almonds may be substituted for the raisins.

Stollen (1922)

Sufficient for 2 - 3 Cakes:

1 qt. of milk
¼ lb. of blanched, ground almonds
6 cents yeast
12 to 15 cups of flour
⅛ lb. of bitter, blanched, ground almonds

1 lb. of sugar
1 lb. of butter
¼ cup of brandy
6 eggs
1½ lbs. of raisins

¼ lb. of cut citron

Preparation: Warm the milk and stir into a smooth batter with 4½ cups of flour, add the yeast dissolved in ½ cup of lukewarm milk and set the sponge to rise. Stir in the melted butter, sugar, eggs, raisins, citron, sweet and bitter almonds, brandy and the rest of the flour to make a pretty stiff dough. Knead it until it will not adhere to the hands. Cut the dough into 3 or 3 parts, as many "stollen" as you wish to have, and shape them nice and round, then set to rise in a warm place. Butter a pan for each cake, double up the dough, place it into the pan and set to rise again. Bake in a medium oven. If the cakes are large, bake them 3 hours, if small, 1½ hours. As soon as you take them out of the oven, brush them with butter and strew them with sugar. These cakes must be prepared in a warm place.

Strawberry Cake with Vanilla Cream (1904)

For this make a puff paste, take plenty of fresh, ripe, sweetened strawberries 6 ounces of sugar, 8 eggs, a little vanilla, ½ teaspoonful of cornstarch and a trifle of gelatine for the cream.
Bake the puff paste; the cream is made as follows: Stir 1 cupful of the cream with the yolks of the eggs, add sugar and vanilla and whip on a medium fire until just before it boils. After taking it from the fire stir in the dissolved gelatine, (when using cornstarch it should be put into the cream before), and then stir the beaten Whites of 6 eggs through the cream until it begins to cool, but not until it is firmly set. Wash the berries carefully and sprinkle plentifully with sugar. When the cake is to be served stir the berries through the cream and pour them over the cake.

Strawberry Short Cake (1893)

Sift together 2 cups of flour and two teaspoons of baking powder; rub through the flour 2 tablespoons of butter, add 2 tablespoons sugar, yolks of 3 eggs, a pinch of Crystaline salt, and milk enough to make a stiff batter. Bake in tin plates, making three cakes when baked. Let cool a little, then spread with mashed berries well sweetened. Add the second and more berries until all is on. Cover with the white of 3 eggs beaten stiff" and sweetened. Stick with the berries. This never fails.

Strawberry Shortcake, No. 1 (1920)

½ cup butter
1 cup sugar
2 eggs

¾ cup milk
2 cups prepared flour

Stir butter and sugar to a cream and add the eggs 1 at a time; next add the sifted flour and milk alternately; bake in two well buttered jelly tins in a medium hot oven; when done remove and lay them on a napkin which has been dusted with sugar; when cold put a layer onto a plate and cover the cake with fresh strawberries; sprinkle over some sugar, lay over the other layer, cover the top with strawberries, dust with sugar and serve with cold cream or vanilla sauce.

Strawberry Shortcake, No. 2 (1920)

1 cup powdered sugar
3 eggs

1 cup sifted flour mixed with 1 teaspoonful baking powder
2 tablespoonfuls water

Stir the yolks and sugar to a cream, add water and flour and lastly the beaten whites; bake in 3 layers; when done lay them over one another with strawberries between, sprinkle top well with sugar and serve with cream or vanilla sauce.

Strawberry Shortcake (1905)

Margaret's mother called this the Thousand Mile Shortcake, because she sent so far for the recipe to the place where she had once eaten it, when she thought it the best she had ever tasted.

1-pint flour	1 teaspoonful baking-powder
1/2 cup butter	1/2 cup milk
1 egg	1 saltspoonful of salt

Mix the baking-powder and salt with the flour and sift all together. The butter should stand on the kitchen table till it is warm and ready to melt, when it may be mixed in with a spoon, and then the egg, well beaten, and the milk.
Divide the dough into halves; put one in a round biscuit-tin, butter it, and lay the other half on top, evenly. Bake a light brown; when you take it out of the oven, let it cool, and then lift the layer apart. Mash the berries, keeping out some of the biggest ones for the top of the cake, and put on the bottom layer; put a small half-cup of powdered sugar on them, and put the top layer on. Dust this over with sugar till it is white, and set the large berries about on it, or cover the top with whipped cream and put the berries on this.

Strawberry Shortcake (1913)

Take a rich sponge cake and slice; spread with whole berries and sweeten with sugar. Make as many layers as desired, and cover all with mashed strawberry sauce.

Strawberry Shortcake (1922)

2 cups flour	¼ cup shortening
1 tablespoon sugar	½ teaspoon salt
4 teaspoons baking powder	2/3 cup milk

Mix dry ingredients, sift twice, cut in shortening and add milk gradually. Toss on floured board. Pat, roll out and bake in well-greased pan about twenty minutes in a quick oven about 450 degrees F. Cap, wash and sweeten berries to taste. Crush berries slightly and put between and on top of shortcake. Cover with whipped cream.

Strawberry Shortcake (1922)

3 cupfuls flour	1 cupful milk
1 egg	3 teaspoonfuls baking powder
½ cupful Crisco	1½ pints strawberries
2 tablespoonfuls sugar	1 cupful whipped cream
½ teaspoonful salt	

Sift the flour with the baking powder, salt and sugar, then cut in the Crisco with a knife, add egg well beaten, and milk. The dough should be a soft one. Roll in two layers, spread in two Criscoed pans and bake, in a hot oven until a light brown colour. Mash and sweeten one cupful of the strawberries, put on one layer, then place second layer on top. Sweeten remainder of strawberries, spread on top layer, and cover with the whipped cream. Decorate with whole ripe strawberries.

Strawberry Short Cake 1 (1893)

Mix a dough nearly as you would for cream-tartar biscuits, only put considerable shortening in. Roll thin; bake in a pan; when done, split it and put the berries (mashed in sugar) between. Whipped cream over the top makes it very nice.

Strawberry Short cake 2 (1893)

Hull and rinse one quart of perfectly ripe berries; put in a bowl with one large cup of granulated sugar; cut – do not mash - with a silver spoon and set away in the ice-box for two hours. Make a rich biscuit dough, adding double quantity of butter; roll out one inch thick and bake in a deep pie-plate. When done, split quickly with a silver knife, using the knife as little as possible; spread the berries on the lower section and cover with the upper; sift on some fine sugar and serve immediately, as this recipe is for hot short cake.

Strawberry Short Cake (1876)

Two quarts of sifted flour, one even teaspoon of soda, and a little salt thoroughly mixed in the flour, one-half cup of butter or lard rubbed in the flour, one pint of sour cream, and, if necessary, sweet milk sufficient to mix a soft dough. Mix the dough as lightly as possible and avoid kneading more than necessary. Bake in a quick oven. When done, split the cake and spread with sweet butter; sugar the strawberries, and put a thick layer between the parts. Serve with sweetened cream.

Strawberry Short Cake (1920)
(Gâteau aux Fraises)

Place in a basin, six ounces of butter with ten ounces of sugar; beat both well together until a creamy preparation is obtained, then add three eggs, one at a time, two gills of milk and vanilla
flavouring. After the whole has been well mixed pour in a pound of sifted flour into which has been added a coffeespoonful of baking powder. Have some round flat molds seven and a half inches in diameter and the edges raised to three-eighths of an inch high; butter and flour these over, then fill them to the top with the mixture and bake in a brisk oven. Unmould on a grate as soon as they are done and leave stand till cold; cover each one of these layers of cake with a vanilla pastry cream, and on it arrange very fine, ripe strawberries, one next to the other; bestrew with sugar and lay two of these garnished cakes one on top of the other; put on a dish and cover the cake with sweetened whipped cream, flavoured with vanilla and pushed through a pocket.

Strawberry Shortcake (1914)

2 cups flour
¼ cup of butter
4 teaspoons baking powder
1 egg
1 tablespoon sugar

⅓ cup milk
½ teaspoon salt
Strawberries
Whipped Cream

Mix and sift flour, baking powder, sugar and salt and work in butter, using tips of fingers. Beat egg until very light and add milk; then combine the mixtures. Toss on a slightly floured board and divide in two parts. Pat, roll out, and bake in a hot oven in round layer cake pans. Split, remove soft part, and spread with butter. Sprinkle strawberries with sugar, place on back of range until warmed, crush slightly and put between and on top of shortcakes. Cover with whipped cream sweetened and flavoured, and garnish with whole berries.

Strawberry Shortcake (1899)

Into two quarts of sifted flour rub thoroughly one and a half teaspoonfuls of baking-powder, half a teaspoonful of salt, and two tablespoonfuls of butter; add enough sweet milk to make a soft dough; roll out slightly and bake in a shallow pan. When done, split open with a sharp, heated knife, and cover the lower half with a generous layer of ripe, crushed, sweetened strawberries; then place the other half of the shortcake on the top of this, cover it with a few of the crushed berries, and serve with cream. Peaches or raspberries may be used in the same manner.

Streusel Coffee Cake (1922)

Preparation of the Streusel:

A piece of butter the size of an egg
1¼ cups of sugar
½ cup of ground almonds
½ cup of flour
Yeast dough like Coffee Cake (1922)
1 tsp. of cinnamon

Preparation: The dough is prepared as given under Coffee Cake (1922). Instead of strewing on sugar, cinnamon and pieces of butter, you make sugar crumbs as follows: Melt the butter, mix flour, sugar, cinnamon and almonds with it and rub to crumbs with the hands. Sprinkle over the cakes before baking.

Streusel Kuchen (1873)
Strewed Cake

Mix a light dough of half a pound of flour and two ounces of yeast, or a cup of brewer's yeast, in lukewarm milk, and put it to rise. Meanwhile, mix together half a pound of warmed butter, three ounces of sugar, six eggs, the grated peel of a lemon, half a nutmeg, a teaspoonful of salt, a pound and a half of flour, and sufficient lukewarm milk to form a soft dough. Add the yeast sponge as soon as it has risen and beat the whole together thoroughly. Dredge a flat tin with flour. The tin must have a raised edge all round. Roll out the cake on it, half an inch thick, and set it to rise. Now work into a paste, two ounces of warmed butter, two ounces of sugar, a teaspoonful of powdered cinnamon, and two ounces of flour. Chop this paste into little lumps the size of a pea, dredging occasionally with sugar and a little flour. This is called the streusel. Strew it over the cake and bake it a nice colour in a quick oven.

Streusselkuchen (1910)

Prepare the dough as in preceding recipe " Blechkuchen," brush it over with a beaten-up egg and tablespoonful of creamed butter, and sprinkle thickly and equally with the following mixture, then baking as quickly as possible.

8 oz. flour
6 oz. butter (melted)
4 oz. sugar
1 teaspoonful cinnamon
2 oz. grated almonds or vanilla (if desired)

Mix the flour and sugar well. Melt the butter and add, mixing so that little lumps are formed; this is best done by rubbing between the palms of the hands.

Striezel (1910)

2 lbs. flour
4 eggs
2 oz. yeast
¾ pint milk
5 oz. sugar
A little grated lemon peel
7 oz. butter
12 grated bitter almonds
½ lb. currants
½ lb. sultanas
2 oz. candied peel

Prepare the yeast with the milk, 1 tablespoonful sugar and 4 tablespoonsful flour as in recipe "Napfkuchen" and allow to rise. Stir the beaten-up eggs into the flour and mix well with the butter (melted), the milk, sugar, almonds, candied and lemon peel and the risen yeast. Knead well and then add the currants and raisins. Form into small, long loaves, place on a buttered sheet of tin, leave to rise further, and then brush over with egg and bake ¾ to 1 hour. On taking out, brush over again with hot butter and sprinkle thickly with sugar.

Suabian Cake (1904)

For this cake take a puff paste, cream or tart crust, a rather thick compote made of green gooseberries, ripe currants, cherries, apples, or plums, and for the icing 6 eggs, ¼ pound of finely pounded almonds, ¼ pound of sifted sugar and the grated peel of half of a lemon, or some nutmeg.

Make a puff paste crust with standing rim, strew over the bottom of the crust some finely rolled crackers, spread the compote over the crust-and over this the following icing: Stir the yolks of the eggs with sugar, almonds and lemon peel for ¼ hour as directed under (General Directions (1904) and mix with it the beaten whites of the eggs. Bake in a moderate oven. When the icing has turned yellow, lay a paper over the cake so that the icing will not become too dark.

Sugar Cakes (1920)
(Gâteaux au Sucre)

Make a ring with two pounds of flour
in the center place one pound of sugar
Half a pound of butter
Two eggs
Four yolks
Three-quarters of an ounce of salaratus
A quarter of an ounce of dissolved carbonate of ammonia
The peel of a lemon
A little milk

Mix all well together to have a smooth paste; lay this aside in a stone crock, and just when ready to use roll it out very thin and cut it into rounds with a two-and-a-half-inch diameter channeled pastry cutter, and from the center remove small pieces with a three-quarter of an inch diameter cutter. Range these rings on a buttered sheet and bake in a hot oven.

Sultana Cake (1898)

Ingredients:

8 oz. flour
4 oz. sultanas
4 oz. castor sugar
3 oz. butter
2 eggs
1 tablespoonful milk

Method: Rub the butter into the flour, add the sultanas, picked, and the sugar. Beat the eggs well, strain them, and add the milk to them. Moisten the cake with these and beat it for 5 minutes. Line a cake-tin with buttered paper, and pour in the mixture, which should half fill it. Bake in a moderate oven, covering the top with a buttered paper when half done.
Time: About 45 minutes.
Sufficient for: a moderate sized cake.

Sultana Tea Cakes (1911)

Into three-quarters of a pound of flour stir a pinch of salt, a teaspoonful of baking powder, three ounces of butter and lard mixed in equal portions, three ounces of sifted sugar and two ounces of sultanas. Chop one and half ounces of candied lemon peel, add that and moisten all with two well beaten eggs and a little milk if necessary. Work these ingredients together, with a wooden spoon turn on to a board and form into round cakes. Place them on a floured baking sheet and cook in a quick oven. Five minutes before the cakes are done brush them over with milk to form a glaze, and when ready to serve cut each through with a knife and spread liberally with butter.

Sunshine Cake (1922)

Make the mixture as for the Angel Cakes (1922), only add from sixteen to twenty-four yolks to the whites of eggs when they are beaten firm before the flour. Flavour lemon or vanilla. Bake in medium heat.

Sunshine Cake No. 1 (1912)

Whites of seven large or eight small eggs
The yolks of six
One teaspoon of cream of tartar

One cup of flour
One cup of sugar

Beat the yolks and whites separately until very light. When the whites are half beaten, add the cream of tartar. Fold the sugar in the stiffly beaten whites, then the yolks, then the flour. Bake in an ungreased pan forty or fifty minutes.

Sunshine Cake No. 2 (1912)

The whites of eight eggs
Yolks of four
One and one fourth cups of granulated sugar

One cup of flour
One-half teaspoon of cream of tartar
Flavour to taste

Mix as Sunshine No. 1. A pinch of salt added to the whites before beating, stiffens the albumen and makes the eggs whip quicker and stand better. Bake thirty-five or forty minutes.

Sunshine Cake No. 3 (1912)

Whites of seven eggs
Yolks of five
One cup of granulated sugar
One-third teaspoon of cream of tartar

A pinch of salt
Flavouring to taste
One cup of flour

Mix as Sunshine No. 1.

Sunshine Cake (1922)

1½ cups sugar
½ teaspoon cream of tartar
½ cup water

1 cup flour
6 eggs
1 teaspoon vanilla

Melt the sugar in the water in a sauce pan and boil until it threads off the end of the spoon.
Separate the eggs, beat the whites stiff and the yolks frothy. Pour the sugar syrup very slowly into the stiff whites and beat until cool. Then add the frothy yolks.
Sift the cream of tartar with the flour and fold into the sugar-egg mixture. Do not stir or beat the mixture at this stage.
Turn into an ungreased sunshine cake tin with a tube in the center and bake in a moderate oven for forty-five minutes to fifty-five minutes.
When done, invert the pan and allow to cool. Remove the cake and serve.

Sunshine Cake (1893)

Yolks of eleven eggs
Two cups of sugar
One cup of butter
One cup of milk
One teaspoonful cream tartar
One-half teaspoonful of soda
Three cups of sifted flour
One teaspoonful of vanilla

Sunshine Cake (1911)

Cream one cup of butter, add two cups of sugar and beat, add one cup of milk, the yolks of eleven eggs beaten until very light and smooth, and three cups of flour sifted with four teaspoons of baking powder three times to make it very light. Turn into a tube baking pan and bake three-quarters of an hour in a moderate oven.

Sunshine Layer Cake (N.D.)

5 egg yolks
1 cup sugar
½ cup sweet milk
½ teaspoon soda and 1 teaspoon cream of tartar added to flour
1⅓ cups flour
1 teaspoon vanilla

White Layer:

5 egg whites beaten stiff with pinch of salt
½ cup pastry flour
1 teaspoon cream of tartar
Scant ¾ cup sugar

Sift flour and cream of tartar several times.

Filling:

1 cup sour cream
3 tablespoons sugar
1 egg
1 teaspoon corn starch

Boil slowly until thick. Add nuts if desired.

Superior Muffins (N.D.)

3 tablespoons sugar
1 rounding tablespoon lard or butter
Cream together and add 1 egg well beaten

Sift together 2 cups flour, ½ teaspoon baking powder. Add alternately to first mixture with one cup of milk. Bake in greased muffin tin in hot oven for about 12 minutes. If corn meal muffins are desired substitute 1 cup of cornmeal for 1 cup of the flour.

Surprise Muffins (N.D.)

2 cups flour or
1 cup flour
1 cup graham flour or 1 cup flour
1 cup cornmeal
2 tablespoons shortening
1 cup milk
3 teaspoons baking powder
1 tablespoon sugar
¼ tsp. salt
2 eggs

Sift flour and mix dry ingredients. Add milk, eggs, and melted shortening. Mix and put tablespoon batter in muffin tin. Drop in center of each 1 teaspoon currant jelly or strawberry jam, or date, etc. Add another spoon of batter and bake 20 to 25 minutes.

Süste (1910)

¼ lb. butter
¼ lb. sugar
4 eggs
4 bitter almonds
2 oz. sweet almonds
¾ lb. flour
1 oz. baking powder

Cream the butter. Stir in the sugar and grated almonds and then alternately a beaten-up egg and a heaped tablespoonful of flour, mixing well. The flour should be mixed with the baking powder and then sifted. Fill a well-buttered cake tin and bake 1 hour.

Süster (1873)
Süster Cake

Stir two tablespoonfuls, or about two ounces, of yeast into half a pint of lukewarm milk; mix in half a pound of flour, cover, and set it to rise. Meanwhile, beat a pound of butter to a cream; add six ounces of sifted sugar, and, by degrees, eighteen eggs, a quarter of a pound of sweet almonds and half an ounce of bitter ones, blanched and pounded, some grated lemon-peel, and a little nutmeg. Having stirred these well, add by degrees a pound of flour, and lastly the batter you have set to rise. Stir all thoroughly. Butter your mould or moulds well. Fill half full. Let them rise again by warmth. Bake about an hour in a moderate oven.

Swedish Batter Cakes (1908)

Sift 1 pint of flour. Add a salt-spoonful of salt, 1 teaspoonful of soda dissolved in a little milk, the yolks of 6 eggs and the whites beaten to a stiff froth and enough milk to make a thin batter. Then bake on a hot greased griddle until done. Serve hot.

Sweet Cake (1904)
(Rodon Kuchen)

1 pound of sifted flour
¾ pound of freshened butter
¼ pound of coarsely pounded almonds
¼ pound of sugar
9 fresh eggs
1 cupful of fresh warm milk
Grated peel of a lemon
½ teaspoonful of salt
Yeast

Stir the butter to a cream, gradually add the eggs, almonds, milk, spices, sugar and the dissolved yeast, constantly stirring, and at last stir in the flour a spoonful at a time and put into a buttered pan sprinkled with grated roll and raise as given under General directions (1904), and bake.
Remark - Instead of taking yeast, baking powder can be used for all of these cakes.

Sweet Corn Griddle-cakes (1905)

These ought to be made of fresh sweet corn, but you can make them in winter out of canned grated corn, or canned corn rubbed through a colander.

1-quart grated corn
1 cup of flour
1 cup of milk
1 tablespoonful melted butter
4 eggs
1/2 teaspoonful of salt

Beat the eggs separately and put the yolks into the corn; then add the milk, then the flour, then the salt, and beat well. Last of all, fold in the whites and bake on a hot griddle.

Sweet Milk Griddle Cakes (1922)

1 cup milk
2 teaspoons baking powder
1 egg 1 teaspoon butter

1 cup flour
¼ teaspoon salt

Beat the egg well, add the milk and the butter melted. Sift the flour, baking powder and salt and stir all together to make a smooth, thin batter. If batter is too stiff, add a little more milk.
Heat and grease an iron griddle. Spoon off batter into hot griddle. Bake until the cake is full of air bubbles, turn over with a pancake turner and brown on other side. Remove all drippings after each cake is browned and wipe griddle off with waxed paper or greased cloth.
Serve hot with butter and syrup.

Swiss Cream Cake (No.1) (1904)

For the dough take ¾ pound of flour, ½ pound of freshened butter, a little more than 2 ounces of sifted sugar, 1 egg, ½ wineglassful of brandy and half as much cold water. Cover the top with 1 heaping soup plateful of sour cherries, ½ pound of sugar, 1 pint of thick sweet cream and a little vanilla.
The butter is broken into pieces, mixed with the flour, make a depression in the center of the flour, put in the egg, sugar, brandy and water, and mix with a knife in a cool place to a dough which can be worked a little with the hands and then set aside for a short time. Then roll out three-fourths of the dough, cut a round cake of the size desired, spread the outer edge with egg, cut the remaining dough into strips, lay on the edge and bake about ¼ hour. In the meantime, stone the cherries, sweeten, lay them on the cake without the juice and keep in the oven with 1 degree of heat, (see General Directions (1904)), until the cherries are tender. Then whip some cream as directed, season with vanilla and spread over the cherries shortly before serving.

Swiss Cream Cake. (No. 2) (1904)

A cream or a good, puff paste, fruit jelly, the whites of 5 - 6 eggs, ¼ pound of sifted sugar and a little vanilla. The under crust is baked like Swiss cream cake, then cover with fruit, or a marmalade which can be made of fresh plums. Beat the eggs to a froth, add sugar and vanilla, constantly beaming, spread the cake with this and set in the oven until the frosting is of a light brown colour.

Swiss Roll (1898)
Ingredients:

3 eggs
6 oz. pounded sugar

3 oz. flour
¼ lb. apricot, raspberry, or greengage jam

Method: Break the eggs, separating the yolks and the whites, beat the yolks, first taking out the specks, and dredge in the sugar and the flour, beating all the time. Whisk the whites of the eggs to as stiff a froth as possible, and stir them gently to the mixture, butter a small baking-tin, and pour in the mixture, it should be about ¼ inch thick, set it in a moderate oven, and bake 6 or 7 minutes. As soon as slightly firm, take it out, spread jam quickly over it, and roll it up, replace in the oven, and bake another 5 or 6 minutes, sift sugar on, and set aside to cool. Practice will only teach the cook the exact moment at which the cake is ready for rolling; it must not be allowed to get too firm, or it will break as it is rolled; it should be just set enough to handle and no more.
Time: Altogether, about 15 minutes.
Sufficient for: 4 or 5 persons.

Part 21: T

Tampa Cake (1909)
Tapioca Breakfast Cakes (1890)
Tausendjahrkuchen (1910)
(Thousand Year Cake)
Tea Cake No, 1 (1912)
Tea Cake No, 2 (1912)
Tea Cake (1876)
Tea Cake (1911)
Tea Cake (1893)
Tea Cakes (1913)
Tea Cakes (1913)
Tea-party Cakes (1905)
Teekuchen (1910)
(Tea Biscuits)
Thanksgiving Corn Cake (1921)
The Deacon's Blueberry Cake (1911)
The Doctor's Cream Cakes (1911)

The Wholesome Parkin (1922)
Tilden Cake (1922)
Tip-Top Cake (1893)
Tipsy Cake (1898)
Top and Filling for Orange Layer Cake (1922)
Tourte a la Royale (1922)
Triester Torte (1910)
Trouvère Cakes (1920)
(Gâteaux Trouvère)
Tumbler Cake (1889)
Twelve Pound Fruit Cake (1913)
"Groom's Cake"
Twenty Minute Coffee Cake (1922)
Twin Elms Date Cake (1911)
Twin Elms Tea-Cake (1911)

Tampa Cake (1909)

Cream 1 cupful of butter with 1 cupful of sugar, add the beaten yolks of three eggs, 1 cupful of milk, 2 cupfuls of flour sifted with 2 level teaspoonfuls of baking-powder, the grated rind of 1 orange and the beaten whites of 3 eggs. Bake in layers and while still warm spread with one cupful of orange marmalade pressed through a sieve and mixed with sherry to a consistency to spread. Ice the top and sides with water icing.

Tapioca Breakfast Cakes (1890)

A teacup of tapioca soaked overnight in a quart of water. In the morning, before mixing, cook gently a few moments until all lumps are dissolved. Add a cup of milk, 2 well-beaten eggs, a- saltspoonful of salt, and 1 scant teaspoonful of baking powder, sifted into a coffee cupful of flour, added just before frying on the griddle.

Tausendjahrkuchen (1910) (Thousand Year Cake)

1 lb. butter	8 eggs
1 lb. sugar	½ lb. currants
¾ lb. flour	2 oz. sweet almonds
¼ lb. potato flour	8 bitter almonds
½ oz. baking powder	2 oz. candied peel
Grated rind of a lemon	1 tablespoon rum

Cream the butter, stir three-fourths of the flour into it and beat for ¾ hour to a froth. In another basin beat, also to a froth, the sugar and yolks. Add the grated lemon peel and then the whites, whisked stiffly. Then mix with the beaten-up flour and butter and finally stir in lightly the well-washed and dried currants. Fill a well-buttered cake tin and bake 1 to 1¼ hour.

Tea Cake No, 1 (1912)

Three eggs	One cup of buttermilk
Three cups of sugar	One teaspoon of soda
One cup of butter and lard mixed	Flour enough to make a stiff dough

Roll thin, bake in a moderate oven a delicate brown. Sprinkle granulated sugar over them just before putting in the oven. After the cakes are rolled, ready for baking, sprinkle over puffed rice and bake until brown.

Tea Cake No. 2 (1912)

One cup of butter	One-half teaspoon each of nutmeg, cloves allspice and cinnamon
Two cups of sugar	
Three eggs	One scant teaspoon of soda dissolved in five tablespoons of cold water
Flavour	
One cup of pecans	As little flour as possible to make a dough stiff enough to roll
One pound of raisins	

Roll thin, cut and bake quickly

Tea Cake (1876)

One cup of sour milk	One cup of sugar
One cup of raisins	A half-cup of butter

One egg
One teaspoon of soda
One teaspoon of spices
Two and a half cups of flour

Tea Cake (1911)

This cake is to be eaten warm with butter. Rub a rounding tablespoon of butter into three cups of flour sifted with a saltspoon of salt, six level teaspoons of baking powder and one-quarter cup of sugar.
Beat one egg light, add one and one-half cups of milk and the dry ingredients and beat well. Pour into a long-buttered pan and bake about twenty minutes. Do not slice this cake but cut through the crust with a sharp knife and break apart. This mixture can be baked in muffin tins, but it saves time to bake it in a loaf.

Tea Cake (1893)

2 eggs
1 cup sugar
½ cup milk
1½ cups flour
4 tablespoons butter
2 level teaspoons baking powder

Line the pan with buttered paper, separate egg, cream, butter and sugar; sift dry ingredients, add the beaten yolks to milk, add a little flour to creamed butter, then the milk, stirring the mixture well, repeat this until all the ingredients are used up; beat whites to stiff froth, fold lightly into mixture. Bake in quick oven; raisins or currants may be added.

Tea Cakes (1913)

Cream together a cup and a half of butter, and two cups and a half of sugar, add to five eggs beaten very light, mix well, then add a cup and a half of buttermilk with a small teaspoonful of soda dissolved in it. Pour upon flour enough to make a soft dough, flavour with nutmeg, roll out a quarter-inch thick, cut with a small, round cutter, and bake in a quick but not scorching oven.

Tea Cakes (1913)

Beat five eggs very light, with five cups of sugar, a heaping cup of lard, well creamed, and two cupfuls of sour milk, with a teaspoonful of soda dissolved in it. Mix through enough flour to make a soft dough, roll half an inch thick, cut out and bake in a quick oven.

Tea-party Cakes (1905)

2 squares of Baker's chocolate
1 teaspoonful of sugar
Bit of butter the size of a pea

Melt the chocolate over the teakettle and stir in the sugar and butter and a couple of drops of vanilla, if you like.
Take little round crackers, and with a fork roll them quickly in this till they are covered; dry on buttered paper. You can also take saltines, or any long, thin cracker, and spread one side with the chocolate.

Teekuchen (1910)
(Tea Biscuits)

½ lb. butter
¼ lb. sugar
1 lb. flour
2 tablespoonsful water
2 eggs
Ground vanilla
Chopped almonds

Cream the butter, add the sugar, eggs, beaten-up, water and plenty of vanilla, and lastly the flour. Roll out very thin, cut into various shapes, brush over with white of eggs, or butter, sprinkle with sugar and chopped almonds and bake a pale brown on a buttered tin.

Thanksgiving Corn Cake (1921)

Sift together two cups of corn meal
Two cups of white flour
Four *heaping* teaspoonfuls of baking powder
One LEVEL teaspoonful of soda
One teaspoonful of salt

One-half a cup of sugar
Add one cup of sour milk (gradually)
Three-fourths cup of sour cream
Four eggs
One-third a cup of a cup of melted butter

The Deacon's Blueberry Cake (1911)

1 egg whipped light
1 cup sweet milk
3 tablespoons sugar
Butter size of an egg

1 teaspoon soda
2 teaspoons cream tartar sifted in 3 cups flour
2 cups berries

To be eaten hot with butter.

The Doctor's Cream Cakes (1911)

Boil together 1 cup water and ½ cup butter, then add 1 cup flour, all at once, and beat vigorously. When mixture cleaves from pan, remove from fire and break in 4 eggs, one at a time, beating for 2 minutes after adding each egg. After the mixture is cool, drop by spoonful into buttered pan and bake 30 minutes in a moderate oven.

Filling for Cakes:

Mix together ¾ cup of sugar, ½ cup of flour, and 2 eggs. Pour on this 1 pt. of hot milk and cook in double boiler. Flavour to taste.

The Wholesome Parkin (1922)

1 cupful flour
1 egg
½ cupful melted Crisco
1 teaspoonful powdered ginger
2 cupfuls fine oatmeal
¼ teaspoonful powdered allspice

¾ cupful molasses
½ teaspoonful powdered cinnamon
3 tablespoonfuls sugar
¼ teaspoonful salt
½ teaspoonful baking soda

Melt Crisco and mix with molasses, then add sugar, egg well beaten, salt, soda, spices, flour, and oatmeal. Mix and pour into small square Criscoed tin and bake in moderate oven thirty-five minutes. This little cake is excellent when a week old.
Sufficient for: one small cake.

Tilden Cake (1922)

Cream ½ cup Crisco with 1½ cups sugar, add 4 well beaten eggs, 1 cup milk, sift in 3 cups flour, ¾ teaspoon salt, ½ cup cornstarch, 2 teaspoons baking powder, and add 2 teaspoons lemon extract.

Tip-Top Cake (1893)

Two Eggs
1½ cups sugar
½ cup butter

2 teaspoons yeast powder
1 cup sweet milk

Tipsy Cake (1898)

Ingredients:

1 medium-sized sponge cake
¼ pint sherry
1 wine-glassful brandy

Custard made with 1-pint milk, and other ingredients in proportion
2 oz. Jordan almonds

Method: Pierce the cake in several places with a wooden skewer and pour in the wine and brandy, pour back any that runs out into the dish, and continue doing this until all the liquid is absorbed. Make a custard by recipe, pour it hot on the cake, spoonful by spoonful, taking care that every part of the cake is equally covered, and set the cake aside to cool. Blanch the almonds, cut them in length-wise strips, stick them all over the cake, and serve the tipsy cake as cold as possible.
Sufficient for: 5 or 6 persons.

Top and Filling for Orange Layer Cake (1922)

Beat stiff the whites of two eggs and add two cups confectioners' sugar. Add the juice of two large oranges and the grated peel of one. Stir together well and spread thick over top and layers.

Tourte a la Royale (1922)

Bake two thin bottoms from the Vienna Almond Tourte; and bake another bottom from the Meringue Paste or Italian Meringue Paste. Spread one of the first bottoms with an apricot marmalade. Place on top of this the meringue layer. Place on the meringue a layer of wine cream (made without the orange flavour) and cover with the other layer. Ice with lemon fondant and decorate with royal icing.

Triester Torte (1910)

½ lb. butter
6 eggs
¼ lb. chocolate

½ lb. almonds, grated with the skins
½ lb. sugar
2 oz. grated roll or dry breadcrumbs

Cream the butter, add the beaten-up yolks and sugar gradually, the grated almonds and chocolate, and finally the grated roll and the whites of eggs, whisked stiffly. Fill a well-buttered tin and bake in a slow oven.

Trouvère Cakes (1920)
(Gâteaux Trouvère)

Lay a pound of flour in a circle on the table and in the center place half a pound of butter, half a pound of sugar, the peel of one orange and two eggs, also a half-inch ball of carbonate of ammonia, having it finely crushed; mix the whole carefully to obtain a smooth and fine paste, watching attentively that it does not crumble; let it rest for half an hour, then roll it to three-sixteenths of an inch in thickness; cut it into inch and a half diameter rounds with a channelled pastry cutter, range them on a baking sheet, egg over, and trace lines on top with a fork; prick the surfaces and bake in a hot oven.

Tumbler Cake (1889)

One large tumbler of butter
One large tumbler sugar
One small tumbler milk
One small tumbler molasses
Five tumblers flour
Four eggs

One and a half teaspoonfuls soda
One-pound raisins
One-pound currants
Half-pound citron
One teaspoonful each of mace, clove, nutmeg, and cinnamon

Twelve Pound Fruit Cake (1913)
"Groom's Cake"

1/2-pound Cottolene
1-pound brown sugar rolled
Yolks 12 eggs well beaten
2 cups N. O. Molasses
1-pound flour
1/2 tablespoon cinnamon
1 teaspoon cloves
1/2 tablespoon mace
1 teaspoon salt

1 teaspoon soda
Whites 12 eggs beaten stiff
2-1/2 pounds seeded raisins
3 pounds currants
1-pound citron thinly sliced and cut in shreds
1/2-pound candied cherries cut in quarters
1/4-pound candied orange peel finely chopped
1/4-pound candied lemon peel finely chopped
1/4 cup brandy

Process: Cream Cottolene, add sugar gradually, stirring constantly; add egg yolks, continue stirring and beating, add molasses, flour mixed and sifted with spices, salt and soda; fold in the whites of eggs and lastly add the fruit except citron. Turn mixture into a well-greased pan lined with several thicknesses of heavy paper, put citron into mixture in layers, having a layer of batter on top. Divide the mixture equally in two tube pans, eight inches in diameter, filling pans two-thirds full.

Twenty Minute Coffee Cake (1922)

1 cup sour milk
2 tablespoons butter
½ teaspoon soda
1 cup sugar

2 cups flour
1¾ teaspoons baking powder
1 egg (well beaten)
½ teaspoon salt

Mix soda and milk. Add egg, salt, sugar, butter, flour, and beat very hard; then add baking powder. Sprinkle on top granulated sugar, cinnamon and bits of butter and nuts. Bake in moderate oven about 20 minutes.

Twin Elms Date Cake (1911)

½ cup soft butter
1⅓ cups brown sugar
2 eggs
½ cup milk
1¾ cups of flour

3 teaspoons baking powder
½ teaspoon each of cinnamon, nutmeg, cloves, and salt
½ lb. dates, cut into pieces

Put all together at once, beat 3 minutes, and bake 40 minutes.

Twin Elms Tea-Cake (1911)

1 egg well beaten

Piece of butter size of an egg

¼ cup sugar
1 cup sweet milk
Salt

2 cups flour, or if baking powder is used, 3 even teaspoons

Part 22: U

Ulm Cake (1904)
Uncle Robertson Cake (1876)

Upside Down Cake (N.D.)

Ulm Cake (1904)

Mix ½ pound of creamed butter, the yolks of 6 eggs, ½ pound of sugar, lemon peel, 6 ounces of cornmeal and the beaten whites of the eggs to a dough, divide into two parts and bake each part in a moderate oven. In the meantime, stir 1 pint of sour cream, 6 eggs, 6 ounces of sugar, 3 ounces of grated almonds and a little vanilla on a slow fire to a thick cream, let it cool and spread one of the layers of the cake with this. Cover with the other layer, pour over the whole a lemon icing, and decorate with preserved fruits.

Uncle Robertson Cake (1876)

Three cups of sugar
One cup of butter
Four eggs
A half pint of milk lukewarm

One teaspoon of soda
Four cups of flour
Spice and raisins to taste

Upside Down Cake (N.D.)

In bottom of round cake pan spread 1½ cups brown sugar and 2 tablespoons butter. Place 5 or 6 slices of pineapple on top and pour over them the following batter and bake slowly one hour.

Batter: Beat 1½ cups sugar and three egg yolks for fifteen minutes. Add alternately ½ cup of water or pineapple juice and 1½ cups of flour until used. Add 1½ teaspoons baking powder, 1 teaspoon vanilla and a pinch of salt. Add beaten egg whites. Invert cake and put Maraschino cherries in centres of pineapple. Serve with whipped cream.

Part 23: V

Vacherin Cake with Cream (1920)
(Gâteau Vacherin à la Crème)
Valentine Cake with Rum (1920)
(Gâteau Valentin au Rhum)
Valentine Cakes (1913)
Vanilla Cream Cake (1920)
Veal Cake (1898)
Velvet Cake (1905)
Velvet Cake (1893)
Velvet Cake (1911)

Velvet Sponge Cake (1917)
Virginia Pone (1869)
Virginia Pone (1876)
Vienna Almond Tourte (1922)
Vienna Bröselcake (1920)
Vienna Cake (1904)
Vienna Cherry Cake (1908)
Vienna Chocolate Tourte (1922)
Vienna Tourte à la Crème (1922)
Volusia Cake (1909)

Vacherin Cake with Cream (1920)
(Gâteau Vacherin à la Crème)

Cut three or four rounds of white paper seven inches in diameter; on the edges of these push through a socket pocket some meringue, to form a ring an inch wide and of the same height; smooth the surfaces of the meringue on both top and sides with the blade of a knife, bestrew with fine sugar and stand each one on a board dampened with water; dry the meringue in a slack oven without letting attain colour. After these rings have been removed invert them on baking sheets and replace them in the oven for ten minutes to dry the meringue that has remained soft, then stand for twenty-four hours in a warm closet. Arrange these rings on top of each other on a layer of frolle paste cut exactly the same dimensions and cover each one with meringue made of cooked sugar, to fasten them together; mask the entire inside with a thin layer of the same meringue; smooth it quickly and dry for two hours in a warm closet. After the meringue is quite cold cover it superficially with a brush dipped in reduced apricot marmalade, not having it too thick; dry this in the air, then decorate the upper ring with a chain of small rings a quarter of an inch thick made of lady finger paste, also to be covered with the marmalade. Fill the center of these small rings with quince jelly or currant jelly. Slip the cake on a folded napkin and at the last moment cover with whipped cream flavoured with vanilla.

Valentine Cake with Rum (1920)
(Gâteau Valentin au Rhum)

Crush one pound of almonds with one pound of sugar and three eggs; make it into a very fine paste; put it into a basin and dilute gradually with thirteen eggs and one gill of rum; beat well until perfectly light. Line a mold with very thin sweet paste; fill it three-quarters full with the preparation and strew over some finely cut-up almonds. Bake in a very slack oven for three-quarters of an hour, then turn the cake out on a grate and allow to cool; when cold glaze with a light frosting flavoured with rum. This cake can be kept for several months if wrapped in tin-foil and left in a dry cool place.

Valentine Cakes (1913)

2/3 cup Cottolene
2 cups sugar
4 eggs
1 cup milk
3-1/4 cups flour

4-1/2 teaspoons baking powder
1 teaspoon rose water
1/4 teaspoon mace
1/2 teaspoon salt

Process: Cream Cottolene, add gradually one cup sugar. Beat egg yolk thick and light, add gradually remaining cup sugar. Combine mixtures. Mix and sift flour, baking powder, mace and salt. Add alternately to first mixture with milk, add rose water. Then cut and fold in the stiffly beaten whites of eggs. Bake in small heart-shaped individual tins. Cover with frosting and outline the edge with tiny red candies.

Vanilla Cream Cake (1920)

Vanilla Cream Cake is made the same as Lemon Cream Cake, using vanilla flavouring instead of lemon.

Veal Cake (1898)

Ingredients:

1 lb. of cold cooked veal
¼ lb. cold boiled bacon

Grated rind of a lemon
Seasoning pepper and salt

Method: Mince the veal and bacon finely, mix them together with the lemon rind, pepper, and salt; press

them into a thickly-buttered cake-tin, raising the cake to a dome shape on top, and bake in a good oven; turn it out of the tin, and serve cold. f preferred hot, \ pint of good veal gravy should be poured over and round the cake.
Time: 1 hour.
Sufficient for: 4 or 5 persons.

Velvet Cake (1905)

This is a large cake, baked in a roasting-pan; it is very light and delicious, and none too large for two luncheons, or for a picnic.

6 eggs
2 cups of sugar
1 cup of boiling water
2 1/2 cups of flour
3 teaspoonfuls of baking-powder

Put the yolks of the eggs in a deep bowl and beat two minutes; then put in the sugar, and beat ten minutes, or fifteen, if you want it perfect. Put in the water, a little at a time, and next the stiffly beaten whites of the eggs. Mix the baking-powder and flour, put these in next, and add the flavouring last. This is a queer way to mix the cake, but it is right.

Velvet Cake (1893)

One-pound sugar
One-pound flour
One-half pound butter
Four eggs
One teacup of cold water
One teaspoonful cream of tartar
One-half teaspoonful soda

Put yolks and whites of eggs in separate vessels; dissolve soda in the water, sift the cream tartar in the flour. Beat the sugar and butter to a white cream; add the flour and water, stirring well. Next add the whites and lastly the yolks, both well beaten. Flavour with lemon and beat all together for three minutes. Bake an hour. Excellent also for a layer cake, with any filling.

Velvet Cake (1911)

One-half cup butter
One and one-half cups sugar
Yolks four eggs
One-half cup milk
One and one-half cups flour
One-half cup corn-starch
Four level teaspoons baking powder
Whites four eggs
One-third cup almonds blanched shredded

Cream the butter, add gradually the sugar, then the egg-yolks well beaten. Beat well and add the milk, the flour, corn-starch, and baking powder sifted together, and egg whites beaten stiff. Beat well and turn into buttered shallow pan. Sprinkle with the almonds, then with powdered sugar and bake forty minutes in a moderate oven.

Velvet Sponge Cake (1917)

2 eggs
1/2 cup pastry flour
1 cup sugar
2 teaspoons baking powder
1/8 teaspoon salt
Grated rind 1 lemon
1/4 cup potato flour
1/3 cup hot milk

Beat eggs until very light, add sugar gradually, and continue beating with the egg beater; mix and sift salt, flour, and baking powder; add half to the eggs and sugar, and beat well; add rest of flour, and beat again; add rind and milk, and beat hard; pour into a deep pan, and bake forty minutes in a slow oven.

Virginia Pone (1869)

Beat three eggs, and stir them in a quart of milk, with a little salt, a spoonful of melted butter, and as much sifted corn meal as will make it as thick as corn batter cakes; grease the pans and bake quick.

Virginia Pone (1876)

Twelve tablespoons of corn meal, add a piece of butter the size of a Brazil nut, and one-half teaspoon of salt. Pour in a little hot water, then add cold water enough to prevent scalding the eggs, two in number; these must be well beaten before putting in. Beat the whole together five minutes. Bake in iron gem-pans in a moderately quick oven, thirty minutes.

Vienna Almond Tourte (1922)

To the mixture Butter Sponge Cake (1922) or Genoise Sponge Cake (1922) add four ounces of dried and ground almonds. Bake three layers and fill with Almond Cream. Ice with Almond Paste Icing. Spread the icing on very smooth, put back in the oven and colour nicely; let cool and ice with a pink fondant flavoured maraschino, and decorate with French fruit in an artistic manner.

Vienna Bröselcake (1920)

4 eggs
5 tablespoonfuls sugar
3 cups flour
1 cup warm milk
½ cup butter

The grated rind of ½ lemon
1 yeast cake
¼ teaspoonful salt
A little vanilla

Dissolve the yeast in 1 cup milk, add 1 cup sifted flour and mix it into a batter; set it in a warm place to rise; as soon as the sponge is very light stir butter and sugar to a cream and add by degrees the eggs, 1 at a time, stirring a few minutes between each addition; next add salt, lemon or vanilla and lastly the remaining 2 cups sifted flour and the sponge alternately; beat the whole thoroughly with a wooden spoon and set it aside to rise; when light beat it again with a spoon and fill it into a cake mould with tube in center, which should be well buttered and dusted with fine bread, cracker or zwieback crumbs; let it rise again to double its height; in the meantime cut 1 handful almonds into small pieces without removing the brown skin and mix them with 1 handful sugar, a little cinnamon, a little grated lemon peel and some melted butter; work this with a fork briskly into the dough; when the cake is ready to bake press little dents in it with the handle of a silver spoon, brush over with beaten egg, spread the almond mixture over the top and bake in a medium hot oven 1 hour.

Vienna Cake (1904)

For the cake use:

½ pound of freshened butter
½ pound of powdered sugar
½ pound of sifted flour

2 ounces of finely pounded almonds
the grated rind of a lemon
10 eggs

For a cream to cover the cake take nice apples, the juice of a lemon, 1 cupful of arrac, 2 heaping tablespoonfuls of sugar, a piece of butter the size of 2 walnuts and the yolks of 3 eggs.

Stir butter, sugar and lemon peel together, gradually add, constantly stirring, the yolks of the eggs and the almonds, and stir for ½ hour as given under General Directions (1904). Then stir into it the flour and the beaten whites of the eggs; this will make 3 - 4 cakes. Grate some sour apples, take the juice and put it into an enamelled kettle, add sugar and cook, stirring often, until it begins to thicken, add lemon juice, butter and the yolks of the eggs, take from the fire and mix through it the arrac. Spread this over the cake and proceed as given under Brides Cake (1904). Instead of this cream different fruit jellies can be used.

Vienna Cherry Cake (1908)

Make a rich biscuit dough; roll out; then put on a well-buttered baking-tin. Stone black cherries. Sprinkle the dough with flour and cover with the cherries. Sprinkle with sugar and let bake until done. Then cover with a sweetened egg custard and bake until brown. Serve cold

Vienna Chocolate Tourte (1922)

One half of a pound of almond paste
Eight ounces of sugar
Eight ounces of butter
Four ounces of chocolate

Twelve yolks
Twelve whites
Four ounces of flour

Cream the sugar and butter with the yolks; add the almond paste rubbed smooth with four whites and the grated chocolate or cocoa powder; beat the other whites of eggs firm and draw in the cream with the flour. Bake in three layers and fill with Chocolate Nut Cream. Ice the center of top chocolate, and the sides with maraschino fondant, and decorate with nuts and glazed almonds.

Vienna Tourte à la Crème (1922)

Bake thin bottoms from Mixture Bottom Paste for Large Cakes and Layers (1922) or German Short Paste (1922); or make a special mixture like this;
Rub twelve ounces of sugar very lightly with seven yolks, and nix with twelve ounces of starch and two ounces of melted butter and bake this to very thin crisp bottoms.
Fill with Vienna Cream. Ice with chocolate or maraschino and decorate with halves of walnuts dipped in caramel and fruit glace.

Volusia Cake (1909)

Beat 1 cupful of butter to a cream with 2 cupfuls of sugar; add 7 eggs, one at a time, beating well after each addition; add the juice and the grated peel of ½ an orange and 3 cupfuls of flour in which 1 teaspoonful of baking-powder has been sifted. Bake in a loaf in a moderate oven for forty minutes.

Part 24: W

Wafer Cakes (1840)
Wafer Cakes (1869)
Waffeln (1910)
(Wafers; French: Gaufres)
Waikiki Shortcake (1909)
Walnut Cake (1876)
Walnut Cake (1893)
Walnut Cake (1894)
Walnut Cake (1893)
Walnut Cakes (1922)
Walnut Torte (1922)
Washington Cake (1876)
Washington Cake (1840)
Washington Cake (1869)
Washington Cake (1894)
Water Pan Cakes (1869)
(A cheap Dessert)
Wedding Cake (1876)
Wedding Cake (1893)
Wedding Cake Pudding (1876)
Weisse Pfefferkuchen (1910)
Weisse Pfeffernüsse (1910)
Weisse runde Pfeffernüsse (1910)
Wellington Cake (1904)
Westphalian Butter, No. 1 (1904)
(Coffee or Sugar Cake)
Westphalian Cake No. 2 (1904)
Westphalian Cake No. 3 (1904)
Wheat Cakes (1920)
(Galettes au Froment)
Wheat Gems (1876)
Whipped Cream Cake (1913)
Whist Cake (1893)
White Cake (1876)
(Marbled)
White Cake 1 (1876)
White Cake 2 (1876)
White Cake (1922)
White Cake (1917)
White Cake (1869)
White Cake (1893)
White Cake (1893)
White Cake (1893)
White Cake 1 (1894)
White Cake 2 (1894)
White Cake (1893)
White Cake (1893)
White Clouds (1876)
White Cocoa-nut Cakes (1840)
White Corn Cake (1894)
White Corn Meal Cakes for Breakfast (1893)
(A Rhode Island Dish)
White Cup Cake (1876)
White Cup Cake (1840)
White Fruit Cake (1820)
White Fruit Cake 1 (1876)
White Fruit Cake 2 (1876)
White Fruit Cake (N.D.)
White Fruit Cake (1913)
White Fruit Cakes (1922)
White Gingerbread (1840)
White Layer Cake (1913)
White Layer Cake (1913)
White Mountain Cake (1889)
White Mountain Cake 1 (1876)
White Mountain Cake 2 (1876)
White Mountain Cake 3 (1876)
White Mountain Cake (1894)
White Mountain Cake (1893)
White Mountain Cake (1890)
White Nut Cake (1913)
White Patty Cakes (1911)
White Sponge Cake (1913)
Whole Wheat Gingerbread (1922)
Whole Wheat Muffins (1922)
Wiener Soufflée (1873)
Vienna Soufflée, a Dinner Dish
Wiener Torte (1910)
Wiener Torte (1873)
Vienna Cake (No. 1)
Wiener Torte (1873)
Vienna Cake (No. 2)
Wild Rose Cake (1920)
Willie C.'s Birthday Cake (1876)
Wine Cakes (No. 1) (1922)
Wine Cakes (No. 2) (1922)
Wine Glazed Cake (1920)
Wine Glazed Cream Cake (1920)
Witch Cake (1913)
Wreath Cake (1922)

Wafer Cakes (1840)

Mix together half a pound of powdered sugar, and a quarter of a pound of butter; and add to them six beaten eggs. Then beat the whole very light; stirring into it as much sifted flour as will make a stiff batter; a powdered nutmeg, and a tea-spoonful of cinnamon; and eight drops of oil of lemon, or a table-spoonful of rose water. The batter must be very smooth when it is done, and without a single lump. Heat your wafer iron on both sides by turning it in the fire; but do not allow it to get too hot. Grease the inside with butter tied in a rag, (this must be repeated previous to the baking of every cake,) and put in the batter, allowing to each wafer two large table-spoonfuls, taking care not to stir up the batter. Close the iron, and when one side is baked, turn it on the other; open it occasionally to see if the wafer is doing well. They should be coloured of a light brown. Take them out carefully with a knife. Strew them with powdered sugar, and roll them up while warm, round a smooth stick, withdrawing it when they grow cold. They are best the day after they are baked.
If you are preparing for company, fill up the hollow of the wafers with whipt cream, and stop up the two ends with preserved strawberries, or with any other small sweetmeat.

Wafer Cakes (1869)

Rub half a pound of lard into two pounds and a half of flour, add a little salt and water sufficient to make a stiff dough: work it well for half an hour, make it in small round lumps, and roll these until they are as thin as possible; bake them with a slow heat and they will look almost white. These are nice cakes for tea either hot or cold.

Waffeln (1910)
(Wafers; French: Gaufres)

¾ lb. flour	3 eggs
2 oz. sugar	4 oz. butter
½ pint milk	½ oz. baking powder
Grated rind of a lemon	4 grated bitter almonds

Cream the butter, mix it with the sugar, beaten up eggs, grated lemon rind and bitter almonds and, lastly, stir in alternately the milk and the flour, which should have been previously sifted and mixed with the baking powder. Heat a Waffeleisen (wafer iron) over a clear fire, rub it with a piece of bacon rind, pour a teaspoonful of the batter into each division and close up the iron again. Let the wafers become a golden colour, turning the iron so that both sides are done. Then take out and sprinkle over at once thickly with sugar.

Waikiki Shortcake (1909)

Rub 4 bananas through a sieve, add the pulp and grated rind of 1 orange and 1 cupful of powdered sugar; mix well and stir in ½ cupful of thick cream beaten stiff. Spread between two layers of sponge cake and serve with sweetened orange juice.

Walnut Cake (1876)

One pound of flour	A half-cup of milk
One pound of sugar	Six eggs
Three-fourths of a pound of butter	The meats from two quarts of walnuts
One and a half pounds of stoned raisins	A half teaspoon of soda
One nutmeg	

Beat the whites to a stiff froth and add them the last thing. Bake in a quick oven, but not too hot.

Walnut Cake (1893)

Three cups of sugar
One cup of butter
Four cups of flour
One and one-half cup of sweet milk
Three cups of walnut or butternut meats
Whites of eight eggs

Cream the butter and sugar; sift two teaspoons of cream tartar into the flour, into which stir the meats. Dissolve one teaspoon of soda in the milk. Salt and extract as you like, adding the thoroughly-whipped whites the last thing before putting into the oven. Half of this rule can be used.

Walnut Cake (1894)

One cup butter
Two cups sugar
Three and a half cups flour
Two-thirds cup milk
Three eggs
One cup chopped raisins
One cup walnuts
Half teaspoon soda

Walnut Cake (1893)

One cup sugar
Scant ½ cup butter, stir till creamy
Add ½ cup sweet milk
1⅔ cups flour
2 teaspoons baking powder mixed with flour
Whites of egg beaten stiff
1 cup walnuts floured a little

Walnut Cakes (1922)

For Cakes:

1 cupful sugar
2 cupfuls flour
½ cupful Crisco
2 teaspoonfuls baking powder
1 cupful milk or water
1 whole egg and 2 yolks of eggs
½ teaspoonful salt
1 cupful chopped walnut meats
1 teaspoonful vanilla extract

For Frosting:

1 cupful sugar
Pinch cream of tartar
1 cupful water
1 teaspoonful lemon juice
2 whites of eggs
1 teaspoonful vanilla extract

For cakes: Cream Crisco and sugar thoroughly together, add eggs well beaten, salt, vanilla, milk or water, baking powder, flour, and nuts. Mix well and divide into Criscoed and floured gem pans and bake ten minutes in moderate oven. When cold cover with boiled frosting.
For frosting: Dissolve sugar and water over fire in a saucepan, add cream of tartar and boil until it forms a soft ball when tried in cold water, or 240° F. Pour on to the beaten whites of eggs, pouring in a steady stream and very slowly, adding, while beating, lemon juice, and vanilla; beat until thick, and use.
Sufficient for fifteen cakes.

Walnut Torte (1922)

7 eggs
½ lb. ground walnut meats

7 tablespoonfuls sugar   Pinch of salt

Beat egg yolks till light. Add sugar, salt and ground walnuts. Stir. Beat egg whites till stiff and add to mixture. Mix all together and bake in slow oven 50 minutes. When cold serve with whipped cream. This recipe will serve 6 persons.

Washington Cake (1876)

One and a half pounds of sugar   One and three- fourths pounds of flour
One and a half pounds of butter   Two pounds of raisins
Seven eggs   Two pounds of currants
One pint of milk   Mace, cinnamon and cloves

Washington Cake (1840)

Stir together a pound of butter and a pound of sugar; and sift into another pan a pound of flour. Beat six eggs very light, and stir them into the butter and sugar, alternately with the flour and a pint of rich milk or cream; if the milk is sour it will be no disadvantage. Add a glass of wine, a glass of brandy, a powdered nutmeg, and a table-spoonful of powdered cinnamon. Lastly, stir in a small tea-spoonful of pearl-ash, or salaeratus, that has been melted in a little vinegar; take care not to put in too much pearl-ash, lest it give the cake an unpleasant taste. Stir the whole very hard; put it into a buttered tin pan, (or into little tins,) and bake it in a brisk oven. Wrapped in a thick cloth, this cake will keep soft for a week.

Washington Cake (1869)

Take a pound and three-quarters of sugar, the same of flour, three-quarters of a pound of butter, eight eggs, a pint of milk, and mix them as a pound-cake; just as it is ready to bake, dissolve a tea-spoonful of salaeratus in a little sour cream, and stir in; season with nutmeg and rose brandy, or essence of lemon; bake it as pound cake.
Some persons put in a tea-spoonful of lemon juice just before baking

Washington Cake (1894)

One-pound brown sugar   One-pound fruit mixed with flour, currants, raisins
One-half pound butter   and citron
Four eggs (well beaten),   One wine glass wine
One cup milk (medium size cup)   One nutmeg
One-pound flour sifted twice   Teaspoon cinnamon
                                              two tablespoons baking powder

Makes one large cake.

Water Pan Cakes (1869)
A cheap Dessert

Stir a quart of warm water in sufficient flour to make a batter of moderate thickness; dissolve a tea-spoonful of salaeratus, with a little salt, into a tea-cupful of butter-milk, or sour cream; beat it well; put a little lard in a frying-pan, and when it is hot, fry them. They are much better to be eaten hot, with sauce, sugar and cream, or anything you may fancy. This is a very cheap dessert, and has been thought nearly equal to pan cakes made with milk and eggs

Wedding Cake (1876)

Ten eggs
One pound of butter
One pound of sugar
One pound of flour
Four pounds of raisins after stoning

Four pounds of currants after washing
Two pounds of citron
One ounce of nutmeg
One ounce of cinnamon
A fourth of an ounce of cloves

Wedding Cake (1893)

Two pounds currants
1-pound raisins
¾ pound citron
1-pound sugar (dry brown)
¾ pound butter
8 eggs

1¼ pounds flour (browned in oven)
1 cup molasses
½ teaspoon soda,
Rind and juice of 1 lemon
cloves, cinnamon and nutmeg

Wedding Cake Pudding (1876)

One cup of molasses
One cup of milk
A half-cup of butter
Four cups of flour
One nutmeg

Two teaspoons of cinnamon
Two teaspoons of cloves
One teaspoon of allspice
A half teaspoon of soda

Weisse Pfefferkuchen (1910)

5 eggs
½ teaspoonful potash dissolved in
2 tablespoonsful milk
1 lb. flour

12 oz. sugar
3 oz. candied peel
10 ground cloves

Beat the sugar and eggs for 30 minutes to a froth. Then add the potash dissolved in milk, the finely chopped candied peel, ground cloves and the flour gradually and stir 30 minutes. Roll out thinly, cut into little shapes and place on a floured tin till the next day. Before baking, brush over with egg and ornament with slices of candied peel and of almonds.
4 oz. grated sweet almonds and 15 bitter almonds may be substituted for the chopped candied peel and ground cloves.

Weisse Pfeffernüsse (1910)

½ lb. sugar
1 lb. flour
4 eggs

4 oz. almonds
Candied peel or vanilla

Beat the sugar and eggs to a froth for half an hour. Then add the flavouring and stir in the flour, kneading well. Make up into little rolls, ½ to 1 inch in thickness. Cut into slices slantingly, place on a buttered tin and bake in a moderate oven.

Weisse runde Pfeffernüsse (1910)

½ lb. butter

1 gill milk

1 lb. sugar.
2 lbs. flour
4 eggs

Spices to taste
½ teaspoonful baking powder

Cream the butter, add the sugar, beaten-up eggs and spices, the baking powder, dissolved in the milk and the sifted flour stirred in gradually. Mix and knead well. Make into little round nuts and bake on a buttered tin till quite dry throughout.

Wellington Cake (1904)

½ pound of flour
¼ pound of butter
¼ pound of grated almonds
¼ pound of sifted sugar

2 eggs for the dough
6 ounces of sweet almonds and 6 bitter ones finely chopped
the whites of 6 eggs

The dough is either rolled or else put into a form and pressed out. Bake until done, beat the whites of the eggs to a stiff froth, mix with sugar and almonds, spread over the cake and set aside to dry.

Westphalian Butter, No. 1 (1904)
(Coffee or Sugar Cake)

3 pounds of flour
Yeast
7 eggs
1 lemon

2 pounds of butter
2 cupfuls of sifted sugar
1 large cupful of milk
½ pound of stoned raisins or currants

Put the flour into a pan, make a depression in the center, put in the eggs, sugar, raisins, the grated peel of a lemon, milk, and the dissolved yeast; and then by degrees the butter, and thoroughly whip the dough, which has been mixed in a warmed pan. Then butter a large cake pan with unsalted butter, put the dough into this about ½ inch thick and let it raise-in a warm place. When this is done, spread the cake with melted butter, strew thickly over it coarse or finely pounded sugar and bake quickly.

Westphalian Cake No. 2 (1904)

All of the following cakes must be pierced with a fork before putting them into the oven, so that they will not blister.
For the dough:

2 pounds of flour warmed and sifted
¾ pound of freshened butter
2 ounces of yeast
2½ ounces of finely sliced citron

1 teaspoonful of salt
2 eggs
1 pint of warm milk

For on the cake:

⅔ pound of coarse sugar
½ pound of butter

2 ounces of finely pounded almonds

For sprinkling the cake:

½ cupful of rosewater, or if this is not liked the same quantity of white wine or sugar water

The flour is put into a warmed dish and mixed thoroughly with the pieces of butter; make a depression in the center of the flour, add the dissolved yeast, milk, 2 ounces of sugar, eggs and spices, and with a wide knife mix the flour and ingredients together quickly, avoiding working the dough too much; this is an essential point to be observed in making this cake. The dough thus made is put into a warmed pan and smoothed with the hand, which should be dusted with a little flour, until it is about ½ inch thick, put over it a warm cloth and set aside in a warm place 1 - 1½ hours to raise.

After the cake has raised pour over it a mixture of sugar, almonds, cinnamon, lay pieces of butter over this and bake the cake in a quick oven for 15 - 20 minutes.

The cake must be of a dark colour, but not brown, nor should it dry in the oven, because it must be soft inside. When taking out sprinkle the cake with rose water, wine or sugar water.

Remark: These cakes are best when fresh. They can, if a day or so old be put into the oven for a few minutes. They are cut into pieces 1 inch wide and three times as long.

Westphalian Cake No. 3 (1904)

For the dough take:

2 pounds of warmed flour
½ pound of washed and stoned raisins
¼ pound of butter and lard slowly melted together
Fresh yeast

1 pint of warm milk
And if you have it 2 tablespoonfuls of thick sour cream

For the top:

¼ pound of melted butter
¼ pound of sugar

A little cinnamon

The dough is stirred in a warm dish and then mixed on the bread board with the necessary flour; proceed as noted under General Directions (1904), then roll out the dough, put it into the cake pan, and after it has raised, spread with butter, sprinkle sugar over it, put into a hot oven and bake quickly.

Wheat Cakes (1920)
(Galettes au Froment)

Mix in a bowl:

Eight ounces of sifted flour
Two ounces of sugar
Two ounces of butter

A little salt
Four eggs
Two gills of milk

Stir all well together to obtain a smooth paste. Beat one teaspoonful of flour with as much baking powder, add it to the other ingredients and when well mingled, cook and finish them the same as buckwheat cakes, serving them very hot.

Wheat Gems (1876)

One tea-cup of milk, one full cup of wheat flour, a little salt, one egg. Bake in gem pans.

Whipped Cream Cake (1913)

Cream together two tablespoons of Armour's Simon-Pure Leaf Lard and one cup of sugar. Add a well-beaten egg and half cup of milk. Stir in two and one fourth cups of sifted flour to which have been added two teaspoons of baking powder, and vanilla. Bake in layers in moderate oven about fifteen minutes. When ready to serve, whip one half pint of cream, add two teaspoons of sugar and a little vanilla. Spread between layers and on top layer. Serve on dessert plate with fork

Whist Cake (1893)

Cup of butter, creamed with two cups of sugar. Break and stir into the mixture, one at a time, 4 eggs. ½ teaspoon vanilla, ½ teaspoon lemon, ⅔ cup of milk. 2¾ cups of flour, with two level teaspoons baking powder sifted in it. Add flour and milk alternately and beat till very light. Bake about 20 minutes.

White Cake (1876)
(Marbled)

One cup of butter
Two cups of sugar
Three cups of flour

Whites of eight eggs
Two-thirds of a cup of sweet milk
One teaspoon of yeast powder

After the cake is made, take out one large teaspoon of the mixture, and drop two drops of fushiene, mixed with alcohol (four drops if you like it darker coloured) into the tablespoon of cake; mix well, and then put a layer of the white cake at the bottom of the pan, and streak the red around in rings; add more white, and more red, till the white is all gone. Bake in a slow oven.

White Cake 1 (1876)

Whites of fourteen eggs
One pound of sugar
A half-pound of butter
A half-cup of milk

One pound of flour
Two teaspoons of baking powder
Flavour to the taste

White Cake 2 (1876)

Whites of seven eggs
One cup of butter
Two cups of sugar
One cup of corn starch

One cup of milk
Two teaspoons of baking powder
One cup of flour

Dissolve the corn starch in the milk; beat the butter and sugar to a cream, and after all is well beaten mix in the whites lightly.

White Cake (1922)

½ cup butter
3 cups pastry flour
1¾ cups granulated sugar
4 teaspoons baking powder
¾ cup milk

6 egg whites
¼ cup hot water
1 teaspoon vanilla
½ teaspoon almond flavouring

Cream the butter, adding the sugar and a tablespoon of milk. Cream very well. Sift the flour and baking powder together several times for lightness. Pour the hot water on the milk and add the flour and milk mixture to the creamed butter, beating constantly. Add the almond and vanilla flavours.
Beat the whites stiff and fold into the batter.

Line two deep square pans with waxed paper and pour in the batter. Start in a low oven and when the cake has risen, increase the heat and bake for about three-quarter hour longer until the cake is done.
Frost and fill with caramel, white or fudge frosting. Or fill with jelly and frost with thin white icing.

White Cake (1917)

Whites of 2 eggs
3 teaspoons baking powder
Melted butter
7/8 cup sugar

Milk
1/2 teaspoon almond extract
1-1/2 cups flour

Break the whites of eggs into a measuring cup; add melted butter to half fill cup; add milk to fill cup. Mix and sift flour, baking powder, and sugar; combine mixtures, add flavouring, and beat for five minutes. Bake in a shallow cake pan half an hour, or in muffin tins about twenty minutes, in a moderate oven.

White Cake (1869)

Beat the whites of twenty eggs; wash the salt out of a pound of butter; sift a pound of flour, roll a pound of loaf-sugar, blanch a pound of almonds; roll them fine with a bottle, and mix them with rose water.
Work the butter, sugar and almonds together till they look like cream; have the eggs beaten very light, and add them and the flour alternately till you get all in; beat the whole together till it is very light; have a pan buttered, and put it in a heated oven to bake; when it begins to brown, put white paper over the top; bake it about three hours; when it is nearly cold, prepare an icing, flavoured with rose water; put it on the top and sides.

White Cake (1893)

Whites of twelve eggs
Five teacups flour
Three teacups sugar

One teacup sweet milk
One full cup butter
Two teaspoonfuls yeast powder

White Cake (1893)

Cream ½ cup butter
Add 1½ cups sugar gradually
1½ cups milk
2 cups flour, with 1½ tablespoons baking powder

¼ teaspoon cream tartar
1 teaspoon vanilla
Whites of 5 eggs beaten stiff

Bake in shallow pans. Spread between marsh-mallow paste, also on top.
Marsh Mallow Paste: Boil ¾ cup sugar and ¼ cup of milk six minutes. Wet ¼ lb. of marsh mallow with 2 tablespoons water; cook over hot water and stir till smooth. Combine the two mixtures and beat till stiff enough to spread, ½ teaspoon vanilla.

White Cake (1893)

Beat to a cream ½ cup sugar
Butter size of an egg
1½ cups flour
1 teaspoon cream tartar

½ teaspoon soda
½ cup milk
Whites of two eggs

Beat to a stiff froth. Bake 20 minutes.

White Cake 1 (1894)

Whites of eight eggs
Two cups sugar
One-half cup butter
Three-quarters cup milk
Three cups flour
One teaspoon cream tartar
Half teaspoon soda

Bake in layers, spread each with icing and grated cocoanut, and when put together cover the whole with the icing and cocoanut.

White Cake 2 (1894)

One cup butter
Two cups sugar
Three and one-half cups flour
Whites of five eggs
One cup milk
teaspoon cream tartar
Half teaspoon soda
Flavour with almond

White Cake (1893)

Beat to a cream ½ cup sugar
Butter size of an egg
1½ cups flour
1 teaspoon cream tartar
½ teaspoon soda
½ cup milk
Whites of two eggs, beat to a stiff froth

Bake 20 minutes.

White Cake (1893)

Two cups pulverized sugar
½ cup butter
1 cup sweet milk
8 cups flour
Whites of 6 eggs beaten to a stiff froth
2 teaspoons of baking powder
1 teaspoon extract lemon

White Clouds (1876)

One and a half cups of white sugar
a half-cup of butter
a half-cup of sweet milk
whites of four eggs
a small half-teaspoon of soda
one teaspoon of cream tartar
two and a half cups of flour
Flavour with almond or rose

White Cocoa-nut Cakes (1840)

Break up a cocoa-nut; peel and wash the pieces in cold water and grate them. Mix in the milk of the nut and some powdered loaf-sugar and then form the grated cocoa-nut into little balls upon sheets of white paper. Make them all of a regular and handsome form and touch the top of each with a spot of red sugar-sand. Do not bake them, but place them to dry for twenty-four hours, in a warm room where nothing is likely to disturb the them.

White Corn Cake (1894)

One cup cold boiled rice beaten, then add three eggs; scald one-quart milk, stir with the milk one and a third cups of white corn meal, a little salt, then beat all together, have a good one-half cup of butter in the dish you bake in. Bake in hot oven.

White Corn Meal Cakes for Breakfast (1893) (A Rhode Island Dish)

One-pint white corn meal, into which you stir two saltspoonfuls salt. Gradually moisten this with boiling water until the mixture is somewhat thicker than hasty pudding. Stir constantly and after the right consistency is attained, beat thoroughly for two minutes. Drop from spoon into boiling lard and fry for five or six minutes. Serve immediately. It is of absolute importance that the water should be *boiling* and *kept* so, and therefore it is wise to bring the mixing dish very near the stove when the teakettle is heated. The same paste may be fried on a griddle like buckwheat cakes, but the first method makes the crispest, nuttiest flavour. This recipe makes bannocks enough for six people.

White Cup Cake (1876)

Two cups of sugar
A half-cup of butter
A cup of sweet milk

Three cups of flour
Whites of four eggs
Three teaspoons of baking powder

White Cup Cake (1840)

Measure one large coffee cup of cream or rich milk, (which, for this cake, is best when sour,) one cup of fresh butter; two cups of powdered white sugar; and four cups of sifted flour. Stir the butter and sugar together till quite light; then by degrees add the cream, alternately with half the flour. Beat five eggs as light as possible, and stir them into the mixture, alternately with the remainder of the flour. Add a grated nutmeg and a large tea-spoonful of powdered cinnamon, with eight drops of oil of lemon. Lastly, stir in a very small tea-spoonful of salaeratus or pearl-ash, melted in a little vinegar or lukewarm water. Having stirred the whole very hard, put it into little tins; set them in a moderate oven, and bake them about twenty minutes.

White Fruit Cake (1820)

2 c. flour
½ tsp. salt
1 c. almonds
¼ tsp. soda
⅔ c. fat
2 tbsp., milk
6 egg whites

1 c. sugar
1 tsp. vanilla
1 tsp. baking powder
1½ c. candied fruits
½ tsp. rose flavouring
½ c. cocoanut

Cream fat and sugar. Add milk and flavouring. Add cocoanut and almonds. Add flour sifted with baking powder, and salt and soda. Reserve ½cup of the sifted flour and dredge the candied fruits in it. Add this with fruits to mixture. Fold in whites. Bake in a loaf pan in a slow oven 1½ hours.
Any combination of the following candied fruits may be used:
Cherries, pineapple, citron, orange peel, lemon peel, apricot. The almonds should be blanched and shredded. Fresh grated cocoanut may be used or dessicated cocoanut soaked in milk and drained before adding to batter.

White Fruit Cake 1 (1876)

Two cups of sugar
One cup of butter

Three-fourths of a cup of sweet milk
Two eggs

One teaspoon of soda
Two teaspoons of cream tartar
One pound of raisins

One pound of currants
Nutmeg
Flour to make quite stiff

Bake slowly.

White Fruit Cake 2 (1876)

Whites of sixteen eggs
One pound of white sugar
One pound of butter
One pound of flour
One teaspoon of extract of bitter almonds

One pound of blanched almonds (sweet)
Two ounces of bitter almonds
One pound of citron cut fine
One cocoanut grated

Pound the almonds in a mortar with a little rose water to prevent boiling. Whisk the eggs until they will stand alone; cream the butter, into which stir the flour until quite stiff; then add alternately egg, sugar and flour, reserving a little for fruit, till all are well combined; flavour with vanilla or extract of bitter almonds; flour the fruit, and stir it in last. Bake in a slow oven, using great caution not to burn it. Frost.

White Fruit Cake (N.D.)

½ cup butter
1 cup sugar
1¾ cups cake flour
1 teaspoon baking powder
¼ teaspoon salt
½ cup chopped almonds

¾ cup grated cocoanut
½ cup finely cut citron
½ cup Sultana raisins
½ teaspoon each almond and vanilla extract
5 egg whites

White Fruit Cake (1913)

Cream together half a cupful of butter and a cupful of sugar and half a cupful of sweet milk. Sift together a heaping cupful of flour and a rounding teaspoonful of baking powder. Take half a pound each of chopped figs, seeded raisins and blanched almonds. Stir the fruit into the flour and mix all the ingredients together thoroughly. Add a spoonful of grated cocoanut and a little finely shaved citron. Beat the whites of five eggs and stir them in last, with a pinch of salt.
Bake in a loaf pan for nearly two hours.

White Fruit Cakes (1922)

Add to Lady Cake (No.3) (1922) three pounds of mixed fruit, consisting of two pounds of sultanas, a half-pound of blanched and shredded almonds, a half-pound of citron and orange peel; also add for ounces more flour.

Mix and bake as usual.
With other fruits the mixture can be made into Fig, Date, Plain Raisin, or Sultana Currant Cakes, etc.

White Gingerbread (1840)

Sift two pounds of flour into a deep pan and rub into it three quarters of a pound of butter; then mix in a pound of common white sugar powdered; and three table-spoonfuls of the best white ginger. Having beaten four eggs very light, mix them gradually with the other ingredients in the pan, and add a small tea-spoonful of pearl-ash melted in a wine glass of warm milk. Stir the whole as hard as possible. Flour your paste-board; lay the lump of dough upon it and roll it out into a sheet an inch thick; adding more flour if necessary. Butter a large shallow square pan. Lay the dough into it and bake it in a moderate oven. When cold, cut it into squares. Or you may cut it out into separate cakes with a jagging iron, previous to baking. You must be careful not to lay them too close together in the pan, lest they run into each other.

White Layer Cake (1913)

Cream together one-third of a cupful of butter and a large cupful of powdered sugar. Add a small cupful of milk and a scant teaspoonful of lemon or vanilla, with a pinch of salt. Sift with a cupful of flour a rounding teaspoonful of baking powder. Stir all together and beat until smooth. Add the well beaten whites of four or five eggs and flour enough to make a stiff batter. Bake in greased layer tins and when cold put together with any preferred filling.

White Layer Cake (1913)

Sift two teaspoonfuls baking powder through three and a half cups flour, measured before sifting. Cream a cup of butter with two and one-half cups sugar, add a cup of rich milk, beat hard, then add gradually the flour, following it with the whites of seven eggs beaten very stiff with a small pinch of salt. Fold in lightly and bake in three layers. Put together with orange filling, or frosting made thick with nuts and minced figs.

White Mountain Cake (1889)

One-pound sugar
Half-pound butter
One-pound flour
Six eggs, beaten separately
Two scant teaspoonfuls Royal baking powder sifted into a little of the flour

One dessertspoonful of vanilla
Half teaspoonful extract of lemon
or a very few drops of extract of bitter almond
A few drops of rose
Half a teaspoonful of vanilla
Two-thirds cup of milk

The quantity of flour in this and all cakes, save sponge cake, may require to be slightly varied, owing to the size of the eggs or the quantity of flavouring. The batter should be thin as prudent for baking in jelly cake pans and may be tested by a small cake. The batter will make two loaves of three cakes each and may be divided before flavouring. The White Mountain Cake being flavoured as directed above, and, when baked, spread with a frosting made in the proportion of one heaping cup of powdered sugar to the white of an egg, and a quarter only of the juice of a lemon, the flavouring to correspond with that of the cake. Spread it as thickly as possible over the cake, and lay the cakes one upon another, frosting the top with slightly stiffer icing.
The other half of the batter may be varied by adding a glass of sherry, a little nutmeg, and ten drops of rose extract, instead of the flavouring used before. This loaf can have jelly between the layers, the top being iced with the frosting used for the first loaf.
If desired, a quarter of a pound of citron, or a half-pound of raisins, can be added to the batter just described, and baked in small patty pans.
The loaves can be filled with many other mixtures with grated orange, made very stiff with sugar, in which case the flavouring of the cake should be a little orange or lemon juice, mixed, with a tiny quantity of the grated peel; or with cocoanut or chocolate.

White Mountain Cake 1 (1876)

One pound of sugar
A half-pound of butter
Six eggs
One teacup of milk

One pound of flour
One small teaspoon of soda
Two small teaspoons of cream tartar

This will make six or seven cakes.

Frosting: Into one-third of a box of gelatine, dissolved in a teacup of boiling water, stir two pounds of sugar; flavour and spread over the top and sides of each cake.

White Mountain Cake 2 (1876)

Two cups of sugar
A half-cup of butter
One cup of milk

Three cups of flour
Whites of ten eggs
Three teaspoons of yeast powder

Icing: Six cups of sugar and the whites of six eggs beaten to a froth. Boil the sugar till it candies in a half cup of water, then add the whites of two beaten eggs.

White Mountain Cake 3 (1876)

Two cups of sugar
One cup of butter
Three cups of flour
Almost one cup of sweet milk

Three-quarters of a teaspoon of soda
One and a half teaspoons of cream tartar
The whites of eight eggs (six will do)
Flavour with lemon

Bake in layers in square tin pans. Put together with the following Frosting:

Whites of six or seven eggs beaten to a stiff froth, and nine full teaspoons of pulverized sugar to one egg, flavour with lemon and beat to a stiff froth. A pleasant change is made by stirring in one cup of dessicated cocoanut.

White Mountain Cake (1894)

One cup butter
Two cups sugar
Four eggs
Three and a half cups flour,

Two-thirds cup milk
Teaspoon cream tartar
Half teaspoon soda
Teaspoon extract of lemon

Bake in four thin sheets and when done put a layer of frosting between each sheet.

White Mountain Cake (1893)

Two cups sugar
⅔ cups of butter,
the whites of 7 eggs well beaten
⅔ cup sweet milk

2 cups flour
1 cup corn starch
2 teaspoons baking powder

Bake in jelly-cake tins.

Frosting: Whites of 3 eggs and one sugar beaten together, not quite as stiff as usual for frosting - about a cupful. Spread over cake; add some grated cocoanut, then put cakes together and put frosting and cocoanut on top. Use the yolks for gold cake.

White Mountain Cake (1890)

Two cupfuls of butter
4 cupfuls of sugar
4 cupfuls of flour

1 cupful of milk
5 eggs

Bake in jelly pans and put icing between each layer.

Three eggs will make icing enough for the quantity, 2 heaping teaspoonfuls of baking powder. Flavour with bitter almonds.

White Nut Cake (1913)

1/3 cup Cottolene
1-1/2 cups fine sugar
3/4 cup cold water
2-1/4 cups pastry flour
4 teaspoons baking powder

1/4 teaspoon salt
Whites 4 eggs beaten until stiff
1/2 teaspoon Almond extract
1 cup English walnut meats broken in pieces

Process: Cream Cottolene, add sugar gradually, beating constantly. Mix and sift flour, baking powder and salt, add alternately to first mixture with water, add nut meats and extract; cut and fold in whites of eggs. Bake in a sheet thirty-five minutes in a moderate oven. Spread with MAPLE FROSTING.

White Patty Cakes (1911)

Cream one-third cup of butter with one cup of sugar, add one-half cup of milk, one and three-quarter cups of flour sifted twice with two and one-half level teaspoons of baking powder, and flavour with a mixture of one-third teaspoon of lemon flavouring and two-thirds teaspoon of vanilla flavouring. Bake in little plain patty pans and cover the top of each with white icing. Garnish with two little leaves cut from angelica and a bit of red candied cherry.

White Sponge Cake (1913)

Beat very stiff six egg-whites, add to them gradually a cup of sugar, and a cup of flour sifted twice with a teaspoonful of baking powder. Do not forget a tiny pinch of salt in the eggs.

Whole Wheat Gingerbread (1922)

4 tablespoonfuls sugar
½ cupful seeded raisins
½ cupful Crisco
½ teaspoonful salt
2 eggs
1½ cupfuls molasses
1 teaspoonful baking soda
½ cupful chopped nut meats

¼ cupful milk
1 teaspoonful powdered ginger
2 cupfuls flour
½ teaspoonful powdered mace
2 cupfuls whole wheat flour
1 teaspoonful powdered cinnamon
3 tablespoonfuls chopped candied lemon peel

Mix flours, then add peel, raisins, nuts, spices, and salt. Melt Crisco, molasses, and sugar, then cool, and add them with eggs well beaten, with, soda mixed with milk. Mix well and turn into Criscoed and floured cake tin. Bake in moderate oven one hour.
Sufficient for: one large cake of gingerbread.

Whole Wheat Muffins (1922)

½ cup whole wheat flour	3 teaspoons baking powder
1 egg	½ cup brown sugar
1½ cups white wheat flour	1 tablespoon butter or substitute
1 cup milk	½ teaspoon salt

Beat the yolk and add to the milk. Sift the dry ingredients and work into the butter. Stir all together until smooth. Fold in the beaten white. Turn into heated, greased muffin pans and bake in a very hot oven (450 degrees F.) for fifteen minutes.

Wiener Soufflée (1873)
Vienna Soufflée, a Dinner Dish

A quarter of a pound of butter must be stirred to a cream, then a quarter of a pound of sifted sugar added, and the yolks of six eggs. When you have stirred this half an hour, add the juice of half a lemon and an inch of vanilla finely pounded. Lastly, add the six egg-whites whipped to a snow; bake the mixture in a buttered form three-quarters of an hour in a slow oven. When it has risen high and is nicely coloured, sift sugar over, and serve it without delay.

Wiener Torte (1910)

1 lb. flour	4 whites of eggs
¾ lb. sugar	Grated rind of a lemon
¾ lb. butter	
6 yolks	

Cream the butter, add sugar and the beaten-up yolks, and stir ¾ hour. Then add the grated lemon peel and alternately the flour and whisked whites of eggs. Roll out in three pieces and bake on buttered tins. Place the layers on each other, spreading jam between.

Wiener Torte (1873)
Vienna Cake (No. 1)

Make four or five white paper plates by stretching the paper over any round utensil - a large dinner or soup-plate will do - plait up an edge an inch deep and tack it round with needle and thread to keep it upright. Butter these papers and lay them on baking-tins. Spread over each a layer of "sand torte" mixture, not thicker than a thin pancake. Bake them in a moderate oven a nice yellow; do not let them tinge brown. When cold, cut away the paper round, turn the cakes over, and peel off the bottom paper without breaking them. Lay one cake over the other, with different coloured preserves and marmalade between, till all are piled up. Dissolve powdered sugar with a little lemon juice; spread it thickly over the top and sides of the cake to make a glazing. Put it in a cool oven to dry, and when cold, ornament the top with preserved fruit or marmalade.

Wiener Torte (1873)
Vienna Cake (No. 2)

Stir half a pound of butter to a cream. Stir in, by degrees, half a pound of sifted sugar, two ounces of pounded almonds, the grated rind of a lemon, half a pound of fine dry flour, and the yolks of ten eggs; these must be stirred in before the flour. Stir all well for half an hour, then add the whites of the eggs whisked to a stiff snow. Of this mass bake, on paper plates, as before described, three or four flat cakes. Peel, core, and slice eight or ten fine apples; put them in an earthen or enamelled stew-pan, with sufficient sugar, the grated rind of half a lemon, and about an ounce of butter; let them stew to a thick conserve, then stir in the yolks of three eggs and the juice of a lemon; stir the conserve for a few seconds over the fire; then turn it out, and stir in directly a glass of arrack or rum. When cold, lay one cake over the other with a fair division of the conserve between, leaving the top one uncovered. Pare the cake smooth all round, and ice it over, or strew it thickly with sifted sugar.

Wild Rose Cake (1920)

1-pound powdered sugar
¾ pound flour
½ pound butter

1 teaspoonful baking powder
The whites of 8 eggs
1 cup white brandy

Sift flour and baking powder together; wash the butter in cold water, to remove the salt, and dry it in a napkin; put butter and sugar in a mixing bowl and stir it with the right hand to a light white cream; beat the whites to a stiff froth and stir them with a spoon in small portions alternately with the flour and brandy into the creamed butter; divide the mixture into 4 equal parts; add to one part a little prepared cochineal, to colour it a delicate pink, and flavour with 2 teaspoonfuls rose water; stir into the second part 2 tablespoonfuls cocoa and 1 teaspoonful vanilla sugar; add to the third part the yolks of 2 eggs and ½ teaspoonful essence of bitter almonds; leave the fourth part white and flavour it with 1 teaspoonful essence of lemon; take some large, deep jelly cake tins, rub them well inside with butter and dust with flour; put each part of cake mixture into a separate pan and spread the batter smooth with a broad-bladed knife; then bake in a medium hot oven to a delicate brown and well done; lay some clean brown paper or a napkin on a table and dust over some powdered sugar; as soon as one cake is done remove from the oven and let it stand 3 minutes; then turn the pan upside down onto the paper; treat the remaining cakes the same way; as soon as the cakes are cooled off prepare a meringue as follows: - Beat the whites of 5 eggs to a stiff froth and mix them with ½ pound powdered sugar; have ready ½ pound blanched almonds, ½ pound blanched walnuts and ½ pound blanched Brazil nuts; chop the nuts fine; when all is prepared put the cakes together and put the white layer upside down on a jelly dish; spread over the layer ⅓ the meringue and sprinkle over ⅓ the chopped nuts; then put on the dark layer; spread again with meringue and sprinkle with nuts; next put on the yellow layer; spread over the remaining meringue and sprinkle over the nuts; lay the pink layer on top, with the right side up, and cover with the following glaze: - Mix ½ pound powdered sugar with a few spoonfuls red fruit juice or fruit syrup, such as red cherry, raspberry or strawberry syrup; stir the sugar to a thick sauce, set it over the fire and stir constantly until the sugar is lukewarm; then pour it by spoonfuls over the cake; lay blanched almonds and blanched walnuts in a circle around the edge of cake and a few in the centre.

Willie C.'s Birthday Cake (1876)

One cup of butter
two cups of sugar
one cup of water
whites of four eggs
yolk of one

three cups of flour
two heaping teaspoons of baking powder
vanilla flavour
a fourth of a pound of citron cut in very thin slices

Reserve a half cup of flour to mix with the baking powder and put that in the last thing.

Wine Cakes (No. 1) (1922)

One pound and eight ounces of sugar
One pound of butter
One pint of eggs
One pint of milk

One ounce of baking powder
Two and one-half pounds of flour
Vanilla flavour

Wine Cakes (No. 2) (1922)

One pound of sugar
Six ounces of butter

A half pint of yolks
One pint of milk

One and one-half pounds of flour Lemon or vanilla flavour
Three quarters of an ounce of baking powder

Bake in the same temperature as New York Pound Cake (No. 2)
Wine cakes are baked generally in the small round or square tins, five and ten cent size.

Wine Glazed Cake (1920)

4 eggs
1 cup flour
½ cup sugar

1 teaspoonful baking powder
the grated rind and juice of ½ lemon

Stir eggs and sugar to a cream; sift the flour and baking powder together and add them with the lemon to the above mixture; butter a round cake pan and dust it with fine bread crumbs; pour in the mixture and bake about ½ hour in a moderate oven; for glazing dissolve ½ cup sugar in ½ cup cold water and put it over the fire to boil until the sugar forms a thread between 2 fingers; then add 1 tablespoonful sherry wine, remove it from the fire and stir until a skin forms on top; then slowly pour it over the cake.

Wine Glazed Cream Cake (1920)

Stir 4 eggs with ½ cup granulated sugar to a cream and add ¾ cup sifted flour in which 1 teaspoonful baking powder has been mixed; bake in a round pan; when done pour over a wine glaze the same as in foregoing recipe and decorate the top with blanched almonds, hazel or walnuts; when cold cut the cake in half with a sharp knife; spread the under half thickly with whipped cream, put the other layer over it and cover the top with whipped cream.
NOTE: This mixture may be baked in a long, shallow pan and before putting it into the oven sprinkle 2 tablespoonfuls granulated sugar over the top. When done cut into squares; or omit the sugar and when done glaze with boiled sugar glaze and cut into squares.

Witch Cake (1913)

Cream one half cupful of butter with one and one half cupfuls of sugar; add three eggs and beat five minutes; add one cupful of milk. Sift together one third cupful of cornstarch, and two cupfuls of flour, one and one half teaspoonfuls of ground mixed spices, and three teaspoonfuls of baking powder; then add to the mixture. Now add one cupful of seeded floured raisins, also one cupful of chopped nuts. Turn into a well-greased loaf cake pan and bake in a moderate oven about forty-five minutes. Frost with a white boiled icing. Melt sweet chocolate to equal one third cupful, flavor with a teaspoonful of lemon juice, add one cupful of boiled chestnuts which have been run through the meat grinder, and enough confectionery sugar to make a paste easily handled. Roll and cut (by pasteboard pattern) black cats or any other Halloween figure, press them into the icing on the sides of the cake.

Wreath Cake (1922)

1 lb. of flour
1½ cents yeast
¾ cup of butter
2 tbsps. of vanilla

4 eggs
½ cup of milk
¼ lb. of sugar

Preparation: Cream the butter, stir in the eggs, sugar, vanilla, the yeast which has been dissolved in 1/2 cup of luke-warm milk and the flour. Roll out the dough quite thick, cut three strips of it and braid it. Then make a wreath of this braid and put it into a buttered pan to rise in a warm place. Brush it with yolks of eggs, strew sugar on and bake in a hot oven to a nice colour.

Part 25: Y

Yankee Cake (1876)
Yeast Batter for German Fruit Cakes (1904)
Yeast Buckwheats (1876)

Yellow Angel Cake (1820)
Yellow Sponge Cake (1912)
Yomoga Ga Shima (1914)

Yankee Cake (1876)

Two cups of sour cream
Two and a half cups of sugar
Two eggs

A piece of butter the size of an egg
three teaspoons of baking powder

Beat the eggs; add the sugar, butter and cream, and beat again; then stir in the flour and bake in two pans three fourths of an hour.

Yeast Batter for German Fruit Cakes (1904)

1 pound of warmed flour
½ pound of freshened butter
1 egg, the yolks of 2 eggs
3 spoonfuls of sugar

1 small cupful of lukewarm milk
2 tablespoonfuls of dissolved yeast

Mix the yeast with a very little sugar and a teaspoonful of salt, stir one-half of the flour with milk and one-half of the yeast, then add the remaining flour, the softened butter, yeast and salt, stir the dough as given under General Directions (1904), roll or press it with the hands and set aside to raise in a warm place.

Yeast Buckwheats (1876)

Take three pints of warm water, even tablespoon of salt; stir in buckwheat flour enough to make a thin batter. Beat it thoroughly, then add one-half pint of yeast. Set the batter in a warm place to rise over night. Put in a small teaspoon of soda just before baking.

Yellow Angel Cake (1820)

1¼ c. sugar
¾ tsp. cream tartar
5 tbsp. water
4 tsp. corn starch

7 eggs
⅛ tsp. salt
1 c. flour
1 tsp. flavouring

Sift dry ingredients four or five times. Beat yolks and whites separately. Boil sugar and water to a thread. Add syrup to stiffly beaten whites. Add yolks. Fold in the flour. Bake one hour in a slow oven. Frost with a white icing to which has been added a little grated rind of an orange.

Yellow Sponge Cake (1912)

Twelve eggs
The weight of ten eggs in sugar and of six eggs in flour

Rind and juice of one lemon
One saltspoon of salt

Beat the eggs separately until very light, add sugar to yolks then the juice and rind of lemon and the salt. Fold in the whites and then the flour. Bake in layers or a mould in an ungreased pan in a moderate oven. Bake fifty or sixty minutes.

Yomoga Ga Shima (1914)

This crisp little Japanese cake also comes prepared in boxes. It acquired fame through its being the favourite cake of the late Mikado.

To make it, boil to a paste fresh or dried (previously soaked) lima beans. When they are cooked, set them aside to cool and thoroughly dry, then pound them to a fine flour. Roll on a floured board into thin crackers and bake in a hot oven till crisp. They can be sweet or not, as desired.

Lily-root candy can be bought at almost any Chinese store. It has the consistency of very stiff gumdrops, and one variety, called Chicken Neck, is peppered over with red seeds.

Part 26: Z

Zimmet Kuchen (1873)
Cinnamon Cake
Zimmetplätzchen (1910)
(Cinnamon Cakes)
Zimmet-Waffeln (1910)
(Cinnamon Wafers)
Zwetschgen Kuchen (No.1) (1873)
Mussel Plum Cake
Zwetschgen Kuchen (No.2) (1873)

Mussel Plum Cake
Zwieback Torte (1873)
Rusk Cake
Zwiebel Kuchen (No. 1) (1873)
Onion Cake
Zwiebel Kuchen (No. 2) (1873)
Onion Cake

Zimmet Kuchen (1873)
Cinnamon Cake

Blanch half a pound of almonds, and pound them with a little rose-water; mix these with a half a pound of powdered sugar, two eggs, a cup of sour cream, a quarter of an ounce of powdered cinnamon, and the grated peel of a quarter of a lemon. Spread a thin mürberteig on a flat tin; pour over the mass, and bake.

Zimmetplätzchen (1910)
(Cinnamon Cakes)

6 oz. butter	6 oz. sugar
2 oz. flour	½ oz. ground ginger
2 eggs	½ lb. cornflour
1 yolk	

Cream the butter, then add the sugar and stir a further 10 minutes. Add the eggs and cinnamon and then mix well with the flour. Make up into little rolls, ½ inch thick and 3 to 4 inches long, and bake on a buttered tin, in a moderate oven.

Zimmet-Waffeln (1910)
(Cinnamon Wafers)

½ lb. butter	1 tablespoonful Maraschino
4 eggs	1 lb. sifted flour
1 oz. cinnamon	

Cream ½ lb. butter, beat up 4 eggs and stir into the butter, beating well. Flavour with 1 oz. cinnamon and 1 tablespoonful Maraschino. Then stir in 1 lb. sifted flour. Mix well. Grease and heat the special Waffeleisen (wafer irons) and proceed as in recipe " Waffeln."

Zwetschgen Kuchen (No.1) (1873)
(Mussel Plum Cake)

Mix a large breakfast-cup full of grated bread, with two ounces of almonds pounded or cut small, three ounces of sugar, a small teaspoonful of powdered cinnamon, and two ounces of butter beaten to a cream. Spread a good tart paste thinly over a shallow tin, and over this half of the mixture. Halve Orlean or mussel plums the long way, and take out the stones; lay the halves, the skin downwards, close together, all over the plate; strew over some sugar, and spread over equally the other half of the crumb-mixture. Bake it in a well-heated oven.

Zwetschgen Kuchen (No. 2) (1873)
(Mussel Plum Cake)

Spread a plain paste over a flat tin, raise an edge by pinching it up, strew over a thick layer of bread-crumbs and sugar, with a dusting of powdered cinnamon. Halve large dark plums the long way and take the stones out; lay the halves close together all over the paste, the blue side downwards. Strew over more crumbs, with cinnamon and plenty of sugar; lay small pieces of butter here and there, and bake.

Zwieback Torte (1873)
(Rusk Cake)

The yolks of fourteen eggs must be well beaten with threequarters of a pound of sifted sugar, six ounces of pounded almonds, six cloves pounded, a drachm of powdered cinnamon, and the grated peel of a lemon. Stir these well for half an hour. Then add the juice of the lemon, and half a pound of rusks, pounded and sifted through a fine cullender. When this is mixed in, add the whites of the eggs whisked to a snow. Stir all rapidly together, turn it into a well buttered mould, and bake it at once in a moderate oven. Avoid moving it while baking.

Zwiebel Kuchen (No. 1) (1873)
(Onion Cake)

Slice thin three large Spanish onions, chop them small, put them in a stew-pan with three ounces of butter to steam a quarter of an hour; do not let them brown; turn them out to cool. Beat three eggs with a cup of milk or sour cream. Add a few caraway-seeds, and three ounces of ham or bacon cut small. Mix the whole with the onions. Roll out a thin tart paste which has salt in it or put a little salt to the onions. Spread the mass over a third of an inch thick and bake it in rather a quick oven.

Zwiebel Kuchen (No. 2) (1873)
(Onion Cake)

Halve and boil half-a-dozen large common onions ten minutes; drain and chop them. Mix with them a piece of butter, two eggs, two or three grated cold potatoes, two rashers of bacon cut small, a few caraways, salt, white pepper, and a teacup of milk. Spread a thin common paste over a large flat tin. Pinch up a little edge. Spread over the mass and bake at once.

Part 27 Index

Part 1: Notes

Cake – Baking Powder (1894)
Reliable Weights and Measures as used. (1922)
Cakes (1922)
Cakes (1899)
Cakes (1913)
Cakes and Icings (1876)
Cakes, Etc. General Observations (1840)
Cakes, Great and Small (1913)
Remarks on Making and Baking Cake (1869)

Cakes (Remarks on) (1898)
Things to be Remembered in Mixing and Baking Cake (1912)
Cakes, General Directions (1820)
Cakes. General Directions (1904)
Observation on Torten Forms (1873)
Kuchen
New Receipts and Points on Cake Making (1922)

Part 2: 0 – A

1-2-3-4 Cake (1922)
A Caramel Cake (1893)
A Caramel Cake Chocolate Filling (1893)
A Caramel Cake Filling (1893)
A Charlotte Polonaise (1840)
A Cheaper Fruit Cake (1869)
A Composition Cake (1869)
A Nice Apple Cake (1904)
A Rich Fruit Cake (1869)
A Sally Lunn (1840)
A Virginia Hoe Cake (1869)
Abgeriebener Napfkuchen (1910)
Africans (1920)
(Africains)
Aepfel Kuchen (No. 1) (1873)
Common Apple Kuchen
Aepfel Kuchen (No. 2) (1873)
Apple Cake
Aepfel Kuchen (No. 3) (1873)
Apple Cake
Aepfel Kuchen (No. 4) (1873)
Apple Cake
Aepfel Kuchen (No. 5) (1873)
Apple Cake
Air Cake (1913)
Alliance Tourte (1922)
Allianz Torte (1873)
Alliance Cake
Almond and Citron Cake (1922)
Almond Biscuit (1920)
(Biscuit aux Amandes)
Almond Cake No. 1 (1904)
Almond Cake with Wheat Bread No. 2 (1904)
Almond Cake No. 1 (1904)
Almond Cake No. 2 (1904)
Almond Cake (1912)
Almond Cake (1898)

Almond Cake (1840)
Almond Cake (1869)
Almond Cake (1920)
(Gâteau d'Amandes)
Almond Cake (1898)
Almond Cake (1876)
Almond Cake 1 (1894)
Almond Cake 2 (1894)
Almond Cake 3 (1894)
Almond Cakes (1890)
Almond Cakes (1914)
Almond Cakes (1911)
Almond Cakes (1898)
(Small for Afternoon Tea)
Almond Cakes (1914)
Almond Cakes Candy (1894)
Almond Cheese Cake (1840)
Almond Cheese Cakes (1911)
Almond Cheese Cakes (1898)
Almond Cream Cake (1893)
Almond Custard Cake (1876)
Almond Gingerbread (1898)
Almond Marzapan (1904)
Almond or White Cake (1894)
Almond Silver Cake (1894)
Almond Roll (1922)
Almond Torte (1820)
Altdeutscher Napfkuchen (1910)
American Fruit Cake (1922)
Angel Cake (1922)
Angel Cake (No. 1) (1922)
Angel Cake (No. 2) (1922)
Angel Cake (No. 3) (1922)
Angel Cake (No. 4) (1922)
Angel Cake (No. 5) (1922)
Angel Cake (1893)
Angel Cake (1920)

(Gâteau des Anges)
Angel Cake (1894)
Angel Cake 1 (1893)
Angel Cake 1 (1893)
Angel Cake (1893)
Angel Cake (1911)
Angel Cake (1889)
Angel Cake (1912)
(with Nut and Whipped Cream Filling)
Angel Food (1820)
Angel Food (1893)
Angel Food Cake (1912)
Angel Marshmallow Cake (1912)
Angel Sponge Cake (1820)
Aniskuchen (1910)
(Aniseed Cakes)
Another Pretty Cake (1876)
Apees (1840)
Apfelkuchen I (1910)
(Apple Cake)
Apfelkuchen II (1910)
(Apple Cake)
Apfelkuchen mit Blätterteig (1910)
(Apple Cake with Puff Paste)
Apfelsinen Torte (No.1) (1873)
Orange Tart or Cake
Apfelsinen Torte (No. 2) (1873)
Orange Cake
Apfel-Torte (1910)

Apple Cake (1904)
Apple Cake (1920)
Apple Cake (1920)
(Gâteau aux Pommes)
Apple Cake (1898)
Apple Cake with Lemon Sauce (1913)
Apple Cakes (1878)
Apple Cake made of puff paste (1904)
Apple Cake with Almond Icing (1904)
Apple Cheese Cakes (1898)
Apple Gems (1876)
Apple Griddle Cakes (1902)
Apple Roll (1922)
Apple Sauce Cake (1820)
Apple Sauce Cake (1912)
Apple Sauce Cake (1911)
Apple Sauce Cake (1917)
(without Butter, Eggs, or Milk)
Apple Sauce Fruit Cake without Milk (1922)
Apple-Sauce Torte (1922)
Apple and Cranberry Shortcake (1917)
Apricot Cake (N.D)
Arrow Root Cakes (Small) (1898)
Arrowroot Cake (1898)
Ash Cake (Pioneer) (1913)
Aunt Amy's Cake (1911)
Aunt Rachel's Flannel Cakes (1876)

Part 3: B

Baba (1881)
Baba (1920)
Baba Syruped or Iced (1920)
(Baba au Sirop ou Glacé)
Baba with Marsala (1920)
(Baba au Marsala)
Babas with Rum-Small (1920)
(Petits Babas au Rhum)
Baked Rice Cake (1902)
Bakers' Lemon Snaps (1876)
Baltimore Cake 1 (1911)
Baltimore Cake 2 (1911)
Banana Cake (N.D.)
Banana Cake (1920)
Banana Cream Cake (1922)
Banana Shortcake (1917)
Banbury Cakes (1913)
Banbury Cakes (1898)
Bangor Corn Cake (1894)
Barneys (1905)
Batter Cakes 1 (1876)

Batter Cakes 2 (1876)
Batter Cakes 3 (1876)
Batter Cakes (Old Style) (1913)
Baum-Torte (1910)
(Tree Spongecake)
Bavarian Cheese Cake (1908)
Beautiful Cake (1893)
Beef and Bacon Cakes (1917)
Beef and Sausage Cakes (1913)
Beef Cake (1898)
Beef Cakes (1840)
Beef Hash Cakes (1911)
Berliner Pfannkuchen (1910)
(Berlin Pancakes)
Berliner Waffeln (1910)
(Berlin Wafers)
Berry Muffins (1911)
Berwick Cake (1893)
Berwick Sponge Cake (1876)
Best Jumbles (1922)
Birthday Cake (1897)

Födelsedags-kaka
Biscuit à la Hernani (1920)
(Biscuit à la Hernani)
Biscuit-Torte (1910)
(Spongecake)
Biscuit Torte (1893)
A Sponge Cake (No. 1)
Biscuit Torte (1893)
Sponge Cake (No. 2)
Blackberry Jam Cake (1820)
Black Cake (1876)
Black Cake (1840)
Black Cake (1869)
Black Cake No. 1 (1889)
Black Cake No. 2 (1889)
Black Cake with Prune Filling (1922)
Black Chocolate Cake (1922)
Black Cake Icing (1840)
Black Clouds (1876)
Black Molasses Fruit Cakes – Cheap (1922)
Blackberry Roll (1922)
Blätter Teig (1873)
Puff Paste (No. 1)
Blätter Teig (1873)
Puff Paste (No. 2)
Blätter Torte, von Linzerteig (1873)
Linzer Leaves
Blätterteig-Bretzel (1910)
(Puff Paste Twists.)
Blechkuchen (1910)
Blitzkuchen (1910)
(Lightning Cake.)
Blitzkuchen (1873)
Blitz Cake
Blueberry Cake (1893)
Blueberry Cake (1893)
(for breakfast)
Blueberry Cake (1894)
Blueberry Cake (1890)
Blueberry Cake 1 (1894)
Blueberry Cake 2 (1894)
Blueberry Muffins (1917)
Blueberry Muffins (1911)
Blueberry Muffins (1922)
Blueberry Muffins (N.D.)
Blueberry Tea Cake (1913)
Boiled Raisin Cake (1912)
Boiled Rice Muffins (1911)
Boiling Water Cake (1922)
Boston Cream Cakes 1 (1876)
Boston Cream Cakes 2 (1876)
Boston Flat Cake (1913)
Boston Gingerbread (1894)

Boston Pound Cake (1876)
Boswell Cake (1889)
Bran Muffins (1917)
Bran Muffins (1922)
Bran Muffins 1 (N.D.)
Bran Muffins 2 (N.D.)
Braune Pfeffernüsse (1910)
(Mecklenburgische)
Braunschweiger Kuchen (1873)
Brunswick Cake
Braut Torte (1873)
Bride Cake
Bread Batter Cakes (1869)
Bread Cake (1904)
Bread Cake (1894)
Bread Cake (1840)
Bread Cake (1893)
Bread Cake (1911)
Breakfast Cake (1894)
Breakfast Cake (1893)
Breakfast Cakes (1876)
Breakfast Cakes (1911)
Breakfast Cakes (1893)
Breakfast Gems (1876)
Bremen Butter Cake (1904)
Breton Cake (1920)
(Gâteau Breton)
Brick House Bride's Cake (1911)
Bride Cake (1864)
Bride's Cake (1904)
Bride's Cake (1913)
Bride's Cake (1911)
Bride's Cake 1 (1894)
Bride's Cake 2 (1894)
Bridgeport Cake (1876)
Bridgeport Cake (1876)
Bridgewater Cake (1894)
Brioche, or Propheten Kuchen (1873)
Brioche
Brioche Cake (1920)
Brod Kuchen (1912)
Brod Torte (1873)
Brown Bread Cake (No. 1)
Brod Torte (1873)
Brown Bread Cake (No. 2)
Brod Torte mit Chocolade (1873)
Bread Cake with Chocolate
Brown Nut Cake (N.D.)
Brown Sugar Cake (1893)
Bublanina Cherry Cake (1920)
Buckwheat Cakes (No. 1) (1904)
Buckwheat Cakes (No, 2) (1904)
Buckwheat Cakes (1922)

Buckwheat Cakes (1864)
Buckwheat Cakes (1913)
Buckwheat Cakes (1840)
Buckwheat Cakes (1869)
Buckwheat Cakes (1894)
Buckwheat Cakes with Baking Powder (1920)
(Galettes de Sarrasin à la Levure en Poudre)
Buckwheat Cakes with Sour Milk (1876)
Buckwheat Cakes with Yeast (1920)
(Galettes de Sarrasin à la Levure)
Butter Cakes (1920)
Butter Cakes (with Baking Powder) (1920)
Butterkuchen (1910)
Butterless-Milkless-Eggless Cake (1922)
Butter-Mandel-Torte (1910)
(Almond Spongecake)
Butter-milk Batter Cakes (1869)
Butter-milk Cake (1911)
Butter-milk Cakes (1869)
Butter-milk Cakes (1869)
Buttermilk Muffins (1911)
Butter Sponge Cake (No. 1) (1922)
Butter Sponge Cake (No.2) (1922)
Butter Sponge Cake (No.3) (1922)
Butter-Zopf (1910)
(Butter Twist)

Part 4: C

Cake (1898)
(A Plain)
Cake (1893)
(an excellent receipt)
Cake (1898)
(Birthday)
Cake, Pound (1898)
(Rich)
Cake for Jelly Roll or Charlotte Russe (1917)
Cake Made with Cream (1893)
Cake Shortcake (1905)
Cakes Stuffed with Apricot (1920)
(Gâteaux Fourrés à l'Abricot)
Cakes with Fat (1820)
Cakes with Fat (1820)
Variations
Cakes without Fat (1820)
Cakes without Fat (1820)
Suggested Variations
California Cake (1920)
(Made with Yolks)
California Cake (1897)
Kalifornia-kaka
Callas (1893)
Callas (1893)
A Creole Cake Eaten Hot with Coffee
Cambridge Muffins (1917)
Canada War Cake (1917)
(without Butter, Eggs, or Milk)
Candy Cake (1820)
Can't Fail Breakfast Muffins (N.D.)
Caramel Cake (1922)
Caramel Cake (1922)
Caramel Cake (1893)
Caramel Cake (1894)
Caramel Pineapple Cake (1922)
(Skillet Cake)
Caraway Cake (1878)
Carmelite Cake (1904)
Carolina Cakes (1876)
Carolina Muffins (1876)
Carrot Cake (1904)
Casinos (1920)
(Casinos)
Cerealine Muffins (1893)
Chamouinx Cake (1920)
(Gâteau Chamounix)
Chaperone Sponge Cake (1893)
Cheap Cake (1893)
Cheap Fruit Cake (1876)
Cheap Fruit Cake (1911)
Cheap Raisin and Currant Cakes (1922)
Cheap Sponge Cake (1893)
Cheese Cake (1920)
Cheesecakes (1864)
Cherry Cake (1898)
Cherry Torte (1922)
Cherry Valley Cake (1876)
Chess Cake (1893)
Chicken Short-cake (1902)
Chocolate Cake (1897)
Chokolad-kaka
Chocolate Cake (1904)
Chocolate Cake 1 (1876)
Chocolate Cake 2 (1876)
Chocolate Cake (1911)
Chocolate Cake (N.D.)
Chocolate Cake (1922)
Chocolate Cake (1905)
Chocolate Cake (1909)
Chocolate Cake (1913)
Chocolate Cake (1893)

Chocolate Cake (1893)
Chocolate Cake 1 (1911)
Chocolate Cake 2 (1911)
Chocolate Cake 3 (1911)
Chocolate Cake 1 (1894)
Chocolate Cake 2 (1894)
Chocolate Cake 3 (1894)
Chocolate Cake No. 1 (1913)
Chocolate Cake No. 2 (1913)
Chocolate Cake (1909)
Or Devil's Food
Chocolate Cake (1890)
Chocolate Cake (1912)
Chocolate Cake (1904)
Chocolate Caramel Cake (1912)
Chocolate Cocoanut Cake (1894)
Chocolate Cocoanut Cakes (1909)
Chocolate Cream Cake (1920)
Chocolate Fudge Cake (1912)
Chocolate Fudge Cake (1922)
Chocolate Gingerbread (1909)
Chocolate Glacé Cake (1909)
Chocolate Ice Box Cake (N.D.)
Chocolate Layer Cake (1909)
Chocolate Layer Cake (1920)
Chocolate Layer Cake (1911)
Chocolate Layer Cake (1913)
Chocolate Loaf Cake (N.D.)
Chocolate Loaf Cakes (1911)
Chocolate Marble Cake 1 (1909)
Chocolate Marble Cake 2 (1909)
Chocolate Nut Cake (1913)
Chocolate Sponge Cake (1913)
Chocolate Surprise Cakes (N.D.)
Chocolade Torte (1893)
Chocolate Cake (No. 1)
Chocolade Torte (1893)
Chocolate Cake (No. 2)
Christmas Cake (1922)
Black Cake
Christmas Cake (1913)
Christmas Pecan Cake (N.D.)
Chrysanthemum Cake (1920)
Cider Cake (1840)
Cider Cake (1869)
Cinderella Cakes (1909)
Cinderella's (1840)
or German Puffs
Citron Cake (1920)
Citron Cake (1894)
Citron or Almond Cake (1876)
Clove Cake (1876)
Clove Cake (1894)
Clove Cake (1893)
Clove Cake (1876)
Cocoa Cake (1909)
Cocoa Cake (1911)
Cocoa Marble Cake 1 (1909)
Cocoa Marble Cake 2 (1909)
Cocoa Sponge Cake 1 (1909)
Cocoa Sponge Cake 2 (1909)
Cocoanut Cake (1889)
Coconut Cake (1912)
Cocoanut Cake (1876)
Cocoanut Cake (1922)
Cocoanut Cake Icing (1922)
Cocoa-nut Cake (1840)
Cocoanut Cake (1913)
Cocoanut Cake 1 (1876)
Cocoanut Cake 2 (1876)
Cocoanut Cake 3 (1876)
Cocoanut Cake 4 (1876)
Cocoanut Cake 1 (1894)
Cocoanut Cake 2 (1894)
Cocoanut Cake 3 (1894)
Cocoanut Cake 4 (1894)
Cocoanut Cake 5 (1894)
Cocoanut Cake 6 (1894)
One, Two, Three, Four.
Cocoanut Cake (1893)
Cocoanut Cakes (1876)
Cocoanut Cakes (1876)
Cocoanut Cakes (1876)
Cocoanut Cheese Cakes (1898)
Cocoanut Cream Cake (1894)
Cocoa-nut Jumbles (1840)
Cocoanut Layer Cake (1922)
Cocoanut Layer Cake (1920)
Cocoanut Layer Cake (1922)
Coffee Cake (1922)
Coffee Cake (1864)
(Old recipe)
Coffee Cake 1 (1876)
Coffee Cake 2 (1876)
Coffee Cake 3 (1876)
Coffee Cake (1913)
Coffee Cake (1893)
Coffee Cake (1890)
Coffee Cake No. 1 (1913)
Coffee Cake No. 2 (1913)
Coffee Cake No. 3 (1913)
Coffee Cream Cakes and Filling (1911)
Coffee Layer Cake (1922)
Cold Water Cake (1894)
Cold Water Pone (1869)
Columbia Muffins (1922)

Columbian Ginger Cake (1893)
Common Cheese Cake (1840)
Common Gingerbread (1840)
Common Jumbles (1840)
Common Wheat Cakes (No. 1) (1904)
Common Wheat Cakes (No. 2) (1904)
Compiègne Cake (1920)
(Gâteau Compiègne)
Composition Cake (1876)
Composition Cake (1894)
Conde Cakes
(Gâteaux Condé (1920)
Connecticut Election Cake (1893)
Cooking-school Muffins (1905)
Corn and Rice Muffins (1917)
Corn Bannock (1860)
Corn Batter Cakes (1869)
Corn Bread or Johnny-Cake (1894)
Corn Cake (1893)
Corn Cake (1893)
Corn Cake 1 (1894)
Corn Cake 2 (1894)
Corn Cake 3 (1894)
Corn Cakes (1922)
Corn Cakes (1913)
Corn Griddle Cakes (1876)
Corn Griddle Cakes (1893)
Old Virginia Slap Jacks
Corn Griddle Cakes with Water (1876)
Corn-Meal Batter Cakes (1899)
Corn Meal Griddle Cakes (1917)
Cornmeal Muffins (1922)
Corn Muffins (1922)
Corn Muffins 1 (1876)
Corn Muffins 2 (1876)
Corn Muffins (1917)
Corn Starch Cake (1894)
Corn Starch Cake 1 (1876)
Corn Starch Cake 2 (1876)
Corn Starch Cake 3 (1876)
Corn Starch Cake (1893)
Corn Starch Cake (1893)
Corn-starch Cake (1902)
Cornstarch Cake (1899)
Corn Starch Loaf Cake (1913)
Cornelia Cake (1909)
Cream Almond Cake (1893)
Cream Cake (1894)
Cream Cake (1876)
Cream Cake (1899)
Cream Cake (1913)
Cream Cake (1893)
Cream Cake 1 (1876)

Cream Cake 2 (1876)
Cream Cake 3 (1876)
Cream Cake 4 (1876)
Cream Cake or Pie (1911)
Cream Cake Paste (1920)
(Pâte à Chou)
Cream Cakes (1840)
Cream Cakes (1911)
Cream Cakes 1 (1894)
Cream Cakes 2 (1894)
Cream Cakes Glassé (1920)
Cream Cakes Iced with Chocolate, Vanilla or Coffee (1920)
(Choux à la Crème Glacés an Chocolat, à la Vanille ou au Café)
Cream Cakes with Burnt Almonds and Glazed Cream Cakes (1920)
(Choux Pralinés et Choux Glacés)
Cream Cakes with Whipped Cream or St. Honore Cream (1920)
(Choux à la Crème Fouettée on à la Crème St. Honoré)
Cream Koch (1920)
(with Sponge Cake)
Cream Layer Cake (1913)
Cream Layer Cake (1911)
Cream Puffs (1922)
Cream Puffs (1911)
Cream Puff Balls (1922)
Cream Sponge Cake (1876)
Cream Sponge Cake (1913)
Cream Sponge Cake (1893)
Cream Sponge Cake 1 (1876)
Cream Sponge Cake 2 (1876)
Crisco Batter Cakes (1922)
Crisco Fruit Cake (1922)
Crisco Sponge Cake (1922)
Crisp Ginger-cake (1869)
Crisp White Corncake (1911)
Crown of Brioche (1920)
(Couronne de Brioche)
Crumb Coffee Cake (N.D.)
Crumb Griddle Cakes (1902)
Crumb Griddle Cakes (1911)
Crumbled Paste Cakes (1920)
(Gâteaux en Pâte Fondante) (1920)
Cup Cake (1904)
Cup Cake 1 (1876)
Cup Cake 2 (1876)
Cup Cake (1869)
Cup Cake (1912)
Cup Cakes (1922)
Currant Cake, (1922)

Citron Cake or Raisin Cake
Currant Cake (1904)
Currant Cake (1913)
Currant Cake (1898)
Currant Cake (1894)
Currant Cake (1893)
Currant Cake (1904)
Currant Cake (1904)
Cushion Cake (1922)
Custard Cake (1876)
Custard Cakes (1840)
Custard Corn Cake (1917)
Custard Pie (Cake Crumbs) (1917)

Part 5: D

Dansk Lagkage (N.D.)
(Danish Layer Cake)
Dark Fruit Cake (N.D.)
Dark Fruit Cake (1820)
D'Artois Cake with Apricot Marmalade or Almond Cream (1920)
(Gâteau D'Artois à la Marmelade d'Abricots ou à la Crème d'Amandes)
Date and Walnut Torte (1922)
Date Cake (1904)
(Arabian Receipt)
Date Cake (1917)
Date Cake (1911)
Date Cake (1912)
Date Loaf (1912)
Davis Cake (1890)
Dayton Cake (1894)
Delicate Cake (1889)
Delicate Cake (1922)
Delicate Cake (1893)
Delicate Cake 1 (1876)
Delicate Cake 2 (1876)
Delicate Cake 3 (1876)
Delicate Cake 4 (1876)
Delicate Cake 5 (1876)
Delicate Cake 6 (1876)
Delicate Cake 1 (1893)
Delicate Cake 2 (1893)
Delicate cake 1 (1894)
Delicate cake 2 (1894)
Delicate Cake 1 (1893)
Delicate Cake 2 (1893)
Delicious Cake (1911)

Delicious Cake (1893)
Delicious Cake 1 (1894)
Delicious Cake 2 (1894)
Denmark Cake (1920)
Delicate Sponge Cake (1920)
Derby Cake (1864)
Dessertbiskuit (1910)
Devil's Cake in Layers (1913)
Devil's Food (1820)
Devil's Food Cake (N.D.)
Devil's Food Cake (1922)
Devil's Food Nut Cake (1922)
Dicker Pfefferkuchen mit Honig (1910)
(Ginger Cake with Honey)
Dominion Apple Cake (1922)
Domino Cake (1905)
Domino Cakes (1922)
Dorbas Torte (1922)
Dorothy Cake (1820)
Dough Cake (1876)
Dover Cake (1876)
Dover Cake (1869)
Dream Cakes (1913)
Dried Apple Cake (1902)
Dried Crumb Griddle Cakes (1917)
Dried Prune Cake (1904)
Drop Ginger Cakes (1876)
Dutch Apple Cake (N.D.)
Dutch Apple Cake (1917)
Dutch Apple Cake 1 (1893)
Dutch Apple Cake 2 (1893)
Dutchess Cake (1920)

Part 6: E

Easy Fruit-cake (1905)
Economy Cake (1820)
Economy Cake 1 (1876)
Economy Cake 2 (1876)
Economy Cakes 3 (1876)
Economy Cake (1913)
Economical Cake (1897)

Ekonomisk kaka
Eggless Cake (1913)
Eggless Cake (1911)
Eggless Chocolate Cake (1922)
Eggless Spice Cake 1 (1922)
Eggless Spice Cake 2 (1922)
Eier Kuchen or Eierwähen (1873)

A Custard Cake
Eierplätzchen (1910)
Elberfeld Krengel (1873)
An Elberfeld Cake
Eleanor's Cakes (1905)
Election Cake No. 1 (1889)
Election Cake No. 2 (1889)
Election Cake No. 3 (1889)
Election Cake No. 4 (1889)
Election Cake No. 5 (1889)
Election Cake No. 6 (1889)
Election Cake No. 7 (1889)
Election Cake No. 8 (1889)
Election Cake No. 9 (1889)
Election Cake No. 10 (1889)
Election Cake No. 11 (1889)
Election Cake 1 (1876)
Election Cake 2 (1876)
Election Cake (1920)
Election Cake (1840)
Election Cake (1893)
(One Hundred Years Old)
Emmy's Cake (1897)
Emmys kaka

English Christmas Cake (1922)
English Fruit Cake (1922)
English Fruit Cake (1893)
English Layer Cake (1908)
English Fruit Cake (1820)
English Muffins (1922)
English Muffins (1908)
English Muffins (1902)
English Muffins (1911)
English Muffins (1890)
English Plum Cake (1904)
English Seed Pound Cake (1922)
English Tea Cake (1820)
English Tea Cakes (1908)
English Walnut Cake (1894)
Engracia Cake (1909)
Entire Wheat Muffins (1911)
Esmé Shortcake (1909)
Esther's Molasses Cake for Lunch (1890)
Excellent Cake (1893)
Exposition Orange Cake (1893)
Exposition Orange Cake Filling (1893)

Part 7: F

Fairy Gingerbread (1820)
Fancy Cakes-Soft (1920)
(Petits Fours Moelleux)
Farina Cake (1904)
Farina Cakes (1876)
Favart Cake (1920)
(Gâteau Favart)
Feather Cake 1 (1876)
Feather Cake 2 (1876)
Feather Cake 3 (1876)
Feather Cake (1922)
Feather Cake (1911)
Feather Cake (1894)
Feather Cake (1893)
Feather Sponge (1820)
(Made with Potato Flour)
Federal Cakes (1840)
Field's Potato Flour Muffins (N.D.)
Fig Cake (1876)
Fig Cake (1922)
Fig Cake (1922)
Fig Cake (1899)
Fig Cake (1911)
Fig Cake (1894)
Fig Layer Cake (1911)
Filbert Cakes with Rum Small (1920)

(Petits Gâteaux d'Avelines au Rhum)
Filled Sand Cake (1904)
Fine Ginger Dessert Cakes (1889)
Fine Sponge Cake (1920)
Five O'Clocks (1889)
Flag Cake (1922)
Flammen Torte (1873)
Flame Cake
Flannel Cakes (1905)
Flannel Cakes (1913)
Flannel Cakes (1840)
Flannel Cakes (1869)
Flannel Cakes (1920)
(Galettes Légères)
Flannel Cakes (1894)
Fleury Cake (1920)
(Gâteau Fleury)
Florida Corn Cake (1902)
Francillon Cakes (1920)
(Gâteaux Francillon)
Franklin Cake (1840)
French Cake (1876)
French Cake (1894)
French Fruit Cake (No. 1) (1922)
French Fruit Cake (No. 2) (1922)
French Loaf Cake (1876)

French Loaf Cake (1893)
French Loaf Cake (1894)
French Pastry Cake (N.D.)
French Tourte a la Crème (1922)
Fried Cakes 1 (1876)
Fried Cakes 2 (1876)
Fried Cakes 3 (1876)
Fried Cakes with Apple Sauce (1922)
Fried Cornmeal Nut Cakes (1922)
Fritters, Cake (1898)
Fruit Cake (1897)
Frukt-kaka
Fruit Cake (1889)
Fruit Cake (1904)
Fruit Cake 1 (1876)
Fruit Cake 2 (1876)
Fruit Cake 3 (1876)
Fruit Cake 4 (1876)
Fruit Cake 5 (1876)
Fruit Cake (1890)
Fruit Cake (1913)
Fruit Cake (1920)
Fruit Cake (1920)
(Gâteau aux Fruits)
Fruit Cake (1911)
Fruit Cake 1 (1893)
Fruit Cake 2 (1893)
Fruit Cake 3 (1893)
Fruit Cake 1 (1893)
Fruit Cake 2 (1893)
Fruit Cake 3 (1893)
Fruit Cake 1 (1894)
Fruit Cake 2 (1894)
Fruit Cake 3 (1894)
Fruit Cake (1912)
Fruit Cake from Bread Dough (1913)
Fruit Drop Cakes (1876)
Fruit Drop Cakes (1922)
Fruit Drop Cakes (1922)
Fruit Layer Cake (1912)
Fruit or Plum Cake (1869)
Fruit Queen Cakes (1840)
Fruit-Nut Loaf Cake (1922)
Fruit Gems (1876)
Fryeburg Sponge Cake (1911)
Fudge Cake (1911)
Fudge Cake (1922)
Fudge Cake (1917)

Part 8: G

Gâteau à la Weckesser (1920)
Gem Cake (1899)
Geneva Cake (1904)
Gennoise Cake (1922)
Genoa Cake (1922)
Genoa Cake (1909)
Genoa Pound Cake (1922)
Genoese Cake (1920)
(Gâteau Génoise)
Genoese Cake-Light (1920)
(Génoise Légère)
Genoeses with Cream Meringued (1920)
(Génoises à la Crème Meringues)
Genoise Sponge Cake (1922)
Génoises (1898)
Georgie's Cake (1893)
German Apple Cake (1908)
German Brod Tourte (1922)
German Cake (1894)
German Cakes (1876)
German Coffee Cake 1 (1913)
German Coffee Cake 2 (1913)
German Plum Cake (1873)
Plum Cake
German Prune Cake (1902)
German Short Paste (1922)
Ginger Apple Cake (1917)
Ginger Bread (1893)
Ginger Bread (1893)
Ginger Bread (N.D.)
Ginger Bread (1893)
Gingerbread (1920)
Gingerbread (1893)
Gingerbread (1905)
Gingerbread (1864)
Ginger Bread (1905)
Gingerbread (1922)
Ginger Bread, (1876)
(Plain)
Ginger Bread (1876)
Ginger-Bread (1898)
Ginger-Bread (1898)
(Another Recipe)
Gingerbread 1 (1894)
(Sugar)
Gingerbread 2 (1894)
(Hard Sugar)
Gingerbread 3 (1894)
(Maggie's)
Gingerbread 4 (1894)

(Molasses)
Gingerbread 5 (1894)
Gingerbread 6 (1894)
(Simplest and Best)
Ginger Cake (1876)
Ginger Cake (1922)
Ginger Cake (1894)
Ginger Cup-cake (1869)
Ginger Plum Cake (1840)
Ginger Sponge Cake (1876)
Glasgow Cakes (1909)
Gold and Silver Cake (1897)
Guld-och Silfver-kaka
Gold and Silver Cake (1893)
Gold Bar Cake (1909)
Gold Cake 1 (1876)
Gold Cake 2 (1876)
Gold Cake (1911)
Gold Cake (1922)
Gold Cake (1911)
Gold Cake (1893)
Gold Cake 1 (1894)
Gold Cake 2 (1894)
Gold Thread Cake (1909)
Golden Cake (1894)
Goldenrod Cake (1909)
Golden Corn Muffins (1922)
Golden Orange Cake (1922)
Good Batter for large Cakes. (1904)
Gooseberry Cake (1904)
Gooseberry Cakes and Tarts (1920)
(Gâteaux et Tartes aux Groseilles Vertes)

Graham Cake (1894)
Graham Cakes (1876)
Graham Cracker Cake (1922)
Graham Flour Muffins (1922)
Graham Gems 1 (1876)
Graham Gems 2 (1876)
Graham Muffins (1911)
Graham Muffins (1890)
Graham Muffins (1876)
Graham Muffins (1876)
Grandmother's Bread Cake (1893)
Grandmother's Little Feather Cake (1905)
Grange Cake (1911)
Granose Fruit-Cake (1899)
Grape Cake (1904)
Greek Cakes (1908)
Green Corn Cakes (1876)
Griddle Cakes (N.D.)
Griddle-cakes (1905)
Gries-Torte (1910)
(Ground Rice Spongecake)
Gugelhopfen (No. 1) (1873)
Savoy Cake, or German Brioche
Gugelhopfen (No. 2) (1873)
Savoy Cake
Gugelhopfen (1920)
(Cougloff)
Gum Lu (1914)
(Golden Cakes)
Guss Torte or Kuchen (1873)
A Fruit Cake (Guss - a creamy mixture)

Part 9: H

Ham Cakes (1893)
Hamilton Chocolate Cake (1820)
Harlequin Cake (1893)
Harrison Cake 1 (1876)
Harrison Cake 2 (1876)
Harrison Cake (1894)
Hartford Election Cake (1894)
Hartford Election Cake (1889)
Yeast
Hasty Cake (1897)
Kaka i hast
Hasty Cake (1922)
Hazel-Nut Cake (1920)
(Gâteau aux Noisettes)
Hazel Nut Cake (1912)
Hazel Nut Torte (1820)
Hefen Teig (1873)
Yeast Dough

Hefen-Waffeln (1910)
(Yeast Wafers)
Henry Cake (1894)
Hickory Nut Cake (1911)
Hickory-Nut Cake 1 (1876)
Hickory-Nut Cake 2 (1876)
Hickory-Nut Cake 3 (1876)
Hickory-Nut Cake (1894)
Himbeer Kuchen (1873)
Raspberry Cake
Hoe Cake (1902)
Hoe Cake (1913)
Hoe Cake (1840)
Hominy Cakes (1911)
Hominy Muffins (1911)
Honey Cake (1820)
Honey Cake Special (1820)
Honey Cakes (1840)

Honey Ginger Cake (1840)
Honey-Cake (1864)
Honey Tea Cakes (1912)
Honigkuchen – I (1910)
(Honey Cakes - I)
Honigkuchen – II (1910)
(Honey Cakes - II)
Horseshoe Cakes (1902)
Hot Lemonade Cake (1820)
Hot Water Gingerbread (1917)
(without Egg)
Hot Water Gingerbread (1917)
(with Egg)
Hot Water Sponge Cake (1893)
Hot Water Sponge Cake (1912)
Huckleberry Cake (1840)
Huckleberry Cakes (1911)
Hungarian Spice Cakes (1908)
Hurry Up Cake (1922)

Part 10: I

Ice Box Cake (1922)
Ice Box Cake 1 (N.D.)
Ice Box Cake 2 (N.D.)
Ice Cream Cake (1876)
Ice Cream Cake (1911)
Ice Cream Cake (1894)
Ice-Water Sponge Cake (1876)
Icing Cake (1876)
Imperial Cake (1897)
Kejsarkaka
Imperial Cake (1889)
Imperial Cake (1894)
Imperial Muffins (1922)
Indian Batter Cakes (1840)
Indian Breakfast Cake (1894)
Indian Cake (1894)
Indian Cakes (1920)
(Galettes Indiennes)
Indian Cakes (1878)
Indian Drop Cake (1894)
Indian Loaf Cake (1840)
Indian Meal Griddle Cakes (1911)
Indian Mush Cakes (1840)
Indian Pound Cake (1840)
Indian Pound Cake (1869)
Indio Cake (1820)
Individual Shortcakes (1911)
Inexpensive Devil's Food (1820)
Irish Batter Cakes (1908)
Italian Batter Cakes (1908)
Italian Sugar Cakes (1908)

Part 11: J

Jam Cake (1922)
Jam Fruit Cake (1912)
Jamaica Cake (1920)
(Gâteau à la Jamaïque)
Japanese Cakes (1920)
(Gâteaux Japonais)
Javaneses (1920)
(Javanais)
Jelly Cake 1 (1876)
Jelly Cake 2 (1876)
Jelly Cake (1840)
Jelly Cake (1894)
Jelly Cake (1869)
Jelly Cake Meringued (1920)
(Gâteau à la Gelée Meringué)
Jelly Cake, No. 1 (1920)
Jelly Cake, No. 2 (1920)
Jelly Cake, No. 3 (1920)
Jelly Roll (1913)
Jelly Roll (1920)
Jelly Roll (1922)
Jenny Lind Cake (1893)
Jewish Purim Cakes (1908)
Johnny Cake (1911)
Johnny Cake (1899)
Johnny Cake (1905)
Johnny Cake (1913)
Johnny Cake (1840)
Johnny Cake (1893)
Johnny Cake (1878)
Johnny Cakes (1864)
Journey Cake (1869)
Julia Cake (1894)
Jumbles 1 (1876)
Jumbles 2 (1876)
Jumbles 3 (1876)
Jumbles 4 (1876)
Jumbles
(Jumbles) (1920)
Jumbles 1 (1894)
Jumbles 2 (1894)
(Soft)

Jumbles (1911)

Part 12: K

Kaffeekringel (1910)
Kaffeekuchen (1910)
Kaiser Kuchen (1873)
Imperial Cake
Kartoffel Torte (1873)
Potato Cake
Käsekuchen (1873)
Cheese Cake (No.1)
Käsekuchen (1873)
Cheese Cake (No.2)
Käsekuchen (1910)
(Cheese Cake)
King's Cake (1904)
Kirschkuchen (1910)
(Cherry Cake)
Kirschen Kuchen (1873)
Cherry Cake (No.1)
Kirschen Kuchen (1873)
Cherry Cake (No.2)
Kirschen Kuchen (1873)
Cherry Cake (No.3)
Kirschen Kuchen (1873)
Plainer Cherry Cake (No.4)
Kirsch-Torte (1910)
(Cherry Cake)
Kleine Biskuittörtchen (1910)
Kleine Kirschtörtchen (1910)
(Cherry Tartlets)
Kleine Sandkuchen (1910)
Königskuchen (1910)
(King Cake)
Krack Torte (1873)
Crack Tart
Kuchen Michel (1873)
A Savoury Cake
Kugelhupf (1920)
Kümmel-Kakes (1910)
(Carraway Biscuits)
Kümmelstangen (1910)
(Carraway Sticks)

Part 13: L

Ladies' Cake (1893)
Lady Baltimore Cake (1922)
Lady Baltimore Cake Filling and Frosting (1922)
Lady Baltimore Cake (1922)
Lady Baltimore (1912)
Lady Cake 1 (1876)
Lady Cake 2 (1876)
Lady Cake 1 (1920)
Lady Cake 2 (1920)
Lady Cake
(Gâteau des Dames) (1920)
Lady Cake (1894)
Lady Cake (1893)
Lady Cake (1840)
Lady Cake (No. 1) (1922)
Lady Cake (No. 2) (1922)
Lady Cake (No. 3) (1922)
Lady Cake (No. 4) (1922)
Lady Finger Cake (1912)
Lady Fingers (1876)
Lady Fingers
(Biscuits à la Cuiller) (1920)
Lafayette Gingerbread (1864)
Lagen-Torte (1910)
Lapland Cakes (1876)
Laplander Cakes (1902)
Large Brioche with Head (1920)
(Grosse Brioche & Tête)
Layer Cake (1904)
Layer Cake (1905)
Layer Cake (1911)
Layer Cake No. 1 (1912)
Layer Cake No. 2 (1912)
Layer Cake, Yellow (No. 1) (1922)
Layer Cake, Yellow (No. 2) (1922)
Layer Cake, Yellow (No. 3) (1922)
Layer Cake, Yellow (No. 4) (1922)
Layer Cake, Yellow (No. 5) (1922)
Layer Cake, White (No.1) (1922)
Layer Cake, White (No.2) (1922)
Layer Fruit-Cake (1876)
Lemon Cake 1 (1876)
Lemon Cake 2 (1876)
Lemon Cake 3 (1876)
Lemon Cake (1913)
Lemon Cake (1893)
Lemon Cake (1898)
Lemon Cake with Icing (1904)

Lemon Cheese – Cake Mixture (1898)
Lemon Cheese-Cakes (1898)
Lemon Cream Cake (1920)
Lemon Currant Cake (1876)
Lemon Ice Box Cake (N.D.)
Lemon Jelly Cake 1 (1876)
Lemon Jelly Cake 2 (1876)
Lemon Jelly Cake 3 (1876)
Lemon Layer Cake (1922)
Lemon Layer Cake (1899)
Lemon Layer Cake (1920)
Lemon or Orange Cake (1876)
Lemon Snaps (1876)
Lemon Snaps (1894)
Lemon Sponge Cake (1899)
Lemon Sponge Cake (1869)
Lightened Pone (1869)
Lightning Cake (1820)
Lightnings (1897)
Blixtar
Lily Cake (1876)
Lily Cake (1893)
Lincoln Cake (1876)
Lincoln Cake (1893)

Linzer Cake (1904)
Linzer Torte (1910)
Linzer Torte (1873)
Linzer Cake, (No. 1)
Linzer Torte (1873)
Linzer Cake, (No. 2)
Linzer Torte (1873)
Linzer Cake, (No. 3)
Linzer Torteletten (1873)
Linzer Tartlets,
Linzer Tourte (1922)
Lise's Sponge Cake (N.D)
Little Indian Cakes (1869)
Little Plum Cakes (1876)
Loaf Cake (1869)
Loaf Ginger Cake (1893)
Löffelbiskuit (1910)
Lord Baltimore Cake (1922)
Love Cake (1904)
Lubec Marzapan (1904)
Lucile Shortcake (1909)
Lunch Cakes (1922)
Luncheon Cake (1913)

Part 14: M

Macaroon Cake (1904)
Macaroon Cream Cake (1904)
Madeira Cakes (No. 1) (1922)
Madeira Cakes (No. 2) (1922)
Madeira Cakes (No. 3) (1922)
Madeira Cake (1898)
Madison Cake (1876)
Madison Cake (1869)
Madison Fruit Cake (1922)
Magdalenen Torte (1873)
Magdalen Cake
Magic Cake (1894)
Mahogany Cake (1820)
Makovy Dort Poppy Seed Cake (1920)
Malted Milk Cake (1922)
Mammy's Ginger Cakes (1913)
Mandarin Cake (1920)
(Gâteau Mandarin)
Mandel or Sudel Torte (1873)
Almond Cake
Mandel Kuchen (1873)
Almond Cake (No.1)
Mandel Kuchen (1873)
Almond Cake (No.2)
Mandelbrötchen (1910)
(Almond Cakes)

Mandelkuchen (1910)
(Almond Cake)
Madelines No.1 (1889)
Madelines No.2 (1889)
Mandelringe (1910)
(Almond Rings)
Mandelspäne (1910)
(Almond Chips)
Mandel-Torte (1910)
(Almond Cake)
Mandel Torte (1893)
Almond Cake (No.1)
Mandel Torte (1893)
Almond Cake (No.2)
Mannheim Apple Cake (1904)
Marble Cake 1 (1876)
Marble Cake 2 (1876)
Marble Cake (1911)
Marble Cake (1922)
Marble Cake (1922)
Marble Cake (1913)
Marble Cake (1920)
Marble Cake (1913)
Marble Cake (1913)
Marble Cake (1894)
Marble Cake 1 (1893)

Marble Cake 2 (1893)
Marble Cakes (1922)
Marbled Chocolate Cake (1894)
Margaret's Own Cake (1905)
Margarettes (1911)
Marillan Cakes (1920)
(Gâteaux Marillan)
Marly Cake (1920)
(Gâteau Marly)
Marmalade Cake (1922)
Marmalade Cake (1840)
Mars Cakes (1920)
(Gâteaux Mars)
Marshall Cake (1894)
Maryland Corn Cakes (1869)
Marzipan (1910)
(Marchpane)
Measure Pound Cake (1913)
Meat Short Cake (1893)
Meringue Cake (N.D.)
Meringue Tourte (1922)
Milan Apple Cake (1904)
Milfoil Cake, Pompadour (1920)
(Gâteau Mille-Feuilles, Pompadour)
Milfoil with Preserves (1920)
(Gâteau Mille-Feuilles aux Confitures)
Millionaire Cake (1920)
Miss Farmer's Chocolate Nougat Cake (1909)
Mocha Cake (1911)
Mocha Cake (1922)
Mocha Cake (1920)
(Gâteau Moka)
Mohn-Striezel (1910)
Mohn-Torte (1910)
(Poppy Cake)
Molasses Cake (1913)
Molasses Cake (1920)
Molasses Cake 1 (1894)
Molasses Cake 2 (1894)
Molasses Cake 3 (1894)
(Drop)
Molasses Cake 4 (1894)
(Mrs. Clark's)
Molasses Drop Cake (1894)
Mor's Sur Fløde Kage (N.D.)
(Mother's Sour Cream Cake)
Moravian Sugar Cake (1840)
Mosaic Cake (1820)
Mother Hubbard Cake (1894)
Mother's Cake (1913)
Mountain Cake 1 (1876)
Mountain Cake (1893)
Mousseline Biscuit (1920)
(Biscuit Mousseline)
Mrs. Black's Orange Cake (1909)
Mrs. Carpenter's Wedding Cake (1876)
Mrs. Dodge's Wedding Cake (1876)
Mrs. Harmon's Fruit Cake (1876)
Mrs. Madison's Whim (1893)
Mrs. Mason's Cake (1876)
Mrs. Rorer's Chocolate Cake (1909)
Mrs. Sherman's Almond Cake (1876)
Mrs. Sibley's Raised Cake (1876)
Mrs. Speed's Layer Cake (1876)
Muffins (1905)
Muffins (1911)
Muffins (1911)
Muffins (1890)
Muffins 1 (1894)
Muffins 2 (1894)
Muffins 3 (1894)
(English)
Muffins 4 (1894)
(Graham)
Muffins 5 (1894)
(Graham)
Muffins 6 (1894)
(Indian Meal)
Muffins 7 (1894)
(Raised)
Muffins 8 (1894)
(Raised)
Muffins 9 (1894)
(Rye)
Muffins 10 (1894)
(White)
Muffins 1 (1876)
Muffins 2 (1876)
Muffins 3 (1876)
Muffins 4 (1876)
Muffins 5 (1876)
Muffins 6 (1876)
Muffins (1864)
Muffins 1 (N.D.)
Muffins 2 (N.D.)
Muffins (1922)
Muffins (1893)
Muffins (1893)
Mürbekuchen – I (1910)
Mürbekuchen – II (1910)
Mürber Teig (No. 1) (1873)
Short Crust for Savoury Pasties
Mürber Teig (No. 2) (1873)
Short Crust
Mürber Teig (No. 3) (1873)
Short Crust

Mürber Teig (No. 4) (1873)
Common Short Crust
Mush (1876)
Mush Batter Cakes (1913)
(For Invalids)

Mush Flannel Cakes (1869)
Mush, Mush Cakes, and Fried Mush (1869)
Muster Gingerbread (1911

Part 15: N

Napfkuchen mit Hefe (1910)
(Plain Yeast Cake)
Neapolitan Cake (1876)
Neapolitan Cake (1920)
Neapolitan Cake (1920)
(Gâteau Napolitain)
Never Fail Devil's Food Cake (N.D.)
New England Election Cake (1913)
New England Raised Loaf Cake (1893)
New Year Cake (1869)
New York Pound Cake (No.1) (1922)
New York Pound Cake (No.2) (1922)
Newport Tea Cakes (1902)
Nice Breakfast Cakes (1876)
Nice Cake (1894)
Nice Griddle Cakes (1876)
Nice Johnny-Cake (1876)
Nice Rice Cake (1904)
North Dakota Sponge Cake (1893)
Nougatine Cake (1920)
(Gâteau Nougatine)
Novelty Cake (1820)

Nugget Cake (1909)
Number Cake (1876)
Nun's Cake (N.D.)
Nuss-Torte (1910)
(Nut Cake)
Nut and Raisin Cake (1913)
Nut Cake (1912)
Nut Cake (1899)
Nut Cake (1920)
Nut Cake 1 (1893)
Very old French recipe
Nut Cake 2 (1893)
Nut Cake 3 (1893)
Nut Cake 1 (1893)
Nut Cake 2 (1893)
Nut Cake 1 (1894)
Nut Cake 2 (1894)
Cream
Nut Cake 3 (1894)
Golden
Nut Layer Cake (1912)

Part 16: O

Oatcakes (1898)
Oat Cakes (1922)
Oat Meal Cakes No. 1 (1912)
Oat Meal Cakes No. 1 (1912)
Oat Meal Cakes (1893)
Oatmeal Cake (1911)
Oat Meal Gems 1 (1876)
Oat Meal Gems 2 (1876)
Occidental Fudge Cake (1820)
Old Fashioned Hickorynut Cake (1922)
Old-Fashioned Pork Cake (1917)
Old Fashioned Raisin Cake (1922)
Old Fashioned Seed Cake (1922)
Old Time Pound Cakes (No. 1) (1922)
Old Time Pound Cakes (No. 2) (1922)
Old Virginia Bread Cake (1893)
One-Egg Cake (1917)
One-Egg Cake (1920)
Orange Cake (1904)
Orange Cake (1912)

Orange Cake 1 (1876)
Orange Cake 2 (1876)
Orange Cake 3 (1876)
Orange Cake (1917)
Orange Cake (1913)
Orange Cake (1893)
Orange Cake (1894)
Orange Cake 1 (1893)
Orange Cake 2 (1893)
Orange Cake 3 (1893)
Orange Cake 4 (1893)
Orange Cake (1890)
Orange Cake (1904)
Orange Cake with Milk Icing (1909)
Orange Cheesecakes (1909)
Orange Cheesecakes (1898)
Orange Fruit Cake (1909)
Orange Gingerbread (1909)
Orange Lady Cake (1909)
Orange Layer Cake (1922)

Orange Layer Cake (1920)
Orange Shortcake (1913)
Orange Short Cake (1893)
Orange Sponge (1909)
Orange Sunshine Cake (1893)

Orange Tourte (1922)
Orange Washington Cake (1909)
Ormond Cake (1909)
Oyster Shortcake (1922)
Oyster Shortcake (1912)

Part 17: P

Pan Cakes (1869)
Parisian Cake (1904)
Parisian Cakes (1920)
(Gâteaux Parisiens)
Peach Cake with Sweetened Cream (1913)
Peach Shortcake (1922)
Peach Shortcake (1920)
Pearl Grit Gems (1876)
Pecan Cake (1893)
Pensacola Cake (1909)
Pfefferkuchen (1910)
(Gingerbread)
Pflaumenkuchen (1910)
Piccolomini Cake (1894)
Pineapple Cake (1913)
Pineapple Cake (1920)
Pineapple Cake (1920)
(Gâteau Ananas)
Pine-apple Sponge (1898)
Pineapple Upside Down Cake (1922)
Pink Cake (1876)
Plain Apple Cake (1904)
Plain Cake (1922)
Plain Cake (1917)
Plain Cake (1920)
Plain Cake (1911)
Plain Cake with Fruit Jelly (1904)
Plain Cider Cake (1840)
Plain Genoa Pound Cake (1922)
Plain Ginger Cakes (1913)
Plain Griddle Cakes (1917)
Plain Jelly Cake (1913)
Plain Layer Cake (1913)
Plain Muffins (1917)
Plain Orange Cake (1909)
Plain Pound Cake (1922)
Plain Pound Cake (1893)
Plain Raisin Cake (1894)
Plain Sponge Cake (No. 1) (1922)
Plain Sponge Cake (No. 2) (1922)
Plain Strawberry Shortcake (1920)
Plain Tea Cake (1911)
Plain White Cake No, 1 (1912)
Plain White Cake No, 1 (1912)
Pleasant Point Eggless Cake (1911)

Plum Cake (1898)
(Plain)
Plum Cake (1898)
(Good)
Plum Cake (1920)
(Gâteau aux Raisins de Corinthe)
Plum Cake (1904)
Plum-Cake (1864)
Plunderbretzel – Kranzkuchen (1910)
Polnischer Krengel (1910)
Pome-de-Terres (1912)
Pomme de Terre Cake (1820)
Poppy Seed Cakes (1922)
Poppyseed Cake (1922)
Pork Cake (1913)
Pork Cake No. 1 (1876)
Pork Cake No. 2 (1876)
(Fruit)
Portuguese Coffee Cake (1904)
Potato Cake (1904)
Potato Cake No. 1 (1912)
Potato Cake No. 2 (1912)
Potato Cakc (1909)
Potato Cake (1836)
Potato Cakes (1876)
Potato Cakes (1922)
Potato Cakes (1899)
Potato Cakes (1905)
Potato Cakes (1913)
Potato Cakes (1920)
(Gateaux de Pommes de Terre)
Potato Cakes (1894)
Potato Cakes with Ham (1920)
(Galettes de Pommes de Terre au Jambon)
Potato Chocolate Cake (1820)
Potato Flour Cake (1911)
Potato Flour Muffins (1922)
Potato Torte (1820)
Pound Cake No. 1 (1889)
Pound Cake No. 2 (1889)
Pound Cake 1 (1876)
Pound Cake 2 (1876)
Pound Cake (1922)
Pound Cake (N.D.)
Pound Cake (1922)

Pound Cake
(Aunt Polly Rives) (1913)
Pound Cake (1840)
Pound Cake (1869)
Pound Cake
(Pound Cake) (1920)
Pound Cake (1894)
Pound Cake (No.1) (1922)
Pound Cake (No.2) (1922)
Poverty Cake (1911)
Princess Cake (1922)
Prune Cake (1820)

Puff Cake (1913)
Pumpernickel-Torte (1910)
(Pumpernickel Spongecake)
Punch Cake, Punch Biscuit, Imitation of Boar's Head, a Book or a Ham (1920)
(Gâteau Punch, Punch Biscuit, Imitation de Hure de Sanglier, d'un Livre ou d'un Jambon)
Punch Layer Cake (1904)
Punsch Torte (1893)
Punch Cake
Punch Tourte (1922)
Pyramid Birthday Cake (1921)

Part 18: Q

Queen Cake (1897)
Drottning-kaka
Queen Cake (1840)
Queen Cake (1869)
Queen Cake (1920)
(Gâteau Reine)
Queen Cakes (1922)
Queen Cakes (1913)

Quick Cake (1911)
Quick Coffee Cake (1922)
Quick Coffee Cake (1917)
Quick Loaf Cake (1889)
Quick Muffins (1922)
Quick Muffins in Rings (1911)
Quince Cakes (1878)

Part 19: R

Rahm Kuchen (1873)
(Cream Cake)
Railroad Cake 1 (1876)
Railroad Cake 2 (1876)
Raised Buckwheat Cakes (1917)
Raised Cake 1 (1876)
Raised Cake 2 (1876)
Raised Corn Muffins (1917)
Raised Fruit-Cake (1899)
Raised Loaf Cake (1894)
Raised Muffins (1917)
Raised Oatmeal Muffins (1917)
(Uncooked Oats)
Raised Plum Cake (1869)
Raisin Cake (1820)
Raisin Cake (1876)
Raisin Cake (1911)
Raisin Cakelets (1913)
Raisin Cup Cakes (1914)
Raspberry Muffins (1922)
Raspberry Short Cake (1876)
Real Gold Cake (1913)
Real Silver Cake (1913)
Rehrücken (1910)
(Saddle of Venison - A Viennese Cake)
Rhode Island Cakes (1913)
Rhode Island Corn Cake (1917)

Ribbon Cake (1904)
Ribbon Cake (1911)
Ribbon Cake (1913)
Ribbon Cake 1 (1893)
Ribbon Cake 2 (1893)
Rice and Lemon Cake (1904)
Rice Cake (1904)
Rice Cake (1898)
Rice Cake (1836)
Rice Cakes (1922)
Rice Cakes (1840)
Rice Cakes (1840)
Rice Cakes (1920)
(Galettes au Riz)
Rice Cakes (1920)
(Gâteaux au Riz)
Rice Cakes (1878)
Rice Cakes (1898)
(Small, for Afternoon Tea)
Rice Flour Cake (1894)
Rice Flour Pound Cake (1869)
Rice Gems 1 (1876)
Rice Gems 2 (1876)
Rice Gems 3 (1876)
Rice Griddle Cakes (1876)
Rice Griddle Cakes (1917)
Rice Johnny Cake (1902)

Rice Muffins (1893)
Rice Sponge Cake (1869)
Rice Tea Cake (1876)
Rich Bride Cake (1897)
Fin brud-kaka
Rich Cake (1876)
Rich Chocolate Cake (1913)
Rich Coffee Cake (1876)
Rich Fruit Cake (1920)
Rock Cake (1876)
Rock Cake (1840)
Rock Cakes (1878)
Rockland Cake (1894)
Rockland Cake (1911)
Rodonkuchen, or Napfkuchen (1873)
Rodon Cake (No.1)
Gerührter Napfkuchen (1873)
Rodon Cake (No. 2)
Rodonkuchen (1873)
Rodon Cake (No. 3)
Roederer Cake (1920)
(Gâteau Roederer)
Roll Cake (1904)
Roll Jelly Cake (1876)
Roll Jelly Cake (1893)
Rose Leaf Cakes (1922)
Round Coffee Cake No. 1 (1922)
Round Coffee Cake (No. 2) (1922)
(with Raisins)
Royal Sponge Cake (1899)
Runaway Cakes (1893)
(for breakfast)
Russian Torte (N.D.)
(Angel Food Cake)
Rye and Corn Cakes (1913)
Rye Breakfast Cakes (1911)
Rye Drop Cakes (1876)
Rye Drop Cakes (1922)
Rye Muffins (1922)
Rye Muffins (1893)
Rye Muffins (1917)

Part 20: S

Saarbruck Puff Paste (1904)
Sacher-Torte (1910)
Salaeratus Cake (1869)
Sally Jewett Cake (1894)
Sally Lunn (1917)
Sally Lunn (1902)
Sally Lunn (1876)
Sally Lunn (1869)
Sally Lunn (1893)
Sally Lunn without Yeast (1876)
Sally White Cake (1893)
Sand Cake (1904)
Sand Cake (1922)
Sand Cake (1920)
(Gâteau Sable)
Sand Cakes (1893)
Sand Tarts (1876)
Sand Torte or Kuchen (1873)
Sand Cake (No. 1)
Sand Torte (1873)
Sand Cake (No. 2)
Sand Tourte (1922)
Santa Barbara Cake (1820)
Saratoga Corn Cake (1902)
Savarin Cake (1920)
Savarin à la Valence (1920)
(Savarin à la Valence)
Savoy Biscuit (1920)
(Biscuit de Savoie)
Schaum Torte (1922)
Schnecken (1922)
(Snails)
Schokoladen-Biscuit (1910)
(Chocolate Spongecake)
Schokoladen-Torte (1910)
(Chocolate Cake)
Scotch Cake (1876)
Scotch Cake (1840)
Scotch Chocolate Cake (1922)
Scotch Cream Muffins (1908)
Scotch Loaf Cake (1908)
Scotch Oat Cakes (1911)
Scotch Queen Cake (1840)
Scotch Shortbread (1922)
Scottish Shortbread (1922)
Scripture Cake (1911)
Seed Cakes (1893)
Seed Cakes (1913)
Seed Cake (1898)
(Plain)
Seed Cake (1898)
(Very Good)
Sexton's Cake (1904)
Sheraton Cake (1909)
Shortbread (1898)
Shortcake (1913)
(Fruit)
Short Cake (1876)

Short Cake (1869)
Short Cakes (1840)
Shortcake (1917)
Shrewsbury Cake (1876)
Shrewsbury Cakes (1902)
Shrewsbury Cakes (1864)
Shrewsbury Cakes (1840)
Shrewsbury Cakes (1913)
Silesian Cheese Cake (1904)
Silver Cake (No.1) (1922)
Silver Cake (No.2) (1922)
Silver Cake 1 (1876)
Silver Cake 2 (1876)
Silver Cake (1911)
Silver Cake (1893)
Silver Cake 1 (1894)
Silver Cake 2 (1894)
Silver Cake (1820)
(Made with Whites)
Silver Nut Cake (1922)
Simnel Cake (1922)
Six Egg Cake (1876)
Skladany Dort s Ovocnymi Rosoly (1920)
Layer Jelly Cake
Small Apple Cakes (1904)
Small Fruit Cake (1913)
Small Royal Cakes 1920)
Small Savarins
(Petits Savarins) (1920)
Small Sponge Cake (1920)
Small Wheat Cakes (1904)
Snippodoodles (1911)
Snow Cake 1 (1876)
Snow Cake 2 (1876)
Snow Cake (1911)
Snow Cake (1894)
Snow Cake (1893)
Snow Cake (1898)
Snowball Cake (1911)
Snowflake Cake (1920)
Snow White Cake (1820)
Soda Cake (1898)
Soft Gingerbread (1905)
(To Be Eaten Hot)
Soft Ginger Bread 1 (1876)
Soft Ginger Bread 2 (1876)
Soft Ginger Bread 3 (1876)
Soft Gingerbread 1 (1893)
Soft Gingerbread 2 (1893)
Soft Ginger Bread (N.D.)
Soft Ginger Bread (1893)
Soft Gingerbread (1921)
Solid Chocolate Cake (1913)

(Mrs. R. Heim)
Sour Cream Cake (N.D.)
Sour Milk Gingerbread (1917)
Sour Milk Griddle Cakes (1922)
Sour Milk Griddle Cakes (1922)
Sour Milk Griddle Cakes (1917)
Sour Milk Griddle Cakes (1913)
Sour Milk Muffins (1917)
Sour Milk Tea Cakes (1922)
Southern Corncake (1911)
Southern Fruit Cake (1922)
Spanish Bun Cake (1913)
Spanish Cake (1922)
Spanish Cake (1908)
Spanish Chocolate Cake (1909)
Spanish Layer Cake (1913)
Spanish Pound Cake (No. 1) (1922)
Spanish Pound Cake (No. 2) (1922)
Spanish Pound Cake (No. 3) (1922)
Spanish Pound Cake (No. 4) (1922)
Speck Kuchen (1873)
Bacon Cake (No.1)
Speck Kuchen mit Kummel (1873)
Bacon Cake with Caraways (No. 2)
Spice Cake (1904)
Spice Cake No. 1 (1912)
Spice Cake No. 2 (1912)
Spice Cake (1876)
Spice Cake (1922)
Spice Cake (N.D.)
Spice Cake (1913)
Spice Cake (1920)
Spice Cake (1913)
Spice Cake (1894)
Spice Cake (1917)
(without Eggs)
Spice Cakes (1876)
Spice Cakes (1911)
Spiced Cake (1913)
(Without Eggs)
Spiced Ginger Bread (1876)
Spiced Ginger Cake (1912)
Spider Cake (1902)
Sponge Cake (1836)
(Called in France Biscuit)
Sponge Cake (1897)
Svamp-kaka
Sponge Cake No. 1 (1889)
Sponge Cake No. 2 (1889)
Sponge Cake No. 3 (1889)
Sponge Cake (1898)
Sponge Cake 1 (1876)
Sponge Cake 2 (1876)

Sponge Cake 3 (1876)
Sponge Cake 4 (1876)
Sponge Cake 5 (1876)
Sponge Cake 6 (1876)
Sponge Cake 7 (1876)
Sponge Cake 8 (1876)
Sponge Cake 9 (1876)
Sponge Cake (1911)
Sponge Cake (1922)
Sponge Cake (1890)
Sponge Cake (N.D.)
Sponge Cake (1899)
Sponge Cake (1905)
Sponge Cake (1905)
Sponge Cake (1864)
Sponge Cake (1913)
Sponge Cake (1920)
(Biscuit Leger)
Sponge Cake (1840)
Sponge Cake (1913)
Sponge Cake (1869)
Sponge Cake (1911)
Sponge Cake (1917)
(Hot Water)
Sponge Cake 1 (1893)
Sponge Cake 2 (1893)
Sponge Cake 3 (1893)
Sponge Cake 4 (1893)
Sponge Cake 5 (1893)
Sponge Cake 6 (1893)
Sponge Cake 7 (1893)
Sponge Cake (1914)
Sponge Cake 1 (1893)
Sponge Cake 2 (1893)
Sponge Cake 3 (1893)
Sponge Cake 1 (1894)
Sponge Cake 2 (1894)
Sponge Cake 3 (1894)
Sponge Cake 4 (1894)
Sponge Cake 5 (1894)
Sponge Cake (1893)
Sponge Cake Croquettes (1911)
Sponge Cake in Small Pans (1869)
Sponge Cake (1922)
Ladyfinger Mixture
Sponge Cakes (1898)
(Small)
Sponge Drop Cakes (1876)
Sponge Gingerbread (1890)
Sponge Layer Cake (1899)
Spritzkuchen (1910)
Squash Griddle Cakes (1902)
Squash Griddle Cakes (1894)

St. Honoré and St. Honoré Sultana (1920)
(St. Honoré et St. Honoré Sultane)
St. Nicholas Cake (1876)
Stachelbeer-Torte (1910)
(Gooseberry Cake)
Stale Bread Cakes (1893)
Steamed Shortcake (1913)
Stolle (1910)
Stollen (1922)
Strawberry Cake with Vanilla Cream (1904)
Strawberry Short Cake (1893)
Strawberry Shortcake, No. 1 (1920)
Strawberry Shortcake, No. 2 (1920)
Strawberry Shortcake (1905)
Strawberry Shortcake (1913)
Strawberry Shortcake (1922)
Strawberry Shortcake (1922)
Strawberry Short Cake 1 (1893)
Strawberry Short Cake 2 (1893)
Strawberry Short Cake (1876)
Strawberry Short Cake (1920)
(Gâteau aux Fraises)
Strawberry Shortcake (1914)
Strawberry Shortcake (1899)
Streusel Coffee Cake (1922)
Streusel Kuchen (1873)
Strewed Cake
Streusselkuchen (1910)
Striezel (1910)
Suabian Cake (1904)
Sugar Cakes (1920)
(Gâteaux au Sucre)
Sultana Cake (1898)
Sultana Tea Cakes (1911)
Sunshine Cake (1922)
Sunshine Cake No. 1 (1912)
Sunshine Cake No. 2 (1912)
Sunshine Cake No. 3 (1912)
Sunshine Cake (1922)
Sunshine Cake (1893)
Sunshine Cake (1911)
Sunshine Layer Cake (N.D.)
Superior Muffins (N.D.)
Surprise Muffins (N.D.)
Süste (1910)
Süster (1873)
Süster Cake
Swedish Batter Cakes (1908)
Sweet Cake (1904)
(Rodon Kuchen)
Sweet Corn Griddle-cakes (1905)
Sweet Milk Griddle Cakes (1922)
Swiss Cream Cake (No.1) (1904)

Swiss Cream Cake (No.2) (1904)　　　Swiss Roll (1898)

Part 21: T

Tampa Cake (1909)
Tapioca Breakfast Cakes (1890)
Tausendjahrkuchen (1910)
(Thousand Year Cake)
Tea Cake No, 1 (1912)
Tea Cake No, 2 (1912)
Tea Cake (1876)
Tea Cake (1911)
Tea Cake (1893)
Tea Cakes (1913)
Tea Cakes (1913)
Tea-party Cakes (1905)
Teekuchen (1910)
(Tea Biscuits)
Thanksgiving Corn Cake (1921)
The Deacon's Blueberry Cake (1911)

The Doctor's Cream Cakes (1911)
The Wholesome Parkin (1922)
Tilden Cake (1922)
Tip-Top Cake (1893)
Tipsy Cake (1898)
Top and Filling for Orange Layer Cake (1922)
Tourte a la Royale (1922)
Triester Torte (1910)
Trouvère Cakes (1920)
(Gâteaux Trouvère)
Tumbler Cake (1889)
Twelve Pound Fruit Cake (1913)
"Groom's Cake"
Twenty Minute Coffee Cake (1922)
Twin Elms Date Cake (1911)
Twin Elms Tea-Cake (1911)

Part 22: U

Ulm Cake (1904)
Uncle Robertson Cake (1876)

Upside Down Cake (N.D.)

Part 23: V

Vacherin Cake with Cream (1920)
(Gâteau Vacherin à la Crème)
Valentine Cake with Rum (1920)
(Gâteau Valentin au Rhum)
Valentine Cakes (1913)
Vanilla Cream Cake (1920)
Veal Cake (1898)
Velvet Cake (1905)
Velvet Cake (1893)
Velvet Cake (1911)

Velvet Sponge Cake (1917)
Virginia Pone (1869)
Virginia Pone (1876)
Vienna Almond Tourte (1922)
Vienna Bröselcake (1920)
Vienna Cake (1904)
Vienna Cherry Cake (1908)
Vienna Chocolate Tourte (1922)
Vienna Tourte à la Crème (1922)
Volusia Cake (1909)

Part 24: W

Wafer Cakes (1840)
Wafer Cakes (1869)
Waffeln (1910)
(Wafers; French: Gaufres)
Waikiki Shortcake (1909)
Walnut Cake (1876)
Walnut Cake (1893)
Walnut Cake (1894)
Walnut Cake (1893)
Walnut Cakes (1922)
Walnut Torte (1922)

Washington Cake (1876)
Washington Cake (1840)
Washington Cake (1869)
Washington Cake (1894)
Water Pan Cakes (1869)
(A cheap Dessert)
Wedding Cake (1876)
Wedding Cake (1893)
Wedding Cake Pudding (1876)
Weisse Pfefferkuchen (1910)
Weisse Pfeffernüsse (1910)

Weisse runde Pfeffernüsse (1910)
Wellington Cake (1904)
Westphalian Butter, No. 1 (1904)
(Coffee or Sugar Cake)
Westphalian Cake No. 2 (1904)
Westphalian Cake No. 3 (1904)
Wheat Cakes (1920)
(Galettes au Froment)
Wheat Gems (1876)
Whipped Cream Cake (1913)
Whist Cake (1893)
White Cake (1876)
(Marbled)
White Cake 1 (1876)
White Cake 2 (1876)
White Cake (1922)
White Cake (1917)
White Cake (1869)
White Cake (1893)
White Cake (1893)
White Cake (1893)
White Cake 1 (1894)
White Cake 2 (1894)
White Cake (1893)
White Cake (1893)
White Clouds (1876)
White Cocoa-nut Cakes (1840)
White Corn Cake (1894)
White Corn Meal Cakes for Breakfast (1893)
(A Rhode Island Dish)
White Cup Cake (1876)
White Cup Cake (1840)
White Fruit Cake (1820)
White Fruit Cake 1 (1876)

White Fruit Cake 2 (1876)
White Fruit Cake (N.D.)
White Fruit Cake (1913)
White Fruit Cakes (1922)
White Gingerbread (1840)
White Layer Cake (1913)
White Layer Cake (1913)
White Mountain Cake (1889)
White Mountain Cake 1 (1876)
White Mountain Cake 2 (1876)
White Mountain Cake 3 (1876)
White Mountain Cake (1894)
White Mountain Cake (1893)
White Mountain Cake (1890)
White Nut Cake (1913)
White Patty Cakes (1911)
White Sponge Cake (1913)
Whole Wheat Gingerbread (1922)
Whole Wheat Muffins (1922)
Wiener Soufflée (1873)
Vienna Soufflée, a Dinner Dish
Wiener Torte (1910)
Wiener Torte (1873)
Vienna Cake (No. 1)
Wiener Torte (1873)
Vienna Cake (No. 2)
Wild Rose Cake (1920)
Willie C.'s Birthday Cake (1876)
Wine Cakes (No. 1) (1922)
Wine Cakes (No. 2) (1922)
Wine Glazed Cake (1920)
Wine Glazed Cream Cake (1920)
Witch Cake (1913)
Wreath Cake (1922)

Part 25: Y

Yankee Cake (1876)
Yeast Batter for German Fruit Cakes (1904)
Yeast Buckwheats (1876)

Yellow Angel Cake (1820)
Yellow Sponge Cake (1912)
Yomoga Ga Shima (1914)

Part 26: Z

Zimmet Kuchen (1873)
Cinnamon Cake
Zimmetplätzchen (1910)
(Cinnamon Cakes)
Zimmet-Waffeln (1910)
(Cinnamon Wafers)
Zwetschgen Kuchen (No.1) (1873)
Mussel Plum Cake

Zwetschgen Kuchen (No.2) (1873)
Mussel Plum Cake
Zwieback Torte (1873)
Rusk Cake
Zwiebel Kuchen (No. 1) (1873)
Onion Cake
Zwiebel Kuchen (No. 2) (1873)
Onion Cake

www.ingramcontent.com/pod-product-compliance
Lightning Source LLC
Chambersburg PA
CBHW060302010526
44108CB00042B/2607